HISTORY OF INDIAN MUSIC

HISTORY OF INDIAN MUSIC

With Particular Reference to Theory and Practice

By
BHAVANRAV A. PINGLE

LOW PRICE PUBLICATIONS
DELHI-110052

Published by
Low Price Publications
A-6, Nimri Commercial Centre,
Near Ashok Vihar Phase-IV,
Delhi-110052
Phones: 27302453
e-mail: lpp@nde.vsnl.net.in
url: www.lppindia.com

Reprinted in **LPP** 1999, 2007
ISBN 978-81-7536-432-5

Printed at
D K Fine Art Press P Ltd.
Delhi-110052

PRINTED IN INDIA

PREFACE

The present monograph neither pretends to be an exhaustive analysis nor aims at giving a complete description of Indian music or demonstration of the phenomena of Sound or of the elaborate history and laws of Music. Those who wish to study these subjects thoroughly, whether from their scientific or artistic aspect, must have recourse to special works and specialised studies.

To show briefly the broad outlines of Indian music as an art, and to test them by the light of Western science, has been the aim and seope of this discussion which, it is hoped, will be received with some interest by the public.

If there be anything acceptable to the general reader in this discussion, it is exclusively due to my drawing on the writings on the phenomena of Sound by Herbert Spencer, Charles Darwin and a few other English authors, which I have been studying for sometime. If there be anything interesting or instructive to the admirer of music, it is wholly due to the characteristics of Indian music itself which I have regularly studied for a long time.

The nomenclature used throughout this discussion, is not pure Sanskrit, but is the popular one among the Indian musicians, and, therefore, no strict rule of spelling is observed.

CONTENTS

CORRECTIONS

Page	37,	line 6	for	Zálás	*read*	Zhálás
"	Do	" 13	"	through	"	though
"	45,	" 24	"	Shodava	"	Shádava
"	53,	" 17	"	carefnl	"	careful
"	Do	" 40	"	alrs	"	airs
"	115	" 35	"	th	"	$\frac{1}{4}$

I.

THE HISTORY OF INDIAN MUSIC AND THE THEORY OF MUSIC IN GENERAL

It is an unwarrantable and speculative presumption to decide positively in the absence of reliable record, whether the singers of former times were much more accomplished than those of the present day, or *vice versa*.

In painting, carving, sculpture, architecture, and in the composition and execution of music, many persons would have us believe that we have, owing to our contact with Western civilizing influences, progressed. A judgment on the former arts can be formed by comparing the old things with the new ones, but a definite opinion on the merits and demerits of the by-gone singers, can only be substantiated by examining the music, its works, and its traditions which have come down to us from time immemorial. It is a fact beyond doubt, that the said music, its works, and traditions of Ancient Indian Aryas underwent alterations and modifications through many vicissitudes to which India has singularly been subjected.

Our judgment on the worth of Indian music is based on the ancient music, works, and traditions. The conclusion thus arrived at, might perhaps be flattering, or otherwise, because, we have no other alternative than to be guided by the aforesaid materials which have been handed down from generation to generation with certain additions and omissions. In such a state of things, it is very difficult to treat the subject with absolute impartiality, because it is a subject with which a considerable part of the Ancient Indian civilization is concerned. Suffice it to say, that the fact that music is a product of civilization, is as manifest as language or means of communication—spoken and silent, or written or otherwise expressed—is a means to education ; for though savages and rustics have their dance-chants and ceremonious vociferations, they are of a nature hardly to be dignified by the title musical.

The Indian musicians in spite of the absence of material encouragement in recent times, have preserved and protected the ancient plant of music from its total annihilation, and havegiven us an ancient legacy, which, though half dead, if properly understood, will considerably assist us to come to a right conclusion.

It is a well-known fact that the art of writing, though known for centuries to Indians, was hardly resorted to as a means to perpetuate their learning. The mode of transmitting knowledge or theory of things was in verses which were committed to memory by personal tuition, or as is said by Sir H. Mayne and others—Indian Aryas expressed their learning in a form of language so concise, as to fasten it on the memory, and finally to the fountain-head of their literature, which is admitted to be the oldest literature of Aryan race. The faculty of recollection (Indians are celebrated for their retentive memory) and the brevity of poetry for which poems are known, were so much developed, as to meet their want for accumlation of science, as an extension of the preception by means of reasoning or organized experience.

Language like an organized being, struggles for life, the better, the shorter, the easier forms gaining the upper hand.

Our by-gone writings are greatly mixed with foreign and imported matters, which have no relevancy whatever with music, but they were brought in, as necessary auxiliaries to it, when the art of music was thought to be a gift from the divinity of Anthropomorphites. In such a deplorable state of our writings, we are forced to depend more on inferences and deductions, than on direct evidence.

Indian traditions abound in instances such as

Haradása, Rámadása, Suradása, Tánasena, Lád, Kapola and their predecessors and successors too many to mention here. These artists in their respective times had made music their life-long study, and had been so much absorbed in it that most of them preferred to lead an ascetic life to worldly enjoyments, and thus became not only men of reverence and genius of their generation, but are even remembered and respected to this day on account of their keenness of sense in composition.

An unusually emotional nature is the general characteristic of musical composers. Stronger feeling produces stronger manifestation, and any cause of excitement will call forth from such a nature, tones and changes of voice more marked than those called forth from an ordinary nature. All music is originally vocal. All sounds are produced by the agency of certain muscles. These muscles in common with those of the body at large, are excited to contraction by pleasurable and painful feelings, and therefore it is, that feelings demonstrate themselves in sounds as well as in movements. Different qualities of voice accompany different mental states, and under states of excitement, the tones are more sonorous than usual. The sounds of common conversation have but little resonance, those of strong feeling have much more.

When we unbiasedly sift the roots of many sources of music, such as religious devotion and ceremonies, social performances, desultory works, and many a family of musicians in which it has so extensively been spread—and when we bring it in a systematized form to tell its own tale—we can safely affirm without fear of exaggeration, that it had once reached a higher stage of development than it is generally credited with.

The above assertion will be looked down upon by many as absurd, and even it will be thought paradoxical by right-thinking men, who justly admit that the Western education has successfully instilled and widely spread a new force of European growth into Indian thoughts and things, which have progressed and are still progressing, under the British supremacy, in refinements, arts, sciences, and in general knowledge.

The validity of the said assertion, however, is not an ideal one, but is based on reliable and reasonable sources, which form the subject-matter of this discussion. It is true, that we have no direct evidence of history in its narrow sense, but this difficulty can be overcome by critically examining the extant and traditional resources which go to form a history.

History, as is said, in its earlier stages, was regarded chiefly as a form of poetry, recording the more fabulous and dramatic actions of Kings, Queens, Heroines, Sages, Poets, Singers &c., and was sung as ballads by bards, and was told as legends or stories by story-tellers. History, as comprehended now, teaches us that the historical or great men were the histories or products of their societies. Without certain antecedents and a certain average national character, they could neither have been generated nor could have had the culture which formed them. If their societies were reinfluenced by them to a certain extent, they were both, before and after birth, influenced by their societies. They were the results of all those influences which fostered the ancestral character they inherited, and the social institutions they imbibed. So that such social changes which were directly attributable to individuals of unusual power, were still indirectly traceable to the social causes which produced these individuals.

Instead of enlarging on the elements of history, let us say that the justification of predicating the proposition—that Indian music was of higher origin and nobler development than it is generally voted to be and it is dying out for want of support—can be shown by reasonable inferences and deductions drawn from solid dara. To do this we commence the discussion historically in its extended sense.

It is said of Tànasena, the famous singer of the latter part of the 16th century, that this wonderfully skiled and gifted artist sang so melodiously and so forcibly charmed the feelings of his hearers with his emotional cadences, that the kind and great Akbar, then Emperor, on hearing his performance styled him as a paragon of cadences. The vocalist was not only raised as one of the Emperor's immediate courtiers, an honour deservedly bestowed on those admitted to be specialists in their respective spheres of vocation, but was adulated as a personification of sound. It is a well-known fact that in our day instances never occur where similar infatuation, if infatuation meant appreciation and admiration, which played so effectively on Akbar, might take place. It is lamentable that we have got no immediate means to fathom how many pious, heroic and noble hearts must have been impressed by different emotions,—how many bright eyes must have been made brighter, and how many fair bosoms must have heaved on hearing the dulcet notes and religious pathos of Suradása, Bhikudása, Kabiradása and other celebrities of past ages. What known and unknown conquests those artists must have performed in their times and places ? But our present public are more circumspect and are taught to keep their feelings more under command than to give way to hasty expressions of delight in public, and they cannot be blamed for so doing, otherwise the world would not perhaps be edified thereby. Therefore the mask worn by the public to screen their emotional expressions may be said to be a necessary evil with which we must remain content, and must bring ourselves to be looked upon, as more intellectual than emotional !

To be dead to any natural expression of emotion is simply impossible from a naturalist's standpoint of view. If any being is devoid of natural expressions, it necessarily follows that it is dead to the impressions which act as stimulants, technically called *reflex action*.

The law of reflex action teaches us, that an impression on the end of an *afferent* (sensory) nerve is conveyed to some ganglionic centre, and is thence usually reflected along an *efferent* (motor) nerve to one or more muscles which it causes to contract ; nervous excitation always tends to beget muscular motion ; and when it rises to a certain intensity, it always does beget it. Those external actions through which we read the feelings of others, show us that under any considerable tension the nervous system in general, discharges itself on the muscular system in general, either with or without the guidance of the will. It is manifest that emotions and sensations tend to generate bodily movements which are forcible in proportion as the emotions or sensations are intense.

It is proved that equal stimulants produce unequal effects on differently constituted and circumstanced species of animal, man included with his different stages of civilisation or advancement to adaptation. It is moreover proved, that as knowledge progresses, the mode of impressions and expressions, metaphysically called objective and subjective, becomes more complex and economical than simple and violent, in obedience the law of the least resistance and greatest traction or the resultant of the two, but none the less impressive and expressive in its total effect.

The following paragraphs, though long and many, completely show how the superfluities or original necessities are cast away and the economical or better adapted ones are acquired and accumulated.

It is an open secret that the art of writing is of later origin than that of speaking. It is said that the arts of writing and printing have descended from picture-language. The most primitive form of permanently symbolizing a thing, was by depicting it on wall, that is by representing something like the thing to be imitated. In process of time, as the symbols grew habitual and extensive, the most necessary became fixed and thus economized, and passing through the hieroglyphic and ideographic stages, the symbols lost all apparent relations to the things signified, just as the verbal language did.

Verbal language, according to H. Spencer, "consists at the beginning of symbols which are alike to the things symbolized as it is practical to make them. The language of signs is a means of conveying ideas by mimicking the actions or peculiarities of the things referred to. Verbal language is also, at the beginning, a mode of suggesting objects or acts, by imitating the sounds which the objects make or with which the acts are accompanied. It needs but to watch the gesticulations with which savage accompanies his speech—to see a Bushman or a Kaffir dramatizing before an audience, his mode of catching game, or to note the extreme paucity of words in primitive vocabularies to infer—that at first attitudes, gestures, and sounds were all combined to produce as good a *likeness* as possible of the things, animals, persons or events described ; and that as the sounds came to be understood by themselves, the gestures fell into disuse leaving traces, however, in the manners of the more excitable civilized races."

With regard to the origin and development of language Charles Darwin says—"After having read on the subject—I cannot doubt that language owes its origin to the imitation and modification of various natural sounds, the voices of other animals, and man's own instinctive cries, aided by signs and gestures. When we treat of sexual selection, we shall see that primeval man, or rather some early progenitor of man, probably first used his voice in producing true musical cadences that is, in singing as do some of the *Gibbon-apes* at the present day ; and we may conclude from a widely spread analogy, that this power would have especially created during the courtship of the sexes and would have expressed various emotions, such as love, jealousy, triumph, and would have served as a challenge to rivals. It is, therefore, probable that the imitation of musical cries by articulate sounds may have given rise to words expressive of various complex emotions. The strong tendency in our nearest allies, the monkeys, in microcephalous idiots, and in the barbarous races of mankind, to imitate whatever they hear, deserves notice as bearing on the subject of imitation. Since monkeys certainly understand much that is said to them by man, and, when wild, utter signal cries of danger to their fellows; and since fowls give distinct warning for danger on the ground, or in the sky, from hawks, may not some unusully wise ape-like animal have imitated the growl of a beast of prey, and thus told his fellow monkeys the nature of the expected danger? This must have been a first step in the formation of a language. As the voice was used more and more, the vocal organs would have been strengthened and perfected through the principle of the inherited effects of use—and this would have reacted on the power of speech. But the relation between the continued use of language and the development of the brain, has no doubt been far more important. The mental powers in some early progenitor of man must have been more highly developed than in any existing ape, before even the most imperfect form of speech could have come into use, but we may confidently believe that the continued use and advancement of this power would have reacted on the mind itself, by enabling and encouraging it to carry on long trains of thought which no more can be carried without the aid of words, whether spoken or silent, than a long calculation without the use of figures or algebra. It appears, also, that even an ordinary train of thought almost requires, or is greatly facilitated by, some form of language. A long succession of vivid and connected ideas may pass through the mind, without the aid of any form of language, as we may infer from the movements of dogs during their dreams. We have also seen that animals are able to reason to a certain extent, manifestly without the aid of language. The intimate connection between the brain, as it is developed in us, and the faculty of speech, is well shewn by those various cases of brain diseases in which speech is especially affected. There is no more improbability in the continued use of the mental and vocal organs leading to inherited changes in their structures and functions, than in the case of hand-writing, which depends partly on the form of the hand and partly on the disposition of the mind, and hand-writing is certainly inherited."

"Several writers have lately insisted that the use of language implies the power of forming general concepts, and that as no animals are supposed to possess this power an impassable barrier is formed between them and man. With respect to animals, I have already endeavoured to shew that they have that power, at least in a rude and incipient degree. As far as infants from ten to eleven months old are concerned, it seems to me. incredible that they should be able to connect certain sounds with certain general ideas, unless such ideas were already formed in their minds. The same remarks may be extended to the more intelligent animals. A dog forms a general conception of cats or speech, and knows the corresponding words as well as a philosopher. And the capacity to understand is as good a proof of vocal intelligence, though in an inferior degree, as the capacity to speak."

"Why the organs now used for speech should have been originally perfected for this purpose rather than any other organs, it is not difficult to see. Ants have considerable powers of intercommunication by means of their antennæ. We might have used our fingers as efficient instruments, for a person with practice can report to a deaf man every word of a speech, rapidly delivered at a public meeting; but the loss of our hands, whlist thus employed, would have been a serious inconvenience. As all the higher mammals possess vocal organs, constructed on the same general plan as ours, and used as a means of communication, it was obviously probable that these same organs would still be further developed if the power of communication had to be improved; and this has been effected by the aid of adjoining and well adapted parts, namely the tongue and lips."

"The fact of the higher apes not using their vocal organs for speech, no doubt depends on their intelligence not having been sufficiently advanced. The possession by them of organs, which with long continued practice might have been used for speech, although not thus used, is paralleled by the case of many birds which possess organs fitted for singing, though they never sing. Thus the nightingale and crow have vocal organs similarly constituted, these being used by the former for diversified song, and by the latter only for croaking."

According to modern researches, the voice is a transformation or equivalent of the respiratory movements. The respiratory mechanism with its adjuncts, in addition to its respiratory function, becomes of service in the case of man, animals, birds, and some insects, as a means of expressing emotion. The respiratory column of air, moreover, in its exit from the chest, is frequently made use of, in a mechanical way to expel bodies from the upper passages. Hence arise a number of peculiarly modified and more or less complicated respiratory movements such as sighing, coughing, laughing &c, to secure special ends, which are not distinctly respiratory. But as we have to confine solely to vocal sound, we of necessity should not enlarge on the movements of the organ of respiration. The vocal organ is nothing more than a wind instrument :—A blast of air, driven by a more or less prolonged expiratory movement, throws into vibrations two elastic membranes, the *Chorde Vocales*. These impart their vibrations to the column of air above them, and so give rise to the sound we call voice.

The emission of sound by the organs of voice in many kinds of animals, man included, is efficient in the highest degree as a means of expressions. When the sensorium is strongly excited, the muscles of the body are generally thrown into violent action, and as a consequence loud sounds are uttered, however silent the animal generally may be.

The phenomenon of sound, which is most interesting and instructive to us, is produced by the organs of voice in man, under different sensations and emotions. The vocal sound, as an indispensable interpreter of our thoughts and feelings, and the peculiar sounds and noises of animals, which express their wants and emotions, pleasurable and painful, are caused by the reflex action.

Charles Darwin philosophically says :—"Through man's power of intellect, articulate language has been evolved, and on this his wonderful advancement mainly depended. A physiological analysis of the faculty of language shews, that even the smallest proficiency in it might require more brain power than the greatest proficiency in any other direction. This faculty has justly been considered as one of the chief distinctions between man and other lower animals. But man is not the only animal that can make use of language to express what is passing in his mind, and can understand more or less, what is expressed by another. A kind of money, when excited, utters at least six distinct sounds, which excite in others of its kind, similar emotions. The movements of the features and gestures of monkeys are understood by us, and they partly understand ours."

"It is a more remarkable fact that the dog, since being domesticated, has learnt to bark in at least four or five distinct tones. Although barking is a new art, no doubt the wild parent species of the dog expressed their feelings by cries of various kinds. With the domesticated dog, we have the bark of eagerness, as in the chase ; that of anger, as when growing ; the yelp or howl of despair, as when shut up ; the baying at night ; the bark of joy, as when starting on a walk with his master, and the very distinctive one of demand or supplication on wishing for a door or window to be opened, How the barking of the dog, which serves to express various emotions and desires, and which is so remarkable from having been acquired since the animal was domesticated, and from being inherited in different breeds, was first learnt, we do not know ; but may we not suspect that imitation has had something to do with its acquisition (to meet new conditions or environments) owing to dogs having long lived in strict association with loquacious an animal as man ?"

"The habitual use of articulate language is, however, peculiar to man, but he uses, in common with the lower animals, inarticulate cries to express his meaning aided by gestures and the movements of the face. This especially holds good with the more simple and vivid feelings, which are but little connected with higher intelligence. Our cries of pain, fear, surprise, anger together with their approximate actions, and the murmur of a mother to her beloved child, are more expressive than any words."

"That which distinguishes man from the lower animals, is not the understanding, for every one knows, dogs understand many words and sentences. It is not the mere articulation which is our distinguishing character, for parrots and other birds possess this power. Nor is it the mere capacity of connecting definite sounds with definite ideas, for it is certain that some parrots, which have been taught to speak, connect unerringly words with things, and persons with events."

"Language is an art. It differs, however, widely from all ordinary arts, for man has an instinctive tendency to brew or bake. Moreover no philologist supposes that any language has been *deliberately* invented. It has been evolved and unconsciously developed by many steps. The sounds uttered by birds offer, in several respects, the nearest analogy, for all the members of the same species utter the same instinctive cries expressive of their emotions ; and all the kinds which sing, exert their power instinctively ; but the actual song, and even call-notes are learnt from their parents or foster-parents. These sounds are no more innate than language is in man. The first attempt to sing may be compared to the imperfect endeavour in a child to babble. The young males continue practising for ten or eleven months. Their first essays show hardly a rudiment of the song. Nestlings which have learnt the song of a distinct species, as with the canary-birds educated in the Tyrol, teach and transmit their new song to their offsprings. The slight material differences of song in the same species inhabiting different districts may be appositely compared to provincial dialects; and the songs of allied, though distinct species may be compared with the languages of distinct races of man."

"The birds appear to be the most æsthetic of all animals, excepting of course man, and they have nearly the same tastes for the beautiful as we have. This is shewn by our enjoyment of the singing of birds."

The foregoing details by H. Spencer and Ch. Darwin show that an instinctive tendency to acquire an art is not peculiar to man; and that the lower animals differ from man solely in his almost infinitely larger power of associating together the most deversified sounds and ideas; and this obviously depends on the higher development of his mental power.

It is evident that mere words are dull sounds if they are not accompanied by different accents and force, and that the same sounds, if differently modulated, produce different ideas. These modifications of voice, produced by feelings in others can be engenderd. Add to this voice, expressions and gestures of face, which give life to the otherwise dead sounds in which the intellect utters its ideas and enable the hearers, not only to understand the state of mind they accompany, but to participate in it. All speech is composed nominally of two elements, but in reality they are so inseparably interwoven that we cannot draw a line, where the words end and the tones, in which they are uttered, begin. But we can say that the words are the signs of ideas and the tones are those of feelings. It is true that certain articulations express the thought, while certain vocal sounds convey more or less of pain or pleasure which the thought gives. Using the phrase "vocal expression" in an extended sense as covering all modifications of vocal sounds, we may say that vocal expression is a means for the conveyance of thoughts and feelings. This double function of even spoken language is dimly recognized, but in practice we invariably find that more weight is attached to the tones than to the words, and the former are more relied upon than the latter.

Professor Max Muller rightly says—"we may speak in singing, and sing in speaking ; we may speak in whispering and whisper in speaking, we may even sing in whispering, and whisper in singing ; in fact we seldom speak without either singing or whispering certain portions of our words."

The tones of speaking, of reciting, and of singing severally exemplify one general principle—that the tones of excited feelings are more sonorous than those of common conversation, because muscular action is directly proportional to mental excitement. Expressiveness of speaking, of reciting, and of singing, is a question of tones, for these three phases of vocal sounds, under which all vocal phenomena are explained, are interchangeable one into other by the admission or dismissal of the variety and duration of tones.

Music, which is said to be the most powerful of all arts, has been evolved from its most primitive function in a great number of animals, man included with his different stages of development—to charm and call the opposite sex ; and that in man's advanced state of civilization it has been evolved to emotionally express the most complex sentiments, which intellectual or articulate language and poetry could not express. To add more to the vocal charms, science began to invent many musical instruments or supplementary senses, which, in animals, are confined to bodily movements, intensely performed during the pairing season on the earth, in the water and in the air.

Dr. Samman most thoughtfully said :— "we can concentrate greater intensity of feeling in a single musical note than any pages of writing."

Our nature is such that feeling and intellect are the two sides of man or the two expressions of the same thing, because there could be no feeling without intellect and intellect without feeling. Every student of philosophy or *unification* of knowledge knows that no thought is possible without things thought of ; and in addition, we may treat intellect and feeling objectively, and infer that no thought or intellect is possible without emotion or feeling of pain or pleasure which is its attribute, and that complexity of thought or intellect involves complexity of emotion or feeling and that complexity of impressions involves complexity of expressions.

It is true that the highest intellectual mânifestations imply a good balance of the highest feeling ; but it is also true that the highest intellect is possible only with the highest feeling. They are so inseparably interwoven that we can not draw a line of *demarcation* where intellect or thought begins, and emotion or feeling proper to that intellect or thought ends, or *vice versa*. The tissue of every thought or feeling resolves itself into affections of consciousness. What we call affections of consciousness are subjective states of objective forces.

Instead of treating the above subject at length, suffice it to say that if higher intellect is a product of civilization, so is also higher emotion of the same agency.

Apart from the above considerations, which belong more to natural sciences and philosophical speculations than to music proper, let us consider what was the state of Indian society in which those wonderful singers, of whom we have spoken before, had lived, and what is the present state in force. From all that can be gathered, it seems, that in former times there were a few fine voices in existence in each generation as is the case now. But in our day there appears to be an amount of affectation, which if dilated upon, would at once seal the fate of many who pass as artists of no mean calibre. Besides, are the present classes so capable of knowing music as they were in former times, and have we got the same opportunities and facilities to indulge in it ? Is it too much to say that music as an art is not at all understood except by a microscopic few, who are probably prejudiced in favour of an artist or two whom they delight to pet and flatter ? Are not our educated men quite indifferent to music, partly for its objectionable surroundings and partly for their want of taste for it ? Nobody cares for its revival and encouragement, because the present well-to-do persons are not generally alive to its charm, and those who like it and practise it, are hardly beyond their immediate wants to compete for the race of life owing to the changed circumstances. Lastly, what steps have been taken to solicit the State patronage towards learning music as such ? To suppose that music will be resuscitated and systematized without the necessary support from State, is too idle a dream to be realized. Owing to the present educational policy of Government and the report of the last Education Commission, no hope is held out of any movement in the direction of State help. Government are quite in the dark about the true value of Indian music. They paid neither attention nor rendered help to it which they did to Indian literature, prose and verse. Unless music forms a part of the curriculum of schools and colleges, as do the classical and vernacular languages and even athletics, and unless some enterprising European scholars of music devote themselves to its regeneration, there will be neither its revival, nor will it be brought to such a system as would meet the wants of modern society. The most elementary way to teach music is to make the pupils recite their poetries to Harmonium or such other instruments as an accompaniment, and thus to cultivate a taste in youths to produce voice musically, and to appreciate it. It is really most rude and rustic to hear poetry recited in our educational institutions without the least regard for concordance. Indians never did any progress independently of the ruling power. Men, who have closely studied the problems of Indian administration, say that the Indians are so unpatriotic as not to be able to do substantial things without assistance from State, because they have been subjected from time immemorial to a despotic Government—a Government in which every thing is done for the people and nothing by them.

It will not be out of place here to mention, that even the Muhammadans partonized Hindu music to the best of their means, notwithstanding the inclemency of their religion to music in any form. It is a fact that the Muhammadans took a liking for music when they were sufficiently tempered by converts, intermarriages, contact with Hindus, and by acclimatization, and when they looked upon India as their adopted home. It is true that the Muhammadans had spoilt and checked every progress of Hindu thoughts and things in the beginning of their conquests and consolidation of their power and authority. But eventually they not only adopted Hindu music as an ennobling art, resorted to it with certain alterations as an additional force to their Marshiàs and Sojas, which are composed and sung in the sacred memory of their Imáms, Hásen and Husen. It is exceedingly probable that the love with which Hindu music inspired the Muhammadans was considerably due to the intolerance of their religion for natural expressions of emotion. They had brought with them their arts and poetry for which they were celebrated, but no music. As a matter of course, their patronage and intercourse were so powerful and forcible that they changed the

2

features of original music, and wonderfully separated it from its parent stock. This fact can be verified by comparing the Sanskrit music (which is very rare in its original purity) of the Southern India with the Hindustani one. Hindustani music is a mixture of the Aryan origin or development and Muhammadan cultivation, and Sanskrit music of the Southern India is a mixture of the Aryan origin or development and Dravidian cultivation. Be this as it may, we find these two principal schools of Indian music, which do not so materially differ from each other, as the Aryan and Dravidian families of languages do.

It is said, that the ancients must have heard an amount of sweet and plaintive voices, because no ceremony, either religious or social, was performed without music. Music was thought to be a necessary part not only of secular enjoyments and of religious devotion, but of boody warfares and funeral ceremonies. Music is said to have been performed by a number of devotees by day and by night. Temples and halls are said to have been thronged by numerous musicians and bards. It is said that music was so much developed and spread that different melodies were fixed for differnt parts of the day and night and even season melodies were invented. Every village of importance had a bard or minstrel of its own who entertained his village patrons by extolling the deeds and personalities of great men and women, or by singing poems of morality inculcated by great sages. Those sages were revered who were more stoic than epecurian. It is believed, that the art of music was the principal enjoyment of the ancient Aryas, because they had a limited number of arts and sciences to attend to.

It is said that there were many musicians in possession of lands free from State imposition. This method of patronizing music was of great antiquity. Rávan of Rámáyan, according to traditions, had given a large province to his musicians, and he was himself proficient in music. Almost all the kings, who governed Ancient Indians, were more or less patrons or artists of music, and they were given special instructions in it. Even Royal ladies were not prohibited from acquiring the arts of singing, dancing and gesticulation.

In short, looking at the historically fabulous number of musicians who were employed in religious, political, and social institutions, and looking at the method of their music, we are forced to admit that the ancients had a considerable taste for music. Arts like comodities are improved only by their corresponding demands. It is said that as a relic of former times, we have many religious and itinerant singers who are spread all over the country, and that they show in a wonderful degree the sweetness and plaintiveness of voices which are attributed to the hereditary transmission and development of them.

Many will be surprised when we say that music is not only a sign of gratified feelings but it is a means to acheive them, and hence the songs of begging are a force to create sympathy. It will, perhaps, be objected that the function of creating sympathy in others allotted to singing, is more reproachful than complimentary, but a thoughtful consideration will lead them to the opposite conclusion. The utilitarian principle or the *summum bonum* is the tendency of civilizations which replaces the individual gratification, by gratification resulting from, or involving the happiness of others.

It is true that the songsters of whom we have just spoken are generally minstrels who sing either to the Ektárá (one-stringed lyre), Morli (made of gourd), or to the Kinri (crude form of Sarangi or fiddle) heroic or religious narratives versified by themselves to music of their own composition, and thus unite the separate offices in advanced societies of poet, composer, and instrumentalist.

We have selected the above case as a typical one of the lowest form of music, to show that the progress from simple to complex was considerably displayed in the multiplied differentiations which each of them underwent in Aryan societies. Instead of dwelling here on the many kinds of dancing, poetry, and music, which must have in the course of Aryan civilization come into use, and instead of occupying space in dilating upon the progress of poetry, of the various forms of metre, of rhyme and of their general culture, let us confine our attention to the immediate subject in hand.

To recur to our subject, we say that we do not find a single class of Indians, however crude it may be in its social institutions, dead and depraved to music of its own. Some of the airs, which are sung by certain classes, are pleasant if musically performed. It was a common practice in former times to teach the youths their lessons in tones of music. This practice was considerably due to the oral transmission and verse literature. Every Hindu of high caste was taught more or less to praise and pray his divinity by certain intonations called, Vratta, Chhand, Prabandh, Gita &c. The Vrattas and Gitas, which have come down to us, are really pleasant if musically expressed, and they give us an idea of the poetical singing of ancient Hindoos. This class of singing has not at all been influenced by the Muhammadan intercourse on account of its religious bearing.

Those who have studied the above subject, pronounce that this class of singing has not been what we call singing, but nearly allied to it; and as such is much less remote from common speech than singing is. For poetical singing is in all respects, intermediate between speech and song. Its average effects are neither so loud nor so low as those of song. Its tones are less sonorous in *timbre* than those of song. Commonly it travels to a smaller extent from the middle notes, and it uses notes neither so high nor so low in pitch. Those intervals habitual to it are neither so wide nor so varied. Its rate of variation is not rapid. And at the same time its primary *rhythm* is less decided ; it has none of the secondary *rhythm*, which is one of the marked characteristics of song. And the last but not the least, its average duration of notes is neither so long nor so short as that of song.

Hindus were such devoted admirers of music that they worshipped it not only as an offshoot of one of the four sacred Vedas, but they composed their Sáma-Veda to be chanted or sung. Their Sutras and Shrutis were attributed to the music of Shiva, who was styled the king of kings of musicians according to Shivasutra Jálum. Ascetic or stoically abstemious Buddhists and Jains, too, were not indifferent to the charm of music. Even now, it is generally believed by Hindus that the royal way to win over the deity is to say its praise and prayer in music. Every religious act is performed either in singing, in bodily movements, or in muttering and in gesticulation. We cannot pass over without remarking that, even in the most advanced nations of the world, the praise and prayer are generally accompanied by music. This class of music, which is called devotional music, is used like an all-absorbing—engrossing and concentrating agency or force—to completely divest oneself of all the affairs of all-powerful and ever-felt secularism, and to impress on him or on her nothing but vague (though believed to be grand and solemn) influence of Him or Unknowable, and to render the possibility of knowing—! In the Chinese annals it is said, "music hath the power of making heavens descend upon earth." People who are religiously inclined, call music a divine art.

It will not be grudged to quote here Herbert Spencer's most thoughtful exposition of the vocal sounds. He says—"That the vocal phenomena have a physiological basis. They are so many manifestations of the general law that feeling is a stimulus to muscular action—a law confirmed throughout the whole economy, not of man only, but of every sensitive creature—a law therefore, which lies deep in the nature of animal organization. The expressiveness of those modifications of voice is therefore innate. Each of us, from babyhood upwards, has been spontaneously making them, when under the various sensations and emotions by which they are produced. Having been conscious of each feeling at the same time we heard ourselves make the consequent sound, we have acquired an established association of ideas between such sound and the feeling which caused it. When the like sound is made by another, we ascribe the like feeling to him ; and by a further consequence we not only ascribe to him that feeling but have a certain degree of it aroused in ourselves : for to become conscious of the feeling which another is experiencing is to have that feeling awakened in us, which is the same thing as experiencing the feeling. Thus these various modifications of voice become not only a language, through which we understand the emotions of others, but also the means of exciting our sympathy with such emotions."

Illustrious Charles Darwin says : "Music and impassioned speech become *intelligible* to a certain extent, if we may assume that musical tones and rhythm were used by our half-human ancestors during the course of courtship, when animals of all kinds are excited not only by the love, but by the strong passion of jealousy, rivalry, and triumph. From the deeply laid principle of inherited associations, music in this case would be likely to call forth vaguely and indefinitely the strong emotions of a long past age. We have every reason to suppose that articulate speech is one of the latest as it certainly is, one of the highest, of the arts acquired by man, and as the instinctive power of producing musical notes and rhythms is developed low down in the animal series, it would altogether be opposed to the principle of evolution, if we were to admit that man's musical capacity has been developed from the tones used in passioned speech. We can thus understand how it is that music, dancing, song and poetry are such ancient arts. We may go further than this, and believe that musical sound afforded one of the bases for the development of language. As the males of several quadrumanous animals have their vocal organs much more developed than in the females, and as a Gibbon, one of the anthropomorphous apes, pours forth a whole octave of musical sounds and may be said to sing, it appears probable that the progenitors of man, either the males or females or both sexes, before acquiring the power of expressing their mutual love in articulate language, endeavoured to charm each other with musical notes and rhythms. So little is known about the use of voice by quadrumana during the season of love, that we have no means of judging whether the habit of singing was first acquired by our male or female ancestors. Women are generally thought to possess sweeter voice than men and, as far as this serves as any guide, we may infer that they first acquired musical power in order to attract the other sex. But if so, this must have occurred long ago, before our ancestors had become sufficiently human to treat and value their women merely as useful slaves. The impassioned orator or bard, or musician, when he with his voiced tones and cadences excites the strongest emotions in his hearers, little suspects that it was the same means by which his half-human ancestors long ago aroused each other's ardent passions during their courtship and rivalry."

"Naturalists are much divided with respect to the object of the singing of birds. Montagu and a few others maintained that the males of song-birds and of many others do not in general search for the female, but on the contrary their business in the spring is to perch on some conspicuous spot, breathing out their full and amorous notes, which by instinct the female knows and repairs to the spot to choose her mate. Jenner Weir informed me that 'this is certainly the case with nightingale.' Beepsteen, who kept birds during life, asserts that 'the female canary always chooses the best singers, and that in a state of nature the female finch selects that male out of a hundred, whose notes please her most.' There can be no doubt that birds closely attend to each other's song. Weir had told me of the case of a bull-finch 'which had been taught to pipe a German Waltz and he was a good performer. When this bird was first introduced into a room where other birds were kept and when he began to sing, all the others consisting of about twenty linets and carriers, ranged themselves on the nearest side of their cages, and listened with the greatest attention to the new performer.' Many naturalists believe that the singing of birds is almost exclusively the effect of "rivalry" and "emulation," and not for the sake of charming their mates. This was the opinion of Daines Burrington and White of Selborne, who both especially attended to this subject. Burrington, however, admitted that 'superiority in song gives to birds an amazing ascendency over others,' as it is well-known to bird-catchers. It is certain that there is an intense degree of rivalry between the males in their singing. Bird-fanciers match their birds to see which will sing longest. I was told by Yarell that a first-rate bird sometimes sings till he drops down almost dead, or according to Beepsteen, quite dead from rupturing a vessel in the lungs. Whatever the case may be, male birds, as I hear from Weir, often die suddenly during the season of song. That the habit of singing is sometimes quite independent of love is clear, for a sterile hybrid canary-bird has been described as singing whilst viewing itself in a mirror, and then dashing at its own image; it likewise attacked with fury a female canary when put in the same cage."

The above facts, which are so philosophically and studiously expounded, show that we do like the sounds which habitually accompany agreeable and pleasurable feelings, and dislike those sounds which invariably accompany disagreeable and painful feelings. Music adopts all the sounds which we like and intensifies them more and more when it ascends to its higher and higher forms, and becomes music or language of emotion simply in virtue of thus intensifying them. Music is rationally supposed to have influenced man in making those involved cadences of common conversation by which he conveys his complex thoughts and feelings.

To return to the subject in hand we say that we have but a very small portion of the ancient music. A large quantity of classic music must ever remain sealed to us, because we neither possess the means to collect and decipher many manuscripts and music which are secreted in different quarters like a sacred and invaluable trust, nor we are conversant with the knowledge of old works and notations, nor we have any standard work and notation of the modern origin in force. These difficulties are partly due to the proverbial selfishness of Indian musicians who do not like to part with the secret of their art, and partly to the want of taste in the public at large. If we attempt to write on Indian music as a science, independently of European researches and resources, we have but very scanty means at our command to produce even a small treatise. Such a treatise can not stand the critical test of a devout student of music and convince an impartial judge that the modern treatment of it is as thoughtful as it was in the times when Shiva, Hanumán, Kanád, Nárad, Bharat, and Parijátak flourished. Kanád was right in saying that sound was propagated by undulations that sent wave after wave in all directions from a central point. Some of the maxims, which we find in some of these authors, are presented in an unorganized form, or they stand as isolated dogmas or empirical generalizations which are neither so clearly apprehended, nor so much respected, as they would be, were they reduced to some intelligible form.

When we unbiasedly look at the researches of Kanád and others we are forced to admit that the ancients had made a considerable progress in music, not only as an art, but as a science in the remotest period of their civilization. It is deplorable that the data, which must have been adópted by Kanád and others to propound their theory of sound, should permanently be lost and nothing left, except the simple generalizations of their researches, to show and prove specifically what were the means which had caused a theory of sound probable at such a remote time of antiquity.

Wilson said : "Music of Sanskrit composition must ever remain inadequately represented by any other tongue."

Max Muller says : "The orthography of Sanskrit is the most complete and the language inflectionable."

When Sanskrit language has been admitted on all hands to be one of the most inflective and grammatically finished languages of the civilized world, it seems inexplicable why its not only co-existent but the parent-stock—the language of emotion—is discarded and condemned as barbarous. It cannot be said to be a sane proposition that Indians were civilized only in expressing their intellect or thought but they were barbarous in expressing their feeling or emotion. These two interwoven elements of vocal expressions are the necessary result of civilized life.

Says Jones :—"Amongst Hindus of early ages music appears to have attained a theoretical precision at a period, when even Greece was little removed from barbarism."

It is not too much it we postulate that the acheivement of the ancients must have been possible only inductively, and not otherwise, because, there is no deduction in the absence of induction. The two have a common root and neither can go without the other.

We assert without fear of contradiction that the music and works on it, which have come down to us, if properly fathomed to the bottom, abound in artistic, scientific, and philosophical speculations. It is a fact that the works have scarcely been brought forward in a connected form, so we are obliged to collect their tenets more from a number of scattered fragments which are dispersed through works on mythology, theology, and literature, than from a treatise exclusively devoted to the subject. When mythology and theology are duly eliminated, it seems simply absurd to deny that the ancients had made a considerable progress in music as an art as well as a science. Their inventions and researches of the musical scale, their treatment of the gamut, their distinction between sound and noise, their composition of so many Vratas, Gitas &c. and their selection of many Rágas and Tálas are too thoughtful to be trifled with.

It was not known only to Pythagoras and early geometers that the length of a free vibrating string influenced the pitch of the note it produced, but the ancient Aryas had discoverd a connection between the pitch and its number of vibrations.

Captain Day, in his notes on Indian music says: "As regards the apparent similarity of the Indian and European scales, it must be remembered that the later were evolved, in process of time, from those of Ancient Greece. * * * The historian Strabo shows that the Greek influence extended to India, and also that Greek musicians of a certain school attributed the greater part of the science of music to India."

We give in the next chapter a comparative ratio of European and Hindu theories of gamut, not with an object to refute the European theory, which is presumed to be correct, but to support the above facts.

It should be borne in mind that, however the ratios may theoretically differ between the European and Hindu theories of (Grám) gamut, practically that is not the case. That which is discordant to one is also to the other. The difference lies only in composing the notes which form a musical piece, but not in the notes themselves.

II

THE THEORY AND PRACTICE OF MUSICAL SOUNDS

The name of "gamut" (Gráma or Saptak) is given to a series of seven sounds which succeed each other, proceeding from the grave to the acute, or *vice versa.* These sounds are comprised between two extreme Notes having the following character, namely, the highest sound is produced by double the number of the vibrations of the lowest. The most acute Note being the eighth of the series, the two extreme Notes are the octave of each other : one being the lower octave, the other higher one. If we now start from eighth Note, considered as the starting-point of a series of Notes similar to the first, and if we take care to strike a new series of Notes having between them the same degree of pitch as the first, it will be noticed that the impression left on the ear by their sucession, has the greatest analogy with that which results from hearing the Notes of the first scale. A melody, thus formed of a succession of Notes taken from the first series, preserves the same character if it is sung or played with the help of Notes of the same order taken in the second series. It would be the same if we formed in a similar manner one or more Gamuts, higher or lower.

A musical scale of the above kind formed of consecutive Gamuts, is unlimited, or at least has no other limits than those of our power of perceiving sounds.

We may remark that the Note from which we start to form a gamut is arbitrary. (In Europe for practical purpose they have conventionally adopted a fixed point of departure), because there is a vast number of similar musical scales placed by nature at the disposal of musicians.

In Europe the seven sounds are called C, D, E, F, G, A, and B. These letters are repeated for each octave. The same sounds are also called by other names, which are derived from the first syllable of each line of a Latin hymn, attributed to Paulus Diaconus.

The European and Hindu theories of Gamut (Saptak), if explained mathematically, stand thus :—

	1	2	3	4	5	6	7	8
European—	Do.	Ri.	Mi.	Fá.	Sol.	Lá.	Si.	Do.
	24	27	30	32	36	40	45	48
	1	2	3	4	5	6	7	8
Hindu	Sá.	Ri.	Gá.	Má.	Pá.	Dhá.	Ni.	Sá.
	22	26	29	31	35	39	42	44

Before going further, we give below the names of the 22 Shrutis (literally heard or perceived) as we find them in old works. The names are tolerably thus :—

(1) Tivrá, (2) Kamudvati, (3) Mandá, (4) Chhandovati, (5) Dayávti, (6) Ranjani, (7) Ratiká, (8) Roudri, (9) Krodhi, (10) Bajriká, (11) Prasárani, (12) Priti, Marjni, (14) Kshiti, (15) Raktá, (16) Sandipini, (17) Alápini, (18) Mandati, (19) Rohini, (20) Rammyá, (21) Ugrá and (22) Kshobhini.

Whatever Note we might conventionally select as a true Sá. (C) having a certain number of vibrations, the relation of all other Notes to it could be expressed mathematically, and this is done in the above theories.

The ratio of one sound to another is the determining cause of consonance and dissonance, or in other words, a musical scale is the melodious relationship of the number of vibrations (per second) of the Notes of which it (musical scale) is formed.

Sá. Ri. Gá, Má. Pá. Dhá. and Ni. are the initial letters of the names by which the seven sounds of Saptak (Gamut) are called, these letters are repeated for each octave. The names of the Notes seem to be as arbitrary as they are in Europe, though attempts have been made by early Hindus to justify them. The names are thus :—1st. Khashṭaja or Kharaja or Shaḍaja, 2nd. Rikhaba, 3rd, Gándhára, 4th. Madhyama, 5th. Pạnchama, 6th. Dhaivat and 7th. Nikháda.

Practically speaking, all the sounds (which are given in the above theories), in spite of their respective differences in the ratio of the number of vibrations per second which correspond to each of them, are classed—Shudh-Svaras (tones) and Komal-Svaras (half-tones or semi-tones). The Saptak (Diatonic scale) consists of seven Notes out of which five are tones—2nd Ri. 3rd. Ga. 5th Pa. 6th Dha. and 7th Ni.—and two are semi-tones 4th Ma. and the 8th or the first Sá. Excepting the 4th and the 8th or the first, which are already Komal (flat) or semi-tones, we can reduce or flatten the remaining five tones to ten semi-tones, and thus get in all twelve Notes (Chromatic Scale).

The above classification is in complete correspondence with the same that is adopted in Europe. But the peculiarity of the Indians is that though the Panchama (Sol. or G), when reduced to a half-tone, ought to be named Komal-Panchama (G Fl.), they in its stead call it Tivra or Kaḍi-Madhyama (F Sh.). All the semi-tones, excepting the two in the Diatonic scale—Sá and Má., are recognized by the name of Komal prefixed to the five tones of the Diatonic scale; and why this half-Panchama (G Fl.) is excluded from the general rule, we do not know. Besides, no reasonable cause is shown in old works for this departure. It seems to be more conventional than logical to call a semi-tone once sharp (Tivra) and once flat (Komal), for we do not raise E (Gá.) and B (Ni.) to E sharp and B sharp, nor do we reduce F (Má.) and C (Sá.) to F flat and C flat

The names of the 12 Notes are these :—

(1) Shaḍja (C), (2) Komal-Rikhab (C Sh.), (3)

Rikhab (D), (4) Komal-Gandhára (D Sh.), (5) Gandhára (E), (6) Madhyam (F), (7) Tivra-Madhyam (F Sh.), (8) Pancham (G), (9) Komal-Dhaivat (G Sh.), (10) Dhaivat (A), (11) Komal-Nikhád (A Sa.) (12) Nikhád (B), and (13) Shaḍja (C, repetition of the first in the second octave).

The so-called sixteen and twenty-seven Shrutis, which are borrowed from some old works with much noise, are more fabulous than thoughtful, and the less we discuss them, the better. They run thus :—

Sá.	Ri.	Ga.	Ma.	Pa.	Dha.	Ni.
1	3	3	2	1	3	3—16
1	5	5	5	1	5	5—27

Physiologically, the range of an ordinary appreciation of tones lies between 40 and 4,000 vibrations a second *i. e.* between the lowest bass (C 33 vibrations) and the highest treble (C^5 4,224 vibrations of the Piano) : tones above and below these, even when audible, being distinguished from each other with great difficulty.

According to Indian idea of music, the limit of a voice (generally matured male) is three Saptaks (scales), one below (Anudátta), the register (Svaritta) and one above (Udátta) it. This is the general arrangement of their instruments. Indians were not satisfied with the 12 Notes (Chromatic scale), but increased the number of Notes under the names of Murchhaná (literally swoon, musically $\frac{1}{4}$th part of a tone) The number of Murchhanás is 21, but it ought to be 12 only. These Murchhanás are distributed over all the Rágas with the greatest advantage. The Indian scale with the aforesaid addition stands thus—5 tones, 2 semi-tones, or 12 Notes and 12 Murchhanás. We shall speak of the latter shortly.

Indian music is divided into two branches, *i. e.* Rágas (literally Ranj to please) and Ráginis or Bháryás (literally females). The characteristic distinction between a Rága and Rágini (diminutive of Rága), is that the former has in additions to tones and semitones, which are the only constituents of the latter, the principles of A'rohan (ascent or going from the grave to the acute), of A'vrohan (descent or going from the acute to the grave), of Murchhaná ($\frac{1}{4}$th part of a tone), of Gamak or Ghrashṭaka (literally that which slips, musically a connection of two or more Notes), of Meenḍ or Minḍ (literally resonant, musically a joining of two or more Notes on certain musical instruments), and of the total absence of accidentals.

Gamak or Ghrashtak—or Meenḍ (now called Minḍ) is a way of sliding from a Note to other or others at a stretch ; it is not jumping, but it is an exceedingly attractive form of connecting two or more Notes. Minḍ or Ghrashṭaka is an impossibility on the Organ, Piano, Harmonium, Concertina and such other instruments, as long as they stand in the condition in which we find them. With due admiration for the real worth of European instruments, we are reluctantly constrained to say that, however slow or fast we may be in traversing from a Note to a Note on these instruments, the impression left on the ear is always of jumping, and not that of connecting two Notes. To give an idea of Minḍ or Ghasiṭ, corruption of Ghrashṭak, we give below a way to show how it is produced.

(1st)—SIMPLE JUMPING OF DIATONIC SCALE :—

1	2	3	4	5	6	7	8
Sá.	Ri.	Gá.	Má.	Pá.	Dhá.	Ni.	Sá.

(2nd)—SIMPLE JUMPING OF CHROMATIC SCALE :—

1	2	3	4	5	6	7	8
Sá.	K.-Ri.	Ri.	K.-Gá.	Gá.	Má.	T.-Má.	Pá.
9	10	11	12	13			
K.-Dhá..	Dhá.	K.-Ni.	Ni.	Sá.			

(3rd)—TRAVERSING BY MIND. DIATONIC SCALE :—

I 2 3 4 5 6 7 8

Sá. —Ri.—Gá.——Má.—Pa'.—Dha'.——Ni.—Sa'.

(4th)—Traversing by Meed : Chromatic scale :—

1 2 3 . 4 5 6 7
Sá.—K.-Ri.——Ri.—K.-Gá.—Gá.—Má.—T.-Má.—

8 9 10 11 12 13
Pá.—K.-Dhá.—-Dhá.—K.-Ni.——Ni.—Sá.

It is not fixed to produce a Meeḍ or Ghasiṭ of a particular Note from a particular Note, but the production depends on the capability of voice and instruments, and on the construction of Rágas. We shall speak of this subject in its proper course. It is not necessary to say that Meeḍ or Ghasiṭ may be an ascent as well as a descent. The line in the third and the fourth diagrams, which connects one Note to other or others, is the Meeḍ or Ghasiṭ. Many persons believe that in traversing by a Meeḍ or a Ghasiṭ from a Note to a Note or others, the intermediate Note or Notes must be touched, in spite of our desire, but practically that is not the case. Suppose, we ascend by a Meeḍ or Ghasiṭ from Sá (C) to Má (F), we can touch Má. (F) from Sá (C) without producing the intermediate Notes —K-Ri. (C-Sh.), Ri. (D), K.-Gá. (D-Sh.) and Gá. (E). The same remark is applicable to a Meeḍ or a Ghasiṭ in descent. This fact can easily be verified on the fretted string instruments, such as Biná, Satára, &c.

Ghasiṭ is a peculiar way of sliding from a point to a point or points on the unfretted string instruments. It is a substitute for Meeḍ, and we shall speak of it presently.

Meeḍ and Ghasiṭ have been so much attended to by the Indian artists that they have constructed special instruments for them, such as Biná (Rudra Biná in Madras, Jantra, a primitive form, in Gujrat), Rabába, Sur-singár (not extant), Saroda, Satára, Sárangi (Indian fiddle), etc. The word Meeḍ, corruption of *Mand* (soft or dim), shows why it is not intended for a large audience, notwithstanding its charming effect. Credulous people fancy that the Biná is played by ten fingers, but only six fingers are used—3 of the right hand and 3 of the left hand. The usual musical limit of touching the Notes from a fret of the Biná or Satára by a Meeḍ, is five Notes, for instance from Sá (C) to Pá. (G). This limit is considerably changed when the artist moves from steal-wire to brazen-wire: this is due to the relative differences of densities, dimensions, and tensions of the respective metals. In Rabába, Saroda, Sárangi and such other instruments, or in the instruments having no frets, the limit of a Ghasiṭ is not fixed, because it can be produced by slipping over the wire from a point to any point, and not by stretching or drawing aside the wire at a point, which is done in the case of a Meeḍ. The characteristic distinction between a Meeḍ and a Ghasiṭ, is that the former connects the Notes by the tension of a wire ; while the latter joins the Notes by reducing the length of a wire. Many artists prefer Meeḍ to Ghasiṭ, but musically speaking, the question seems to be more of taste than that of any intrinsic value ; besides, certain instruments are fit only for Meeḍ, and certain for Ghasiṭ. The instruments, which are used for Meeḍ are long, fretted, (excluding Táus) and not played by a bow, and those, which are used for Ghasiṭ, are short, unfretted, stringed (not always metalic) and generally played by a bow. It may be remarked in passing that the Ghasiṭ can be produced on Biná and Satára, despite their frets ; but the impression left on the ear, is not the same like the one produced by the Meeḍ.

The male voice is more adapted to Meeḍ or Ghasiṭ than the female voice. This is due to the relative shortness of the female vocal cords. We are not in a position to say that Meeḍ and Ghasiṭ are produced by the voice, but we are sure tnat the Ghasit is produced by it.

Since we want to speak at some length on Meeḍ or Ghasiṭ, we may describe the vocal sound in a few words.

In the voice, as in other sounds, we distingnish (1) Loudness. This depends on the strength of the expiratory blast. (2) Pitch. This depends on the length and tension of the vocal cords. Their length may be regarded as constant, or varying only with age. It consequently determines the range only of the voice, and not the particular Note given out at any time. The shrill voice of the child is determined by the shortness of the cords in infancy, and the voices of a soprano, tenor, and baritone are all dependent on the respective lengths of their vocal cords. Their tension is, on the contrary, variable ; and the chief problem connected with the voice, refers to variations in the tension of the vocal cords. (3) Quality or *Timbre*. This depends on the number and character of the over-tones accompanying any fundamental Note sounded, and it is determined by a variety of circumstances, chief among which is the physical quality of the cords.

According to Max Muller, "the average length of the vocal cords in man is $18\frac{1}{2}$ m. m. when relaxed, $23\frac{1}{2}$ m. m. when stretched ; in woman, $12\frac{2}{3}$ m. m. when relaxed, $15\frac{2}{3}$ m. m. when stretched : thus giving a difference of about one-third between the two sexes, which accounts for the different pitch of male and female voice."

Music with Meeḍ requires more exertion than without it, and such music is also slow. The same may be said of Ghasiṭ. Excellence in Meeḍ or Ghasiṭ is measured by the number of Notes connected in a given time.

It is accordingly probable, that the Meeḍ or Ghasiṭ is developed to express energy, resolution and decision. The action of the vocal muscles, which produces the Meeḍ or Ghasiṭ, is analogous to the muscular action which produces the energetic, resolute, and decisive movements of the body indicating these states of mind. Meeḍ or Ghasiṭ is so impressive and touching that it is redundant to say, that emotions are equally, if not better, expressed by connecting one Note to other or others, as by simple jumping from a Note to other or others.

Indian music appears to have been formed in two branches—Aláp (resonant) or Joḍ (literally joint, musically something like prelude) and Dhrupad (literally settled or moderate, musically a poetry set to music in Rágas and in certain Tálas, but not in Rágiṇis). The difference between Joḍ and Dhrupad, is that the former is completely free from poetry, and it is less restricted by a Tála (time-measure); the latter is fully restricted by a Tála, and it has less Meeḍs or Ghasiṭs. Joḍ can be sung or played only in Bilambpad (slow-going or *largo*) and Madhya (middle-moderate or *adante*) but not in Palut or Drut (fast or *presto*); while Dhrupad can pass through these three stages. Joḍ cannot be sung or played very fast, because it is simply impracticable to connect Notes with a rapidity which Palut (fast) presupposes. For instance—

Meeḍ—	1	3	5	5	6	8	8	10	12
	Sá.—	Ri.—	Gá.,	Gá.-	Má.-	Pá.,	Pá.—	Dhá.—	Ni.
Jamping—	1	3	5	5	6	8	8	10	12
	Sá.	Ri.	Gá.,	Ga.	Má.	Pá.,	Pá.	Dhá.	Ni.

Joḍ music is a later or advanced form of Dhrupad, and Dhrupad is a later form of the original Pads or Bhajans (prayer or praise). The Toma or Noma, the first word of Jod, looks to be an alteration of the Sanskrit "Oma," the letters Ṭ, Ḍ, T, Th, D, N, R, L, &c., and their peculiar combinations in Joḍ, are either arbitrary, or they are borrowed from the vocabulary of drum. Joḍ music is really charming for its fulness in Meeḍ or Ghasiṭ, and for its Murchhanás, in spite of the absence of words and of the technicalities of Tála (time). But now-a-days this class of music is very rare, it is found to a limited extent in the instrumental music, such as Biná, Saroda, Satára, &c.

The string instruments, which are not handled by a bow, are played very fast without Meeḍ or Ghasiṭ by Javá (a triangle piece of bone or ivory used on Rabába and Sarod) and Mijráfa or Nakhi (a triangle ring of wire used on Biná and Sátar). The Javá and Nakhi require but a very short time to give a stroke out and into a tensed cord of the aforesaid instruments. This facility of giving the strokes swiftly, has been taken advantage of by the instrumentalists to compose their own tunes, called Zálás and Gats. The former are played with Joḍ in Madhya (moderate time) like its accompaniment or complement on the last wire of Biná (in this instrument the last finger of the left hand is also used to touch a Chikárá), Sarod, and Satára ; the latter are played in Rágas and Ra'ginis. The Gats are nicely formed through they have only four technicalities, *i.e.* Da' Ḍa', Did, and Ḍid or Ḍada'. The stroke which is given in, is named Da', and the out one is called Ḍa'. When the in and out strokes are combined and produced at the same time which Da' or Ḍa' takes, the combination is called Diḍ ; and this process of giving the strokes in and out if reversed, goes by the name of Ḍid or Ḍada'. There are hundreds of Gats in Sarod and Sata'ra music which are really artistic on account of their Meeḍ, Ghasiṭ, Murchhana' and Murki—an advanced form of the trill.

Murki (a collective name of Giṭakaḍi, Jam-jama', Khaṭka' and Sa'sa or A'sa) is less valued and respected than Meeḍ and Ghasiṭ. Musically speaking, Murki is eqnally, if not more, attractive as Meeḍ and Ghasiṭ. The cause of this disparagement seems to be that it is of later formation, and the female voice is better adapted to it than the male voice. This is due to the relative shortness of the female vocal cords. The differeuce in adaptations to Meeḍ or Ghasiṭ and Murki by the male and the female voices respectively, is a subject which admits of a generalization :—*All things being equal, no longer and the thicker the sonorous body, the better the Meeḍ or Ghasiṭ.—All things being equal, the shorter and the thinner the sonorous body, the better the Murki.*

To render the above proposition more rigorous, we must define the intensity or loudness and the pitch of sound in the words of Acoustics. The intensity of sound is determined by the amplitude of the vibrations : the greater the disturbance of the air or other medium, the intenser the sound. The pitch of sound is ascertained by the wave-length of the vibrations : the shorter the wavelength, the larger the number of consecutive vibrations which fall upon the ear in a second—the higher the pitch.

All things being equal, the longer the wave-length of the sonorous vibrations, the better the Meeḍ or Ghasiṭ—All things being equal, the shorter the wave-length of the sonorous vidrations, the better the Murki.

The above proposition can easily be verified by changing the length and thickness of the wire of a string instrument. Even the change of thickness will give us an idea of it. It is probable that Murki is expressive of gentler and less active feelings, and that is so because, it implies the smaller muscular vivacity, due to a lower mental energy. Murki has wonderfully progressed in recent times owing to a special branch of music called Ṭappá (literally stage). They have considerably lessened the rigidity of Tála in order to encourage Murki. Music with Murki is slower than with Meeḍ or Ghasiṭ. Excellence in Murki is measured by the rapidity of strokes on two or three Notes in a given time. When this motion is moderate it is called Gitakaḍi or Jam-jamá, and when it is the lowest it is called Khaṭká or Sás or A'sa.

The distinction between Ṭappá and Khyál (literally attention, musically a later form of Dhrupad), is that in the former there are more Murkis than Meeds or Ghasiṭs, and it generally consists of Rágnis ; while the latter is always sung in Rágas, and it has more Ghasiṭs or Meeds than Murkis. The above distinction is not strictly observed now-a-days, for any kind of Chija (poetry set to music) is sung in Rágas as well as in Ráginis.

There is a class of singing which goes by the

name of Tirvaṭ-Taráná and Chatarang. The former is formed only of the drum technicalities, or is a form of long-past poetry ; the latter is a combination of poetry and the drum technicalities. This kind of singing is performed very swiftly, and Tála (time measures) seems to be the principal item to it, though it is sung in Rágas as well as in Ráginis.

The singing of Sargams (the initial letters of the Notes to be touched are set to music in Rágas and Ra'ginis—this way of singing seems to be ancient) is more accurate in Karnatic music than in Hindustani one, so far as the names of the Notes sung are concerned, but so far as the composition of Notes goes, Karnatic music cannot be said with impartiality to be superior to Hindustani.

Pada or Bhajan (oldest form of praise and prayer, or love-song of Krishna) Ṭhumri (love-song), Gazal, Rekta', &c. &c. are very common though musical. They are identical more with Nrtya (dancing) and Ha'va-Bha'va or A'rath (gesticulation) than with classical music. There are many songs of this description which are really lovely for their poetry and music.

The shaking of the body is one of the necessary results of certain passions, or perhaps all passions when pushed to an extreme. It is superfluous to remind ourselves that we have the trembling of anger, of fear, of hope, of joy ; and that the vocal muscles being implicated with the rest of the body, the voice too becomes tremulous. This trembling (*Kamp*) of voice is not only taken advantage of by the Indian musicians, but its opposite—the principle of steadiness (Sthirata' or Thairna')—is marvellously observed by them.

The Principle of Ta'na (literally stretching or extending musically variation) is the common property of Khya'l, Ṭappa', Ṭhumri, Pada, &c. &c.

Ta'na or variability of pitch (simple jumping) is a characteristie of emotional speech. Instead of discussing this subject with its metaphysics, we must be content with the knowledge that the muscular excitement is shown not only in the strength of contraction, but also in the rapidity with which different muscular adjustments succeed each other.

The principle of A'rohan (ascent) and A'vrohan (descent) is so strict that even a slight change alters the Ra'ga into other Ra'ga or Ra'gini, as the case may be. Instead of treating this principle at length, suffice it to say that while speech is comparatively monotonous, singing makes use of wider intervals. Speaking voice seldom wanders over more than three (in some cases four) notes, above or below its medium, and that too by small steps, but the singing voice not only wanders over higher and lower Notes of its register, but goes from one Note to others by larger intervals.

Before going further, we must not omit to say that those which ordinarily go by the names of Ráginis are, practically speaking, Rágas. They are called Ráginis simply because their names end in "*I*," or possibly they may have been composed by women, or probably they may have been formed by men and sung in praise or love of women, as some names of the Ra'ginis suggest, such as Goudi or Gouri, Renki, Dhánashri or Dhànyastri, Shri or Stri, Lalita', Ma'lashri &c. The real Ráginis—diminutive of Ra'gas—are known by the name of Dhun or Jilhá. The characteristic distinction between a Rág or Rágini and a Dhun or Jilhá, is that the former has a fixed number of Notes, no accidentals, a regulated arrangement of traversing the Notes upwards and downwards, and above all a number of Murchhanás (¼ part of a tone) ; while the latter is free from so many restrictions.

The Murchhanás (¼ part of a tone) are so charmingly distributed over different Ra'gas, that if taken away from them they (Ra'gas) considerably lose their effect. Murchhaná is always touched by Meed or Ghasit, but not otherwise. Those who have practised Indian Ra'gas, can easily understand why Darbári-

Kánaḍa is reduced to Sind-Bhairvi (a Jilhá) by eliminating only the Murchhanás. A mere taking away of the Murchhanás changes Sáhána:Kánáḍá into Káfi (a Jilhá), Jogia into Bhairvi (a Jilhá), Bágeshri-Kánáḍá into Báhár (a Jilhá) &c.

It is really a very difficult, if not an impossible, task to deal with the above facts without entering deeply into the primary and secondary composition of Rágas. The scope of this discussion does not allow us to do so, which would turn it into a treatise on Indian music. However, without unnecessarily swelling the body of this discussion, we shall briefly treat this subject in its proper place.

It is an open secret to those who have practised music (as an art), that the second stage of their progressive and successful study in the Saptak (Gamut), is the acquisition of a wonderful power to perceive the least difference between the unision (first acquirement) and the 8th Note of the Chromatic scale, or between Sá. (C) and Pa. (G). The third stage is generally Ga. (E). Broadly speaking, the unison and its octave are not separate Notes, but the latter reinforces some of the harmonics of the former. The wonderful sympathy of Sá. (C) with Gá. (E) and Pá. (G), which is called in Acoustics simple ratio or Harmony, is not only known to Physicists, but it is experienced by keen musicians to a great advantage as a test of the accuracy of a musical scale.

In place of the tuning-forks, which are used in Europe to adjust a musical scale, Indians use their acquisition of the perception of relation or sympathy of Sá. (C) with Ga (E) and Pá. (G) in the following simple but certain method to attune a musical scale with the greatest possible precision. First they adjust Sá. (C), Gá. (E), and Pá, (G), or A B C of Indian music (the perfect major chord), and then the remaining four notes—Ri. (D), Má (F), Dha'. (A), and Ni. (B) are tested thus :—Ri. (D) is tested with Dha. (A), Ma'. (F) with Sá. (C), and Gá. (E) with Ni. (B).

The sympathy between Ri. (D) and Dha. (A), Ma.

(F) and Sá. (C), Gá. (E) and Ni. (B), artistically speaking, is the same which exists between Sá. (C) and Pá. (G).

The above method teaches us that the 12 Notes (Chromatic scale) stand in sympathy with each other in the following way :—

	1		8	1		5
1	Sá. (C)	with	Pá. (G)	Sá. (C)	with	Gá. (E)
2	K. Ri.	„	K. Dha	K.-Ri.	„	Má.
3	Ri.	„	Dhá.	Ri.	„	T.-Má.
4	K.-Gá.	„	K.-Ni.	K.-Gá.	„	Pá.
5	Gá.	„	Ni.	Gá.	„	K.-Dhá.
6	Má.	„	Sá.	Má.	„	Dhá.
7	T.-Má.	„	K.-Ri.	T.-Má.	„	K.-Ni.
8	Pá.	„	Ri.	Pá.	„	Ni.
9	K.-Dhá.	„	K.-Ga′.	K.-Dhá.	„	Sá.
10	Dhá.	„	Ga′.	Dhá.	„	K.-Ri.
11	K.-Ni.	„	Ma.	K.-Ni.	„	Ri.
12	Ni.	„	T. Ma.	Ni.	„	K.-Gá.
13	Sá. (C)	„	Pa. (G)	Sá. (C)	„	Gá. (E)

The above method is called, in practical music, Sur-Bevrá or Bevdá,—this word (literally signifying double) is not an appropriate term.

The above description is a practical illustration of the *nodes* and *ventral segments* of the science of Acoustics, or of the perfect major chord, as it is called by some scientists.

We shall be wanting in doing justice to our immediate subjet in hand if we do not speak a word about the variety intensity and velocity of sound, and a word about noise.

The variety of sound depends on the forms and nature of the sonorous body, and on the way in which the sound is conveyed to our ears. The intensity of sound varies according to the density of the medium which propagates it. The velocity of sound is uniform at every portion of the distance traversed, and it is the same with sharp and dull sounds. Neither the line, nor the precision of a piece of music, is altered whatever may be its distance from the listener; when the distance increases, all the sounds are lessened in the same degree.

Noise frequently proceeds from a confused mixture of different sounds, which the ear can scarcely distinguish from each other; or in other words, noise is nothing but a sound the vibrations ot which do not last long enough to enable the hearer to appreciate the relative pitch.

Max Muller says :—"Noise is produced by irregular impulses imparted to the air, and tone is produced by regular periodical (issochronous) vibrations of elastic air."

According to N. Lockyer :—When two melodious sounds follow each other at a sufficiently short interval, the sensations are fused into one. When two sounds not quite in tune are struck together, the interference of the vibrations gives rise to an alternating rise and fall of the sound, known in Acoustics as "beats." When the beats follow each other, as rapidly as 132 in a second, they cease to be recognized, that is to say, the sensations which they cause, become fused. Before they disappear, they give a peculiar disagreeable roughness to the sound. The pleasure, which is given by musical sounds, depends largely on the absence of this incomplete fusion of the sensations

P Blaserna says :—" In the music of all nations two unfailing characters are found, rythmic movement and procedure by determinate intervals. The first appertains also to the speech and the other acts of man as walking, swimming, dancing, etc.; the second belongs exclusively to music."

" All nations have selected notes to be used, have collected together those intended to be together, and have thus created one or more *musical scales.*"

" By musical scale is meant the collection of all the notes, comprised between the fundamental note and its octave. * * The study of the musical scale gives one of the most important and concise means of judging of the musical state of a nation. * * * "

"It seems strange that a few notes put together in a musical scale should be able to acquire a true importance in the study of music. If it were a question of an assemblage of notes made at hazard or capriciously, the matter would be of no importance; but the musical scale is always the product of the musical activity of many centuries. It is not established before music, but is developed with it. A very perfect form of music must have a perfect scale; an imperfect and primitive form of music, on the other hand, will have a scale of little value."

"A musical sound is always a compound sound, its vibrations are more or less complicated, and it by itself constitutes a true harmony. * * It follows that in combining two, three, or more musical sounds in order to form a chord, it is not enough that the fundamental notes should bear simple ratios to each other, but it is also necessary that the harmonies should obey this law.".

A Bain says:—"Since a sweet note is already a harmony, the influence of the recognized musical concords is not something absolutely new, but an extension of the same harmonizing process. * * * The simple musical ratios ($\frac{2}{1}$ $\frac{3}{2}$ $\frac{4}{3}$ &c.) express the best chords, and, as the ratios are further removed from simplicity, the harmonious effect gives place to discord, which is at last painful."

We give in the next chapter an analysis of a few simple and compound Rágas.

III

THE RĀGAS AND THEIR FORMATIONS

The object of selecting the following Rágas for our discussion, is to show that there is but very little difference of opinion on their respective Sargams or skeletons. These Rágas, which are familiar to many, admit of being explained in the following tables without intricate technicalities. There are many finished compound Rágas, but they cannot be explained without exhaustive details, which do not form the subject-matter of this discussion. However, it should be borne in mind, that whatever conclusions we may arrive at after discussing the Rágas given below, they will hold good with all Rágas. which are practised, and not simply theorized.

It will not be out of place here to state, that there is a slight difference of opinion in the Sargams or skeletons of some of the Rágas which are practised by artistes of different schools. This difference is considerably due to the oral transmission af Rágas for many generations, although they were once committed in writing, and not orally taught, as they are done even at the present day.

All Rágas are divided into four divisions—1st Odava (consisting of 5 Notes), 2nd Kha'ḍava or Shoḍava (consisting of 6 Notes), 3rd Sanipurná (consisting of 7 Notes), and the 4th Sankirna (literally gleaned, consisting of seven or more Notes, and their arrangement of ascent and descent is not the same which is in the first three divisions, and, therefore, we call them Misra, or compound Rágas),

In order to understand the following three tables, let us refresh our memory by saying that the Saptak (Diatonic scale) consists of 5 tones and 2 semitones, or 12 Notes (Chromatic scale), the 13th is the repetition of the first in the second octave ; and that the

Indians call the 7th Note (which is a semitone, and ought to be named Komal-Komal-Pancham (G Fl.) Tivra or Kaḍi-Madhyam (F Sh.)

The arrangement, which is adopted in the following tables, is so simple that no lengthy explanation is needed. The Rágas are not arranged in an alphabetical order, but they are given under the four heads Oḍhava, Khaḍava, Sampurna, and Sankirna with the numbers and names of the Notes which they cover. In the first three classes, which are given in the first table, the order of ascent and descent is the same. In the fourth class (Sankirna), which is given in the second table, the order of descent is different from that of ascent, and some of them contain more than 7 Notes. In the third table, the order of ascent and descent is not the same, and, therefore, they are separated from the Sankirna in the second table. Those who are acquainted with the first two tables, will find no material change in the third table, except Sá (C)—second which is introduced on the second line to indicate the orders of ascent and descent.

The initial letters, which are used in the following tables, and in the subsequent discussion, are these :—(1) S for Shaḍja, (2) K-R for Komal-Rikhab, (3) R for Rikhab, (4) K-G for Komal-Gándhár. (5) G for Gàndhár, (6) M for Madhyam, (7) T-M for Tivra Madhyam, (8) P for Pancham, (9) K-Dh for Komal-Dhaivat, (10) Dh for Dhaivat, (11) K-N for Komal Nikhád, (12) N for Nikhád, and (13) S for Shaḍ which is the repetition of the first in the second octave (Ashṭak).

Since we have concisely defined the artistic meaning of the word Rága in the last chapter, we need not interest ourselves, at this stage of our discussion, with its dialectics ; nor can we venture to trace its origin historially. The most that we can say concerning the word "Rága" (Ranj to please), is that it is intended, from time immemorial for certain combinations of the musical notes with certain elaborations, which we have already briefly stated.

We shall dilate on the subject a little, after studying the skeletons of the Rágas. It is neeessary to say that many of the Rágas, which are given in the table are too old, as their names imply.

However several the above Rágas may appear at first sight, in reality they show formations of certain combinations (chords) of Notes, which we class under the following eleven groups. The groups run thus :—

1st -Rágas with Komal-Rikhab (C Sh), followed by Komal-Gandhára (D Sh.) in ascent, and *vice versa* in descent, are—Jogia or Jilhá-Bhairvi, Gurjari, Toḍi and Mul-táni (K-R, not in ascent).

2nd—Rágas with Komal-Rikhab (C Sh.), followed by Gandhára (E) in ascent, and *vice versa* in descent are—Bibhása, Kámkali or Gunkali, Lalat, Lalita or Lalat, Jaita, Puriá or Renki, Márvá or Dipak, Soheni, Basant, Kálangḍá-Jilhá, Purvi. Dipak or Puriá-Kalyána, Paraja, and Purvi-Hindi.

3rd—Rágas with Komal-Rikhab (C Fl.), preceded by Gandhára (E) in descent, are—Jogiá, Shri, Bhairava or Jilhá-Kalangḍá, Jaitáshri, and Málava.

4th—Rágas with Rikhab (D), followed by Komal-Gandhára (D Sh.) in ascent, and *vice versa* in descent are—Nàyaki-Kánaḍa, Madhur-Kánaḍá, Darbári Kánaḍá or Jilhá Sind-Bhairvi, Sáhánà-Kánaḍá or Jilhá-Ka'fi, Dha'ni Ka'náḍa', Sind-Ka'náḍa' or Jilha'-Ka'fi, and Jejevanti-Kána'ḍ or Jilha'-Sindora'.

5th—Ra'gas with Rikáab (D), Preceded by Komal Gàndha'r (E Fl.) in descent, are—Gàndha'r or Jilhà Sind-Bhairvi, Miàki or Ta'nsen's Malha'r. Pala'sa or Jilhà-Sind-Bhiarvi or Jilha', Dhana'shri or Jilhà Kafi, Jounpuri, Ba'geshri Kànaḍa' or Jilhà-Ba'ha'r, and Bhim pala's or Jilha' Sind Bhairvi.

6th—Ra'gas with Rikhab (D), followed by Ga'ndha'ra (E) in ascent, and *vice versa* in descent, are—Bhupa or Bibha'sa, Bhupáli, Jangalà, Kalyána Bilával Alaiá Bilával Yaman Kalyàna Hàmir, and Nàṭa.

7th—Ra'gas with Rikhab (D), preceded by Ga'ndhára (E) in descent, are—Deshási, Soraṭa or

Jilhá Khamách, Desa, Gounḍ, Kámoḍa, Bhyágaḍá, Bhyága, Shankara′ Bharan, Shankara′, Keda′rà, Chha′ya′, Gounḍ Malha′r, and Gouḍ Sa′rang (G or E is seldom touched in descent.)

8th—Ra′gas with Rikhab (D), followed by Madhyam (F) in ascent, and *vice versa* in descent, are—Megh or Sur-Malha′r, Brinda′bani-Sa′rang, Sur-Sarang, Baḍahans Sa′rang, Madhuma′t Sa′rang, Ra′mada′shi Sa′rang, and Gouḍ-Sa′rang (the last is a misnomer, as it has but very little similarity with other Sa′rangs

9th—Ra′gas without Komal (flat) or Shudha (Diato nic) Rikhab (D), but with Komal Gandha′ra (D Sh.), fol lowed by Madhyam (F) in ascent, and *vice versa* in descent, are—Ma′lkosa and Koushi.

10th—Ra′gas without Komal (flat) or Shudha (Dia tonic) Rikhab (D), but with Gandha′ra (E) follow ed by Madhyam (F) in ascent, and *vice versa* in descent, are—Banga′li Tilanga or Banga′li, Khamba′ti, Deshi and Khamàcha.

11th—Ra′gas without Komal (flat) or Shudha (Diatonic) Rikhab (D), but with Gandha′ra (E), followed by Tivra-Madhyam (F Sh.) in ascent, and *vice versa* in descent, are—Màleshri Hindola, and Pancham.

The classification of all the Rágas into eleven groups, is not quite scientific, but it helps us to draw the following conclusions :—

1st—There is not a Rága, simple (Oḍhava, Khoḍava and Sampurna) or compound (Sankirna), which covers the 12 Notes (Chromatic scale).

2nd—There is not a Rága which has less than six Notes from the register or fundamental S (C) to the S (C) in the second octave.

3rd—There is no Rága which has two Rikhabs (Ds), Komal (flat) and Shudha (Diatonic), or two Dhaivats (As), Komal (flat) and Shudha (Diatonic).

4th—There is a Ra′ga which has two Ga′ndha′rs (Es), Komal (flat) and Shudha (Diatonic)—5th in the second table.

5th—There are Ra'gas which have two Panchams (Gs) or Tivra-Madhyam (F Sh. or G Fl.) and Pancham (G)—9th, 14th, 25th, 26th, 29th, 33rd, 34th, and 39th in the first table, 1st, 3rd, 13th, 17th, 19th, 21st, 23rd, 24th, and 25th in the second table, and 1st, 2nd, 6th, and 9th in the third table.

6th—There are Rágas which have two Nikháds (Bs), Komal (flat) and Shudh (Diatonic)—40th, 41st, and 42nd in the first table, 4th, 6th, 9th, 12th, and 25th in the second table, and 2nd and 3rd in the third table.

7th—Every Rága must have either G (E), M (F), or P (G); and that there is not a Rága which has Shudh-Rikhab (D) without Pancham (G); and that there is not a Rága which has Shudh-Rikhab (D) and Komal-Dhaivat (G Sh) without the intercession of Komal-Gandhára (E Fl).

Instead of giving a long dissertation on the composition of the above Rágas, we allow them to stand as they are. If we attempt to analyse each and every Rága, we are sure to exceed the limits of this discussion, and to launch into deep technicalities, which, from the beginning of our discussion, we have tried our best to avoid without compromising it.

It will be too far to presume to find out a reasonable cause to show why two Rikhabs (Ds), or two Dhaivats (As) were thought to be incongruous or incompatible for a Rága, when two Gandhárs (Es), two Panchams (Gs), and two Nikháds (Bs) were selected to be harmonious or artistic for a Rága. The omission of two Rikhabs (Ds), or of two Dhaivats (As) for a Rága, properly speaking, seems to be a question of mere accident or non-occurrence. However, it can positively be said that most of the Rágas, which are given in the above tables, are highly melodious. These Rágas show a wonderful degree of the thought and labour spent by the by-gone generations in combining the Notes to form so many Rágas without allowing them to be confounded one with the other. It cannot be denied that the said Rágas are quite disṭinct from each other, and that they are highiy finished. It cannot be said with fairness that so many Rágas were the formation of arithmetical calculus, but in reality, they were the necessary manifestation anḍ results of the antiquated Aryan invention and Mahomedan cultivation of music, as an art.

It is opportune to say that instead of simply traversing along the Notes of a Rága in a given time from one octave to other or others, they begin their Rága first in Kharaja (one octave below the register), then they go to A'sthái, corruption of Sthái (the register octave), thence to Antará (one octave above the regisṭer), and finally they end it in S (C or tonic) of the first or register octave : thus covering three octaves, one below (Anudátt) and one above (Udátt) the register (Svaritt) octave.

The ordinary class of singing, which deals in Chija (poetry set to music), and with which we very often come in contact in ordinary performances, is not extended beyond the register (Svaritt) octave. The Chija-singing, as a class, contains more words than music, and the words are done away with in Tána (variatian), in Murki (an advanced form of ṭhe trill), and in Minḍ or Ghasiṭ (not jumping). It is true that Chija-singing of some of the Rágas does not always begin from the register (Svaritt) S or tonic, for instance, in Hámir and Bhupa or Bibhás. These two Rágas generally begin from Dh (A).

To extend the variation of the Notes in a Rága, without breaking through the rigid principle of ascent and descent they go in this way, for instance, in Bhupa or Bibhása (2nd, in the first table) :—

1	3	1	3	5	3	5	8	8	10	13	13	10	8	10	8
S	R	S	R,	G	R	G	P,	P	Dh	S	S,	Dh	P	Dh	P,
10	8	5	8	10	8	5	3	5	3	5	3	1			
Dh	P	G	P,	Dh	P	G	R,	G	R	G	R,	S.			

Bindra'bani-Sa'rang (4th in the first table) :—

1	3	6	8	6	3	3	6	8	8	11	13	13	11
S	R	M	P,	M	R	R	M,	P	P	K-N	S,	S	K-N

8	11	8	6	3	6	3	6	3	1
P	K-N,	P	M	R	M,	R	M	R	S.

Bana'gli (7th in the first table) :—

1	5	6	8	6	5	6	8	11	8	11	13	13	11
S	G	M	P,	M	G	M	P,	K-N	P	K-N	S,	S	K-N

8	6	5	5	6	8	6	8	6	5	1
P	M,	G	G	M	P,	M	P	M	G,	S.

Jogi or Jilha'-Bhairvi (27th in the first table) :—

1	2	4	6	6	8	9	8	8	9	11	13	13	11
S	K-R	K-G	M,	M	P	K-Dh	P,	P	K-Dh	K-N	S,	S	K-N

9	8	9	8	6	4	6	4	2	2	1
K-Dh	P,	K-Dh	P	M	K-G,	M	K-G	K-R	K-R,	S.

Kalya'na (39th in the first table) :—

1	3	5	3	5	7	8	8	10	12	10	12	13	13	12
S	R	G	R,	G	T-M	P	P,	Dh	N	Dh	N,	S	S	N

10	8	10	8	7	5	5	3	1
Dh,	P	Dh	P	T-M,	G	G	R	S.

Alaia'-Bila'val (6th in the second table) :—

1	3	5	8	10	11	12	13	13	12	11	10	8
S	R	G	P,	Dh	K-N	N	S,	S	N	K-N	Dh,	P

10	11	10	10	8	6	5	3	5	8	6	5	5	3	1
Dh	K-N	Dh,	Dh	P	M	G,	R	G	P	M,	G	G	R	S.

Gouḍ-Sa'rang (6th in the third table) :—

1 3 6 5 5 7 8 8 3 1 1 3 6 5 5
S R M G, G T-M P P, R S S R, M G G

7 8 8 10 12 10 12 13 13 12 10
T-M, P P Dh N, Dh N S S, N Dh

8 3 6 5 8 3 1
P R, M G P R, S.

The above extensions, which are purposely made most simple, and without regard for Tála (time), strictly preserve the principle of ascent and descent, and show a way as to how Rágas can be extended. It is not necessary to stick to the above formations. Any formations, with due regard to the principle of ascent and descent, would do as well. As there is a legitimate liberty in the Poetry to slightly disregard the Grammar, so is the case with the Rágas in their extensions.

We give below a common formation of some of the Rágas by Minḍ or Ghasiṭ, to show how an artistic formation is effected. The formations are not set to Tála (time).

Bhupa or Bibhása (2nd in the first table) :—

1 3 5 3 5 8 5 3 5 8 10 13 13 10 8 5
S R-G R, G-P-G R, G P-Dh S, S-Dh-P G,

3 5 3 1
R-G-R S.

Darbári Kánaḍá (35th in the first Table) :—

1 3 3 4 3 4 6 8 9 11 13 13 11
S R R-K-G, R-K-G-M-P, P-K-Dh-K-N-S, S K-N

9 11 9 8 6 8 8 6 6 4 3 4 3
K-Dh-K-N, K-Dh-P M-P, P-M M-K-G, R-K-G-R

1
S.—(This Ra'ga, if deprived of its Minds or Ghasits, will be reduced to Jilha'-Sind-Bhairvi. We shall speak of this subject in its proper place).

Desa (10th in the second table) :—

1	3	6	5	3	3	6	8	8	10	12	13	13	12	10	8	6
S	R-	M-	G,-	R	R-	M-	P,	P	Dh-	N-	S,	S	N	Dh	P,	M

5	3	6	6	5	3	1
G	R-	M,	M-	G	R	S.

The above three formations of Bhupa or Bibha'sa, of Darbári-Kanadá, and of Desa, if reproduced either by voice or by instruments, will give us an idea, though not a complete one, as to how an artistic performance of the Mind or Ghasit is effected.

The artistic execution of Rágas belongs more to the domain of the art than to the subject of this discussion. However, a carefnl study of the above formations, along with their preceding and succeeding dlscussion with a little knowledge of the art, will show a way to extend, to adorn, and to set to music any Rága. As a matter of fact no Rága is complete without its Murchhanás being touched by Mind or Ghasit.

It is superfluous to say that all Rágas admit of being extended, though in different degrees, on account of their difference in the number of Notes which they (Ra'gas) cover. This extension is called Prastára,

When they touch a Note or Notes and its or their corresponding Note or Notes in the octaves, one below (Anudátt), or one above (Udátt) the register (Svaritt) octave, they call the touching in the register octave Vádi, and in the other two octaves Samvádi, for instance, in Kalyána (39th in the first table) :—

Samvádi Below or Anudátt.			Vádi, Register or Svaritt.			Samvádi. Above or Udátt.		
1	3	5	1	3	5	1	3	5
S	R	G.	S	R	G	S	R	G

Samvádi Below or Anudátt	Vádi, Register or Svaritt	Samaàdi Above or Uda'tt

7	8	10	7	8	10	7	8	10
T-M	P	Dh.	Г-M	P	Dh,	T-M	P	Dh.

Instead of touching the corresponding Note of a Rága in the other two octaves, they touch other Notes of the same Rága in the said octaves. This process goes by the same of Anuvádi, for example, in Kalyana (39th in the first table) ;—

Anuvádi. Below or Anudutt.	Vádi. Register or Svaritt.	Anuvadi. Above or Udátt.

7	8	10	1	3	5	7	8	10
T-M	P	Dh.	S	R	G	T-M	P	Dh.

It is not compulsory to touch first Va'di, and then Samvádi and thence Anuva'di, but any arrangement with due regard to the principle of ascent and descent, will be acceptable. It is also not necessary to touch the equal numbers of Va'di, Samvadi, and of Anuvadi, for instance, in Kalyàna (39th in the first table) :—

Anuvádi. Below or Anuda'tt.	Vádi. Register or Svaritt.	Samvádi. Above or Udátt.

7	8	10	12	1	3	5	1	3	8	5	7	8
T-M	P	Dh.	N.	S	R	G.	S	R	G	T-M	P	

It is hardly necessary to say that Va'di, Samva'di, and Anuvadi are not only touched in simple jumping, but, also, in Mind or Ghasit, and seldom in Murki. A Selection of the Viva'di for a Ràga, is condemned and discarded, as most unmusical, for instance in Kalya'na (39th in the first table) :—

Vivádi. Below or Anudátt.			Vádi. Register or Svaritt.			Vivádi. Above or Udátt.		
2	6	9	1	3	5	2	4	7
K-R	M	K-Dh.	S	R	G.	K-R	K-G	T-M,
2	3	4	7	8	10	4	7	9
K-R	R	G.	T-M	P	Dh.	K-G	T-M	K-Dh,

The subject of Va'di, Samva'di, Anuva'di, and of Viva'di, is a controversial one. There are some who say that the Vádi, Samva'di, Anuvadi, and Viva'di are the names given to the Notes of Ràgas according to their (Notes') relative arrangement, and, therefore, they have nothing to do with the change of octaves. But as we are not guided exclusively by the musical scriptures, we need not discuss anything that is vague and meaningless. If the Va'di, Samvadi, and Anuva'di do not imply the change of octaves, then what do they signify? The word Viva'di only shows that a certain arrangement of the Notes is not thought to be acceptable even by a change of octaves, as it (Viva'di) creates inartistic or unæsthetic effect. We have found the true meaning of the subject in practice, which is an ample and reasonable justification for our view of the matter.

The definition—(which is generally accepted) ot the three Gra'mas, namely, Shadja, Madhyam, and Pancham, and of their respective names—Nandyá-Vratt (Nandi is an emblem of the earth), Subhadra (very good or higher), and Jimuta (cloud hence celestial)—is too unintelligible or fabulous to be of any use in this discussion. The definitions of Bhoga, Abhoga, and Samsthái or Sancha'i are more hair-splitting than descriptive, and we omit them as such from this discussion.

It is certainly more charming than pleasant (for the practised ear) to listen to distinct Ra gas clearly preserved by strictiy confiniug to the number of Notes and to the rigid but distinctive principle of ascent and descent. This principle along with others, admirably preserves the individual Rágas and prevents confounding one with the other.

The confusion of Rágas invariably generates (in the practised ear) a chaotic group (like the Vivádi) of Notes, however skilful and regular in time they (Notes) may be. It is a truism that with the increase of progress in music, the number of Rágas must necessarily be increased, but it is also true that the increase in the number of Rágas involves definiteness of the distinctive signs. The number of Rágas in recent times, has not been increased, but it has been decreased. Increase, if there is any, has partly been on the side of Chijas (poetry set to music) in a Rága, and wholly on the side of Chijas in a Jilhá or Dhun.

Before dismissing this side of our discussion, let us say that one of the most artistic characteristics of Indian Rágas, is the Murchhanà (literally swoon)—¼th part of a tone.

We have said before [in the second chapter] that the 12 Murchhanás are distributed over all the Rágas, and that they (Murchhanás) are touched only in Mind or Ghasiṭ. Now let us add that each Rága consists of two Murchhanás, the first is called "Graha" (literally place), and the second is named "Nyása" (literally distance or interval), and that there is no Murchhaná in a Jilhá or Dhun (diminutive of Rága). This number of Murchhanás in a Rága has admirably been increased in later times not only in the compound Rágas but also in the simple Rágas of Komal-Svaras (semitones) and the effect has simply been charming.

Artistically speaking, simple production of the Notes of a Rága in a given time does not give a complete idea of the Rága so produced, unless its Murchhanás are added to the Notes of which they (Murchhanás) form parts. The Murchhaná is touched first or next to the Note of which it forms a part, and never separately. No stand (pause) is made on a Murchhaná which is never produced without a Mind or Ghasiṭ. If this arrangement is not strictly observed, the Murchhana' will be regarded as a discordant and violently shaky *note*, but that is not the case with it. Artistically speaking, the Murchhana' is a ¼th part of a tone, and it is always produceḍ in Minḍ or Ghasiṭ along with the Note of which it forms a part, and its number is limited in each Ra'ga. There are many Rágas of which the characteristics are the Murchhana's, as distinguishing marks. An omission of the distinctive signs, is the destruction of the Rágas so characterized : this is the reason which confounds Jogia' with Jilha'-Bhairvi (27th in the first table), Darbàri-Kanaḍà with Jilhà-Sind-Bhairvi (35th in the first table), Sáhànà-Kánáḍa with Jilhà-Kàfi (36th in the first table), Sind-Kánaḍá with Jilhá-Sindora (5th in the second table), Jejevanti-Kánaḍa' with Jilha'-Sindora' (5th in the second table), Gándhár with Jilha-Sind-Bhairvi (7th in the second table), Sora'ṭa with Jilha'-Kha'mách (9th in the second table), Palás with Jilhá-Barva' (14th in the second table), Dhanáshri with Jilhá-Ka'fi (15th in the second table), Bhairava with Jilhá-Kálangḍá (18th in the second and 32nd in the first table), Bágeshri-Kánáḍá with Jilhá-Báhár (7th in the third table), and Bhimpalás with Jilhá-Sind Bhairvi (8th in the third table).

The fact of the above confusion simply proves as we have said before, that the Rágas, if deprived of their Murchhana's, and of their principle of ascent and descent, result in Dhuns (not complete) or Jilha's of those Ra'gas : this is the reason why Jilha' or Dhun is recognized as diminutive of Ra'ga, for the former is not so distinctive as the latter. It is hardly necessary to say that even the touching of the Notes of a Ra'ga with Minḍ or Ghasiṭ, without covering its Murchhana's, results in Dhun of that Ra'ga. When the production of Notes of a Ra'ga, is devoid of Minḍ or Ghasiṭ, it results in a simple Jilha' or jumping. It is not to be understood that by implication we disparage simple jumping of the Notes, which has its own charms. We have used the word

"Jumping" simply as opposed to the Mind or Ghasit which means connection. Even in a complete form of a Ra'ga, we do not encumber each and every Note of it with Mind or Ghasit and Murchhana'; if we want to have the music of that Ra'ga, and not to have an impracticable, if not an impossible, feat. If the Murki, trill, shake, and other principles adorn the Notes, the Mind or Ghasit, and the Murchhana' do the same thing, if not more.

To render the above facts clear, we give below the 12 Murchhana's with the 12 Notes (Chromatic scale) on which they (Murchhana's) depend. The Murchhana's are the chief if not the only, item of Indian Raga's, and they are also called Tartivra (double sharp or sharper) or Ati-Komal (double flat or very flat). There is another minuter but none the less perceptible division of the Murchhana', but as it comes under the principle of shaking, we need not treat it separately. In shaking a Note the action, however skilful it may be, is always either of raising or of lowering a Note, but generally the former. The artistic way of shaking a Note cannot be called discordant and violent.

Instead of showing the utility of the Murchhana' (¼th part of a tone) we simply quote the following paragraphs.

P. Blaserna says :—" Certain notes adopted by the Greeks at a period of decline—as, for example, quarter tones—are decisively rejected by us. It is therefore an error which many commit, to think that music, and especially modern music, has absolute character and values, and therefore to reject every musical system which does not agree with ours. There is nothing absolute in it but the laws of notes and their combinations, but the application of these laws is rather vague, and there remains a very wide and indeterminate field, which will be traversed in very different ways by different nations at various historical epochs."

* * * "It may be well believed that even twenty-four keys well arranged would not offer insurmountable difficulties of execution, and even if musical complications and arabesques had to be abandoned, true aud serious music would only be the gainer."

Helmholtz, in suggesting some reforms in the temperate scale, says :—" That by starting from somewhat different considerations, it is possible to provide for everything in a very satisfactory manner, with twenty-four notes per octave."

Instead of giving a table to show the 12 Notes (Chromatic) on which the 12 Murchhanás ($\frac{1}{4}$th part of a tone) depend, we simply say that the first Murchhaná is between S (C) and K-R (C Sh.), the second stands between Ḳ-R (C Sh.) and R (D), the third between R (D) and K-G (D Sh.), the fourth is between K-G (D Sh.) and G (E), and so on. According to this arrangement, the first Murchhaná is between S (C) and K-R (C Sh.), and the 12th between N (B) and S (C).

The above description shows that to produce a Murchhaná in a Minḍ or Ghasiṭ we must touch the Note on which it depends. If we want to produce, for instance, the first Murchhaná, we can do it only by two ways – first, we may touch the Note S(C) and then the Murchhaná, or we may touch first the K-R (C Sh. or D Fl.) from the S (C) and then the Murchhaná. It is hardly necessary here to remind ourselves that to touch the S (C) by a Minḍ or Ghasiṭ, we must go first to N (B) or to K-N (B Fl. or a Sh.) to Dh (A) or to K-Dh (A Fl. or G Sh.), as the case may be, for we know that there are Rágas from which the three Notes—N (B), K-N (B Fl. or A Sh.), and Dh (A) are excluded, as in the cases of Bibhása (1st in the first table) and Rámkali or Gunkali (11th in the first table).

What does an artist do when he wants to touch the first Murchhaná, which is a Murchhaná of Purvi and such other Rágas ? He first touches the Note S (C) from N (B) or from any other Note, as it suits his convenience, then the Murchhaná, and thence the

K-R (D Fl.), and finally he reverts to the S (tonic); or he goes first to the K-R (C Sh.) from S (C) and then the Murchhanà, before reverting to the S (C).

In showing the second Murchhaná, which is a Murchhaná of Bibhàsa and such other Rágas, the performer gives the Murchhaná first, and then the K-R (D Fl), on the reverse. The third Murchhanà is a Murchhaṇá of Sárangs and such other Ra'gas. Instead of swelling the body of this discussion, we give below the Ra'gas according to the order of the number of Murchhana' which they possess for their first Murchhana', and the number of their second Murchhana' is given at the end of each name.

Ra'gas with the first Murchhana', are :—Jaita 8th, Puria' or Renki 7th, Ma'rva' or Dipak 7th, Purvi 8th, Dipak or Purvi-Kalya'na 8th, Shri 8th, Jaita'shri 8th, Ma'lava 8th and Purvi-Hindi 8th.

Ra'gas with the 2nd Murchhana', are :—Bibha'sa 9th, Ra'mkali or Gunkali 9th, Lalat 9th, Lalita' or Lalat 10th, Jogia 9th, Gurjari 9th, Toḍi 9th, Sohini 9th, Basant 10th, Paraja 9th, Jogia' 9th, and Bhairava 9th.

Ra'gas with the third Murchhana's, are :—Bhupa or Bibha'sa 10th, Megh or Sur-Malha'r 10th, Brinda'-bani-Sa'rang 11th, Sur-Sa'rang 12th, Baḍhans-Sarang 10th, Madhuma't- Sa'rang 12th, Bila'val 10th, Ra'ma-da'shi-Sarang 10th, Ala'ia-Bilaval 10th, Desha'si 10th, Suraṭa 10th, Desa 10th, Gounḍ 10th, Miaki or Ta'na-sen's Malhár 10th (Ta'nsen's Malhar is wonderfully finished for its Murchhana's. It has the Murchhana's of Megh or Sur-Malha'r, of Ka'naḍa's and of other Ra'gas. Whoever hears this Ra'ga, in its true form, will have an idea as to the wonderful gift of the celebrated singer for composing Ra'gas), Gounḍ-Malha'r 10th, and Gouḍ-Sa'rang 10th

Ra'gas with the fourth Murchhana', are :—Ma'lkosa 11th, Koushi 11th, Na'yaki-Ka'naḍa' 11th, Madhur-Ka'naḍa' 12th, Darba'ri-Ka'naḍa'11th, Sa'ha'ná-Kánaḍá 11th, Dha'ni-Ka'naḍa 12th, Sind-Ka'naḍa' 11th, Jeje-vanti-Ka'naḍa'11th, Gandha'r 11th, Pala's 11th, Dhana'-

shri 11th, Jounpuri 12th, Multa'ni 12th, Ba'geshri-Ka'naḍa' 11th, and Bhimpala's 11th.

Ra'gas with the fifth Murchhana', are :—Ba'nga'li 11th, Tilanga or Banga'li 12tḍ, Ma'leshri 12th, Hindola 12th, Bhupa'li 12th, Khamba'bati 11th, Deshi 12th, Ṭankika' 12th, Pancham 12th, Jangala' 12th, Kalya'na 12th, Khama'cha 11th, Biha'ga 12th, Shankara' 12th, Shankara'-Bharan 12th, Yaman-Kalya'na 12th, Ha'mir 12th, Na'ṭa 12th, and Chha'ya' 12th.

Ra'gas with the sixth Murchhana' are :—Ka'moda 12th, Biha'gaḍa' 12th, and Keda'ra' 12th.

Ka'langḍa' is a Jilha', and, therefore, it has no Murchhana'.

Without dilating on the distribution of the 12 Murchhana's, suffice it to say that with the progress of Minḍ or Ghasiṭ the touching of the Murchhana's is marvellously developed. Even in a simple Ra'ga', the number of the Murchhana's is increased. This increase in Murchhana's in a Ra'ga, is in proportion to the number of the Komal-Svaras (semitones) which that Ra'ga covers.

We give below a common formatiou, without Ta'la (time), of Kalya'na (39th in the first table) to show how the two Murchhana's of it are covered, It is hardly necessary to say that the Murchhana' is a ¼th part of a tone, and it is produced only in a Minḍ or Ghasiṭ, and no stand (pause) is made on it.

1 3 5 3 5 3 5 7 8 8 10
S R G, R—G-¼—-R—G—T-M—-P, P Dh.

10 12 10 12 13 13 12 10 10 8
Dh—N-¼——-Dh—-N—-S S, N—Dh Dh—-P,

7 5 5 3 1
T-M G, G—R—S,

The above formatiou, which is an ordinary piece for an artistic singer or player of Joḍ-music, may not be reproduced either by voice or by instrument by a novice without a long practice. Therefore, we do not wish to treat the subject of Murchhanás further. However, in concluding the subject we say, as we have said before, that with the progrsss in Minḍ or Ghasiṭ the number of Murchhana's is increased in a Rags of Komal-Svaras (Semitones) ; for instance, in Kalya'na (39th in the first table) there is a room for a third Murchhana' between Tivra-Madhyam (F Sh. or G Fl.) and Pancham (G), aad the number of the third Murchhana', is 7. In an artistic performance of a Ra'ga, the artist does not show a Murchhana' only once, but at a stretch he shows the Murchhana' along with the Note on which it depends, more than once, and the effect, thus produced, is simply entrancing. When a Minḍ or Ghasiṭ does not show a Murchhana', it goes by the name of Khaḍi, and when it shows it, it is called Suda.

Now is the proper time to say that each Ra'ga has certain Notes as its Pradha'na or Pramukha (principal) on which a comparatively long stand is made. This snbject is exclusively an artistic one, and, therefore, we should not pass it over without speaking a word concerning it.

Those who are practised to the Ra gas give a preponderance to certain Notes, which are the principal (ornamental) Notes of that Ra'ga, and its remaining Notes are thought to be subordinate ones.

Apart from the artistic considerations, the object of selecting particular Notes to make a stand on, seems to be that when many Ra'gas blend with each other considerably there must be as many distinctive marks as possible, and the subject of "Pradha'na" is one of them.

As a general guidance, we say that the principal Notes of a Ra'ga are generally the Notes, on which the Murchhana's of that Ra'ga depend.

Before dismissing this side of our discussion, let us mention that there is a custom of long standing to sing or play particular Ra'gas at particular time of the day and night. This custom has got such a stronghold over the mind of those who are practised to the Indian Ra'gas, that a departure from it is regarded by them as most unseasonable and unenjoyable. But the above analysis, though not a scientific one, does not support the custom. Nor does it seem to be warranted by any intrinsic influence of musical sounds. Neither does it seem to be justifiable on the ground of any distinctive Note or Notes which go to form the above Ra'gas. The most that can be brought forward to maintain the conventionality, is that there are certain Ra'gas—such as Bhairava and Sur-Sa'rang, Jogia and Megh, Toḍi and Gounḍ-Malha'r, Puria' and Gouḍ-Sa'rang, Sohini and Desa, Lalit and Kalya'na, &c., &c.—which are distinct from each other in Murchhana's, in tones and in semitones, and which above all produce different efforts on account of their different formations. But difference in impression does not follow difference in time. If it is assumed that the effect produced by Bhairva, Jogia, Toḍi, Puria', Lalat and by such other Ra'gas, is softer or less excitable or less lively than the one produced by Sa'rangs, Ka'naḍa's, Malha'rs, Kalya'ns and such other Ra'gas, still liveliness or dullness has nothing whatever to do with any particular time in itself. It cannot be presumed that a particular time of the day or night by itself changes pleasureable feelings into painful ones, or *vice versa.*

In order to sing or play any Ra'ga at any time and to thereby break through the ancient custom, many old celebrities seem to have mixed, more ingeniously than musically, two Ra'gas of quite different melodies, such as Hinḍola-Ba'ha'r, Bhairava-Ba'har—otherwise called Pancham (not of our table), and many others, and they have called others by misnomers, such as Gouḍ-Sa'rang, Ra'tki-Puria, Dinki-Puria', Kukab-Bilaval, Sarfarda'-Bilavala, &c,

Instead of refuting the so-called theory of a particular Ra'ga for a particular time at length and of bringing forth good many arguments against it, we may challenge any advocate of the custom to reasonably explain, out of many instances, why " Toḍi " (29th in the first table) is fixed for the *morning* and why " Multa'ni " (17th in the second table) is meant only for the *afternoon* ?

It is sheer madness to think that the Toḍi shows any sign of the diurnal revolution of the earth, and when its second Note (C Sh.) is omitted only in ascent, which is done in the case of Multa'ni, it shows the mean or extreme difference from 6 to 8 hours chronometrically. These remarks are equally applicable to the *Season-Ra'gas.*

To speak anything in abstract concerning Time is to leap into "mystery" which H. Spencer describes thus :—"It results therefore that Space and Time are wholly incomprehensible. The immediate knowledge which we seem to have of them, proves, when examined, to be total ignorance. While our belief in their objective reality is insurmountable, we are unable to give any rational account of it. And to posit the alternative belief (possible to state but impossible to realize) is to multiply irrationalities."

To realize time (Ta'la) in concrete is to experience "rhythm" or pulsation which is a marked distinction of music, and as such we treat it in the next chapter.

IV

THE TA'LAS AND THEIR FORMATIONS

A. Bain says :—"In his very subtle and original analysis, Sully traces the attribute of unity in variety through all the various guises assumed in musical compositions. First and most conspicuous, as a means of unity, is Time. To make a sequence of tone all equal in time, gives the simplest impression of unity, in variety. Next is a sequence where the tones are alternated with their sub-divisions—a semi-breve with two crotchets, and so on. This is carried up to the Foot or Bar, which confers on music its distinguishing rhythmic character, as triple, quadruple, &c."

Tála (Time-measures), which is an important factor of every school of music (even barbarian vociferation), regulates the relative durations of musical sounds, and as such seems to have considerably engrossed the Indian mind.

That which the Indians call Mátrá (metre), is an unit of Tála. For the sake of simplification, we call 1, 2, 3, 4, 5, 6, 7, 8, 9, &c, when counted or pronounced at a regular and uniform interval ("Laya"), as Mátrás. Tála is an aggregate of the Mátrás or equal lengths of a piece of music. The number of Mátrás in each Tála is fixed. If we repeat the figure 1 (one) and adjust a stroke either by the hands, or by any other means with the first letter of the word one, we get A'ditála (primary), which is ordinarily known by the name of Dádrá (literally ladder). The A'ditála is the foundation on which other Tálas are based. If we repeat 1, 2, and strike only at the first letter of the word one, we get Jhaptála. In repeating 1, 2, 3, and striking the first letter of the word one, we get Gajaltála or Dipchandi (practically, this is like a treble and it is used extensively). In repeating 1, 2, 3, and striking the first letters of the words one and two, we realize Rupaktála (this Tála also covers 3½ Mátrás and called Jhampá). Before going further, we must say that in order to increase the number of Mátrás in a Tála, they have called them by the name of Avasána, of tála, and of kála (rest). The first (Avasán) is the beginning or end of a Tála, and it is also the point of meeting of musicians and drummers—and of receiving applause from audience. The second is the point of a stroke (tála), and the third is that of an absence of stroke (rest).

When a Tála is repeated, each repetition is called Avarda', correction of A'vritti (repetition). A number of repetitions does not change a Ta'la, but it shows the number of repetitions.

In Jhapta'la, Gajaltála or Dipchandi, and in Rupaktala the point of Avasána is not a tála (stroke), but a kála (rest). No cause is shown for this deviation.

To simplify our immediate subject in hand, we allot the Avasána (storke)—otherwise called "Sama" —the *first place* in the serial order of the Mátrás in a Tála. We give a *serial figure* to the tála (stroke, but not the Avasána) which is called "Bhari" (not empty). We show the kála (rest)—otherwise called "Kháli" (empty)—by a serial *figure in a bracket*. This process at once teaches us that the first figure stands for the Avasána, the figure without a bracket, is the sign of tála, and the figure in a bracket, is the mark of kála.

If we go by the above method, we reproduce the Titála or Tirvaṭtála (4 Mátrás, but 3 strokes) in the following way :—

1, 2, (3), 4. Here are the Surfáktála (5 Mátrás, but 3 strokes)—1, (2), 3, 4, (5), Choutála or Ekká (6 Mátrás, but 4 strokes)—1, (2), 3, (4), 5, 6, and A'ḍa'chouta'la (7 Ma'tra s, but 4 strokes)—1, 2, (3), 4, (5), 6, (7).

The above Ta'las are the principal ones, and others are their specializations. The special Ta'las are effected simply by doubling or quadrupling the number of Ma'tra's of the original Tálas and by simply changing the order of strokes and rests. For example, the Dhamàr or Hori (difficult and seldom practised : its Avasàna is not on a stroke) is neither more nor less than the A'ḍáchoutála doubled, and its strockes and rests changed.

A'ḍàchoutála—1, 2, (3), 4, (5), 6, (7).

Dhama'r—1, (2), (3), (4), (5), 6, (7), (8), (9), (10), 11, (12), (13), (14).

The big-named Brahmatála and Rudratála are no other Tálas than the Titála and Surfa'kta'la quardrupled, and their order of strokes and rests changed.

Tita'la— 1, 2, .(3),

Brahmta'la—1, (2), 3, (4), 5, (6), 7, 8, (9), 10, 11, 12,

4.

(13), 14, 15, I

Surfa'kta'la - *(figs. 1st & 3rd lines)*

1, 2, 3,

Rudratála—1, (2), 3, (4), 5, 6, (7), 8, 9, 10, (11), 12, 13,

4, (5)

14, 15, (16), 17, 18, 19, 20.

The Savárітála or Kaid (literally hampered) is no other Tála than the Titála, but the real Savári is not used now. It has 7 Mátrás and a half, and this is the reason why it is difficult. This Savári when doubled and its strokes and rests changed, goes by the name of Brahmatála (another form of the original Brahmatála).

Saváritála—1, 2, (3), 4, (5), 6,

Brahmtála—1, (2), 3, (4), 5, (6), 7, 8, (9), 10, 11,(12),

(7), (½)·

13, 14, 15.

The peculiarity of Tála is that instead of going at a regular interval (Laya), the singer or player in competing with the drummer at times changes the point of Avasán to $\frac{1}{2}$ or $\frac{1}{4}$ of that Mátrá. The former is called A'ghát or Atit (no stroke), and the latter is named Anughát (after the stroke).

To break up the monotony or the dead uniformity of time, the singer or player (who deals more with simple jumping than with Minḍ or Ghasiṭ and Murki) at times, reduces the original time (Barobari) or speed to one-half (Ṭha'), or at times he doubles (Dvigunі or Duni) it, or quadruples (Chougun) it. And, as a matter of course, the drummer adopts the same course. Thá (one-half), Barobari (equal), Duni (double), and Chougun (quadruple) are the relative terms, and their relation to each other stands thus :—

Thá is equal to a Semibreve, Barobari is equal to a Minim, Duni is equal to a Crotchet, and Chougun is equal to a Quaver ; or in other words, Thá is equal to 8 Annas, Barobari is equal to 16 Annas, Duni is equal to 32 Annas, and Chougun is equal to 64 Annas or equal parts of a Rupee. Thay also double the Chougun in Tàn (variation), but they never go further than this ; or in other words, they use a semi-quaver, but not a demisemi-quaver.

They at times accelerate the original time (Barobari) or speed to $1\frac{1}{2}$ (A'ḍa or Deḍi), or to $1\frac{1}{4}$ (Kuáḍa or Savái), but this is very difficult. To realize this difficulty we suggest to our readers an attempt to produce instantaneously with the hands—Titála with Choutála (A'ḍa or $1\frac{1}{2}$) and Tita'la with Surfa'kta'la (Kua'ḍa or $1\frac{1}{4}$) ; or in other words, the Tita'la and Chouta'la and Tita'la and Surfa'kta'la should be regulated in such a way as to converge their respective Avasa'ns. This attempt is sure to be attended with an abnormal difficulty in the absence of a key, which we have invented and have given at the end of the description of Ta'las.

Indians seem to have taken great pains to form the technical vocabulary of their drumming, as an art. The peculiarity of Indian Pakha'vaja (Paksha-A'va'ja means sounded by two sides) or Tabla'-Ba'ya' (detached Pakhavaja), is that it is generally attuned (few drummers know how to adjust it completely) to the fundamental (Svaritt) note - S (C or tonic) of the musicians. It is played by the palms and fingers of both the hands at the edge, at the middle, and on the centre of the two circles into which it is divided. The right-hand side (not of a left-handed drummer), which is besmeared with iron to make it resonant, is called Daina' or Dakshan ; and the left-hand side, which is also made resonant by pressing it with wheat-flour to adjust it with the right side, is called B'ya' or Va'ma. The instrument (artistic excluded) is too common and noisy to need any description. The right-hand fingers are used more freely than those of the left hand. The stroke, which is produced in the middle of the right side by the right palm, is named Ta'l ; and the stroke by the same palm on the centre (iron), is called Ti or Tin, The stroke, which is produced at the edge by the index finger of the right hand, goes by the name of Na'. The similar (four fingers, excepting the thumb) arrangement, if manipulated by the left hand on the left side, is named Ga, Ghi or Ghin, and Ka respectively. When the right palm and the left-hand fingers produce a stroke jointly in the middle of their respective circles, the stroke thus produced goes by the name of Dha'—the usual, but not an invariable, sign of the Avasa'na. It is not necessary to say that the Dha' is a compound stroke of the Ta' and Ga. A compound stroke of the Ti or Tin and Ghin, is named Dhin. This arrangement is slightly changed on Tabla'-Ba'ya' (detached Pakha'vaja. There is but very little difference between Pakha'vaja and Tabla'-Ba'ya' instrumentally. The former is handled more with the palms and the joint fingers of the left hand (sometimes only three fingers, excepting the thumb and the last, are used separately) than with separate fingers of the hands ; while the latter is played more by the fingers than by the palms, and even the left-hand fingers (three excepting the thumb and the last) are used more freely and separately. Pakhavaja is generally played with Dhrupada and Dhama'r (music set to Dhama'rta'la), and Tabla'ba'ya' regulates (not in Madras) the Khya'l, Ṭappa', Ṭhunri, Gazal and Dance.

By adjusting the palms and the fingers at different points on the right and left sides of Pakhavaja or Tabla'-ba'ya', we get in all (artistic and practical drumming) 13 letters or technicalities as elements composing the Ṭheka's and Parands (we shall speak of these in their proper place), which are played in accompaniment of music. The letters are these :—

Ka, Ga, Gha, Ṭa, Ḍa, Ta, Tha, Da, Dha, Na, Ma, Ra, and La (the last is obsolete).

A combination of the above letters, is formed thus :—1st.—Ka or Ka' Kḍa'n, Kiṭ and Kiḍ.

2nd.—Ga or Gi, Gan and Gadi or Gdi.

3rd.—Ghḍa'n, Ghiṭ, Ghiḍ, and Ghin.

4th.—Ta or Ta', Ti or Tu, Tak, Tag, Tiṭ, Tin or Tun, Tir and Ṭra'n.

5th.—Tho and Thun.

6th.—Di and Dag or Dig.

7th.—Dha or Dha', Dhḍa'n, Dhig, Dhiṭ, Dhiḍ, Dhin, Dhir, Dhla'ng (obsolete), and Dhum.

8th—Na or Na', Nak, or Nag.

The one Ma'tra' combinations (or monosyllables), which are given above, show that out of the 12 (13th is absolete) letters 8 are used as initial as well as final (Ghi is not final), and the remaining four (Ṭ, Ḍ, M and R.) are used only as final. The ways in which the above combinations are made, and the addition of nasal sounds—M and N (in Kḍa'n, Gan, Gha'ḍn, Ghin, Tin, Tra'n, Thun, Dha'ḍn, Dhin, Dhum, &c.) only in pronouncing and not in playing, and the substitution of R for Ḍ (in Tra'n and not Tḍa'n) in pronounciug and not in playing seem to be either arbitrary, or probably they are a modification or a part of the 14 Sutras, which are attributed to Siva thus—" (Siva) The King of Kings of musicians

(" Nata ") in order to gratify the desire of Sanaka and other Rishis (sages) played fourteen times on the Ḍamaru when he was in an elevated state of feeling (Nritya or dancing) and these collections are known as Shiva Sutras." The 14 Sutras, for our purpose, are tolerably these :—

1st. A I Un, 2nd. Ri Lrik, 3rd. E On, 4th. Ai Auch, 5th. Ha'ya Vara'ṭa, 6th. Lana, 7th. Yaman Nanam, 8th. Zabha Ghaḍ Dhak, 9th. Jab Gaḍ Dash, 10th. Khap Chhaṭ Tha,. 11th. Chaṭ Tav, 12th. Ka Pain, 13th. Shakh Sar, and the 14th. Hal.

We shall be wanting in doing justice to our discussion if we do not speak a word about the "Damaru," which is said to have been used as an instrument to produce the 14 Sutras. With due respect to the Sutras, we are most painfully constrained to say that the " Damaru," which we know, and which is played by our aboriginal tribes or brothers with a stick and a little pressure by a few fingers of the left hand, is a primitive form of the advanced Pakha'-vaja of our day. We cannot bring ourselves to believe that the Damaru can admit of so admirable Sutras, which are said to be the fundamental basis of Aryan philosophy aud religion. But as this subject is a religious one, we leave it to abler heads and religious hearts, more especially as it in no way furthers our discussion. What little we have said concerning the " Damaru " should not be interpreted into an indirect attack on the Sutras. In tracing the identity or origin of the drum technicalities, we have touched the " Damaru " only in passing.

As we have given one Mátra' combinations, we give now two Ma'tra' combinations to show how they are formed in Theka's and Parands, which are extant :—

1st.—Ka-Ta', Ka-Dha', .Kḍa'n-Ta', Kḍa'n-Dha', Kiṭ-Ta, Kiḍ-Tak, Kiṭ-Thun, Kiḍ-Dhum, Kiḍ-Na' and Kid-Na'g.

2nd.—Ga-Ta', Ga-Dhá, Ga-Dhin, and Gdi-Gan or Gadi-Gan,

3rd.—Ghiṭ-Tak, Ghiḍ-Tit, Ghiḍ-Nag, Ghḍa'n-Ta', Ghḍa'n-Dha', and Ghiṭ-Thun,
4th.—Ta-Kiṭ, Ta'-Thun, Tag-Tiṭ, and Tir-Kiṭ.
5th. - Tho-Kiṭ, Thun Ga', Thun-Ta', Thun-Thun, Thun-Dha', and Thun-Na'.
6th.—Dig-Ta', Dig-Dhá, and Dig-Nag.
7th.—Dha-Kiṭ, Dhá-Tiṭ, Dhig-Nag, Dhir-Kiṭ, Dhi-Láng (obsolete), and Dhum-Kiṭ.
8th.—Na-Kiṭ, Nag-Tiṭ, Nag-Dhiṭ, Nag-Thun, Nag-Dhun or Dhum.

When the above combinations are given the same time, which is given to the proceding ones (one Mátrá combinations), the speed ("Laya") will be relatively double (Duni).

There are certain other combinations, but we have selected the best according to our taste of drumming, and they also serve as specimens. The beauty of a combination is that it not only sounds well, but it admits of being played swiftly with comparative ease. In short, the above technicalities and their combinations are so exquisitely formed in different divisions of Tála, and they are played so smoothly and artistically that to become an excellent drummer would require a life-long practice. Mathematically Ta'las are of no great consequence, but musically they are of the greatest use.

We give below commonplace Theka's of the principal Ta'las we have spoken of, and also give a few Parands to show how the technicalities are combined. It will be observed that the above specimens and the following combinations, if properly read, will assist us in forming new Theka's and Parands.

The distinction between a Theka' (the word is purely a technical one, literally it signifies contract or license) and a Parand (purely technical), is that the former is a limited and a repeated combination to keep up the Ta'la ; the latter is an extended and generaily changed combination to swell (variation in time, that is to say, combinations are not of uniform speed) the Ta'la.

Before giving the Thekás and Parands, it is opportune to say that Pakhávaja deals more in resonant words as Dhá and its combinations, Ghi and its combinations, and Tho and its combinations, than Tablá-báyá which generally deals in Ga and its combinations, Tá and its combinations, Dig and its combinations, and Ná and its combinations. This is in a great measure due to the palms being used more freely in the former than in the latter.

Our reading of the aforsaid combinations, teaches us that "t," when preceded by "i" is always to be pronounced as "ṭ" and not "t." When "d" is preceded either by "i," or by K, Gh, T, or Dh, it is invariably "ḍ" and not "d." This description may do away with the special letters in the Ṭhekás and **Parands by allowing the use of the ordinary ones.**

Ṭhekás on Tablá-báyá.

(1), 2.
Jháptála - Ghin Tá Tá, Tin Tá Tá (Avasán on the rest and the first is rest),

1, 2, (3),
Tirvaṭtála—Ná Dhin Dhina, Ná Dhin Dhiná Ná
4.
Tin Tiná, Ná Dhin Dhina'.

1 2, (3), 4,
Tirvaṭ or Tita'la—Dhin Dhin, Dha Tit, Tu Na', Kit Ta',

1, (2), 3, 4,
Surfa'kta'la—Dhin Dhin, Dha' Tit, Tu Na', Ka Tá,
(5).
Kit Ta'.

1, (2), 3,
Ekka' or Chauta'la—Dhin Dhin, Dha' Tit, Tu Na',
(4) 5, 6.
Ka Ta', Dhag Tit, Dhi Na'.

1, 2,
Aḍá (not straight) Chautála—Dhin Dhin, Dhá Tit,
(3) 4, (5) 6, (7),
Tu Na', Ka, Ta' Dhin Dhin, Na' Dhin, Dhin Na'.

1, 2, (3),
Sava'ri or Kaid—Dhin Ghin, Dha' Tit, Dhin Ghin
4, (" ½ "),(5) 6, (7)
Tuna' Kata', Dha', Dhin Dhin, Na'-Dhin, Na' Dhin.

If the Dhá (½) is taken away from the Sava'ri it is reduced to Aḍáchautála in another Theká, and if the Dhá (½) or its equivalent is added to the A'ḍáchautála it will serve the purpose of Savári, It is not necessary to stick to the Thekás which we have given above. The same Ta'las can be represented by any other combinations. The object of giving simple Thekàs with a slight alteration in order to meet the different Tálas, is to simplify description, and to give an idea as to how Thekàs are ordinarily composed. There are, and can be made, excellent Thekás of artistic combitions, but want of space does not permit us to do so.

A peculiar kind of combination, which is familiarly known by the name of A'ḍa, is as follows on Tablá-báyá :—

1 2 (3)
Tirvaṭ or Titàla—Dhá Ghi Nag, Takit Ghi Nag, Dhà
4 1, 2,
Trak Dhá Kit, Ghi Nag Tin, Ná Gin Ná Gin, Ka
(3) 4
Tak Dhá Kit, Dhá Trak Dhàkit, Ghi Nag Tagan.

Here are common but artistic Parands on Ta'bla'-báyá,

1. 2,
Tirvaṭ or Titála—Dhinà Kdadhán, Dag Nag Dig
(3) 4 1,
Nag, Tirkit Dag Nag, Dhig Nag Tirkit, Dhag Tit
2 (3)
Tag Tit, Dha' Trak Dhakit Ghid, Nag Dhit Kit Tak,
4, 1, 2,
Nag Tit Kdán, Dhà Dha' Dhi Gan, Dha' Dhi Gan
(3) 4,
Dhà, Kid Nag Tarkit Tak Dhir Kit Tak, Dhag Nag
Thag Tit.

1, 2,
Tirvat or Titála—Ta Kit Thunkit Ghid, Nag Dhit
(3) 4, 1,
Kit-Tàk, Nag Tit Kdán, Dhá Dhà Dhi Gan, Dhá Dhi
2, (3)
Gan Dhá, Kid Nag Tar Kit Thir Kit Tak, Dhag Nag
4,
Dhag Tit, Dhag Tit Dhag Tit.

Thekàs on Pakha'vaja.—

(1) 2, 3
Rupakta'la—Dha' Dha', Tit Kata', Gadigan. (Ava-sa'na on rest).

1, 2 (3), 4
Tita'la –Dha' Dha', Dhin Ta, Gadi Gan Dha', Tit Ta'.

1, (2) 3,
Surfa'kta'la—Dha' Dha' Dhin Ta', Gadi Gan Dha',
4, (5)
Dhin Ta', Kit Ta'.

1, (2) 3,
Chauta'la—Dha' Dha', Dhin Tá, Gaḍi Gan Dha',
(4) 5, 6.
Dhin Ta' Tit Ka Ta', Gadi Gan.

The following is a common Theka' for Dhama'r, and a careful perusal of it will show how nicely it is composed.

(1),(2), (3), (4), (5), 6,(7), (8), (9),(10),(11),(12),
Dhamár – Dh———a' Dhi-t Dha' Ga Dhi-n Ti—ta
(13), (14).
T——a' (Avsa'na on rest).

It the Theka's of Tita'la and Surfa'kta'la are quadrupled, they will serve the purpose of Brahmatála and Rudrata'la respectively. When the Theka' of Sava'ri is doubled, it will represent the Brahmatála in other form.

Now we give Parands (common but artistic) on Pakhávaja, which are familiarly known by the name of A'ḍa :—

1, (2),
Chauta'la—Takk Dha' Kit, Ta' Kit Tho Kit,
3, (4), 5,
Dhigan Nagan, Digg Gadi Gan, Katit Dha' Dhin Ta',
6.
Ta' Kit Dha'n.

1, (2), 3,
Chauta'la—Nakit Takit, Katak Dhakit, Dha'n Na'n,
(4), 5, 6.
Dha' Dhinta' Katt, Dhda'n, Nagan Dha'n.

1, (2),
Chauta'la—Dha' Kit Takk, Takk Thokit,
3, (4), 5,
Katt Ghinag, Ka Tit Dha'kit, Nakit Tan,
6.
Kda'n Dha'n.

It is necessary to say that the Dvitt (double) K, G, T and N are accents. Wherever any Dvitt comes, it should be considered as an accent. The accents are beautifully shown in an artistic drumming.

Parands on Pakha'vaja in Chauta'la :—

1, (2), 3, (4),
1st.—Takit Tho, Kit Tak, Dhig Tag, Tag Tit
5, 6, 1, (2),
Ka Tit Ta, Gan Ghi Ghi, Nag Dhigg, Ghda'n
3, (4), 5,
Dhag Na' Na', Kit Takk Thunn, Taka' Thun Thun,
6.
Kit Takk Gadi Gan—(This Parand is in one Avarda', that is to say, in 6 Matra's, but we have given it in two Avarda's, that is in 12 Ma'tra's).

1, (2),
2nd.—Ghin Tir Kit Tak Ta', Ka Ta' Ghi Ghi Dhinn,
3, (4), 5, 6.
Nag Dhitt Ta', Ghin Tda'n Dha', Dhin Ta' Ka Tit,

Dha' Kit Tak Gadi Gan.

1, (2),
3rd.—Dhit Tit Kit Tak, Dhig Tag Tit Ka Ta',
3, (4),
Ghin Tir Kit Tak Tag Tit, Tag Tit Dhag Tit,
5, 6.
Ka Tit Ta Gan Dhag Dhitt, Dhda'n Na Gan Dha'n.
1, (2),
4th.- Dhit Tit Trak Dhit, Dhir Kit Ta' Ghin Dhi Ka
3 (4),
Ta, Kit Tag Tag Tit, Kit Takk Thun Ga' Takk Thun
5, 6.
Ga', Tir Kit Ta. Dhir Kit Ta', Dha Gi Gi Dha Gi Gi.

The few examples given above, though short and not the best, will, however, give an idea as to how the Ṭheka's and Parands are formed. There has been a general belief, and seems to be well-founded, among the Indian musicians that to become an artist one must necessarily and sufficiently appreciate the real beauty of Theka's and Parands as a guide to compose and execute music.

We give below a formula by the aid of which we can easily give out any Ta'la by the left hand and its Duni or double by the right hand at a time. It is unusually difficult to practise this without the support of a process we now speak of. In order to know the formula a few words are necessary :— A stroke by the left hand, should be named—"Ka," and by the right hand—"Ta'." The joint strokes by the left and right hands at a time, should be called—"Dha'," and the absence of a stroke should be signed —"a'." This process teaches us to produce the following Ta'las :—

Tita'la—Dha', Ta', Ka, Ta', Ta', Ta', Ka, Ta'.

Surfa'kta'la—Dha', a', Ta', Ta', Ka, Ta', Ka, Ta', Ta', á.

Chauṭa'la—Dha', a', Ta', a', Dha', Ta', Ta', a', Dha', a', Dha', Ta'.

Aḍa'chauta'la—Dha', Ta', Ka, Ta', a', Ta', Ka, Ta, Ta', a', Dha', a', Ta', a'.

Instead of giving the strokes and rests, we give below the key which has rendered the process so easy and practical. It is hardly necessary to say that the key will work with all the Ta'las.

Tịta'la—1, 2, (3), 4.
Duni— 1, 2, (3), 4, 1, 2, (3) 4.
Dha', Ta', Ka, Ta', Ta', Ta', Ka, Ta'

Surfa'kta'la—1, (2), 3, 4, (5).
Duni—1, (2) 3, 4, (5), 1, (2), 3, 4, (5)
Dha', a', Ta', Ta', Ka, Ta', Ka, Ta', Ta', a'.

Chauta'la – 1, (2), 3, (4), 5,
Duni—1, (2), 3, (4), 5, 6, 1, (2), 3, (4),
Dha', a', Ta', a', Dha', Ta, Ta, a', Dh a', a',
6.
5, 6.
Dha, Ta'.

Aḍa'chauta'la— 1, 2, (3), 4,
Duni—1, 2, (3), 4, (5), 6, (7), 1,
Dha, Ta' Ka, Ta', a', Ta, Ka, Ta',
(5) 6, (7).
2, (3), 4, (5), 6, (7).
Ta', a', Dha', a', Ta', a'.

A careful perusal of the above process shows that when two strokes meet together, we call them Dha'. When there is a stroke on the Duni or double, we term it Ta'; and when there is a stroke on the Ta'la, we name it Ka. It is not necessory to say that "a'" stands for an absence of stroke, and whenever it comes it is always on the Duni or double. The only thing to be done in producing the Ta'las and their Dunis at a time, is to give equal and uniform time ("Laya") to the "signs."

As a novelty, the Chauta'la and Tita'la can be produced by the hands and by a foot at a time in such a way as to converge their (the said Ta'las') respective Avasa'nas. Those who havc seen the way, have admired it much. First, give the Ta'la and Duni of the Chauta'la by the hands as shown above, and adjust the three strokes (rest excluded) of Tita'la by a foot in the following way :—

Hands—Dha', a', Ta', a', Dha', Ta', Ta', a', Dha,
A foot—1, 2, (3),
a', Dha', Ta.
4. (a foot)

In finishing the description of Ta'las we give below, as we have promised, a key by the aid of which Tita'la and Chauta'la (A'ḍa or $1\frac{1}{2}$), and Tita'la and Surfa'kta'la) (Kuaḍa or $1\frac{1}{4}$), can be produced by both the hands at a time in such a way as to converge their respective Avasa'nas.

Suppose we take a series of 12 consecutive figures beginning from 1 and ending with 12. Now in Chauta'la there would be 4 strokes and 2 rests. The strokes will be on 1, 5, 9 and 11 and the rests will be on 3 and 7. The reader must already have seen from the general description that the 1st stroke on 1, is the Avasa'na. In the same manner as regards Tita'la the series will divide itself in 4 points (Ma'tra's) composed of 3 strokes and 1 rest—the strokes coming on 1, 4 and 10, and the rest coming on 7, the stroke on 1 being of course the Avasa'na. The following is a demonstratson of what we are saying :—

Chauta'la—	1,		(2),		3,		(4),		5,		6,	
series—	1,	2,	3,	4,	5,	6,	7,	8,	9,	10,	11,	12
Tita'la—	1,			2,			(3)			4		

The 12 figures are to be counted at a regular and uniform interval and the strokes and rests should be adjusted as shown above.

The above being understood, it is clear that the Titála and Surfákta'la may also be similarly realized.

As the later is $1\frac{1}{4}$ times the former, instead of 12 figures, we shall have to take the series of 20 figures. The result will be that as regards Tita'la there will be strokes on 1, 6 and 16, and the rest on 11 ; and as regards Surfa'kta'la the strokes will be on 1, 9 and 13, and the rests on 5 and 17,

The reader must have seen from the above description and demonstration that the thing to be done, is to take any common multiple of the units (Ma'tra's) contained in the different Ta'las to be produced simultaneously by the hands and their strokes and rests are to be adjusted in the manner aforesaid.

Before dismissing this side of our discussion, it is absolutely necessary to say that we have purposely omitted the subject of giving a mode of setting to the Ta'las the Ra'gas we have spoken of. We cannot do this artistically in the absence of a *notation* of general and recognized acceptance. The ancient notations are too complicated to be clearly understood for a practical purpose, and those which are invented by our present writers on Indian music, are too crude and many to be of general use. We, therefore, strongly recommend our authors to adopt the European *notation* with certain additions to meet the peculiarities of Indian music as a whole. Such a system of *notation* is sure to lay open a way to the advanced music of Europe, and to serve as a channel of exchange.

To secure the above object with least trouble, we must introduce it first in schools and colleges as a means to reduce to writing the music of Indian poems, and it will establish itself in process of time. The dramatists (Náṭakválás) probably be the first to adopt it in their printed programmes and pamphlets (on account of their favourable situation), as a guide to their patrons if they wish to improve their singing,

Our discussion will be incomplete if we do not devote a separate chapter to dancing, as an art, because it is, in its earlier stages (as is the case in barbarian races), co-ordinate with poetry and music., Rhythm in speech, rhythm in sound and rhythm in motion are the elements out of which music or language of emotions or feelings has been evolved. The secret of the great impression which music makes upon the human heart, wholly resides *in rhythmic movements, in determinate intervals, in simple ratios, in rich harmonics, in different sequences and in different shades.*

Spencer says :—"The several kinds of *rhythm,* characterizing æsthetic expression, are not, in the common sense of the word, artificial, but are intenser forms of an undulatory movement habitually generated by feelingin its bodily discharge. It is shown by the fact that they are all traceable in ordinary speech ; which in every sentence has its primary and secondary emphases, and its cadence containing a chief rise aud fall complicated with subordinate rises and falls ; and which is accompanied by a more or less oscillatory action of the limbs when the motion is great."

V
THE THEORY OF DANCING

Dancing, which has all over the civilized world been recognized as an art, is dependent on the muscular action generated by elevated feeling. Feelings are the concomitants of nervous changes. There is a recognized relation between the quantity of feeling (pleasurable or painful) and the amount of motion generated. This mode of expressing emotions, is not performed only by the civilized races, but it is considerably exhibited by birds and animals.

The curious love gestures of some kinds of birds, have remarkably been observed by some naturalists.

Audubon describes thus :—"The males of heron (*audea herodius*) walk about on their long legs with great dignity before the females, and bid defiance to their rivals. With one of the disgusting carron vultures the gesticulations and the parade of the males at the beginning of love season are extremely ludicrous."

Darwin says:—"In Northern America large numbers of grouse meet every morning during the breeding season on a selected level spot, and here they run round and round in a circle of about 15 to 20 feet in diameter, so that the ground is worn quite bare like a fairy-ring. In these partridge dances (called by the hunters) the birds assume the strangest attitudes, and run round and round, some to the left and some to the right. Certain kinds of birds often rise a few feet or yards in the air above some bush, and flutter with a fitful and fantastic motion, singing all the while."

There may be very few of us who have not watched and enjoyey the Chandol (lark), Bulbul (big lark), Dayar and a few other birds undergoing manœuvres of the above description. The dancing of peacock, which is depicted by our poets, is admirable only for the show of its beautiful feathers, and for nothing more.

A. Bain says:—"Next to the experience of Feelings, is the experience of the signs. These are—the recognized expression of human and other sentient beings, by Voice, Movement, Gesture, and Demonstration of every kind."

"Probably the foremost place among the associated signs of feeling should be given to the voice. In the first place, the emission of sound is the most widespread of all the significant signs of the mental states of animals and human beings. Under a stimulation of the senses, as music, our strong favourite emotions are resuscitated ; and the pleasure is a complex product of present sensation and ideal feelings. We, therefore, infer that, when music or other genial stimulation wakens up past occasions of pleasure, these echoes do greatly increase the emotional glow ; and the highly educated emotional man is necessarily much more elated under the circumstance than the poor, the outcast, the emotionally famished man.

"We might carry on the exposition of imitation into all the postures, gesticulations, and motions of the body at large. As regards the lower limbs and the trunk, there is no essential difference from the case already dwelt upon. The feet seem much less prepared originally for varied voluntary movements than the hands ; their accomplishment is both more limited and more laborious, as we see in dancing.

W. D. Whitney says :—"Language is expression for the sake of communication. The instrumentalities capable of being used for this purpose and actually more or less used, are various ; gesture and grimace, pictorial or written signs, and uttered or spoken signs. The first two addressed to the eye, the last to the ear."

It is hardly necessary to say that many of our most important expressions, when exhibited by those who are unhappily born blind, prove that they are innate or not individually learnt. It is strictly true that to perform certain expressive actions in a regular and perfect way, is to imitate and practise them individually.

It is exceedingly regrettable that so natural an expression of delighted feelings,—dancing which is, and has been, manifested by the ideal nations of the world, present and past, has been totally ignored and discarded by ourselves and by our predecssors as a debasing art, and hence its confinement to the female (noble) sex. It is strictly true that the ancient Hindus used to take delight in dancing, not only in religious devotion but in social ceremonies, not only up to the time of Krishna but long after it. Dancing was so much held in reverence by early Hindus that their Sutras were thought to be the result of the dancing of Siva.

Our present dancing, social and professional, though performed by a few male artists, is exclusively feminine. In Madras-dancing there are certain male attributes, but they are so much overpowered by the feminine attributes that we look upon them as exclusively feminine. Social (non-professional) dancing, which is performed in the higher families, and even in the most secluded part of "Zenana" is unsæsthetic. The Rásaḍá, an antiquated name of dancing by males and females, are but now danced by females only. Ladies catch each other's hands as a support, and bow and move round and round in a regulated motion of the feet in a circle, slow in the beginning and fast in the end ; when separated or not supporting each other by the hands, they perform a zig-zag motion, and clap and flourish the hands. Those who possess a sweet voice, take the lead, and others follow in their train. A female drummer or regulator of the voice and of the metre of the feet, sits in the centre. Hámchi (in Guzerat a circle dance and jumping by ladies and seldom by males around an image. This is a crude form of Rásaḍá), Fera (in Southern Maratha country a rude form of Rásaḍá), Fugaḍi (two females support each other by crossed hands, and revolve with a tremendous speed), etc. are miserably crude and rustic. The professional (of course not tom-tom Nách) or artistic dancing is good, though objectionably surrounded.

Artistic dancing has less technicalities than the drumming. It is worked out with the soles and the big toes of the feet, the right foot performs the major part of it, and "parands" are resorted to as a means to an artistic performance. The ordinary technicalities are few, and they are these:—Tá, Tak, Tad, Thai Tho, Thun, etc.

An artistic way of dancing has not only to look to Tálas (time), but it has to adorn the whole body in regulation with the metres of the feet in combination with different emotions by the features, attitudes, postures, and by gestures. The flourishing of the hands is a necessary condition of the body showing emotions in their full strength. To understand the meaning of flourishing the hands in dancing, as a necessray condition, cannot be completely comprehended by simply reminding ourselves that the acrobatic feats are facilitated by flourishing the hands or the poles to gravitate the body. We, therefore, deviate a little from our immediate subject to study the actions of the arms in walking.

If we place our arms close to our sides, and keep them there while walking with some rapidity, we will unavoidably fall into a backward and forward motion of the shoulders of a wriggling (ungraceful) character. After persevering in this for a space, until we find, as we must, that the action is not only ungraceful but fatiguing, let us suddenly allow our arms to swing as usual. The wriggling of the shoulders will cease, the body will be found to move equably forward, and comparative ease will be felt. On analysing this fact, we may perceive that the backward motion of each arm is simultaneous with the forward motion of the corresponding leg, and, if we will attend to our muscular sensations we will find that this backward swing of the arm is a counterbalance to the forward swing of the leg ; and that it is easier to produce that counterbalance by moving the arms than by contorting the body, as we otherwise must do.

The action in the arms in walking being thus understood, it will be clear that the graceful employment of the hands in dancing, is simply an advancement of the same thing.

An artistic dancer is one not only having so acute a muscular sense as at once to feel in what direction the flourishing of the hands should be moved to most readily counterbalance any motion of the body or leg, but having an artistic sense to gracefully adjust them in such a way as to add to the general effect of different postures, of attitudes, and of movements. Those who fail to adjust the hands in an artistic way, give to the audience, of course not an unthoughtful one, the impression that their hands are a trouble to them ; they are held stiffly in a meaningless attitude, they are checked from swinging in the directions in which they would naturally swing, ; or they are so moved, that instead of helping to maintain the gracefulness (the principal aim in a dance) they endanger it. A good dancer, on the contrary, makes us feel that, so far from the hands being in the way, they are of great use. Each motion of them, while it seems naturally to result from a previous motion of the body, is turned to some advantage. We perceive that it facilitates instead of hindering the general action of the body or the gracefulness of dancing. As in walking nobody praises a walk that is irregular and jerking, and as nobody sees any gracefulness or beauty in the waddling of a fat man or the trembling step of an invalid ; so in dancing nobody admires the dancing that is speedy, perfectly *unrhythmical*, and accompanied by violent swings of the hands.

The reference to walking and dancing suggests that graceful motion, as is said by Spencer, might be defined as motion in curved lines, certainly zig-zag movements are excluded from the suggestion. He says : "The sudden stoppages and irregularities which angular movements imply, are its antithesis : for a leading element of grace is continuity—flowingness"

It will be found that the above saying is merely another aspect of the same truth which we have said before. That as knowledge progresses the mode of impressions and expressions becomes more complex and economical (better adapted, that is, to obtain *the maximum of result with the minimum of energy or force*. This is a fundamental law of nature) in obedience to the law of least resistance and greatest traction or the resultant of the two, which governs motion, physical, psychological and sociological. And in addition to this we say that motion is undulatory or *rhythmical* ; and that motion in curved lines is an economical motion. Instead of giving the metaphysics of motion, we simply refresh our memory by saying that our daily walks, the flights of birds, the paces of graceful dancers, the drills of soldiers, the lines of railways, the foot-paths, the currents of streams, the cadences of orators, poets and singers, etc, are rhythmical or undulatory.

Instead of treating the subject of dancing at length, suffce it to say that the movements or locomotions of the feet, of the hands, of the features, and of the whole body, which we always use in a comparatively irregular form in our daily life, are regulated and advanced as a means to express emotions or centrally-initiated feelings.

If dancing in itself like an art, is debasiug, so are, also, the rhetoric, poetry, and music. Regarded from this point of view, it is unaccountable why the present agitation is directed against dancing wholesale. The same agitation would be better directed, if it were against, or in improving, the Nách and Kairbá of dancing-girls, of Tamásháválas, of Bhavaiás, and of many others. This sort of fun is not only ludicrous but is an eye-sore.

We cannot pass over without saying a few words on the gesticulations (Háva-Bháva or Arath) or the expressions of emotion by the features and by the movements of the body in artistic dancing. In dancing the expressions of emotion of pain or pleasure, suitable to words (this class of singing always deals more with poetry than with music), are exhibited more vividly by bodily movements than by voice. Certainly, the violent or inordinate emotions of a maniac and the horrible pangs of a sufferer are excluded from this description. Pleasurable feelings are attempted by voice, by flourishing the whole body, by brightening the eyes and by a gentle or graceful smile.

It is hardly necessary to say that while standing, we commonly economize power by throwing the weight chiefly on one leg, which we straighten to make it serve as a column, while we relax the other; and to the same end, we allow the head to lean some. what on one side. Instead of showing the necessity of using the neck in expressions of emotion, we simply remind ourselves that—that which the photographer does with our sitting, standing, and with adjusting our neck and sight, is better and done more artisically.

In dancing, painful feelings are shown more skilfully than the pleasurable ones, because the muscular action of this kind is much more decided to be imitated. A convulsive start of the whole body (not regardless of Tála or time), is shown by a sudden twinge. A pain is shown by a knitting of the brows, by a biting of the lips, and by the contraction of the features generally. A persistent pain is shown by different attitudes and postures, the body is made to swing to and fro (consistently with the general time of the piece of music), and the hands are clenched. Grief is shown by a wringing of the hands, the shedding of tears and by sighing. And even a pretended action of tearing the hair, cloths and ornaments or adornments, is restored to. A pretended mode of rubbishing the body and of committing suicide by poisons and by every instrument of Asiatic warfare is adopted. Anger is shown in frowns, in distended nostrils, in compressed lips, and in stamping the ground. And even the action of clenching the fingers, of blows of the shoulders, and of elbows and throwing about the clothes and ornaments, is not left in the cold. Discontent is shown by raised eyebrows and by wrinkled forehead. Disgust is shown by a curl of the lips, and offence is shown by a pout. In short, some of the natural expressions of emotion are so artistically performed (there are very few of this description), with due regard to decency and to music, that they give to a patient observer many materials, which a painter or a sculptor may turn to advantage. It is true that the majority of the painful expressions, is a result of the pretended grief, pain, disgust, discontent etc. but it shows in a degree the most unhappy result of poligamy. It is really irreconcilable with the notion of the performer to condemn poligamy, but it is a sentiment of the progressive humanity, and, therefore it predominates in spite of its objectionable surroundings. It is too much to say that monogamy is exclusively human, because there are many kinds of birds and animals, who practise it persistently.

To show the utility of certain gesticulations which we unconsciously practise in our daily life, we draw directly on the most thoughtful writings of Spencer, who is in one with the illustrious Darwin. Spencer says: "How truly language must be regarded as a hindrance to thought, though the necessary instrument of it, we shall clearly perceive on remembering the comparative force with which simple ideas are communicated by signs. To say 'Leave the room,' is less expressive than to point to the door. Placing a finger on the lips is more forcible than whispering 'Do not speak.' A beck of the hand is better than 'come here.' No phrase can convey the idea of surprise so vividly as opening the eyes and raising the eyebrows. A shrug of the shoulders would lose much by translation into words."

To add to the above subject we say "A nodding of the neck with a slight *ye* or *hn* or *hun*" is more expressive than any words of affirmation and approval. "A slight shaking of the neck with a slight *n* or *an* or *un* or *hn*" is more impressive than any words of negation and disapproval. "A slight wrinkle of the nose and of the forehead and a little raising of the cheeks and closing of the eyes with a slight *ish* or *hish* (or something expelling out)" is stronger than any amount of words of disgust and disapprobation. In short, there are numerous but impressive expressions of simple feelings which no form of orthography and of articulate language attempts to imitate. They are too short and inaudible to be covered by music. That branch of grammar, which is called interjection, and which condenses entire sentences into syllables, is too incomplete to give them due justice.

Darwin says that "from the excitement of pleasure the circulation becomes more rapid, the eyes are bright, and the colour of the face rises; and that the brain being stimulated by the increased flow of blood, reacts on the mental power. A man in this state holds his body erect, his head upright, and his eyes open; and that there is no drooping of the features, and no contraction of the eyebrows. To unwrinkle means to be cheerful or merry; and that the whole expression of a man in good spirit is exactly the opposite of that of suffering from sorrow."

C. Bell says: "In all the exhilarating emotions the eyebrows, eyelids, the nostrils, and the angles of the mouth are raised. In the depressing passions it is the reverse. Under the influence of the latter the brow is heavy, the eyelids, cheeks, mouth, and the whole body droop, the eyes are dull, the countenance pallid, and the respiration slow. In joy the face expands, in grief it lengthens."

The subject of dancing and gesticulations cannot be treated at length for want of space. But we can safely pronounce that, that which expresses feelings by bodily actions and movements to which the human flesh is heir, is the manifestation of the waves of nervous influence, which (waves) are the correlative of feelings, presentative, representative and re-representative.

Instead of treating the law of *reflex action* again, let us point out that from that pursuing of the mouth indicative of slight displeasure of a *Savant* in avoiding a false deduction upto the roaring of anger of a savage, and from that mechanism of the muscle (commonly-called) in weaping of a sufferer, —and from that contraction of the zigomatic muscles in a smile of a civilized upto the paroxysm of laughter of a rude man, and from that mechanism of the vocal cords in a whisper of a scandal-monger upto the most complex song of a singer—we find that mental excitement exhibits itself in bodily activity.

Spencer says:—"Before proceeding to the synthetic interpretation, it may be well to remark that even in our ordinary experience, the impossibility of dissociating the psychical states classed as intellectual from those seemingly most unlike psychical states classed as emotional, may be discerned. While we continue to compare such extreme forms of the two as an inference and a fit of anger, we may fancy that they are entirely distinct. But if we examine intermediate modes of consciousness, we shall quickly find some which are both cognitive and emotive.."

In closing this chapter we trust that the broad outlines of Indian music which are given in this and the proceeding chapters, cannot be said to have been accidental and to have been progressed when the said music was in its infancy, neither they can be said to have been borrowed by the ancient Hindus from their contemporary nations. Unhappily that part of Indian music, which is more interesting and instructive from a scientific point of view, has been entirely neglected by ourselves and by our predecessors. We give no theory, but confine our sphere and investigation to the narrower limits of calculating Svaras (notes). Tálas (time), Nritya (dancing) and Háva'-bháva (gesticulation), and thus degrade our music from its higher aspirations to lower pleasures. However, we believe that the evidence, which has been brought forward in our discussion, though of a small magnitude, is sufficient to warrant the leading proposition that Indian music was of higher development than it is generally voted to be and has been dying out for want of support.

Our task will be complete if we now turn our attention to the present state of Indian music.

VI

THE PRESENT STATE OF INDIAN MUSIC

It is neither with a pessimistic notion nor with a sarcastic object we remark that the striking defect of our present singers, is that very few of them are properly trained. This defective training is due, partly to the proverbial unwillingness of Indian musicians to part with their skill unreservedly, and partly to the want of ambition on the part of learners because of the lack of encouragement by the public. No sooner is a voice of some sweetness discovered than it is forced into a hurried drill for a time, the possessor of it is taught to sing a few Chijas (poetry set to music), and is straight way thrust before the public with as much trumpeting as his circumstances can admit of. The singer, after spluttering for a time, gradually subsides into a dead level of mediocrity ; or supposing him to be possessed of taste and perseverance, continues practising, and learns to sing by the time he has lost the major portion of the sweetness of his voice. In good many instances, the possession of a sweet voice is regarded by the owner as amply sufficient for his purpose, and he discards any attempt to acquire an artistic management of it. It is really puzzling that there are many vocalists who did not think it worth their while, to consult a sweetness of the voice as the necessary instrument to singing. There are now, and will no doubt always remain, a few not able exceptions to the above rule; but with the generality of singers there is not the remotest realization of concordance and no endeavour is made to hide defects by a careful and well-considered practice. It is enough that mere accident has given them a sweet voice, and henceforth let indiscriminate praise and patronage do their worst. Smooth and easy singing and graceful and finished phrasing go for nothing, and in their place an amount of shouting, shrieking, violent gesticulations, and comic grimaces are performed. Natural means are always preferable, but the necessary cultivation is of great utility. It is rigorously true, as is said by J. S. Mill and others, that natural is as artificial as artificial is natural, because art has no means independent of Nature. Art is a part and parcel of Nature. The words nature, art, and science, when properly interpreted into thought, are heriditarily transmitted,. accumulated and organized experiences of the continuous adjustment of subjective to objective relations which constitute life.

Other false methods of splitting the ear of the groundlings, have also come into vogue, namely, the introduction of high notes screamed out to the fullest extent of the singer's lungs and the practice of Tána (variation or swift jumping) has reached such a tremendous speed, that it can hardly be known by the performer himself, or followed by an artistic ear. Such a tremendous velocity is evidently inadmissible for the want of consonance in Svaras (notes) and in Rágas. It is ridiculous to presume that with such an undue haste of producing the notes, we can maintain a complete preservation of the Svaras (notes), of the principle of ascent and descent, of the Murchhanás and of the distinction of the Rágas. The practical ear is so much accustomed to the principles of Sura (concordance), of Komal-Tivra (half or sharp notes), of Arohan (ascent), of Avarohan (descent), of Minḍ (connection of notes by tension), of Ghasit (connection of notes by shortening the length of a sonorous body), of Ta'na (variation or jumping), of Murchhana' (¼th part of a tone), of Murki (an advanced form of the trill), of Kamp (shaking or *vibrato* tones), and of Ta'la (time or sequnce) that a slight breach in them is made out, and the performance is regarded not only as inartistic, but most unmusical.

In addition to the aforesaid defects of high notes

and speedy Ta'nas, there is one, which is very intolerable, namely, the introduction of the most complicated, slowest, and of fastest Ta'las. What earthly advantage could there be to the singers who pay more of their attention to the intricate branches of Ta'la, than to the Svaras ?

The Ta'las if normally kept, add to the charm of sound, but if handled most technically they are more puzzling than charming. However, such screaming-notes, speedy Ta nas and chronometric Ta'las are supposed to be the highest aim of the vocal art.

Notes that are too high, are shrill and lose entirely that sweet quality which constitutes the principal characteristic of musical notes. It is strictly true that the aesthetic principles to which the art of music successively confirms, have no absolute value. But it may be said with certainty that no single innovation will ever be accepted, which is clearly in conflict with the broad principles of music, which are reduced by Western philosophers and scientists to one single principle, viz. that musical notes must satisfy the laws of *harmony* and this is the more perfect, the more the notes of *a chord reinforce the fundamental note.*

Sound of fine *timbre* and harmonies of sound have in common the character, that they result from vibrations so related as to cause in the auditory apparatus the least conflict of action and the greatest amount of co-operation, thus producing the largest total of normal excitement in the nerve elements affected.

The high notes, swift Tánas and puzzling Tálas of claptrap are wholly undeserving the attention and support they receive; yet some of the highly praised singers do bring in these sensational means to pander to the liking of the un-deserving and shallow portion of their hearers. Stooping to such an unworthy device to obtain applause and patronage from the unthoughtful audience, which, unhappily, too often form the modern patrons of music, should be repudiated and shaken off by the singers who are capable of better things, and whose artistic conscience must cry shame at such slidings and presumptuous fallacies. Moreover, those on the topmost round of the ladder, should set a noble example to their brethern below. These abnormally high notes and undue liberties in music are always more or less disagreeable to the ear. It may justly be observed that there should be no violation of nearly the only rule in singing, which admits of no excuse—that two unsympathetic (like Vivadi) sounds must not be sounded successively or instantaneously. Such sounds never make a complete fusion, and hence are totally incompatible with music which is a pleasure-giving art.

In order that a chord, produced by three or more notes, may be consonant, it is necessary that the different notes that compose it bear, in respect of the number per second of the vibrations, simple ratios, not only to the fundamental note, but also to each other. It is rigorously true that music, if confined only to consonant chords, and it if does not adopt dissonant chords, would by extremely poor (monotonous).

P. Blaserna says : "Strictly speaking, much greater satisfaction is felt when a dissonant chord is resolved into a consonant chord than when nothing but consonant chord has been heard. It is the force of contrast which produces these sensations in us, just as we doubly appreciate a calm after a storm."

"There can be no absolute rule for the admission of dissonance, and for determining the limit up to which it may be used. All this depends on the degree of musical culture and on habit. Discords which now are perfectly permissible would have appeared monstrosities in the time of Palestrina"

It is necessary to remind the reader that the aforesaid description in no way affects the notes or determinate intervals of a musical scale, but it relates to a composition of those notes or intervals.

Again, how seldom singers are met with who can sing the ancient and old composers' florid music with clearness and flexibility? And how few, even in the simplest passages of Kirtan (something like *oratorio*), are capable of singing with sufficient religious pathos and fervency, to reach the hearts of their hearers, and thus create in them those agreeable and pleasurable sensations (peripherally-initiated feelings) and emotions (centrally-initiated feelings), which are the most coveted and even called *Nirvána* (total absorption or eternal happiness), the principal ambition and end of all religious beliefs. This want of skill to produce certain notes in a given time, is sadly observable in our day, and yet instances have been known of the astounding effect and influence, which some of the great singers of past ages had had over their hearers.

It is said of Tansen that when he sang before Haridás, the latter after hearing him with admiration told him :—"Whilst singing you neither stood, nor moved like a human being. This is supernatural, because you have concentreted the whole spirit of your body and mind into the voice. But I tell you these gigantic Gamaks (not jumping), Tánas, Paltás (a kind of variation), Bolatáns (variation of the poetical words in sound and in Tàla. In ordinary singing they do away with the words in Tàna and never-ending notes are only astonishing. Now it is time that you should think of pleasing your audience. You are too young to know your gift, and if you wish to reach the innermost heart, you must take a plainer and a simpler road." These few but most thoughtful words taught the singer a lesson which he never unlearnt, and thenceforth he studied to be effective and pathetic as well as grand and powerful. It is pitiful that many of our much-made-of singers could not receive a similar hint and profit by it.

It was observed more than once that when the late Haddu Khan of Gwallior used to sing to his satisfaction, his band (accompaniment) which consist-

7

ed of two Tànapurás, or Tamburás (four-stringed lyre), two Sárengis (fiddles), two boys or assistants (his sons) and a drummer, left off playing, and, when called attention, confessed that they were so much overpowered with admiration as to be unable to accompany him. No such effects are produced in our day, perhaps, we are getting more artistic than touching !

Haddukhán had held an undisputed sway over his contemporary Khya'l-singers and was credited with having preserved some of the cadences and Khya'ls of Ta'nsen and his successors, though he (Haddukhán) belonged to another family of the great singers of the 19th century. The cadences of Ta'nsen and of many others of the by-gone generations, were transmitted by generation to generation as a patrimony or heritage to the trustworthy and deserving relatives. This mode of confining the transmission and diffusion of music within the limited families and of dealing with it as an article of monopoly, had and has been so strict that it had and has been very difficult, though not impossible, for other families and amateurs to compete on terms of equality. This check has told very heavily on the circulation of Indian music and not only has it stopped further progress of the labour and thought of the by-gone generations, but has injured the art most vitally.

In connection, with the last prodigies of the Hindustani music we cannot pass over without enumerating, out of many, the names of the following artists :—

Vajirkha'n—Dhama'r-singer. Hasukha'n, Haddukha'n and Ta'nraskha'n—Khya'l-singers. Alija'n, Tasduk-Husen and Devaji—Ṭappa' and Tirvaṭ-Tara na -singers. Ba'bu Jotsingji, Kudousing, Joravarsing and Nasarkhán—drummers, Ghula'mali—Swarod-player. Va'rasalikhán—Bina'-player. Sa'dakalikha n—Raba'b-player. Ba'ha'dersenkha'nsa'heb—Raba b and Sursinga'r-player. And the last but not the least the late Gosva'mi Maha ra ja Shri Jivanla'lji (an amateur Sata'r and Bina'-player. The Ma'ha'ra'ja' was an artist in Joḍa in Bilambpada and in Madhya).

The aforesaid artists and a few others were the real artists in our time and whoever heard them and knew their real worth, was never left untouched and unmoved. These artists are not only dead and buried or burnt, but along with them many Ra'gas, cadences, songs, tunes and Parands of the Aryan design and Mahomedan improvement are irretrievably lost, never to reappear in their true form and force.

Language, intellectual or emotional, like organic beings, when once extinct, never reappears. The same language, as has been said by Western philosophers, never has two birthplaces. Distinct languages may be crossed or blended together, but the dominant (not, invariably superior in every respect) languages spread widely and lead to the gradual extinction of other languages.

The Rágas, which are composed by Hardás, (Tánsen's last Usta'd or teacher) Ra mda's, Surda's, Ta'nsen, Bila'skha'n and others, and called after their names, indicate a remarkable degree of the power of composition. The Ra'gas composed by these artists, are not new, but consisted of more than one old Ra'ga melodiously combined. There has been a general belief among the Indian musicians that however new and accomplished a composition of the notes may be, it can be classed under the names of the old Ra'gas, singly or combined.

Oh, but where are our Ta'nsens, Ba'ha'darsenkhánsáhebs and Máhárájás Shri Jivanláljis now? Alas, neither the pathos nor the Joḍas exist. It is true that occasionally some of the imitative pieces of the great vocalists and instrumentalists, are heard, but nothing unusual occurs except a fair execution of a few Rágas and Tánas.

Many vocalists get a name solely for the so called *musical literature* and *Ta'la-Prasta'r* (extension), others are liked for Rágas and Tánas, others are praised for Minḍ or Ghasiṭ, others are valued for Murki and Giṭakaḍi, and others are patronized *for vigour and vocal fire-works*. But is there ever heard a mastery of beautiful style combined with a sweet and forcible voice, skill in the management of it, purity of intonations, clearness of phraseology and above all, a capability to entrance the feelings of the hearers, the only object and aim of the evolution of music?

It is regretable to say that the recitative singing in Nátak (drama), is abnormally degenerated and hybridized. It is true that there are certain mixed airs of the so-called Indian and European music, but they cannot be classed as musical and are also very remote from any kind of perfection. This branch of music seems to be quite misunderstood because of there being no heart, no earnestness and no intelligence thrown into a true state of the legitimate singing. The deplorable fault in Nátak-singing, will not be magnified if it be said that it is the rule and not an exception, that we find but very few actors who can in singing, adjust their voices to the musical instruments and thus save the audience from the discordant and incoherent clatter which counts for singing. Such actors are anything but musical and artistic in expressing the genuine expression of Emotions. And yet such performers are allowed to act in singing and are patronized to become not only troublesome to a degree to the audience appreciating music and emotions, but to spread their so-called airs like a wild-fire throughout their patrons. It is simply ridiculous to see a parade of lads, in female costume, exhibiting fortuitous female feelings and charms.

Again, these interlopers in music think that by reciting their poems aloud or *falsetto* and by a lower or a higher tone at times or alternately, they execute the artistic modulations of voice. Many actors sing as if they have been taught to do certain things without understanding the motive for so doing. Any intelligent critic has only to attend a Nátak (Drama) to see the above facts fully demonstrated. Will the newly-started and much made of Gáyan Samájas (musical congresses of clubs) and schools of music at different quarters, tend to mitigate and alliviate the evil by assuring such actors that what they perform as singing, is no more than a sort of musical declamation of an ordinary type? The answer must, it is feared at the present at all events, remain in abeyance. If the Samájas and schools are unable to improve the Nátak-music, which is the more valued and appreciated, how are they to be credited to regenerate the music which is unalloyed by poetry and stage scenery?

The less we say, the better of our modern poets who unnecessarily mar their, otherwise good, poetries by encumbering them with their big-named Rágas and Tálas.

We know all vocal sounds, when considered by themselves, are musical sounds caused by the vibrations of the vocal cords. Vowels are, as their name implies, the only real vocal sounds; it is only in a vowel that a note can be said or sung. Our speech however is made up not only of vowels, but also of consonants, *i.e.*, of sounds which are produced not by the vibrations of the vocal cords, but by the expiratory blast being in various ways interfered or otherwise modified in its course through the throat and mouth. It is true that distinction between the vowels and consonants is, however, not an absolute one, as the characters of the several vowels depend on the form of the mouth and in the production of some consonants vibrations of the vocal cords do form a necessary though adjutant factor. Whenever we hear a note sounded by the larynx, we are able to recognize in its features one or other of the "vowels" as being uttered. Vowel sounds are in fact only extreme cases of quality, extreme prominence of certain overtones brought about by the shape assumed by the buccal and pharyngeal passages and orifices, as the vibrations pass through them. Each vowel has its approximate and causative disposition of these parts. Each of the "vowel" forms of the mouth possesses a note of its own, one towards which it acts as a resonance chamber.

Max Muller says : "The vowels are produced by the form of the vibrating air. They vary like the *timbre* of different instruments, and we in reality change the instrument on which we speak when we modify the buccal tubes in order to pronounce a, e, i, o and u.

G. P. Field says : "Vowel sounds are rich in overtones and can therefore be heard at a much longer distance. Hence whispering, in which, as the vowel sounds are abated, the consonants are relatively strengthened."

Woolf shows : "The broad A is heard further than any other vowel ; and also that, H without an added vowel, is the weakest of all the consonants."

As one of the great triumphs of the present science of Europe, Helmholtz has actually demonstrated the relative pitches and *timbres* of the vowels and has succeeded in making the fundamental pipe *speak* the different vowels in a clearly pronounced manner.

For the high notes singers prefer the "e" and "i" and find it impossible to pronounce "a" and "u" on the highest.

Do our poets know that there are many difficulties in their way to render their poems to the big-named Rágas and Tálas.

Strictly speaking, the laws of music, which are being accumulated and systematized by Western philosophers and scientists and which we have been using throughout our discussion, were certainly not known to our genius-poets and musicians of olden times, who have left an imperishable mark in their respective works. They were guided in their works by feelings, fancy and artistic inspirations.

As the most profound knowledge of Grammar, Syntax and Prosody is not sufficient to make even a mediocre *poet*, so no complex study of the laws of harmony and instrumentation would be sufficient to create a *musician*. Science is directive and art is executive ; the former systematizes, while the latter accumulates.

Singing, when developed to its higher stage of perfection, does away with words as its adjuncts, and produces not only the same influence but better effect.

To return to the thread of our immediate subject, we remark that another cause of deterioration in singing of our day is the strength of Sáth (band or accompaniment) which is the principal hindrance. It is perfectly useless for a best singer in the world to attempt to make himself heard through a number of voices, strings, pipes, bells and parchments played. No human lungs could do such a feat with ease and grace. And yet the experiment of many instruments as accompaniments, is continuously being tried. Most singers think, as if it were a necessity, highly of their band which appears to claim their attention and in good many instances they appear to study nothing else.

With the majority of singers we find 2 boys or assistants, 2 big Tánpurás or Tamborás, 2 big fiddles with as many strings and holes as the instrument can bear and a noisy Pakhávaj or Tablábáyá. In some performances the above list is greatly swelled as a means to melodies by the incoherent and unsympathetic instruments. It should be borne in mind that the audience like to hear the vocalists as well as the instrumentalists. Singers, in making their headway against so many odds and so much power brought literally to play upon them, are seen opening their mouths and we are led to fancy that they are singing ; but, honestly speaking, nothing comes out of their mouths, except the pantomimic action, contortion of the features and above all the most funny and comic expressions of the different phases of anthropomorphous animals, the band efiectually drowning whatever vocal effect might be intended.

Nothing is more pleasurable, elevating and ennobling than to listen to melodies and harmonies produced by trained and sweet voices ; and nothing is gained by overpowering them, when it can so easily be avoided.

Singers ought to contrive to keep their band in playing with as little din and noise as possible and to enhance the pleasure of their audience and thus be appreciated. It is necessary for an artistic performance to have an accompaniment of a few instruments as a support and addition to the voice, but it is also very desirable that the instrumentalists should rest satisfied with their opportunity for displaying their skill without attempting to ruin the voice of their co-operator.

It is self-evident that the organ of voice is a musical instrument by the aid of which we communicate our emotional and intellectual feelings and thoughts in their most intimate and delicate shade an instrument so flexible and complete that the most perfect artificial contrivance cannot imitate it in the diversity of shades and qualities, which enable the human voice to express the most varied sentiments and passions.

Spencer says :—"It is generally agreed that the tones of the human voice are more pleasing (because they are very rich in harmonics) than any others. Grant that music takes its rise from the modulations of the human voice under emotion, and it becomes a natural consequence that the tones o that voice should appeal to our feelings more than others ; and so should be considered more beautiful than any others."

The most that can be said of the instrumental music, is that it is supplementary. In an advanced stage of musical culture the instrumental music is specialized, and has its own charms.

It will create a capital effect if some of our airs and tunes of artistic value, which are peculiarly adapted to be played by a number of instruments at a time, are widened, extended and reduced to the European *notation*, and are heard through their *bands*. The so-called Native airs, which are played by the bands, and which are selected for the musical boxes, are too unmusical to charm the culvitated ear. Some of the Native princes, no doubt, have their bands taught to play Native airs, and the impression is pleasant, but the airs selected are inartistic. If any enterprising artist of high culture and test were to devote himself to compose new airs and tunes of certain simple and compound Ra'gas and of certain Dhuns with due regard to Tála, and get them performed by the European band, the result cannot be otherwise than charming. As a matter of fact, all the technicalities of Indian classic music, cannot be done adequate justice to by the European instruments as they stand now. We must, however, frankly admit and admire that the European instruments as a class, are superior to the Indian instruments in every respect, except the individual string-instruments which are specialized to execute Mind, Ghasit, Murchhaná and Murki, which are the real artistic peculiarities and the charming influences of Indian music.

Apart from the above consideration, we pronounce that on the whole it is easy to perceive that many of the defects of our modern singing, may be ascribed to the increased dimensions of the Sáth (band) and its difficult and fortuitous ways of playing. In this connection we cannot pass over without strongly condemning the false notion of drummers that their aid is required to test the vocalist's or instrumentalist's steadiness (Laya) in Tála (time) by harassing him with the most abstruse technicalities of drumming, as if he had to attend only to Tálas and not to Svaras (notes). A vocalist is a real prodigy when assisted by instrumentalists, but is a helpless victim in the hands of instrumentalists when assailed in sounds by them and in time by the drummer. These beatings of drums, clapping of hands, clashing of cymbals, playing of instruments, and these bowing and blowing with might and main by the instrumentalists, lead to shouting, shrieking, screaming and to the roughness of style on the part of singers, to say nothing of the loss of the purity of tone and the spoiling of voices. It would have puzzled our by-gone celebrities to have their voices driven through a tremendous force which is not uncommonly employed as an accessary to the charm of voice.

It is true that the civilized nations of the West have advanced their music to such a degree of perfection, according to their standard of taste, that they utilize different melodies and harmonies to be sung or played by different voices or instruments simultaneously and successively, and produce an effect which to our ear, is too complex to know and judge. But it may safely be said that the Europeans as nations, are really civilized, progressive and con-considerably free to shake off the old ways which on examination prove to be of no use, and to take to new ones or the better ones. It is, therefore, to be presumed that the effect produced by singing and playing of so many voices and instruments at a time, might not be unmusical, but might be a necessary consequence of constructive, distributive and collective skill which progress involves. Broadly speaking, the present music of Europe seems to be on the ascending branch of the parabola.

It is absurd to say that every form or school of music is absolutely charming to all humanity, but is relatively so—to those who have imbibed from their infancy and have been taught individually, socially, and above all hereditarily. Heriditary transmission applies to psysical as well as phychical peculiarities.

Hence the difference even in the Christan nations of accents and music.

Generally speaking, the Italian music is called simple, intelligible, and melodious; while the German music is studied, obsure and transcendental. In short, every nation has its special marks in national music.

Doctor Saman, in some interesting remarks on the subject of music, doubts "whether even amongst the nations of Western Europe, intimately connected as they are by close and frequent intercourse, the music of the one is interpreted in the same sense by the others."

In returning to the subject in hand, we say that on enquiries it is found that even Europeans, with all knowledge and notation, are, at times, helpless to reduce to writing the most touching and charming cadences of their great singers. Every art has its own secrets which are taught by personal tuition and apprenticeship. This difficulty stands in the way, as we have said more than once, of many musicians whose performance does not go, as a rule, beyond tom-tom music, and confounds with music proper. Tom-tom music is as separate from the Indian classic music as vulgar language is from Sanskrit.

In connection with the overstraining of voice of which we have said before, the subject of Kharaja or Anuda'tt (grave or bass sound), perhaps, deserves a little attention. That the Kharaja has gradually been lowered to a pitch, which to singers is almost beyond endurance, is an unmistakeable fact; and it is within the bounds of possibility that further lowering may yet be made. Lowering of voice to the pitch, when its natural harmonics are hardly appreciable to the ear, is not a vocal charm; but it is a kind of voice considerably shorn, though skilful and difficult, of the harmonics which alone adorn the voice as an indispensable medium to express our thoughts and feelings in their most complex shades. It is true that the tones, in which feelings express themselves, are not always high, but are also deep in comparison with the register or Svaritt.

The tendency to produce a tone of *a very low* pitch, is an established and well-understood sign of anger eventually being used consciously as a threat. The low pitch is indicative of disagreeable feelings such as growling, grumbling, indignation, etc. It is true that disagreeable feelings are also shown in screams and shouts.

When our by-gone artists composed Chijas (poetry set to music in Rágas and Jilhás) they knew that they (Chijas) were within the reach of most voices, and could be delivered without violent efforts ; but transpose them either to a higher or a lower pitch and see how mighty is the differnce. The result in most cases is neither pleasant to the hearer, nor graceful to the performer, but very often greatly tends to bring splendid natural means to premature decay. Whom are we to blame for such intolerable transpositions of high and low pitches ? The former fault must, we think, be laid at the door of instrumentalists. It is a well-known fact that the higher the pitch, the greater the brilliancy of tone produced on most instruments. The latter fault lies with the singers who in the heat of competing with the instrumentalists, lower the pitch to such a depth that most instruments are incapable of following the voice. It is, however, to be hoped that further steps in the above directions may be stayed and discouraged. One of the best indications to that effect, is the adoption of European wind-instruments (the only defect in them is that they get out of tune soon) to replac the string-instruments which do not give a long current of sound unless produced by a bow, and that too is not in unity or quality with the voice. It is absolutely necessary that the accompanying instruments, excepting the drum, must not be only in *unision,* but must be in quality or *timbre.*

To secure the above end in the best possible way, is to adopt "voice" as an accompaniment with some wind-instruments as support. The accompanying voice should only support and intensify the performing one when it makes a stand. Such an effect will not only be capital, but most touching and impressive. It is rigorously true that the wind instruments are wanting in Ghasiṭ but the performing voice can do its Ghasiṭ without support after a long practice. The present mode of accompaniments, is an anomaly, because the singer and player do not do the same general thing with their means, which the word Sa th (accompaniment) implies.

The high and low pitches the swift Ta'nas (variation) and difficult Ta'las (time) have enormonsly contributed to ruin many a voice and to spoil music. It is most intolerable that musicians as a class try to test the capability of their andience instead of consciously trying to please them. In attempting to overwhelm their audience (who in retaliation frightens the performer with the big-named Ra'gas and Ta'las) with the abstruse technicalities they miserably overlook the pleasurable effect of their art. This stratagem leads to many difficult branches of music, which are more astonishing or frightful than pleasant. Any attempt to cast off the above defects should, we hope, be supported by true lovers of music.

Before dismissing this side of our discussion, we give below a few popular hints, which, if properly adhered to, will considerably improve the present defects of our singing and playing :—

1st.—There should be a sweetness of voice and instruments, and a complete concordance of all the notes to be touched in a piece of music.

2nd.—There should be a sympathetic correspondence of the voice and its accompaniments, and the drummer should try to keep up his time with as delicate a handling as possible and to keep his instrument in tune.

3rd.—The number of the notes of a Ra'ga should be scrupulously preserved even in Minḍ or Ghasiṭ, in

Murki, in Tána, or in each and every way of going from a note to a note with due regard to the principle of ascent and descent.

4th.—The Murchhanás should be touched by a Minḍ or Ghasiṭ along with the notes on which they depend and never separately, and there should be no stand made on them.

5th.—There should be moderation in pitch, in Minḍ or Ghasiṭ, in Murki, in Tána and in Tála, and the activities wasted away by bodily actions and movements, should be concentrated on the voice and instruments.

Our final task is to treat the present literature on Indian music.

VII

MODERN AUTHORS AND CRITICS ON INDIAN MUSIC

In concluding our discussion, a question of a somewhat delicate natue, concerning music, now crops up, but as it is of great importance, and the remaining vitality of the half-dead Indian music solely depends upon it, the question should not be fearfully shirked under any amount of odium. Such a meterial question cannot at any cost be evaded in this discussion. It may be asked, are not most of our so-called authors and critics of music answerable and responsible for much of the false taste and gross ignorance so palpably displayed and betrayed by our audience ? It is really uncharitable not to presume and not to admit that there are a few able, experienced, and impartial authors and critics, who are capable of doing their self-imposed duty with admiration and authority ; but it is also a fact that there are many more who cannot, with honesty, be classed in the above category.

In the majority of published works and criticisms on Indian music, it is not difficult to discover numberless instances of the gross laxity of the primary laws of music, as an art or a science ; and the main object appears to be to write with pedantic exaggeration something without any knowledge, practical or theoretical, under the proverbially revered and impunitive cloth of an author with the object of praising or dispraising a particular school (form) of music. According to such writers, everything is good or bad as the case may be ; and it is not an uncommon occurrence to find two accounts directly opposed to each other of the same Rága and Tála, not only in ideal judgment, but in matter-of-fact particulars. It is proverbial that tastes vary and differ, but that is no excuse why certain canons of a particular school of music should be entirely respected or disregarded. A few out of many inconsistencies, above referred to, combined with a certain amount of flippancy, unhappily in nine cases out of every ten, appear to constitute the sum and substance of modern works and criticisms on Indian music.

There is no standard work on Indian music in any of the spoken languages of the present age, no school is regularly constituted, no competent masters to teach music unreservedly, no examinations are held by professors of music, and in fact no knowledge of the art ; but as equivalent of so many conditions which progress presupposes, we have good deal of impudence and conceit, a vast amount of assumptions and presumptions, and these together with much of the ordinary gloss of the present age, seem to make up the sum total of an author or critic as a recognized stock-in-trade. There is firing and throwing together of words and intricate phraseology, culled from old works of music, or from a Sanskrit Kosha (Dictionary), which, on an artistic or scientific examination, mostly turn out to be simply meanningless grandiloquence that ever soiled a paper. And yet such nonsenses are printed and quoted to help to mislead and to misguide our otherwise enlightened and not easily to be deceived public opinion.

Anybody with a commonplace knowledge of the subject, with a literal insight into the technicalities of Suddha (Diatonic), of Komala (Chromatic), of Tar Tivra (sharper), of Ati-Komala (very flat), of Oḍhava (Rága with 5 notes), of Khaḍava (6 notes), of Sampurna (7 notes), of Sankirna (gleaned or compounded), of A'rohan (ascent), A'varohan (descent), of Shrutis (ratio of the Saptak or scale), of Murchhaná ($\frac{1}{4}$th part of a tone), of Gráma (collection, musically meaningless), of Prastára (extension), of Tála (sequence) of Minḍ or Ghrashaṭak (sliding), and a knowledge of the Sanskrit literature, thinks himself amply justified in giving to the public his works and opinions, and would write with all the airs, as if he had all the intricacies of the art or science, as the case may be, at his finger's end. These so called authors and critics have not the least idea of the theory of musical sounds, nor have they the knowledge of how to produce voice musically. They do not know the real distinction between velocity, intensity, pitch and quality of sound. Nor have they a clear comprehension of the construction and capability of musical instruments. They are unable to realize a Ra'ga or possibly a sound correctly when emitted by voice or by instruments, and are utterly ignorant of the science of melody and its later off-spring harmony. In short, such writers are perfect strangers to the physical, psychological, and socio-logical evolution of sound. And yet these so-called authors and critics presume to pass an elaborate judgment, not only on music of the Hindu design and Mahomadan improvement, as well as on the musicians who have devoted their whole life to study their art, but on also the European music which is one of the real wonders of the 19th century. These self-constituted professors and authors fancy that, by reading a little literature on music and by mere attempts at learning it, they are sufficiently qualified to say whatever they like on it.

Practical experience and theoretical perception in every branch of knowledge, are commonly unattain-able by an individual to a very great extent, and the want may be allowed for, if it is not exclusive of each other, but there is a fair proportion so as not to be prejudicial to each other. To make oneself a practical artist, it is desirable that he should know the primary laws of the scientific aspect of his art, but at the same time it is not necessary that he should master the most complex scientific details to learn singing and know how to reach the heart with sweet and skilled voice. History and the living ins-tances of Europe amply confirm the above fact.

P. Blaserna says : " I will content myself by saying that in our modern music art has outstripped science with rapid strides, and it is only quite recently that the latter has been able to give complete and rational explanation of what the former has effected by means of delicate æsthetic feeling. Science cannot desire to be substituted for art."

N. Lockyer, in his translation of the "Forces of Nature", says—" If we mean by musical sounds those which an artist thinks right to introduce into his work to add to the desired effect, not only must those sounds be closely connected by bonds, which are determined by the pitch and duration, but they must unite certain particular qualities, the examination of which pertains more to the domain of art than that of seience."

A. Bain says: " But high scientitic knowledge manifestly transcends the sphere of Art, just as a highly artistic form transcends the sphers of science. If it were otherwise, we should be great gainers. If what give us knowledge and certainty as regards the world were also of easy comprehension, and the source of light and fascinating amusement, we should be saved from many pains, and take much higher strides of advancement in the happiness and security of life."

Spencer says that among men a vague notion prevails that the scientific knowledge differs in nature from common knowledge. He conclusively shows that there is no absolute line of demarcation between the two, because the same faculties are employed in both cases and their mode of operation is fundamentally the same. Even the common actions of man presuppose facts colligated, inferences drawn, resuits expected, and general success of these actions proves the data by which they were guided to have been correctly put together. He, after analysing the subject at length, which for want of space we cannot bring out here, says:—"It is a difference not between common knowledge and scientific knowledge, but between the successive phases of science itself, or knowledge itself—whichever we choose to call. In its earlier phases science attains only to certainty of knowledge, in its later phases it further attains to completeness. We begin by discovering a relation: We end by discovering the relation. Our first achievement is to foretell the kind of phenomena which will occur under specific conditions: our last achievement is to foretell not only the kind but the amount. Or, to reduce the proposition to most definite form—undeveloped science is qualitative prevision: developed science is quantitative prevision. . . . And this is the difference which leads us to consider certain orders of knowledge as scientific when contrasted with knowledge in general." . . .

"So close, indeed, is the relationship, that it is impossible to say where science begins and art ends. All the instruments of the natural philosopher are the products of art; the adjusting one of them for use is an art; there is art in making an observation with one of them; it requires art properly to treat the facts ascertained; nay, even the employing established generalizations, to open the way to new generalizations, may be considered as art. In each of these cases previously organized knowledge becomes the implement by which new knowledge is got at: and whether that previously organized knowledge is embodied in a tangible apparatus or in a formula, matters not in so far as its essential relation to the new knowledge is concerned. If as, no one will deny, art is applied knowledge, then such portion of the scientific investigation as consists of applied knowledge is art. So that we may even say that as soon as any prevision in science passes out of its originally passive state, and is employed for reaching other previsions, it passes from theory into practice—becomes science in action—becomes art. And when we thus see how purely conventional is the ordinary distinction, how impossible it is to make any real separation—when we see not only that science and art were originally one; that the arts have perpetually assisted each other; that there has been a constant reciprocation of aid between the sciences and arts, but that the sciences act as arts to each other, and that the established part of each science becomes an art to the growing part—when we recognize the closeness of these associations, we shall the more clearly perceive that as the connexion of the arts with each other has been ever becoming more intimate, as the help given by sciences to arts and by arts to sciences, has been age by age increasing; so the interdependence of the sciences themselves has been ever growing greater, their mutual relations more involved, their *consensus* more active.

In returning to the subject in hand, we remark that the so-called authors and critics are increasing now-a-days at the expense of the artists and the public at large.

It is true that composition and criticism are diametrically opposite operations of the human mind: they ought to go hand in hand, and as far as possible with a common agreement, and be complementary one to the other; but the critic will never be a great composer, nor the composer a true critic.

Clever artists must laugh when they read—if they ever do—the mass of stuff written concerning their art, of which they have made a life-long study; and yet their experience and knowledge do not allow them to presume and pretend to promulgate a practice or theory of sound, and to impose and practise on public credulity. It is amply justifiable and not too much to pronounce that, if the so-called authors and critics are called upon to submit to an examination to adjust or to find out the difference between the four strings but two notes of Tamborá (four-stringed lyre) —the A B C of the Indian musician, we shall find the percentage of success not only microscopic, but their presumptions and pretensions are sure to vanish in the air.

What bitterness must arise in the mind of artists at times when they cogitate over the power that is wielded by these misleaders of the public opinion?

Power used with discretion, is a desideratum, but becomes a nuisance when used recklessly, at random, and now and then for a motive worthy of nothing but misplaced confidence in one's own abilities.

Again, are not works ever and anon written to propound a particular practice of the Rágas and Tálas, which was never in existence? The major portion of the published music contains a substance which, if reproduced as a vocal or instrumental art, would hardly please the cultivated ear for which it has professedly been published and trumpeted. Many of these authors are fabulous, others are superstitious, and others are full with mythology. None of them, even after a great deal of verbosity, can answer the needful treatment of music, as an alluring and ennobling art, and of its grand evolution to rejoice an innumerable species of animals, man included, with complex sensations (peripherally-initiated feelings), and emotions (centrally-initiated feelings), peculiar to each species and special to each race and its sub-divisions, and of its formation to constitute a part of that whole—a whole which is instrumental in increasing the average length and happiness of individual, family, tribal, national, and human life—a whole which is the force (human activities in their individual and social welfare) that governs and promotes civilization as a means to an end.

Whatever ascetic morality may say, pleasures and pains are the incentives and restrictions by which life is prolonged and multiplied. No contemptuous title of pig-philosophy, as is said by Western philosophers, will alter the eternal law, (so long as life exists), that Misery is the high way to death; while happiness is added Life, and the giver of life. Life, individual and social, on a rational plan, is not of an asceticism; but of full enjoyment in the performance of function and the gratification of senses without endangering the equal happiness of other men. It is an established induction of, and deduction from, the hypothesis of Evolution that pains are the correlatives of actions injurious to the organism, while pleasures are the correlatives of actions conducive to its welfare.

A. Bain says :—"It is a fact of great practical importance that fellow-feeling requires us to have a certain regard to our own happiness in the first instance. If our lot contains but a small share of pleasure, or, if by an ascetic culture we are made to set little value on the enjoyment of life, we part with the very basis of sympathy. Thus, while a large amount of self-regard excludes sympathy, self-abnegation and misery extinguish it. There is a certain middle point between the two extremes, where fellow-feeling is most likely to flourish."

J. S. Mill says : - "That men need not be comfortable themselves in order to enter into discomforts of others ; virtue and wretchedness are incompatible."

H. Spencer says :—"Here, as in every case, there can be no altruistic feeling but what arises by sympathetic excitement of a corresponding egoistic feeling ; and hence there can never be a sense of justice to others when there is not a sense of justice to self, at least equally great. . . . Societies, past and present, supply ample evidence of these relations. At the one extreme, we have the familiar truth that the type of nature which readily submits to slavery, is a type of nature equally ready to play the tyrant when occasion serves. At the other extreme, we have the fact well-illustrated in our own society, that along with the increasing tendency to resist aggression, there goes a diminishing tendencv on the part of those in power to aggress." . . .

"The conflict that has hitherto gone on in every society between the predatory life and the industrial life, has necessitated a corresponding conflict between modes of feelings appropriate to the two, and there have similarly been necessitated conflicting standards of right. But now that the pain-inflicting activities are less habitual, and the repression of the sympathies less constant, the altruistic sentiments, which find their satisfaction in conduct that is regardful of others and so conduces to harmonious co-operation, are becoming stronger. The sacredness of life, of liberty, of property, are more and more vividly felt as civilization advances."

Again, none of our so-called and much-made of authors are scientific, however boasting and noisy they may be, to explain and convince that Sound is a transformation or equivalent of Heat or molecular motion, and in itself is a wave of sonorous vibrations caused by the purcussion and friction or by both of solids, liquids and gasses against each other or between themselves. Such authors cannot give us a tangible theory of the phenomenon of sound and prove that it is not universal like gravitation, but is confined to the earth within the limits of atmosphere although in various degrees in torrid, tropical and temporate zones. They also cannot teach us to explain—that sound is conspicuously absent from the antartic, arctic and frigid regions, and is totally absent from a complete vacuum and inter-stellar spaces due to the absence of elastic bodies and tangible media—the necessary condition for the expenditure of heat or manifestation of *Sound* and to explode to pieces the "Nádo-Brahm" notion of the early Hindus.

Do our so-called psychologists know that what we call feelings, sensational, perceptional, and emotional, are the concomitant nervous changes or the waves of nervous influence? Do they also know that by virtue of the general law of nervo-motor action, every feeling has for its primary concomitant a diffused nervous discharge, which excites the muscles at large, including those of the vocal organs, in a degree proportionate to the strength of feeling, and therefore muscular activity increases in amount—be the nature of feeling what it may? Again, do our misnomers comprehend that deep down in the nervo-muscular structures, as they have been evolved by converse between the organism and its environment, are to be found the cause of all the manifestations; and that in the nature of things there have grown up these connexions between internal feelings and external manifestations? It is beyoud the reach of our so-calied psychologists to grasp that a secondary concomitant of feeling in general as it rises in intensity, is an excitement by the diffused discharge, first of the small muscles attached to easily-moved parts, afterwards of morenumerousand large muscles moving heavier parts, and eventually of the whole body.

In short, such self-styled and self-praised philosophic and scientific authors and critics are incapable of comprehending that the production of Sound by animals, is a necessary manifestation of the nervous and muscular force generated and expended by the impressions and expressions which constitute life—as continuous adjustment of internal (subjective) to external (objective) relations—philosophically called ***Natural Selection*** or ***Survival of The Fittest***; and that the intensity of Sound demonstrates the strength of feelings involved; and that the change of Sound is an indicator of the variety of sentiments and passions aroused.

Through the instrumentality of such sham writers and critics many a talented artist has hopelessly been driven out of the patronage which he otherwise richly deserves, and the cause of regenerating Indian music, is not only retrograded and obscured, but the music of Hindu design and Mahomedan improvement of many centuries, is shamelessly forced to die an accelerated death.

That the cultivation of music has no effect on the mind, few will be absurd enough to contend. Every civilized nation (past and present) rationally believes that in its bearing upon human happiness, the emotional language, which musical culture develops and refines, is second to none; and that music has an effect beyond the immediate pleasure it produces, because every class of rational enjoyment does not end with itself, but ministers to bodily and mental well-being. Our nature is such that in fulfilling each desire we in some way facilitate the fulfilment of the rest.

Music in which we discover the synthesis of one of the grandest evolutions of human feeling—is an evolution that in itself forms one of the most brilliant pages in the history of human culture.

The illustrious Darwin, in his "Expression of Emotions" says : "That the chief expressive actions exhibited by man and the lower animals, are now innate or inherited—that is, have not been, learnt by the individual—is admitted by everyone. So little has hearing or imitation to do with several of them that they are from the earliest days and throughout life quite beyond our control, for instance, the relaxation of the certain muscles of the skin in blushing and the increased action of the heart in anger. We may see children, and even these born blind blushing from shame, and the naked sculp of every young infant reddens from passions. If infants scream from pain or frown disapproval, we readily perceive sympathy in others by their expression, our sufferings are thus mitigated aud our pleasure increased, and mutual good feeling is thus strengthened. The movements of expression give vividness and enegy to our spoken words. They reveal the thoughts and intentions of others more truly than do words which may be falsified. The first expression of our outward signs of an emotion, intensifies it. Ou the other hand, the repression, as far as this is possible, of all outward signs softens our emotion. These results follow partly from the intimate relation which exists between almost all the emotions and their outward manifestations ; and partly from the direct influence of exertion on the heart, and consequently on the brain. Even the simulation of an emotion tends to arouse it in our minds. We also know that expression in itself..., is certainly of importance for the welfare of man kind."

Illustrious Herbert Spencer, in his finishing remark on the principles of psychology, philosophically says :—"The æsthetic feelings and sentiments are not, as our words and phrases lead us to suppose, feelings and sentiments that essentially differ in origin and nature from the rest. They are nothing else than particular modes of excitement of the faculties, sensational, perceptional, and emotional—faculties which, otherwise excited, produce those other modes of consciousness constituting our ordinary impressions, ideas, and feelings. The same agencies are in action ; and the only difference is in the attitude of consciousness towards its resulting states."

"Throughout the whole range of sensations, perceptions, and emotions which we do not call as æsthetic, the states of consciousness serve simply as aids and stimuli to guidance and action. They are transitory, or if they persist in consciousness some time, they do not monopolize the attention : that which monopolizes the attention is something ulterior, to the effecting of which they are instrumental. But in the states of mind we class as æsthetic, the opposite attitude is maintained towards the sensations, perceptions, and emotions. They are no longer links in the chain of states which prompt and guide conduct. Instead of being allowed to disappear with merely passing recognition, they are kept in consciousness and dwelt upon : their natures being such that their continued presence in consciousness is agreeable."

"Before this action of the faculties can arise, it is necessary that the needs to be satisfied through the agency of sensational, perceptional, and emotional excitements shall not be urgent. So long as there exist strong cravings arising from bodily wants and unsatisfied lower instincts, consciousness is not allowed to dwell on these states that accompany the actions of the higher faculties : the cravings continually exclude them."

"The activities of this order begin to show themselves only when there is reached an organization so superior, that the energies have not to be wholly expended on the fulfilment of material requirements from hour to hour."

..."When, however, a long discipline of social life decreasingly predatory and increasingly peaceful, has allowed the sympathies and resulting altruistic sentiments to develop, these, too, begin to demand spheres of superfluous activity. Fine art of all kinds takes forms more and more in harmony with these sentiments."

"A final remark worth making is, that the æsthetic activities in general may be expected to play an increasing part in human life as evolution advances. Greater economization of energy, resulting from superiority of organization, will have in the future effects like those it has had in the past. The order of activities to which the æsthetics belong, have been already initiated by this economization, will hereafter be extended by it: the economization being achieved both directly through the improvement of all appliances, mechanical, social, and other. A growing surplus of energy will bring a growing proportion of the æsthetic activities and gratifications, and while the forms of art will be such as yield pleasurable exercise to the simpler faculties, they will in a greater degree than now appeal to the higher emotions."

To a patriotic Indian nothing is more mournful than to see the dying out of Indian music which in its grandeur must have attracted innumerable heads and hearts at times and places.

Oh, why are not our public equally, if not more, thoughtful as they are in matters, political and educational? And why are they so easily led away by the so-called authors and critics on Indian music, in spite of their patriotism which is the most marked trait of modern civilization? And above all, why do not those of the professional and amateur musicians critics and authors, who are capable of better things than those aforesaid, set their feet on the shameful system of bogus writings and criticisms, and thus save and revive the half-dead Indian music from its total annihilation or transformation to a hybrid class—a music that must have in its glory rejoiced many a generation of the ancient and old Indians by its solacing, ennobling, and, above all, charming influence—an influence for which music as a whole has been brought into requisition, not only by the civilized Europeans, Americans, Asiatics and Africans, but by the human race as a whole—a whole composed of the most horrible savage of the forest and the most thoughtful philosopher of the world—the world in which savages transform into families, families into tribes, tribes into communities, communities into nationalities, and nationalities into internationalities, and internationalities in their turn concentrate their collective knowledge or experience into philosophers and philosophers i their turn, after exhausting all possible knowledge in explaining the immutable laws of the inorganic, organic and superorganic evolution and dissolution, stop and conclude :—To *think* is to *condition* ; and conditional limitation is the fundamental law of the possibility of thought. For as the greyhound cannot outstrip his shadow, nor the eagle outsoar the atmosphere in which he floats, and by which alone he may be supported, so the mind cannot transcend that sphere of limitation, within and through which exclusively the possibility of thought is realized. Thought is only of the conditioned, because to think is simply to condition. The *absolute* is conceived merely by a negation of conceivability, and all that we know, is only known as—Won From the Void And Formless Infinite.

FINIS

Robust Safety-Critical Control

IEEE Press
445 Hoes Lane
Piscataway, NJ 08854

Robust Safety-Critical Control

Theory, Application and Experiments

Tengfei Liu
Northeastern University, China

Si Wu
Northeastern University, China

Zhi Liu
Northeastern University, China

Zhong-Ping Jiang
New York University, USA

IEEE*Press*
WILEY

Published by John Wiley & Sons, Inc., Hoboken, New Jersey.

Library of Congress Cataloging-in-Publication Data has been applied for:

Print ISBN: 9781394400188
ePDF ISBN: 9781394400201
ePub ISBN: 9781394400195
oBook ISBN: 9781394400218

Cover Design: Wiley
Cover Image: Zitong Lin, College of Arts, Northeastern University, China

To our families

Contents

List of Figures

List of Table

About the Authors

Tengfei Liu received his Ph.D. from the Australian National University, Canberra, Australia, in 2011. From 2011 to 2013, he was a postdoctoral fellow at the Polytechnic Institute of New York University. Since 2014, he has been with Northeastern University, China, where he is currently a full professor. His research focuses on the stability and control of interconnected nonlinear systems. He leads the first cohort of the NSFC Innovative Research Group Project, the only award of its kind in the control discipline. He has served as an Associate Editor for IEEE Transactions on Automatic Control since 2022.

Si Wu received his Ph.D. from Northeastern University, Shenyang, China, in 2025, where he currently serves as a Postdoctoral Fellow and an Associate Research Fellow. His research interests focus on nonlinear control theory and applications to vehicles and robotic systems. He was a leading team member winning the IMAV 2019 outdoor competition.

Zhi Liu received his B.E. degree in Automation from Northeastern University, China, in 2021. He is currently pursuing a Ph.D. in Control Science and Engineering at Northeastern University. His research interests include safety-critical control theory and its applications to Euler–Lagrange systems. He was a recipient of the Zhang Si-Ying (CCDC) Youth Paper Award in 2023.

Zhong-Ping Jiang received the M.Sc. degree in statistics from the University of Paris XI, France, in 1989, and the Ph.D. degree in automatic control and mathematics from ParisTech-Mines, France, in 1993, under the direction of Prof. Laurent Praly.

Currently, he is an Institute Professor in the Department of Electrical and Computer Engineering at the Tandon School of Engineering, New York University. His main research interests include stability theory, robust/adaptive/distributed nonlinear control, robust adaptive dynamic programming, reinforcement learning, and their applications to information, mechanical, transportation, and biological systems. In these fields, he has written seven books and is the author/co-author of about 600 peer-reviewed journal and conference papers.

Prof. Jiang is currently serving the IEEE Intelligent Transportation Systems Society's Board of Governors, and has served as Deputy Editor-in-Chief, Senior Editor, and Associate Editor for numerous journals. He is among the Clarivate Analytics Highly Cited Researchers and Stanford's Top 2% Most Highly Cited Scientists. In 2022, he received the Excellence in Research Award from the NYU Tandon School of Engineering. Prof. Jiang is a foreign member of the Academia Europaea (Academy of Europe) and an ordinary member of the European Academy of Sciences and Arts, and is also a Fellow of the IEEE, IFAC, CAA, AAIA, and AAAS.

Preface

Over the past decades, substantial research has been devoted to addressing the inherent challenges associated with the safety of vehicles, robots, human–machine interaction, and multi-agent systems. The application of systems and control methodologies to enhance safety performance has become an increasingly important and stimulating research direction, aiming to improve not only the assurance of safety but also flexibility, adaptability, and reliability.

Within the context of dynamical systems, the distinction and relationship between stability and safety are well understood. Stability ensures that the system state remains close to an equilibrium or a trajectory of interest, whereas safety guarantees that the state stays within a desired safe set. Under this interpretation, classical research on stability and stabilization with respect to an equilibrium or a nominal trajectory may be regarded as special instances of a broader, safety-centric paradigm. Yet the general framework of safety-critical control remains largely uncharted, presenting formidable but fascinating challenges for future research.

This book focuses on the safety-critical control of nonlinear dynamical systems subject to dynamic uncertainties and multiple safety constraints. It addresses two fundamental questions: (1) How do dynamic uncertainties and safety-critical controllers interact? (2) How can one redesign controllers that mitigate the adverse effects of dynamic uncertainties while maintaining feasible safety for the closed-loop system?

When safety reduces to stability, the corresponding problem naturally falls within the classical framework of robust control, a field that has already achieved considerable theoretical and practical maturity. However, the simultaneous enforcement of multiple state constraints often lies beyond the capability of conventional robust control techniques and is substantially more complex than merely combining constraints algebraically or adopting a switching mechanism. Although heuristic methods may work in practice, they often lack rigorous theoretical justification, and, when applied to closed-loop systems, can lead to unsafe dynamic behaviors. For example, Lipschitz continuity of the closed-loop dynamics is generally required to ensure well-posedness and robustness, yet it is frequently overlooked when designing practical safety-critical controllers.

Extending the idea of robust control, it is quite intuitive to characterize the interaction between dynamic uncertainties and controlled safety using gain functions and to ensure closed-loop safety through small-gain analysis. However, doing so is far from trivial. In safety-critical control systems, gain properties typically hold locally, and dynamic uncertainties are often influenced by the rate of change of the underlying safety indicator functions. For such systems, existing formulations of the small-gain theorem cannot be directly applied to assess closed-loop safety without a renewed, system-specific proof.

The associated technical challenges become increasingly pronounced when one must address the following requirements:

- The fine-tuning of safety-critical controllers to effectively accommodate dynamic uncertainties;
- The real-time integration of multiple safety constraints while maintaining robustness;
- The direct processing of constraint information derived from real-time, set-valued measurements in uncertain environments;
- The decentralized enforcement of safety constraints within cooperative multi-agent systems;
- The design of safety-critical controllers for systems preserving energy conservation; and
- The systematic development of safety-critical controllers that exploit and preserve the intrinsic structure of the plant.

This book integrates systematic results from nonlinear control, such as input-to-state stability (ISS), the small-gain theorem, and constructive nonlinear control techniques, with the latest developments in safety-critical control, including barrier functions and optimization-based real-time constraint satisfaction, to develop a comprehensive and constructive framework for the safety-critical control of nonlinear systems. The major contributions include:

- the synthesis of refined small-gain conditions to govern the interaction between the nominal closed-loop dynamics and dynamic uncertainties;
- the feasible-set reshaping technique to enable the optimization-based integration of multiple constraints while preserving robustness;
- the regularization of set-valued measurement models for safe operation in cluttered or uncertain environments;
- comprehensive controller design based on feasible-set reshaping, constraint relaxation, and nonlinear small-gain synthesis;

- the integration of safety certificate functions with storage functions for the safety-critical control of Euler–Lagrange systems; and
- recursive design methodologies for robust, safety-critical control in cascaded nonlinear systems.

These developments are presented sequentially from Chapter 2 through Chapter 7. Throughout this book, experiments are designed and conducted to verify the effectiveness of the proposed designs. The source code files for the numerical simulations and experiments in the book are available at https://github.com/EXPSIN/ROBUST_SAFETY_CRITICAL_CONTROL.

From a broader theoretical perspective, the study of safety-critical control provides a fresh lens through which to deepen our understanding and extend the conceptual boundaries of modern control theory. This book represents only a partial and preliminary exploration of robust safety-critical control. Many questions remain open, including those related to time-varying environments, cooperative and competitive multi-agent interactions, and human–machine collaboration.

The publication of this book coincides with the 60th birthday of Professor Jiang, one of its esteemed authors. As members of Professor Jiang's academic family, the younger co-authors are honored to dedicate this work to him, with heartfelt congratulations and warm wishes for continued health, inspiration, and a long, flourishing journey of scholarly achievement.

The authors are grateful to the editorial staff at Wiley, especially John Linglei Meng, Becky Cowan, and Kavipriya Ramachandran, for their efforts in publishing this book. The authors also thank the anonymous reviewers, whose feedback has been invaluable in improving the book. This work was supported in part by the National Natural Science Foundation of China (62325303, 62333004, 62521001) and the National Science Foundation of the United States, whose support is gratefully acknowledged.

Shenyang, China
December, 2025

Tengfei Liu, Si Wu, Zhi Liu

Notations

This book adopts, wherever possible, the notation conventionally used in the analysis and control of nonlinear systems. Unless otherwise specified, all physical quantities in this textbook are expressed in the International System of Units (SI). Frequently used symbols are listed below.

Common Symbol Conventions

t	Time
x, z	States
y	Outputs
u, v	Control inputs
d, w	Disturbance inputs
A, B	System matrix and input matrix of a linear time-invariant system
f, g	Dynamics of a nonlinear system
h	Output mapping of a nonlinear system
V	A Lyapunov function
m, n, p, N	Dimension of a vector, matrix, or space, or the number of subsystems, etc.
i, j, k	Index of elements, variables, or subsystems, or the step number in iterative analysis or design, etc.
r	An arbitrary real number
s	An arbitrary non-negative real number

Set and Logical Symbols

$\{x_1, \dots, x_m\}$	The set composed of elements $x_1, \dots, x_m$
$\in$	Belongs to (the former is an element of the latter)

$\notin$	Does not belong to (the former is not an element of the latter)
$\subseteq$	Subset of (the former is a subset of the latter)
$\forall$	For all
$\Rightarrow$	Implies
$\Leftrightarrow$	If and only if (equivalent to)
s.t.	Subject to
$\text{Int}(\mathcal{S})$	The interior set of $\mathcal{S}$
$\text{Cl}(\mathcal{S})$	The closure set of $\mathcal{S}$

Real Numbers and Sequences

$\mathbb{R}$	Set of real numbers
$\mathbb{R}_+$	Set of non-negative real numbers
$\mathbb{R}^n$	n-dimensional Euclidean space
$\mathbb{R}^{m\times n}$	Set of $m \times n$ real matrices
$\mathbb{Z}$	Set of integers
$\mathbb{Z}_+$	Set of non-negative integers
$=$	Equals
$\equiv$	Identically equal to
$\approx$	Approximately equal to
$:=, =:$	Defined as
$<, >$	Less than, greater than
$\leq, \geq$	Less than or equal to, greater than or equal to
$\rightarrow$	Tends to
max, min	Maximum, minimum
sup, inf	Supremum, infimum
ess sup	Essential supremum
lim	Limit
limsup	Upper limit
liminf	Lower limit

Vectors and Matrices

x^T	Transpose of vector x
A^T	Transpose of matrix A
$[a_1, \dots, a_n]$	Row vector with elements $a_1, \dots, a_n$
$\text{diag}\{a_1, \dots, a_n\}$	$n \times n$ diagonal matrix with diagonal entries $a_1, \dots, a_n$
I_n or simply I	$n \times n$ identity matrix
$\mathbf{1}_n$	n-dimensional column vector of all ones
$\mathbf{1}_{m\times n}$	$m \times n$ matrix of all ones

$[a_{ij}]_{m\times n}$	$m \times n$ matrix with (i, j)-th entry a_{ij}
$\otimes$	Kronecker product
$\text{span}\{x_1, \dots, x_m\}$	Subspace spanned by column vectors $x_1, \dots, x_m$: $\{[x_1, \dots, x_m]A : A \in \mathbb{R}^m\}$
$\|x\|$	Euclidean norm of real vector x: $\|x\| = (x^T x)^{1/2}$
$\|A\|$	Induced 2-norm of real matrix A: $\|A\| = \max_{\|x\|=1} \|Ax\|$
$\lambda_{\max}(A), \lambda_{\min}(A)$	Maximum and minimum eigenvalues of real symmetric matrix A
$\det(A)$	Determinant of real square matrix A
$P > 0$	Matrix $P \in \mathbb{R}^{n\times n}$ is positive definite: $x^T P x > 0$ for all nonzero $x \in \mathbb{R}^n$
$P \geq 0$	Matrix $P \in \mathbb{R}^{n\times n}$ is positive semi-definite: $x^T P x \geq 0$ for all $x \in \mathbb{R}^n$

Functions

$f: \mathcal{X} \to \mathcal{Y}$	Function f mapping $\mathcal{X}$ to $\mathcal{Y}$
$f \circ g$	Composition of functions f and g: $f \circ g(x) = f(g(x))$
f^{-1}	Inverse of function f
$\partial f(x)/\partial x$	First-order derivative (Jacobian matrix) of $f: \mathbb{R}^n \to \mathbb{R}^m$ at x
$\partial f(x_1, \dots, x_n)/\partial x_i$	First-order partial derivative of f at $(x_1, \dots, x_n)$ with respect to x_i
∇f	Gradient (row vector) of $f: \mathbb{R}^n \to \mathbb{R}$
$\nabla^T f$	Transpose of ∇f
$D^+ f$	Right upper Dini derivative of $f: \mathbb{R} \to \mathbb{R}^n$
$L_f h$	Lie derivative: $L_f h(x) = (\partial h(x)/\partial x) f(x)$
$[f, g]$, $\text{ad}_f g$	Lie bracket: $[f, g](x) = (\partial g(x)/\partial x) f(x) - (\partial f(x)/\partial x) g(x)$
$\text{ad}_f^k g$	$[f, \text{ad}_f^{k-1} g]$, where $\text{ad}_f^1 g = \text{ad}_f g$
$\dot{x}$	First derivative of x with respect to time
$\ddot{x}$	Second derivative of x with respect to time
$\dddot{x}$	Third derivative of x with respect to time
$x^{(i)}$	i-th order time derivative of x
Id	Identity function: for any $r \in \mathbb{R}$, $\text{Id}(r) = r$
$\text{argmax} f(x)$	Value(s) of x where f attains its maximum
$\text{argmin} f(x)$	Value(s) of x where f attains its minimum
$\|\|d\|\|_T$	Essential supremum: $\|\|d\|\|_T = \text{ess sup}_{t\in T} \|d(t)\|$, where $d: \mathbb{R} \to \mathbb{R}^n$, $T \subseteq \mathbb{R}$
$\|\|d\|\|_\infty$	$\|\|d\|\|_{[0,\infty)}$
$\sum$	Summation
$\prod$	Product

$\mathrm{Re}(z)$	Real part of complex number z
sin, cos	Sine function, cosine function
tan, arctan	Tangent function, arctangent function
tanh	Hyperbolic tangent: $\tanh x = (e^x - e^{-x})/(e^x + e^{-x})$
ln	Natural logarithm
sign	Sign function: if $r > 0$, then $\mathrm{sign}(r) = 1$; if $r = 0$, then $\mathrm{sign}(r) = 0$; if $r < 0$, then $\mathrm{sign}(r) = -1$
sat	Saturation function: $\mathrm{sat}(r) = \max\{-1, \min\{r, 1\}\}$, where $r \in \mathbb{R}$
$\cap$	Intersection: $S_1 \cap S_2 = \{x:\ x \in S_1 \text{ and } x \in S_2\}$
$\cup$	Union: $S_1 \cup S_2 = \{x:\ x \in S_1 \text{ or } x \in S_2\}$
$\setminus$	Set difference: $S_1 \setminus S_2 = \{x:\ x \in S_1 \text{ and } x \notin S_2\}$
$\times$	Cartesian product: $S_1 \times S_2 = \{(x_1, x_2):\ x_1 \in S_1 \text{ and } x_2 \in S_2\}$
∂S	Boundary of set S
$\mathrm{dist}(x, S)$	Distance from point x to set S: $\mathrm{dist}(x, S) = \inf_{s \in S} \lvert x - s \rvert$, where $x \in \mathbb{R}^n$, $S \subseteq \mathbb{R}^n$

Acronyms

AS	Asymptotic stability, asymptotically stable
CBF	Control barrier function
CLF	Control Lyapunov function
EL	Euler–Lagrange
GAS	Global asymptotic stability, globally asymptotically stable
IOS	Input-to-output stability, input-to-output stable
ISS	Input-to-state stability, input-to-state stable
LICQ	Linear independence constraint qualification
OAS	Output asymptotic stability
QCQP	Quadratically constrained quadratic programming
QP	Quadratic programming, quadratic program

About the Companion Website

This book is accompanied by a companion website.

http://www.wiley.com/go/liu/robustsafety-1

To access the website materials, click on the link under Related Resources on the book's page on wiley.com. You can also find this by searching www.wiley.com for the ISBN 9781394400188.

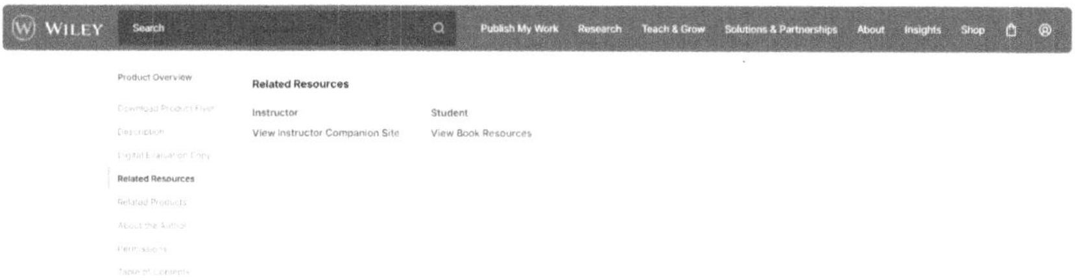

The website includes:

- MATLAB source code, together with supporting data and auxiliary functions, for reproducing the main examples and the corresponding simulation and experimental figures in each chapter.

1

Introduction

The study presented in this book is motivated by practical needs. Despite the exceptionally high level of automation achieved in industrial processes, many operations on manufacturing equipment still rely on operators performing tasks manually in accordance with established protocols and multiple layers of safety protection. These manual procedures are not only labor-intensive but also entail substantial safety risks, where even minor errors can lead to serious injuries and significant economic losses.

Replacing manual operations with mobile agents equipped with actuators offers a compelling alternative. These agents can be monitored or controlled remotely by human operators or intelligent decision-making systems, either independently or in coordination. For effectiveness, mobile agents must satisfy safety, configuration, and task-related constraints throughout operation. The associated questions can be formulated as problems of safety-critical control.

In idealized settings, control commands (e.g., reference trajectories) are specified in advance, the operating environment is fixed, and all mobile agents are centrally controlled. When these assumptions are fully or partially satisfied, safety-critical control can be addressed within the standard planning-and-tracking paradigm.

In more advanced settings, mobile agents must exhibit greater autonomy. Consider a typical case in which a mobile agent is teleoperated to inspect the exterior wall of a building or shut off a valve in a hazardous area. During this process, the agent must avoid obstacles, maintain safe standoff distances from surrounding equipment, and complete the assigned task while complying with all operational constraints. While human operators may focus on task-specific directives, complex safety considerations are often overlooked, underscoring the need for agents to autonomously enforce and satisfy these constraints. In even more challenging situations, the operating environment may evolve over time, and dynamic interactions may arise among multiple agents. These considerations motivate the study of robust safety-critical control. Figure 1.1 illustrates a conceptual block diagram

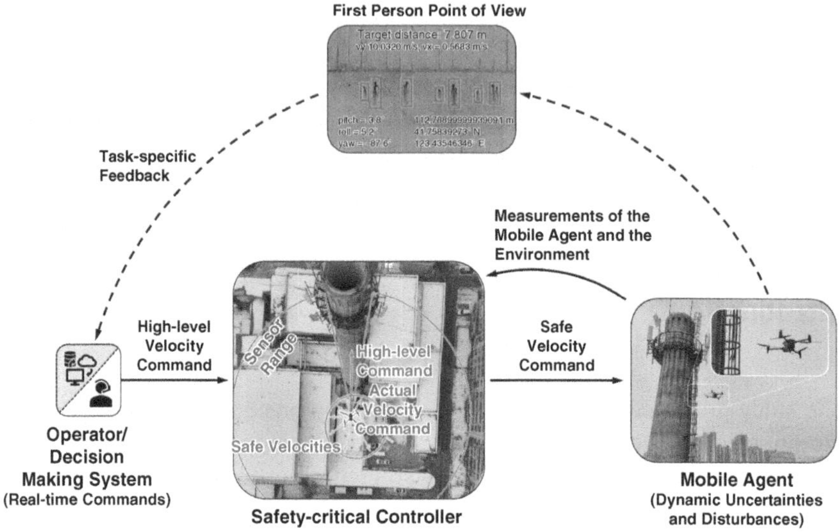

Figure 1.1 Safety-critical control schematic for a teleoperated quadrotor performing vision-based building inspection.

in which a quadrotor UAV, teleoperated by a human operator, uses a vision sensor to inspect an industrial building while autonomously ensuring safety-critical control based on its onboard perception of the environment.

This book develops a systematic framework for addressing robust safety-critical control problems under dynamic uncertainties. To sharpen the theoretical insights, the scope is intentionally limited to safety constraints induced by obstacles, with particular emphasis on safety-critical control strategies for obstacle avoidance. These scenarios are highly representative in industrial systems and naturally generalize to a broad range of practical applications.

This chapter reviews the foundational concepts of safety-critical control, including set-invariance-based notions of safety, control barrier functions, robust safety, and the optimization-based safety-critical control structure. Through illustrative examples, this chapter also examines the practical relevance and theoretical challenges of robust safety-critical control, particularly under dynamic uncertainties and multiple constraints.

1.1 Characterization of Safety for Dynamical Systems

Consider the autonomous system

$$\dot{x} = f(x), \tag{1.1}$$

where $x \in \mathbb{R}^n$ denotes the state and $f : \mathbb{R}^n \to \mathbb{R}^n$ specifies the dynamics. Throughout this chapter, unless stated otherwise, assume that f is locally Lipschitz. Then, for each initial condition, there exists a unique (maximal) trajectory defined on a nontrivial time interval; see [98, Theorem 3.1].

1.1.1 Safety Defined by Set Invariance

The safety property of a dynamical system of the form (1.1) is characterized by the positive invariance of a set that constrains the system's evolution.

Definition 1.1 ***(Safe Set Defined by Positive Invariance [228])*:** A closed set $\mathcal{S}$ is called a safe set (i.e., a positively invariant set) for the system (1.1) if

$$x(0) \in \mathcal{S} \quad \Rightarrow \quad x(t) \in \mathcal{S}, \quad \forall t \in [0, T_{\max}), \tag{1.2}$$

where $[0, T_{\max})$, with $T_{\max} > 0$ possibly infinite, is the interval on which the unique solution $x(t)$ is right-maximally defined.

Nagumo's theorem [150] (see also [25]) provides a necessary and sufficient condition, known as the sub-tangentiality condition, for weak positive invariance[1] of a set $\mathcal{S}$ for a dynamical system of the form (1.1), under the assumption that for each initial condition $x(0)$ in an open set $\mathcal{X}$, the system admits a solution (not necessarily unique in the absence of local Lipschitz continuity of f) defined for all $t \geq 0$. With an additional uniqueness assumption on solutions, Nagumo's theorem yields a necessary and sufficient condition for positive invariance, and hence for safety as in Definition 1.1 with $T_{\max} = \infty$. The theorem has been revisited in several equivalent formulations; here, we adopt the version in [228], which addresses systems with locally Lipschitz dynamics.

Theorem 1.1 ***(Sub-tangentiality Condition for Positive Invariance)*:** *Consider the system* (1.1) *with f locally Lipschitz. A closed set $\mathcal{S} \subseteq \mathbb{R}^n$ is positively invariant for* (1.1)*, that is, property* (1.2) *holds, if and only if*

$$f(x) \in \mathcal{T}_{\mathcal{S}}(x), \quad \forall x \in \mathcal{S}, \tag{1.3}$$

where $\mathcal{T}_{\mathcal{S}}(x)$ denotes the tangent cone to $\mathcal{S}$ at x, defined by

$$\mathcal{T}_{\mathcal{S}}(x) = \left\{ z \in \mathbb{R}^n : \liminf_{\tau \downarrow 0} \frac{\mathrm{dist}(x + \tau z, \mathcal{S})}{\tau} = 0 \right\}, \tag{1.4}$$

and dist *is the distance function,* $\mathrm{dist}(\xi, \mathcal{S}) = \inf_{s \in \mathcal{S}} |\xi - s|$.

---

1 Informally, weak positive invariance means that at least one solution of (1.1) satisfies (1.2); see [25, Definition 4.2]. Reference [25, Chapter 4] also provides nice illustrations of weak positive invariance.

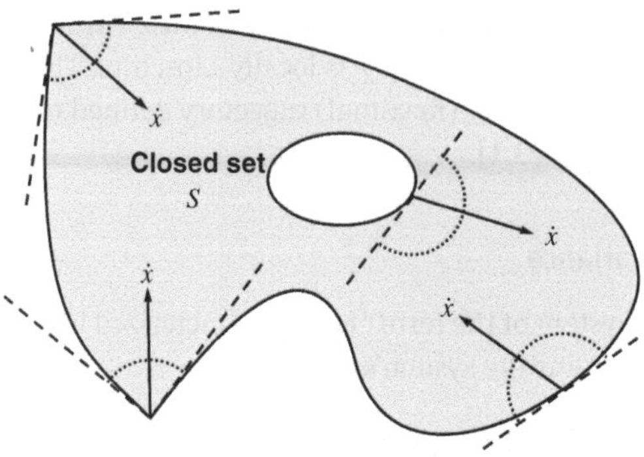

Figure 1.2 A safe set and the sub-tangentiality condition.

A quite detailed discussion on the tangentiality condition for set invariance can be found in [25, Section 4.2]. Figure 1.2, motivated by [25, Figure 4.1], illustrates a safe set and the sub-tangentiality condition.

For the system (1.1), existence and uniqueness of the solution $x(t)$ for all $t \geq 0$ are guaranteed under either of the following conditions:

- f is Lipschitz continuous on $\mathbb{R}^n$ (see [98, Theorem 3.2]);
- $\mathcal{S}$ is compact, and f is locally Lipschitz on an open, connected set $\mathcal{X}$ containing $\mathcal{S}$.

Since $\mathcal{T}_{\mathcal{S}}(x) = \mathbb{R}^n$ for any interior point x of $\mathcal{S}$, it suffices to verify (1.3) only for $x \in \partial\mathcal{S}$. Thus, condition (1.3) can be replaced by

$$f(x) \in \mathcal{T}_{\mathcal{S}}(x), \quad \forall x \in \partial\mathcal{S}. \tag{1.5}$$

Suppose $\mathcal{S}$ is given as the c-sublevel set of a function $h : \mathbb{R}^n \to \mathbb{R}$:

$$\mathcal{S} = \{x \in \mathbb{R}^n : h(x) \leq c\}, \tag{1.6}$$

where c is a constant ensuring that $\mathcal{S}$ is nonempty. Then, the safety property (1.2) is equivalent to

$$h(x(0)) \leq c \quad \Rightarrow \quad h(x(t)) \leq c, \quad \forall t \in [0, T_{\max}). \tag{1.7}$$

Assume that h is continuously differentiable. For any $x \in \partial\mathcal{S}$, if $\nabla h(x) \neq 0$, then the tangent cone in (1.4) admits the equivalent characterization

$$\nabla h(x)z \leq 0 \quad \Leftrightarrow \quad z \in \mathcal{T}_{\mathcal{S}}(x). \tag{1.8}$$

A proof is given in [16, pp. 123–124]. See also Appendix A.7 for a discussion of the related notion of "practical sets."

The next proposition specializes Nagumo's sub-tangentiality condition (1.3) to level sets.

Proposition 1.1 ***(Sub-tangentiality Condition for Level Sets of Functions)*****:** Consider $\mathcal{S}$ as in (1.6). If h is continuously differentiable and satisfies

$$\nabla h(x) \neq 0, \quad \forall x \in \partial\mathcal{S}, \tag{1.9}$$

then condition (1.5) is equivalent to

$$\nabla h(x) f(x) \leq 0, \quad \forall x \in \partial\mathcal{S}. \tag{1.10}$$

Condition (1.10) is commonly referred to as the half-space condition, as it requires $f(x)$ to lie in the half-space[2] $\{z : \nabla h(x) z \leq 0\}$ determined by $\nabla h(x)$. The preceding discussion thus motivates the introduction of safety indicator functions.

Definition 1.2 ***(Safety Indicator Functions)*****:** For the dynamical system (1.1), a continuously differentiable function h that characterizes a safe set as in (1.6) and satisfies properties (1.9) and (1.10) is called a safety indicator function.

This notion is closely related to other concepts, such as barrier functions, which are widely used in the recent literature of safety-critical control [3]. Here, we refer to h as a safety indicator function rather than a barrier function, because it is quite common that strict safety guarantees, as typically formulated via barrier functions, cannot be ensured. For example, with the employment of safety indicator functions, we account for the influence of uncertain dynamics (which induce transient responses) and perturbations.

By treating safety indicator functions directly as output maps, one can address safety-critical control problems by imposing safety constraints on the outputs of the plants; see Section 1.3. Moreover, for plants with specific structures, feasible sets of safety-oriented control inputs can be constructed using the gradients of the safety indicator functions.

By defining

$$h_z(x) = -h(x) + c, \tag{1.11}$$

the safe set $\mathcal{S}$ in (1.6) can be expressed as the 0-superlevel set of h_z:

$$\mathcal{S} = \{x \in \mathbb{R}^n : h_z(x) \geq 0\}. \tag{1.12}$$

Clearly, the boundary of $\mathcal{S}$ in (1.12) consists of all states x satisfying $h_z(x) = 0$.

Under condition (1.9), namely

$$\nabla h_z(x) \neq 0, \quad \forall x \in \partial\mathcal{S}, \tag{1.13}$$

---

2 A half-space is a set of the form $\{x : a^T x \leq b\}$ with $a \neq 0$.

using h_z in place of h to characterize safety, one readily verifies that condition (1.10) is equivalent to

$$\nabla h_z(x) f(x) \geq 0, \quad x \in \partial \mathcal{S}. \tag{1.14}$$

Under the condition that $\mathcal{S}$ is compact, the following proposition establishes the existence of a class $\mathcal{K}$ function that describes a dissipation-like inequality for $h_z(x(t))$, with $x(t)$ evolving within $\mathcal{S}$.

Proposition 1.2 *(Zeroing Barrier Functions [6])*: Consider the safe set $\mathcal{S}$ in (1.12) with h_z continuously differentiable and satisfying condition (1.13). Suppose that $\mathcal{S}$ is nonempty and compact. Then, property (1.14) implies the existence of $\alpha_z \in \mathcal{K}$ such that

$$\nabla h_z(x) f(x) \geq -\alpha_z(h_z(x)), \quad \forall x \in \mathcal{S}. \tag{1.15}$$

The function h_z in Proposition 1.2 is called a zeroing barrier function. A proof of Proposition 1.2 is given in [6] using continuity arguments. In particular, one may construct $\alpha_z \in \mathcal{K}$ as an upper bound of

$$\alpha_z'(r) = - \inf_{\{x \in \mathbb{R}^n :\ 0 \leq h_z(x) \leq r\}} \nabla h_z(x) f(x). \tag{1.16}$$

Reference [127] established necessary and sufficient conditions for the existence of zeroing barrier functions for safety verification of nonlinear systems.

From the preceding discussion, if a compact set $\mathcal{S}$ defined in (1.12) is safe in the sense of Definition 1.1, and h_z is continuously differentiable and satisfies the constraint qualification $\nabla h_z(x) \neq 0$ for all $x \in \partial \mathcal{S}$, then there exists a function $\alpha_z \in \mathcal{K}$ such that h_z is a zeroing barrier function satisfying (1.15). The notion of zeroing barrier functions has been widely used for safety-critical control. Figure 1.3, motivated by [145], shows a zeroing barrier function with its associated safe set and trajectories outside and inside the safe set.

Recalling (1.11) and substituting $h_z(x) = -h(x) + c$ into (1.15) yield an equivalent condition

$$\nabla h(x) f(x) \leq \alpha_z(-h(x) + c), \quad \forall x \in \mathcal{S}. \tag{1.17}$$

1.1.2 Transient-aware Safety Described by Generalized Safety Indicator Functions

In the presence of transient dynamics (intuitively, overshoot arising from the initial-state response), the strict safety property (1.7) characterized by the safety indicator function h may fail to hold, motivating a transient-aware relaxation of the notion.

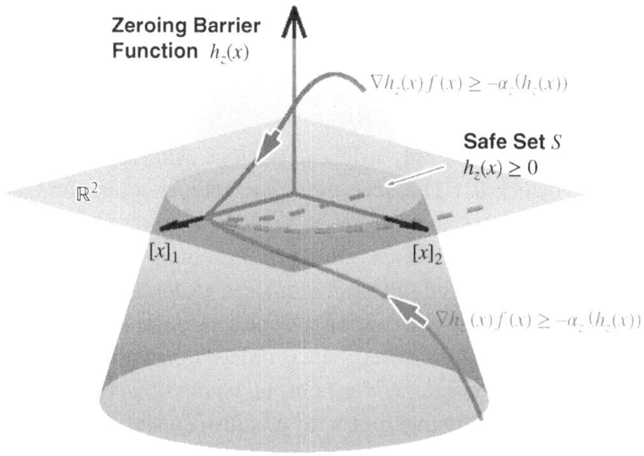

Figure 1.3 An illustration of a zeroing barrier function with its associated safe set and trajectories outside and inside the safe set.

Note that for any $h : \mathbb{R}^n \to \mathbb{R}$, one can always find a strictly increasing map $\rho : \mathbb{R} \to (0, \infty)$ such that

$$\bar{h}(x) = \rho(h(x)) \tag{1.18}$$

takes values in $(0, \infty)$ and likewise serves as a safety indicator function in the sense of (1.19) with the constant c replaced by $\bar{c} = \rho(c)$. Therefore, without loss of generality, we restrict attention to safety indicator functions taking values in $(0, \infty)$. This convention is convenient when employing $\mathcal{KL}$ functions to describe transient-aware safety, in a manner analogous to their use in standard stability notions.

The following definition of transient-aware safety is inspired by practical stability [71, 111].

Definition 1.3 ***(State-independent Transient-aware Safety)*:** The dynamical system (1.1) is said to be state-independent, transient-aware safe with a generalized safety indicator function $h : \mathbb{R}^n \to (0, \infty)$ if there exist $\beta \in \mathcal{KL}$ and a constant $c > 0$ such that, for any initial state $x(0)$, the trajectory $x(t)$ satisfies

$$h(x(t)) \leq \max\{\beta(h(x(0)), t), c\}, \quad \forall t \in [0, T_{\max}), \tag{1.19}$$

where $[0, T_{\max})$, with $T_{\max} > 0$ possibly infinite, is the interval on which the unique solution $x(t)$ is right-maximally defined.

Intuitively, β quantifies the transient response. In the special case where $\beta(s, 0) = s$ for all $s \geq 0$, property (1.19) recovers the strict safety property (1.7):

$$h(x(0)) \leq c \quad \Rightarrow \quad h(x(t)) \leq \max\{\beta(c, t), c\} \leq c, \quad \forall t \in [0, T_{\max}). \tag{1.20}$$

In general, property (1.19) does not imply strict safety, since $\beta(h(x(0)), 0)$ is not necessarily bounded above by $h(x(0))$. This accommodates overshoot phenomena in the transient response.

If $h(x)$ is interpreted as the output of the system (1.1), property (1.19) means that only the output $h(x)$, instead of the full state x, is used to describe the transient response. This is the reason why the transient-aware safety is called state-independent, though the influence of the initial state is indeed taken into account. The concept is consistent with state-independent output asymptotic stability, up to a practical offset (Lagrange stability together with practical convergence), and with output-Lagrange input-to-output stability with c viewed as an input. See [193] for further discussion on the relevant concepts.

Following the Lyapunov formulation of IOS [193], a Lyapunov-like function can be used to establish state-independent transient-aware safety.

Proposition 1.3 ***(A Lyapunov-like Formulation of State-independent Transient-aware Safety)*****:** Consider the system (1.1) with f locally Lipschitz. Given a continuously differentiable function $h : \mathbb{R}^n \to (0, \infty)$, if there exists a continuously differentiable function $V : \mathbb{R}^n \to (0, \infty)$ such that

$$\underline{\alpha}(h(x)) \leq V(x) \leq \bar{\alpha}(h(x)), \tag{1.21}$$

$$V(x) \geq \underline{\alpha}(c) \quad \Rightarrow \quad \nabla V(x) f(x) \leq -\alpha(V(x)), \tag{1.22}$$

with $\underline{\alpha}$ and $\bar{\alpha}$ of class $\mathcal{K}_\infty$, α continuous and positive definite, and constant $c > 0$, then there exists $\beta \in \mathcal{KL}$ such that, for any initial state $x(0)$, the trajectory $x(t)$ satisfies (1.19).

Indeed, along any trajectory $x(t)$ of (1.1), condition (1.22) guarantees $\mathrm{d}V(x(t))/\mathrm{d}t \leq -\alpha(V(x(t)))$ until $V(x(t)) < \underline{\alpha}(c)$, as long as $x(t)$ is defined. The bounds in (1.21) then yield property (1.19).

A notable special case of Proposition 1.3 occurs when $\underline{\alpha} = \bar{\alpha} = \mathrm{Id}$, so $V(x) = h(x)$. In this case, (1.21)-(1.22) ensure strict safety in the sense of (1.7).

Broader generalizations of safety indicator functions can also be considered to describe how safety constraints are influenced by full states of dynamical systems. When a generalized safety indicator function h is defined as a function of part of the state x but influenced by the full state x, the following generalized transient-aware safety property would be meaningful.

Definition 1.4 ***(Transient-aware Safety)*****:** The dynamical system (1.1) is said to be transient-aware, safe with a generalized safety indicator function $h : \mathbb{R}^n \to$

$(0, \infty)$ if there exist $\beta \in \mathcal{KL}$ and constants $b \geq 0$ and $c > 0$ such that, for any initial state $x(0)$, the trajectory $x(t)$ satisfies

$$h(x(t)) \leq \max\{\beta(|h(x(0))| + |x(0)| + b, t), c\}, \quad \forall t \in [0, T_{\max}), \tag{1.23}$$

where $[0, T_{\max})$, with $T_{\max} > 0$ possibly infinite, is the interval on which the unique solution $x(t)$ is right-maximally defined.

Viewing $h(x)$ as the output map, this definition extends output asymptotic stability (OAS; see [188]) by incorporating offset constants b and c to describe the influence of the initial value of the full state.

1.2 Robust Safety

In this section, we address the more general setting in which external disturbances are nonnegligible, and we analyze their impact on safety-critical control performance.

We consider the system

$$\dot{x} = f(x, d) \tag{1.24}$$

where $x \in \mathbb{R}^n$ is the state, $d \in \mathbb{R}^m$ represents external disturbance inputs, and $f : \mathbb{R}^n \times \mathbb{R}^m \to \mathbb{R}^n$ specifies the plant dynamics. Throughout this chapter, unless stated otherwise, f is assumed to be locally Lipschitz. The disturbance d, viewed as a function of time, is assumed to be piecewise continuous and bounded. These assumptions on f and d may be relaxed, provided local existence of solutions to the system (1.24) is guaranteed. For a detailed discussion of existence and uniqueness for systems with external inputs, see [187, Appendix C].

1.2.1 Input-to-state Safe Set

Robust safety in the presence of disturbances has been studied extensively in the literature [168, 87, 104]. Introducing an offset to the safe set of the disturbance-free case is a common approach to incorporating disturbance effects into a set-invariance-based definition of safety.

In the disturbance-free case, i.e., $d \equiv 0$, for (1.24), one may employ a zeroing barrier function $h_z : \mathbb{R}^n \to \mathbb{R}$ to define the safe set

$$\mathcal{S} = \{x \in \mathbb{R}^n : h_z(x) \geq 0\}. \tag{1.25}$$

When d is nonzero, robustness with respect to d is captured by an enlarged set, leading to the notion of an input-to-state safe set [104].

Definition 1.5 ***(Input-to-state Safe Set):*** The set $\mathcal{S}$ in (1.25) with $h_z : \mathbb{R}^n \rightarrow \mathbb{R}$ is an input-to-state safe set for the system (1.24) if there exist $\gamma \in \mathcal{K}$ and $\bar{d} \geq 0$ satisfying

$$\inf_{x \in \mathbb{R}^n} h_z(x) < -\gamma(\bar{d}), \tag{1.26}$$

such that for any input d satisfying

$$|d(t)| \leq \bar{d}, \quad \forall t \geq 0, \tag{1.27}$$

the trajectory $x(t)$ satisfies

$$x(0) \in \mathcal{S}_d \quad \Rightarrow \quad x(t) \in \mathcal{S}_d, \quad \forall t \in [0, T_{\max}) \tag{1.28}$$

with

$$\mathcal{S}_d = \{x \in \mathbb{R}^n : h_z(x) \geq -\gamma(\|d\|_\infty)\} \tag{1.29}$$

where $[0, T_{\max})$, with $T_{\max} > 0$ possibly infinite, is the interval on which the unique solution $x(t)$ is right-maximally defined.

Accordingly, the system (1.24), with x as the state and d as the input, is called input-to-state safe (ISSf) with respect to $\mathcal{S}$. Figure 1.4 presents an illustration of an input-to-state safe set and its associated zeroing barrier function.

The idea of Proposition 1.1, which invokes the sub-tangentiality condition to assess the safety of a set $\mathcal{S}$, extends to the disturbed setting by verifying that the dynamics $f(x, d)$ lie in the tangent cone of $\mathcal{S}_d$.

Proposition 1.4 ***(A Sufficient Condition of an Input-to-state Safe Set):*** Consider the system (1.24) with f locally Lipschitz. The closed set $\mathcal{S}$ defined by a

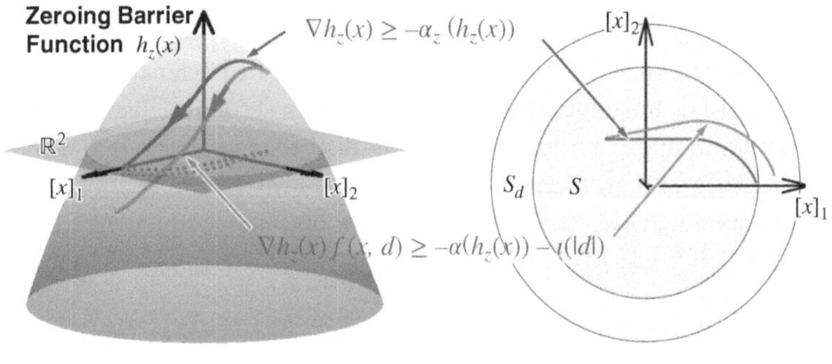

Figure 1.4 Illustrations of an input-to-state safe set and its associated zeroing barrier function.

continuously differentiable function $h_z : \mathbb{R}^n \to \mathbb{R}$ in (1.25) is input-to-state safe, if there exist $\alpha \in \mathcal{K}^e$, $\iota \in \mathcal{K}$, and $\bar{d} \geq 0$ such that

$$\alpha\left(\inf_{x \in \mathbb{R}^n} h_z(x)\right) < -\iota(\bar{d}) \tag{1.30}$$

$$\nabla h_z(x) f(x, d) \geq -\alpha(h_z(x)) - \iota(|d|) \tag{1.31}$$

for all $x \in \mathbb{R}^n$ and $|d| \leq \bar{d}$.

Proposition 1.4 follows by showing that $\mathcal{S}_d$ defined in (1.29), with $\gamma(s) = -\alpha^{-1}(-\iota(s))$ for $s \in [0, \bar{d}]$, satisfies (1.28). This is achieved by comparing $h_z(x(t))$ with the solution $\eta(t)$ of the initial-value problem

$$\dot{\eta}(t) = -\alpha(\eta(t)) - \iota(\|d\|_\infty), \qquad \eta(0) = h_z(x(0)) \tag{1.32}$$

over the interval on which $x(t)$ is defined. See, for example, [71, Section 24.E] for scalar trajectory analysis and [98, Lemma 3.4] for the comparison principle.

1.2.2 Transient-aware Safety Subject to External Disturbances

When transient effects are nonnegligible, the safety notion based on input-to-state safe sets in Definition 1.5 may fail to hold. Moreover, in typical safety-critical control scenarios, it is quite demanding to investigate robustness with respect to state-dependent perturbations $d = \Delta(x)$, for which one may not determine in advance an upper bound $\bar{d}$ for $\|d\|_\infty$. This motivates a modification of the transient-aware safety in Definition 1.4 for disturbance-free systems.

We propose a trajectory-based safety property, inspired in part by input-to-state stability (ISS) [184, 188], input-to-output stability (IOS) [92, 193], and their practical variants. The trajectory-based formulation emphasizes signal interactions and mitigates reliance on nonsmooth analysis for nonlinear systems with uncertain perturbations.

Definition 1.6 ***(Disturbed Transient-aware Safety)*****:** The system (1.24) is said to be disturbed, transient-aware safe with a generalized safety indicator function $h : \mathbb{R}^n \to (0, \infty)$ if there exist $\beta \in \mathcal{KL}$, $\gamma \in \mathcal{K}$, and constants $b \geq 0$ and $c > 0$ such that, for any initial state $x(0)$ and any piecewise continuous, bounded disturbance d, the trajectory $x(t)$ satisfies

$$h(x(t)) \leq \max\{\beta(|h(x(0))| + |x(0)| + b, t), \gamma(\|d\|_\infty), c\}, \quad \forall t \in [0, T_{\max}) \tag{1.33}$$

where $[0, T_{\max})$, with $T_{\max} > 0$ possibly infinite, is the interval on which the unique solution $x(t)$ is right-maximally defined.

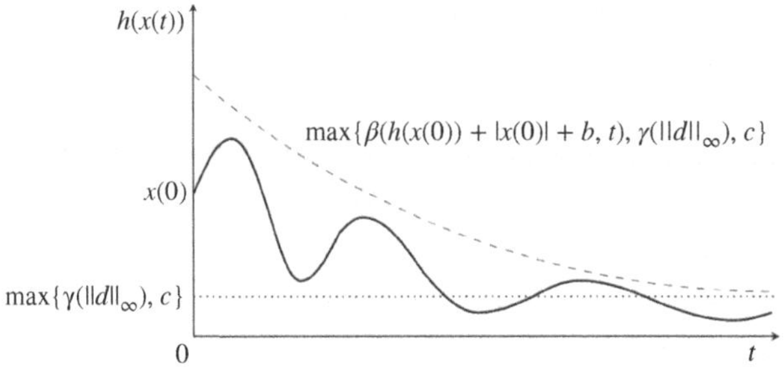

Figure 1.5 An illustration of transient-aware safety in the presence of disturbances.

An illustration of transient-aware safety in the presence of disturbances is shown in Figure 1.5.

Quite often, the generalized safety indicator function h is defined only on an open set $\mathcal{X} \subset \mathbb{R}^n$. In such cases, safety is expected only while $x(t)$ stays in some domain inside $\mathcal{X}$. Specifically, one expects the existence of $\beta \in \mathcal{KL}$, $\gamma \in \mathcal{K}$, and constants $b \geq 0$ and $c > 0$ such that, for any initial state $x(0) \in \mathcal{X}$ and any piecewise continuous, bounded d, the trajectory $x(t)$ satisfies condition (1.33) on the maximal forward interval $[0, T_{\max})$ on which the solution is defined and remains in $\mathcal{X}$.

For the remainder of the book, we will refer to generalized safety indicator functions simply as safety indicator functions, for brevity.

Existing work on robust stability has extensively studied robustness to external disturbances and state-dependent perturbations (also known as dynamic uncertainties). It is therefore natural to extend robust-stability notions to safety-critical systems. This monograph presents new theoretical results motivated by practical considerations, focusing on specific classes of state-dependent perturbations, and analyzing their impact on the performance of safety-critical systems.

1.3 Safety-critical Control: A Quadratic Programming Approach

In this section, we consider an elementary safety-critical control problem and briefly outline the fundamental ideas underlying the recently developed quadratic programming (QP) approach to safety-critical control.

1.3.1 A Typical Safety-critical Control Problem

Consider a plant (a dynamical system with control input) given by

$$\dot{x} = f(x, u), \tag{1.34}$$

where $x \in \mathbb{R}^n$ is the state, $u \in \mathbb{R}^m$ is the control input, and $f : \mathbb{R}^n \times \mathbb{R}^m \to \mathbb{R}^n$ denotes the plant dynamics, assumed locally Lipschitz.

For safety-critical control, one seeks a feedback control law of the form

$$u = \rho(x), \tag{1.35}$$

with $\rho : \mathbb{R}^n \to \mathbb{R}^m$, such that the closed-loop system

$$\dot{x} = f(x, \rho(x)) \tag{1.36}$$

satisfies a specified safety property, as discussed in Section 1.2. In particular, consistent with (1.17), one may require the existence of a safety indicator function $h : \mathbb{R}^n \to (0, \infty)$ satisfying

$$\nabla h(x) f(x, \rho(x)) \leq \alpha_z(-h(x) + c), \quad \forall x \in \mathcal{S} \tag{1.37}$$

with $\alpha_z \in \mathcal{K}$ and a constant c satisfying $0 < c < \sup_{x \in \mathbb{R}^n} h(x)$, so that $\mathcal{S}$, defined as in (1.6), is a safe set for the closed-loop system. Incorporating robustness considerations, it is natural to consider a larger region (for simplicity, take $\mathbb{R}^n$) such that every element of $\mathcal{S}$ is its interior point, and to require that (1.37) hold on this region. In this case, α_z should be chosen as a class $\mathcal{K}^e$ function.

When the safety-critical control problem reduces to stabilization, there are systematic methods to explicitly construct ρ; see, for example, [98, 80, 174, 107].

1.3.2 Feasible Control Inputs Under Safety Constraints

For systems subject to multiple safety constraints, rather than specifying the controller as a single-valued function as in (1.35), it can be advantageous to introduce a set-valued map from x to u. A set-valued map can encode the set of admissible control inputs that ensure safety, thereby providing greater flexibility in synthesizing controllers to satisfy multiple constraints simultaneously.

For the plant (1.34), given a safety indicator function $h : \mathbb{R}^n \to (0, \infty)$ and a constant $c > 0$, with u considered as a value to be determined, in accordance with (1.37), we define the following set-valued map:

$$\mathcal{F}(x) = \{u \in \mathbb{R}^m : \nabla h(x) f(x, u) \leq \alpha_z(-h(x) + c)\} \tag{1.38}$$

for $x \in \mathbb{R}^n$, where α_z is of class $\mathcal{K}^e$. If $\mathcal{F}(x) \neq \emptyset$ for all states of interest, one may choose

$$u = \rho(x) \in \mathcal{F}(x) \tag{1.39}$$

to meet the safety requirement (1.19).

This construction extends to multiple safety constraints. Given $h_j : \mathbb{R}^n \to (0, \infty)$ and constants $c_j > 0$ for $j = 1, \dots, n_c$ with n_c representing the number of constraints, define

$$\mathcal{F}(x) = \{u \in \mathbb{R}^m : \nabla h_j(x) f(x, u) \leq \alpha_j(-h_j(x) + c_j),\ j = 1, \dots, n_c\} \tag{1.40}$$

for $x \in \mathbb{R}^n$, where each α_j is of class $\mathcal{K}^e$.

If $u = \rho(x) \in \mathcal{F}(x) \neq \emptyset$ on a domain of interest, then following the standard discussion for ISS (see, e.g., [184, Lemma 6.1]), for each $j = 1, \dots, n_c$, there exist $\beta_j \in \mathcal{KL}$ and $c'_j > c_j$ such that

$$h_j(x(t)) \leq \max\{\beta_j(h_j(x(0)), t), c'_j\}, \quad \forall t \in [0, T_{\max}) \tag{1.41}$$

where $[0, T_{\max})$, with $T_{\max} > 0$ possibly infinite, is the interval on which the solution $x(t)$ of the closed-loop system is right maximally defined. To ensure uniqueness of solutions, one would select a locally Lipschitz selection ρ from the set-valued map $\mathcal{F}$, which yields locally Lipschitz closed-loop dynamics.[3]

1.3.3 Quadratic Programming Incorporating Safety Constraints and the Primary Control Objective

When a control system is tasked with achieving a primary objective subject to multiple safety constraints, the controller should be able to integrate these safety constraints with the main control objective.

Let us continue with the plant (1.34). Suppose that a controller

$$u = \rho_0(x), \tag{1.42}$$

referred to as the primary controller in this book, has been designed to achieve a primary control objective, but the resulting control input u may violate safety constraints.

With $\mathcal{F}(x)$ in (1.40) being the set of feasible control inputs that ensure safety, it is desirable to design a controller

$$u = \rho(x) \in \mathcal{F}(x) \tag{1.43}$$

so that all safety constraints are satisfied while deviating as little as possible from the primary controller (1.42). This naturally leads to a controller formulated as an optimization problem:

$$u = \underset{u}{\operatorname{argmin}} |u - \rho_0(x)|^2, \tag{1.44a}$$

$$\text{s.t.} \quad u \in \mathcal{F}(x). \tag{1.44b}$$

3 See [16] for notions of set-valued analysis.

Here, the control input u is treated as the optimization variable.

If the plant (1.34) admits the control-affine form:

$$\dot{x} = f(x) + g(x)u, \tag{1.45}$$

then the feasible set $\mathcal{F}(x)$ defined in (1.40) becomes

$$\mathcal{F}(x) = \{u \in \mathbb{R}^m : \nabla h_j(x)(f(x) + g(x)u) \leq \alpha_j(-h_j(x) + c_j),\ j = 1, \dots, n_c\}, \tag{1.46}$$

which consists of affine constraints; that is, the constraints are given by linear functions of u with offsets independent of u. Accordingly, (1.44) reduces to the QP:

$$u = \underset{u}{\operatorname{argmin}} |u - \rho_0(x)|^2, \tag{1.47a}$$

$$\text{s.t.} \quad \nabla h_j(x)g(x)u \leq -\nabla h_j(x)f(x) + \alpha_j(-h_j(x) + c_j), \quad j = 1, \dots, n_c. \tag{1.47b}$$

If the QP (1.47) is feasible (i.e., $\mathcal{F}(x)$ is nonempty) for each x in some domain of interest, then solving it yields a map ρ from x to u, thereby defining a controller as in (1.35). Generally speaking, a QP with multiple constraints does not admit a closed-form, explicit solution. In this book, a controller implicitly defined by a QP is called a QP-based controller.

Beyond feasibility, it is important to ensure (Lipschitz) continuity of the resulting controller to guarantee robustness under perturbations. Consider the following safety-oriented QP whose data depend on the external state x (typically the plant state):

$$u = \underset{u}{\operatorname{argmin}} |u - \rho_0(x)|^2 \tag{1.48a}$$

$$\text{s.t.} \quad A_c(x)u \leq b_c(x) \tag{1.48b}$$

where $u \in \mathbb{R}^m$ represents the optimization variable, $\rho_0 : \mathbb{R}^n \to \mathbb{R}^m$ is the primary controller, and $A_c : \mathbb{R}^n \to \mathbb{R}^{n_c \times m}$, $b_c : \mathbb{R}^n \to \mathbb{R}^{n_c}$ encode the safety constraints.

The Lipschitz continuity of solution maps for optimization problems has been investigated in [70] and several other fundamental works. For each x, let

$$\breve{A}_c(x)u \leq \breve{b}_c(x) \tag{1.49}$$

denote constraints that directly affect the optimal solution. That is, changing such constraints would alter the optimal solution[4] of the QP (1.48). Under feasibility and boundedness assumptions, if A_c, b_c, and ρ_0 satisfy suitable Lipschitz and

4 Note that the number of rows of $\breve{A}_c$ cannot exceed m, since otherwise the rows of $\breve{A}_c$ would be linearly dependent, contradicting the fact that removing any row changes the solution.

boundedness conditions, then the solution map from x to u is Lipschitz continuous, provided that $\breve{A}_c(x)$ has full row rank for all x [70, Theorem 3.1]; see also Theorem B.1. If only local Lipschitz continuity is required, it suffices that A_c, b_c, and ρ_0 are locally Lipschitz, and the boundedness requirement can be omitted.

The full-row-rank condition for $\breve{A}_c(x)$ essentially asserts linear independence of the "binding constraints" [70], which can be guaranteed by the well-known linear independence constraint qualification (LICQ) in general optimization [161, 37]. In [148], LICQ is employed to guarantee differentiability of certain minimizers in feedback control design via nonlinear programming.

Note that continuity can still be ensured even if the coefficient matrix becomes singular at some points. We illustrate this with a simple example. Consider the specialization of (1.48) with a single constraint:

$$u = \operatorname{argmin} |u|^2 \tag{1.50a}$$

$$\text{s.t.} \quad a(x)u \leq b(x) \tag{1.50b}$$

where $a : \mathbb{R}^n \to \mathbb{R}^{1\times m}$ and $b : \mathbb{R}^n \to \mathbb{R}$ are continuous. As shown in [21, Example 2.1.5], the solution map is given explicitly by

$$u = \begin{cases} a^T(x)\dfrac{b(x)}{|a(x)|^2}, & \text{if } a(x) \neq 0 \text{ and } b(x) < 0, \\ 0, & \text{otherwise} \end{cases} \tag{1.51}$$

provided that

$$\lim_{x\to x^*} \frac{|b(x)|}{|a(x)|} < \infty \tag{1.52}$$

for any x^* with $a(x^*) = 0$. Moreover, the map in (1.51) is continuous if

$$\lim_{x\to x^*} \frac{|b(x)|}{|a(x)|} = 0 \tag{1.53}$$

whenever $a(x^*) = 0$; see Theorem B.2.

In QP-based safety-critical control systems, the safety constraints depend on the real-time state of the plant, and it is generally infeasible to verify *a priori* whether the coefficient matrix of the constraints that directly affect the optimal solution always satisfies the full-row-rank condition. This poses a substantial challenge for safety-critical control, particularly when robustness is paramount. A detailed discussion is given in Section 1.5.

1.3.4 A Discussion on the Relationship with Feedback Stabilization

For the plant (1.34), assume $f(0, 0) = 0$, so the zero-input system has an equilibrium at the origin. Constructing feasible sets for safety-critical control based on safety indicator functions, discussed in Section 1.3.2, generalizes asymptotic stabilization based on control Lyapunov functions (CLFs). Relevant discussions can be found in [87, 138].

Intuitively, if the function h in (1.38) is replaced by a positive definite, continuously differentiable function $V : \mathbb{R}^n \to \mathbb{R}_+$, and if the set-valued map $\mathcal{F}$ defined therein (with a positive definite α_z and constant $c = 0$) is nonempty, then there exists a feedback control law $u = \rho(x)$ that asymptotically stabilizes (1.34) at the origin, with V serving as a Lyapunov function for the closed-loop system.

A function V is a CLF for (1.34) if

$$\inf_u \nabla V(x) f(x, u) < 0 \tag{1.54}$$

for all $x \neq 0$ in a neighborhood containing the origin. Intuitively, (1.54) asserts the existence of a feedback control law with u as the control input such that V is a Lyapunov function of the closed-loop system.

For the control-affine plant (1.45), condition (1.54) becomes

$$\inf_u \nabla V(x)(f(x) + g(x)u) < 0 \tag{1.55}$$

for all $x \neq 0$. Moreover, (1.55) is equivalent to

$$\nabla V(x) g(x) = 0 \quad \Rightarrow \quad \nabla V(x) f(x) < 0 \tag{1.56}$$

for all $x \neq 0$; see [183] for detailed discussions on CLFs.

Given a CLF V as in (1.55), assuming that V, f, and g are smooth, Sontag constructed an explicit controller $u = \rho(x)$, continuous at the origin and smooth elsewhere, that globally asymptotically stabilizes (1.45) at the origin [183]. The result is known as Sontag's formula, originally developed to provide a constructive proof of Artstein's theorem [15], which states that a smooth CLF implies smooth stabilizability.

We now show that the continuity property of the solution to the QP (1.50), under condition (1.53), yields a continuous stabilizing controller for (1.45) based on the CLF V; the resulting controller coincides with Sontag's formula.

Consider the QP-based controller

$$u = \operatorname{argmin} |u|^2 \tag{1.57a}$$

$$\text{s.t.} \quad \nabla V(x) g(x) u \leq -\nabla V(x) f(x) - \phi(x), \tag{1.57b}$$

where $\phi(x)$ is chosen as specified below. Clearly, (1.57) matches (1.50) with

$$a(x) = \nabla V(x) g(x), \tag{1.58}$$

$$b(x) = -\nabla V(x) f(x) - \phi(x). \tag{1.59}$$

We require ϕ to satisfy:

- $\lim_{x\to x^*} b(x)/a(x) = 0$ at any x^* with $a(x^*) = 0$, which ensures feasibility and continuity of the controller (see (1.52) and (1.53));
- $\phi(x) > 0$ whenever $a(x) \neq 0$ (i.e., $\nabla V(x)g(x) \neq 0$), which guarantees $\nabla V(x)(f(x) + g(x)u) < 0$ for $x \neq 0$, hence asymptotic stabilization (consistent with (1.55)).

The conditions can be satisfied by choosing

$$\phi(x) = \sqrt{\left(\nabla V(x)f(x)\right)^2 + \left(\nabla V(x)g(x)\right)^4}. \tag{1.60}$$

Applying (1.51), the QP-based controller (1.57) is explicitly given by

$$u = \begin{cases} a^T(x)\dfrac{b(x)}{|a(x)|^2}, & \text{if } a(x) \neq 0 \text{ and } b(x) < 0, \\ 0, & \text{otherwise,} \end{cases} \tag{1.61}$$

which coincides with Sontag's formula for global asymptotic stabilization. This elucidates the intrinsic link between safety-critical control and feedback stabilization.

1.4 A Practical Scenario of Robust Safety-critical Control

This section presents an elementary robust safety-critical control problem. The principal technical challenges, arising primarily from dynamic uncertainties and multiple constraints, will be discussed in the next section.

1.4.1 Plant: A Mobile Agent Subject to Uncertain Actuation Dynamics

We consider a common class of mobile agents modeled as a cascade of a nominal kinematic system and an uncertain actuation system (corresponding to the controlled dynamics). An example is given by Example 1.2. The nominal system is

$$\dot{p} = v, \tag{1.62}$$

where $p \in \mathbb{R}^n$ denotes position and $v \in \mathbb{R}^n$ denotes velocity. The velocity v is generated by an actuation system of the form

$$\dot{z} = f(z, v^*), \tag{1.63a}$$

$$v = g(z, v^*), \tag{1.63b}$$

where $z \in \mathbb{R}^m$ is the state, $v^* \in \mathbb{R}^n$ is a velocity-reference input, and $f : \mathbb{R}^m \times \mathbb{R}^n \to \mathbb{R}^m$ and $g : \mathbb{R}^m \times \mathbb{R}^n \to \mathbb{R}^n$ are functions specifying the dynamics and the

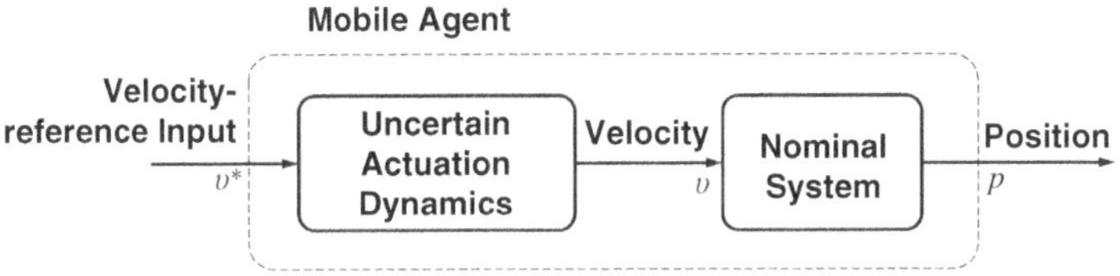

Figure 1.6 Cascade connection of a nominal system and an uncertain actuation system.

output map of the actuation system. Both f and g are assumed to be locally Lipschitz, which guarantees that the trajectories of the actuation system (1.63) are uniquely defined. In our problem setting, we consider the case where f and g are unknown functions, so their explicit expressions are not available for controller design. Figure 1.6 shows a block diagram of a mobile agent subject to uncertain actuation dynamics.

Because of dynamical response of the actuation system, the actual velocity v generally differs from the velocity-reference input v^*. To highlight the influence of the velocity-tracking error

$$\tilde{v} = v - v^*, \tag{1.64}$$

we rewrite the nominal system (1.62) as

$$\dot{p} = v = v^* + \tilde{v}. \tag{1.65}$$

In practice, the actuation system should be intrinsically stable and capable of tracking velocity-reference inputs. For the class of systems considered in this book, we adopt the following standing assumptions:

- For any constant velocity-reference input v^*, the actual velocity v asymptotically converges to v^*;
- For any time-varying but locally Lipschitz v^*, the magnitude of the velocity-tracking error $\tilde{v}$ is determined by the changing rate of v^*.

The following assumption characterizes the reference-tracking capability of the actuation system.

Assumption 1.1 ***(Reference-tracking Capability of the Actuation System)*:** Consider the actuation system (1.63). There exist functions $\beta_{\tilde{v}} \in \mathcal{KL}$ and $\alpha_{z1}, \alpha_{z2}, \gamma_{\tilde{v}} \in \mathcal{K}$ such that for any $z(0)$ and any locally Lipschitz v^*,

$$|\tilde{v}(t)| \leq \max\{\beta_{\tilde{v}}(|z(0)| + |v^*(0)|, t), \gamma_{\tilde{v}}(\|D^+ v^*\|_t)\} \tag{1.66}$$

$$|z(t)| \leq \max\{\alpha_{z1}(|z(0)|), \alpha_{z2}(\|v^*\|_t)\} \tag{1.67}$$

for all $t \geq 0$.

In our safety-critical control system setup, the velocity-reference input υ^* is typically generated by optimization-based controllers and may not be differentiable in time. For this reason, Assumption 1.1 takes υ^* to be locally Lipschitz. Note that for a locally Lipschitz υ^*, the upper right Dini derivative $D^+\upsilon^*$ is always well defined [95, Theorem 3.6.5].

Property (1.66) employs the notion of IOS to characterize the reference-tracking performance, considering the upper right Dini derivative of the velocity-reference input υ^* as the input and the velocity-tracking error $\tilde{\upsilon}$ as the output:

- $\beta_{\tilde{\upsilon}}$ captures the transient behavior, and
- $\tilde{\upsilon}$ ultimately enters a neighborhood of the origin whose size is determined by $\gamma_{\tilde{\upsilon}}(\|D^+\upsilon^*\|_t)$.

Additionally, property (1.67) ensures boundedness of z for any bounded υ^*.

If the dynamics of the actuation system are negligible, i.e., $\upsilon^* \equiv \upsilon$, the plant model (1.62)-(1.63) reduces to a single integrator, a case extensively studied in safety-critical control. A double-integrator model also fits (1.62)-(1.63) by introducing a virtual controller to the inner velocity loop; see [108] for the notion of virtual control in backstepping-based nonlinear control of cascaded systems, and Chapter 7 for constructive safety-critical controller designs. This idea is illustrated in Figure 1.7, which presents an equivalent representation of the cascade connection between a nominal system and an uncertain actuation system.

The following example shows that, under mild conditions, an uncertain actuation system modeled as a stable linear time-invariant system satisfies Assumption 1.1.

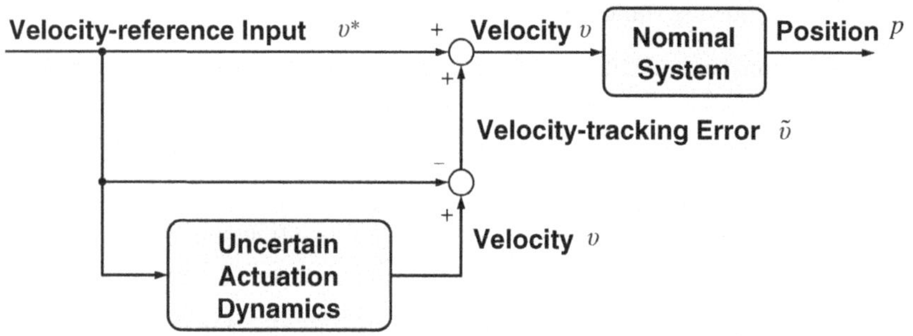

Figure 1.7 An equivalent representation of the cascade connection of a nominal system and an uncertain actuation system.

Example 1.1 ***(Reference-tracking Capability of a Linear Time-invariant System):*** *Suppose that the uncertain actuation system* (1.63) *takes the linear time-invariant form:*

$$\dot{z} = Az + Bv^*, \tag{1.68a}$$

$$v = Cz, \tag{1.68b}$$

where $z \in \mathbb{R}^m$ *is the state,* $v \in \mathbb{R}^n$ *is the actual velocity,* $v^* \in \mathbb{R}^n$ *is the velocity-reference input, and* A, B, C *are real matrices of compatible dimensions. Assume that* A *is Hurwitz and*

$$CA^{-1}B = -I_{n\times n}. \tag{1.69}$$

Let $v^* : [0, \infty) \to \mathbb{R}^n$ *be locally Lipschitz. By [98, Theorem 3.2], for any initial condition* $z(0)$*, the model* (1.68) *uniquely defines a trajectory* $z(t)$ *for all* $t \geq 0$.

Define the velocity-tracking error

$$\tilde{v} = v - v^*. \tag{1.70}$$

Since A *is Hurwitz, for any constant velocity-reference input* v^**, condition* (1.69) *ensures*

$$\lim_{t\to\infty} \tilde{v}(t) = 0. \tag{1.71}$$

To analyze the transient performance, set

$$\zeta = Az + Bv^*. \tag{1.72}$$

Under condition (1.69)*, using [61, equation (1c)], a direct computation gives*

$$D^+\zeta = A\dot{z} + BD^+v^* = A\zeta + BD^+v^*, \tag{1.73}$$

$$\tilde{v} = Cz - v^* = CA^{-1}(\zeta - Bv^*) - v^* = CA^{-1}\zeta. \tag{1.74}$$

Because A *is Hurwitz, the Lyapunov method for linear time-invariant systems [34, Theorem 5.5] guarantees that for any positive definite symmetric* $Q \in \mathbb{R}^{m\times m}$*, there exists a unique positive definite symmetric* $P \in \mathbb{R}^{m\times m}$ *solving*

$$A^TP + PA = -Q. \tag{1.75}$$

Fix $Q > 0$*, let* $P > 0$ *solve* (1.75)*, and define*

$$V(\zeta) = \zeta^TP\zeta. \tag{1.76}$$

As long as $\zeta(t)$ satisfies (1.73), *the upper right Dini derivative of $V(\zeta(t))$ with respect to t satisfies*[5]

$$\begin{aligned} D^+V(\zeta(t)) &= \nabla V(\zeta(t))A\zeta(t) + \limsup_{\Delta\to 0+} \nabla V(\zeta(t))B\frac{\upsilon^*(t+\Delta)-\upsilon^*(t)}{\Delta} \\ &= \zeta^T(t)(A^TP+PA)\zeta(t) + 2\limsup_{\Delta\to 0+} \zeta^T(t)PB\frac{\upsilon^*(t+\Delta)-\upsilon^*(t)}{\Delta} \\ &= -\zeta^T(t)Q\zeta(t) + 2\limsup_{\Delta\to 0+} \zeta^T(t)PB\frac{\upsilon^*(t+\Delta)-\upsilon^*(t)}{\Delta} \\ &\le -\lambda_{\min}(Q)|\zeta(t)|^2 + 2|PB||\zeta(t)|D_L^+\upsilon^*(t) \end{aligned} \tag{1.77}$$

for all $t \ge 0$, where $D_L^+\upsilon^*(t)$ denotes the right Lipschitz derivative of υ^* at $t \in \mathbb{R}_+$ (see [38, Definition 2.2.19] for details), which is defined by

$$D_L^+\upsilon^*(t) = \limsup_{\Delta\to 0+}\left|\frac{\upsilon^*(t+\Delta)-\upsilon^*(t)}{\Delta}\right|. \tag{1.78}$$

Since $\upsilon^*(t)$ is locally Lipschitz, $D_L^+\upsilon^*(t)$ is measurable and locally essentially bounded. Fix $\epsilon \in (0, \lambda_{\min}(Q))$. Using (1.76),

$$\begin{aligned} D^+V(\zeta(t)) &\le -\lambda_{\min}(Q)|\zeta(t)|^2 + \epsilon|\zeta(t)|^2 + \frac{1}{\epsilon}|PB|^2|D_L^+\upsilon^*(t)|^2 \\ &\le -\frac{\lambda_{\min}(Q)-\epsilon}{\lambda_{\max}(P)}V(\zeta(t)) + \frac{1}{\epsilon}|PB|^2|D_L^+\upsilon^*(t)|^2 \end{aligned} \tag{1.79}$$

for all $t \ge 0$.

To analyze the dynamical behavior of $V(\zeta(t))$, we apply the comparison principle. Specifically, consider the following scalar system for comparison:

$$\dot{\eta}(t) = -\frac{\lambda_{\min}(Q)-\epsilon}{\lambda_{\max}(P)}\eta(t) + \frac{1}{\epsilon}|PB|^2|D_L^+\upsilon^*(t)|^2, \tag{1.80}$$

with initial state $\eta(0)$, whose solution is

$$\eta(t) = e^{-\frac{\lambda_{\min}(Q)-\epsilon}{\lambda_{\max}(P)}t}\eta(0) + \frac{1}{\epsilon}|PB|^2\int_0^t e^{-\frac{\lambda_{\min}(Q)-\epsilon}{\lambda_{\max}(P)}(t-\tau)}|D_L^+\upsilon^*(\tau)|^2\,d\tau. \tag{1.81}$$

By applying elementary inequality techniques, we have

$$\eta(t) \le e^{-\frac{\lambda_{\min}(Q)-\epsilon}{\lambda_{\max}(P)}t}\eta(0) + \frac{\lambda_{\max}(P)|PB|^2}{\epsilon(\lambda_{\min}(Q)-\epsilon)}\|D_L^+\upsilon^*\|_\infty^2 \tag{1.82}$$

for all $t \ge 0$.

---

5 See Proposition A.26 in Appendix A.6 for the chain rule for Dini derivatives.

Choosing $\eta(0) = V(\zeta(0))$ *and applying the comparison lemma [98, Lemma 3.4] to* (1.79) *and* (1.80), *we obtain*

$$V(\zeta(t)) \le e^{-\frac{\lambda_{\min}(Q)-\epsilon}{\lambda_{\max}(P)}t} V(\zeta(0)) + \frac{\lambda_{\max}(P)|PB|^2}{\epsilon(\lambda_{\min}(Q)-\epsilon)} \|D_L^+ v^*\|_\infty^2 \tag{1.83}$$

for all $t \ge 0$.

Using the definitions of $\tilde{v}$ *and* ζ *in* (1.74) *and* (1.72), *respectively, we have*

$$|\tilde{v}(t)| \le |CA^{-1}||\zeta(t)| \le \frac{|CA^{-1}|}{\sqrt{\lambda_{\min}(P)}} \sqrt{V(\zeta(t))} \tag{1.84}$$

$$\begin{aligned} |\zeta(t)| &= |Az(t) + Bv^*(t)| \le |A||z(t)| + |B||v^*(t)| \\ &\le \max\{|A|, |B|\}(|z(t)| + |v^*(t)|) \end{aligned} \tag{1.85}$$

for all $t \ge 0$. *Substituting* (1.83) *into* (1.84) *and evaluating* $\zeta(0)$ *via* (1.85) *at* $t = 0$, *we obtain*

$$\begin{aligned} |\tilde{v}(t)| \le |CA^{-1}| \sqrt{\frac{2\lambda_{\max}(P)}{\lambda_{\min}(P)}} \max \Bigg\{ &\max\{|A|, |B|\}(|z(0)| \\ &+ |v^*(0)|) e^{-\frac{\lambda_{\min}(Q)-\epsilon}{2\lambda_{\max}(P)}t}, \frac{|PB|}{\sqrt{\epsilon(\lambda_{\min}(Q)-\epsilon)}} \|D_L^+ v^*\|_\infty \Bigg\} \end{aligned} \tag{1.86}$$

for all $t \ge 0$.

Since v^* *is locally Lipschitz continuous on* $\mathbb{R}_+$, *by [38, Theorem 3.4.1 and Remark 3.4.2],* $v^*(t)$ *is differentiable almost everywhere on* $\mathbb{R}_+$. *Hence, for almost every* $t \in \mathbb{R}_+$,

$$D^+ v^*(t) = \dot{v}^*(t) \ \text{ and } \ D_L^+ v^*(t) = |\dot{v}^*(t)|. \tag{1.87}$$

Therefore,

$$|D^+ v^*(t)| = D_L^+ v^*(t) \tag{1.88}$$

for almost every $t \in \mathbb{R}_+$, *which means that* $\{t \in \mathbb{R}_+ : |D^+ v^*(t)| \ne D_L^+ v^*(t)\}$ *is a set of measure zero. Then, by the definition of essential supremum [17, Definition 7.1],*

$$\|D^+ v^*\|_\infty = \operatorname*{ess\ sup}_{t\in[0,\infty)} |D^+ v^*(t)| = \operatorname*{ess\ sup}_{t\in[0,\infty)} D_L^+ v^*(t) = \|D_L^+ v^*\|_\infty. \tag{1.89}$$

This, together with (1.86), *ensures the satisfaction of the form* (1.66).

To verify property (1.67), *consider* (1.68). *Since* A *is Hurwitz, standard ISS results (see, e.g., [188]) guarantee the existence of* $\beta_z \in \mathcal{KL}$ *and* $\gamma_z \in \mathcal{K}$ *such that, for any* $z(0)$ *and any locally Lipschitz* v^*,

$$|z(t)| \le \max\{\beta_z(|z(0)|, t), \gamma_z(\|v^*\|_\infty)\} \tag{1.90}$$

for all $t \geq 0$. *Hence,* (1.67) *holds with* $\alpha_{z1}(s) = \beta_z(s, 0)$ *and* $\alpha_{z2}(s) = \gamma_z(s)$ *for all* $s \in \mathbb{R}_+$.

Note that the arguments above are still valid if one replaces $\|\cdot\|_\infty$ *with* $\|\cdot\|_t$. *Overall, this example establishes Assumption 1.1 for the linear time-invariant system* (1.68) *with A being Hurwitz and satisfying* (1.69).

Interestingly, a data-identified model of the dynamics of a velocity-controlled quadrotor can be cast in the form (1.68) and satisfies Assumption 1.1.

Example 1.2 ***(Velocity-reference-tracking Capability of a Quadrotor)*****:** *Consider a Crazyflie 2.0,*[6] *whose velocity is governed by a PID controller designed with MATLAB*[7] *Control System Designer and implemented via ROS*[8] *on a laptop computer. The kinematics model describing the position-velocity relation is given by* (1.62). *We suppose that the controlled dynamics of the quadrotor, which generates the velocity* v, *takes the form* (1.68). *The experimental system for model identification and algorithm verification is composed of a quadrotor (Crazyflie 2.0 with original onboard attitude controller, as shown in Figure 1.8), an optical motion capture system (OptiTrack), and a laptop computer running ROS. The motion capture system measures the real-time positions and velocities of the quadrotors. Data transmission from the laptop computer to the quadrotor is based on Crazyradio PA, and that from the motion capture system to the laptop computer is through TCP/IP Ethernet. System identification for the velocity-controlled quadrotor is performed using the MATLAB System Identification Toolbox, based on indoor experimental data (as shown in Figure 1.9).*

The identified model, with the velocity-reference input v^* *as input and the actual velocity* v *as output, takes the form* (1.68), *where*

$$A = \text{diag}\{A_{11}, A_{22}, A_{33}, A_{44}\}, \tag{1.91a}$$

$$B^T = \begin{bmatrix} B_{11}^T & B_{21}^T & 0 & 0 \\ 0 & 0 & B_{32}^T & B_{42}^T \end{bmatrix}, \tag{1.91b}$$

$$C = \begin{bmatrix} C_{11} & 0 & C_{13} & 0 \\ 0 & C_{22} & 0 & C_{24} \end{bmatrix} \tag{1.91c}$$

---

6 Crazyflie 2.0 is a lightweight, open-source flying development platform based on a nano quadrotor, developed and manufactured by Bitcraze.
7 MATLAB is a commercial mathematical software developed by MathWorks.
8 ROS (Robot Operating System) is a collection of software libraries and tools for building robotic applications.

Figure 1.8 Nano quadrotor Crazyflie 2.0.

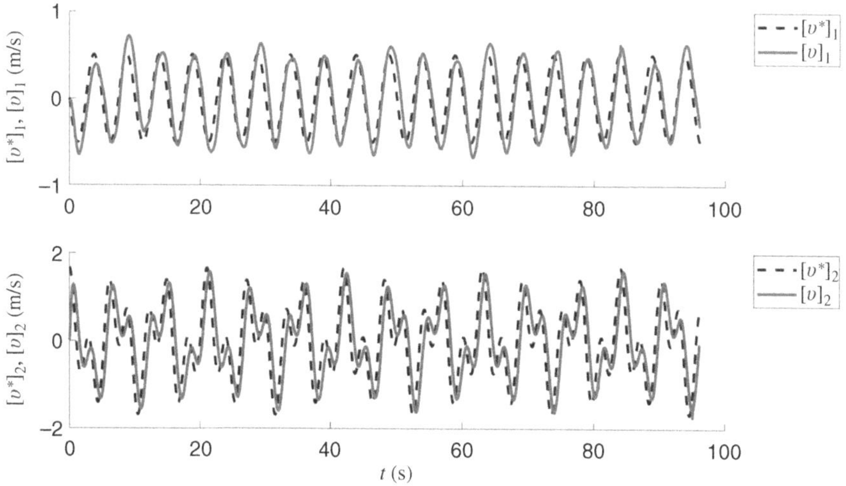

Figure 1.9 The influence of the uncertain actuation system: comparison between the velocity-reference input and the measured velocity of a Crazyflie 2.0 in an indoor experiment.

with component matrices

$$A_{11} = [-1.58, 2.92; -2.92, -1.58], \qquad A_{22} = [-2.68, 7.18; -7.18, -2.68] \tag{1.92a}$$

$$A_{33} = [-2.56, 6.86; -6.86, -2.56], \qquad A_{44} = [-2.14, 3.71; -3.71, -2.14] \tag{1.92b}$$

$$B_{11}^T = [\ 1.65,\ \ 0.65], \qquad B_{21}^T = [\ 1.50,\ \ 0.92], \tag{1.92c}$$

$$B_{32}^T = [\ 1.58,\ \ 0.84], \qquad B_{42}^T = [\ 1.51, -2.29], \tag{1.92d}$$

$$C_{11} = [\ 0.78, -1.98], \qquad C_{13} = [\ 2.13,\ \ 2.41], \tag{1.92e}$$

$$C_{22} = [-2.20, -2.82], \qquad C_{24} = [-1.51, -0.99]. \tag{1.92f}$$

It is straightforward to verify that A is Hurwitz and satisfies (1.69)*. Based on the arguments in Example 1.1, we can prove that the identified quadrotor model satisfies Assumption 1.1.*

When internal states are subject to saturation, the IOS property in (1.66) may not be valid globally, and a local IOS property becomes more appropriate. In such cases, one must delineate the region where IOS holds, which can substantially complicate the closed-loop analysis.

1.4.2 Safety Constraints Caused by Obstacles

Consider a mobile agent operating in an environment with n_o stationary spherical obstacles indexed by

$$\mathcal{N}_o = \{1, \dots, n_o\}. \tag{1.93}$$

For each $i \in \mathcal{N}_o$, let $o_i \in \mathbb{R}^n$ denote the center position of the i-th obstacle.

Define a safety indicator function $h : \mathbb{R}^n \setminus \{0\} \rightarrow (0, \infty)$ by

$$h(\tilde{p}_i) = \mu(|\tilde{p}_i|), \tag{1.94}$$

where $\mu : (0, \infty) \rightarrow (0, \infty)$ is an $\mathcal{M}^-\mathcal{C}$ function,[9] and for each $i \in \mathcal{N}_o$,

$$\tilde{p}_i = p - o_i, \tag{1.95}$$

is the relative position of the mobile agent with respect to obstacle i. The origin is usually considered a singular point, and excluded from the domain of h, because $\tilde{p}_i = 0$ corresponds to a collision with obstacle i.

---

9 A function $\mu : (-a, \infty) \rightarrow (0, b)$ with constants $a, b \in \mathbb{R}_+ \cup \{\infty\}$ is said to be of class $\mathcal{M}^-\mathcal{C}$, denoted by $\mu \in \mathcal{M}^-\mathcal{C}$, if it is strictly decreasing, strictly convex and continuously differentiable, and satisfies $\lim_{r\rightarrow\infty} \mu(r) = 0$ and $\lim_{r\rightarrow\infty} \mathrm{d}\mu(r)/\mathrm{d}r = 0$.

To quantify safety with respect to all obstacles, define

$$\bar{h}(p) = \max_{i \in \mathcal{N}_o} h(\tilde{p}_i). \tag{1.96}$$

Given a predetermined safe distance $D > 0$, the agent modeled by (1.62)-(1.63) under a suitably designed controller, is deemed safe if there exist $\beta \in \mathcal{KL}$ and constants $h_0, z_0, b_0, \bar{z} \geq 0$ such that, for any initial conditions $p(0)$ satisfying $\bar{h}(p(0)) \leq h_0$ and $z(0)$ satisfying $|z(0)| \leq z_0$, the following properties hold for all $t \geq 0$:

$$\bar{h}(p(t)) \leq \max\{\beta(\bar{h}(p(0)) + |z(0)| + b_0, t), \mu(D)\}, \tag{1.97a}$$

$$|z(t)| \leq \bar{z}. \tag{1.97b}$$

The safety requirement (1.97a) aligns with Definition 1.6 on transient-aware safety. In addition, property (1.97b) requires that the internal state z of the actuation system remains bounded, as is standard in normal control designs.

To ensure feasibility of the safety-critical control problem, we impose a separation condition on the obstacles.

Assumption 1.2 ***(Separation Condition on the Obstacles)***: There exists $D_o > D$ such that

$$|o_i - o_j| \geq 2D_o \tag{1.98}$$

for all $i, j \in \mathcal{N}_o$ with $i \neq j$.

1.4.3 A Safety-critical Control System Structure

We denote by $v^c \in \mathbb{R}^n$ the velocity-command signal associated with the primary control objective. In practice, v^c is typically generated by a higher-level planner or a primary controller.

We aim to design a safety-critical controller that incorporates the command v^c while enforcing the safety constraints induced by the obstacles o_i for $i \in \mathcal{N}_o$. An expected structure of the safety-critical control system is shown in Figure 1.10.

Without loss of generality, we impose the following condition on v^c.

Assumption 1.3 ***(Boundedness of the Velocity-command Signal and Its Time Derivative)***: The velocity-command signal v^c is continuously differentiable in time, and there exist positive constants $\bar{v}^c$ and $\bar{v}^{cd}$ such that

$$|v^c(t)| \leq \bar{v}^c, \quad |\dot{v}_i^c(t)| \leq \bar{v}^{cd} \tag{1.99}$$

for all $t \geq 0$.

In the presence of dynamic uncertainty and multiple safety constraints, the safety-critical control problem becomes substantially challenging. The next section highlights two major difficulties through illustrative examples.

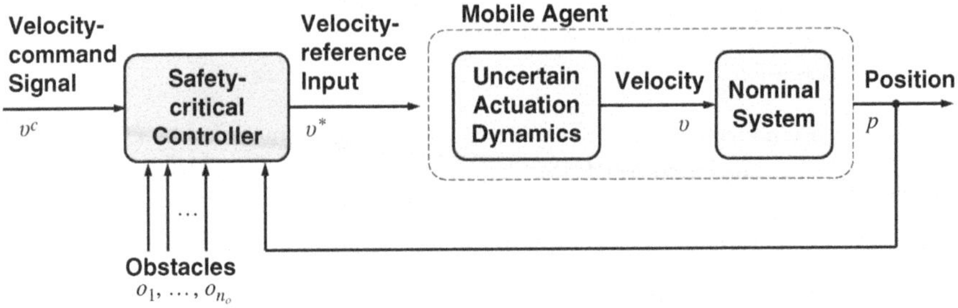

Figure 1.10 An expected structure of the safety-critical control system.

1.5 Challenges

1.5.1 Dynamic Uncertainties

Consider a specific instance of the safety-critical control problem introduced in Section 1.4. In particular, consider a mobile agent modeled by (1.62)-(1.63) and a stationary spherical obstacle with center at $o \in \mathbb{R}^n$.

If the velocity-tracking error $\tilde{v}$, defined in (1.70), is negligible, then following the discussion in Section 1.3.3, a safety-critical controller for the system (1.65) may be specified by the following QP:

$$v^* = \underset{v^* \in \mathbb{R}^n}{\operatorname{argmin}} |v^* - v^c|^2, \tag{1.100a}$$

$$\text{s.t.} \quad -\frac{\tilde{p}^T}{|\tilde{p}|} v^* \leq -\alpha_h(h(\tilde{p}) - \mu(D)), \tag{1.100b}$$

where $\tilde{p} \in \mathbb{R}^n$ defined by $\tilde{p} = p - o$ is the relative position between the agent and the obstacle, $h : \mathbb{R}^n \setminus \{0\} \to \mathbb{R}_+$ is the safety indicator function defined in (1.94), $\alpha_h \in \mathcal{K}^e$ is a locally Lipschitz function, $v^c : [0, \infty) \to \mathbb{R}^n$ represents the velocity-command signal, and $D > 0$ is the desired safe distance. This controller is nonsingular as long as $p \neq o$.

Compared with (1.38), replacing $\nabla h(\tilde{p})$ by $-\tilde{p}^T/|\tilde{p}|$ in (1.100b) is meaningful provided that the function μ used to define $h(\tilde{p})$ admits negative slopes. Intuitively, whenever $\tilde{p} \neq 0$, the v^* generated by (1.100) steers the mobile agent away from the obstacle (i.e., $\tilde{p}^T v^* > 0$) as long as $h(\tilde{p}) > \mu(0)$, or equivalently $|\tilde{p}| < D$.

When the velocity-tracking error $\tilde{v}$ is nonnegligible, a natural approach to ensure safety is to introduce an enlarged safety margin in the constraint (1.100b):

$$v^* = \underset{v^* \in \mathbb{R}^n}{\operatorname{argmin}} |v^* - v^c|^2, \tag{1.101a}$$

$$\text{s.t.} \quad -\frac{\tilde{p}^T}{|\tilde{p}|} v^* \leq -\alpha_h(h(\tilde{p}) - \mu(D_s)), \tag{1.101b}$$

where $D_s > D$ is a positive constant specifying the safety margin.

However, as indicated in Assumption 1.1, the velocity-tracking error $\tilde{v}$ depends on the upper right Dini derivative D^+v^*, whereas v^* is generated by the QP-based controller based on the feedback of the real-time value of the safety indicator function $h(\tilde{p})$. Conversely, the value of $h(\tilde{p})$ is affected by $\tilde{v}$. The coupling between $h(\tilde{p})$ and $\tilde{v}$ makes it difficult to assume a uniform upper bound on $\tilde{v}(t)$ for all $t \geq 0$ for the controller design, and hence to directly select a constant D_s that is guaranteed to attenuate the effect of $\tilde{v}$. In other words, to ensure safety, the values of α_h, μ and D_s must be selected in a coordinated manner.

We illustrate the impact of dynamic uncertainties on safety via a numerical simulation.

Example 1.3 ***(Impact of Dynamic Uncertainties on Safety)***: *Consider the safety-critical altitude control problem for an unmanned aerial vehicle (UAV).*

In the altitude direction, the motion of the UAV is modeled by (1.62)-(1.63). *In particular, the actuation system takes the form* (1.63) *with*

$$f(z, v^*) = \begin{bmatrix} -2 & -2 \\ 1 & 0 \end{bmatrix} z + \begin{bmatrix} 2 \\ 0 \end{bmatrix} v^*, \tag{1.102a}$$

$$g(z, v^*) = [-1, 1]z. \tag{1.102b}$$

Following the discussion in Example 1.1, one verifies that the actuation system possesses velocity-tracking capability (1.66).

Model the ground as an obstacle at $o = 0$, *and let the desired safe distance be* $D = 0.5$. *We use the safety indicator function* $h(\tilde{p})$ *to quantify safety:*

$$h(\tilde{p}) = \frac{1}{|\tilde{p}|} = \frac{1}{|p - o|}. \tag{1.103}$$

Our goal is to design a safety-critical controller that, in the presence of uncertain actuation dynamics, prevents ground collision while tracking the operator's velocity-command signal v^c *as closely as possible. Specifically, in the altitude direction, we consider*

$$v^c \equiv -1, \tag{1.104}$$

which basically forces the UAV to the ground.

We employ the safety-critical controller (1.101) *and choose* $\alpha_h(s) = k_h s$ *(with constant* $k_h > 0$*) and* $\mu(D_s) = 1/D_s$. *Consider the following controller parameter choices:*

$$\text{Parameter set 1:} \quad k_h = 0.5, \; D_s = 1.0; \tag{1.105a}$$

$$\text{Parameter set 2:} \quad k_h = 1.0, \; D_s = 1.0; \tag{1.105b}$$

$$\text{Parameter set 3:} \quad k_h = 1.0, \; D_s = 2.0. \tag{1.105c}$$

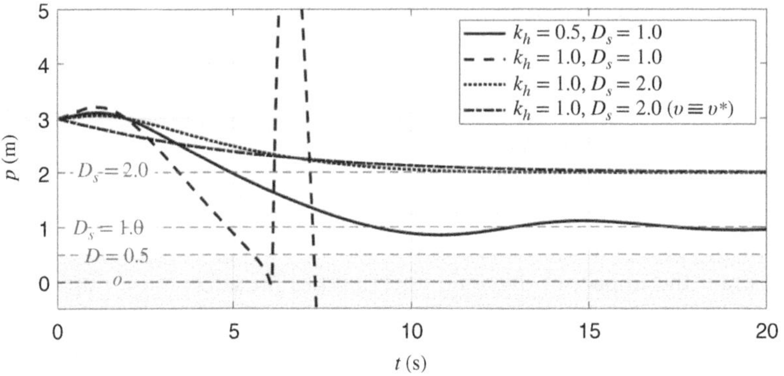

Figure 1.11 Altitude trajectories of a UAV corresponding to different controller parameter sets.

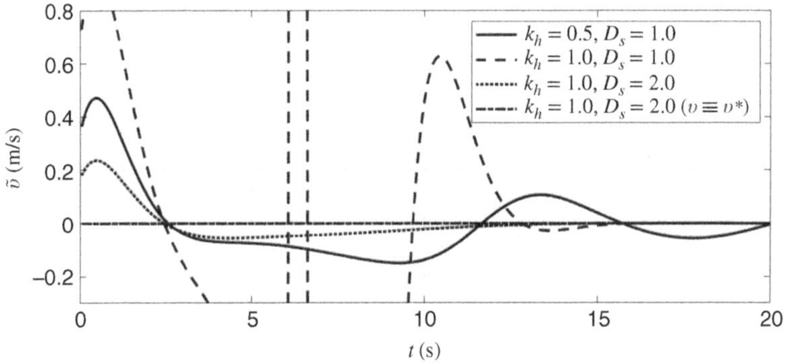

Figure 1.12 Velocity-tracking error trajectories of a UAV corresponding to different controller parameter sets.

Figures 1.11 and 1.12 show the altitude trajectories and velocity-tracking error trajectories corresponding to different parameter sets. In Figure 1.11, a comparison between parameter sets 1 and 2 shows that increasing k_h may lead to violation of the safety constraint (contrary to intuition), whereas comparing the trajectories of Sets 2 and 3 reveals that a larger safety margin D_s enhances safety. Meanwhile, Figure 1.12 indicates that an upper bound for the tracking error $\tilde{v}$ cannot necessarily be determined in advance, implying that D_s cannot be chosen based on a predetermined bound on $|\tilde{v}|$. For comparison, Figure 1.11 also shows the altitude trajectory of the controlled UAV model with $v \equiv v^*$, using controller parameters from Parameter set 3. The impact of dynamic uncertainties on safety is quite clear.

From the trials in Example 1.3, one expects a quantitative method to appropriately tune the safety-critical controller in the presence of dynamic uncertainties (see Chapter 2).

1.5.2 Multiple Constraints

Consider again the safety-critical control problem formulated in Section 1.4. Specifically, examine a scenario with a mobile agent modeled by (1.62)-(1.63) and n_o stationary spherical obstacles located at positions $o_i \in \mathbb{R}^n$ for $i \in \mathcal{N}_o$.

When the velocity-tracking error $\tilde{v}$ defined in (1.70) is nonnegligible, the QP-based safety-critical controller (1.47) from Section 1.3.3 motivates the design

$$v^* = \underset{v^* \in \mathbb{R}^2}{\operatorname{argmin}} |v^* - v^c|^2 \tag{1.106a}$$

$$\text{s.t.} \quad A(p)v^* \leq b(p) \tag{1.106b}$$

with

$$A(p) = \left[-\frac{\tilde{p}_1}{|\tilde{p}_1|}, \dots, -\frac{\tilde{p}_{n_o}}{|\tilde{p}_{n_o}|} \right]^T, \tag{1.107a}$$

$$b(p) = [-\alpha_h(h(\tilde{p}_1) - \mu(D_s)), \dots, -\alpha_h(h(\tilde{p}_{n_o}) - \mu(D_s))]^T \tag{1.107b}$$

where $\tilde{p}_i \in \mathbb{R}^n$, defined by $\tilde{p}_i = p - o_i$, is the relative position between the mobile agent and the i-th obstacle at $o_i \in \mathbb{R}^n$ for $i \in \mathcal{N}_o$, $h : \mathbb{R}^n \setminus \{0\} \to \mathbb{R}_+$ is the safety indicator function defined in (1.94), $\alpha_h \in \mathcal{K}^e$ is a locally Lipschitz function, $v^c : [0, \infty) \to \mathbb{R}^n$ represents the velocity-command signal, and $D_s > 0$ is a constant that introduces an enlarged safety margin.

In the presence of multiple safety constraints, the safety-critical control problem becomes more challenging if dynamic uncertainties cannot be neglected. In particular, the control input directly generated by a QP may fail to be Lipschitz locally with respect to the state of the plant. This, in turn, can drive the closed-loop dynamics, under dynamic uncertainty, beyond the scope of standard robustness analysis. The requirement of Lipschitz continuity for ensured robustness of QP-based safety-critical controllers is well documented in the literature [137, 87, 148, 219, 157, 33]. We employ a numerical example to illustrate these points.

Example 1.4 ***(Robustness Issues in the Presence of Multiple Constraints)***: *Consider the safety-critical control problem formulated in Section 1.4 with the mobile agent's position $p \in \mathbb{R}^2$, and two obstacles at $o_1 \in \mathbb{R}^2$ and $o_2 \in \mathbb{R}^2$. In this example, take $o_1 = [0.5; 0.5]$, $o_2 = -[0.5; 0.5]$, $v^c = [1; -1]$, and $D = 0.68$.*

Let $h(\tilde{p}_i) = 1/|\tilde{p}_i|$ and $\alpha_h(s) = k_h s$ (with constant $k_h > 0$). Consider the safety-critical controller with an enlarged safety margin, as defined in (1.101):

$$v^* = \underset{v^* \in \mathbb{R}^2}{\operatorname{argmin}} |v^* - v^c|^2 \tag{1.108a}$$

$$\text{s.t.} \quad -\frac{\tilde{p}_i}{|\tilde{p}_i|} v^* \leq -k_h \left(\frac{1}{|\tilde{p}_i|} - \frac{1}{D_s} \right), \quad i = 1, 2. \tag{1.108b}$$

Directly addressing the safety-critical control problem by stacking constraints can render the QP infeasible at certain states. For example, if $D_s > \sqrt{2}/2$, the feasible set defined in (1.108b) *is empty at* $p = [0; 0]$.

Even if the parameters are appropriately chosen such that the QP (1.108) *remains feasible over a domain of interest, the presence of the two constraints may cause the controller map from p to* υ^* *to lose local Lipschitz continuity. For the QP* (1.108) *with* $D_s = \sqrt{2}/2$ *and* $k_h = 1$, *Figure 1.13 shows the dependence of* $|\upsilon^*|$ *on p, where darker shading indicates larger values of* $|\upsilon^*|$. *One observes sharp changes in* $|\upsilon^*|$ *near* $p = [0; 0]$.

Now incorporate the actuation system. Consider an actuation system in the form of (1.63) *with*

$$f(z, \upsilon^*) = \begin{bmatrix} -5 & 0 \\ -10 & -5 \end{bmatrix} z + \begin{bmatrix} 5 & 0 \\ 10 & 5 \end{bmatrix} \upsilon^*, \tag{1.109a}$$

$$g(z, \upsilon^*) = \begin{bmatrix} 1 & 0 \\ 0 & 1 \end{bmatrix} z. \tag{1.109b}$$

Set initial states $p(0) = [-0.5; 0.5]$ *and* $z(0) = [0; 0]$. *Figure 1.14 shows the position trajectories of the mobile agent under the QP-based controller* (1.108) *with* $D_s = \sqrt{2}/2.01$ *and* $k_h \in \{0.05, 0.5, 2.0\}$. *Owing to the non-Lipschitz continuity of the QP-based controller, the corresponding trajectories exhibit adverse transient behavior near* $p = [0; 0]$, *resulting in collisions with one of the obstacles.*

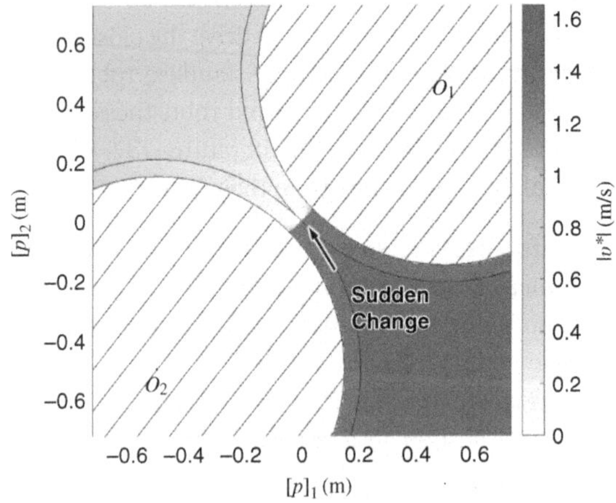

Figure 1.13 The dependence of the velocity-reference input $|\upsilon^*|$ on the position p under the QP-based controller (1.108).

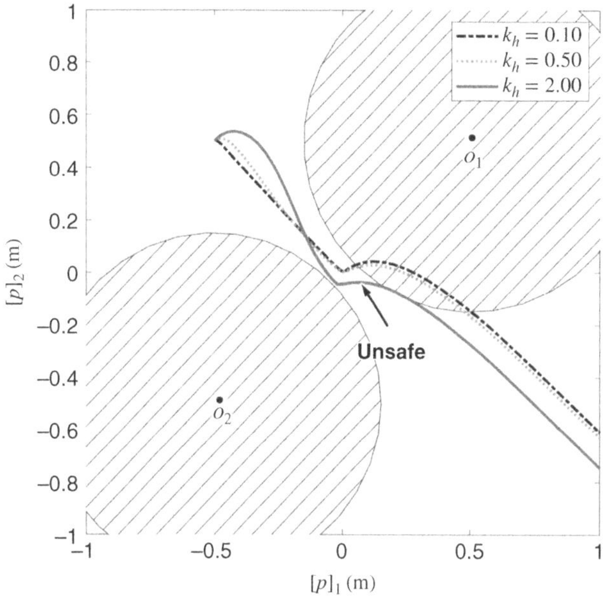

Figure 1.14 Position trajectories of the mobile agent under the QP-based controller (1.108).

As noted in Section 1.3.3, establishing Lipschitz continuity for a QP-based controller typically entails verifying that the coefficient matrix of the constraints that directly affect the optimal solution always satisfies the full-row-rank condition. Clearly, this condition is difficult to guarantee *a priori*, since the set of constraints varies along with the state trajectories.

New methods and tools are needed to address this issue and ensure safety in the presence of dynamic uncertainties.

1.6 Outline of this Book

This book presents a systematic study of safety-critical control for nonlinear systems subject to dynamic uncertainties and multiple safety constraints. The ubiquity of dynamic uncertainties underscores the need for robustness in the design of safety-critical controllers. Moreover, the requirement to accommodate multiple safety constraints often exceeds the capabilities of conventional, explicit-form stabilizing controllers and introduces additional robustness challenges for standard optimization-based methodologies.

In response, this book develops a constructive framework for robust safety-critical control of nonlinear uncertain systems, building on recent advances in the field.

1.6.1 Safety-critical Control Subject to Dynamic Uncertainties

Dynamic uncertainties are pervasive in industrial systems. A mobile agent modeled as a cascade of an integrator and an uncertain actuation subsystem, as in Section 1.5.1, provides a simple yet representative example. Many higher-order systems, such as Euler–Lagrange (EL) systems, can likewise be transformed into a cascade comprising a kinematic module (modeled by an integrator) and a controlled dynamic module (viewed as the actuation subsystem).

As discussed in Section 1.5, dynamic uncertainties pose significant challenges to the robustness of QP-based controllers. A systematic methodology is therefore required to assess the interaction between the controlled nominal system and the dynamic uncertainties, particularly in the context of safety-critical control.

Chapter 2 introduces the idea of nonlinear small-gain theorem to safety-critical control and develops a small-gain-based approach to robust safety-critical control under dynamic uncertainties.

1.6.2 Real-time Integration of Multiple Safety Constraints

Unlike standard stabilizing and tracking controllers, a practical safety-critical controller must address not only nonlinear uncertain dynamics involved in the plant but also multiple safety constraints, which poses substantial technical challenges. A sufficiently smooth (at least locally Lipschitz) outer-loop control law is considered to be crucial for feasibility and robustness with respect to controlled inner-loop dynamics. However, directly employing QPs to integrate multiple safety constraints (often described by safety indicator functions) can yield a non-Lipschitz control law or a control law with extremely large Lipschitz constants, leading to chattering and oscillations and thereby jeopardizing closed-loop safety when dynamic uncertainties are not neglectable (see Section 1.5.2).

Chapter 3 introduces a feasible-set reshaping technique for the QP-based integration of multiple constraints. Building on this, one can design QP-based, locally Lipschitz safety-critical controllers with improved robustness.

1.6.3 Safety-critical Control with Set-valued Feedback

Consider designing a safety-critical controller for a mobile robot that receives a velocity-command signal for its primary objectives and enforces safety constraints directly constructed from real-time obstacle measurements in cluttered environments (e.g., LiDAR-based laser scans). This problem is motivated by practical applications such as operator-assistance systems and safety-critical learning-based control, where primary velocity commands can be adjusted in real time by higher-level algorithms or human operators. In such cases, planning-based methods that rely on predetermined targets or reference trajectories may not be directly applicable. Moreover, set-valued and possibly discontinuous feedback of the obstacle positions induces constraints that shift with the robot's position, which can result in discontinuous control inputs when standard optimization-based control methods are used. If dynamic uncertainties are non-neglectable, safety constraints may be violated.

Chapter 4 proposes a refined regularization method which, together with feasible-set reshaping, resolves the safety-critical control problem for mobile agents navigating in cluttered environments.

1.6.4 Coordination of Multi-agent Systems Subject to Safety Constraints

As the number of mobile agents increases, safety constraints arise not only from agent-obstacle interactions but also from interactions among agents. The ability to enforce pairwise safety constraints between the mobile agents depends on the control of all the agents. Ensuring overall safety therefore requires the coordinated design of safety-critical controllers for all agents.

Chapter 5 extends the techniques of Chapter 3 on multiple safety constraints to multi-agent systems, addressing both agent-agent and agent-obstacle constraints.

1.6.5 Safety-critical Control of Mechanical Systems Featuring Conservation of Energy

The Euler–Lagrange (EL) equation models a broad class of physical systems and is widely used in the control of mechanical systems. Systematic safety-critical control strategies for EL systems are therefore of significant interest. A representative example arises in the safe operation of industrial robotic manipulators, where safety requires that every point on the manipulator's body maintain sufficient distance from both cooperative and noncooperative objects. Notably, a single obstacle point in the workspace typically results in obstacles in the configuration (joint) space.

Unlike standard stabilizing and tracking controllers, a well-designed safety-critical controller for an EL system must exploit the plant's inherent energy properties while handling multiple safety constraints, which precludes the direct application of standard energy-based methods.

Chapter 6 discusses the integration of energy storage functions and safety indicator functions in the design of safety-critical controllers for EL systems.

1.6.6 Constructive Safety-critical Control Leveraging System Structure

Consistent with engineering practice, constructive nonlinear control exploits structural properties in the design of controllers for nonlinear uncertain systems. In particular, backstepping and forwarding methods have been developed for benchmark systems in lower-triangular, upper-triangular, and interlaced forms [108, 174]. These techniques enable joint controller design and stability analysis in a recursive, stepwise manner. However, for systems subject to multiple safety constraints, results in constructive nonlinear control remain limited. In particular, for lower-triangular systems, a principal challenge is the potentially non-Lipschitz nature of virtual control laws and the lack of robustness of subsystems when standard optimization-based algorithms are used to enforce multiple constraints.

Chapter 7 presents a recursive design for the safety-critical control of nonlinear uncertain systems with cascade structures.

The overall relationship among the chapters is illustrated in Figure 1.15.

Supplementary materials, including topics on QPs, Lyapunov stability theory, ISS, the nonlinear small-gain theorem, and other mathematical preliminaries, are provided in the appendix.

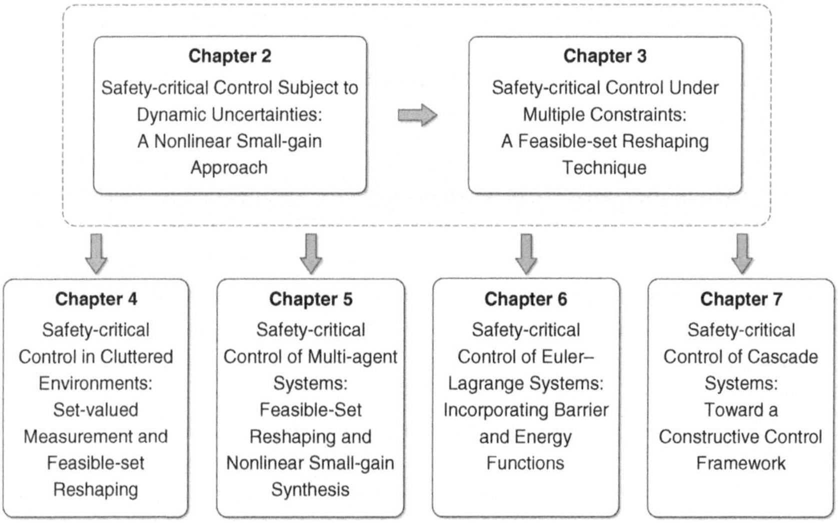

Figure 1.15 Organization of the book.

1.7 Notes

Accomplishing complex control tasks while guaranteeing safety is a central theme in the controls and robotics community. Theory and methods for safety-critical control have been investigated for several decades [112, 14, 36, 166, 31, 136], and a solid foundation has been established for autonomous and cooperative control across a broad range of vehicles and robots [6, 53, 178, 10, 211, 11, 3, 210]. Applications include humanoid robots [53], manipulators [176], human–robot interaction [10], nonholonomic mobile robots [215], autonomous driving [226], life-support systems [62], single-agent systems [225], multi-agent systems [211, 233], aerial vehicles [134, 231, 236, 75], and marine vessels [160]. Within this landscape, several research directions have emerged: planning and tracking under constraints, reachability analysis, velocity obstacles, barrier functions and control barrier functions, and real-time optimization-based methods. We briefly summarize the core ideas.

1.7.1 Planning and Tracking Under Constraints

Classical motion planning and robot control provide foundational algorithms in graph search and sampling-based planning, geometric navigation in configuration space, and feedback-based trajectory tracking with closed-loop motion synthesis [112, 14, 36, 166, 31, 136, 124, 182]. Planning and tracking under constraints [236, 35, 177, 22] typically follow a path-trajectory-tracking paradigm: first synthesize a feasible path that satisfies safety constraints using environmental information; next perform trajectory optimization to enforce system dynamics; finally, design a tracking controller to achieve accurate tracking and thereby maintain safety constraints in closed loop. These methods excel in global performance optimization and constraint consistency. Recent work emphasizes adaptability in dynamic environments and reduced computational cost, together with tighter integration of planning and control: constraints are embedded at the planning stage and sustained through closed-loop tracking under time-varying conditions [35].

1.7.2 Reachability Analysis

Reachability analysis [207, 143, 60] evaluates safety and attainability by solving Hamilton–Jacobi equations over the state space to compute reachable sets. A reachable set characterizes all states that can be attained within a specified time horizon from a given initial or target state. With respect to time direction, one distinguishes forward and backward reachable sets. For a system $\dot{x} = f(x, u)$, the forward reachable set from $x(0)$ comprises all states that can be reached within time $T \geq 0$ under admissible inputs $u(t)$. The backward reachable set comprises all initial states that can be driven to a target state $x(0)$ within time $T \leq 0$. Mature software toolboxes are available [12, 142], and the methodology has been widely applied to safety-constrained control problems [35, 19, 56]. Nevertheless, real-time computation of Hamilton–Jacobi PDEs under limited computational resources remains challenging.

1.7.3 The Velocity-obstacle Method

The velocity-obstacle method [72, 208, 55] is a velocity-geometry approach to collision avoidance, widely used for multi-agent safety in dynamic, crowded environments. Based on real-time relative positions and velocities of the agents, it constructs, for each agent, a set of relative velocities that can lead to collisions. If the current relative velocity lies within this set, collision risk is present and the agent's velocity must be adjusted to exit the set. Conceptually, it converts position constraints into velocity constraints, which is intuitive and easy to implement. However, it often relies on idealized assumptions such as piecewise-constant, switching velocities, which can preclude continuity of control inputs in state space and induce chattering or undesirable transients. For refinements that mitigate these issues, see, e.g., [172].

1.7.4 Barrier Functions and CBFs

Barrier functions originate in constrained optimization [21, 26]. By defining a safe set and exploiting invariance, they establish safety [162, 214, 153, 200, 213, 163, 5, 216, 167]. Inspired by control Lyapunov functions [15, 183], CBFs were proposed in [213] to connect safety constraints directly with control inputs and have become a central tool in safety-critical control. CBFs define safe sets via invariance and enforce pointwise input constraints that guarantee positive invariance [213, 5, 167]. For control-affine plants, CBFs are advantageous in transforming (possibly nonconvex) state constraints into affine constraints on the control input. Extensions include zeroing and reciprocal barrier functions and higher relative-degree generalizations, improving robustness and applicability [3, 198, 154, 222, 29, 220]. The framework has progressed from continuous-time single-agent systems to hybrid/switching systems [155, 121], interconnected systems [125, 126], and uncertain systems with disturbances and modeling errors [225, 87, 42, 1, 197]. Compared with artificial potential fields [99] and velocity obstacles [55, 208], CBFs provide formal invariance guarantees and a stronger characterization of robust safety [179].

1.7.5 Safety-critical Control via Real-time Optimization

Integrating safety constraints with a primary control objective through constrained optimization, such as QPs, offers an effective means to address control problems with complex constraints [151, 53, 134, 4]. Combining CBFs with control Lyapunov functions [15] yields multi-objective controllers that balance performance and safety [6]. The prototypical CBF-CLF-QP controller minimizes deviation from the primary objective subject to safety constraints, thereby achieving both safety and performance [6, 52]. This methodology has been widely adopted in autonomous driving, legged locomotion, teleoperation, networked robotics, and human–robot interaction [6, 148, 176, 211, 63, 215, 180, 221, 234, 224]. By extending workspace constraints to configuration-space constraints, the CBF-QP framework accommodates platforms with high degrees of freedom and intricate task geometries [178]. Furthermore, effective integrations with model predictive control, adaptive control, and inverse optimal control enhance the method's flexibility to handle diverse specifications [67, 223, 156, 106].

These developments mark a shift from purely performance-driven design to safety-first principles. The shift is especially pronounced in domains involving contact, nonconvex constraints, and interactive dynamics. Representative examples include humanoid balance and locomotion [53], dexterous manipulation [178], human–robot interaction [10], and distributed multi-agent coordination [211, 139]; for which ensuring closed-loop safety is paramount.

2

Safety-critical Control Subject to Dynamic Uncertainties: A Nonlinear Small-gain Approach

Dynamic uncertainties are ubiquitous in engineering control systems. They may arise from unmodeled plant dynamics, uncertain actuator dynamics, imperfections in perception and information processing, or interactions with the environment. In safety-critical systems, such uncertainties can compromise safety constraints, necessitating systematic methodologies to characterize and mitigate their effects.

This chapter considers a typical scenario comprising a mobile agent and a stationary spherical obstacle. The agent is modeled as a cascade of an integrator (the kinematic system) and an actuation system (corresponding to controlled dynamics) that exhibits dynamic uncertainty. The integrator describes the position-velocity relationship, while the actuation system captures the dynamic response of the actual velocity to the velocity-reference input (serving as the control input). Consistent with practical implementations, the actuation system is assumed to possess reference-tracking capability: the velocity-tracking error converges to a neighborhood of zero whose size is determined by the time derivative of the velocity-reference input. This reference-tracking property, as discussed in Section 1.4.1, is formalized by using input-to-output stability (IOS) [92, 192].

The proposed framework encompasses a broad class of practical control systems. For instance, the identified dynamics of a quadrotor (see Example 1.2) conform to this model. When actuation dynamics are negligible, the overall model reduces to an integrator, which has been extensively studied in the literature of safety-critical control. Moreover, systems such as the double integrator and Euler–Lagrange (EL) systems can be cast into the present structure by introducing appropriate virtual control laws.

For safety-critical control of this class of nonlinear systems, the principal technical challenge stems from the interaction between the nominal integrator and the uncertain actuation dynamics. As elaborated in Section 1.5, uncertain actuation dynamics induce unanticipated feedback links that couple safety indicator function and the uncertain actuation dynamics, potentially degrading robustness properties described by half-space conditions.

The nonlinear small-gain theorem is recognized as a powerful tool for stability analysis and control of interconnected nonlinear systems. We develop a nonlinear small-gain framework to address the challenge caused by interconnections appearing in safety-critical control systems. First, we synthesize a safety-critical controller for the integrator by considering the velocity-reference input as the control input and regarding the velocity-tracking error as an exogenous disturbance. Next, leveraging the reference-tracking property of the actuation system, we quantify how the value of the safety indicator function affects the reference-tracking error. Finally, we exploit the fundamental relationship between stability and safety and extend the nonlinear small-gain methodology to robust safety-critical control. Specifically, we use gain functions to characterize the interaction between safety indicator function and the uncertain actuation dynamics, and propose a nonlinear small-gain condition to tune the safety-critical controller for ensured safety of the resulting closed-loop system.

2.1 Problem Formulation

In this chapter, we study a safety-critical control problem for a single mobile agent operating in the presence of a stationary spherical obstacle. The problem considered in this chapter is a special case of the problem in Section 1.4 (let $n_o = 1$).

2.1.1 System Setup

The mobile agent is modeled as a cascade of a nominal kinematic system and an uncertain actuation system. The kinematics are

$$\dot{p} = v, \tag{2.1}$$

where $p \in \mathbb{R}^n$ is the position and $v \in \mathbb{R}^n$ is the velocity. The velocity v is produced by an actuation system of the form

$$\dot{z} = f(z, v^*) \tag{2.2a}$$

$$v = g(z, v^*) \tag{2.2b}$$

where $z \in \mathbb{R}^m$ is the state, $v^* \in \mathbb{R}^n$ is the velocity-reference input, and f and g are locally Lipschitz continuous functions specifying the dynamics and the output map of the actuation system. In our problem setting, we consider the case where f and g are unknown functions, which means that they cannot be directly used for controller design.

Suppose that the center of the spherical obstacle is located at $o \in \mathbb{R}^n$.

2.1.2 Safety-critical Control Objective and Desired Control System Structure

To analyze safety with respect to the stationary obstacle, the relative position between the mobile agent and the obstacle is defined as

$$\tilde{p} = p - o, \tag{2.3}$$

which satisfies

$$\dot{\tilde{p}} = v. \tag{2.4}$$

To characterize safety, we consider a safety indicator function $h : \mathbb{R}^n \setminus \{0\} \to (0, \infty)$ defined by

$$h(\tilde{p}) = \mu(|\tilde{p}|), \tag{2.5}$$

where $\mu : (0, \infty) \to (0, \infty)$ is an $\mathcal{M}^{-}\mathcal{C}$ function.

Given a desired safe distance $D > 0$, the system composed of (2.2) and (2.4) with a suitable controller is said to be safe if there exist $\beta \in \mathcal{KL}$ and constants $h_0, z_0, b_0, \bar{z} \geq 0$ such that for any initial state $\tilde{p}(0)$ satisfying $\mu(|\tilde{p}(0)|) \leq h_0$ and $z(0)$ satisfying $|z(0)| \leq z_0$, the following properties hold for all $t \geq 0$:

$$h(\tilde{p}(t)) \leq \max\{\beta(h(\tilde{p}(0)) + |z(0)| + b_0, t), \mu(D)\}, \tag{2.6a}$$

$$|z(t)| \leq \bar{z}. \tag{2.6b}$$

The safety requirement in (2.6a) is consistent with Definition 1.6 of transient-aware safety. As illustrated in Figure 2.1, uncertain actuation dynamics can lead to collisions even when the ideal path is collision-free. Moreover, it is desirable that the state z of the actuation system remains bounded for well-posedness of the closed-loop system.

Let $v^c \in \mathbb{R}^n$ denote the velocity-command signal associated with the primary objective. In practice, v^c is provided by a higher-level planner or primary controller. Treating the velocity-reference input v^* as the control input, with $\tilde{p}$ available to feedback, the goal is to design a controller that maintains a sufficient

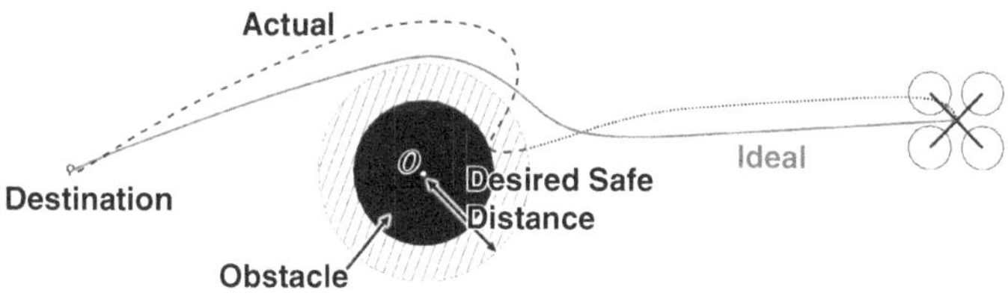

Figure 2.1 The ideal path is collision-free, whereas uncertain actuation dynamics may lead to collisions.

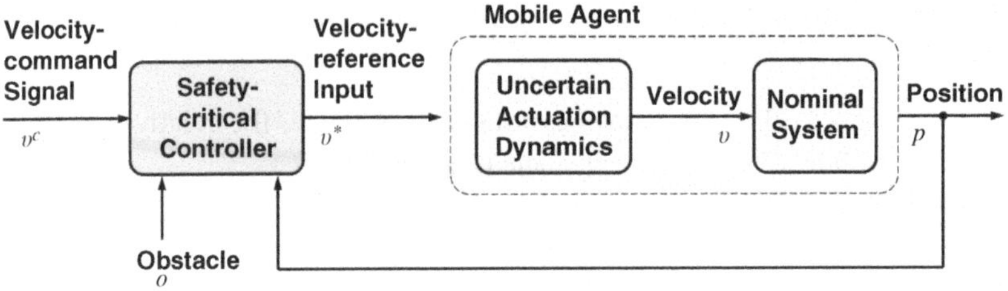

Figure 2.2 Structure of a safety-critical control system subject to uncertain actuation dynamics.

distance between the mobile agent and the obstacle in the sense of (2.6), while ensuring that v^* minimally displaces v^c. The desired structure of the safety-critical control is illustrated in Figure 2.2.

2.1.3 Assumptions

Due to uncertain actuation dynamics, the actual velocity v may not coincide with the velocity-reference input v^*. Define the velocity-tracking error

$$\tilde{v} = v - v^*. \tag{2.7}$$

Assume that for constant v^*, the velocity v converges asymptotically to v^*, while for time-varying v^*, the magnitude of the velocity-tracking error $\tilde{v}$ depends on the changing rate of v^*. Suppose that $v^*(t)$ is locally Lipschitz in t.

Assumption 2.1 ***(Reference-tracking Capability of the Actuation System)*:** For the actuation system (2.2), there exist $\beta_{\tilde{v}} \in \mathcal{KL}$ and $\gamma_{\tilde{v}}, \alpha_{z1}, \alpha_{z2} \in \mathcal{K}$ such that for any $z(0)$ and any locally Lipschitz v^*,

$$|\tilde{v}(t)| \leq \max\{\beta_{\tilde{v}}(|z(0)| + |v^*(0)|, t), \gamma_{\tilde{v}}(\|D^+v^*\|_t)\} \tag{2.8}$$

$$|z(t)| \leq \max\{\alpha_{z1}(|z(0)|), \alpha_{z2}(\|v^*\|_t)\} \tag{2.9}$$

for all $t \geq 0$.

The practical aspects of Assumption 2.1 are discussed in Section 1.4.1.

Without loss of generality, assume that the velocity-command signal v^c is bounded and continuously differentiable in time.

Assumption 2.2 ***(Boundedness of the Velocity-command Signal and Its Time Derivative)*:** The signal v^c is continuously differentiable, and there exist positive constants $\bar{v}^c$ and $\bar{v}^{cd}$ such that

$$|v^c(t)| \leq \bar{v}^c, \quad |\dot{v}^c(t)| \leq \bar{v}^{cd} \tag{2.10}$$

for all $t \geq 0$.

2.2 Robust Safety-critical Controller Design

2.2.1 Ideal Case: Neglecting Uncertain Actuation Dynamics ($\upsilon \equiv \upsilon^*$)

If the mobile agent is free of uncertain actuation dynamics (i.e., $\upsilon \equiv \upsilon^*$), then the model (2.1)–(2.2) reduces to

$$\dot{p} = \upsilon = \upsilon^*, \tag{2.11}$$

and the relative position $\tilde{p}$ between the agent and the obstacle satisfies

$$\dot{\tilde{p}} = \dot{p} - \dot{o} = \upsilon^*. \tag{2.12}$$

In this ideal setting, QP-based safety-critical controller designs (see e.g., [3] for a tutorial, and also see the discussion in Section 1.3) are directly applicable. In particular, inspired by (1.47), consider the safety-critical controller

$$\upsilon^* = \underset{\upsilon^* \in \mathbb{R}^n}{\operatorname{argmin}} |\upsilon^* - \upsilon^c|^2, \tag{2.13a}$$

$$\text{s.t.} \quad A_{\text{ideal}}(\tilde{p})\upsilon^* \leq b_{\text{ideal}}(\tilde{p}) \tag{2.13b}$$

with

$$A_{\text{ideal}}(\tilde{p}) = -\frac{\tilde{p}^T}{|\tilde{p}|}, \tag{2.14a}$$

$$b_{\text{ideal}}(\tilde{p}) = -\alpha_h(h(\tilde{p}) - \mu(D)), \tag{2.14b}$$

where $\alpha_h \in \mathcal{K}^e$ is a continuously differentiable function, and $h(\tilde{p})$ is defined in (2.5). To avoid singularities, the controller requires $\tilde{p} \neq 0$. Here, we define $A_{\text{ideal}}(\tilde{p})$ as $-\tilde{p}^T/|\tilde{p}|$ instead of $\nabla h(\tilde{p})$ for an intuitive understanding, that the υ^* generated by (2.13) steers the mobile agent away from the obstacle (in accordance with $\tilde{p}^T\upsilon^* > 0$) as long as $h(\tilde{p}) > \mu(0)$, or equivalently $|\tilde{p}| < D$.

Indeed, the constraint (2.13b) can be equivalently written as

$$-\frac{\tilde{p}^T}{|\tilde{p}|}\upsilon^* \leq -\alpha_h(h(\tilde{p}) - \mu(D)). \tag{2.15}$$

The validity of the design can also be verified by studying the dynamical behavior of the safety indicator function $h(\tilde{p})$:

$$\nabla h(\tilde{p})\dot{\tilde{p}} = \frac{\mathrm{d}\mu(|\tilde{p}|)}{\mathrm{d}|\tilde{p}|}\frac{\tilde{p}^T}{|\tilde{p}|}\upsilon^* \leq \frac{\mathrm{d}\mu(|\tilde{p}|)}{\mathrm{d}|\tilde{p}|}(\alpha_h(h(\tilde{p}) - \mu(D))). \tag{2.16}$$

By Definition A.28, any class $\mathcal{M}^-\mathcal{C}$ function is strictly decreasing and hence admits negative slopes. Since $\mu \in \mathcal{M}^-\mathcal{C}$, we have $\mathrm{d}\mu(s)/\mathrm{d}s < 0$ for all s in the domain of μ. Applying the comparison principle [98, Lemma 3.4], one can prove $h(\tilde{p}(t)) \leq \mu(D)$ for all $t \geq 0$ whenever $h(\tilde{p}(0)) \leq \mu(D)$.

Moreover, the QP-based controller (2.13) selects the velocity-reference input v^* as close as possible to the velocity-command signal v^c.

2.2.2 Controller Design in the Presence of Uncertain Actuation Dynamics

In the presence of uncertain actuation dynamics, the velocity-tracking error $\tilde{v}$ defined in (2.7) must be taken into account:

$$\dot{p} = v = v^* + \tilde{v}, \tag{2.17}$$

which implies

$$\dot{\tilde{p}} = v = v^* + \tilde{v}. \tag{2.18}$$

If the controller (2.13) is implemented without modification, then the nonzero velocity-tracking error $\tilde{v}$ may invalidate the property (2.16) and thus compromise the safety of the closed-loop system. This issue has been briefly discussed in Section 1.5.1.

A natural way to accommodate the velocity-tracking error is to introduce an additional safety margin into the constraints in (2.13b). This leads to the following refined QP-based safety-critical controller:

$$v^* = \underset{v^* \in \mathbb{R}^n}{\operatorname{argmin}} |v^* - v^c|^2, \tag{2.19a}$$

$$\text{s.t.} \quad A(\tilde{p})v^* \leq b(\tilde{p}) \tag{2.19b}$$

with

$$A(\tilde{p}) = -\frac{\tilde{p}^T}{|\tilde{p}|}, \tag{2.20a}$$

$$b(\tilde{p}) = -\alpha_h(h(\tilde{p}) - \mu(D_s)), \tag{2.20b}$$

where $h(\tilde{p})$ is defined in (2.5), $\alpha_h \in \mathcal{K}^e$ is a continuously differentiable function, and D_s is a positive constant representing the enlarged safety margin.

The refined controller (2.19) and (2.20) closely follows the initial design (2.13) and (2.14), except that $\mu(D_s)$ is used in (2.20b) instead of $\mu(D)$ in (2.14b).

For the position-error system (2.18), if v^* satisfies the constraint (2.19b), then the following inequality holds:

$$-\frac{\tilde{p}^T}{|\tilde{p}|}v^* \leq -\alpha_h(h(\tilde{p}) - \mu(D_s)). \tag{2.21}$$

Consequently,

$$\begin{aligned}\nabla h(\tilde{p})\dot{\tilde{p}} &= \frac{\mathrm{d}\mu(|\tilde{p}|)}{\mathrm{d}|\tilde{p}|}\frac{\tilde{p}^T}{|\tilde{p}|}(v^* + \tilde{v}) \\ &\le \frac{\mathrm{d}\mu(|\tilde{p}|)}{\mathrm{d}|\tilde{p}|}(\alpha_h(h(\tilde{p}) - \mu(D_s))) + \frac{\mathrm{d}\mu(|\tilde{p}|)}{\mathrm{d}|\tilde{p}|}\frac{\tilde{p}^T}{|\tilde{p}|}\tilde{v} \\ &\le \frac{\mathrm{d}\mu(|\tilde{p}|)}{\mathrm{d}|\tilde{p}|}(\alpha_h(h(\tilde{p}) - \mu(D_s)) - |\tilde{v}|).\end{aligned} \tag{2.22}$$

Note that for each $\tilde{p} \neq 0$ and each v^c, the QP (2.19) and (2.20) admits a unique solution v^*. Let $\phi : (\mathbb{R}^n \setminus \{0\}) \times \mathbb{R}^n \to \mathbb{R}^n$ denote the map from $(\tilde{p}, v^c)$ to v^* resulting form solving the QP. The following proposition gives an explicit expression of ϕ and presents properties on the boundedness of ϕ and the changing rate of the velocity-reference input v^*.

Proposition 2.1 ***(Properties of the QP-based Safety-critical Controller)*:** Consider the kinematics model (2.17) and the QP-based controller (2.19)-(2.20). The following properties hold:

a. **Explicit Expression of the Controller:** The function ϕ is given by

$$\phi(\tilde{p}, v^c) = v^c + A^T(\tilde{p})\min\{b(\tilde{p}) - A(\tilde{p})v^c, 0\}, \tag{2.23}$$

for all $\tilde{p} \neq 0$ and all $v^c \in \mathbb{R}^n$.

b. **An Upper Bound of the Controller:** For all $\tilde{p} \neq 0$ and all $v^c \in \mathbb{R}^n$, it holds that

$$|\phi(\tilde{p}, v^c)| \le |v^c| - \min\{b(\tilde{p}), 0\}. \tag{2.24}$$

c. **Lipschitz Continuity of the Controller:** The function ϕ is Lipschitz continuous on any compact subset of $(\mathbb{R}^n \setminus \{0\}) \times \mathbb{R}^n$.

d. **Changing Rate of the Velocity-reference Input:** Under Assumption 2.2, for any piecewise continuous $\tilde{v}$, on any time interval $[0, T)$ on which $\tilde{p}(t)$ is defined and nonzero, it holds that

$$\|D^+v^*\|_t \le \max\{\gamma_d(\|h(\tilde{p})\|_t), \gamma_d(\|\tilde{v}\|_t), c_d\} \tag{2.25}$$

for all $t \in [0, T)$, where γ_d is a class $\mathcal{K}_\infty$ function, and c_d is a positive constant, which are given by

$$\begin{aligned}\gamma_d(s) = 2\sqrt{n}\big(&\alpha_{h,\mu}(s) + \alpha_p(s)\,(2\bar{v}^c + \max\{\alpha_h(s - \mu(D_s)), 0\})\big) \\ &\times (s + \max\{\alpha_h(s - \mu(D_s))), 0\} + \bar{v}^c),\end{aligned} \tag{2.26a}$$

$$c_d = 4\sqrt{n}\bar{v}^{cd}, \tag{2.26b}$$

respectively, with

$$\alpha_{h,\mu}(s) = \sup_{s' \in [0,s]} \left| \frac{\mathrm{d}\alpha_h(s' - \mu(D_s))}{\mathrm{d}(s' - \mu(D_s))} \alpha_\mu(s') \right| \text{ for } s \geq 0, \tag{2.27a}$$

$$\alpha_\mu(s) = \begin{cases} -\dfrac{\mathrm{d}\mu(\mu^{-1}(s))}{\mathrm{d}\mu^{-1}(s)}, & \text{for } s > 0, \\ 0, & \text{for } s = 0, \end{cases} \tag{2.27b}$$

$$\alpha_p(s) = \begin{cases} \dfrac{1}{\mu^{-1}(s)}, & \text{for } s > 0, \\ 0, & \text{for } s = 0. \end{cases} \tag{2.27c}$$

Proof. The properties are proved one-by-one.

(a) Explicit expression of the controller: For all $\tilde{p} \neq 0$ and all $v^c \in \mathbb{R}^n$, the functions $A(p)$ and $b(p)$ are well defined. Then, for the QP (2.19)-(2.20), the explicit expression (2.23) can be proved following the discussion in [21, Example 2.1.5] and applying the projection theorem. In particular, if v^c is the solution to the QP (2.19)-(2.20), then $b(p) - A(p)v^c \geq 0$, and hence

$$\begin{aligned} v^* &= v^c \\ &= v^c + A^T(p)\min\{b(p) - A(p)v^c, 0\}. \end{aligned} \tag{2.28}$$

Otherwise, if v^c is not the solution to the QP (2.19)-(2.20), then v^* is the point satisfying $A(p)v^* = b(p)$ that is closest to v^c. By [21, Example 2.1.5], the explicit expression for QPs with equality constraints implies that

$$\begin{aligned} v^* &= v^c - A^T(p)A(p)v^c + A^T(p)b(p) \\ &= v^c + A^T(p)\min\{b(p) - A(p)v^c, 0\}. \end{aligned} \tag{2.29}$$

Then, (2.23) is proved based on (2.28) and (2.29).

(b) An upper bound of the controller: The projection theorem guarantees that $\phi(\tilde{p}, v^c)$, as the solution to the QP (2.19)-(2.20), is continuous and nonexpansive with respect to v^c [21, Proposition B.11 (c)], that is,

$$|\phi(\tilde{p}, v^c) - \phi(\tilde{p}, 0)| \leq |v^c|. \tag{2.30}$$

Then, applying the triangle inequality [13, Theorem 3.3 (e)] and using the fact that $A(\tilde{p})$ defined in (2.20a) is a unit vector for all $\tilde{p} \neq 0$, we have

$$\begin{aligned} |\phi(\tilde{p}, v^c)| &\leq |v^c| + |\phi(\tilde{p}, 0)| \\ &= |v^c| + |A^T(\tilde{p})\min\{b(\tilde{p}), 0\}| \\ &\leq |v^c| + |A^T(\tilde{p})||\min\{b(\tilde{p}), 0\}| \\ &= |v^c| - \min\{b(\tilde{p}), 0\}. \end{aligned} \tag{2.31}$$

(c) Lipschitz continuity of the controller: Consider the explicit expression (2.23) of the controller. From their definitions in (2.20), one can verify that the functions A and b are Lipschitz on any compact subset of $(\mathbb{R}^n \setminus \{0\}) \times \mathbb{R}^n$. Consequently, using standard properties of algebraic combinations of Lipschitz functions [98, Propositions 2.3.3 and 2.3.4], we can verify that the function ϕ is Lipschitz on any compact subset of $(\mathbb{R}^n \setminus \{0\}) \times \mathbb{R}^n$.

(d) Changing rate of the velocity-reference input: On any time interval $[0, T)$ on which $\tilde{p}(t)$ is defined and nonzero, υ^* is defined. Thus, for any $t \in [0, T)$, $D^+\upsilon^*(\tau)$ is defined for all $\tau \in [0, t)$. Then, by using properties of the essential supremum and the Lipschitz norm, we have

$$\|D^+\upsilon^*\|_t = \operatorname*{ess\,sup}_{\tau\in[0,t)} |D^+\upsilon^*(\tau)| \leq \sup_{\tau\in[0,t)} |D^+\upsilon^*(\tau)| \leq \sqrt{n}L_{[0,t)}(\upsilon^*), \tag{2.32}$$

where $L_{[0,t)}(\upsilon^*)$ represents the Lipschitz norm of υ^* on $[0, t)$:

$$L_{[0,t)}(\upsilon^*) = \sup_{\tau,\tau'\in[0,t),\, \tau\neq\tau'} \frac{|\upsilon^*(\tau) - \upsilon^*(\tau')|}{|\tau - \tau'|}, \tag{2.33}$$

with υ^* considered a signal of time. The validity of the last inequality in (2.32) is guaranteed by Proposition A.25.

Recall that $\upsilon^* = \phi(\tilde{p}, \upsilon^c)$ is explicitly given by (2.23). By using properties of algebraic combinations of Lipschitz functions [38, Propositions 2.3.3 and 2.3.4], we have

$$\begin{aligned} L_{[0,t)}(\upsilon^*) &= L_{[0,t)}(\upsilon^c + A^T(\tilde{p}) \min\{b(\tilde{p}) - A(\tilde{p})\upsilon^c, 0\}) \\ &\leq L_{[0,t)}(\upsilon^c) + L_{[0,t)}(A^T(\tilde{p}) \min\{b(\tilde{p}) - A(\tilde{p})\upsilon^c, 0\}) \\ &\leq L_{[0,t)}(\upsilon^c) + L_{[0,t)}(\min\{b(\tilde{p}) - A(\tilde{p})\upsilon^c, 0\}) \sup_{\tau\in[0,t)} |A^T(\tilde{p}(\tau))| \\ &\quad + L_{[0,t)}(A^T(\tilde{p})) \sup_{\tau\in[0,t)} |\min\{b(\tilde{p}(\tau)) - A(\tilde{p}(\tau))\upsilon^c(\tau), 0\}|. \end{aligned} \tag{2.34}$$

Now, we find an upper bound for each term on the right-hand side of inequality (2.34).

- Under Assumption 2.2, υ^c is continuously differentiable with respect to time. Thus, we have

$$L_{[0,t)}(\upsilon^c) = \sup_{\tau\in[0,t)} |\dot{\upsilon}^c(\tau)| \leq \bar{\upsilon}^{cd}. \tag{2.35}$$

- The definition of $A(\tilde{p})$ in (2.20a) directly implies

$$\sup_{\tau\in[0,t)} |A^T(\tilde{p}(\tau))| = 1. \tag{2.36}$$

- From the definition in (2.20a), $A(\tilde{p})$ is continuously differentiable with respect to $\tilde{p}$ as long as $\tilde{p} \neq 0$. From the original model (2.1)-(2.2), the continuity of $\upsilon(t)$ with respect to t implies the continuous differentiability of $\tilde{p}(t)$ with respect to t. Then, we have

$$\begin{aligned}
L_{[0,t)}(A^T(\tilde{p})) &= \sup_{\tau\in[0,t)} \left| \frac{\partial A^T(\tilde{p}(\tau))}{\partial \tilde{p}(\tau)} \dot{\tilde{p}}(\tau) \right| \\
&= \sup_{\tau\in[0,t)} \left| \frac{1}{|\tilde{p}(\tau)|} \left(I - \frac{\tilde{p}(\tau)\tilde{p}^T(\tau)}{|\tilde{p}(\tau)|^2} \right) \dot{\tilde{p}}(\tau) \right| \\
&\leq \sup_{\tau\in[0,t)} \left| I - \frac{\tilde{p}(\tau)\tilde{p}^T(\tau)}{|\tilde{p}(\tau)|^2} \right| \left| \frac{\dot{\tilde{p}}(\tau)}{|\tilde{p}(\tau)|} \right| \\
&\leq \sup_{\tau\in[0,t)} \left| \frac{\dot{\tilde{p}}(\tau)}{|\tilde{p}(\tau)|} \right| \\
&\leq \alpha_p \left(\sup_{\tau\in[0,t)} h(\tilde{p}(\tau)) \right) \sup_{\tau\in[0,t)} |\dot{\tilde{p}}(\tau)|, \\
&= \alpha_p (\| h(\tilde{p}) \|_t) \sup_{\tau\in[0,t)} |\dot{\tilde{p}}(\tau)|,
\end{aligned} \tag{2.37}$$

where α_p is defined in (2.27c). For the last inequality in (2.37), we have used the definition of $h(\tilde{p})$ in (2.5). An upper bound for the term $\sup_{\tau\in[0,t)} |\dot{\tilde{p}}(\tau)|$ on the right-hand side of inequality (2.37) is given by

$$\begin{aligned}
\sup_{\tau\in[0,t)} |\dot{\tilde{p}}(\tau)| &= \|\tilde{\upsilon} + \upsilon^*\|_t \\
&\leq \|\tilde{\upsilon}\|_t + \max\{\alpha_h(\|h(\tilde{p})\|_t - \mu(D_s)), 0\} + \bar{\upsilon}^c.
\end{aligned} \tag{2.38}$$

- From the definitions of $A(\tilde{p})$ and $b(\tilde{p})$ in (2.20), we have

$$\begin{aligned}
&\sup_{\tau\in[0,t)} |\min\{b(\tilde{p}(\tau)) - A(\tilde{p}(\tau))\upsilon^c(\tau), 0\}| \\
&\leq \sup_{\tau\in[0,t)} \max\{-b(\tilde{p}(\tau)) + A(\tilde{p}(\tau))\upsilon^c(\tau), 0\} \\
&\leq \sup_{\tau\in[0,t)} \{\max\{-b(\tilde{p}(\tau)), 0\} + |A(\tilde{p}(\tau))\upsilon^c(\tau)|\} \\
&\leq \sup_{\tau\in[0,t)} \{\max\{\alpha_h(h(\tilde{p}(\tau)) - \mu(D_s)), 0\} + |\upsilon^c(\tau)|\} \\
&\leq \max\{\alpha_h(\|h(\tilde{p})\|_t - \mu(D_s)), 0\} + \bar{\upsilon}^c,
\end{aligned} \tag{2.39}$$

where we have used the boundedness of υ^c given in (2.10) in Assumption 2.2 together with the strictly increasing property of $\alpha_h \in \mathcal{K}^e$ for the last inequality.

- By using algebraic properties of Lipschitz functions, we have

$$\begin{aligned}
&L_{[0,t)}\big(\min\{b(\tilde{p}) - A(\tilde{p})v^c, 0\}\big) \\
&\leq L_{[0,t)}(b(\tilde{p}) - A(\tilde{p})v^c) \\
&\leq L_{[0,t)}(b(\tilde{p})) + L_{[0,t)}(A(\tilde{p})v^c) \\
&\leq L_{[0,t)}(b(\tilde{p})) + L_{[0,t)}(A(\tilde{p})) \sup_{\tau\in[0,t)} |v^c(\tau)| + L_{[0,t)}(v^c) \sup_{\tau\in[0,t)} |A(\tilde{p}(\tau))| \\
&\leq L_{[0,t)}(b(\tilde{p})) + L_{[0,t)}(A(\tilde{p}))\bar{v}^c + L_{[0,t)}(v^c) \\
&\leq \sup_{\tau\in[0,t)} \left| \frac{d\alpha_h(h(\tilde{p}(\tau)) - \mu(D_s))}{d(h(\tilde{p}(\tau)) - \mu(D_s))} \frac{d\mu(\mu^{-1}(h(\tilde{p}(\tau))))}{d\mu^{-1}(h(\tilde{p}(\tau)))} \frac{\tilde{p}^T(\tau)}{|\tilde{p}(\tau)|} \dot{\tilde{p}}(\tau) \right| \\
&\quad + \bar{v}^c \sup_{\tau\in[0,t)} \left| \frac{\dot{\tilde{p}}^T(\tau)}{|\tilde{p}(\tau)|} \right| + \bar{v}^{cd} \\
&\leq (\alpha_{h,\mu}(\|h(\tilde{p})\|_t) + \bar{v}^c \alpha_p(\|h(\tilde{p})\|_t)) \sup_{\tau\in[0,t)} |\dot{\tilde{p}}(\tau)| + \bar{v}^{cd},
\end{aligned} \tag{2.40}$$

  where we have used [38, Propositions 2.3.9, 2.3.3 and 2.3.4] for the first, second, and third inequalities, respectively, used the boundedness of v^c and $\dot{v}^c$ given in (2.10) in Assumption 2.2 for the fourth inequality, used the definitions of $A(\tilde{p})$ and $b(\tilde{p})$ in (2.20) for the fifth inequality, and used the definitions of $\alpha_{h,\mu}(s)$ and $\alpha_p(s)$ in (2.27) for the last inequality.

Substituting (2.35)–(2.40) into (2.34), we have

$$\begin{aligned}
L_{[0,t)}(v^*) &\leq \bar{v}^{cd} + (\alpha_{h,\mu}(\|h(\tilde{p})\|_t) + \bar{v}^c \alpha_p(\|h(\tilde{p})\|_t)) \sup_{\tau\in[0,t)} |\dot{\tilde{p}}(\tau)| + \bar{v}^{cd} \\
&\quad + \alpha_p(\|h(\tilde{p})\|_t) \sup_{\tau\in[0,t)} |\dot{\tilde{p}}(\tau)| \big(\bar{v}^c + \max\{\alpha_h(\|h(\tilde{p})\|_t - \mu(D_s)), 0\}\big) \\
&= (\alpha_{h,\mu}(\|h(\tilde{p})\|_t) + \alpha_p(\|h(\tilde{p})\|_t)(2\bar{v}^c + \max\{\alpha_h(\|h(\tilde{p})\|_t - \mu(D_s)), 0\})) \\
&\quad \times \sup_{\tau\in[0,t)} |\dot{\tilde{p}}(\tau)| + 2\bar{v}^{cd} \\
&\leq (\alpha_{h,\mu}(\|h(\tilde{p})\|_t) + \alpha_p(\|h(\tilde{p})\|_t)(2\bar{v}^c + \max\{\alpha_h(\|h(\tilde{p})\|_t - \mu(D_s)), 0\})) \\
&\quad \times (\|\bar{v}\|_t + \max\{\alpha_h(\|h(\tilde{p})\|_t - \mu(D_s)), 0\} + \bar{v}^c) + 2\bar{v}^{cd} \\
&= \alpha_d(\|h(\tilde{p})\|_t, \|\bar{v}\|_t) + 2\bar{v}^{cd},
\end{aligned} \tag{2.41}$$

where

$$\begin{aligned}
\alpha_d(s_1, s_2) = &\big(\alpha_{h,\mu}(s_1) + \alpha_p(s_1)\big(2\bar{v}^c + \max\{\alpha_h(s_1 - \mu(D_s)), 0\}\big)\big) \\
&\times \big(s_2 + \max\{\alpha_h(s_1 - \mu(D_s)), 0\} + \bar{v}^c\big),
\end{aligned} \tag{2.42}$$

with $\alpha_{h,\mu}$ and α_p defined in (2.27).

Using (2.32), we have

$$\|D^+ v^*\|_t \le \sqrt{n}(\alpha_d(\|h(\tilde{p})\|_t, \|\tilde{v}\|_t) + 2\bar{v}^{cd}). \tag{2.43}$$

Now, we show that γ_d defined by

$$\gamma_d(s) = 2\sqrt{n}\alpha_d(s, s) \tag{2.44}$$

for $s \in \mathbb{R}_+$ is of class $\mathcal{K}_\infty$ and ensures the satisfaction of property (2.25).

For this purpose, we show that γ_d admits the following properties:

- $\boldsymbol{\gamma_d(0) = 2\alpha_d(0,0) = 0}$**.** From the definitions of α_p and α_μ and $\alpha_{h,\mu}$ given in (2.27), together with the continuous differentiability of α_h, one can verify that

$$\alpha_p(0) = 0, \qquad \alpha_\mu(0) = 0, \qquad \alpha_{h,\mu}(0) = \left.\frac{\mathrm{d}\alpha_h(s - \mu(D_s))}{\mathrm{d}(s - \mu(D_s))}\right|_{s=0} \alpha_\mu(0) = 0. \tag{2.45}$$

  Then, using the definition of α_d in (2.42), we have $\alpha_d(0, 0) = 0$.
- $\boldsymbol{\gamma_d(s)}$ **is continuous for all** $\boldsymbol{s \ge 0}$**.** From the definition of γ_d in (2.44), $\gamma_d(s)$ is continuous with respect to $s \ge 0$ if $\alpha_d(s, s)$ is continuous with respect to $t \ge 0$, for which, from the definition of α_d in (2.42), we show the continuity of α_h, α_p and $\alpha_{h,\mu}$. Specifically,
  - The continuity of α_h directly follows from $\alpha_h \in \mathcal{K}^e$, as clarified right after (2.20).
  - $\alpha_p(s)$ is continuous for all $s \ge 0$. From the definition of α_p in (2.27c), we have $\alpha_p(s) = 1/\mu^{-1}(s)$ for $s > 0$ and $\alpha_p(0) = 0$. Since $\mu \in \mathcal{M}^-\mathcal{C}$ (see Definition A.28), $\mu(s)$ is continuous for all $s > 0$ and satisfies $\lim_{r\to\infty} \mu(r) = 0$, which implies that $\alpha_p(s)$ is continuous for all $s > 0$ and that $\lim_{s\to 0+} \alpha_p(s) = 0$, respectively. Therefore, $\alpha_p(s)$ is continuous for all $s \ge 0$.
  - $\alpha_\mu(s)$ is continuous for all $s \ge 0$. From the definition of α_μ in (2.27b), we have $\alpha_\mu(s) = -\mathrm{d}\mu(\mu^{-1}(s))/\mathrm{d}\mu^{-1}(s)$ for $s > 0$ and $\alpha_\mu(0) = 0$. Since $\mu \in \mathcal{M}^-\mathcal{C}$, $\mu(s)$ is continuously differentiable for all $s > 0$, which implies that $\mathrm{d}\mu(s)/\mathrm{d}s$ is continuous for $s > 0$ and thus $\alpha_\mu(s)$ is continuous for $s > 0$. Moreover, $\mu \in \mathcal{M}^-\mathcal{C}$ has the properties that $\lim_{r\to\infty} \mu(r) = 0$ and $\lim_{r\to\infty} \mathrm{d}\mu(r)/\mathrm{d}r = 0$, which in turn implies that $\lim_{s'\to 0+} \alpha_\mu(s') = 0$. Therefore, $\alpha_\mu(s)$ is continuous for all $s \ge 0$.
  - $\alpha_{h,\mu}(s)$ is continuous for all $s \ge 0$. From the definition of $\alpha_{h,\mu}$ in (2.27a), $\alpha_{h,\mu}(s)$ is continuous for all $s \ge 0$ if $\alpha_\mu(s)$ and $\mathrm{d}\alpha_h(s)/\mathrm{d}s$ are continuous for all $s \ge 0$. The continuity of α_μ has been verified above, while the continuity of $\mathrm{d}\alpha_h(s)/\mathrm{d}s$ with respect to s directly follows the continuous differentiability of α_h as clarified right after (2.20).

- $\gamma_d(s_1) > \gamma_d(s_2)$ **for any** $s_1 > s_2 \geq 0$. Recall the definitions of α_d and γ_d in (2.42) and (2.44), respectively. Specifically, it can be directly checked that both $(\alpha_{h,\mu}(s) + \alpha_p(s)(2\bar{v}^c + \max\{\alpha_h(s - \mu(D_s)), 0\}))$ and $(s + \max\{\alpha_h(s - \mu(D_s)), 0\} + \bar{v}^c)$ are nonnegative for $s \geq 0$ by using the definitions of α_h, α_p and $\alpha_{h,\mu}$. Then, the strictly increasing property of γ_d can be proved by showing that (A) $\alpha_h(s_1) > \alpha_h(s_2)$, (B) $\alpha_p(s_1) > \alpha_p(s_2)$ and (C) $\alpha_{h,\mu}(s_1) \geq \alpha_{h,\mu}(s_2)$ for all $s_1 > s_2 \geq 0$. Property (A) is obvious, as $\alpha_h \in \mathcal{K}^e$. Property (B) can be verified by using the definition of α_p in (2.27c) and the strict decreasing property of $\mu \in \mathcal{M}^-\mathcal{C}$. The increasing property of $\alpha_{h,\mu}$ defined in (2.27a) can be verified by using the fact that the supremum of a signal over $[0, s_1]$ is greater than or equal to that over $[0, s_2]$ if $s_1 > s_2$.
- $\max\{\gamma_d(s_1), \gamma_d(s_2)\} \geq 2\sqrt{n}\alpha_d(s_1, s_2)$ **for any** $s_1, s_2 \in \mathbb{R}_+$. Based on the discussion above, this property can be proved through direct calculation:

$$\begin{aligned}
\alpha_d(s_1, s_2) &= (\alpha_{h,\mu}(s_1) + \alpha_p(s_1)(2\bar{v}^c + \max\{\alpha_h(s_1 - \mu(D_s)), 0\})) \\
&\quad \times (s_2 + \max\{\alpha_h(s_1 - \mu(D_s)), 0\} + \bar{v}^c) \\
&\leq (\alpha_{h,\mu}(s_*) + \alpha_p(s_*)(2\bar{v}^c + \max\{\alpha_h(s_* - \mu(D_s)), 0\})) \\
&\quad \times (s_* + \max\{\alpha_h(s_* - \mu(D_s)), 0\} + \bar{v}^c) \\
&= \alpha_d(s_*, s_*) \\
&= \frac{1}{2\sqrt{n}}\gamma_d(s_*) \\
&= \frac{1}{2\sqrt{n}} \max\{\gamma_d(s_1), \gamma_d(s_2)\},
\end{aligned} \tag{2.46}$$

  for $s_1 > s_2 \geq 0$ with $s_* = \max\{s_1, s_2\}$, where we have used:
  - the definition of α_d in (2.42) for the first and second equalities;
  - the proved fact that $\alpha_{h,\mu}(s)$, $\alpha_p(s)$, $\max\{\alpha_h(s - \mu(D_s)), 0\}$ and Id are increasing and nonnegative for $s \geq 0$, and that $\bar{v}^c \geq 0$ for the inequality;
  - the definition of γ_d in (2.44) for the third equality;
  - the proved fact that $\gamma_d(s_1) > \gamma_d(s_2)$ for any $s_1 > s_2 \geq 0$ for the last equality.
- $\gamma_d(s) \to \infty$ **as** $s \to \infty$. This property follows directly since each term in $\alpha_{h,\mu}(s) + \alpha_p(s)(2\bar{v}^c + \max\{\alpha_h(s - \mu(D_s)), 0\})$ is nonnegative for all $s \geq 0$, and $s + \max\{\alpha_h(s - \mu(D_s)), 0\} + \bar{v}^c \to \infty$ as $s \to \infty$.

Then, from (2.43), it is a direct consequence that

$$\begin{aligned}
\|D^+v^*\|_t &\leq \sqrt{n}(\alpha_d(\|h(\tilde{p})\|_t, \|\tilde{v}\|_t) + 2\bar{v}^{cd}) \\
&\leq \sqrt{n}\max\{2\alpha_d(\|h(\tilde{p})\|_t, \|\tilde{v}\|_t), 4\bar{v}^{cd}\} \\
&\leq \max\left\{\gamma_d(\|h(\tilde{p})\|_t), \gamma_d(\|\tilde{v}\|_t), 4\sqrt{n}\bar{v}^{cd}\right\}.
\end{aligned} \tag{2.47}$$

This proves the property (2.25) on D^+v^* with γ_d and c_d as defined in (2.26). □

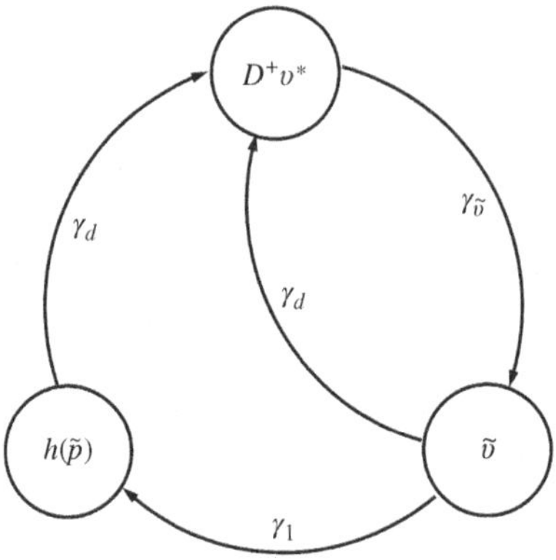

Figure 2.3 Gain interconnection among $h(\tilde{p})$, $\tilde{v}$ and D^+v^*.

For the closed-loop safety-critical system, property (2.25) indicates how $h(\tilde{p})$ and $\tilde{v}$ influence D^+v^*. Within the closed loop, one may also recognize that $h(\tilde{p})$ is influenced by $\tilde{v}$ as $\tilde{v}$ appears in the safety-critical controller (also see Proposition 2.2 in the following section) and $\tilde{v}$ is influenced by D^+v^* as indicated in Assumption 2.1. This means a nontrivial interaction among $h(\tilde{p})$, $\tilde{v}$ and D^+v^*, as shown in Figure 2.3.

Even with $D_s > D$, it is still challenging for the refined QP-based controller (2.19)-(2.20) to ensure safety in the presence of nonzero $\tilde{v}$, as the boundedness of $\tilde{v}$ cannot be guaranteed *a priori* due to the interaction. In the following sections, we carefully analyze the interaction and introduce a nonlinear small-gain method to select the functions α_h and μ as well as the constant D_s for the controller (2.19)-(2.20) such that the closed-loop system admits the desired safety property (2.6).

2.3 Interaction Between Velocity Tracking and Safety

To illustrate how the velocity-tracking error and uncertain actuation dynamics affect the safety property, the closed-loop system is reformulated as an interaction between two subsystems. As shown in Figure 2.4, one subsystem represents the controlled nominal system influenced by the velocity-tracking error, while the other characterizes the velocity-tracking error induced by the uncertain actuation dynamics.

In this section, we discuss the interaction between the velocity-tracking error $\tilde{v}$ and the safety indicator function $h(\tilde{p})$ within the closed-loop system. The interaction is characterized by Propositions 2.2 and 2.3.

Proposition 2.2 ***(The Influence of $\tilde{v}$ on $h(\tilde{p})$):*** Consider the kinematics model (2.17) and the QP-based safety-critical controller (2.19)-(2.20). Under

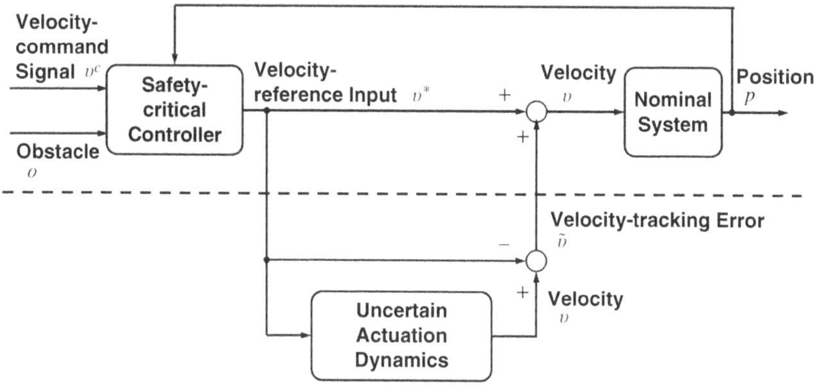

Figure 2.4 An equivalent representation of the safety-critical control system illustrating the interaction between the velocity-tracking error $\tilde{v}$ and the safety indicator function $h(\tilde{p})$ within the closed-loop system.

Assumption 2.2, given any $\gamma_1 \in \mathcal{K}_\infty$, constant $c_0 \in \mathbb{R}_+$ and constant $c_1 \in (\mu(D_s), \mu(D))$, select $\alpha_h : (-\mu(D_s), \infty) \to \mathbb{R}$ to be of class $\mathcal{K}^e$ and in the specific form

$$\alpha_h(s) = (1 + c_0)\gamma_1^{-1}\left(\frac{c_1}{c_1 - \mu(D_s)} s\right), \quad \forall s \geq 0. \tag{2.48}$$

Then, there exists $\beta_1 \in \mathcal{KL}$ such that, for any $\tilde{p}(0) \neq 0$ and any locally Lipschitz $\tilde{v}$ satisfying $\gamma_1(\|\tilde{v}\|_\infty) < \sup_{s>0} \mu(s)$, the inequality

$$h(\tilde{p}(t)) \leq \max\{\beta_1(h(\tilde{p}(0)), t), \gamma_1(\|\tilde{v}\|_t), c_1\} \tag{2.49}$$

holds over any time interval $[0, T)$ on which $\tilde{p}(t)$ is defined and nonzero.

Proof. We first establish the existence of the solution of the closed-loop $\tilde{p}$-system composed of (2.18), (2.19), and (2.20):

$$\dot{\tilde{p}} = \phi(\tilde{p}, v^c) + \tilde{v} \tag{2.50}$$

where ϕ is defined by (2.23). Under Assumption 2.2, for any locally Lipschitz $\tilde{v}$, $\phi(\tilde{p}, v^c(t)) + \tilde{v}(t)$ is defined for all $\tilde{p} \neq 0$ and all $t \geq 0$, and is locally Lipschitz continuous with respect to $\tilde{p}$ and t, which is ensured by Proposition 2.1. Thus, by [98, Theorem 3.1], for any $\tilde{p}(0) \neq 0$ and any locally Lipschitz $\tilde{v}$, there exists $\tau > 0$ such that $p(t)$ is defined for all $t \in [0, \tau)$.

We now prove the existence of $\beta_1 \in \mathcal{KL}$ such that for any $\tilde{p}(0) \neq 0$ and any locally Lipschitz $\tilde{v}$ satisfying $\gamma_1(\|\tilde{v}\|_\infty) < \sup_{s>0} \mu(s)$, the inequality (2.49) holds over any time interval $[0, T)$ on which $\tilde{p}(t)$ is defined and nonzero. To this end, we use the property established in (2.22): For any $\tilde{p} \neq 0$,

$$\nabla h(\tilde{p})\dot{\tilde{p}} \leq \alpha_\mu(h(\tilde{p}))(-\alpha_h(h(\tilde{p}) - \mu(D_s)) + |\tilde{v}|), \tag{2.51}$$

where α_μ is defined in (2.27b). Based on (2.51), given any $\gamma_1 \in \mathcal{K}_\infty$ and any $c_1 \in (\mu(D_s), \mu(D))$, with α_h chosen to satisfy (2.48), we show the existence of a positive definite function $\tilde{\alpha}$ such that for any $\tilde{p} \neq 0$,

$$h(\tilde{p}) \geq \max\{\gamma_1(|\tilde{v}|), c_1\} \tag{2.52a}$$

$$\Rightarrow \nabla h(\tilde{p})\dot{\tilde{p}} \leq -\tilde{\alpha}(h(\tilde{p})). \tag{2.52b}$$

Indeed, when $\tilde{p}$ satisfies (2.52a), from (2.51), we have

$$\begin{aligned}
\nabla h(\tilde{p})\dot{\tilde{p}} &\leq \alpha_\mu(h(\tilde{p}))\left(-\alpha_h\left(h(\tilde{p}) - \frac{h(\tilde{p})}{c_1}\mu(D_s)\right) + |\tilde{v}|\right)\\
&= \alpha_\mu(h(\tilde{p}))\left(-\alpha_h\left(\frac{c_1 - \mu(D_s)}{c_1}h(\tilde{p})\right) + |\tilde{v}|\right)\\
&= \alpha_\mu(h(\tilde{p}))\left(-(1+c_0)\gamma_1^{-1}\left(\frac{c_1}{c_1 - \mu(D_s)}\frac{c_1 - \mu(D_s)}{c_1}h(\tilde{p})\right) + |\tilde{v}|\right)\\
&= \alpha_\mu(h(\tilde{p}))\left(-c_0\gamma_1^{-1}(h(\tilde{p})) - \gamma_1^{-1}(h(\tilde{p})) + |\tilde{v}|\right)\\
&\leq \alpha_\mu(h(\tilde{p}))\left(-c_0\gamma_1^{-1}(h(\tilde{p})) - \gamma_1^{-1}(\gamma_1(|\tilde{v}|)) + |\tilde{v}|\right)\\
&= -c_0\alpha_\mu(h(\tilde{p}))\gamma_1^{-1}(h(\tilde{p}))\\
&= -\tilde{\alpha}(h(\tilde{p})),
\end{aligned} \tag{2.53}$$

where

$$\tilde{\alpha}(s) = c_0\alpha_\mu(s)\gamma_1^{-1}(s) \tag{2.54}$$

for $s \geq 0$. Clearly, $\tilde{\alpha}$ is positive definite as $\gamma_1 \in \mathcal{K}_\infty$ and α_μ are positive definite. For the derivations of (2.53), we have used the properties that α_μ is positive definite (as established in the proof of Property 2.1 of Proposition 2.1), $\alpha_h \in \mathcal{K}^e$ and $h(\tilde{p}) \geq c_1$ for the first inequality, used the definition of α_h in (2.48) for the second equality, used $h(\tilde{p}) \geq \gamma_1(|\tilde{v}|)$ for the second inequality, and used (2.54) for the last equality.

For any time interval $[0, T)$ over which $\tilde{p}(t)$ is defined and nonzero, the velocity-reference input $v^*(t)$ solving the QP (2.19)-(2.20) is defined for all $t \in [0, T)$. This means that the closed-loop signals of the $\tilde{p}$-system are defined for all $t \in [0, T)$. Following standard argument for ISS-Lyapunov functions [184, 188], we can prove the existence of $\beta_1 \in \mathcal{KL}$ for the validity of the property given by (2.49). This ends the proof of Proposition 2.2. □

Proposition 2.3 ***(The Influence of $h(\tilde{p})$ on $\tilde{v}$)*:** Under Assumptions 2.1 and 2.2, given the velocity-reference input v^* generated by the QP-based controller (2.19)-(2.20), consider the mobile agent modeled by (2.1)-(2.2), as well as the velocity-tracking error $\tilde{v}$ defined in (2.7). For any $z(0) \in \mathbb{R}^m$, any $v^c(0) \in \mathbb{R}^n$ and any locally Lipschitz, nonzero $\tilde{p}$,

$$|\tilde{v}(t)| \leq \max\{\beta_2(|z(0)| + |\phi(\tilde{p}(0), v^c(0))|, t), \gamma_2(\|\tilde{v}\|_t), \gamma_2(\|h(\tilde{p})\|_t), c_2\} \tag{2.55}$$

holds over any time interval $[0, T)$ on which $\tilde{v}(t)$ is defined, where $\beta_2 \in \mathcal{KL}, \gamma_2 \in \mathcal{K}$ and constant $c_2 \geq 0$ are given by

$$\beta_2(s, t) = \beta_{\tilde{v}}(s, t), \tag{2.56a}$$
$$\gamma_2(s) = \gamma_{\tilde{v}} \circ \gamma_d(s), \tag{2.56b}$$
$$c_2 = \gamma_{\tilde{v}}(c_d), \tag{2.56c}$$

with γ_d and c_d defined in (2.26).

Proof. Substituting inequality (2.25) in Proposition 2.1 (which is valid under Assumption 2.2) into inequality (2.8) given by Assumption 2.1 implies that for any $z(0) \in \mathbb{R}^m$, any $v^c(0) \in \mathbb{R}^n$ and any locally Lipschitz, nonzero $\tilde{p}$,

$$\begin{aligned} |\tilde{v}(t)| &\leq \max\{\beta_{\tilde{v}}(|z(0)| + |\phi(\tilde{p}(0), v^c(0))|, t), \gamma_{\tilde{v}}(\|D^+v^*\|_t)\} \\ &\leq \max\{\beta_{\tilde{v}}(|z(0)| + |\phi(\tilde{p}(0), v^c(0))|, t), \\ &\quad \gamma_{\tilde{v}} \circ \gamma_d(\|\tilde{v}\|_t), \gamma_{\tilde{v}} \circ \gamma_d(\|h(\tilde{p})\|_t), \gamma_{\tilde{v}}(c_d)\} \end{aligned} \tag{2.57}$$

holds over any time interval $[0, T)$ on which $\tilde{v}(t)$ is defined. This ends the proof of Proposition 2.3. □

Propositions 2.2 and 2.3 naturally give rise to two interacting subsystems, with $\tilde{v}$ and $h(\tilde{p})$ considered as the outputs, respectively. Moreover, the interconnection between $\tilde{v}$ and $h(\tilde{p})$ are defined by gain functions (see Figure 2.5). One should note the existence of a self-loop from $\tilde{v}$ to itself corresponding to the term $\gamma_2(\|\tilde{v}\|_t)$ in (3.73).

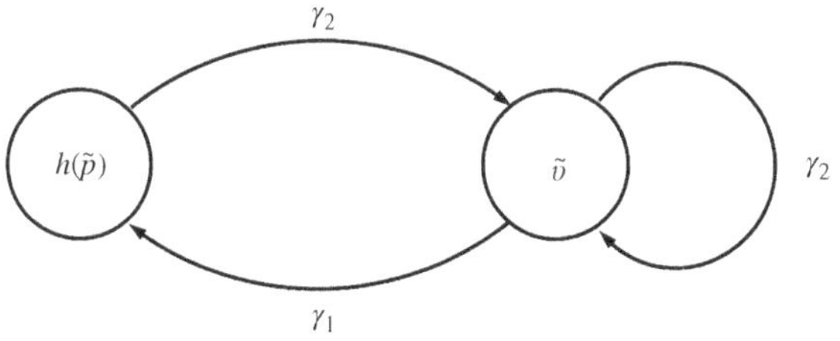

Figure 2.5 Gain interconnection between $h(\tilde{p})$ and $\tilde{v}$.

2.4 Small-gain Synthesis for Safety of the Closed-loop System

The nonlinear small-gain theorem has been recognized to be a natural tool for stability analysis and controller design of interconnected nonlinear systems. Since the closed-loop safety-critical control system resulting from the above controller design has already been transformed into an interconnected system with the interconnection naturally described by gain functions, it is intuitive to perform a nonlinear small-gain analysis to guarantee desired safety properties for the closed-loop system.

Given the interconnection gains between the two subsystems, we impose the following small-gain-type condition to ensure safety:

$$\gamma_1 \circ \gamma_2(s) < s, \quad \gamma_2 \circ \gamma_1(s) < s, \quad \gamma_2(s) < s, \tag{2.58}$$

for all $s \in [0, \bar{s}]$, with

$$\bar{s} = \mu\left(\frac{D_s + D}{2}\right), \tag{2.59}$$

where D and D_s are positive constants representing the desired safe distance and an additional safety margin, respectively.

It is well-known that $\gamma_1 \circ \gamma_2 < \mathrm{Id}$ is equivalent to $\gamma_2 \circ \gamma_1 < \mathrm{Id}$. However, the commutative property may not be valid when the small-gain condition is only required to hold on some bounded region. That is, $\gamma_1 \circ \gamma_2(s) < s$ for $s \in [0, \bar{s}]$ does not necessarily imply $\gamma_2 \circ \gamma_1(s) < s$ for $s \in [0, \bar{s}]$. For example, check $\gamma_1(\gamma_2(s))$ and $\gamma_2(\gamma_1(s))$ on the interval $[0, 3/2]$ with $\gamma_1(s) = s + s^2$ and $\gamma_2(s) = s/2$. Also see Figure 2.6.

Theorem 2.1 shows cases in which one can design a safety-critical controller in the form of (2.19)-(2.20) such that the nonlinear small-gain condition (2.58) is satisfied, and the closed-loop system admits desired safety properties. It should be noted that the nonlinear small-gain theorem was primarily developed for stability

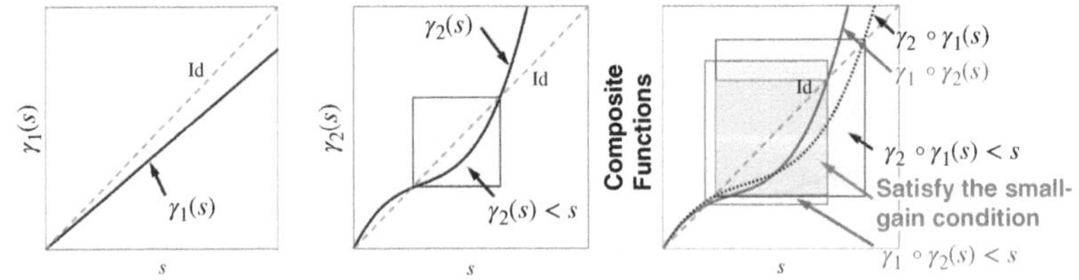

Figure 2.6 An example of local satisfaction of the small-gain condition.

analysis and stabilizing controller design. It is far from standard to extend small-gain arguments to safety-critical control. Techniques used for the proof of the nonlinear small-gain theorem (see e.g., [92]) should be re-evaluated for safety-critical control.

Theorem 2.1 ***(Small-gain-ensured Transient-aware Safety)*****:** *Under Assumptions 2.1 and 2.2, consider the mobile agent described by (2.2), (2.4), and (2.5), and the controller given by (2.19)-(2.20). The following two conclusions hold:*

A. *For any desired safe distance $D > 0$, any additional safety margin $D_s > D$, any $\mu \in \mathcal{M}^{-}\mathcal{C}$, and any function $\alpha_h : (-\mu(D_s), \infty) \to \mathbb{R}$ that is of class $\mathcal{K}^e$, if $\bar{v}^c$ is sufficiently small, by appropriately choosing $\gamma_{\tilde{v}} \in \mathcal{K}$, there exist $\beta \in \mathcal{KL}$ and constants $h_0, z_0, b_0, \bar{z} \geq 0$ such that for any initial state $\tilde{p}(0)$ satisfying $\mu(|\tilde{p}(0)|) \leq h_0$ and $z(0)$ satisfying $|z(0)| \leq z_0$, property (2.6) holds for all $t \geq 0$.*

B. *Given any $\gamma_{\tilde{v}} \in \mathcal{K}$ satisfying*

$$\gamma_{\tilde{v}}(s) \leq k_{\tilde{v}} s \tag{2.60}$$

with some constant $k_{\tilde{v}} > 0$, for any desired safe distance $D > 0$, if $\bar{v}^c$ and $\bar{v}^{cd}$ are sufficiently small, by appropriately choosing $\mu \in \mathcal{M}^{-}\mathcal{C}$, $\alpha_h \in \mathcal{K}^e$ and $D_s > D$, there exist $\beta \in \mathcal{KL}$ and constants $h_0, z_0, b_0, \bar{z} \geq 0$ such that, for any initial state $\tilde{p}(0)$ satisfying $\mu(|\tilde{p}(0)|) \leq h_0$ and $z(0)$ satisfying $|z(0)| \leq z_0$, property (2.6) holds for all $t \geq 0$.

Proof. We first verify that the small-gain condition (2.58)-(2.59) can be satisfied in both of the cases considered in Theorem 2.1. Then, with the satisfaction of the small-gain condition, we show that the closed-loop signals are defined and bounded on the timeline. Finally, we prove the desired safety property.

1. **The satisfaction of the nonlinear small-gain condition** (2.58)-(2.59).

   Recall the definition of γ_2 in (2.56b). Condition (2.58)-(2.59) is equivalent to

$$\gamma_1 \circ \gamma_{\tilde{v}} \circ \gamma_d(s) < s, \quad \gamma_{\tilde{v}} \circ \gamma_d \circ \gamma_1(s) < s, \quad \gamma_{\tilde{v}} \circ \gamma_d(s) < s, \tag{2.61}$$

for all $s \in [0, \bar{s}]$.

Consider Case (A). For any $\alpha_h : (-\mu(D_s), \infty) \to \mathbb{R}$ of class $\mathcal{K}^e$, and any constants $D_s > D$, $c_0 > 0$ and $c_1 \in (\mu(D_s), \bar{s})$, we choose $\gamma_1 \in \mathcal{K}_\infty$ according to (2.48) as

$$\gamma_1(s) = \frac{c_1}{c_1 - \mu(D_s)} \alpha_h^{-1}((1 + c_0)s), \quad \forall s \geq 0. \tag{2.62}$$

Then, for any γ_1 of the forms (2.62) and any $\gamma_d \in \mathcal{K}_\infty$ of the form (2.26a), we choose $\gamma_{\bar{v}} \in \mathcal{K}$ such that

$$\gamma_{\bar{v}}(s) < \gamma_1^{-1} \circ \gamma_d^{-1}(s), \qquad \forall s \in [0, \gamma_d(\bar{s})], \tag{2.63a}$$

$$\gamma_{\bar{v}}(s) < (\gamma_d \circ \gamma_1)^{-1}(s), \qquad \forall s \in [0, \gamma_d \circ \gamma_1(\bar{s})], \tag{2.63b}$$

$$\gamma_{\bar{v}}(s) < \gamma_d^{-1}(s), \qquad \forall s \in [0, \gamma_d(\bar{s})]. \tag{2.63c}$$

The function $\gamma_{\bar{v}}$ can be constructed by taking the minimum of the right-hand-side functions in (2.63), all of which are of class $\mathcal{K}$. Then, condition (2.61) is satisfied.

For Case (B), we choose

$$\mu(s) = \frac{1}{s} \tag{2.64}$$

for $s > 0$, and choose α_h in the form of (2.62) with

$$\alpha_h(s) = k_h s \tag{2.65}$$

for $s \in \mathbb{R}_+$, where k_h is a positive constant to be determined later, c_0 is any positive constant, and $c_1 = \mu(D_1)$ with $D_1 = (5D_s + D)/6$. Clearly, $c_1 > 0$. Such α_h and γ_1 automatically satisfy condition (2.48). Then, from the definitions of α_μ, α_p and $\alpha_{h,\mu}$ in (2.27), we have

$$\alpha_\mu(s) = s^2, \qquad \alpha_p(s) = s, \qquad \alpha_{h,\mu}(s) = k_h s^2 \tag{2.66}$$

for $s \in \mathbb{R}_+$. Then, using to the definition of γ_d in (2.26a), we have

$$\begin{aligned} \gamma_d(s) &= 2\sqrt{n}\left(k_h s^2 + (2\bar{v}^c + k_h \max\{s - \mu(D_s), 0\})\, s\right) \\ &\quad \times (s + k_h \max\{s - \mu(D_s), 0\} + \bar{v}^c) \end{aligned} \tag{2.67}$$

for $s \in \mathbb{R}_+$.

With γ_1 and γ_d given by (2.62) and (2.67), respectively, and with $\gamma_{\bar{v}}$ satisfying (2.60), we show the existence of k_h, D_s and $\bar{v}^c$ for the satisfaction of condition (2.61).

Let

$$k_h = \bar{v}^c, \qquad D_s \geq \frac{2}{k_h}. \tag{2.68}$$

Then, we have

$$\gamma_1(s) = \frac{6(1 + c_0)}{k_h(1 - D/D_s)} s \leq \frac{12(1 + c_0)}{k_h(2 - k_h D)} s \tag{2.69}$$

for all $s \in \mathbb{R}_+$, and

$$
\begin{aligned}
\gamma_d(s) &\le 2\sqrt{n}\,(k_h s + (2\bar{\upsilon}^c + k_h s))\,(s + k_h s + \bar{\upsilon}^c)\,s \\
&\le 4\sqrt{n}\,(k_h \bar{s} + \bar{\upsilon}^c)(\bar{s} + k_h \bar{s} + \bar{\upsilon}^c)s \\
&= 4\sqrt{n}\left(k_h \frac{2}{D_s + D} + \bar{\upsilon}^c\right)\left(\frac{2}{D_s + D} + k_h \frac{2}{D_s + D} + \bar{\upsilon}^c\right)s \\
&\le 4\sqrt{n}\left(k_h \frac{2}{D_s} + \bar{\upsilon}^c\right)\left(\frac{2}{D_s} + k_h \frac{2}{D_s} + \bar{\upsilon}^c\right)s \\
&\le 4\sqrt{n}\,(k_h^2 + k_h)(k_h + k_h^2 + k_h)s \\
&\le 4\sqrt{n}k_h^2(k_h + 2)^2 s,
\end{aligned}
\tag{2.70}
$$

for $s \in [0, \bar{s}]$. For the inequality (2.69), we have used the definition of c_1 as given below (2.65) for the first equality, and used (2.68) for the last inequality. For the inequality (2.70), we have used the definition of γ_d in (2.67) for the first inequality, used the definitions of $\bar{s}$ and μ in (2.59) and (2.64) for the first equality, and used (2.68) for the fourth inequality.

Viewing the right-hand sides of (2.69) and (2.70) as upper bounds for γ_1 and γ_d, respectively, and substituting them into the left-hand sides of the inequalities in condition (2.61), we obtain

$$\gamma_1 \circ \gamma_{\bar{\upsilon}} \circ \gamma_d(s) \le (48(1 + c_0)k_{\bar{\upsilon}}\sqrt{n}) \frac{k_h(k_h + 2)^2}{2 - k_h D} s, \tag{2.71a}$$

$$\gamma_{\bar{\upsilon}} \circ \gamma_d \circ \gamma_1(s) \le (48(1 + c_0)k_{\bar{\upsilon}}\sqrt{n}) \frac{k_h(k_h + 2)^2}{2 - k_h D} s, \tag{2.71b}$$

$$\gamma_{\bar{\upsilon}} \circ \gamma_d(s) \le 4k_{\bar{\upsilon}}\sqrt{n}k_h^2(k_h + 2)^2 s \tag{2.71c}$$

for $s \in [0, \bar{s}]$. Clearly, by choosing k_h sufficiently small, e.g.,

$$k_h < \min\left\{1, \frac{1}{D}, \frac{1}{432(1 + c_0)k_{\bar{\upsilon}}\sqrt{n}}\right\}, \tag{2.72}$$

we can guarantee the satisfaction of condition (2.61) and thus condition (2.58)-(2.59).

2. **Existence and uniqueness of $[\tilde{p}(t); z(t)]$ for all $t \ge 0$ and boundedness of $h(\tilde{p}(t))$ and $|\bar{\upsilon}(t)|$ for all $t \ge 0$.**

   2.1. **Existence, uniqueness and local Lipschitz continuity of $\tilde{p}(t)$ and $z(t)$ over a (possibly infinite) time interval.**

   The closed-loop system, composed of (2.2), (2.4), (2.5), (2.19), and (2.20), is described by

$$\dot{\tilde{p}} = g(z, \phi(\tilde{p}, \upsilon^c)), \tag{2.73a}$$

$$\dot{z} = f(z, \phi(\tilde{p}, \upsilon^c)). \tag{2.73b}$$

It should be noted that the function ϕ is not defined at $\tilde{p} = 0$. With the local Lipschitz continuity of f, g, ϕ and v^c, we can verify the local Lipschitz continuity of $[g(z, \phi(\tilde{p}, v^c(t))); f(z, \phi(\tilde{p}, v^c(t)))]$ with respect to $(\tilde{p}, z, t)$ on $(\mathbb{R}^n \setminus \{0\}) \times \mathbb{R}^m \times \mathbb{R}_+$. Using [187, Theorem 54], we have, for any initial state $\tilde{p}(0) \neq 0$ and $z(0)$ and any input v^c satisfying Assumption 2.2, the system (2.73) admits a unique trajectory $[\tilde{p}(t); z(t)]$ over some time interval starting at $t = 0$. Moreover, since $[g(z, \phi(\tilde{p}, v^c(t))); f(z, \phi(\tilde{p}, v^c(t)))]$ is locally Lipschitz with respect to t, using [206, Theorem 2.2], we can verify that the trajectory $[\tilde{p}(t); z(t)]$ is continuously differentiable and thus, locally Lipschitz continuous with respect to t as long as it is defined.

2.2. Existence, uniqueness, and local Lipschitz continuity of $\tilde{p}(t)$ and $z(t)$ for all $t \geq 0$.

We denote by $[0, T_*)$ with $0 < T_* \leq \infty$ the time interval over which the trajectory is right maximally defined. Based on the discussion in (2.1), $\tilde{p}(t)$ and $z(t)$ are locally Lipschitz continuous for all $t \in [0, T_*)$. When $\mu(|\tilde{p}(0)|)$, $|z(0)|$, $\bar{v}^c$ and $\bar{v}^{cd}$ are sufficiently small, we show $T_* = \infty$ by contradiction: if $T_* < \infty$, then there exists a continuous function $B : [0, T_*] \to \mathbb{R}_+$ such that

$$\max\{|\tilde{p}(t)|, 1/|\tilde{p}(t)|, |z(t)|\} \leq B(t) \tag{2.74}$$

for all $t \in [0, T_*)$.

Specifically, we consider the case in which $\mu(|\tilde{p}(0)|)$, $|z(0)|$, $\bar{v}^c$ and $\bar{v}^{cd}$ satisfy

$$\beta_1(h(\tilde{p}(0)), 0) < \bar{s}_0, \tag{2.75a}$$

$$\beta_2(|z(0)| + |\phi(\tilde{p}(0), v^c)|, 0) < \bar{s}_0, \tag{2.75b}$$

$$\gamma_2 \circ \beta_1(h(\tilde{p}(0)), 0) < \bar{s}_0, \tag{2.75c}$$

$$\gamma_1 \circ \beta_2(|z(0)| + |\phi(\tilde{p}(0), v^c)|, 0) < \bar{s}_0 \tag{2.75d}$$

for all $|v^c| \leq \bar{v}^c$, and

$$\max\{\gamma_{\tilde{v}}(4\sqrt{n}\bar{v}^{cd}), \gamma_1 \circ \gamma_{\tilde{v}}(4\sqrt{n}\bar{v}^{cd})\} < \bar{s}_0 \tag{2.76}$$

with constant $\bar{s}_0$ satisfying $c_1 < \bar{s}_0 < \bar{s}$. Note that, the satisfaction of condition (2.76) is guaranteed by choosing $\gamma_{\tilde{v}}$ for Case (A) and choosing $\bar{v}^{cd}$ for Case (B).

Note that the result of Proposition 2.2 only hold when $\|\tilde{v}\|_\infty$ is small enough (i.e., $\gamma_1(\|\tilde{v}\|_\infty) < \sup_{s>0} \mu(s)$), and the small-gain condition (2.58) only holds in a local range. When $\mu(|\tilde{p}(0)|)$, $|z(0)|$, $\bar{v}^c$ and $\bar{v}^{cd}$ satisfy (2.75), we verify that all the relevant signals indeed keep within the specific ranges during the time interval $[0, T_*)$. For this purpose, we define

$$T = \sup\{t \in [0, T_*) : \max\{\|h(\tilde{p})\|_t, \|\tilde{v}\|_t, \gamma_1(\|\tilde{v}\|_t)\} < \bar{s}\} \tag{2.77}$$

with $\bar{s}$ defined in (2.59), and show that $T = T_*$.

Recall Proposition 2.2. Condition (2.48) is satisfied following the definition of γ_1 in (2.62). Using the definitions of $\tilde{\upsilon}$, υ and ϕ in (2.7), (2.2), and (2.23), respectively, we can verify that

$$\tilde{\upsilon}(t) = g(z(t), \phi(\tilde{p}(t), \upsilon^c(t))) - \phi(\tilde{p}(t), \upsilon^c(t)), \tag{2.78}$$

and it is locally Lipschitz continuous in t on $[0, T_*)$. The definition of T in (2.77) ensures that $\gamma_1(\|\tilde{\upsilon}\|_T) \leq \bar{s} < \sup_{s>0}\mu(s)$. Due to causality, there exists $\beta_1 \in \mathcal{KL}$ such that

$$h(\tilde{p}(t)) \leq \max\{\beta_1(h(\tilde{p}(0)), t), \gamma_1(\|\tilde{\upsilon}\|_t), c_1\} \tag{2.79}$$

holds for all $t \in [0, T)$. Here, according to the discussion in (1) and the selection of $\bar{s}_0$, the constant c_1 satisfies $c_1 \in (\mu(D_s), \bar{s}_0)$.

Also, from Proposition 2.3, it holds that

$$|\tilde{\upsilon}(t)| \leq \max\{\beta_2(|z(0)| + |\phi(\tilde{p}(0), \upsilon^c(0))|, t), \gamma_2(\|\tilde{\upsilon}\|_t), \gamma_2(\|h(\tilde{p})\|_t), c_2\}, \tag{2.80}$$

for all $t \in [0, T)$, where β_2, γ_2 and c_2 are defined in (2.56). In particular, $c_2 = \gamma_{\tilde{\upsilon}}(4\sqrt{n}\bar{\upsilon}^{cd})$.

From (2.79) and (2.80), taking the supremum of $h(\tilde{p}(t))$ and $\tilde{\upsilon}(t)$ over $[0, T)$, we obtain

$$\|h(\tilde{p})\|_T \leq \max\{\beta_1(h(\tilde{p}(0)), 0), \gamma_1(\|\tilde{\upsilon}\|_T), c_1\}, \tag{2.81a}$$

$$\|\tilde{\upsilon}\|_T \leq \max\{\beta_2(|z(0)| + |\phi(\tilde{p}(0), \upsilon^c(0))|, 0), \gamma_2(\|\tilde{\upsilon}\|_T), \gamma_2(\|h(\tilde{p})\|_T), c_2\}. \tag{2.81b}$$

Substituting the right-hand side of (2.81a) for $\|h(\tilde{p})\|_T$ into (2.81b), we obtain

$$\begin{aligned}\|\tilde{\upsilon}\|_T \leq \max\{&\beta_2(|z(0)| + |\phi(\tilde{p}(0), \upsilon^c(0))|, 0), \gamma_2\circ\beta_1(h(\tilde{p}(0)), 0), \gamma_2(c_1), c_2,\\ &\gamma_2(\|\tilde{\upsilon}\|_T), \gamma_2\circ\gamma_1(\|\tilde{\upsilon}\|_T)\}.\end{aligned} \tag{2.82}$$

With $\|\tilde{\upsilon}\|_T \leq \bar{s}$, using condition (2.58), we have

$$\gamma_2(\|\tilde{\upsilon}\|_T) < \|\tilde{\upsilon}\|_T, \quad \gamma_2\circ\gamma_1(\|\tilde{\upsilon}\|_T) < \|\tilde{\upsilon}\|_T. \tag{2.83}$$

Thus,

$$\|\tilde{\upsilon}\|_T \leq \max\{\beta_2(|z(0)| + |\phi(\tilde{p}(0), \upsilon^c(0))|, 0), \gamma_2\circ\beta_1(h(\tilde{p}(0)), 0), \gamma_2(c_1), c_2\}. \tag{2.84}$$

With $\beta_1(h(\tilde{p}(0)), 0) \leq \bar{s}_0$ and $c_1 < \bar{s}_0$, using condition (2.58), we have

$$\gamma_1 \circ \gamma_2 \circ \beta_1(h(\tilde{p}(0)), 0) < \beta_1(h(\tilde{p}(0)), 0), \quad \gamma_1 \circ \gamma_2(c_1) < c_1. \tag{2.85}$$

Thus,

$$\gamma_1(\|\tilde{v}\|_T) \leq \max\{\gamma_1 \circ \beta_2(|z(0)| + |\phi(\tilde{p}(0), v^c(0))|, 0), \beta_1(h(\tilde{p}(0)), 0), c_1, \gamma_1(c_2)\}. \tag{2.86}$$

Substituting inequality (2.86) for $\gamma_1(\|\tilde{v}\|_T)$ into (2.81a), we have

$$\|h(\tilde{p})\|_T \leq \max\{\beta_1(h(\tilde{p}(0)), 0), \gamma_1 \circ \beta_2(|z(0)| + |\phi(\tilde{p}(0), v^c(0))|, 0), c_1, \gamma_1(c_2)\}. \tag{2.87}$$

From inequalities (2.87), (2.86) and (2.84), together with conditions (2.75), (2.76), as well as $c_1 \in (\mu(D_s), \bar{s}_0)$ and $\gamma_2(c_1) < \bar{s}_0$, it can be verified that

$$\max\{\|h(\tilde{p})\|_T, \|\tilde{v}\|_T, \gamma_1(\|\tilde{v}\|_T)\} < \bar{s}_0. \tag{2.88}$$

This, together with $\bar{s}_0 < \bar{s}$ and the definition of T in (2.77), implies that $T = T_*$.

We show that if $T_* < \infty$, then there exists a continuous function B : $[0, T_*] \to \mathbb{R}_+$ satisfying (2.74). In particular, an upper bound of $|z(t)|$ over $[0, T_*)$, denoted by $\bar{z}$, can be derived from the property (2.9), together with the boundedness of $z(0)$ (guaranteed by (2.75)) and the boundedness of $|v^*(t)|$ on $[0, T_*)$ (ensured by combining (2.10), (2.24), and (2.88)). An upper bound of $1/|\tilde{p}(t)|$ over $[0, T_*)$ is given by $1/\mu^{-1}(\bar{s}_0)$, which follows from the definition of $h(\tilde{p})$ in (2.5), $\mu \in \mathcal{M}^-\mathcal{C}$, as well as the boundedness of $h(\tilde{p}(t))$ for all $t \in [0, T_*)$ (ensured by (2.88)). An upper bound of $|\tilde{p}(t)|$ is given by $|\tilde{p}(0)| + \bar{v}t$ for $t \in [0, T_*)$, which can be obtained by solving (2.4) with the initial condition $\tilde{p}(0)$ and the velocity bound $\bar{v}$, where $\bar{v}$ can be established from the boundedness of $|\tilde{v}(t)|$ and $|v^*(t)|$ over $[0, T_*)$. This proves $T_* = \infty$.

3. **Transient-aware safety** (2.6).
Property (2.6) can be proved by substituting the boundedness property (2.88) on the trajectories into (2.79) and (2.80), and setting $T = \infty$. This ends the proof of Theorem 2.1. □

We now propose an algorithm (Algorithm 1) to determine D_s and α_h in a parametric form. We specify α_h in the form of $\alpha_h(s) = k_h s$, where $k_h > 0$ is a tunable coefficient. Based on this choice, we formulate the controller-tuning problem as an optimization problem that treats D_s and k_h as decision variables. The objective is to minimize D_s while maximizing k_h, under constraints induced by the small-gain conditions (2.58).

Algorithm 1: An Algorithm for Tuning the Safety-critical Controller

Require: Assumptions 2.1 and 2.2; safety-critical controller $\upsilon^* = \phi(\tilde{p}, \upsilon^c)$ with a parameterized function $\alpha_h \in \mathcal{K}^e$ (e.g., $\alpha_h(s) = k_h s$ with $k_h > 0$); desired safe distance D; upper bounds of υ^c and $\dot{\upsilon}^c$, denoted $\bar{\upsilon}^c$ and $\bar{\upsilon}^{cd}$.

Ensure: Optimized parameters D_s and k_h.

1: **Initialization:** Set $c_1 = \mu((5D_s + D)/6)$ and $c_0 = 1 \times 10^{-3}$.

2: **Constraint Construction:**

- Calculate the gain function γ_1 in property (2.49):

$$\gamma_1(s) = \frac{c_1(1 + c_0)}{c_1 - \mu(D_s)} k_h^{-1} s. \tag{2.89}$$

- Estimate an upper bound of $|\upsilon^*|$:

$$|\upsilon^*| \leq \bar{\upsilon}^c + k_{\upsilon^*} h(\tilde{p}), \tag{2.90}$$

where $k_{\upsilon^*} = \sup_{|\tilde{p}| \geq D} |\phi(0, \tilde{p})|/h(\tilde{p})$.

- Calculate the Lipschitz constant L_ϕ of the controller ϕ:

$$L_\phi = \sup_{x_1, x_2 \in \mathcal{L}, x_1 \neq x_2} \frac{|\phi(x_1) - \phi(x_2)|}{|x_1 - x_2|}, \tag{2.91}$$

where $x \triangleq [\upsilon^c; \tilde{p}]$ and $\mathcal{L} = \{[\upsilon^c; \tilde{p}] : |\upsilon^c| \leq \bar{\upsilon}^c, |\tilde{p}| \geq D\}$. This implies that the inequality in (2.25) holds with

$$\gamma_d(s) = 3\sqrt{n} L_\phi \max\{k_{\upsilon^*}, 1\} s, \quad c_d = \sqrt{n} L_\phi(\bar{\upsilon}^{cd} + \bar{\upsilon}^c). \tag{2.92}$$

- Calculate the gain function and corresponding constant in property (2.55):

$$\gamma_2(s) = \gamma_{\tilde{\upsilon}} \circ \gamma_d(s), \quad c_2 = \gamma_{\tilde{\upsilon}}(c_d). \tag{2.93}$$

- Construct the constraints based on the above calculations to ensure the satisfaction of the small-gain-type conditions (2.58):

$$\gamma_1 \circ \gamma_2(s) < s, \quad \gamma_2 \circ \gamma_1(s) < s, \quad \gamma_2(s) < s, \quad \max\{c_2, \gamma_1(c_2)\} < \bar{s}, \tag{2.94}$$

for $s \in [0, \bar{s}]$, where $\bar{s} = \mu((D + D_s)/2)$.

3: **Objective:** Minimize D_s and maximize k_h.

4: **Optimization:** Solve the resulting nonlinear optimization problem to obtain the optimized parameters D_s and α_h.

5: **Output:** Return the optimized parameters D_s and k_h, along with the associated gain functions.

2.5 Simulation and Experiment

2.5.1 Numerical Simulation

To assess the effectiveness of the method proposed in this chapter, we revisit the safety-critical altitude control problem for a UAV introduced in Example 1.3 of Section 1.5.1. The objective is to design a safety-critical controller for a UAV involving uncertain actuation dynamics, such that the UAV tracks the velocity-command signal as closely as possible while avoiding ground contact.

Specifically, the dynamic model in the altitude direction takes the form (2.1)-(2.2). For readability, we rewrite the model (2.1)-(2.2) here:

$$\dot{p} = v, \tag{2.95}$$

where $p \in \mathbb{R}^n$ is the position and $v \in \mathbb{R}^n$ is the velocity. The velocity v is produced by an actuation system of the form

$$\dot{z} = f(z, v^*) \tag{2.96a}$$

$$v = g(z, v^*) \tag{2.96b}$$

where $z \in \mathbb{R}^m$ is the state, $v^* \in \mathbb{R}^n$ is the velocity-reference input. In accordance with Example 1.3, we consider

$$g(z, v^*) = \begin{bmatrix} -2 & -2 \\ 1 & 0 \end{bmatrix} z + \begin{bmatrix} 2 \\ 0 \end{bmatrix} v^*, \tag{2.97a}$$

$$h(z, v^*) = [-1, 1]z. \tag{2.97b}$$

Intuitively, the z-subsystem, though called actuation system, models the controlled dynamics of the UAV. Following the analysis in Example 1.1, one verifies that the actuation system satisfies Assumption 2.1 and exhibits the reference-velocity tracking property (1.66), where

$$\gamma_{\tilde{v}}(s) = 2.33s. \tag{2.98}$$

Set the velocity-command signal v^c to

$$v^c \equiv -1. \tag{2.99}$$

Clearly, Assumption 2.2 is readily satisfied.

Model the ground as an obstacle $o = 0$ with $n_o = 1$, set the desired safe distance $D = 0.5$, and choose $\mu(s) = 1/s$. Use the safety indicator function $h(\tilde{p})$ to encode safety in the altitude direction:

$$h(\tilde{p}) = \frac{1}{|\tilde{p}|}. \tag{2.100}$$

Consider the safety-critical controller defined in (2.19) and select $\alpha_h(s) = k_h s$ with constant $k_h > 0$. By inequality (2.72) in the proof of Theorem 2.1, one should select k_h sufficiently small and choose $D_s \geq 2/k_h$ to enlarge the safety margin such that the small-gain condition (2.58)-(2.59) holds, thereby guaranteeing closed-loop safety.

Consider the following cases where the controller parameters k_h and D_s take different values:

$$\text{Parameter set 1:} \quad k_h = 1.0, \quad D_s = 2.0, \tag{2.101a}$$

$$\text{Parameter set 2:} \quad k_h = 1.0, \quad D_s = 1.0, \tag{2.101b}$$

$$\text{Parameter set 3:} \quad k_h = 4.0, \quad D_s = 2.0. \tag{2.101c}$$

Consider initial states $p(0) = 3$ and $z(0) = [0; 0]$. Figures 2.7 and 2.8 show, respectively, the altitude trajectories and the velocity-tracking error trajectories under the safety-critical controller (2.19) with the above parameter sets. From Figure 2.7, it can be observed that, when comparing the trajectories corresponding to Parameter Sets 1 and 2, reducing D_s leads to $D_s < 2/k_h$, which violates the small-gain condition and ultimately breaches the safety constraint. In contrast, comparing the trajectories for Parameter Sets 1 and 3 shows that increasing k_h likewise invalidates the small-gain condition, and even a larger safety margin D_s cannot reestablish safety.

2.5.2 Experiment

To further validate the effectiveness of the method proposed in this chapter, we design and carry out a physical experiment.

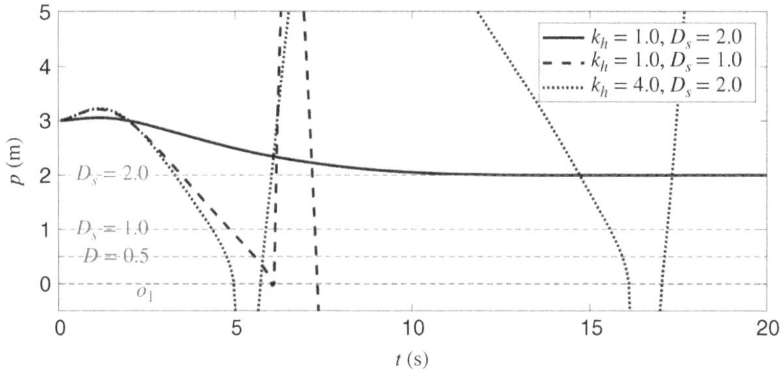

Figure 2.7 Altitude trajectories of a UAV under safety-critical controller (2.19) with different parameter sets: safety can be ensured by choosing a smaller k_h and a larger D_s.

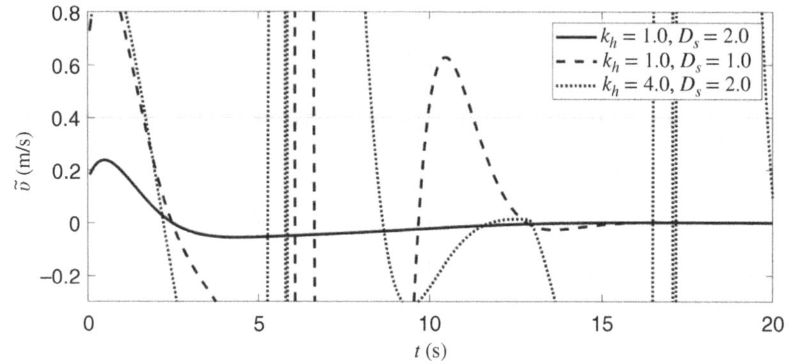

Figure 2.8 Velocity-tracking error trajectories of a UAV under safety-critical controller (2.19) with different parameter sets.

We consider a scenario in which a UAV is controlled to avoid a single static, disc-shaped obstacle. The overall experimental setup is illustrated in Figure 2.9. The plant is a DJI RoboMaster TT quadrotor, whose position and attitude are measured by an indoor optical motion-capture system. Cameras record the UAV's position in real time, and the measured data are transmitted through a network switch to Motive for processing, before being forwarded to the ground-station computer via the NatNet interface. The ground station runs a MATLAB program that implements the safety-critical controller based on real-time position feedback and generates a velocity-reference input for the velocity-tracking controller. The attitude command signal is then transmitted to the UAV over Wi-Fi, thereby achieving closed-loop control.

The velocity-reference tracking capability is established as follows. First, using the MATLAB System Identification Toolbox, a dynamic model is identified between the dimensionless stick (attitude) commands and the UAV's body-frame tri-axial accelerations. Then, with the MATLAB Control System Designer, a velocity-tracking controller is designed and tuned. A schematic diagram of the experimental system is shown in Figure 2.9.

The experiment focuses on the motion of the UAV in the horizontal plane ($n = 2$). A circular obstacle is positioned at $[0; 0]$, and the desired safe distance is set to $D = 0.3$. It is desired that the controlled UAV avoids the obstacle and reaches a designated target point. The velocity-command signal generated by the primary controller is

$$v^c = -(p - [1.5; 0.05]) \min\left\{\frac{1}{|p - [1.5; 0.05]|}, 2\right\}, \tag{2.102}$$

so that the magnitude of the velocity-command signal does not exceed 1. The safety-critical controller is defined in (1.101), with $\alpha_h(s) = k_h s$ (where $k_h > 0$ is

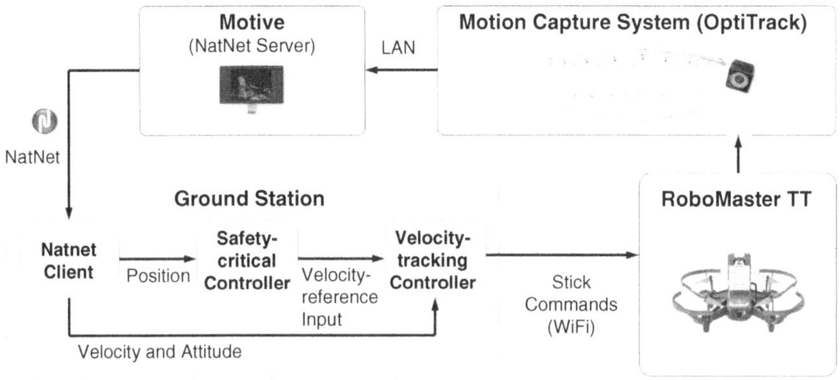

Figure 2.9 Schematic diagram of the experimental setup based on an indoor optical motion capture system and the RoboMaster TT.

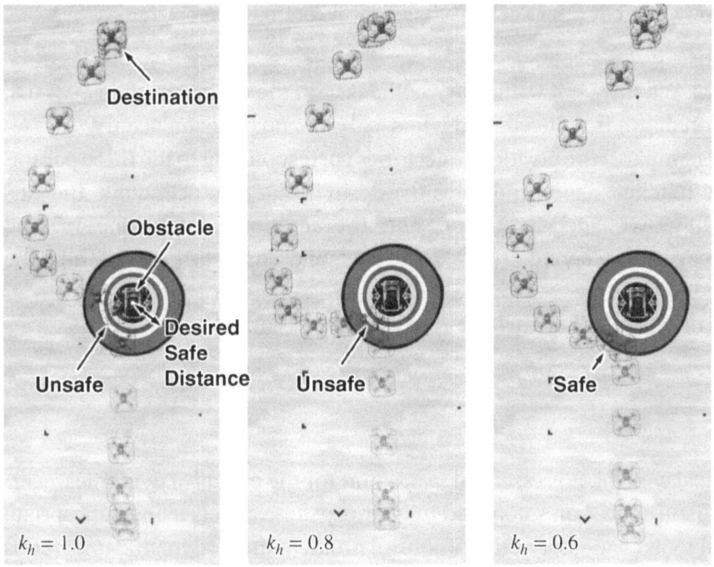

Figure 2.10 Position trajectories of the RoboMaster TT in experiments under the safety-critical controller (1.101) with the parameter k_h taking different values.

a constant) and $D_s = 0.45$. Three parameter sets are tested in the experiments: $k_h = 1.0$, $k_h = 0.8$, and $k_h = 0.6$.

During the experiment, a camera records the UAV's motion on the horizontal plane, capturing images every 0.5 seconds. The UAV is initially positioned at [1.5; 0]. Figure 2.10 shows the UAV position trajectories corresponding to the three

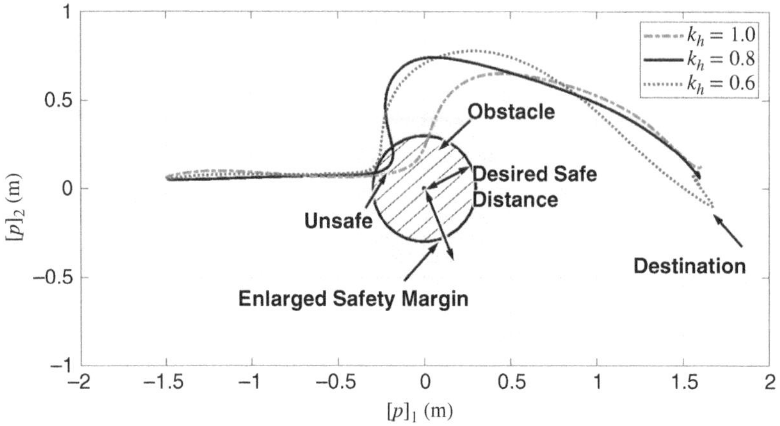

Figure 2.11 Comparison of the position trajectories of the RoboMaster TT in experiments with different values of the safety-critical controller parameter k_h.

parameter sets. When $k_h = 1.0$, the UAV collides with the obstacle; when $k_h = 0.8$, the penetration depth is reduced; and when $k_h = 0.6$, no collision occurs.

Figure 2.11 compares the position trajectories corresponding to the three parameter sets. The hatched region indicates the desired safe distance, while the surrounding light-gray shaded area represents the additional safety margin. The dash-dotted curve corresponds to $k_h = 1.0$, the solid curve to $k_h = 0.8$, and the dashed curve to $k_h = 0.6$.

Evolutions of several other variables are shown in Figure 2.12.

2.6 Notes

In safety-critical control, it is essential to account for the effects of dynamic uncertainties and disturbances on safety and to quantify these effects using appropriate mathematical tools. The safety-critical control problem under dynamic uncertainties considered in this chapter is basically a robust control problem.

2.6.1 Input-to-state Safety

Inspired by input-to-state stability (ISS), developed by E. D. Sontag in the 1990s [184, 190], the notion of input-to-state safety (ISSf) was introduced in [168] and provides a powerful analytic framework for robust safety. Whereas ISS quantifies the impact of external inputs on stability, ISSf extends this viewpoint to safety

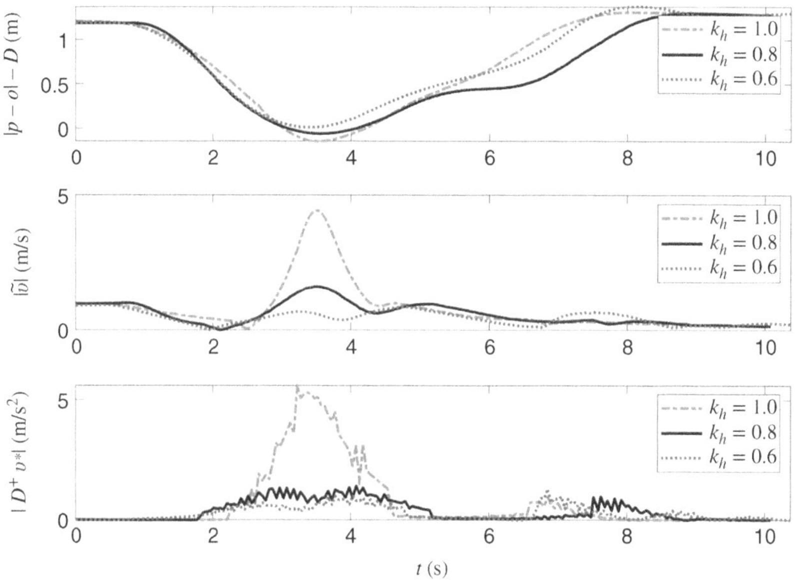

Figure 2.12 The safety measure $|p - o| - D$ of the quadrotor with respect to the obstacle, the norm of the velocity-tracking error $|\tilde{v}|$, and the norm of the changing rate of the velocity-reference input $|D^+v^*|$ in experiments with the safety-critical controller parameter k_h taking different values.

analysis by quantifying how disturbances affect safety margins. Building on the level-set characterization of ISSf in [168, 169], reference [104] combined ISSf with control barrier functions to formulate dissipative input-to-state control barrier functions. For robust safety, this approach preserves positive invariance of a designated set which allows disturbance-induced deviations, with the magnitude of the derivation monotonically depends on that of the disturbance and thus provides an effective way to characterize robust safety. Implemented within a unified QP framework, ISSf-CBFs coordinate safety and stability and provide reliable, robust control strategies for real-time safety in mobile robotics, autonomous driving, and multirobot systems [1]. Characterized through barrier functions, the concept of ISSf also enables the extension of the classical ISS small-gain theorem [92, 93] to safety-critical interconnected systems. In [125, 126], this is achieved by carefully analyzing the boundedness and convergence properties of the barrier functions associated with the subsystems, whose interactions are described by gain functions.

2.6.2 Robust Safety-critical Control

Robust safety-critical control aims to ensure that the closed-loop states always satisfy prescribed safety constraints, despite the presence of modeling uncertainties [137], external disturbances [87], and measurement errors [42]. To address the robustness issue when the system dynamics involve perturbations, reference [225] extended the conventional notion of control barrier functions, and proposed ISS conditions for ensured positive invariance when disturbances are present. The notion of robust CBF [87, 42] has also been developed for ensured robustness of the safety property by enforcing control inputs within robust margins to attenuate different types of perturbations. References [225, 154, 87, 104, 42, 175, 198, 1, 29, 137] addressed the challenges arising from robust safety-critical control for various plants subject to uncertainties in plant dynamics and/or disturbances. Among these, references [198, 154, 87, 137] specifically considered uncertainties in the plant dynamics, and references [175] and [29] focused on Euler–Lagrange systems and satellite, respectively, and handled the coexistence of multiple constraints and high-order nonlinear dynamics, as well as accounting for bounded disturbances or sampling-time effects.

3

Safety-critical Control Under Multiple Constraints: A Feasible-set Reshaping Technique

This chapter extends the discussion in Chapter 2 to systems that must keep safe with respect to multiple obstacles. As in Chapter 2, we consider a mobile agent modeled as a cascade of an integrator (nominal subsystem) and an actuation subsystem subject to dynamic uncertainties. The velocity-tracking capability of the actuation subsystems is again characterized by a modified notion of input-to-output stability (IOS).

From the discussion in Chapter 2, it is evident that Lipschitz continuity plays a crucial role in ensuring the robustness of safety-critical controllers under dynamic uncertainties. Figure 3.1 illustrates a scenario in which the coexistence of uncertain actuation dynamics and multiple constraints can lead to collisions, even if the nominal (ideal) path is collision-free. However, directly adopting the design from Chapter 2 to handle multiple safety constraints may lead to controllers with extremely large Lipschitz constants or even loss of Lipschitz continuity. This issue arises because the constraint matrix corresponding to the constraints (formed directly from safety indicator functions) that directly affect the optimal solution may fail to satisfy the full-row-rank condition, which is commonly required to ensure the Lipschitz continuity of constrained optimization solutions (see the discussion in Section 1.3.3).

To address the challenges of robust safety-critical control in the presence of multiple constraints, this chapter introduces a new approach termed feasible-set reshaping, for the purpose of constructing a (locally) Lipschitz continuous safety-critical controller by reconstructing a feasible set of safety-oriented control inputs based on the original safety constraints. Specifically, we develop a positive-span model to perform feasible-set reshaping. The key idea is to project the constraints of the original feasible set onto a suitably chosen constant matrix with row vectors positively spanning the space of the control input. It is shown that the newly constructed feasible set is nonempty (ensuring feasibility), contained within the original feasible set (ensuring safety), and associated with a constant constraint

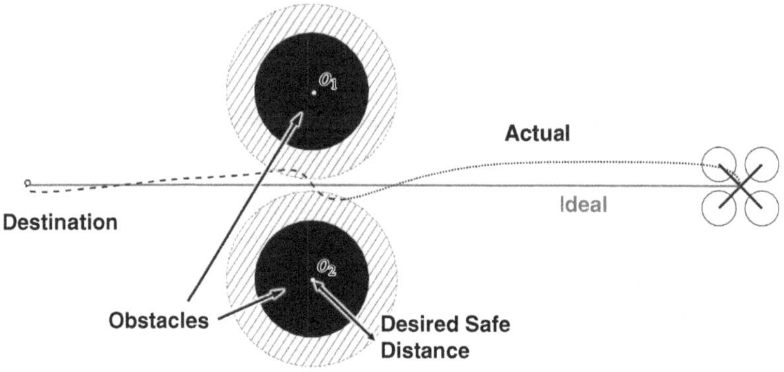

Figure 3.1 The ideal path is collision-free, whereas the coexistence of uncertain actuation dynamics and multiple constraints may lead to collisions.

matrix that satisfies the above-mentioned full-row-rank condition. Consequently, the safety-critical controller constructed based on the reshaped feasible sets features feasibility, Lipschitz continuity, and robust safety properties.

The closed-loop system is then viewed as an interconnection of two subsystems: one representing the controlled nominal dynamics subject to velocity-tracking errors, and the other capturing the uncertain actuation dynamics. The feasible-set reshaping technique enables using gain functions to characterize the interconnection between these subsystems, thereby allowing the application of nonlinear small-gain analysis (as in Chapter 2) to study their interaction and guarantee safety of the closed-loop system.

3.1 Problem Formulation

In this chapter, we study the scenario involving a single mobile agent and multiple stationary obstacles.

3.1.1 System Setup

We consider a mobile agent modeled as a cascade connection of a nominal system and an uncertain actuation system. Specifically, the nominal system is described by

$$\dot{p} = v, \tag{3.1}$$

where $p \in \mathbb{R}^n$ and $v \in \mathbb{R}^n$ represent the position and the velocity, respectively.

The actual velocity v is produced by an actuation system of the form

$$\dot{z} = f(z, v^*), \quad v = g(z, v^*) \tag{3.2}$$

where $z \in \mathbb{R}^m$ is the state of the actuation system, $v^* \in \mathbb{R}^n$ is the velocity-reference input, and $f : \mathbb{R}^m \times \mathbb{R}^n \to \mathbb{R}^m$ and $g : \mathbb{R}^m \times \mathbb{R}^n \to \mathbb{R}^n$ are locally Lipschitz continuous functions. Note that the explicit forms of f and g are not assumed to be known for the purpose of controller design.

There are n_o stationary spherical obstacles, indexed by

$$\mathcal{N}_o = \{1, \dots , n_o\}. \tag{3.3}$$

For each $i \in \mathcal{N}_o$, let $o_i \in \mathbb{R}^n$ denote the position of the i-th obstacle's center.

3.1.2 Safety-critical Control Objective

To analyze the safety property of the mobile agent with respect to the obstacles, for $i \in \mathcal{N}_o$, define the relative position between the agent and the i-th obstacle as

$$\tilde{p}_i = p - o_i. \tag{3.4}$$

Accordingly, to characterize safety, define a safety indicator function $h : \mathbb{R}^n \setminus \{0\} \to (0, \infty)$ as

$$h(\tilde{p}_i) = \mu(|\tilde{p}_i|), \tag{3.5}$$

where $\mu : (0, \infty) \to (0, \infty)$ is an $\mathcal{M}^-\mathcal{C}$ function.

To encode the overall safety with respect to all the obstacles, define

$$\bar{h}(p) = \max_{i \in \mathcal{N}_o} h(p - o_i). \tag{3.6}$$

In practice, given a desired safe distance $D > 0$, the mobile agent modeled by (3.1)–(3.2) with an appropriately designed controller is said to be safe if there exist constants $h_0, z_0, \bar{z} \geq 0$ such that for any initial state $p(0)$ satisfying $\bar{h}(p(0)) \leq h_0$ and $z(0)$ satisfying $|z(0)| \leq z_0$, the following properties hold for all $t \geq 0$:

$$\bar{h}(p(t)) \leq \mu(D), \tag{3.7a}$$

$$|z(t)| \leq \bar{z}. \tag{3.7b}$$

Let $v^c \in \mathbb{R}^n$ denote the velocity-command signal for the primary control objective. In practice, v^c can be generated by a higher-level planner or a primary controller.

With the velocity-reference input v^* considered the control input, the objective of this chapter is to design a controller such that the position p of the mobile agent remains sufficiently far from the obstacle positions o_i for $i \in \mathcal{N}_o$ (in the sense of

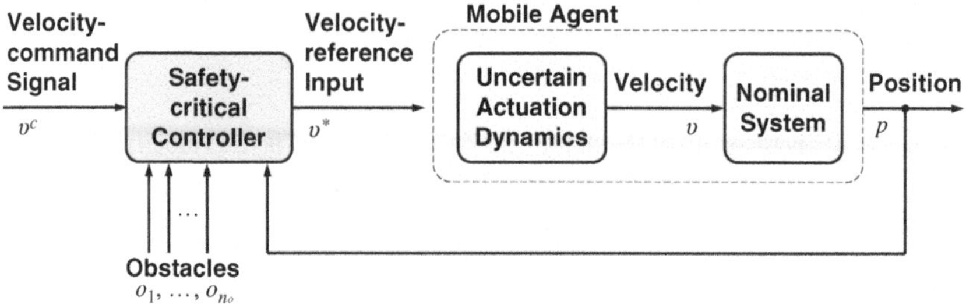

Figure 3.2 Structure of a safety-critical control system subject to multiple constraints.

(3.7a)), and the velocity-reference input v^* deviates from the velocity-command input v^c as little as possible. The proposed structure of the safety-critical control system is depicted in Figure 3.2.

3.1.3 Assumptions

In the presence of uncertain actuation dynamics, the actual velocity v may not coincide with the velocity-reference input v^*. Define the velocity-tracking error as

$$\tilde{v} = v - v^*. \tag{3.8}$$

We assume that when v^* is constant, the actual velocity v asymptotically converges to v^*. Moreover, when v^* is time-varying, the velocity-tracking error $\tilde{v}$ depends on the rate of change of v^*. Suppose that $v^*(t)$ is locally Lipschitz in time.

Assumption 3.1 ***(Reference-tracking Capability of the Actuation System)*:** Consider the actuation system (3.3). There exist $\beta_{\tilde{v}} \in \mathcal{KL}$ and $\gamma_{\tilde{v}}, \alpha_{z1}, \alpha_{z2} \in \mathcal{K}$ such that for any $z(0)$ and any locally Lipschitz v^*,

$$|\tilde{v}(t)| \leq \max\{\beta_{\tilde{v}}(|z(0)| + |v^*(0)|, t), \gamma_{\tilde{v}}(\|D^+v^*\|_t)\} \tag{3.9}$$

$$|z(t)| \leq \max\{\alpha_{z1}(|z(0)|), \alpha_{z2}(\|v^*\|_t)\} \tag{3.10}$$

hold for all $t \geq 0$.

Without loss of generality, we assume that v^c is continuously differentiable in time, and that v^c and its time derivative are bounded.

Assumption 3.2 ***(Boundedness of the Velocity-Command Signal and Its Time Derivative)*:** The velocity-command signal v^c is continuously differentiable in time, and there exist positive constants $\bar{v}^c$ and $\bar{v}^{cd}$ such that

$$|v^c(t)| \leq \bar{v}^c, \qquad |\dot{v}^c(t)| \leq \bar{v}^{cd} \tag{3.11}$$

for all $t \geq 0$.

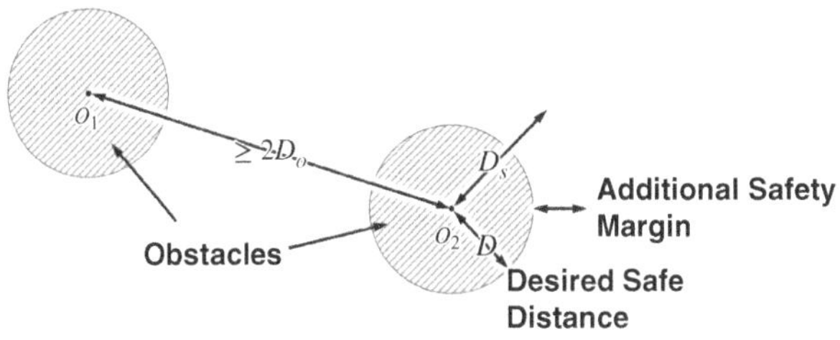

Figure 3.3 An illustration of the separation condition among obstacles.

To ensure the feasibility of the safety-critical control problem, it is reasonable to assume that the distances between obstacles are sufficiently large relative to the desired safe distance D. An illustrative example is shown in Figure 3.3.

Assumption 3.3 ***(Separation Condition Among Obstacles)*****:** There exists a constant $D_o > D$ such that

$$|o_i - o_j| \geq 2D_o \tag{3.12}$$

for all $i, j \in \mathcal{N}_o$ with $i \neq j$.

3.2 Trial of Directly Extending the Safety Margin

In this section, we try designing a safety-critical controller by directly extending the safety margin of the controller introduced in Chapter 2.

In the presence of uncertain actuation dynamics, the velocity-tracking error $\tilde{v}$ (defined in (3.8)) needs to be incorporated in the controller design. For $i \in \mathcal{N}_o$, from (3.1) and (3.8), taking the time-derivative of $\tilde{p}_i$ yields

$$\dot{\tilde{p}}_i = \dot{p} - \dot{o}_i = v^* + \tilde{v}. \tag{3.13}$$

As a natural extension of the safety-critical controller (2.19) proposed in Chapter 2, we incorporate multiple safety constraints into (2.19b). This leads to a QP-based safety-critical controller subject to multiple constraints:

$$v^* = \underset{v^* \in \mathcal{V}(p)}{\operatorname{argmin}} |v^* - v^c|^2 \tag{3.14}$$

where

$$\mathcal{V}(p) = \{v^* \in \mathbb{R}^n : A(p)v^* \leq b(p)\} \tag{3.15}$$

is the feasible set, with

$$A(p) = \left[-\frac{\tilde{p}_1}{|\tilde{p}_1|}, \dots, -\frac{\tilde{p}_{n_o}}{|\tilde{p}_{n_o}|} \right]^T, \tag{3.16a}$$

$$b(p) = [-\alpha_h(h(\tilde{p}_1) - \mu(D_s)), \dots, -\alpha_h(h(\tilde{p}_{n_o}) - \mu(D_s))]^T \tag{3.16b}$$

forming a polyhedron.[1] Here, α_h is a continuously differentiable class $\mathcal{K}^e$ function whose domain contains $[-\mu(D_s), \infty)$, $h : \mathbb{R}^n \setminus \{0\} \to (0, \infty)$ is defined in (3.5), and D_s is a positive constant introducing an additional safety margin. The difference between the QP-based controllers (3.14)–(3.16) and (2.13)–(2.14) lies in the number of constraints.

As discussed in Section 1.5.2, with an inappropriately chosen α_h, the QP (3.14)–(3.16) may become infeasible at certain points within the safe set

$$\mathcal{S} = \{p \in \mathbb{R}^n : |p - o_i| \geq D, i \in \mathcal{N}_o\}. \tag{3.17}$$

The following proposition gives a condition on α_h to ensure the feasibility of the QP-based controller for all $p \in \mathcal{S}$. Although an enlarged safety margin D_s is imposed on the refined QP-based controller, we can still guarantee the feasibility of the controller in the desired safe set $\mathcal{S}$ defined by the original safe distance D.

Proposition 3.1 *(Feasibility)*: Given the desired safe distance $D > 0$, suppose that the obstacles satisfy Assumption 3.3 with $D_o > D$. Consider the QP (3.14)–(3.16) with $\alpha_h \in \mathcal{K}^e$, $\mu \in \mathcal{M}^-\mathcal{C}$ and constant $D_s \in [D, D_o]$. With α_h chosen to satisfy

$$\alpha_h(\mu(2D_o - s) - \mu(D_s)) \leq -\alpha_h(\mu(s) - \mu(D_s)) \tag{3.18}$$

for all $s \in [D, D_s]$,

$$\nu_s(p) = \sum_{i \in \mathcal{N}_o} [A(p)]_{i,:}^T \min\{[b(p)]_i, 0\} \tag{3.19}$$

is a feasible point of the QP with $\mathcal{V}(p)$ defined in (3.15) representing the feasible set, i.e.,

$$\nu_s(p) \in \mathcal{V}(p), \tag{3.20}$$

for all $p \in \mathcal{S}$ with $\mathcal{S}$ being the safe set defined in (3.17).

Proof. Note that one can always find an $\alpha_h \in \mathcal{K}^e$ satisfying (3.18) by evaluating the ranges of α_h that are considered on the two sides of inequality (3.18): $\mu(2D_o - s) - \mu(D_s) \leq 0$ and $\mu(s) - \mu(D_s) \geq 0$ for $s \in [D, D_s]$.

---

1 A polyhedron is defined as the intersection of a finite number of half-spaces and hyperplanes [26].

The following discussions are carried out for any $p \in \mathcal{S}$ with $\mathcal{S}$ defined in (3.17). Note that $p \in \mathcal{S}$ implies that

$$|p - o_i| \geq D, \qquad \forall i \in \mathcal{N}_o. \tag{3.21}$$

Also, under Assumption 3.3,

$$|\tilde{p}_i| = |p - o_i| = |o_j - o_i + p - o_j| \geq |o_j - o_i| - |\tilde{p}_j| \geq 2D_o - |\tilde{p}_j| \tag{3.22}$$

Moreover, with α_h satisfying (3.18), it holds that

$$[b(p)]_i \geq -[b(p)]_j, \qquad \forall i, j \in \mathcal{N}_o, i \neq j. \tag{3.23}$$

Indeed, if $[b(p)]_i < -[b(p)]_j$ for some $i \neq j$, then at least one of $[b(p)]_i$ and $[b(p)]_j$ would be negative. Without loss of generality, assume that $[b(p)]_j$ is the smaller one (and hence $[b(p)]_j < 0$). Then, the definition of $b(p)$ in (3.16b) implies $|\tilde{p}_j| < D_s$. Also, since $\alpha_h \in \mathcal{K}^e$ and $\mu \in \mathcal{M}^-\mathcal{C}$, using (3.22) and (3.16b), we have

$$\begin{aligned}
[b(p)]_i &= -\alpha_h(\mu(|\tilde{p}_i|) - \mu(D_s)) \\
&\geq -\alpha_h(\mu(2D_o - |\tilde{p}_j|) - \mu(D_s)) \\
&\geq \alpha_h(\mu(|\tilde{p}_j|) - \mu(D_s)) \\
&= -[b(p)]_j.
\end{aligned} \tag{3.24}$$

With $|\tilde{p}_j| < D_s$ as $[b(p)]_j < 0$ and $|\tilde{p}_j| \geq D$ according to (3.21), the validity of the second inequality in (3.24) is ensured by condition (3.18). Note that property (3.23) means that at most one of $[b(p)]_i$ for $i \in \mathcal{N}_o$ is negative.

Now, we prove $\nu_s(p) \in \mathcal{V}(p)$. Using the definition of $\nu_s(p)$ in (3.19) and the fact that each row of $A(p)$ defined in (3.16a) is a unit vector, we have

$$\begin{aligned}
[A(p)]_{j,:}\nu_s(p) &= \min\{[b(p)]_j, 0\} + \sum_{i\in\mathcal{N},i\neq j} [A(p)]_{j,:}[A(p)]_{i,:}^T \min\{[b(p)]_i, 0\} \\
&\leq [b(p)]_j + \min\{-[b(p)]_j, 0\} + \sum_{i\in\mathcal{N}_0,i\neq j} - \min\{[b(p)]_i, 0\} \\
&= [b(p)]_j + \min\{-[b(p)]_j, 0\} - \min\left\{\min_{i\in\mathcal{N}_0,i\neq j} [b(p)]_i, 0\right\} \\
&\leq [b(p)]_j
\end{aligned} \tag{3.25}$$

for any $j \in \mathcal{N}_o$, where the last inequality holds as $\min\{-[b(p)]_j, 0\} \leq \min\{[b(p)]_i, 0\}$ for $i \neq j$, which is ensured by (3.23). This ends the proof of Proposition 3.1. □

Nevertheless, even if an appropriately chosen α_h helps retain the feasibility of the QP-based controller with an enlarged safety margin, it remains challenging to guarantee the achievement of the safety-critical control objective due to the presence of dynamic uncertainties. As shown later in this chapter, the boundedness of the velocity-tracking error $\tilde{v}$ cannot be guaranteed *a priori* due to the uncertain actuation dynamics. In fact, $\tilde{v}$ is influenced by D^+v^*, as indicated in Assumption 3.1, and D^+v^* itself is affected by the values of the safety indicator functions $h(\tilde{p}_i)$. In Chapter 2, we have already discussed the challenge caused by the interaction between the safety indicator function and the velocity-tracking error for the single-obstacle case.

Moreover, directly applying the QP design may lead to the map from the position p to the control input v^*, corresponding to the QP-based controller, admitting extremely large Lipschitz constants or even losing Lipschitz continuity. Indeed, the coefficient matrix of the constraints that directly affect the optimal solution may violate the full-row-rank condition discussed in Section 1.5.2. A fast-changing velocity-reference input induces a large gain from the safety indicator function to the velocity-tracking error and may cause undesirable responses of the actuation system, probably violating the safety constraints.

3.3 A Feasible-set Reshaping Technique for Robust Safety-critical Control

In this section, we present a novel technique that reshapes the feasible set to address the Lipschitz continuity issue with QP-based safety-critical controllers. Our basic idea is to project the constraints onto a predefined constant matrix that positively spans the space of the control input (see, e.g., [47] and also Appendix A.2 for notions of positive span), which results in a feasible set as an intersection of the newly constructed affine constraints. Under mild conditions, by appropriately choosing the matrix, we can ensure that the coefficient matrix of the constraints that directly affect the optimal solution always satisfies the full-row-rank condition discussed in Section 1.5.2 and the QP-based safety-critical controller with the reshaped feasible set is Lipschitz continuous.

The new technique consists of four main steps:

- Step 1: Find an Element (Called Feasible Point) from the Original Feasible Set;
- Step 2: Select a Constant Matrix that Positively Spans $\mathbb{R}^n$;
- Step 3: Project Each Constraint of the Original Feasible Set onto the Selected Matrix;
- Step 4: Integrate the Projected and Corrected Constraints.

A step-by-step development of the new technique is presented below.

3.3.1 Step 1: Find an Element (Called Feasible Point) from the Original Feasible Set

A QP-based safety-critical controller determines the value of the velocity-reference input υ^* by choosing the element closest to υ^c from the feasible set $\mathcal{V}(p)$ defined in (3.15) and (3.16). To ensure that the map of the controller, which is a selection function of the set-valued map[2] $\mathcal{V}$, is locally Lipschitz with respect to both p and υ^c over some specific domain, it is necessary that $\mathcal{V}$ admit a selection function that is locally Lipschitz continuous over the domain.

As shown in Proposition 3.1, given the feasible set $\mathcal{V}(p)$ defined in (3.15) and (3.16), a function $v_s : \mathcal{S} \to \mathbb{R}^n$ satisfying $v_s(p) \in \mathcal{V}(p)$ for all $p \in \mathcal{S}$ can be explicitly constructed as in (3.19).

Furthermore, due to the (locally) Lipschitz continuity of $A : \mathcal{S} \to \mathbb{R}^{n_o \times n}$ and $b : \mathcal{S} \to \mathbb{R}^{n_o}$, the algebraic properties of Lipschitz functions [38, Section 2.3] ensure that the function v_s defined in (3.19) is (locally) Lipschitz continuous over $\mathcal{S}$.

Example 3.1 ***(Step 1 of Feasible-set Reshaping: Find a Feasible Point from the Original Feasible Set)***: *Consider two disc-type obstacles with centers located at* $o_1 = [-1; 1]$ *and* $o_2 = [1; -1]$, *with the desired safe distance* $D = 1.0$. *Choose* $D_s = \sqrt{2}/1.01$. *The feasible set* $\mathcal{V}(p)$ *takes the form* (3.14) *with* $A(p)$ *and* $b(p)$ *defined by*

$$A(p) = \left[-\frac{p - o_1}{|p - o_1|}, -\frac{p - o_2}{|p - o_2|}\right]^T, \tag{3.26a}$$

$$b(p) = [|p - o_1| - D_s, |p - o_2| - D_s]^T \tag{3.26b}$$

for all $|p - o_i| \geq D$, $i = 1, 2$. *For this feasible set* $\mathcal{V}(p)$, *using Proposition 3.1, we can construct a function* $v_s(p)$ *in the form of* (3.19) *such that* $v_s(p) \in \mathcal{V}(p)$ *for all* $|p - o_i| \geq D$, $i = 1, 2$.

Figure 3.4 shows the original feasible set $\mathcal{V}(p)$ *and the feasible point* $v_s(p)$ *in the space of velocity-reference inputs for* $p = [-1; 0]$, *along with the obstacles in the space of positions.*

3.3.2 Step 2: Select a Constant Matrix that Positively Spans $\mathbb{R}^n$

Given any constant $c_A \in (0, 1)$, define a constant matrix $A_L \in \mathbb{R}^{n_l \times n}$ with integer $n_l > n$, where the rows of A_L positively spans $\mathbb{R}^n$[3] satisfying the following conditions:

(PB1) Each $[A_L]_{i,:}$ is a unit vector, i.e., $|[A_L]_{i,:}| = 1$;
(PB2) Any n rows of A_L are linearly independent;

2 See [16] for relevant notions of set-valued maps.
3 See Appendix A.2 for the concept of positive span.

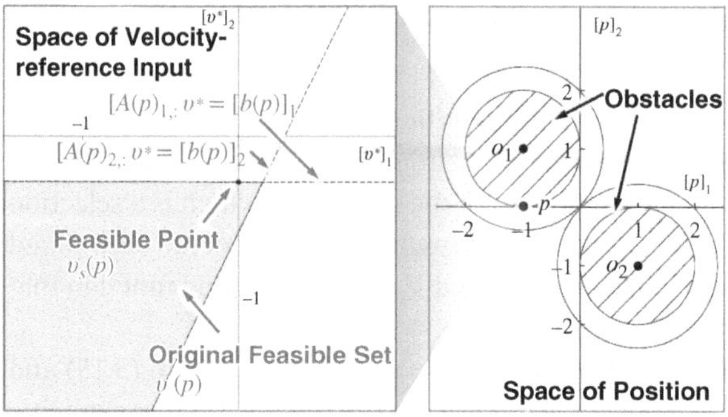

Figure 3.4 Step 1 of feasible-set reshaping: find a feasible point from the original feasible set.

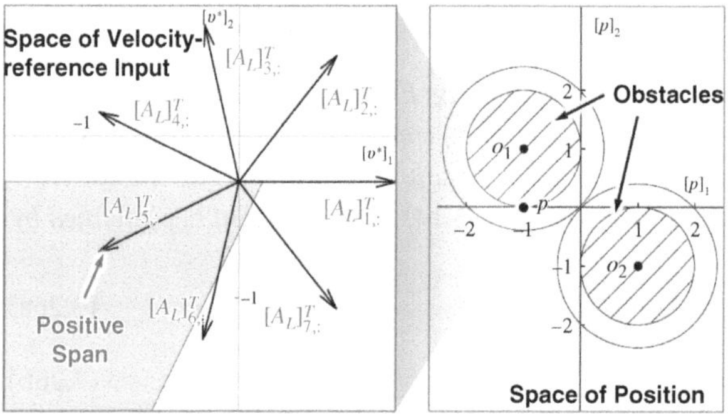

Figure 3.5 Step 2 of feasible-set reshaping: select a constant matrix that positively spans $\mathbb{R}^n$.

(PB3) Any unit vector $l_0 \in \mathbb{R}^n$ is a positive combination of the elements of $\{[A_L]_{i,:}^T : [A_L]_{i,:} l_0 \geq c_A, i = 1, \dots, n_l\}$, whose cardinality is not less than n.

For any constant $c_A \in (0, 1)$, the existence of such A_L is guaranteed by Proposition A.14 in Appendix A.2.

Example 3.2 ***(Step 2 of Feasible-set Reshaping: Select a Constant Matrix That Positively Spans $\mathbb{R}^n$):*** *Continue Example 3.1. Given $c_A = 2\pi/n_l$ with $n_l = 7$, we define*

$$[A_L]_{k,:} = \left[\cos\frac{2\pi(k-1)}{n_l}, \sin\frac{2\pi(k-1)}{n_l}\right] \tag{3.27}$$

for $k = 1, \dots, n_l$. It can be checked that the resulting matrix A_L satisfies conditions (PB1), (PB2) and (PB3). Figure 3.5 illustrates the rows of A_L, which positively span $\mathbb{R}^2$.

3.3.3 Step 3: Project Each Constraint of the Original Feasible Set onto the Selected Matrix

The i-th constraint of the original feasible set $\mathcal{V}(p)$ defined in (3.15) is given by

$$\mathcal{V}_i(p) = \{v^* \in \mathbb{R}^n : [A(p)]_{i,:} v^* \leq [b(p)]_i\}. \tag{3.28}$$

For $i = 1, \dots, n$, we "project" the vector $[A(p)]_{i,:}^T [b(p) - A(p)\nu_s(p)]_i$, associated with the i-th constraint, onto the rows $[A_L]_{j,:}$ for $j = 1, \dots, n_l$ satisfying $[A_L]_{j,:}[A(p)]_{i,:}^T \geq c_A$, and perform a correction for Lipschitz continuity. In particular, the reshaped feasible set associated with the i-th constraint is given by

$$\mathcal{V}_{L,i}(p) = \{v^* \in \mathbb{R}^n : A_L(v^* - \nu_s(p)) \leq \psi([A(p)]_{i,:}, [b(p) - A(p)\nu_s(p)]_i)\}, \tag{3.29}$$

where $\psi : \mathbb{R}^{1\times n} \times \mathbb{R}_+ \to \mathbb{R}_+^{n_l}$ is chosen such that $\mathcal{V}_{L,i}(p) \subseteq \mathcal{V}_i(p)$ for all $p \in \mathcal{S}$. Specifically, one may choose

$$\psi(A, b) = b \max\{A_L A^T, c_A\} + k_\psi \max\{c_A - A_L A^T, 0\} \tag{3.30}$$

where k_ψ is a nonnegative constant.

From the definition of ψ in (3.30), it can be observed that

- for each such j, the j-th element of $\psi([A]_{i,:}, [b - A\nu_s]_i)$ equals $[b - A\nu_s]_i \cdot [A_L]_{j,:}[A]_{i,:}^T$, which represents the length of the projection of the vector $[A]_{i,:}^T[b - A\nu_s]_i$ onto the based vector corresponding to the j-th row of A_L;
- for $j' \neq j$, the j'-th element of $\psi([A]_{i,:}, [b - A\nu_s]_i)$ is given by $[b]_i c_A + k_\psi(c_A - [A_L]_{j',:}[A]_{i,:}^T)$, which increases as $[A_L]_{j',:}[A]_{i,:}^T$ decreases preventing the reshaped feasible set from becoming too small.

The "projection" process is illustrated in Example 3.3. Intuitively, for specific $[A]_{i,:}$ and $[b]_i$, with larger c_A and k_ψ, the reshaped constraint approximates the original constraint better.

Example 3.3 ***(Step 3 of Feasible-set Reshaping: Project Each Constraint of the Original Feasible Set onto the Selected Matrix)***: *Continue Example 3.2. We use the function ψ defined in (3.30) with $k_\psi = 1$ to reshape the original feasible set $\mathcal{V}(p)$ at $p = [-1; 0]$. The left subfigure of Figure 3.6 illustrates the "projection" process, while the right subfigure illustrates the "extension" that prevents the reshaped feasible set from becoming too small.*

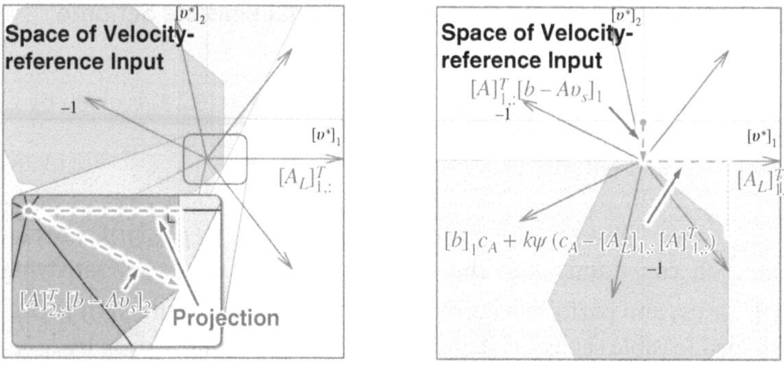

Figure 3.6 Step 3 of feasible-set reshaping: project each constraint of the original feasible set onto the selected matrix.

3.3.4 Step 4: Integrate the Projected and Corrected Constraints

All the projected and corrected constraints of the original feasible set are integrated by taking their intersection, resulting in the reshaped feasible set:

$$\mathcal{V}_L(p) = \{v^* \in \mathbb{R}^n : A_L(v^* - \nu_s(p)) \leq b_L(p)\}, \tag{3.31}$$

where $\nu_s : \mathcal{S} \to \mathbb{R}^n$ is defined in (3.19) and $b_L : \mathcal{S} \to \mathbb{R}^n_+$ is given by

$$[b_L(p)]_j = \min_{i \in \mathcal{N}_0} [\psi([A(p)]_{i,:}, [b(p) - A(p)\nu_s(p)]_i)]_j, \quad j = 1, \dots, n_l, \tag{3.32}$$

with $A(p)$ and $b(p)$ defined in (3.16).

Based on the reshaped feasible set, we construct a QP-based safety-critical controller as

$$v^* = \underset{v^* \in \mathcal{V}_L(p)}{\operatorname{argmin}} |v^* - v^c|^2. \tag{3.33}$$

For each fixed p, the QP (3.33) admits no more than n constraints that directly affect the optimal solution, as long as $\mathcal{V}_L(p) \neq \emptyset$. With A_L chosen to satisfy conditions (PB1), (PB2), and (PB3) in Section 3.3.2, the coefficient matrix of any n constraints of the reshaped feasible set is of full row rank. Thus, the coefficient matrix of the constraints that directly affect the optimal solution of the QP (3.33) is always full row rank. If the QP (3.33) is feasible on some domain of interest, then the map from p to v^* resulting from solving the QP admits local Lipschitz continuity [70, Theorem 3.1 and Equation (3.1)] (see also Theorem B.1 and the discussion in Section 1.3.3).

Example 3.4 ***(Step 4 of Feasible-Set Reshaping: Integrate the Projected and Corrected Constraints)***: *Continue Example 3.3. We can directly construct the*

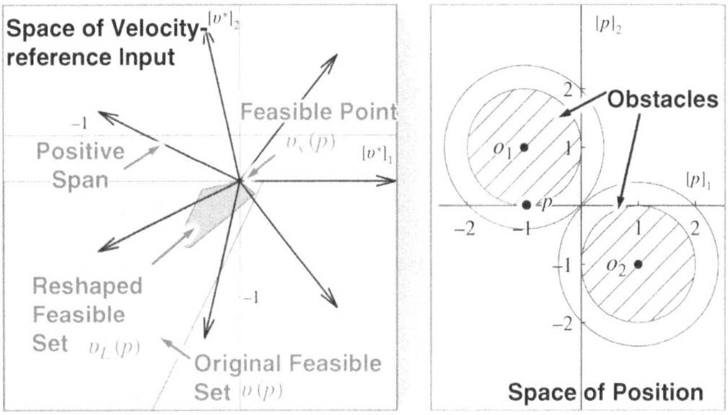

Figure 3.7 Step 4 of feasible-set reshaping: integrate the projected and corrected constraints.

reshaped feasible set $\mathcal{V}_L(p)$ as defined in (3.31). *Figure 3.7 illustrates the comparison of the original feasible set $\mathcal{V}(p)$ and the reshaped feasible set $\mathcal{V}_L(p)$ at $p = [-1; 0]$. It can be observed that the reshaped feasible set $\mathcal{V}_L(p)$ contains the feasible point $v_s(p)$ and is a subset of the original feasible set $\mathcal{V}(p)$.*

The following proposition shows that, for any $p \in \mathcal{S}$, the reshaped feasible set $\mathcal{V}_L(p)$ contains the point $v_s(p)$ for ensured feasibility and is a subset of the original feasible set $\mathcal{V}(p)$ for ensured safety.

Proposition 3.2 ***(Feasibility and Safety Retained by the Reshaped Feasible Set):*** Given an original feasible set $\mathcal{V}(p)$ defined in (3.15) and a function $v_s : \mathcal{S} \to \mathbb{R}^n$ satisfying

$$v_s(p) \in \mathcal{V}(p) \tag{3.34}$$

for all $p \in \mathcal{S}$, the reshaped feasible set $\mathcal{V}_L(p)$ defined in (3.31)–(3.32) satisfies

$$v_s(p) \in \mathcal{V}_L(p) \subseteq \mathcal{V}(p) \tag{3.35}$$

for all $p \in \mathcal{S}$.

Proof. Throughout the proof, the discussions are made for any $p \in \mathcal{S}$.

We first prove $v(p) \in \mathcal{V}_L(p)$. From the definition of $\mathcal{V}(p)$ in (3.15), with $v_s(p) \in \mathcal{V}(p)$, we have $b(p) - A(p)v_s(p) \geq 0$. Then, using the definitions of $b_L(p)$ and $\psi(A, b)$ in (3.32) and (3.30), respectively, we have $b_L(p) \geq 0$, which implies that $v^* = v_s(p)$ directly satisfies $A_L(v^* - v_s(p)) \leq b_L(p)$, and thus $v(p) \in \mathcal{V}_L(p)$ according to the definition of $\mathcal{V}_L(p)$ in (3.31).

We now prove $\mathcal{V}_L(p) \subseteq \mathcal{V}(p)$ by showing that any $v^* \in \mathcal{V}_L(p)$ also belongs to $\mathcal{V}(p)$. For this purpose, a convenient property is that each row of $A(p)$ defining

$\mathcal{V}(p)$ can be represented as a positive combination of certain rows of A_L defining $\mathcal{V}_L(p)$. In particular, for any $i \in \mathcal{N}_o$, with A_L satisfying condition (PB3) given in Section 3.3.2, the vector $[A(p)]_{i,:}^T$ is a positive combination of some n elements from the set $\{[A_L]_{j,:}^T : [A_L]_{j,:}[A(p)]_{i,:}^T \geq c_A, j = 1, \dots, n_l\}$, and can be written as

$$[A(p)]_{i,:} = k_{L,i}^T A_{L,i} \tag{3.36}$$

with constant $k_{L,i} \in \mathbb{R}_+^n$. Corresponding to these n elements, the n constraints in (3.31) are denoted by

$$A_{L,i}(\upsilon^* - \nu_s(p)) \leq b_{L,i}(p), \tag{3.37}$$

which is equivalent to

$$A_{L,i}\upsilon^* \leq A_{L,i}\nu_s(p)) + b_{L,i}(p). \tag{3.38}$$

Then, for any υ^* satisfying (3.37), it holds that

$$\begin{aligned} [A(p)]_{i,:}\upsilon^* &= k_{L,i}^T A_{L,i}\upsilon^* \\ &\leq k_{L,i}^T A_{L,i}\nu_s(p) + k_{L,i}^T b_{L,i}(p) \\ &\leq k_{L,i}^T A_{L,i}\nu_s(p) + k_{L,i}^T A_{L,i}[A(p)]_{i,:}^T([b(p)]_i - [A(p)]_{i,:}\nu_s(p)) \\ &= [b(p)]_i - [A(p)]_{i,:}\nu_s(p) + [A(p)]_{i,:}\nu_s(p) \\ &\leq [b(p)]_i, \end{aligned} \tag{3.39}$$

where we have used $A_{L,i}[A(p)]_{i,:}^T \geq c_A$ along with the definitions of $b_L(p)$ and $\psi(A, b)$ in (3.32) and (3.30), respectively, for the second inequality. Therefore, any $\upsilon^* \in \mathcal{V}_L(p)$ satisfies all the constraints defining $\mathcal{V}(p)$. This ends the proof of Proposition 3.2. □

By Proposition 3.2, for any $p \in \mathcal{S}$ and any $\upsilon^c \in \mathbb{R}^n$, the QP (3.33) with the feasible set defined in (3.31)–(3.32) admits a unique solution. Let $\phi : \mathcal{S} \times \mathbb{R}^n \to \mathbb{R}^n$ denote the map from (p, υ^c) to υ^* resulting from solving the QP (3.33). The following proposition presents properties on the boundedness and Lipschitz continuity of ϕ and the changing rate of the velocity-reference input υ^*.

Proposition 3.3 *(Properties of the QP-based Safety-Critical Controller with the Reshaped Feasible Set)*: Under Assumption 3.3, consider the kinematics model (3.13) and the QP-based safety-critical controller (3.33) with the feasible set defined in (3.31). The following properties hold:

a. **An Upper Bound of the Controller**: The function ϕ satisfies

$$|\phi(p, \upsilon^c)| \leq |\nu_s(p)| + |\upsilon^c|, \tag{3.40}$$

for all $p \in \mathcal{S}$ and all $\upsilon^c \in \mathbb{R}^n$, where ν_s is defined in (3.19).

b. Lipschitz Continuity of the Controller: The function $\phi(p, \upsilon^c)$ is Lipschitz continuous in (p, υ^c) on any compact subset of $\mathcal{S} \times \mathbb{R}^n$. Moreover, under Assumption 3.2, $\phi(p, \upsilon^c)$ is Lipschitz continuous in (p, υ^c) on $\mathcal{S} \times \{\upsilon^c \in \mathbb{R}^n : |\upsilon^c| \leq \bar{\upsilon}^c\}$.

c. Changing Rate of the Velocity-reference Input: Under Assumption 3.2, for any piecewise continuous $\tilde{\upsilon}$, there exist $\gamma_d \in \mathcal{K}$ and a constant $c_d \in \mathbb{R}_+$ such that

$$\|D^+\upsilon^*\|_t \leq \max\{\gamma_d(\|\bar{h}(p)\|_t), \gamma_d(\|\tilde{\upsilon}\|_t), c_d\} \tag{3.41}$$

holds on any time interval $[0, T)$ on which $p(t)$ is defined and satisfies $p(t) \in \text{Int}(\mathcal{S})$.

Proof. The properties are proved one-by-one.

(a) An upper bound of the controller: This property is proved by applying the projection theorem [21, Proposition B.11] to the QP (3.33). Specifically, as the solution of the QP (3.33), $\phi(p, \upsilon^c)$ satisfies

$$|\phi(p, 0)| \leq |\nu_s(p)| \tag{3.42a}$$
$$|\phi(p, \upsilon^c) - \phi(p, 0)| \leq |\upsilon^c| \tag{3.42b}$$

for all $p \in \mathcal{S}$ and $\upsilon^c \in \mathbb{R}^n$. In particular, (3.42a) is guaranteed by $(\nu_s(p) - \phi(p, 0))^T(0 - \phi(p, 0)) \leq 0$, which follows from [21, Property (b) of Proposition B.11] together with the fact that $\nu_s(p)$ satisfies the constraints of the QP (3.33) (ensured by Proposition 3.2); (3.42b) is guaranteed by [21, Property (c) of Proposition B.11].

From (3.42), using the triangle inequality [13, Theorem 3.3], we have

$$\begin{aligned} |\phi(p, \upsilon^c)| &= |\phi(p, 0) + \phi(p, \upsilon^c) - \phi(p, 0)| \\ &\leq |\phi(p, 0)| + |\phi(p, \upsilon^c) - \phi(p, 0)| \\ &\leq |\nu_s(p)| + |\upsilon^c| \end{aligned} \tag{3.43}$$

for all $p \in \mathcal{S}$ and $\upsilon^c \in \mathbb{R}^n$.

(b) Lipschitz continuity of the controller: We prove the Lipschitz continuity of the controller (3.33) by using [70, Theorem 3.1] (also see Theorem B.1 in the appendix).

We first consider the following QP:

$$\upsilon^{*\prime} = \underset{\upsilon^* \in \mathbb{R}^n}{\text{argmin}} |\upsilon^* - \upsilon^{c\prime}(p, \upsilon^c)|^2, \tag{3.44a}$$
$$\text{s.t. } A_L \upsilon^* \leq b_L(p) \tag{3.44b}$$

for $p \in \mathcal{S}$ and $\upsilon^c \in \mathbb{R}^n$, where $\upsilon^{c\prime}(p, \upsilon^c) = \upsilon^c - \nu_s(p)$. It can be verified that 0 always satisfies (3.44b) as $b_L(p) \geq 0$ for all $p \in \mathcal{S}$, according to the definitions of b_L in (3.32) and ψ in (3.30). By comparing the QPs (3.33) and (3.44), we have

$$\phi(p, \upsilon^c) = \nu_s(p) + \phi'(p, \upsilon^c), \tag{3.45}$$

where ϕ' is the map from (p, υ^c) to $\upsilon^{*\prime}$ resulting from solving the QP (3.44).

We verify the satisfaction of the conditions required by Theorem B.1. For any $p \in \mathcal{S}$ and $\upsilon^c \in \mathbb{R}^n$, let $\breve{A}_L \upsilon^* \leq \breve{b}_L(p)$ represent the constraints that directly affect the optimal solution of the QP (3.44) at the optimal solution υ^*. It can be directly checked that the values of $\upsilon^{c\prime}(p, \upsilon^c)$, A_L and $b_L(p)$ are elements of $\mathbb{R}^n$, $\{A_L\}$ and $\mathbb{R}^{n_l}_+$, respectively, for all $p \in \mathcal{S}$ and $\upsilon^c \in \mathbb{R}^n$. Then, it can be verified that:

- The sets $\mathbb{R}^n$, $\{A_L\}$ and $\mathbb{R}^{n_l}_+$ are convex.
- For each $p \in \mathcal{S}$, by the projection theorem [21, Property (a) of Proposition B.11] and the fact that 0 always satisfies the constraints in (3.44b), the QP (3.44) is feasible and admits a unique solution.
- Property (PB1) of A_L, given below (3.31), guarantees the boundedness of $|\breve{A}_L|$.
- Property (PB2) of A_L, given below (3.31), guarantees the existence of a constant $c_{A_L} > 0$ satisfying $\lambda^{1/2}_{\min}(\breve{A}_L \breve{A}_L^T) \geq c_{A_L}$ and thus $|\breve{A}_L^T \xi| \geq c_{A_L} |\xi|$ for all ξ.

Applying Theorem B.1, we can prove the existence of a constant $L_{\phi'} > 0$, depending on A_L, such that

$$\begin{aligned} |\phi'(p_1, \upsilon^c_1) - \phi'(p_2, \upsilon^c_2)| &\leq L_{\phi'}(|\upsilon^{c\prime}(p_1, \upsilon^c_1) - \upsilon^{c\prime}(p_2, \upsilon^c_2)| + |b_L(p_1) - b_L(p_2)|) \\ &\leq L_{\phi'}(|\nu_s(p_1) - \nu_s(p_2)| + |\upsilon^c_1 - \upsilon^c_2| + |b_L(p_1) - b_L(p_2)|) \end{aligned} \tag{3.46}$$

for all $p_1, p_2 \in \mathcal{S}$ and all $\upsilon^c_1, \upsilon^c_2 \in \mathbb{R}^n$. Then, the relationship between $\phi(p, \upsilon^c)$ and $\phi'(p, \upsilon^c)$ given in (3.45) ensures that

$$\begin{aligned} |\phi(p_1, \upsilon^c_1) - \phi(p_2, \upsilon^c_2)| \leq{}& (L_{\phi'} + 1)|\nu_s(p_1) - \nu_s(p_2)| \\ &+ L_{\phi'}(|\upsilon^c_1 - \upsilon^c_2| + |b_L(p_1) - b_L(p_2)|). \end{aligned} \tag{3.47}$$

Inequality (3.47), together with the closedness of $\mathcal{S}$ and the local Lipschitz continuity of ν_s and b_L (as ensured by their definitions in (3.19) and (3.32), respectively), ensures that ϕ is Lipschitz continuous in p and υ^c on any compact subset of $\mathcal{S} \times \mathbb{R}^n$.

Based on (3.47), we show that $\phi(p, \upsilon^c)$ is Lipschitz continuous in (p, υ^c) on $\mathcal{S} \times \{\upsilon^c \in \mathbb{R}^n : |\upsilon^c| \leq \bar{\upsilon}^c\}$.

Denote

$$\mathcal{P} = \{p \in \mathcal{S} : c_A[b(p)]_i \leq \bar{\upsilon}^c, \exists i \in \mathcal{N}_o\}, \tag{3.48}$$

and consider the following two cases: $p \in \mathcal{S} \setminus \mathcal{P}$ and $p \in \mathcal{P}$.

In the case of $p \in \mathcal{S} \setminus \mathcal{P}$, we have $b(p) \geq \bar{v}^c$ by using the definition of $\mathcal{P}$ in (3.48). This, together with the definition of $\nu_s(p)$ in (3.19), implies that $\nu_s(p) = 0$. Thus, we have

$$\begin{aligned}
[b_L(p)]_j &= \min_{i \in \mathcal{N}_o} [\psi([A(p)]_{i,:}, [b(p) - A(p)\nu_s(p)]_i)]_j \\
&= \min_{i \in \mathcal{N}_o} [\psi([A(p)]_{i,:}, [b(p)]_i)]_j \\
&= \min_{i \in \mathcal{N}_o} \Big[[b(p)]_i \max\{A_L [A(p)]_{i,:}^T, c_A\} \\
&\quad + k_\psi \max\{c_A - A_L [A(p)]_{i,:}^T, 0\}\Big]_j \\
&\geq \min_{i \in \mathcal{N}_o} c_A [b(p)]_i \\
&> \bar{v}^c
\end{aligned} \tag{3.49}$$

for all $j = 1, \dots, n_l$, where we have used the definition of $b_L(p)$ in (3.32) for the first equality, used $\nu_s(p) = 0$ for the second equality, used the definition of ψ in (3.30) for the third equality, used $c_A > 0$, $k_\psi \geq 0$ as well as $[b(p)]_i > 0$ ensured by $p \in \mathcal{S} \setminus \mathcal{P}$ for the first inequality, and used $c_A[b(p)]_i > \bar{v}^c$ for all $i \in \mathcal{N}_o$ ensured by $p \in \mathcal{S} \setminus \mathcal{P}$ for the last inequality. Property (3.49) implies that v^c is a feasible point of the QP (3.33), and thus $\phi(p, v^c) = v^c$ for $p \in \mathcal{S} \setminus \mathcal{P}$ and $v^c \in \{v^c \in \mathbb{R}^n : |v^c| \leq \bar{v}^c\}$.

In the case of $p \in \mathcal{P}$, based on the definitions of $\nu_s(p)$ and $b_L(p)$ in (3.19) and (3.32), respectively, we rewrite $\nu_s(p)$ and $b_L(p)$ as

$$\nu_s(p) = f_{\nu_s} \circ f_{Ab}(p), \qquad b_L(p) = f_{b_L} \circ f_{Ab}(p), \tag{3.50}$$

where $f_{\nu_s} : \mathcal{X}_{Ab} \to \mathbb{R}^n$, $f_{b_L} : \mathcal{X}_{Ab} \to \mathbb{R}^{n_l}$, and $f_{Ab} : \mathcal{P} \to \mathcal{X}_{Ab}$ are defined by

$$f_{\nu_s}([A, b]) = \sum_{i \in \mathcal{N}_o} [A]_{i,:}^T \min\{[b]_i, 0\}, \tag{3.51a}$$

$$\begin{aligned}
[f_{b_L}([A, b])]_j = \min_{i \in \mathcal{N}_o} \{&[b - A f_{\nu_s}([A, b])]_i \max\{[A_L]_{j,:}[A]_{i,:}^T, c_A\} \\
&+ k_\psi \max\{c_A - [A_L]_{j,:}[A]_{i,:}^T, 0\}\},
\end{aligned} \tag{3.51b}$$

$$f_{Ab}(p) = [A(p), b(p)], \tag{3.51c}$$

with $A(p)$ and $b(p)$ defined in (3.16), and

$$\mathcal{X}_{Ab} = \left\{ [A, b] \in \mathbb{R}^{n_o \times (n+1)} : \begin{array}{l} |[A]_{i,:}| = 1, \ i \in \mathcal{N}_o, \\ b \geq -\alpha_h(\mu(D) - \mu(D_s)), \\ b \leq \min\{-\alpha_h(-\mu(D_s)), c_A^{-1}\bar{v}^c\} \end{array} \right\}. \tag{3.52}$$

It can be easily verified that $\mathcal{X}_{Ab}$ is compact and $[A(p), b(p)] \in \mathcal{X}_{Ab}$ for all $p \in \mathcal{S}$.

We now establish the Lipschitz continuity of the functions f_{ν_s}, f_{b_L} and f_{Ab} as follows:

- By standard results for algebraic operations with Lipschitz functions [38] and the fact that $\mathcal{X}_{Ab}$ is a compact set, $f_{\nu_s}([A, b])$ and $f_{b_L}([A, b])$ are Lipschitz continuous in $[A, b]$ on $\mathcal{X}_{Ab}$.
- We establish the Lipschitz continuity of $f_{Ab}(p)$ with respect to p on $\mathcal{P}$ by analyzing the Lipschitz continuity of $A(p)$ and $b(p)$ separately.
  - Recall the definition of $A(p)$ in (3.16a). One can verify that $[A(p)]_{i,:}^T$ for $i \in \mathcal{N}_o$ is Lipschitz in p on $\mathcal{P}$ as

$$\left| \frac{\partial \frac{p-o_i}{|p-o_i|}}{\partial p} \right| = \left| \frac{1}{|p-o_i|} \left(I - \frac{(p-o_i)(p-o_i)^T}{|p-o_i|^2} \right) \right| \leq \frac{1}{|p-o_i|} \leq \frac{1}{D} \quad (3.53)$$

    for all $p \in \mathcal{S}$. Thus, $A(p)$ is Lipschitz continuous in p on $\mathcal{P}$.
  - Recall the definition of $b(p)$ in (3.16b). We show that $b(p)$ is Lipschitz continuous in p on $\mathcal{P}$ by considering that: $|p - o_i|$ for $i \in \mathcal{N}_o$ are greater than D and are Lipschitz continuous in p on $\mathcal{P}$; $\mu(s)$ is Lipschitz on $[\mu(D), \infty)$ as $\mu \in \mathcal{M}^-\mathcal{C}$, with its convexity and strict monotonicity ensuring $d\mu(s)/ds$ is increasing and bounded on $[D, \infty)$, and $\mu(|p - o_i|) \in (0, \mu(D)]$ for all $p \in \mathcal{P}, i \in \mathcal{N}_o$; $-\alpha_h(s - \mu(D_s))$ is Lipschitz in s on $[0, \mu(D)]$ due to the continuous differentiability of α_h as clarified below (3.16).

Based on the above analysis, the functions $f_{\nu_s} \circ f_{Ab}(p)$ and $f_{b_L} \circ f_{Ab}(p)$ are Lipschitz in p on $\mathcal{P}$ and consequently $\nu_s(p)$ and $b_L(p)$ are Lipschitz continuous in p on $\mathcal{P}$. Together with Eq. (3.47), this ensures the existence of a positive constant L_ϕ such that

$$|\phi(p_1, v_1^c) - \phi(p_2, v_2^c)| \leq L_\phi \max\{|p_1 - p_2|, |v_1^c - v_2^c|\}, \quad (3.54)$$

for $p_1, p_2 \in \mathcal{S}$ and $v_1, v_2 \in \{v^c \in \mathbb{R}^n : |v^c| \leq \bar{v}^c\}$.

(c) Changing rate of the velocity-reference input: We prove the validity of (3.41) by combining the Lipschitz property of $\phi(p, v^c)$ with (3.11) and (3.47).

On any time interval $[0, T)$ on which $p(t)$ is defined and satisfies $p(t) \in \text{Int}(\mathcal{S})$, Proposition 3.2 ensures that $v^*(t)$ is defined. Thus, for any $t \in [0, T)$, $D^+v^*(\tau)$ is defined for all $\tau \in [0, t)$. Then, by using properties of the essential supremum and the Lipschitz norm, we have

$$||D^+v^*||_t = \text{ess} \sup_{\tau \in [0,t)} |D^+v^*(\tau)| \leq \sup_{\tau \in [0,t)} |D^+v^*(\tau)| \leq \sqrt{n} L_{[0,t)}(v^*), \quad (3.55)$$

where $L_{[0,t)}(v^*)$ represents the Lipschitz norm of v^* on $[0, t)$:

$$L_{[0,t)}(v^*) = \sup_{\tau,\tau' \in [0,t),\ \tau \neq \tau'} \frac{|v^*(\tau) - v^*(\tau')|}{|\tau - \tau'|}, \quad (3.56)$$

with v^* considered as a signal of time. The validity of the last inequality in (3.55) is guaranteed by Proposition A.25.

We then estimate an upper bound of $L_{[0,t)}(v^*)$. By $v^*(t) = \phi(p(t), v^c(t))$ for $t \in [0, T)$ and (3.54), we have

$$|v^*(\tau) - v^*(\tau')| \le L_\phi \max\{|p(\tau) - p(\tau')|, |v^c(\tau) - v^c(\tau')|\} \tag{3.57}$$

for any $\tau, \tau \in [0, T)$. Substituting (3.57) into (3.55), we obtain

$$\begin{aligned}
\|D^+ v^*\|_t &\le \sqrt{n} \sup_{\tau,\tau' \in [0,t), \tau \neq \tau'} \frac{|v(\tau) - v(\tau')|}{|\tau - \tau'|} \\
&\le \sqrt{n} \sup_{\tau,\tau' \in [0,t), \tau \neq \tau'} L_\phi \max\left\{\frac{|p(\tau) - p(\tau')|}{|\tau - \tau'|}, \frac{|v^c(\tau) - v^c(\tau')|}{|\tau - \tau'|}\right\} \\
&\le \sqrt{n} L_\phi \max\left\{\sup_{\tau \in [0,t)} |\dot{p}(\tau)|, \bar{v}^{cd}\right\} \\
&\le \sqrt{n} L_\phi \max\{\|\tilde{v}\|_t + \bar{v}^c + \max\{\alpha_h(\|\bar{h}(p)\|_t - \mu(D_s)), 0\}, \bar{v}^{cd}\} \\
&\le \sqrt{n} L_\phi \max\{2\|\tilde{v}\|_t + 2\max\{\alpha_h(\|\tilde{v}\|_t - \mu(D_s)), 0\}, \\
&\quad 2\|\bar{h}(p)\|_t + 2\max\{\alpha_h(\|\bar{h}(p)\|_t - \mu(D_s))), 0\}, 2\bar{v}^c, \bar{v}^{cd}\},
\end{aligned} \tag{3.58}$$

where we have used (3.11) for the third inequality, and used

$$\begin{aligned}
\sup_{\tau \in [0,t)} |\dot{p}(\tau)| &= \|\tilde{v} + v^*\|_t \\
&\le \|\tilde{v}\|_t + \|v^c\|_t + \|\nu_s(p)\|_t \\
&\le \|\tilde{v}\|_t + \bar{v}^c + \max\{\alpha_h(\|\bar{h}(p)\|_t - \mu(D_s)), 0\}.
\end{aligned} \tag{3.59}$$

for the fourth inequality, and used $\alpha_h \in \mathcal{K}^e$ for the last inequality. For inequality (3.59), we have used (3.1) and (3.8) for the first equality, used the triangle inequality [13, Theorem 3.3] and inequality (3.40) for the first inequality, and used (3.11) together with $|\nu_s(p)| \le \max\{\alpha_h(\bar{h}(p) - \mu(D_s)), 0\}$ for $p \in \mathcal{S}$ (which follows from the definition of (3.11) and the fact that at least one element of $b(p)$ is negative, as shown in the proof of Proposition 3.1) for the last inequality.

Based on (3.58), property (3.41) can be proved by choosing

$$\gamma_d(s) = 2\sqrt{n} L_\phi (s + \max\{\alpha_h(s - \mu(D_s)), 0\}), \qquad c_d = \sqrt{n} L_\phi \max\{2\bar{v}^c, \bar{v}^{cd}\}. \tag{3.60}$$

This completes the proof of Proposition 3.3. □

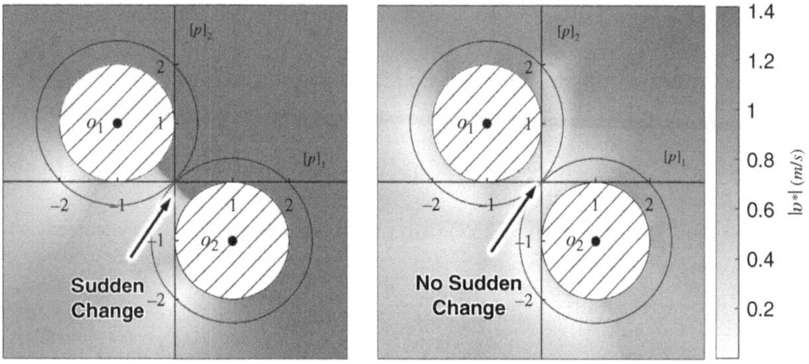

Figure 3.8 Lipschitz continuity of QP solutions ensured by feasible-set reshaping.

In the following example, we examine the proposed QP-based safety-critical controller (3.33) with the feasible set defined in (3.31) in the same scenario as in Section 1.5.

Example 3.5 *(Comparison of the Original and Reshaped Feasible Sets)*: *For the QP with the original feasible set defined in* (3.14)–(3.16), *we consider* $D = 1.0$, $D_s = \sqrt{2}/1.01$, $v^c = [1; 1]$, $o_1 = [-1; 1]$, $o_2 = [1; -1]$, $\mu(s) = 1/s$, *and*

$$\alpha_h(s) = \begin{cases} s, & s \geq 0, \\ 2s, & s < 0. \end{cases} \tag{3.61}$$

Denote $k_\psi = 1$, $n_l = 5$ *and* $c_A = \cos(2\pi/n_l)$. *Then, we construct the constant matrix* A_L *as*

$$[A_L]_{j,:} = \left[\cos\frac{2\pi j}{n_l}, \sin\frac{2\pi j}{n_l}\right], j = 1, \ldots, n_l, \tag{3.62a}$$

$$c_A = \cos\frac{2\pi}{n_l}, \tag{3.62b}$$

with $n_l = 5$ *for the QP* (3.33) *with the reshaped feasible set* (3.31).

Figure 3.8 illustrates the influence of p *on* $|v^*|$. *It can be observed that, for the QP with the original feasible set, the solution changes abruptly as* p *crosses zero, whereas for the reshaped feasible set, the solution varies continuously around* $p = 0$.

3.4 Interaction Between Velocity Tracking and Safety

Within the closed-loop system composed of the mobile agent (3.1)–(3.2) and the QP-based safety-critical controller (3.33) constructed based on the reshaped feasible set (3.31), we analyze how the velocity-tracking error $\tilde{v}$ and the value of the safety indicator function $\bar{h}(p)$ affect each other. The properties are given by Propositions 3.4 and 3.5.

Proposition 3.4 ***(The Influence of $\tilde{v}$ on $h(\tilde{p}_i)$ for $i \in \mathcal{N}_o$):*** Consider the kinematics model (3.13) and QP-based safety-critical controller (3.33) with the feasible set defined in (3.31). Under Assumptions 3.2 and 3.3, given any $\gamma_1 \in \mathcal{K}_\infty$, any constants $c_0 \in \mathbb{R}_+$ and $c_1 \in (\mu(D_s), \mu(D))$, select $\alpha_h \in \mathcal{K}^e$ whose domain includes $[-\mu(D_s), \infty)$ such that it satisfies condition (3.18) and is of the form

$$\alpha_h(s) = (1 + c_0)\gamma_1^{-1}\left(\frac{c_1}{c_1 - \mu(D_s)}s\right), \quad \forall s \geq 0. \tag{3.63}$$

Then, there exists $\beta_1 \in \mathcal{KL}$ such that for each $i \in \mathcal{N}_o$, any $p(0) \in \text{Int}(\mathcal{S})$, and any locally Lipschitz $\tilde{v}$ satisfying $\gamma_1(\|\tilde{v}\|_\infty) < \mu(D)$,

$$h(\tilde{p}_i(t)) \leq \max\{\beta_1(h(\tilde{p}_i(0)), t), \gamma_1(\|\tilde{v}\|_t), c_1\}, \tag{3.64}$$

holds over any interval $[0, T)$ on which $p(t)$ is defined.

Proof. The basic idea of the proof of this proposition is similar to that of Proposition 2.2. We highlight the new issues caused by multiple constraints.

We first establish the existence of the solution of the closed-loop p-system composed of (3.13) and (3.33):

$$\dot{p} = \phi(p, v^c) + \tilde{v}, \tag{3.65}$$

where $\phi(p, v^c)$ denotes the map from (p, v^c) to v^* resulting from solving the QP (3.33). With the satisfaction of Assumption 3.3 and condition (3.18), using Propositions 3.1 and 3.2, we can verify that ϕ is defined for all $p \in \mathcal{S}$ and $v^c \in \mathbb{R}^n$. Moreover, by Proposition 3.3, $\phi : \mathcal{S} \times \mathbb{R}^n \to \mathbb{R}^n$ is locally Lipschitz with respect to p and v^c on any compact subset of $\mathcal{S} \times \mathbb{R}^n$. This, together with Assumption 3.2, ensures that, for any locally Lipschitz $\tilde{v}$, $\phi(p, v^c(t)) + \tilde{v}(t)$ is defined for all $p \in \mathcal{S}$ and all $t \geq 0$, and is locally Lipschitz continuous with respect to p and t. Thus, by [98, Theorem 3.1], for any $p(0) \in \text{Int}(\mathcal{S})$, and any locally Lipschitz $\tilde{v}$, there exists $\tau > 0$ such that $p(t)$ is defined for all $t \in [0, \tau)$.

We now prove the existence of $\beta_1 \in \mathcal{KL}$. To this end, using $v^* \in \mathcal{V}_L(p) \subseteq \mathcal{V}(p)$ (ensured by (3.35) in Proposition 3.2) and the definition of $\mathcal{V}(p)$ in (3.15), we have

$$-\frac{\tilde{p}_i^T}{|\tilde{p}_i|}v^* \leq -\alpha_h(h(\tilde{p}_i) - \mu(D_s)), \qquad i \in \mathcal{N}_o \tag{3.66}$$

for all $p \in \mathcal{S}$. Consequently, we have

$$\begin{aligned} \nabla h(\tilde{p}_i)\dot{\tilde{p}}_i &= \frac{\mathrm{d}\mu(|\tilde{p}_i|)}{\mathrm{d}|\tilde{p}_i|}\frac{\tilde{p}_i^T}{|\tilde{p}_i|}(v^* + \tilde{v}) \\ &\le \frac{\mathrm{d}\mu(|\tilde{p}_i|)}{\mathrm{d}|\tilde{p}_i|}(\alpha_h(h(\tilde{p}_i) - \mu(D_s))) + \frac{\mathrm{d}\mu(|\tilde{p}_i|)}{\mathrm{d}|\tilde{p}_i|}\frac{\tilde{p}_i^T}{|\tilde{p}_i|}\tilde{v}, \\ &\le \frac{\mathrm{d}\mu(|\tilde{p}_i|)}{\mathrm{d}|\tilde{p}_i|}(\alpha_h(h(\tilde{p}_i) - \mu(D_s)) - |\tilde{v}|) \\ &= \alpha_\mu(h(\tilde{p}_i))(-\alpha_h(h(\tilde{p}_i) - \mu(D_s)) + |\tilde{v}|), \end{aligned} \tag{3.67}$$

where

$$\alpha_\mu(s) = \begin{cases} -\dfrac{\mathrm{d}\mu(\mu^{-1}(s))}{\mathrm{d}\mu^{-1}(s)}, & \text{for } s > 0, \\ 0, & \text{for } s = 0. \end{cases} \tag{3.68}$$

Given any $\gamma_1 \in \mathcal{K}_\infty$ and any $c_1 \in (\mu(D_s), \mu(D))$, with α_h chosen to satisfy (3.63), we consider the case of $h(\tilde{p}) \ge \max\{\gamma_1(|\tilde{v}|, c_1)\}$. In this case, the derivation based on (3.67) yields

$$\begin{aligned} \nabla h(\tilde{p}_i)\dot{\tilde{p}}_i &\le \alpha_\mu(h(\tilde{p}_i))\left(-\alpha_h\left(h(\tilde{p}_i) - \frac{h(\tilde{p}_i)}{c_1}\mu(D_s)\right) + |\tilde{v}|\right) \\ &= \alpha_\mu(h(\tilde{p}_i))\left(-\alpha_h\left(\frac{c_1 - \mu(D_s)}{c_1}h(\tilde{p}_i)\right) + |\tilde{v}|\right) \\ &= \alpha_\mu(h(\tilde{p}_i))\left(-(1 + c_0)\gamma_1^{-1}\left(\frac{c_1}{c_1 - \mu(D_s)}\frac{c_1 - \mu(D_s)}{c_1}h(\tilde{p}_i)\right) + |\tilde{v}|\right) \\ &= \alpha_\mu(h(\tilde{p}_i))(-c_0\gamma_1^{-1}(h(\tilde{p}_i)) - \gamma_1^{-1}(h(\tilde{p}_i)) + |\tilde{v}|) \\ &\le \alpha_\mu(h(\tilde{p}_i))(-c_0\gamma_1^{-1}(h(\tilde{p}_i)) - \gamma_1^{-1}(\gamma_1(|\tilde{v}|)) + |\tilde{v}|) \\ &= -c_0\alpha_\mu(h(\tilde{p}_i))\gamma_1^{-1}(h(\tilde{p}_i)) \\ &= -\tilde{\alpha}(h(\tilde{p}_i)), \end{aligned} \tag{3.69}$$

where

$$\tilde{\alpha}(s) = c_0\alpha_\mu(s)\gamma_1^{-1}(s) \tag{3.70}$$

for $s \ge 0$. Clearly, $\tilde{\alpha}$ is a positive definite function as $\gamma_1 \in \mathcal{K}_\infty$ and α_μ are positive definite. For the derivations of (3.69), we have used the properties that α_μ is positive definite (as established in the proof of Property 2.1 of Proposition 2.1), $\alpha_h \in \mathcal{K}^e$ and $h(\tilde{p}_i) \ge c_1$ for the first inequality, used the definition of α_h in (3.63) for the second equality, used $h(\tilde{p}_i) \ge \gamma_1(|\tilde{v}|)$ for the second inequality, and used (3.70) for the last equality. Thus, along the trajectories of the closed-loop p-system (3.65), we have

$$h(\tilde{p}_i) \geq \max\{\gamma_1(|\tilde{v}|), c_1\} \Rightarrow \nabla h(\tilde{p}_i)\dot{\tilde{p}}_i \leq -\tilde{\alpha}(h(\tilde{p}_i)) \tag{3.71}$$

for all $i \in \mathcal{N}_o$.

Then, following the standard argument for ISS-Lyapunov functions [184, 188], we can prove the existence of $\beta_1 \in \mathcal{KL}$ for the validity of the property given in (3.64). This ends the proof of Proposition 3.4. □

According to Propositions 3.1 and 3.4, the function α_h used to define the safety constraints is required to satisfy conditions (3.18) and (3.63) simultaneously. To fulfill this requirement, one may first determine the value of $\alpha_h(s)$ for $s \geq 0$ to satisfy condition (3.63). Then, to satisfy condition (3.18), one chooses

$$\alpha_h(s) \leq -\alpha_h(\mu(2D_o - \mu^{-1}(s + \mu(D_s))) - \mu(D_s)) \tag{3.72}$$

for $s \in [\mu(2D_o - D) - \mu(D_s), \mu(2D_o - D_s) - \mu(D_s)]$. Finally, one may arbitrarily choose the value of $\alpha_h(s)$ for $s < \mu(2D_o - D) - \mu(D_s)$ as long as α_h is ensured to be strictly increasing.

Proposition 3.5 ***(The Influence of $\bar{h}(p)$ on $\tilde{v}$)*****:** Under Assumptions 3.1–3.3, consider the mobile agent modeled by (3.1)–(3.2), the velocity-reference input v^* generated by the QP (3.33), as well as the velocity-tracking error $\tilde{v}$ defined in (3.8). For any $z(0) \in \mathbb{R}^m$ and any p which is locally Lipschitz continuous on the timeline and satisfies that $p(t) \in \mathrm{Int}(\mathcal{S})$ for all $t \geq 0$, the inequality

$$|\tilde{v}(t)| \leq \max\{\beta_2(|z(0)| + \bar{h}(p(0)) + \tilde{v}^c, t), \gamma_2(\|\tilde{v}\|_t), \gamma_2(\|\bar{h}(p)\|_t), c_2\} \tag{3.73}$$

holds over any time interval $[0, T)$ on which $\tilde{v}(t)$ is defined, where $\beta_2 \in \mathcal{KL}, \gamma_2 \in \mathcal{K}$ and constant $c_2 \geq 0$ are given by

$$\beta_2(s, t) = \beta_{\tilde{v}}(s + \max\{\alpha_h(s - \mu(D_s)), 0\}, t), \tag{3.74a}$$

$$\gamma_2(s) = \gamma_{\tilde{v}} \circ \gamma_d(s), \tag{3.74b}$$

$$c_2 = \gamma_{\tilde{v}}(c_d), \tag{3.74c}$$

with γ_d and c_d defined in Proposition 3.3.

Proof. To prove property (3.73), we combine (3.40) and (3.41) in Proposition 3.3 with (3.9) in Assumption 3.1.

Under Assumption 3.3, with $p(t) \in \text{Int}(\mathcal{S})$ for all $t \geq 0$, $\phi(p(t), v^c(t))$ is defined for all $t \geq 0$, according to Propositions 3.1 and 3.2. Thus, we have

$$\begin{aligned}
|v^*(t)| &= |\phi(p(t), v^c(t))| \\
&\leq |v^c(t)| + |\nu_s(p(t))| \\
&= |v^c(t)| + \left| \sum_{i \in \mathcal{N}_o} [A(p)]_{i,:}^{\mathsf{T}} \min\{[b(p)]_i, 0\} \right| \\
&\leq |v^c(t)| + \max\{-\min_{i \in \mathcal{N}_o} [b(p)]_i, 0\} \\
&\leq |v^c(t)| + \max\{\alpha_h(\bar{h}(p(t)) - \mu(D_s)), 0\} \\
&\leq \bar{v}^c + \max\{\alpha_h(\bar{h}(p(t)) - \mu(D_s)), 0\}
\end{aligned} \tag{3.75}$$

for all $t \geq 0$, where we have used property (3.40) for the first inequality, used the definition of $\nu_s(p)$ in (3.19) for the second equality, used the fact that at most one of $[b(p)]_i$ for $i \in \mathcal{N}_o$ is negative (see the proof of Proposition 3.1) for the second inequality, used the definition of $b(p)$ in (3.16b), $\bar{h}$ in (3.6), and $\alpha_h \in \mathcal{K}^e$ for the third inequality, and used condition (3.11) in Assumption 3.2 for the last inequality.

Substituting (3.41) into (3.9) (note that (3.41) is valid under Assumptions 3.2 and 3.3, and under the condition that $p(t)$ is well-defined and satisfies $p(t) \in \text{Int}(\mathcal{S})$ for all $t \geq 0$) and substituting (3.75) into (3.9) in Assumption 3.1, we have that for any $z(0) \in \mathbb{R}^m$ and any p which is locally Lipschitz continuous on the time line and satisfies $p(t) \in \text{Int}(\mathcal{S})$ for all $t \geq 0$,

$$\begin{aligned}
|\tilde{v}(t)| &\leq \max\{\beta_{\tilde{v}}(|z(0)| + |v^*(0)|, t), \gamma_{\tilde{v}}(\|D^+v^*\|_t)\} \\
&\leq \max\{\beta_{\tilde{v}}(|z(0)| + |v^*(0)|, t), \gamma_{\tilde{v}} \circ \gamma_d(\|\tilde{v}\|_t), \gamma_{\tilde{v}} \circ \gamma_d(\|\bar{h}(p)\|_t), \gamma_{\tilde{v}}(c_d)\} \\
&\leq \max\{\beta_{\tilde{v}}(|z(0)| + \bar{v}^c + \max\{\alpha_h(\bar{h}(p(0)) - \mu(D_s)), 0\}, t), \\
&\qquad \gamma_{\tilde{v}} \circ \gamma_d(\|\tilde{v}\|_t), \gamma_{\tilde{v}} \circ \gamma_d(\|\bar{h}(p)\|_t), \gamma_{\tilde{v}}(c_d)\} \\
&\leq \max\{\beta_2(|z(0)| + \bar{h}(p(0)) + \bar{v}^c, t), \gamma_{\tilde{v}} \circ \gamma_d(\|\tilde{v}\|_t), \gamma_{\tilde{v}} \circ \gamma_d(\|\bar{h}(p)\|_t), \gamma_{\tilde{v}}(c_d)\}
\end{aligned} \tag{3.76}$$

holds over any time interval $[0, T)$ on which $\tilde{v}(t)$ is defined. Note that we have used the definition of β_2 in (3.74) and $\beta_{\tilde{v}} \in \mathcal{KL}$ for the last inequality in (3.76).

This ends the proof of Proposition 2.3. □

Propositions 3.4 and 3.5 naturally give rise to two interacting subsystems, with the interconnection between their outputs, $\tilde{v}$ and $\bar{h}(p)$, characterized by gain functions (see Figure 3.9). Furthermore, there is also a self-loop from $\tilde{v}$ to itself (see property (3.73)).

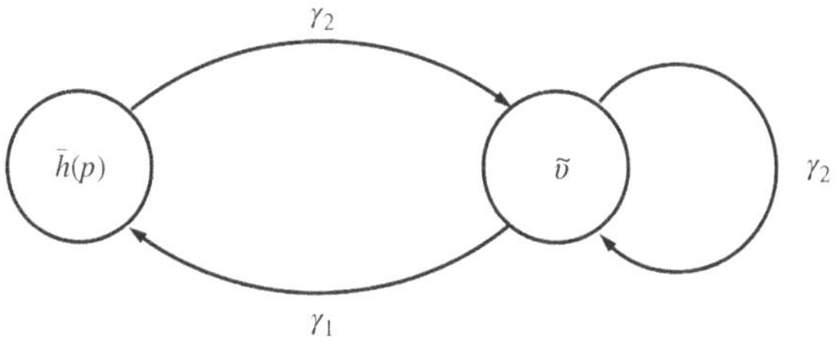

Figure 3.9 Gain interconnection between $\bar{h}(p)$ and $\tilde{v}$.

3.5 Small-gain Synthesis for Safety of the Closed-loop System

Motivated by the discussion in Chapter 2, we perform a nonlinear small-gain analysis to ensure the safety of the closed-loop system when multiple obstacles should be handled.

With the interconnection characterized by gain functions, following an approach similar to the small-gain method developed in Chapter 2, we propose the following small-gain-type condition to ensure safety:

$$\gamma_1 \circ \gamma_2(s) < s, \quad \gamma_2 \circ \gamma_1(s) < s, \quad \gamma_2(s) < s \tag{3.77}$$

for all $s \in [0, \bar{s}]$, where

$$\bar{s} = \frac{D + D_s}{2}. \tag{3.78}$$

We present the main result of this chapter in Theorem 3.1, which is established based on a nontrivial refinement of the techniques used in the proof of the nonlinear small-gain theorem [92].

Theorem 3.1 *(Small-gain-ensured Safety)*: *Under Assumptions 3.1, 3.2, and 3.3, consider the mobile agent described by* (3.1)–(3.2) *and the controller given in* (3.31)–(3.33). *For any desired safe distance $D > 0$, any $D_o > D$, any additional safety margin $D_s \in (D, D_o)$, any $\mu \in \mathcal{M}^{-}\mathcal{C}$ and any $\alpha_h \in \mathcal{K}^e$ whose domain includes $[-\mu(D_s), \infty)$ such that it satisfies conditions* (3.18) *and* (3.63), *if $\tilde{v}^c$ is sufficiently small, then by appropriately choosing $\gamma_{\tilde{v}} \in \mathcal{K}$, there exist $\beta \in \mathcal{KL}$ and constants $h_0, z_0, \bar{z} \geq 0$ such that for any initial $p(0)$ satisfying $\bar{h}(p(0)) \leq h_0$ and $|z(0)| \leq z_0$, property* (3.7) *holds for all $t \geq 0$.*

Proof. We prove the theorem by first showing that the closed-loop signals are defined and bounded on the time line. Then, we prove the desired safety property. Note that the small-gain conditions (3.77) and (3.78) can be verified in a similar manner as in the proof of Theorem 2.1. In particular, given any $\mu \in \mathcal{M}^{-}\mathcal{C}$ and any

$\alpha_h \in \mathcal{K}^e$ whose domain includes $[-\mu(D_s), \infty)$ and satisfies conditions (3.18) and (3.63), we choose any $c_1 \in (\mu(D_s), \bar{s})$ and subsequently determine γ_1 according to (2.62). Then, we choose $\gamma_{\bar{v}} \in \mathcal{K}$ to satisfy conditions (3.77)–(3.78).

(1) Existence and uniqueness of $[p(t); z(t)]$ for all $t \geq 0$ and boundedness of $\bar{h}(p(t))$ and $|\tilde{v}(t)|$ for all $t \geq 0$.

(1.1) Existence, uniqueness and local Lipschitz continuity of $p(t)$ and $z(t)$ over a (possibly infinite) time interval.

The closed-loop system (composed of (3.1) and (3.2) and (3.31)–(3.33)) can be written in the form of

$$\dot{p} = g(z, \phi(p, v^c)), \tag{3.79a}$$
$$\dot{z} = f(z, \phi(p, v^c)). \tag{3.79b}$$

Note that ϕ may be undefined for $p \notin \mathcal{S}$. With the local Lipschitz continuity of f, g, ϕ, and v^c, we can verify the local Lipschitz continuity of $g(z, \phi(p, v^c(t)))$ and $f(z, \phi(p, v^c(t)))$ with respect to (p, z, t) on $\mathcal{S} \times \mathbb{R}^m \times \mathbb{R}_+$. Using [187, Theorem 54], we have, for any initial state $p(0) \in \text{Int}(\mathcal{S})$ and $z(0) \in \mathbb{R}^m$ and any input v^c satisfying Assumption 3.2, the system (3.79) admits a unique trajectory $[p(t); z(t)]$ over some time interval starting at $t = 0$. Moreover, since $g(z, \phi(p, v^c(t)))$ and $f(z, \phi(p, v^c(t)))]$ are locally Lipschitz with respect to t, using [206, Theorem 2.2], we can verify that the trajectory $[p(t); z(t)]$ is continuously differentiable and thus, locally, Lipschitz continuous with respect to t as long as it is defined.

(1.2) Existence, uniqueness and local Lipschitz continuity of $p(t)$ and $z(t)$ for all $t \geq 0$.

We denote by $[0, T_*)$ with $0 < T_* \leq \infty$ the time interval over which the trajectory is right maximally defined. Based on the discussion in (1.1), $p(t)$ and $z(t)$ are locally Lipschitz continuous for all $t \in [0, T_*)$. When $\bar{h}(p(0))$, $|z(0)|$, $\bar{v}^c$ and $\bar{v}^{cd}$ are sufficiently small, we show $T_* = \infty$ by contradiction in the sense that if $T_* < \infty$, then there exists a continuous function $B : [0, T_*] \to \mathbb{R}_+$ such that

$$\max\{|\tilde{p}_i(t)|, 1/|\tilde{p}_i(t)|, |z(t)|\} \leq B(t) \tag{3.80}$$

for all $t \in [0, T_*)$ and $i \in \mathcal{N}_o$.

Specifically, we consider the case in which $\bar{h}(p(0))$, $|z(0)|$, $\bar{v}^c$ and $\bar{v}^{cd}$ satisfy

$$\beta_1(\bar{h}(p(0)), 0) < \bar{s}_0, \tag{3.81a}$$
$$\beta_2(|z(0)| + \bar{h}(p(0)) + \bar{v}^c, 0) < \bar{s}_0, \tag{3.81b}$$
$$\gamma_2 \circ \beta_1(\bar{h}(p(0)), 0) < \bar{s}_0, \tag{3.81c}$$
$$\gamma_1 \circ \beta_2(|z(0)| + \bar{h}(p(0)) + \bar{v}^c, 0) < \bar{s}_0 \tag{3.81d}$$

and

$$\max\{\gamma_{\bar{v}}(c_d), \gamma_1 \circ \gamma_{\bar{v}}(c_d)\} < \bar{s}_0 \tag{3.82}$$

with constant $\bar{s}_0$ satisfying $c_1 < \bar{s}_0 < \bar{s}$, and

$$c_d = \sqrt{n} L_\phi \max\{2\bar{v}^c, \bar{v}^{cd}\}, \tag{3.83}$$

where L_ϕ denotes a Lipschitz constant of $\phi(p, v^c)$ with respect to (p, v^c) over $\mathcal{S} \times \{v^c \in \mathbb{R}^n : |v^c| \leq \bar{v}^c\}$. The satisfaction of condition (3.82) is guaranteed by appropriately choosing $\gamma_{\tilde{v}}$.

Note that the result of Proposition 3.4 only hold when $\|\tilde{v}\|_\infty$ is small enough (i.e., $\gamma_1(\|\tilde{v}\|_\infty) < \sup_{s>0} \mu(D)$), and the small-gain condition (3.77) only holds in a local range. When $\bar{h}(p(0))$, $|z(0)|$, $\bar{v}^c$ and $\bar{v}^{cd}$ satisfy (3.81) and (3.82), we verify that all the relevant signals indeed keep within the specific ranges during the time interval $[0, T_*)$. For this purpose, we define

$$T = \sup\{t \in [0, T_*) : \max\{\|\bar{h}(p)\|_t, \|\tilde{v}\|_t, \gamma_1(\|\tilde{v}\|_t)\} < \bar{s}\} \tag{3.84}$$

with $\bar{s}$ defined in (3.78), and show that $T = T_*$.

Recall Proposition 3.4. Conditions (3.18) and (3.63) can be satisfied according to the guideline provided below the proof of Proposition 3.4. Using the definitions of $\tilde{v}$ and v in (3.8) and (3.2), respectively, and noting that $v^* = \phi(p, v^c)$, we can verify that

$$\tilde{v}(t) = g(z(t), \phi(p(t), v^c(t))) - \phi(p(t), v^c(t)), \tag{3.85}$$

and that $\tilde{v}(t)$ is locally Lipschitz continuous in t on $[0, T_*)$. The definition of T in (3.84) ensures that $\gamma_1(\|\tilde{v}\|_T) \leq \bar{s} < \sup_{s>0} \mu(s)$. Due to causality, there exists $\beta_1 \in \mathcal{KL}$ such that

$$h(\tilde{p}_i(t)) \leq \max\{\beta_1(h(\tilde{p}_i(0)), t), \gamma_1(\|\tilde{v}\|_t), c_1\}, \qquad i \in \mathcal{N}_o \tag{3.86}$$

holds for all $t \in [0, T)$. Then, by the definition of $\bar{h}(p)$ in (3.6), we have

$$\bar{h}(p(t)) \leq \max\{\beta_1(\bar{h}(p(0)), t), \gamma_1(\|\tilde{v}\|_t), c_1\} \tag{3.87}$$

for all $t \in [0, T)$.

Also, from Proposition 3.5, we have

$$|\tilde{v}(t)| \leq \max\{\beta_2(|z(0)| + \bar{h}(p(0)) + \bar{v}^c, t), \gamma_2(\|\tilde{v}\|_t), \gamma_2(\|\bar{h}(p)\|_t), c_2\}, \tag{3.88}$$

for all $t \in [0, T)$, where β_2, γ_2 and c_2 are defined in (3.74). In particular, $c_2 = \gamma_{\tilde{v}}(c_d)$.

From (3.86) and (3.88), taking the supremum of $\bar{h}(p(t))$ and $\tilde{v}(t)$ over $[0, T)$, we obtain

$$\|\bar{h}(p)\|_T \leq \max\{\beta_1(\bar{h}(p(0)), 0), \gamma_1(\|\tilde{v}\|_T), c_1\}, \tag{3.89a}$$

$$\|\tilde{v}\|_T \leq \max\left\{\beta_2(|z(0)| + \bar{h}(p(0)) + \bar{v}^c, 0), \gamma_2(\|\tilde{v}\|_T), \gamma_2(\|\bar{h}(p)\|_T), c_2\right\}. \tag{3.89b}$$

Substituting the right-hand side of (3.89a) for $\|\bar{h}(p)\|_T$ into (3.89b), we obtain

$$\begin{aligned}\|\tilde{v}\|_T \leq \max\{&\beta_2(|z(0)| + \bar{h}(p(0)) + \bar{v}^c, 0), \gamma_2\circ\beta_1(\bar{h}(p(0)), 0), \gamma_2(c_1), c_2,\\ &\gamma_2(\|\tilde{v}\|_T), \gamma_2\circ\gamma_1(\|\tilde{v}\|_T)\}.\end{aligned} \tag{3.90}$$

With $\|\tilde{v}\|_T \leq \bar{s}$, using condition (3.77), we have

$$\gamma(\|\tilde{v}\|_T) < \|\tilde{v}\|_T, \quad \gamma_2\circ\gamma_1(\|\tilde{v}\|_T) < \|\tilde{v}\|_T. \tag{3.91}$$

Thus,

$$\|\tilde{v}\|_T \leq \max\{\beta_2(|z(0)| + \bar{h}(p(0)) + \bar{v}^c, 0), \gamma_2\circ\beta_1(\bar{h}(p(0)), 0), \gamma_2(c_1), c_2\}. \tag{3.92}$$

With $\beta_1(\bar{h}(p(0)), 0) \leq \bar{s}_0$ and $c_1 < \bar{s}_0$, using condition (3.77), we have

$$\gamma_1\circ\gamma_2\circ\beta_1(\bar{h}(p(0)), 0) < \beta_1(\bar{h}(p(0)), 0), \quad \gamma_1\circ\gamma_2(c_1) < c_1. \tag{3.93}$$

Thus,

$$\begin{aligned}\gamma_1(\|\tilde{v}\|_T) \leq \max\{&\gamma_1\circ\beta_2(|z(0)| + \bar{h}(p(0)) + \bar{v}^c, 0),\\ &\beta_1(\bar{h}(p(0)), 0), c_1, \gamma_1(c_2)\}.\end{aligned} \tag{3.94}$$

Substituting (3.94) into (3.89a), we have

$$\|\bar{h}(p)\|_T \leq \max\{\beta_1(\bar{h}(p(0)), 0), \gamma_1\circ\beta_2(|z(0)| + \bar{h}(p(0)) + \bar{v}^c, 0), c_1, \gamma_1(c_2)\}. \tag{3.95}$$

From inequalities (3.95), (3.94), and (3.92), under conditions (3.81), (3.82), as well as $c_1 \in (\mu(D_s), \bar{s}_0)$ and $\gamma_2(c_1) < \bar{s}_0$, it can be verified that

$$\max\{\|\bar{h}(p)\|_T, \|\tilde{v}\|_T, \gamma_1(\|\tilde{v}\|_T)\} < \bar{s}_0. \tag{3.96}$$

This, together with $\bar{s}_0 < \bar{s}$ and the definition of T in (3.84), implies that $T = T_*$.

We show that if $T_* < \infty$, then there exists a continuous function $B : [0, T_*] \to \mathbb{R}_+$ satisfying (3.80). In particular, an upper bound of $|z(t)|$ over $[0, T_*)$, denoted by $\bar{z}$, can be derived from the property (3.10), together with the boundedness of $z(0)$ (guaranteed by (3.81)) and the boundedness of $|v^*(t)|$ on $[0, T_*)$ (ensured by combining (3.11), (3.40), and (3.96)). An upper bound of $1/|\tilde{p}_i(t)|$ for $i \in \mathcal{N}_o$ over $[0, T_*)$ is given by $1/\mu^{-1}(\bar{s}_0)$, which follows from the definition of $\bar{h}(p)$ in (3.6), $\mu \in \mathcal{M}^-\mathcal{C}$, as well as the boundedness of $\bar{h}(p(t))$ for all $t \in [0, T_*)$ (ensured by

(3.96)). An upper bound of $|\tilde{p}_i(t)|$ for $i \in \mathcal{N}_o$ is given by $|\tilde{p}_i(0)| + \bar{\upsilon}t$ for $t \in [0, T_*)$, which can be obtained by solving (3.13) with the initial condition $\tilde{p}_i(0)$ and the velocity bound $\bar{\upsilon}$, where $\bar{\upsilon}$ can be established from the boundedness of $|\tilde{\upsilon}(t)|$ and $|\upsilon^*(t)|$ over $[0, T_*)$. This proves $T_* = \infty$.

This ends the proof of Theorem 3.1. □

3.6 Simulation and Experiment

3.6.1 Numerical Simulation

In this section, we consider the scenario presented in Example 3.5. The identified quadrotor model given in Example 1.2 is utilized for the numerical simulations. To validate the effectiveness of the proposed design, we make comparisons between the safety-critical controller (3.33) with the reshaped feasible set (3.31) and the safety-critical controller (3.14) with the original feasible set (3.15).

The simulations are conducted for the following three cases:

Case 1: The actuation dynamics of the quadrotor are assumed to be negligible, and the model for controller design is given by $\dot{p} = \upsilon$, where $\upsilon = \upsilon^*$ and υ^* is the velocity-reference input generated by the safety-critical controller based on the original feasible set (3.14)–(3.16).

Case 2: The quadrotor is modeled as a cascade of an integrator and uncertain actuation dynamics. The identified quadrotor model in Example 1.2 is employed, and the controller is still constructed based on the original feasible set (3.14)–(3.16).

Case 3: The same model as in Case 2 is employed. However, the safety-critical controller is now designed with the reshaped feasible set (3.31).

We consider the velocity-command signal

$$\upsilon^c(t) \equiv [5; 5], \quad \forall t \geq 0. \tag{3.97}$$

Clearly, Assumption 2.2 is satisfied with $\bar{\upsilon}^c = 5\sqrt{2}$ and $\bar{\upsilon}^{cd} = 0$.

For the safety-critical controllers in the three scenarios, select

$$\mu(s) = s^{-1}, \qquad h(\tilde{p}) = |\tilde{p}|^{-1}, \qquad D = 1.0 \tag{3.98}$$

$$\alpha_h(s) = \begin{cases} s, & s \geq 0 \\ 2s, & s < 0 \end{cases} \qquad D_s = \frac{\sqrt{2}}{1.01} \tag{3.99}$$

For the safety-critical controller with the reshaped feasible set, additionally set $k_\psi = 5.0$, and use the constant matrix A_L defined in (3.62b) with $n_l = 11$, so that $c_A = \cos(2\pi/n_l)$.

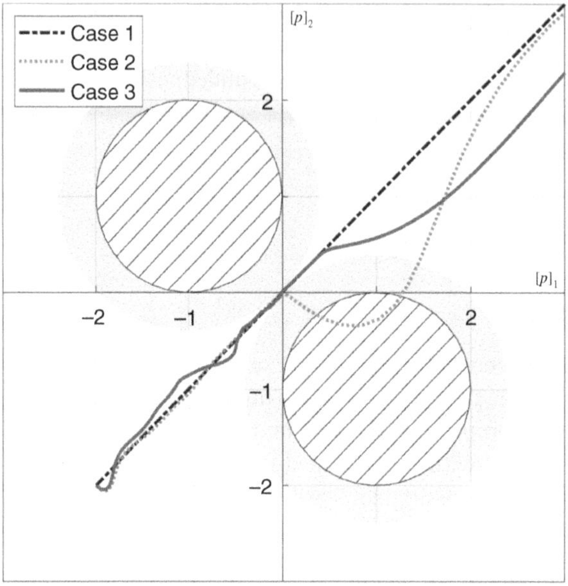

Figure 3.10 Quadrotor position trajectories in the three cases: the feasible-set reshaping technique can ensure safety of the quadrotor in the presence of multiple constraints and dynamic uncertainties.

Consider the initial condition with $p(0) = [-2; -2]$ and $z(0) = 0$. Figure 3.10 shows the quadrotor position trajectories in the three cases. Corresponding to Case 3, the feasible-set reshaping technique can ensure safety of the quadrotor in the presence of multiple constraints and dynamic uncertainties.

Figure 3.11 shows the evolutions of the velocity-reference input in the three cases. Corresponding to Case 3, the velocity-reference input generated by the proposed controller (3.33) changes continuously on the time line.

Figure 3.12 depicts the relationship among control input, safety, and tracking error. It can be observed that under the proposed controller (3.33), the quadrotor maintains the desired safe distance from the two obstacles, with a smaller velocity-tracking error and a lower change rate of the velocity-reference input.

Figure 3.13 illustrates the comparison of the original feasible set $\mathcal{V}(p)$ and the reshaped feasible set $\mathcal{V}_L(p)$. It can be observed that the reshaped feasible set $\mathcal{V}_L(p)$ is a subset of the original feasible set $\mathcal{V}(p)$ at each time instant.

Source codes for the simulation are available at https://github.com/EXPSIN/safety-unmanned-systems.

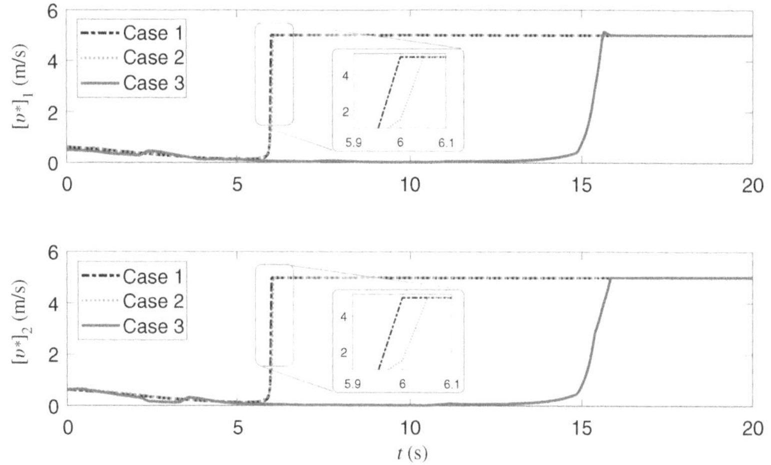

Figure 3.11 The evolutions of the velocity-reference input in the three cases: the velocity-reference input generated by the proposed controller (3.33) changes continuously on the time line.

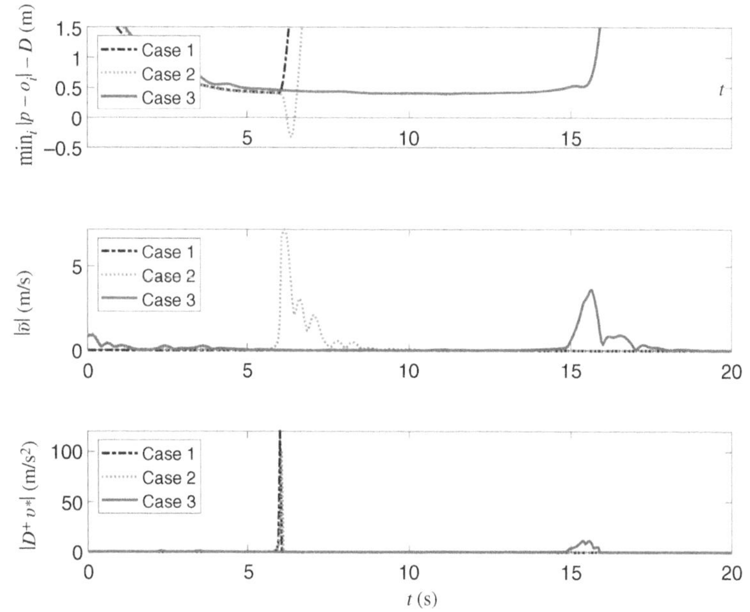

Figure 3.12 The safety measure $\min_i |p - o_i| - D$ of the quadrotor with respect to the obstacles, the norm of the velocity-tracking error $|\tilde{v}|$, and the norm of the changing rate of the velocity-reference input $|D^+ v^*|$ in simulations under three cases.

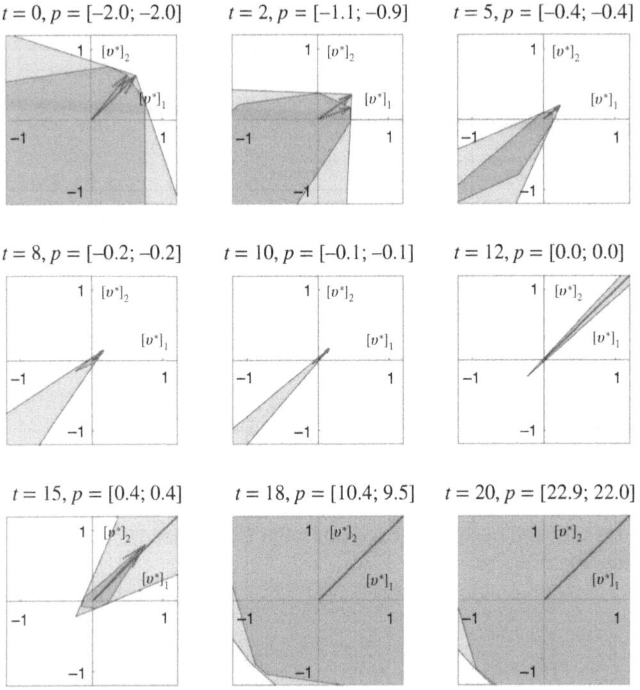

Figure 3.13 Comparison of the evolution of the original and reshaped feasible sets.

3.6.2 Experiment

To further verify the effectiveness of the proposed design, we conduct a physical experiment using a quadrotor UAV. The hardware platform matches that of Section 2.5.2, comprising a DJI RoboMaster TT quadrotor, an OptiTrack motion-capture system, and a ground-station computer. In the experimental scenario, there are two static obstacles located at $o_1 = [0; -0.42]$ and $o_2 = [0; 0.42]$. The UAV is required to move from its initial position $[-1.5; 0]$ to the target point $[1.5; 0]$ while maintaining safety. The initial velocity of the UAV is set to zero. The primary controller for target-reaching is

$$v^c = -(p - [1.5; 0.05]) \min\left\{\frac{1}{\|p - [1.5; 0.05]\|}, 0.5\right\}, \tag{3.100}$$

which means that the magnitude of the velocity-command signal does not exceed 1.

We compare the proposed safety-critical controller with a usual safety-critical controller:

Usual safety-critical controller (UC) defined in (3.14)–(3.16), with

$$\mu(s) = s^{-1}, \qquad h(\tilde{p}) = |\tilde{p}|^{-1}, \qquad D = 0.35, \tag{3.101a}$$

$$\alpha_h(s) = -k_h\left(\frac{1}{s + D_s^{-1}} - D_s\right), \qquad k_h = 1.0, \qquad D_s = 0.4. \tag{3.101b}$$

Proposed safety-critical controller (PC) defined in (3.31), with μ, h, α_h, D and k_h chosen as in (3.101), and the parameters of feasible-set reshaping chosen as

$$k_\phi = 1.0, \quad n_l = 9, \quad c_A = \cos\frac{2\pi}{n_l}. \tag{3.102}$$

Figures 3.14 and 3.15 present the UAV's position trajectories under the two safety-critical controllers. With the **UC** controller, the UAV intrudes into the vicinity of the obstacles and violates the safety constraint, whereas with the PC controller, the UAV successfully avoids the obstacles and safely reaches the target. Curves of several other variables are shown in Figure 3.16.

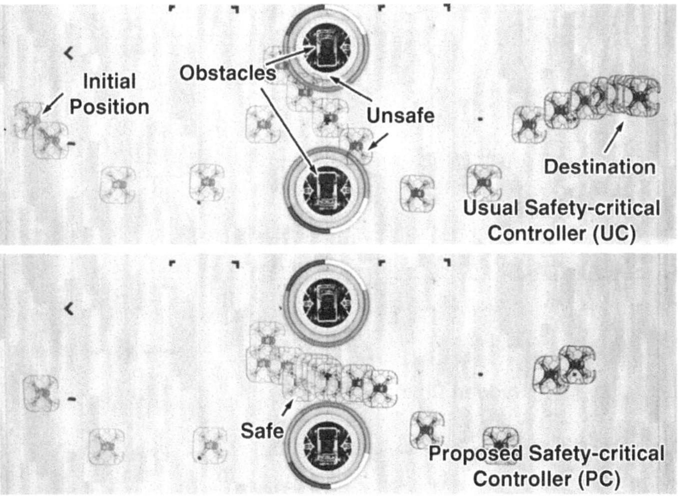

Figure 3.14 Position trajectories of the RoboMaster TT in experiments under a usual safety-critical controller and the proposed safety-critical controller.

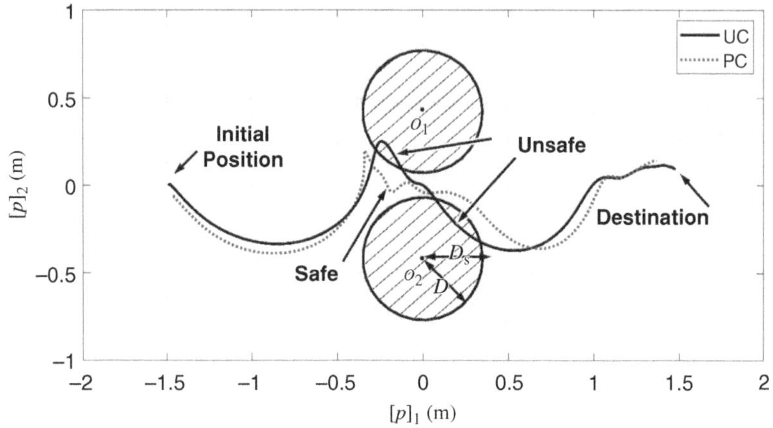

Figure 3.15 Comparison of the position trajectories of the RoboMaster TT in experiments under the usual safety-critical controller and the proposed safety-critical controller.

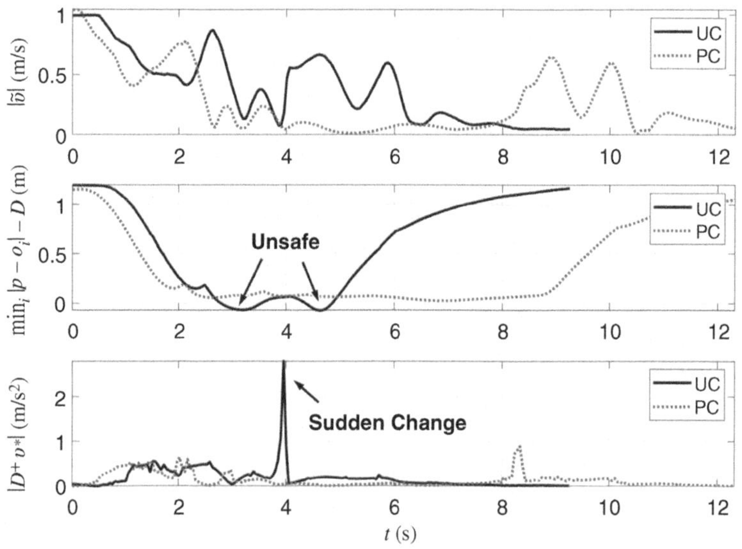

Figure 3.16 The norm of the velocity-tracking error $|\tilde{v}|$, the safety measure $\min_i |p - o_i| - D$ of the quadrotor with respect to the obstacles, and the norm of the changing rate of the velocity-reference input $|D^+ v^*|$ in experiments under the usual safety-critical controller and the proposed safety-critical controller.

3.7 Notes

Safety-critical control under multiple safety constraints has attracted substantial attention in recent years. Practical interest of the study can be found in systems where multiple safety constraints, input limits, and task-performance requirements must be satisfied simultaneously. In particular, composite and multi-barrier-function approaches, such as nonsmooth barrier functions [63], composite control barrier functions [144, 27], soft-minimum and soft-maximum barrier constructions [165], and multiple control barrier functions [41] have been developed to address multiple constraints appearing from safety-critical control. The results in [175, 29] provide safety guarantees for Euler–Lagrange systems and satellite dynamics under multiple constraints, higher-order nonlinearities, and sampling.

3.7.1 Safety-critical Control via Real-time Optimization Under Multiple Safety Constraints

Safety-critical control subject to multiple safety constraints seeks to ensure that the system state remains within the safe set in the simultaneous presence of multiple safety constraints, input bounds, and disturbances [175]. However, the concurrent action of multiple barrier functions and constraints may shrink the feasible set, potentially rendering it empty. The challenge is heightened by higher relative-degree constraints, input saturation, and external disturbances, which complicate real-time optimization-based safety-critical control. To address these issues for multi-robot systems, reference [211] employed decentralized control to handle inter-robot and robot-obstacle collision avoidance, implementing real-time optimization via local control barrier functions and decentralized quadratic programs. Reference [29] proposed an inner-safe-set method that contracts the original safe set to a control-invariant set that remains positively invariant under input constraints, and combined it with optimal and switching control to achieve safety control objectives. Reference [79] analyzed feasibility and continuity issues of QP-based safety-critical controllers when multiple barrier functions act simultaneously, identifying causes of infeasibility such as conflicting constraints and empty feasible sets, and proposed design guidelines that guarantee feasibility and continuity under multiple barrier functions. Reference [27] introduced new decomposition strategies and feasible-set construction methods to address the feasible-set degradation issue caused by input constraints.

3.7.2 Composite and Nonsmooth Control Barrier Functions

Studies on composite and nonsmooth control barrier functions have provided essential analytical and verification tools for safety-critical control under complex, multitask, and time-varying constraints. Composite CBF methods synthesize multiple safety constraints (e.g., multi-obstacle avoidance, velocity limits, task-space constraints) through logical composition into a single equivalent constraint, enabling multiobjective safety-critical control within a unified framework [27, 144]. Early approaches relied on smooth Boolean compositions (e.g., minimum for intersection, maximum for union), which can induce nonsmooth behavior when performing set operations. To mitigate this, reference [165] proposed smooth approximations such as soft-min and soft-max that preserve differentiability. Alternatively, nonsmooth CBFs directly employ min/max operators to implement set operations and utilize nonsmooth analysis tools (differential inclusions and Clarke Generalized gradient generalized gradients) to establish set invariance when the boundaries of the set are not necessarily differentiable. Furthermore, hybrid nonsmooth barrier functions have been developed to extend these ideas to systems with jumps, supporting safety in dynamic environments and integrating effectively with primary controllers for real-time handling of abrupt constraint changes (e.g., sudden obstacle appearance) [63]. These methods have seen extensive engineering application. For example, reference [180] realized collision avoidance among robotic manipulators in food-processing settings. For nonlinear control-affine systems, reference [144] proposed composite CBFs to combine multiple state-based safe sets and constructed a unified safe set via Boolean logic. Although this approach effectively integrates multiple safety constraints, it appears that formal guarantees of controller feasibility and Lipschitz continuity have not been fully established.

3.7.3 Feasibility and Lipschitz Continuity

QP integrates control barrier functions with performance objectives or a primary controller to construct implicit safety-critical controllers [6], and has become a central method for real-time safety-critical control. In this framework, the QP solution, i.e., the control variable generated by the QP-based safety-critical controller, must enforce safety constraints while deviating minimally from the nominal input, thereby balancing safety and performance. When a control system features multiple potentially conflicting constraints and uncertain actuator dynamics, a QP based on nominal CBFs may fail to be feasible at specific states. Reference [227] proposed a feasible region iteration method to achieve the maximum feasible region. Beyond feasibility, the regularity of QP-based controllers, especially Lipschitz continuity, plays a pivotal role in the design and analysis of safety-critical controllers. From the perspective of nonlinear systems, a Lipschitz feedback law guarantees the existence and uniqueness of closed-loop solutions [39, 98, 204, 64]. These properties underpin robust safety-critical control in the presence of external disturbances and model uncertainty. In practice, continuous control laws mitigate input jitter and high-frequency switching. Prior studies also indicate that controller regularity enhances the stability, durability, and overall performance of electromechanical systems [219, 114, 100]. Evidently, the continuity requirements on control inputs in safety-critical control align with established results in nonlinear and nonsmooth control [204, 39, 64]. As early as the late 1970s, reference [70] provided sufficient conditions for continuity and existence of QP solutions, which form a theoretical foundation for QP-based safety-critical control [148, 6, 87, 79, 49, 137]. In multi-constraint scenarios, abruptly changing active constraints can destroy the smoothness of the QP [114, 100], yielding non-Lipschitz control inputs. To remedy this, references [219, 114, 100] introduced slack variables and redesigned the CBF-based QP to avoid switching among multiple active constraints, thereby guaranteeing (Lipschitz) continuity of the feedback law. Appropriate control system structures (e.g., hierarchical architectures) have also been developed to reduce chattering to solve specific safety-critical control problems [114, 100].

4

Safety-critical Control in Cluttered Environments: Set-valued Measurement and Feasible-set Reshaping

This chapter extends the study in this book to the scenario of a mobile robot navigating cluttered environments. Obstacles are modeled as a closed set, and a direction-distance function is employed to describe the obstacle measurement model. With the robot's velocity considered as the control input, based on real-time obstacle measurements, a safety-critical controller is needed to maintain a safe distance between the robot and surrounding obstacles, while ensuring that the robot's velocity tracks a predetermined velocity-command signal as closely as possible. Furthermore, for improved robustness with respect to perturbations, the proposed controller is required to be locally Lipschitz continuous with respect to the robot's position. In this chapter, we focus on the challenges induced by cluttered environments and neglect the influence of dynamic uncertainties.

The motivation for this study arises from practical applications such as operator-assistance systems and safety-critical, learning-based control systems, in which velocity-command signals are updated in real time by higher-level algorithms or human operators. Under such circumstances, planning-based methods that depend on predefined target positions or specified trajectories may not be directly applicable. Additionally, in cluttered environments, discontinuous feedback from obstacle positions leads to discontinuous constraints, which may result in nonsmooth solutions when standard gradient-based algorithms are used.

This chapter presents a nontrivial extension of the techniques introduced in the previous chapters, and proposes a class of continuous safety-critical controllers that can be implemented in the body-fixed coordinate frame. In particular, a Lipschitz-truncated regularization term is introduced as a replacement for the conventional quadratic term used in the standard Moreau–Yosida method [146, 229]. The revised regularization retains both safety and feasibility. Subsequently, a continuous and reactive safety-critical controller is developed that relies solely on real-time obstacle measurements from the environment. The feasible-set reshaping technique plays an essential role in constructing a feasible set with a carefully selected constant matrix that positively spans the space of the control inputs, ensuring that the coefficient matrix of the constraints that directly affect the optimal solution always satisfies the full-row-rank condition. Finally, both safety constraints and the velocity-command signal are incorporated by QP.

4.1 Problem Formulation

Consider a mobile robot with translational and rotational kinematics described by

$$\dot{p} = Rv, \tag{4.1a}$$

$$\dot{R} = R\Omega, \tag{4.1b}$$

where $p \in \mathbb{R}^n$ is the position vector in the earth-fixed frame, $v \in \mathbb{R}^n$ is the velocity vector in the body-fixed frame, $R \in \mathbb{SO}(n)$[1] denotes the rotation matrix between the body-fixed and earth-fixed frames, and $\Omega \in \mathbb{R}^{n\times n}$ is the angular velocity matrix, which satisfies $\Omega = -\Omega^T$.

The model (4.1) is widely adopted for planning and control of various mobile robots and vehicles [164, 195, 113]. In our problem setting, (p, R) and (v, Ω) are regarded as the state and the control input, respectively.

Let $\mathcal{O}$ denote the set of positions of all the obstacle points in an earth-fixed frame. The unit vector $l_w \in \mathbb{R}^n$ represents measurement directions in the earth-fixed frame. The obstacle-measurement model is given by a direction-distance function

$$r(p, l_w) = \min\{|o - p| : o \in \mathcal{O} \cup \mathcal{B}(p), l_w^T(o - p) = |o - p|\}, \tag{4.2}$$

for $p \in \mathbb{R}^n$ and $|l_w| = 1$, where

$$\mathcal{B}(p) = \{o \in \mathbb{R}^n : |o - p| = D_B\} \tag{4.3}$$

with constant $D_B > 0$ being the maximum measurement range (which ensures that the minimum in (4.2) is well defined).

The obstacle-measurement model (4.2) returns the distance from position p to the nearest obstacle point in the direction of l_w. Accounting for the robot's rotation, the set of all the measured obstacle points is described by the set-valued map[2]:

$$\mathcal{M}(p, R) = \{[l; r(p, Rl)] : |l| = 1, l \in \mathbb{R}^n\}, \tag{4.4}$$

for $p \in \mathbb{R}^n$ and $R \in \mathbb{SO}(n)$, where $l \in \mathbb{R}^n$ represents measurement directions in the body-fixed frame.

An illustrative scenario considered in this chapter is depicted in Figure 4.1.

---

1 Special orthogonal group of degree n, defined as $\mathbb{SO}(n) = \{R \in \mathbb{R}^{n\times n} : R^T R = I_n, \det(R) = 1\}$.
2 See [16] for relevant notions of set-valued maps.

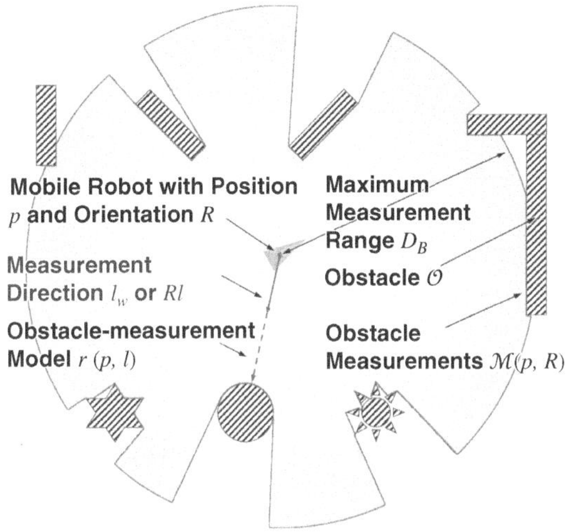

Figure 4.1 A scenario of safety-critical control in a cluttered environment.

The measured obstacles given by the set $\mathcal{M}(p, R)$ defined in (4.4) are consistent with engineering practice. In practical applications, obstacle measurements (i.e., the real-time feedback of the image of $\mathcal{M}(p, R)$) can be acquired using standard sensing and data acquisition interfaces, as long as appropriate sensors such as laser scanners, RGB-D cameras, and stereo cameras are available. For example, in control architectures developed with the Robot Operating System (ROS), the set $\mathcal{M}(p, R)$ can be accessed through the `sensor_msgs\LaserScan` message, which provides distance measurements from a planar laser range-finder.[3] For DJI multirotors that support the Mobile SDK, $\mathcal{M}(p, R)$ can be obtained via member methods of the `ObstacleData` class, which supplies real-time obstacle ranging data from onboard sensors,[4] as illustrated in Figure 4.2.

In this chapter, the mobile robot is considered safe if its position p remains sufficiently far from obstacles. Specifically, with a constant $D > 0$ representing the desired safe distance, the robot is safe if p remains within the safe set

$$\mathcal{S} = \{p \in \mathbb{R}^n : \inf_{o\in\mathcal{O}} |o - p| \geq D\}. \tag{4.5}$$

Suppose that a higher-level controller generates a velocity-command signal $v^c \in \mathbb{R}^n$ in the body-fixed frame, representing some primary control objective.

3 See https://docs.ros.org/en/noetic/api/sensor_msgs/html/msg/LaserScan.html.
4 See https://developer.dji.com/cn/api-reference-v5/android-api/Components/IPerceptionManager/IPerceptionManager_ObstacleData.html.

Figure 4.2 An illustration of direction-distance measurement of obstacles by onboard sensors of a DJI Matrice 3TD multirotor operating in a cluttered environment.

Our goal is to design a continuous safety-critical controller using only the obstacle measurements $\mathcal{M}(p, R)$ and the velocity-command signal v^c, which is of the form:

$$v = \rho_{\mathcal{M}}(\mathcal{M}(p, R), v^c), \tag{4.6}$$

where $\rho_{\mathcal{M}} : \mathbb{R}^{n+1} \times \mathbb{R}^n \to \mathbb{R}^n$, or equivalently,

$$v = \rho(p, R, v^c), \tag{4.7}$$

with $\rho : \mathbb{R}^n \times \mathbb{SO}(n) \times \mathbb{R}^n \to \mathbb{R}^n$.

By appropriately designing the safety-critical controller, we expect that for the closed-loop system composed of (4.1) and (4.7) is safe in the sense that for any initial state $p(0) \in \mathcal{S}$ and $R(0) \in \mathbb{SO}(n)$, the position trajectory satisfies $p(t) \in \mathcal{S}$ for all $t \geq 0$. Additionally, it is required that the actual velocity v deviate from the velocity-command signal v^c as little as possible.

The following standing assumptions are made on the obstacles and the velocity-command signal.

Assumption 4.1 ***(Closeness of the Obstacle Set)***: The obstacle set $\mathcal{O} \subset \mathbb{R}^n$ is closed.

Assumption 4.2 ***(Boundedness of the Primary Velocity-command Signal)***: The velocity-command signal v^c satisfies

$$|v^c(t)| \leq \bar{v}^c \tag{4.8}$$

for all $t \geq 0$, where $\bar{v}^c$ is a positive constant.

The following example presents a safety-critical controller that directly employs the obstacle-measurement model and discusses the non-Lipschitz issue.

Example 4.1 ***(Non-Lipschitz Issue of a Safety-critical Controller Based on the Obstacle-measurement Model):*** *The obstacle-measurement model directly yields safety constraints, based on which one might intuitively consider the following QP-based safety-critical controller:*

$$v = \operatorname*{argmin}_{v} |v - v^c|^2 \tag{4.9a}$$

$$\text{s.t.} \quad l_w^T R v \leq \alpha(r(p, l_w) - D), \quad |l_w| = 1, \tag{4.9b}$$

where $\alpha \in \mathcal{K}^e$, and D is the desired safe distance. It can be verified that $r(p, l_w) \geq D$ for any $p \in \mathcal{S}$ and any $l_w \in \mathbb{R}^n$ satisfying $|l_w| = 1$. Also, $v = 0$ always satisfies the constraints in Eq. (4.9b). *Therefore, the QP (4.9) is feasible for all $p \in \mathcal{S}$ and $v^c \in \mathbb{R}^n$.*

We first show that for any Lipschitz continuous angular velocity matrix Ω, the set $\mathcal{S}$ defined in (4.5) is positively invariant for the closed-loop system composed of (4.1) and (4.9). Consider any fixed obstacle point $o \in \mathcal{O}$. Define

$$h_o(p) = |o - p| - D \tag{4.10}$$

for all $p \in \mathbb{R}^n \setminus \{o\}$. Along the closed-loop trajectories determined by (4.1) and (4.9), we have

$$\begin{aligned} \nabla h_o(p)\dot{p} &= -\frac{(o-p)^T}{|o-p|} R v \\ &\geq -\alpha\left(r\left(p, \frac{o-p}{|o-p|}\right) - D\right) \\ &\geq -\alpha(\min\{|o-p|, D_B\} - D) \\ &\geq -\alpha(|o-p| - D) \\ &= -\alpha(h_o(p)), \end{aligned} \tag{4.11}$$

where the first equality follows from (4.1), the first inequality is based on the constraint in (4.9b) with $l_w = (o-p)/|o-p|$, and the second inequality is derived from (4.2).

From the definition of $h_o(p)$ in (4.10), we observe that

$$\nabla h_o(p) \neq 0, \quad \forall p \in \partial\mathcal{S}, \tag{4.12a}$$

$$\nabla h_o(p) R \rho'(p, R, v^c) \geq 0, \quad \forall p \in \partial\mathcal{S}, \tag{4.12b}$$

where ρ' represents the map from (p, R, v^c) to v resulting from solving the QP (4.9). The satisfaction of the condition (4.12) ensures the satisfaction of the subtangentiality condition (1.4) in Theorem 1.1. Consequently, for any initial condition $p(0) \in \mathcal{S}$, the corresponding trajectory stays within $\mathcal{S}$, i.e., $p(t) \in \mathcal{S}$ whenever it is defined.

However, for some $p \in \mathcal{S}$, the coefficient matrix of the active constraints of the QP (4.9) may lack full row rank. According to the discussion in Section 1.3.3, this implies that the solution to the QP (4.9) may not be Lipschitz continuous with respect to p. See Section 4.5.1 for a comparative illustration based on numerical simulations.

4.2 A Continuous, Reactive Safety-critical Controller

This section presents a two-step design to construct a continuous, reactive safety-critical controller:

- Step 1: Regularization of the Measurement Model;
- Step 2: Construction of a QP-Based Safety-critical Controller.

A step-by-step development of the design is presented below.

4.2.1 Step 1: Regularization of the Measurement Model

Moreau–Yosida regularization is a standard method that can be used to ensure the Lipschitz continuity (and stronger smoothness) of the measurement model defined by $r(p, Rl)$ in (4.2). In particular, one may consider

$$r_{MY}(\mathcal{M}(p, R), l) = \inf_{|l'|=1} \{r(p, Rl') + \mu |l - l'|^2\}, \tag{4.13}$$

for all $p \in \mathbb{R}^n$, $R \in \mathbb{SO}(n)$ and $|l| = 1$, where $\mu |l - l'|^2$ is the regularization term with μ being a positive constant. Recall the equivalent measurement model given by $\mathcal{M}(p, R)$ in (4.4). For an intuitive understanding, one may rewrite r_{MY} in (4.13) as

$$r_{MY}(\mathcal{M}(p, R), l) = \inf_{[r';l']^T \in \mathcal{M}(p,R)} \{r' + \mu |l - l'|^2\}. \tag{4.14}$$

However, with the standard Moreau–Yosida method, the safety constraints may be violated when one constructs the feasible set of safety-oriented control inputs by only using a finite number of constraints. See Section 4.5.1 for a numerical illustration.

To address the above-mentioned issue, we employ a Lipschitz-truncated term $\phi(l^T l')$ to replace the quadratic term $\mu |l - l'|^2$ in (4.14). In particular, we propose the following regularized measurement model:

$$r_c(\mathcal{M}(p, R), l) = \inf_{[r';l']^T \in \mathcal{M}(p,R)} \{r' + \phi(l^T l')\} \tag{4.15}$$

for all $p \in \mathbb{R}^n$, $R \in \mathbb{SO}(n)$ and $|l| = 1$, where $\phi : [-1, 1] \to \mathbb{R}_+$ is a decreasing, Lipschitz continuous function representing the regularization term. In this chapter,

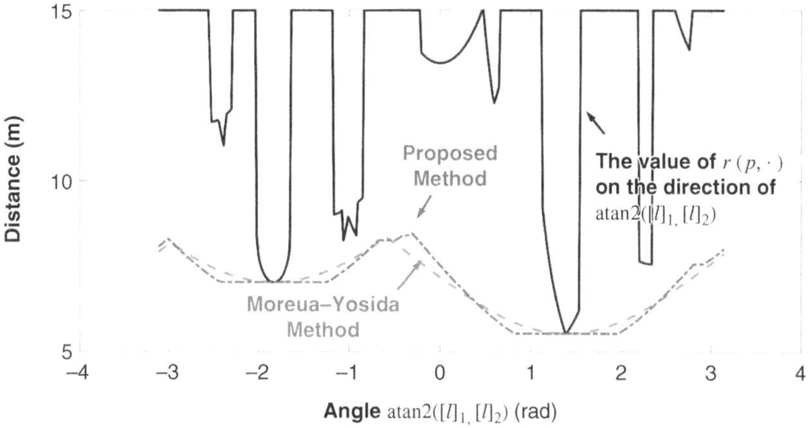

Figure 4.3 Comparison between the Moreau–Yosida regularization method and the proposed regularization method.

the function r_c is called the regularized measurement model. Figure 4.3 compares the values of $r_{MY}(\mathcal{M}(p, R), l)$ and $r_c(\mathcal{M}(p, R), l)$ with l satisfying $|l| = 1$, evaluated at the measured obstacle points $\mathcal{M}(p, R)$ for a specific (p, R) in the scenario depicted in Figure 4.1.

The following lemma shows that the regularized measurement model r_c with an appropriately chosen ϕ admits Lipschitz continuity and boundedness properties as long as some mild conditions are satisfied.

Lemma 4.1 ***(Boundedness and Lipschitz Continuity of the Regularized Measurement Model)*****:** *Consider the regularized measurement model r_c defined in* (4.15) *with the obstacle set $\mathcal{O}$, the obstacle-measurement model r defined in* (4.2), *and the obstacle measurements $\mathcal{M}$ defined in* (4.4). *Under Assumption 4.1, for any constant $c_A \in (0, 1)$, if the regularization term ϕ in* (4.15) *satisfies*

$$\phi(s) = 0, \quad \forall s \in [c_A, 1], \tag{4.16}$$

then we have that:

1. *the regularized measurement model r_c satisfies*

$$\inf_{|l'|=1} r(p, l') \leq r_c(\mathcal{M}(p, R), l) \leq r(p, Rl) \tag{4.17}$$

for all $p \in \mathbb{R}^n$, $R \in \mathbb{SO}(n)$ and $|l| = 1$;

2. *for any $\tau > 0$, the map from p, R and l to $r_c(\mathcal{M}(p, R), l)$, denoted by $r_c'(p, R, l)$, is Lipschitz continuous with respect to $p \in \mathcal{O}_\tau$, $R \in \mathbb{SO}(n)$, and $l \in \mathbb{R}^n$ satisfying $|l| = 1$, and satisfies*

$$|r_c'(p_1, R, l) - r_c'(p_2, R, l)| \leq (1 + 2k_\phi \tau^{-1})|p_1 - p_2|, \tag{4.18a}$$

$$|r_c'(p, R_1, l) - r_c'(p, R_2, l)| \leq k_\phi |R_1 - R_2|, \tag{4.18b}$$

$$|r_c'(p, R, l_1) - r_c'(p, R, l_2)| \leq k_\phi |l_1 - l_2| \tag{4.18c}$$

for all $p, p_1, p_2 \in \mathcal{O}_\tau$ with $\mathcal{O}_\tau = \{p : \inf_{o \in \mathcal{O}} |p - o| \geq \tau\}$, $R, R_1, R_2 \in \mathbb{SO}(n)$ and $l, l_1, l_2 \in \{l \in \mathbb{R}^n : |l| = 1\}$, where k_ϕ is a Lipschitz constant of ϕ.

Proof. The two properties in Lemma 4.1 are proved one-by-one.

Property 1. We prove the first inequality in (4.17) by showing that

$$r_c(\mathcal{M}(p, R), l) \geq \inf_{[r'; l']^T \in \mathcal{M}(p,R)} r' = \inf_{|l'|=1} r(p, l'), \tag{4.19}$$

where we have used the non-negativity of ϕ for the first inequality, and used the definition of $\mathcal{M}$ in (4.4) for the last equality. Now, we prove the second inequality in (4.17) by showing that

$$\begin{aligned} r_c(\mathcal{M}(p, R), l) &\leq \inf_{[r'; l']^T \in \mathcal{M}(p,R), l^T l' \geq c_A} \{r' + \phi(l^T l')\} \\ &= \inf_{[r'; l']^T \in \mathcal{M}(p,R), l^T l' \geq c_A} \{r'\} \\ &\leq \inf_{l^T l' \geq c_A, |l'|=1} r(p, Rl') \\ &\leq r(p, Rl), \end{aligned} \tag{4.20}$$

where we have used (4.16) for the first inequality, used the non-negativity of ϕ for the first equality, and used the definition of $\mathcal{M}$ in (4.4) for the second inequality.

Property (4.17) can be proved by using (4.19) and (4.20) together.

Property 2. Rewrite the regularized measurement model given in (4.15) as

$$\begin{aligned} r_c'(p, R, l) &= r_c(\mathcal{M}(p, R), l) \\ &= \inf_{|l_w|=1} \{r(p, l_w) + \phi(l_w^T R l)\} \\ &= \min\left\{D_B, \inf_{x \in \mathcal{O}} \left\{|x - p| + \phi\left(\frac{(x - p)^T}{|x - p|} Rl\right)\right\}\right\} \end{aligned} \tag{4.21}$$

for all $|l| = 1$, $p \in \mathcal{O}_\tau$ and $R \in \mathbb{SO}(n)$.

For any $p, p_1, p_2 \in \mathcal{O}_\tau$ and $R, R_1, R_2 \in \mathbb{SO}(n)$, direct calculation yields

$$
\begin{aligned}
r_c'(p_1, R, l) &= \min\left\{D_B, \min_{x\in\mathcal{O}}\left\{|x - p_2 - p_1 + p_2| + \phi\left(\frac{(x-p_2)^T}{|x-p_2|}Rl\right)\right.\right. \\
&\quad \left.\left. + \phi\left(\frac{(x-p_1)^T}{|x-p_1|}Rl\right) - \phi\left(\frac{(x-p_2)^T}{|x-p_2|}Rl\right)\right\}\right\} \\
&\le \min\left\{D_B, \min_{x\in\mathcal{O}}\left\{|x-p_2| + \phi\left(\frac{(x-p_2)^T}{|x-p_2|}Rl\right) + |p_1 - p_2|\right.\right. \\
&\quad \left.\left. + k_\phi\left|\frac{x-p_1}{|x-p_1|} - \frac{x-p_2}{|x-p_2|}\right|\right\}\right\} \\
&= \min\left\{D_B, \min_{x\in\mathcal{O}}\left\{|x-p_2| + \phi\left(\frac{(x-p_2)^T}{|x-p_2|}Rl\right) + |p_1 - p_2|\right.\right. \\
&\quad \left.\left. + k_\phi\left|\frac{((x-p_1)-(x-p_2))|x-p_2| + (x-p_2)(|x-p_2| - |x-p_1|)}{|x-p_1||x-p_2|}\right|\right\}\right\} \\
&\le \min\left\{D_B, \min_{x\in\mathcal{O}}\left\{|x-p_2| + \phi\left(\frac{(x-p_2)^T}{|x-p_2|}Rl\right) + |p_1 - p_2| + k_\phi\frac{2|p_1-p_2|}{|x-p_1|}\right\}\right\} \\
&\le \min\left\{D_B, (1 + 2k_\phi\tau^{-1})|p_1 - p_2| + \min_{x\in\mathcal{O}}\left\{|x-p_2| + \phi\left(\frac{(x-p_2)^T}{|x-p_2|}Rl\right)\right\}\right\} \\
&\le (1 + 2k_\phi\tau^{-1})|p_1 - p_2| + r_c'(p_2, R, l) \\
&\Rightarrow \quad |r_c'(p_1, R, l) - r_c'(p_2, R, l)| \le (1 + 2k_\phi\tau^{-1})|p_1 - p_2|,
\end{aligned}
\tag{4.22}
$$

which verifies property (4.18a). In (4.22), we have used (4.21) for the first equality, used the triangle inequality and the Lipschitz continuity of ϕ for the first inequality, used the triangle inequality and reverse triangle inequality for the second inequality, and used the definition of $\mathcal{O}_\tau$ below (4.18) for the third inequality. The properties of reverse triangle inequality and triangle inequality can be found in [13, Theorem 3.3] and its proof.

Then, properties (4.18b) and (4.18c) can be proved similarly. This ends the proof of Lemma 4.1. □

Property (4.17) means the boundedness of the regularized measurement model r_c, which is useful for the subsequent design of the safety-critical controller. Specifically, the lower bound demonstrates that r_c is greater than the minimum distance between the mobile robot and obstacle points, ensuring the feasibility of the safety-critical controller within the safe set. On the other hand, the upper bound shows that r_c is less than the distance to the nearest obstacle along the direction of Rl, which ensures safety when the regularized measurement model is used instead of the original obstacle-measurement model.

4.2.2 Step 2: Construction of a QP-based Safety-critical Controller

As discussed in Section 1.5.2, the full-row-rank condition on the coefficient matrix of the constraints that directly affect the optimal solution is critical to guarantee the Lipschitz continuity of the solution with respect to the parameters of a QP. From this perspective, we use a specific constant matrix to reconstruct a feasible set for QP-based safety-critical controller design.

Based on the regularized measurement model (4.15), we design a QP-based safety-critical controller to incorporate the velocity-command signal v^c:

$$v = \underset{v}{\operatorname{argmin}}\ |v - v^c|^2 \tag{4.23a}$$

$$\text{s.t.}\quad A_L v \leq b_L(\mathcal{M}(p, R)) \tag{4.23b}$$

where $A_L \in \mathbb{R}^{n_l \times n}$ is a constant matrix whose rows positively span $\mathbb{R}^n$ and satisfies the following conditions:

1. Each $[A_L]_{i,:}$ is a unit vector, i.e., $|[A_L]_{i,:}| = 1$;
2. Any n rows of A_L are linearly independent;
3. Any unit vector $l_0 \in \mathbb{R}^n$ is a positive combination of the elements of $\{[A_L]_{i,:}^T : [A_L]_{i,:} l_0 \geq c_A, i = 1, \dots, n_l\}$, whose cardinality is not less than n, with $c_A \in (0, 1)$ being a positive constant;

and $b_L : \mathbb{R}^{n+1} \to \mathbb{R}^{n_l}$ is defined by

$$[b_L(\mathcal{M}(p, R))]_i = \alpha(r_c(\mathcal{M}(p, R), [A_L]_{i,:}) - D), \quad i = 1, \dots, n_l \tag{4.24}$$

with $\alpha \in \mathcal{K}^e$ being a locally Lipschitz continuous function.

The existence of A_L satisfying the conditions above is guaranteed by Proposition A.14 in Appendix A.2, and a script developed to generate the required positive bases is available at https://github.com/EXPSIN/constructive_safety_critical_control.

It can be directly verified that the constraint matrix A_L associated with the QP does not depend on the state of the mobile robot, which helps simplify the complexity of analyzing the Lipschitz continuity of the controller. The block diagram of the proposed safety-critical control system is shown in Figure 4.4.

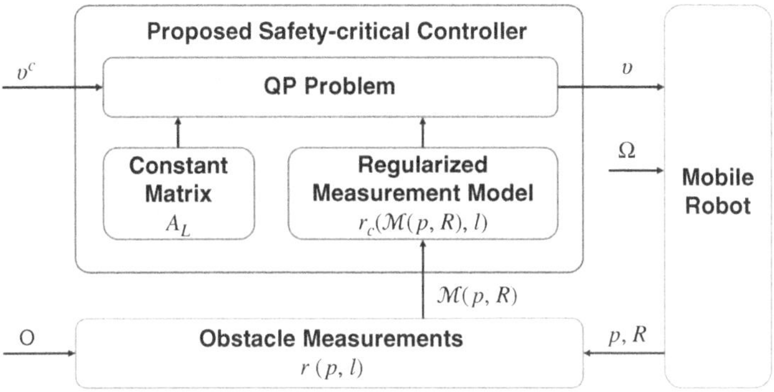

Figure 4.4 Proposed system structure for safety-critical control in cluttered environments.

4.3 Safety of the Closed-loop System

Theorem 4.1 establishes the feasibility, Lipschitz continuity, and safety of the proposed controller.

Theorem 4.1 ***(Safety of the Closed-loop System)*****:** *Consider a mobile robot modeled in* (4.1)*. Suppose that Assumptions 4.1 and 4.2 are satisfied. Choose the function* ϕ *to satisfy condition* (4.16)*. Then, the following properties hold:*

1. *The QP* (4.23) *is feasible and admits a unique solution for all* $p \in \mathcal{S}$, $R \in \mathbb{SO}(n)$, *and* $\upsilon^c \in \mathbb{R}^n$.
2. *The map resulting from solving the QP* (4.23)*, denoted by* $\rho : \mathbb{R}^n \times \mathbb{SO}(n) \times \mathbb{R}^n \to \mathbb{R}^n$, *is Lipschitz continuous with respect to* $p \in \mathcal{S}$, $R \in \mathbb{SO}(n)$, *and* $|\upsilon^c| \leq \bar{\upsilon}^c$. *Furthermore,*

$$|\rho(p, R, \upsilon^c)| \leq |\upsilon^c|, \tag{4.25}$$

   holds for all $p \in \mathcal{S}$, $R \in \mathbb{SO}(n)$ *and* $\upsilon^c \in \mathbb{R}^n$.
3. *The closed-loop system, consisting of* (4.1) *and* (4.23)*, is safe in the sense that, for any* $p(0) \in \mathcal{S}$, $R(0) \in \mathbb{SO}(n)$, *and any Lipschitz continuous* $\Omega : \mathbb{R}_+ \to \mathbb{R}^{n \times n}$ *satisfying* $\Omega(t) = -\Omega^T(t)$ *for all* $t \geq 0$, *the trajectory satisfies* $p(t) \in \mathcal{S}$ *for all* $t \geq 0$.

Proof. The properties stated in Theorem 4.1 are established below.

Property 1 (feasibility). For any $p \in \mathcal{S}$ and $R \in \mathbb{SO}(n)$, feasibility of the QP (4.23) follows from verifying $b_L(\mathcal{M}(p,R)) \geq 0$, which ensures that $\upsilon = 0$ always belongs to the feasible set. In particular, from the definitions of r_c and b_L in (4.15) and (4.24), respectively, for any $i = 1, \dots, n_l$, we have

$$[b_L(\mathcal{M}(p,R))]_i \geq \alpha\left(\inf_{|l'|=1} r(p,l') - D\right) \geq 0, \tag{4.26}$$

where the first inequality uses property (4.17), and the second follows from $|p - x| \geq D$ for all $x \in \mathcal{S}$.

Uniqueness of the solution is guaranteed by the projection theorem [21, Proposition B.11] (also see Proposition A.16).

Property 2 (Lipschitz continuity and boundedness). Consider the QP (4.7). Denote the constraints that directly affect the optimal solution by

$$\breve{A}_L \upsilon \leq \breve{b}_L(\mathcal{M}(p,R)), \tag{4.27}$$

where $\breve{A}$ and $\breve{b}(p)$ are the corresponding submatrices of A and $b(p)$, respectively.

Based on [70, Theorem 3.1] (also see Theorem B.1), the Lipschitz continuity of the QP-based controller is established as follows:

- From Property 1, the QP is feasible for all $p \in \mathcal{S}$, has a convex and closed feasible set, and admits a unique solution.
- Since $\breve{A}$ is comprised of unit vectors, its norm is bounded.
- As any n rows of A are linearly independent, there exists $c_\lambda > 0$ such that

$$\lambda_{\min}^{1/2}(\breve{A}\breve{A}^T) \geq c_\lambda, \tag{4.28}$$

and thus, for all ξ,

$$|\breve{A}^T \xi| \geq c_\lambda |\xi|. \tag{4.29}$$

Therefore, with the conditions of Theorem B.1 satisfied, the QP solution is Lipschitz continuous with respect to $b_L(\mathcal{M}(p,R)) \in \mathbb{R}_+^{n_l}$ and $|\upsilon^c| \leq \bar{\upsilon}^c$.

Additionally, the Lipschitz continuity and boundedness of r_c (given by Lemma 4.1), together with the local Lipschitz continuity of α, ensure that $b_L(\mathcal{M}(p,R))$ is Lipschitz continuous in $p \in \mathcal{S}$ and $R \in \mathbb{SO}(n)$. Using standard results for algebraic operations with Lipschitz functions [38], the controller (4.23) is Lipschitz continuous with respect to $p \in \mathcal{S}$, $R \in \mathbb{SO}(n)$, and $\upsilon^c \in \mathbb{R}^n$.

Applying the projection theorem (see Proposition A.16), we have, for any feasible υ satisfying (4.23b) and any $\upsilon^c \in \mathbb{R}^n$,

$$(0 - \upsilon)^T (\upsilon^c - \upsilon) \leq 0, \tag{4.30}$$

which implies $|\upsilon| \leq |\upsilon^c|$. Thus, property (4.25) holds for all $p \in \mathcal{S}$, $R \in \mathbb{SO}(n)$, and $\upsilon^c \in \mathbb{R}^n$.

Property 3 (safety). For any $o \in \mathcal{O}$, define the candidate zeroing barrier function

$$h_o(p) = |o - p| - D. \tag{4.31}$$

Following the definition of zeroing control barrier functions [3] (also see Section 1.1.1), the set $\mathcal{S}$ is positively invariant if there exists $\alpha_c \in \mathcal{K}^e$ such that the control input υ satisfies

$$\frac{(o-p)^T}{|o-p|} R\upsilon \le \alpha_c(|o-p| - D), \tag{4.32}$$

for all $p \in \mathcal{S}$ and $o \in \mathcal{O}$.

Recall (4.17) and (4.2), which guarantee that for any $o \in \mathcal{O}$ and $p \in \mathcal{S}$,

$$|o-p| \ge r(p, Rl_o(p,R)) \ge r_c(\mathcal{M}(p,R), l_o(p,R)), \tag{4.33}$$

where $l_o(p,R) = R^T(o-p)/|o-p|$. Then, safety is guaranteed if there exists $\alpha_c \in \mathcal{K}^e$ such that

$$l_o^T(p,R)\upsilon \le \alpha_c(r(p, Rl_o(p,R)) - D). \tag{4.34}$$

Given any $|l_*| = 1$, for any unit vector l'_* satisfying $l_*^T l'_* \ge c_A$, we have

$$\begin{aligned} r_c(\mathcal{M}(p,R), l'_*) &= \inf_{[r';l']^T \in \mathcal{M}(p,R)} \{r' + \phi(l'^T_* l')\} \\ &\le \inf_{[r';l']^T \in \mathcal{M}(p,R), l_*^T l' \ge c_A} \{r' + \phi(l'^T_* l')\} \\ &= \inf_{[r';l']^T \in \mathcal{M}(p,R), l_*^T l' \ge c_A} r(p,l') \le r(p, l_*), \end{aligned} \tag{4.35}$$

where we have used the definition (4.15) for the first equality, and used condition (4.16) for the second equality.

For any $l_o \in \mathbb{R}^n$ satisfying $|l_o| = 1$, Property 3 of A_L ensures the existence of n rows of A_L, denoted by A_{L,l_o}, and a nonnegative vector $k_{l_o} \in \mathbb{R}^n_+$ such that $l_o^T [A_{L,l_o}^T]_{i,:} \ge c_A$ for $i = 1, \dots, n$, and

$$A_{L,l_o}^T k_{l_o} = l_o. \tag{4.36}$$

Therefore,

$$l_o^T l_o = l_o^T A_{L,l_o}^T k_{l_o} = \sum_{i=1}^n l_o^T [A_{L,l_o}^T]_{:,i} [k_{l_o}]_i \ge c_A \sum_{i=1}^n [k_{l_o}]_i, \tag{4.37}$$

and

$$
\begin{aligned}
l_o^T v &= k_{l_o}^T A_{L,l_o} v \\
&\leq \sum_{i=1}^{n} [k_{l_o}]_i \alpha(r_c(\mathcal{M}(p,R), [A_{L,l_o}]_{i,:}) - D) \\
&\leq n c_A^{-1} \alpha(r_c(\mathcal{M}(p,R), [A_{L,l_o}]_{i,:}) - D) \\
&\leq n c_A^{-1} \alpha(\inf_{[r';l']^T \in \mathcal{M}(p,R), l_o^T l' \geq c_A} \{r' + \phi(l_o^T l')\} - D) \\
&\leq n c_A^{-1} \alpha(r(p, R l_o(p,R)) - D),
\end{aligned} \tag{4.38}
$$

for all $R \in \mathbb{SO}(n)$ and $p \in \mathcal{S}$, where we have used (4.36) for the first equality, used the constraints in (4.23b) for the first inequality, used (4.37) for the second inequality, used the definition of r_c in (4.15) for the third inequality, and used the condition (4.35) for the last inequality.

Thus, any v satisfying (4.23b) also satisfies (4.32) with $\alpha_c(s) = n c_A^{-1} \alpha(s)$ for $s \in \mathbb{R}$. Using [98, Theorem 3.3], we can prove that for any $p(0) \in \mathcal{S}$, $R(0) \in \mathbb{SO}(n)$ and any Lipschitz continuous Ω satisfying $\Omega = -\Omega$, the closed-loop system consisting of (4.1) and (4.23) admits a unique trajectory for all $t \geq 0$. Furthermore, the controller guarantees the safety of the mobile robot. This concludes the proof of Theorem 4.1. □

4.4 Special Case: An Integrator-like Mobile Robot

Consider a simplified scenario of the mobile robot modeled by (4.1) with $R \equiv I_n$ and $\Omega \equiv 0_{n \times n}$. In this case, the model (4.1) reduces to

$$\dot{p} = v. \tag{4.39}$$

Following the controller design procedure in Section 4.2, we construct a safety-critical controller $v = \varphi(p, v^c)$ defined by the following QP:

$$v = \operatorname{argmin} |v - v^c|^2 \tag{4.40a}$$

$$\text{s.t.} \quad A_L v \leq b(p), \quad v \in \mathbb{R}^n \tag{4.40b}$$

where $A_L \in \mathbb{R}^{n_l \times n}$ is a constant matrix satisfying the conditions stated below (4.23), and

$$[b(p)]_i = \alpha(r_c(p, [A_L]_{i,:}^T) - D), \quad i = 1, \ldots, n_l, \tag{4.41}$$

with α being a Lipschitz continuous, class $\mathcal{K}^e$ function, $D > 0$ representing the desired safe distance, and the function r_c defined by

$$r_c(p, l) = \min_{|l_0|=1} \{r(p, l_0) + \phi(l_0^T l)\} \tag{4.42}$$

for $p \in \mathbb{R}^n$ and $l \in \mathbb{R}^n$ with $|l| = 1$, where $\phi : [-1, 1] \to \mathbb{R}_+$ is a Lipschitz continuous, nonnegative, decreasing function and satisfies $\phi(s) = 0$ for $s \in [c_A, 1]$ with constant c_A satisfying $0 < c_A < 1$.

The following theorem establishes the properties of the proposed safety-critical controller for the simplified model (4.1), without accounting for body rotations.

Theorem 4.2 ***(Safety of the Closed-loop System)*****:** *Under Assumptions 4.1 and 4.2, consider the mobile robot* (4.39) *with the safety-critical controller defined in* (4.40)*. Then, the following statements hold:*

1. *The QP* (4.40) *is feasible for all $p \in \mathcal{S}$ and $v^c \in \mathbb{R}^n$.*
2. *The map φ from (p, v^c) to v, generated by solving the QP* (4.40)*, is bounded and Lipschitz continuous.*
3. *For any $p(0) \in \mathcal{S}$, the trajectory $p(t)$ is defined for all $t \geq 0$, and the set $\mathcal{S}$ is positively invariant; that is, for any $p(0) \in \mathcal{S}$, $p(t) \in \mathcal{S}$ for all $t \geq 0$.*

Theorem 4.2 is a special case of Theorem 4.1.

4.5 Simulation and Experiment

This chapter validates the preceding theoretical results through numerical simulations and physical experiments.

4.5.1 Numerical Simulations

4.5.1.1 Scenarios and Methods

Consider the scenario involving one mobile robot modeled by (4.1) with $n = 2$, and three triangular obstacles whose vertices are located at

$$([0; 1], [0; 3], [-2; 3]), \quad ([0; 0], [0; -2], [-2; -2]), \quad ([7; 0.5], [9; 1], [9; 0]), \tag{4.43}$$

respectively; see Figure 4.5. In the numerical simulations, we consider a maximum measurement range $D_B = 10.0$.

To evaluate the performance of the proposed safety-critical controller, we compare the safety-critical controller with a usual safety-critical controller and a safety-critical controller using Moreau–Yosida regularization, which are described as follows:

- **Usual safety-critical controller (UC)** defined in (4.9), which directly employs the obstacle-measurement model.

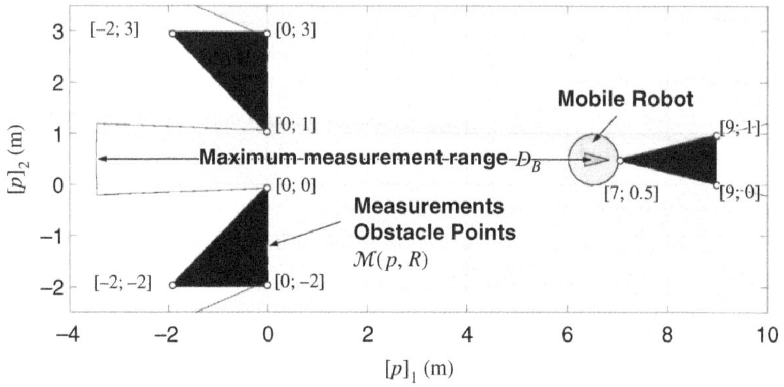

Figure 4.5 A cluttered environment setup considered in the numerical simulations.

- **Safety-critical controller using Moreau–Yosida regularization (MYC)**, which is given by

$$v = \underset{v}{\operatorname{argmin}} |v - v^c|^2 \tag{4.44a}$$

$$\text{s.t.} \quad [A_L]_{i,:} v \leq \alpha(r_{MY}(\mathcal{M}(p, R), [A_L]_{i,:}) - D), \quad i = 1, \dots, n_l \tag{4.44b}$$

where $\alpha \in \mathcal{K}^e$, r_{MY} is defined in (4.14) with $\mu = 1$, D is the expected safe distance, and

$$[A_L]_{i,:} = \left[\cos \frac{(2i+1)\pi}{n_l}, \sin \frac{(2i+1)\pi}{n_l} \right] \tag{4.45}$$

with n_l a positive odd integer.

- **The proposed safety-critical controller [PC]** defined by (4.23) with

$$\phi(s) = 2 \max\{c_A - s, 0\} \tag{4.46a}$$

$$c_A = \cos(2\pi / n_l) \tag{4.46b}$$

For the three controllers, we select the following parameters:

$$\alpha(s) = s, \quad D = 0.48, \quad n_l = 9 \tag{4.47}$$

Note that for controller **PC**, the parameters and functions in (4.45), (4.46), and (4.47) are selected per Section 4.2 to satisfy all assumptions required by Lemma 4.1 and Theorem 4.1:

- The map $\phi : [-1, 1] \to \mathbb{R}_+$ is Lipschitz and satisfies condition (4.16);
- α is any Lipschitz class-$\mathcal{K}^e$ function;
- $A_L \in \mathbb{R}^{n_l \times n}$ and $c_A \in (0, 1)$ satisfy the conditions listed below (4.23);
- The constant $D > 0$ is chosen according to the desired safe distance.

4.5.1.2 Simulation Results and Discussion

Set constant velocity-command signal $v^c(t) = [3; 0]$ and angular velocity $\Omega(t) \equiv [0, 0;\ 0, 0]$ for all $t \geq 0$. Consider the initial conditions $p(0) = [-2; 0]$ and $R(0) = [1, 0;\ 0, 1]$. Figures 4.6 and 4.7 show the position trajectories and the velocity $[v]_1$ under the three controllers. The solid curve (**PC**) maintains the expected safe distance from obstacles, as intended. By contrast, the dashed curve (**UC**) exhibits a jump in the velocity curve at $t = 4.0$, and the dotted curve (**MYC**) violates the safety constraint.

The safety violation observed in Figure 4.6 for the controller **MYC** is caused by the employment of only a finite number of constraints. In particular, when $p = [7 - D;\ 0]$, the constraints corresponding to the last two rows of A_L, as generated

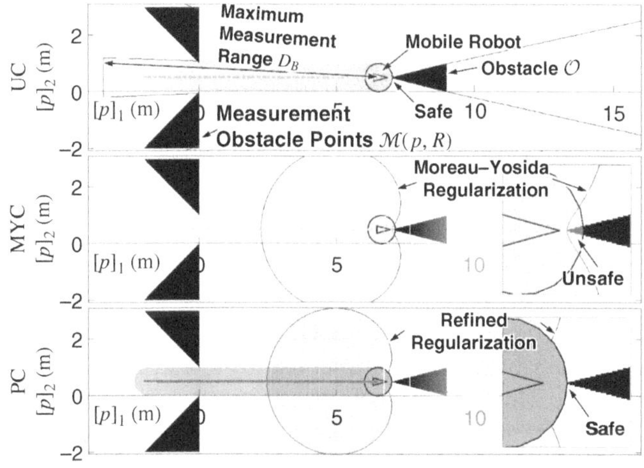

Figure 4.6 Trajectories of the position p of the mobile robot under the three controllers.

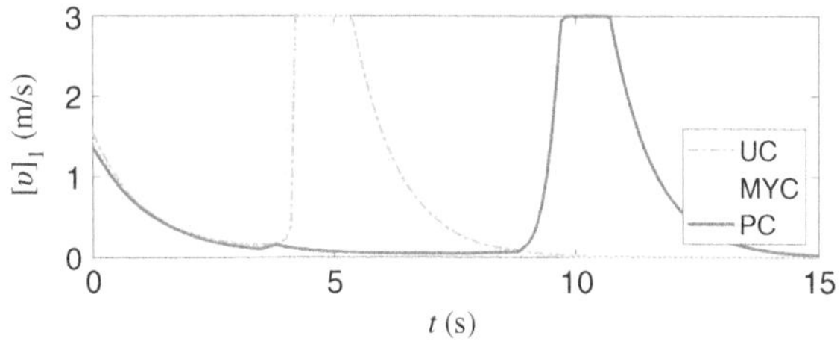

Figure 4.7 Evolution of the velocity $[v]_1$ under the three controllers.

by the **MYC** and **PC** controllers, are given by

$$\begin{bmatrix} \cos\theta_0 & \sin\theta_0 \\ \cos\theta_0 & -\sin\theta_0 \end{bmatrix} \upsilon \le \begin{bmatrix} 2-2\cos\theta_0 \\ 2-2\cos\theta_0 \end{bmatrix}, \quad \begin{bmatrix} \cos\theta_0 & \sin\theta_0 \\ \cos\theta_0 & -\sin\theta_0 \end{bmatrix} \upsilon \le \begin{bmatrix} 0 \\ 0 \end{bmatrix} \tag{4.48}$$

respectively, where $\theta_0 = \pi/n_l$. For any $0 < \upsilon_l < 2/\cos\theta_0 - 2$, the vector $[\upsilon_l; 0]$ satisfies the constraints on the left in (4.48), but violates the constraints on the right in (4.48). Note that such a control input $[\upsilon_l;\ 0]$ leads to a collision in this scenario.

We also conduct a numerical simulation to validate the robustness of the proposed safety-critical controller. The mobile robot in the simulation is modeled as a cascade of a nominal system and an actuation system, described by the following equations:

$$\dot{p} = R\upsilon_a, \qquad \dot{R} = R\Omega, \qquad \text{(nominal system)} \tag{4.49a}$$

$$\dot{z} = Az + B\upsilon, \qquad \upsilon_a = Cz, \qquad \text{(actuation system)} \tag{4.49b}$$

where $\upsilon_a \in \mathbb{R}^2$ is the actual velocity, $z \in \mathbb{R}^2$ is the state of the actuation system, $\upsilon \in \mathbb{R}^2$ is the safety-critical control input, and the constant matrices $A \in \mathbb{R}^{2\times 2}$, $B \in \mathbb{R}^{2\times 2}$, and $C \in \mathbb{R}^{2\times 2}$ are defined as:

$$A = \begin{bmatrix} -5 & 0 \\ -c_c & -5 \end{bmatrix}, \quad B = -A, \quad C = \begin{bmatrix} 1 & 0 \\ 0 & 1 \end{bmatrix} \tag{4.50}$$

where $c_c = -8$ represents the coupling term between $[z]_1$ and $[z]_2$. In the presence of the uncertain actuation dynamics, the actual velocity υ_a may not equal the safety-critical control input υ. However, it can be directly verified that the actual velocity υ_a asymptotically tracks any constant υ, and the norm of the tracking error $\upsilon_a - \upsilon$ depends on the changing rate of υ.

Considering the scenarios discussed in Section 4.5.1.1. Consider the initial state $z(0) = 0$. Figures 4.8 and 4.9 show the simulation results. In the presence of actuation dynamics, the proposed safety-critical controller (corresponding to the position trajectory shown by the solid line) helps to maintain a safe distance from obstacles, as expected. In contrast, the position trajectories of the other two controllers are unsafe around $p = [0; 0.5]$, as non-Lipschitz control inputs may lead to unexpected transient responses of the uncertain actuation system (4.49b).

4.5.2 Experimental Validation of the Body-frame Safety-critical Controller

4.5.2.1 Experimental Setup

An experimental system is designed to validate the proposed safety-critical controller in an environment with a ladder and potted plants arranged as obstacles along a corridor.

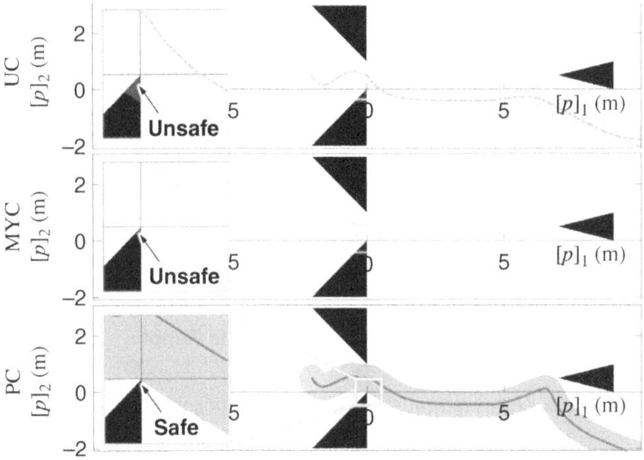

Figure 4.8 Trajectories of the position p of the mobile robot (4.49) with different controllers: the proposed safety-critical controller helps handle actuation dynamics.

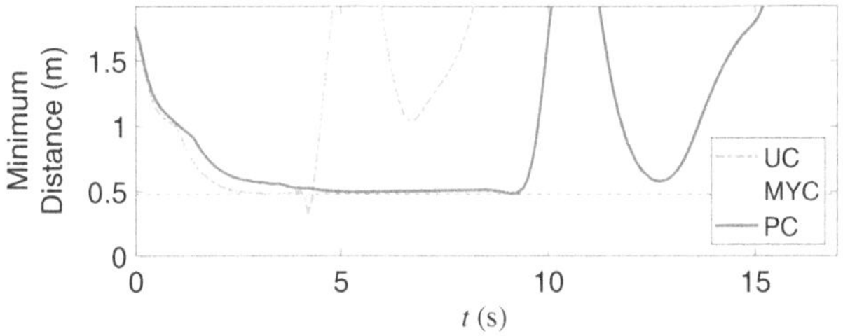

Figure 4.9 Curves of the minimum distance between the mobile robot and the cluttered environment with respect to time in the numerical simulation.

In the experiment, the mobile robot is steered to move through the corridor while avoiding the obstacles. As shown in Figures 4.10 and 4.11, the mobile robot is equipped with a four-wheeled omnidirectional chassis, a LiDAR (SLAMTEC RPLIDAR A3), and an Intel® NUC onboard computer with an i5-8260U CPU. The onboard computer runs Ubuntu 16.04 with a ROS environment to implement the safety-critical controller, log data using rosbag, and share real-time data with the supervisor. The supervisor laptop, running Windows 11, employs MATLAB to generate velocity-command signals and visualizing data in real-time.

The sampling period of the safety-critical controller is 0.05 s. The QP for safety-critical control is solved by the Goldfarb–Idnani active-set dual method [66] with a package available at https://github.com/liuq/QuadProgpp.

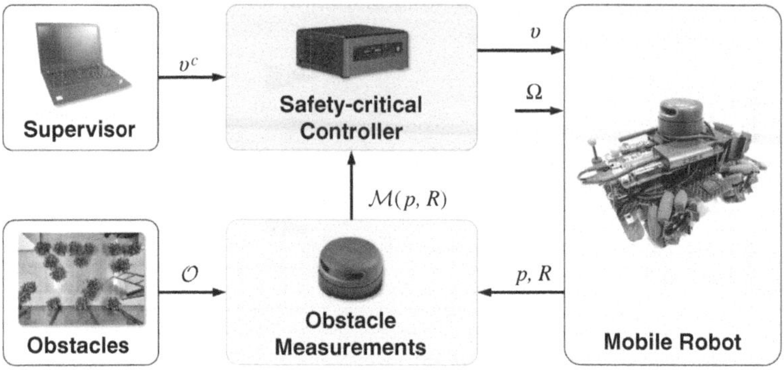

Figure 4.10 Block diagram of the experimental system for a mobile robot in a cluttered environment.

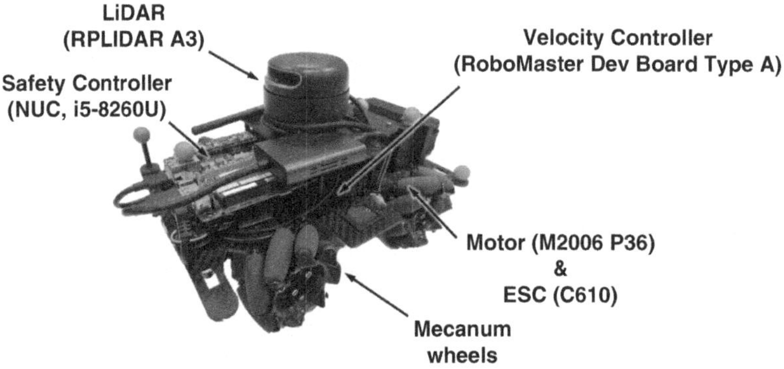

Figure 4.11 A close-up of the four-wheeled omni-direction chassis.

The parameters used in the experiment align with those in Section 4.5.1.1, except for the following updates:

$$\alpha(s) = 2.1s, \quad D = 0.26, \quad n_l = 21, \quad \phi(s) = \max\{c_A - s, 0\}. \tag{4.51}$$

The velocity-command signal v^c, generated by the supervisor computer, is designed to guide the chassis through the cluttered corridor, but may result in collisions. The angular velocity matrix Ω, which is Lipschitz continuous with respect to time t, drives the chassis to rotate while moving through the corridor. In particular, the angular velocity matrix Ω is specified as

$$\Omega(t) = \begin{bmatrix} 0 & -\dfrac{\pi}{2}\sin\dfrac{\pi t}{10} \\ \dfrac{\pi}{2}\sin\dfrac{\pi t}{10} & 0 \end{bmatrix} \tag{4.52}$$

Figure 4.12 The trajectory of the position p of the chassis moving in a corridor.

so that the robot rotates while moving. Note that this rotation does not aid collision avoidance.

4.5.2.2 Experimental Results and Discussion

The results are shown in Figures 4.12–4.15. Figure 4.12 shows that the robot starts on the left and moves rightward along the corridor; the trajectory indicates successful traversal of the cluttered environment without collision. Figure 4.13 reports a minimum distance of 0.24 m between the robot and obstacles, slightly smaller than the desired safe distance 0.26 m. This discrepancy may arise from the robot's dynamic response or LiDAR measurement inconsistencies.

Figure 4.14 compares the velocity-command signal v^c with the safety-critical control input v and confirms the Lipschitz continuity as established in Theorem 4.1. Figure 4.15 illustrates the angle and angular velocity corresponding to the orientation R and the control input Ω, respectively, demonstrating that the time-varying orientation angle does not violate the safety of the mobile robot with the proposed safety-critical controller.

4.5.3 Experimental Comparison with Other Methods Based on the Integrator Model

This section validates the proposed method based on the integrator model, through experimental comparisons with other approaches.

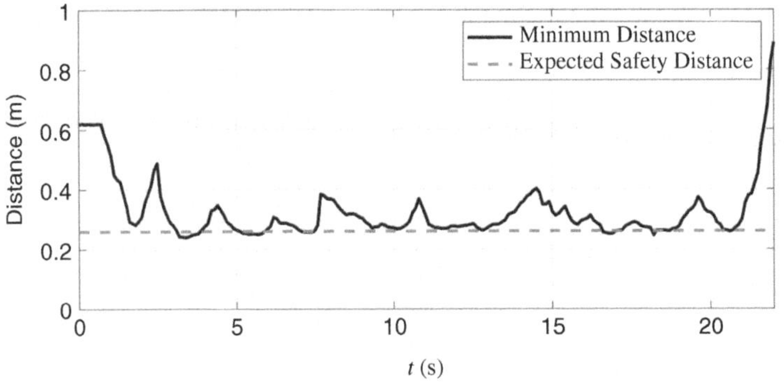

Figure 4.13 The minimum distance between the position p of the chassis and all the obstacle points in $\mathcal{O}$.

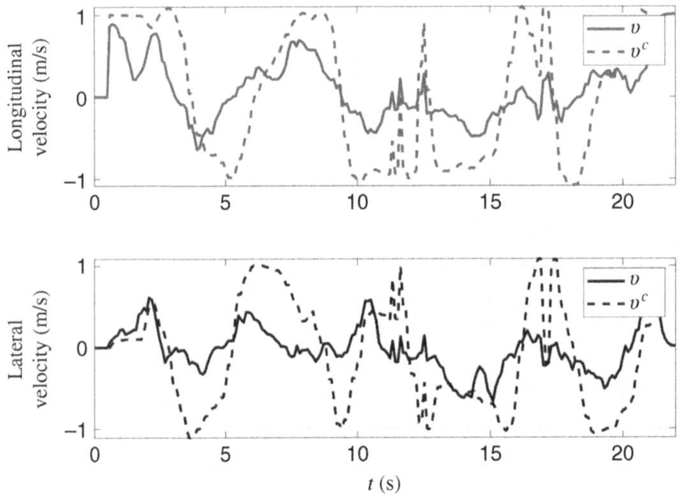

Figure 4.14 The velocity-command signal v^c and the safety-critical control input v.

4.5.3.1 Experimental System

The system setup comprises a four-wheel omnidirectional mobile robot (the one used in Section 4.5.2.1), an OptiTrack motion capture system with Motive, and a supervisor laptop; see Figures 4.16 and 4.17. The supervisor laptop runs Ubuntu 16.04 with ROS, generates paths, implements a pure-pursuit method to produce velocity commands, and monitors robot state data in real time. Figure 4.18 presents a top view of the environment. The narrowest part of the passage in the experimental setup is approximately 0.42 m wide, comparable to the robot's size.

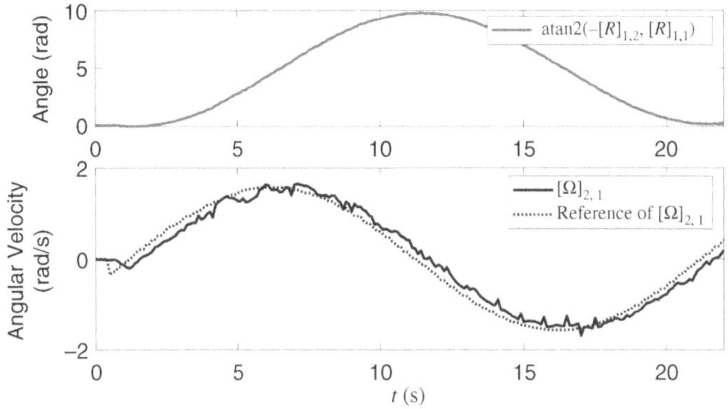

Figure 4.15 The evolution of atan2($-[R]_{1,2}, [R]_{2,1}$) and $[\Omega]_{2,1}$.

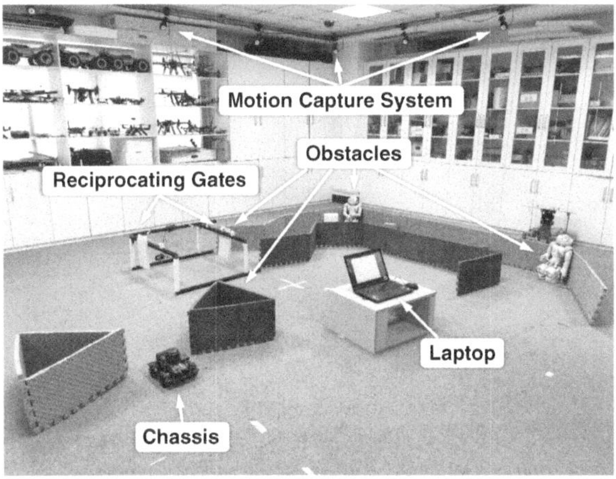

Figure 4.16 The experimental setup for the safety-critical control of an integrator mobile robot in a cluttered environment.

4.5.3.2 Methods

Safety-critical controllers are designed for the integrator model (4.39). The proposed controller is given in (4.40). In addition to the controller **R** defined in (4.40) in Section 4.4, two benchmark designs are considered for comparison:

- **Full-obstacle avoidance A:** The controller features the form (4.40) with constraints

$$A = \begin{bmatrix} \cos\theta_1 & \sin\theta_1 \\ \vdots & \vdots \\ \cos\theta_{n_S} & \sin\theta_{n_S} \end{bmatrix}, \quad b = \begin{bmatrix} \alpha(r_1 - D) \\ \vdots \\ \alpha(r_{n_S} - D) \end{bmatrix}$$

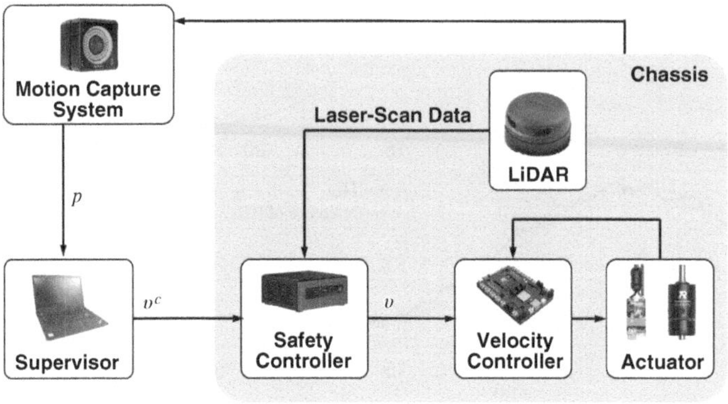

Figure 4.17 Block diagram of the experimental system for the safety-critical control of an integrator mobile robot in a cluttered environment.

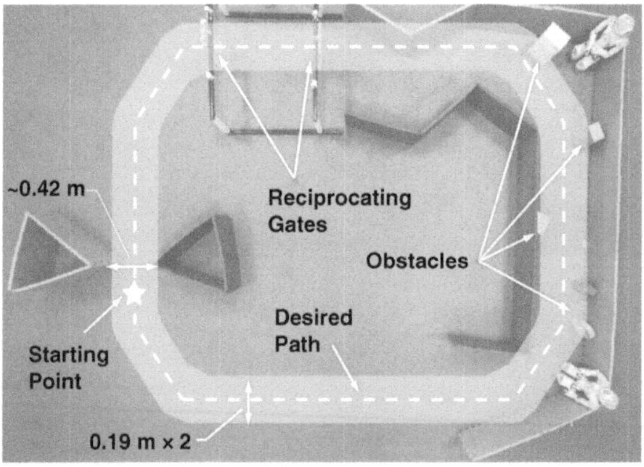

Figure 4.18 Top view of the experimental setup for safety-critical control of an integrator-like mobile robot in a cluttered environment.

where $[\theta_j, r_j]^T$ denotes the j-th element of $\mathcal{F}_B$, and n_S is the cardinality of $\mathcal{F}_B$. This method uses the positions of all the obstacle points to construct the safety constraints.

- **Nearest-obstacle avoidance N:** The controller follows (4.40) with constraints

$$A = \begin{bmatrix} \cos\theta_1 & \sin\theta_1 \\ \vdots & \vdots \\ \cos\theta_{n'_S} & \sin\theta_{n'_S} \end{bmatrix}, \quad b = \begin{bmatrix} \alpha(r_1 - D) \\ \vdots \\ \alpha(r_{n'_S} - D) \end{bmatrix}$$

where $[\theta_j, r_j]^T$ denotes the j-th element of $\mathcal{F}'_B$, and n'_S is the cardinality of $\mathcal{F}'_B$. Here,

$$\mathcal{F}'_B = \left\{[\theta, r]^T \in \mathcal{F}_B : r - \epsilon \leq \min_{[\theta', r']^T \in \mathcal{F}_B} r'\right\}$$

with a small $\epsilon > 0$.

We set the desired safe distance $D = 0.19$ m (equal to the robot radius) and choose $\alpha(s) = 2.1s$. For the controller proposed in this chapter, select

$$[A_L]_{k,:} = [\cos(2\pi(k-1)/n_l), \sin(2\pi(k-1)/n_l)] \tag{4.53}$$

with $n_l = 21$, and

$$\phi(s) = \max\left\{\cos\left(\frac{\pi}{m}\right) - s, 0\right\}. \tag{4.54}$$

4.5.3.3 Experimental Results and Discussion

Figure 4.19 shows the longitudinal velocity-loop response, revealing a discrepancy between the reference and actual velocities. In light of the analyses in Chapters 2 and 3, this discrepancy indicates uncertain actuation dynamics, which may lead to violations of the safety constraints. The lateral response is analogous to the longitudinal response and is omitted here.

Figures 4.20 and 4.21 show the robot trajectories and the curves of the minimum distances to obstacles under the different controllers. The total traversal

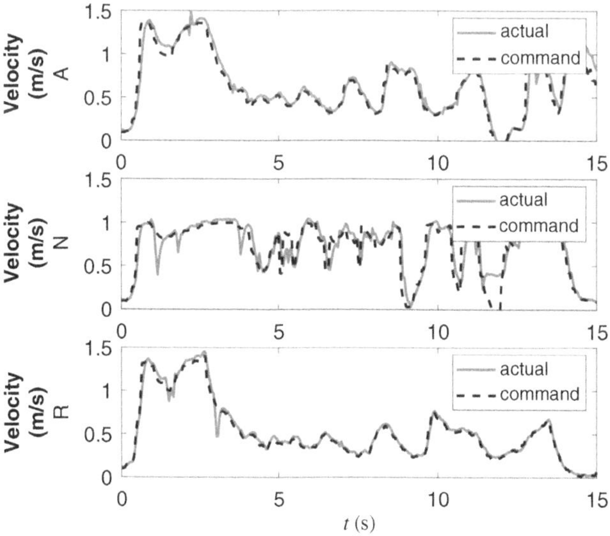

Figure 4.19 Dynamic response of the longitudinal velocity-loop of the chassis.

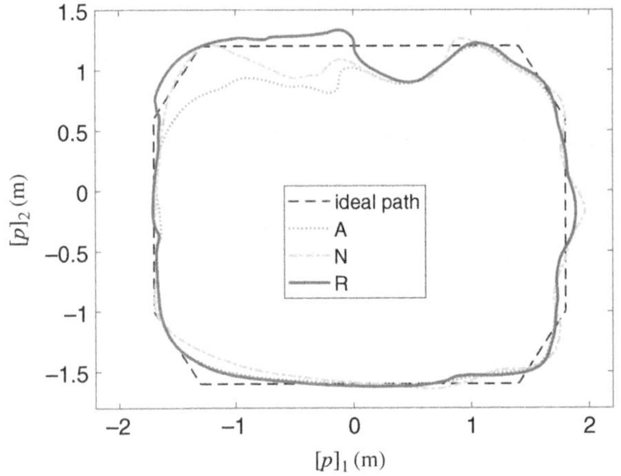

Figure 4.20 Actual paths of the integrator-like mobile robot under different safety-critical controllers.

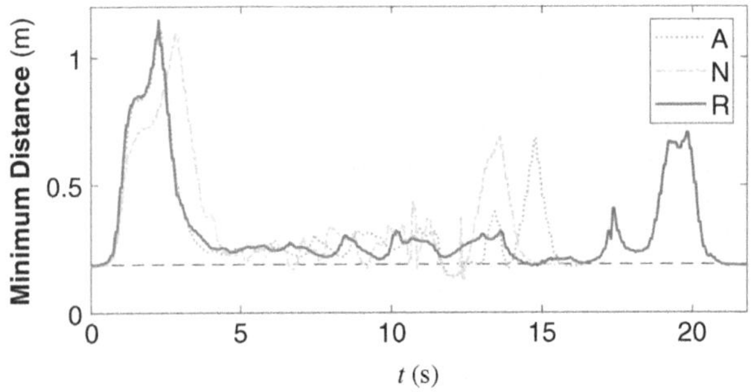

Figure 4.21 Minimum distances between the obstacles and the integrator-like mobile robot under different safety-critical controllers.

times under controllers **A**, **N**, and **R** are 16.4 s, 15.45 s, and 21.8 s, respectively. Note that the techniques of regularization and feasible-set reshaping proposed in this chapter reduce the feasible set of the safety-critical controller. Although controller **N** achieves the shortest traversal time, it frequently violates the safety constraint $D = 0.19$ m.

Due to dynamic uncertainty, the safe distance $D = 0.19$ m may not be perfectly fulfilled. For any $d_s > 0$, let n_s denote the number of time instants at which the robot-obstacle minimum distance is less than d_s. The d_s-n_s relations for all controllers are shown in Figure 4.22. Clearly, for $d_s < 0.19$, controller **R** produces a significantly smaller n_s than the other controllers, indicating improved safety.

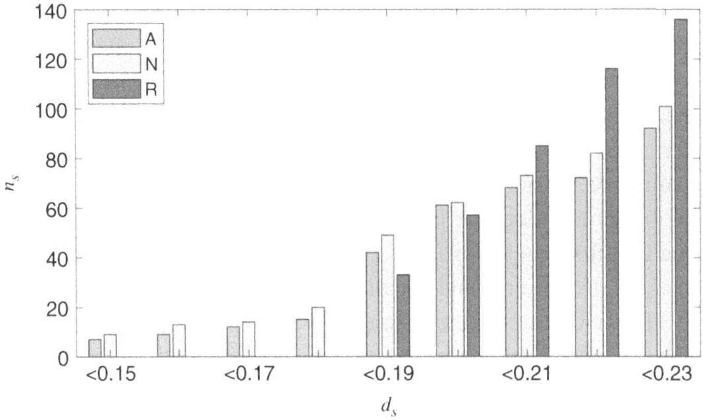

Figure 4.22 Number of time instants when the minimum distance between the mobile robot and the obstacle is less than d_s.

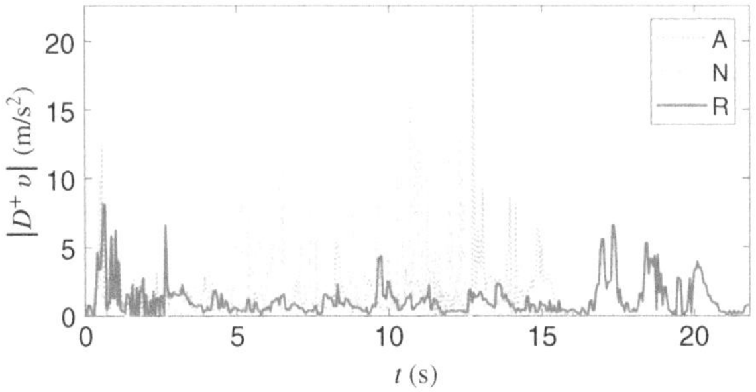

Figure 4.23 Derivatives of the velocity commands.

Figure 4.23 shows that the Dini derivative of the velocity-reference input under controller **R** is markedly smaller than under the other controllers. A smaller Dini derivative ensures a smaller velocity-tracking error and thereby enhances safety with respect to obstacles in the cluttered environment.

A video of the experiment is available at https://youtu.be/1ZYH-ydpLhw.

4.6 Notes

The objective of safety-critical control in cluttered environments is to accomplish real-time collision avoidance and stable trajectory tracking in spaces populated by unknown obstacles. To this end, reference [77] proposed a distributed coordination strategy for cooperative collision avoidance of multiwheeled robots operating in unknown complex environments, leveraging onboard sensing and shared communication to maintain safe inter-robot distances and to plan paths that achieve global obstacle avoidance. Reference [86] incorporated multiple control barrier functions into navigation in cluttered environments by designing distinct barrier functions for different obstacles and safety requirements, thereby ensuring system safety under multiple simultaneous constraints. For micro aerial vehicles in dense indoor environments, reference [131] developed a reactive model predictive control scheme that fuses stereo vision with inertial measurements to enable online three-dimensional mapping and localization, and combines linear analytic trajectory tracking with an efficient discretized collision-avoidance strategy, achieving low computational load and high real-time performance on embedded platforms. Reference [59] proposed a complete and robust system, which considered unmapped or moving obstacles, for the aggressive flight of autonomous quadrotors.

Ensuring continuity of control inputs in cluttered environments is a core challenge in safety-critical control of mobile agents. First, obstacle measurement errors can induce discontinuities in feedback signals [140], which cause gradient-based methods (e.g., artificial potential fields [179] and control barrier functions [63]) to yield discontinuous control laws. A further difficulty in guaranteeing continuity arises at the optimization layer. Regularity of QP solutions typically hinges on constraint qualifications, particularly the linear independence constraint qualification (LICQ), which requires that the coefficient matrix of the constraints that directly affect the optimal solution is of full row rank [161, 70]. In cluttered environments with multiple nearby obstacles and constraints, even if the feedback signal is continuous, the linear independence condition may be violated when the active constraints induced by cluttered environments become linearly dependent [148].

5

Safety-critical Control of Multi-agent Systems: Feasible-set Reshaping and Nonlinear Small-gain Synthesis

This chapter extends the study in Chapters 2 and 3 to multi-agent systems, for which the agents are required to keep safe with respect to each other as well as stationary obstacles. As in Chapter 2, each mobile agent is modeled as a cascade connection of an integrator (the nominal system) and an actuator exhibiting dynamic uncertainties. The velocity-tracking capability of the actuator is still characterized by input-to-output stability (IOS).

In the multi-agent system setup, the separation property assumption on the obstacles (as made in Assumption 3.3 in Chapter 3) cannot be guaranteed in advance if, for each agent, the other agents are considered as moving obstacles. As demonstrated by illustrative examples in this chapter, the presence of uncertain actuation dynamics poses feasibility and Lipschitz continuity challenges when standard safety-critical controllers based on quadratic programming (QP) are directly applied.

This chapter introduces a nontrivial refinement of the feasible-set reshaping technique for seamless integration with relaxation parameters (RPs), resulting in a new class of safety-critical controllers that are implemented in a decentralized manner and ensure feasibility, local Lipschitz continuity, and robust safety (Figure 5.1).

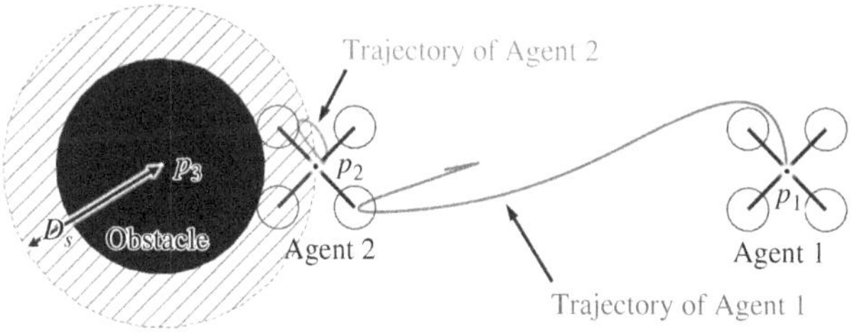

Figure 5.1 A scenario of safety-critical control of multiple mobile agents.

5.1 Problem Formulation

Consider a scenario involving n_a mobile agents and n_o obstacles with the indices given by

$$\mathcal{N}_a = \{1, \dots, n_a\}, \qquad \mathcal{N}_o = \{n_a + 1, \dots, n_a + n_o\}, \tag{5.1}$$

respectively. Define $\mathcal{N}_{ao} = \mathcal{N}_a \cup \mathcal{N}_o$, and let $n_{ao} = n_a + n_o$. For each $i \in \mathcal{N}_{ao}$, use $p_i \in \mathbb{R}^n$ to denote the position of either an agent or an obstacle, and use

$$p = [p_1, \dots, p_{n_{ao}}] \tag{5.2}$$

to represent the positions of all agents and obstacles.

For $i \in \mathcal{N}_a$, each agent i is modeled as a cascade connection of a nominal system and an uncertain actuation system. The nominal system is described by

$$\dot{p}_i = v_i, \tag{5.3}$$

where $v_i \in \mathbb{R}^n$ is the agent's velocity. The velocity v_i is generated by an actuation system of the general form:

$$\dot{z}_i = f(z_i, v_i^*), \qquad v_i = g(z_i, v_i^*), \tag{5.4}$$

where $z_i \in \mathbb{R}^m$ is the actuation system state, $v_i^* \in \mathbb{R}^n$ is the velocity-reference input, and f and g are locally Lipschitz functions.

In this chapter, with appropriately designed controllers, the multi-agent system modeled by (5.3) and (5.4) is said to be safe if, under suitable initial conditions

$$\min_{i\in\mathcal{N}_a,\, j\in\mathcal{N}_{ao}\setminus\{i\}} |p_i(0) - p_j(0)| \geq \underline{D}_0, \qquad \max_{i\in\mathcal{N}_a} |z_i| \leq \bar{z}_0, \tag{5.5}$$

with $\underline{D}_0, \bar{z}_0 > 0$, the relative positions of the mobile agents satisfy

$$\min_{i\in\mathcal{N}_a,\, j\in\mathcal{N}_{ao}\setminus\{i\}} |p_i(t) - p_j(t)| \geq D \tag{5.6}$$

for all $t \geq 0$, where $D > 0$ is the safety margin.

For each agent i, let $v_i^c \in \mathbb{R}^n$ denote the velocity-command signal for the primary objective. For each agent, a safety-critical controller is to be designed to incorporate both the velocity-command signal and the safety constraints. The expected structure of the safety-critical control system is depicted in Figure 5.2.

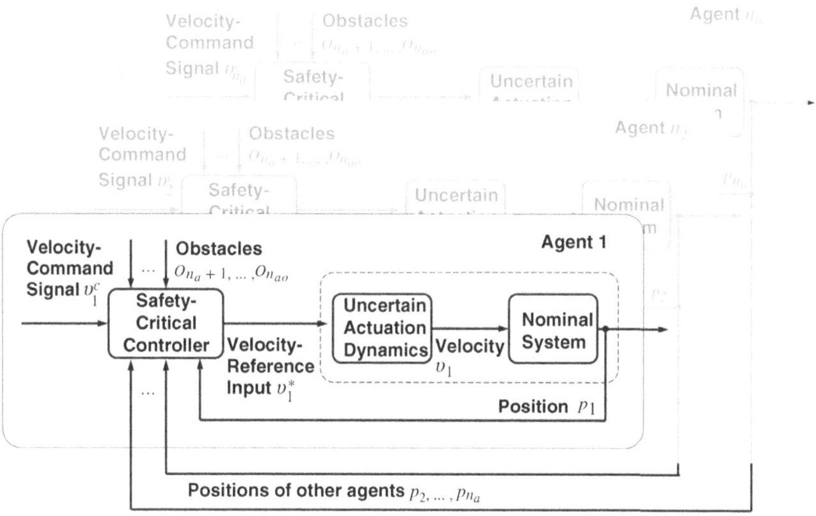

Figure 5.2 Safety-critical control system structure of a mobile agent in a multi-agent system.

5.1.1 Assumptions on the Uncertain Actuation System and Velocity-command Signals

In the presence of uncertain actuation dynamics, the actual velocity v_i may not coincide with the velocity-reference input v_i^*. Define the velocity-tracking error as

$$\tilde{v}_i = v_i - v_i^*. \tag{5.7}$$

The nominal dynamics (5.3) can thus be rewritten as

$$\dot{p}_i = v_i = v_i^* + \tilde{v}_i. \tag{5.8}$$

It is crucial that the actuation system is inherently stable and exhibits the velocity-tracking property. We assume that for any constant velocity-reference input v_i^*, the actual velocity v_i asymptotically converges to v_i^*, and for any time-varying v_i^*, the tracking error $\tilde{v}_i$ depends on the changing rate of v_i^*.

In particular, we impose the following assumption on the uncertain actuation system.

Assumption 5.1 (*Reference-tracking Capability of the Actuation System*): Consider the actuation system (5.4). There exist locally Lipschitz functions $\alpha_{z1}, \alpha_{z2}, \gamma_{\tilde{v}}^{v^{*d}} \in \mathcal{K}$ and constants $c_{\tilde{v}} \geq 1$, $\lambda > 0$ such that, for any initial state $z_i(0)$

and any locally Lipschitz velocity-reference input v_i^*,

$$|\tilde{v}_i(t)| \leq \beta_{\tilde{v}}(|z_i(0)| + |v^*(0)|, t) + \gamma_{\tilde{v}}^{v^{*d}}(\|D^+ v_i^*\|_t) \tag{5.9}$$

$$|z_i(t)| \leq \alpha_{z1}(|z_i(0)|) + \alpha_{z2}(\|v_i^*\|_t) \tag{5.10}$$

for all $t \geq 0$, where $\beta_{\tilde{v}}(s,t) = c_{\tilde{v}} e^{-\lambda t} s$ for $s, t \in \mathbb{R}_+$.

In practice, v_i^c can be generated by a high-level planner or primary controller. Without loss of generality, we impose the following assumption on v_i^c.

Assumption 5.2 (*Boundedness of Velocity-command Signals and Their Derivatives*): For each $i \in \mathcal{N}_a$, v_i^c is continuously differentiable in time, and there exist constants $\bar{v}^c, \bar{v}^{cd} > 0$ such that

$$|v_i^c(t)| \leq \bar{v}^c, \qquad |\dot{v}_i^c(t)| \leq \bar{v}^{cd} \tag{5.11}$$

for all $t \geq 0$.

5.1.2 Characterization of Safety

For the multi-agent system (5.3) and (5.4), define the relative positions as

$$\tilde{p}_{ij} = p_i - p_j \tag{5.12}$$

for $i, j \in \mathcal{N}_{ao}$, $i \neq j$. From (5.8), it follows that

$$\dot{\tilde{p}}_{ij} = v_i - v_j = v_i^* - v_j^* + \tilde{v}_i - \tilde{v}_j. \tag{5.13}$$

To characterize the safety of agent i with respect to another agent or obstacle j, define

$$h(\tilde{p}_{ij}) = \mu(|\tilde{p}_{ij}|), \tag{5.14}$$

where $\mu : (0, \infty) \to \mathbb{R}_+$ is an $\mathcal{M}^-\mathcal{C}$ function. If the velocity-reference inputs v_i^* and v_j^* satisfy

$$-\frac{\tilde{p}_{ij}^T}{|\tilde{p}_{ij}|}(v_i^* - v_j^*) \leq -\alpha_h(h(\tilde{p}_{ij}) - \mu(D_s)) \tag{5.15}$$

with $\alpha_h \in \mathcal{K}^e$ and $D_s > 0$ being a constant that introduces an additional safety margin, then, along the trajectories of (5.13),

$$\nabla h(\tilde{p}_{ij})\dot{\tilde{p}}_{ij} \leq \frac{\partial \mu(|\tilde{p}_{ij}|)}{\partial |\tilde{p}_{ij}|}\left(\alpha_h(h(\tilde{p}_{ij}) - \mu(D_s)) + \frac{\tilde{p}_{ij}^T}{|\tilde{p}_{ij}|}(\tilde{v}_i - \tilde{v}_j)\right), \tag{5.16}$$

and hence,

$$h(\tilde{p}_{ij}) \geq \alpha_h^{-1}(|\tilde{v}_i| + |\tilde{v}_j|) + \mu(D_s) \quad \Rightarrow \quad \nabla h(\tilde{p}_{ij})\dot{\tilde{p}}_{ij} \leq 0. \tag{5.17}$$

If the initial states satisfy $h(\tilde{p}_{ij}(0)) \leq \mu(D)$ and the velocity-tracking errors satisfy $\|\tilde{v}_i\|_\infty + \|\tilde{v}_j\|_\infty \leq \alpha_h(\mu(D) - \mu(D_s))$, then, under the assumption that $p_{ij}(t)$ is defined for all $t \geq 0$,

$$h(\tilde{p}_{ij}(t)) \leq \mu(D) \tag{5.18}$$

holds for all $t \geq 0$, following an argument analogous to that for ISS-Lyapunov functions [184, 188], which establishes safety according to (5.6).

5.2 Trials with Standard Designs

If the agents are free of uncertain actuation dynamics, then the safety-critical control problem would be readily solvable by applying barrier-function-based QP designs [167] and using the idea of positive invariance [6, Theorem 1].

In this section, we try to address the technical difficulties caused by the uncertain actuation dynamics for safety-critical control of multi-agent systems based on standard QP designs.

5.2.1 A QP-based Controller with an Extended Safety Margin

This section directly extends the discussion in Example 1.4 to the safety-critical control of multi-agent systems.

For convenience of notations, denote

$$h_{ij} = h(\tilde{p}_{ij}). \tag{5.19}$$

Given the velocity-command signal v_i^c, with the velocity-reference input v_i^* considered as the control input, we consider a QP-based safety-critical controller:

$$v_i^* = \operatorname*{argmin}_{v_i^* \in \mathcal{P}_i^o(p)} |v_i^* - v_i^c|^2, \tag{5.20}$$

where

$$\mathcal{P}_i^o(p) = \{v_i^* \in \mathbb{R}^n : A_i^o(p)v_i^* + a_i^o(p) \leq 0\} \tag{5.21}$$

is the feasible set with

$$A_i^o(p) = \left[-\frac{\tilde{p}_{i1}}{|\tilde{p}_{i1}|}, \dots, -\frac{\tilde{p}_{i(i-1)}}{|\tilde{p}_{i(i-1)}|}, -\frac{\tilde{p}_{i(i+1)}}{|\tilde{p}_{i(i+1)}|}, \dots, -\frac{\tilde{p}_{in_{ao}}}{|\tilde{p}_{in_{ao}}|} \right]^T, \tag{5.22}$$

$$\begin{aligned} a_i^o(p) = [&\alpha_h(h_{i1} - \mu(D_s)), \dots, \alpha_h(h_{i(i-1)} - \mu(D_s)), \dots \\ &\alpha_h(h_{i(i+1)} - \mu(D_s)), \dots, \alpha_h(h_{in_{ao}} - \mu(D_s))]^T. \end{aligned} \tag{5.23}$$

Here, α_h is a continuously differentiable class $\mathcal{K}^e$ function. The controller (5.20) is valid as long as $\tilde{p}_{ij} \neq 0$ for $i \in \mathcal{N}_a$ and $j \in \mathcal{N}_{ao} \setminus \{i\}$.

For the multi-agent system, if $\tilde{v}_i \equiv 0$, then the QP-based controller (5.20) ensures safety and at the same time selects the velocity-reference input v_i^* as close to the velocity-command signal v_i^c as possible. However, when $\tilde{v}_i$ cannot be neglected, safety could be violated. An intuitive solution is to extend the safety margin [57]; however, this may cause the QP-based controller infeasible when the total number of the constraints is larger than one; see Example 5.1.

Continuing the discussion in Section 1.5.2, we recall the discussion in Example 1.4 in the context of multi-agent systems.

Example 5.1 (*Infeasibility of a Safety-critical Controller with Enlarged Safety Margins*): *Consider the scenario involving one mobile agent with position p_1 and two obstacles with positions p_2 and p_3. In this example, we consider $p_2 = [0.5; 0.5]$, $p_3 = -[0.5; 0.5]$, and $v_1^c = [1; -1]$. If the velocity-tracking error $\tilde{v}$ is neglectable, then one may consider*

$$v_1^* = \underset{v_1^* \in \mathcal{P}_1^o(p)}{\operatorname{argmin}} |v_1^* - v_1^c|^2, \tag{5.24}$$

where $\mathcal{P}_1^o = \{v_1^* \in \mathbb{R}^n : A_1^o v_1^* + a_1^o \leq 0\}$ with $A_1^o = [-\tilde{p}_{12}/|\tilde{p}_{12}|, -\tilde{p}_{13}/|\tilde{p}_{13}|]^T$ and $a_1^o = [|\tilde{p}_{12}|^{-1} - D^{-1}, |\tilde{p}_{13}|^{-1} - D^{-1}]^T$.

When the velocity-tracking error $\tilde{v}_1$ is nonzero, one may consider extending the safety margin and redesigning the safety-critical controller with a new $a_1^o = [|\tilde{p}_{12}|^{-1} - D_s^{-1}; |\tilde{p}_{13}|^{-1} - D_s^{-1}]$. But, such a treatment may result in an empty feasible set at specific positions inside the desired safe regions. For example, in the case of $D = 0.6$ and $D_s = 1$, when $p_1 = [0; 0]$, the feasible set $\mathcal{P}_1^o$ in (5.21) should satisfy $\sqrt{2}^{-1}[1, 1; -1, -1]v_1^* \leq (\sqrt{2} - 1)[1; 1]$, and thus is empty.

5.2.2 Introducing a Relaxation Parameter

As an alternative solution, we introduce a RP [6, 87, 211] to the QP-based controller as

$$\begin{bmatrix} v_i^* \\ \delta_i \end{bmatrix} = \underset{[v_i^*;\delta_i] \in \mathcal{P}_i^s(p)}{\operatorname{argmin}} \frac{1}{2} \begin{bmatrix} v_i^* \\ \delta_i \end{bmatrix}^T \begin{bmatrix} v_i^* \\ \delta_i \end{bmatrix} - \begin{bmatrix} v_i^c \\ \delta \end{bmatrix}^T \begin{bmatrix} v_i^* \\ \delta_i \end{bmatrix}, \tag{5.25}$$

where δ_i is the RP, $\delta \in \mathbb{R}_+$ is a positive constant,

$$\mathcal{P}_i^s(p) = \{[v_i^*; \delta_i] : A_i^s(p) v_i^* + a_i^s(p)\delta_i \leq 0, \delta_i \geq 0\} \tag{5.26}$$

is the feasible set with $A_i^s(p) = A_i^o(p)$ defined in (5.22), and without loss of generality, we choose

$$a_i^s(p) = \frac{1}{\delta} a_i^o(p) \tag{5.27}$$

with $a_i^o(p)$ defined in (5.23).

Clearly, if $\tilde{p}_{ij} \neq 0$ for $i \in \mathcal{N}_a$ and $j \in \mathcal{N}_{ao} \backslash \{i\}$, then 0 is always an element of $\mathcal{P}_i^s(p)$ and thus the QP-based controller is always feasible. From the studies in the previous chapters, the importance of Lipschitz continuity for robust safety-critical control has already been established, particularly when uncertain actuation dynamics cannot be neglected. However, QP-based controllers with feasible sets constructed directly from the safety constraints may not be Lipschitz continuous, even when modifications such as enlarging the safety margin or introducing RPs are made.

Example 5.2 (*Non-Lipschitz Continuity of the Relaxed Safety-critical Controller*): *Still consider the case in Example 5.1. Consider the QP* (5.25)*, we use* $(\breve{A}_i^s, \breve{a}_i^s)$ *to represent the constraints that directly affect the optimal solution, with* $\breve{A}_i^s$ *and* $\breve{a}_i^s$ *being submatrices of* A_i^s *and* a_i^s*, respectively. From [21, Example 2.1.5], the solution to the QP is*

$$v_1^* = v_1^c - \breve{A}_1^{sT}(\breve{A}_1^s \breve{A}_1^{sT} + \breve{a}_1^s \breve{a}_1^{sT})^{-1}(\breve{A}_1^s v_1^c + \breve{a}_1^s \delta). \tag{5.28}$$

Suppose that the constraints that directly affect the optimal solution are not changed in some domain of p*. Then, in this domain, taking the partial derivative of* v_1^* *with respect to* $\breve{a}_1^s$ *yields*

$$\begin{aligned} \frac{\partial v_1^*}{\partial \breve{a}_1^{sT}} &= \frac{\delta \Lambda_2 (2\Lambda_3 \Lambda_0^{-1} - \Lambda_1) - 2\Lambda_2 \Lambda_3 \Lambda_2^T v_1^c \breve{a}_1^{sT} \Lambda_0^{-1}}{\Lambda_1^2} \\ &+ \frac{(v_1^{cT} \Lambda_2 \breve{a}_1^s) \otimes \Lambda_2 + (v_1^{cT} \Lambda_2) \otimes (\Lambda_2 \breve{a}_1^s)}{\Lambda_1}, \end{aligned} \tag{5.29}$$

where $\Lambda_0 = \breve{A}_1^s \breve{A}_1^{sT}$*,* $\Lambda_1 = (1 + \breve{a}_1^{sT} \Lambda_0^{-1} \breve{a}_1^s)$*,* $\Lambda_2 = \breve{A}_1^{sT} \Lambda_0^{-1}$*, and* $\Lambda_3 = \breve{a}_1^s \breve{a}_1^{sT}$*. Here,* $\breve{A}_1^s$ *consists of the relative positions between the agent and the obstacles. Thus,* $\sigma_{\min}(\breve{A}_1^s)$ *cannot be guaranteed to be lower bounded by a positive constant. This means that the solution to the QP may not be Lipschitz with respect to* $a_i^s(p)$*. Indeed, [70, Theorem 3.1] (also see Theorem B.1) requires a positive lower bound of* $\sigma_{\min}(\breve{A}_1^s)$ *to guarantee the Lipschitz continuity of the QP. In this numerical example, we consider* $D = 0.6$*,* $D_s = 0.68$*,* $v_1^c = [1; -1]$*,* $p_1 \in \{p_1 : |\tilde{p}_{1j}| \geq D, j = 2, 3\}$*,* $p_2 = [0.5; 0.5]$*,* $p_3 = -[0.5; 0.5]$*,* $\delta = 100$*,* $A_1^s(p) = [-\tilde{p}_{12}/|\tilde{p}_{12}|, -\tilde{p}_{13}/|\tilde{p}_{13}|]^T$*, and*

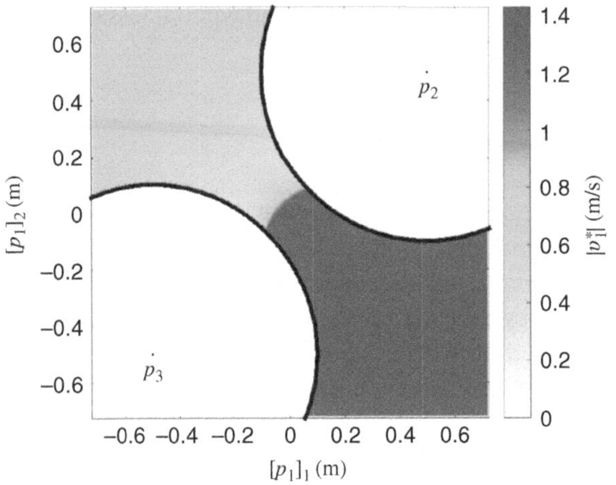

Figure 5.3 $|v_1^*|$ with respect to different p_1: Lipschitz continuity of the solution to the QP cannot be guaranteed by simply adding RPs.

$a_1^s(p) = \delta^{-1}\left[|\tilde{p}_{12}|^{-1} - D_s^{-1}, |\tilde{p}_{12}|^{-1} - D_s^{-1}\right]^T$. *Figure 5.3 shows how* p_1 *influences* $|v_1^*|$. *One may observe sudden changes of* $|v_1^*|$ *when* p_1 *is close to zero.*

5.3 Feasible-set Reshaping and Controller Design

In this section, we introduce a new class of QP-based controllers that incorporate RPs and a refined feasible-set reshaping technique to address the non-Lipschitz issue highlighted in Section 5.2. Compared with the feasible-set reshaping technique presented in Chapter 3, the refined design still projects the original safety constraints onto an appropriately chosen constant matrix to retain both feasibility and Lipschitz continuity. The key difference is that it explicitly accounts for the influence of the RPs.

Specifically, the proposed safety-critical controller is in the form of

$$\begin{bmatrix} v_i^* \\ \delta_i \end{bmatrix} = \underset{[v_i^*;\delta_i]\in\mathcal{P}_i^r(p)}{\operatorname{argmin}} \frac{1}{2}\begin{bmatrix} v_i^* \\ \delta_i \end{bmatrix}^T \begin{bmatrix} v_i^* \\ \delta_i \end{bmatrix} - \begin{bmatrix} v_i^c \\ \delta \end{bmatrix}^T \begin{bmatrix} v_i^* \\ \delta_i \end{bmatrix}, \tag{5.30}$$

where

$$\mathcal{P}_i^r(p) = \{[v_i^*;\delta_i] : A_i^r v_i^* + a_i^r(p)\delta_i \le 0, \delta_i \ge 0\} \tag{5.31}$$

is the reshaped feasible set. Here, $A_i^r \in \mathbb{R}^{n_l \times n}$ is a constant matrix admitting the following properties:

1. Each $[A_i^r]_{i,:}$ is a unit vector, i.e., $|[A_i^r]_{i,:}| = 1$;
2. Any n rows of A_i^r are linearly independent;
3. Any unit vector $l_0 \in \mathbb{R}^n$ is a positive combination of the elements of $\{[A_i^r]_{i,:}^T : [A_i^r]_{i,:} l_0 \geq c_A, i = 1, \dots, n_l\}$, whose cardinality is not less than n, with $c_A \in (0, 1)$ being a positive constant.

We choose $a_i^r : \mathbb{R}^{n \times n_{ao}} \to \mathbb{R}^{n_l}$ as

$$a_i^r(p) = \max\left\{\varphi\left(A_i^s(p), a_i^s(p), \frac{c_P}{\delta}\right)\right\} \tag{5.32}$$

with

$$\begin{aligned}\varphi\left(A_i^s, a_i^s, \frac{c_P}{\delta}\right) &= A_i^r A_i^{sT} \odot a_i^{sT} \\ &\quad - \mathrm{sat}(c_K(c_A - A_i^r A_i^{sT})) \odot (A_i^r A_i^{sT} \odot a_i^{sT} + \frac{c_P}{\delta}),\end{aligned} \tag{5.33}$$

where $c_K \geq 1/c_A$ and c_P can be any positive constants, and δ, A_i^s, and a_i^s are defined in (5.25)–(5.26). When tuning the controller, one may first choose c_A, and then select A_i^r and c_K based on c_A. The existence of A_i^r satisfying the above conditions is guaranteed by Proposition A.14 in Appendix A.2, and a script developed to generate the required A_i^r is available at https://github.com/EXPSIN/constructive_safety_critical_control.

In Example 5.3, we evaluate the refined QP-based controller (5.30) in the same scenario as in Examples 5.1 and 5.2.

Example 5.3 (*Comparison of Safety-critical Controllers in Terms of Lipschitz Continuity*): *Continuing from Example 5.2, we construct $\mathcal{P}_i^r$ in the form of* (5.31) *and analyze the solution to the QP* (5.30) *with a reshaped feasible set. For any odd integer $n_l \geq 5$, a typical $A_i^r \in \mathbb{R}^{n_l \times 2}$ is composed of the outward normal vectors of a regular polygon with an odd number of sides; explicitly, each row of A_i^r is $[\cos(2\pi j/n_l), \sin(2\pi j/n_l)]$ for $j = 1, \dots, n_l$. Accordingly, $c_A = \cos(2\pi/n_l)$.*

In the numerical simulation, we set $n_l = 5$, $c_K = 1$, $c_P = 5/2$, and $c_A = \cos(2\pi/5)$. Figure 5.4 shows the original and reshaped feasible sets for $p_1 = [-0.4;\ 0.4]$. Figure 5.5 shows how p_1 influences $|v_1^*|$, which aligns with our expectation of Lipschitz continuity.

When the RP δ_i approaches zero, robustness with respect to the velocity-tracking error $\tilde{v}_i$ is diminished (see (5.74) in the proof of Proposition 5.3). In this scenario, following the approach in [211], we set $v_i^* = 0$. Consequently, the implemented safety-critical controller is defined as

$$\begin{bmatrix} v_i^*(t) \\ \delta_i(t) \end{bmatrix} = \begin{cases} \underset{[v_i^*;\delta_i]\in\mathcal{P}_i^r(p)}{\operatorname{argmin}} \ \frac{1}{2}\begin{bmatrix} v_i^* \\ \delta_i \end{bmatrix}^T \begin{bmatrix} v_i^* \\ \delta_i \end{bmatrix} - \begin{bmatrix} v_i^c \\ \delta \end{bmatrix}^T \begin{bmatrix} v_i^* \\ \delta_i \end{bmatrix}, & \text{if } \inf_{\tau\in[0,t)} \delta_i(\tau) \neq 0, \\ 0, & \text{if } \inf_{\tau\in[0,t)} \delta_i(\tau) = 0, \end{cases} \tag{5.34}$$

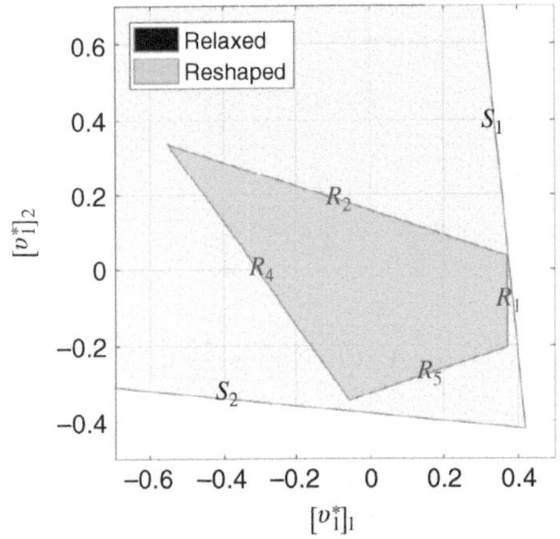

Figure 5.4 Relaxed and the reshaped feasible sets with $S_i : [A_s^1]_{i,:} v^* = -[a_s^1]_i \delta_1$ for $i = 1, 2$ and $R_i : [A_r^1]_{i,:} v^* = -[a_r^1]_i \delta_1$ for $i = 1, \ldots, 5$. R_3 corresponds to a redundant constraint, and is outside the range of the figure.

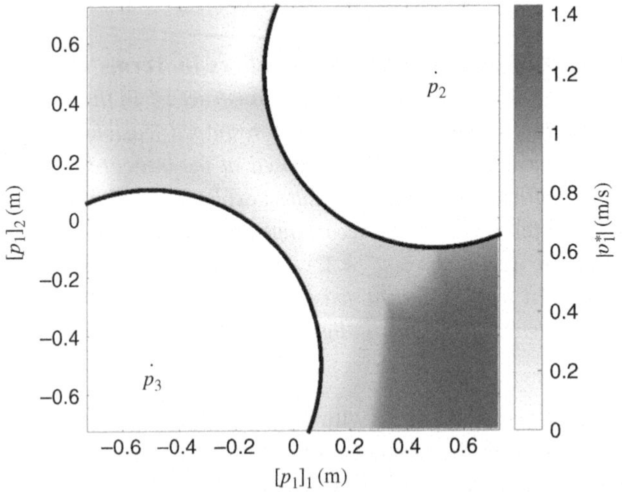

Figure 5.5 $|v_1^*|$ with respect to different p_1. In the scenario of Example 5.1, the Lipschitz continuity of the solution to the QP can be guaranteed by adding RPs and reshaping the feasible set.

where $\mathcal{P}_i^r$ is as defined in (5.30).

For convenience in later discussions, we define

$$T_i = \min\{t \in \mathbb{R}_+ : \delta_i(t) = 0\} \tag{5.35}$$

as the braking time of mobile agent i, and set $T_i = 0$ for $i \in \mathcal{N}_o$. We denote

$$\mathcal{N}_s(t) = \{i = 1, \dots, n_a : \delta_i(t) = 0\} \tag{5.36}$$

as the set of braking agents, and furthermore define

$$h_m = \max_{i \in \mathcal{N}_a, j \in \mathcal{N}_{ao} \setminus \{i\}} h_{ij}, \tag{5.37a}$$

$$h_R = \max_{i \in \mathcal{N}_a \setminus \mathcal{N}_s, j \in \mathcal{N}_{ao} \setminus \{i\}} h_{ij}, \tag{5.37b}$$

$$h_S = \max_{i \in \mathcal{N}_s, j \in (\mathcal{N}_s \cup \mathcal{N}_o) \setminus \{i\}} h_{ij}, \tag{5.37c}$$

$$\tilde{v}_m = \arg\max_{x \in \{\tilde{v}_i : i \in \mathcal{N}_a\}} |x|, \tag{5.37d}$$

$$z_m = \arg\max_{x \in \{z_i : i \in \mathcal{N}_a\}} |x|, \tag{5.37e}$$

$$v_m^* = \arg\max_{x \in \{v_i^* : i \in \mathcal{N}_a\}} |x|. \tag{5.37f}$$

The main result of this chapter is stated in Theorem 5.1.

Theorem 5.1 (*Safety of the Controlled Multi-Agent System*): *Under Assumptions 5.1 and 5.2, consider the multi-agent system* (5.3) and (5.4) *governed by the safety-critical controller* (5.30)–(5.34). *There exist $\mu \in \mathcal{M}^-\mathcal{C}$, $\alpha_h \in \mathcal{K}^e$ and positive constants δ, D, D_s, $\bar{v}^c$, $\bar{v}^{cd}$, $\bar{z}_{m0}$, and $\bar{h}_{m0}$, such that for any initial state satisfying $|z_m(0)| \leq \bar{z}_{m0}$ and $h_m(0) \leq \bar{h}_{m0}$, property* (5.6) *holds for all $t \geq 0$.*

The proof of Theorem 5.1 is provided in Section 5.4.

5.4 Properties of the Proposed Design and Proofs

This section proves Theorem 5.1 by observing new properties of the refined QP-based controller. We first prove that the reshaped feasible set is a subset of the original feasible set (Section 5.4.1). Then, we use gains to describe the interconnections between the controlled nominal systems and the uncertain actuation systems (Sections 5.4.2 and 5.4.3) and present a nonlinear small-gain analysis to guarantee the safety of the controlled multi-agent system (Section 5.5).

5.4.1 Reshaped Feasible Set Belonging to the Original Feasible Set

The following proposition shows that the reshaped feasible set $\mathcal{P}_i^r$ is a subset of the relaxed feasible set $\mathcal{P}_i^s$.

Proposition 5.1(*Retained Safety*): Consider $\mathcal{P}_i^s(p)$ defined in (5.26) and $\mathcal{P}_i^r(p)$ defined in (5.31). We have $\mathcal{P}_i^r(p) \subseteq \mathcal{P}_i^s(p)$.

Proof. With $v_i^* \in \mathbb{R}^n$ and $\delta_i \in [0, \delta]$, we define

$$\mathcal{H}_{ik}^s(p) = \{[v_i^*; \delta_i] : [A_i^s(p)]_{k,:} v_i^* + [a_i^s(p)]_k \delta_i \leq 0\} \tag{5.38}$$

$$\mathcal{H}_{ik}^r(p) = \{[v_i^*; \delta_i] : A_i^r v_i^* + \varphi([A_i^s(p)]_{k,:}, [a_i^s(p)]_k, c_P/\delta)\delta_i \leq 0\} \tag{5.39}$$

for $k = 1, \dots, n_{ao} - 1$, where φ is defined in (5.33).

Obviously, $\mathcal{H}_{ik}^s(p)$ corresponds to the k-th constraint of the feasible set $\mathcal{P}_i^s(p)$, and thus

$$\mathcal{P}_i^s(p) = \bigcap_{k=1}^{n_{ao}-1} \mathcal{H}_{ik}^s(p). \tag{5.40}$$

The definition of $\mathcal{P}_i^r$ in (5.31) implies that

$$A_i^r v_i^* + a_i^r(p)\delta_i \leq 0 \tag{5.41}$$

holds for any $[v_i^*; \delta_i]$ in $\mathcal{P}_i^r(p)$. We rewrite φ defined in (5.33) as

$$\varphi(A_i^s(p), a_i^s(p), c_P/\delta) = \begin{bmatrix} \varphi^T([A_i^s(p)]_{1,:}, [a_i^s(p)]_1, c_P/\delta) \\ \vdots \\ \varphi^T([A_i^s(p)]_{n_{ao}-1,:}, [a_i^s(p)]_{n_{ao}-1}, c_P/\delta) \end{bmatrix}^T, \tag{5.42}$$

which together with the definition of a_i^r in (5.32) implies that

$$\varphi([A_i^s(p)]_{k,:}, [a_i^s(p)]_k, c_P/\delta) \leq a_i^r(p). \tag{5.43}$$

for all $k \in \{1, \dots, n_{ao} - 1\}$. Then, using $\delta_i \in [0, \delta]$ and combining (5.41) and (5.43), we have $\mathcal{P}_i^r(p) \subseteq \mathcal{H}_{ik}^r(p)$ and thus

$$\mathcal{P}_i^r(p) \subseteq \bigcap_{k=1}^{n_{ao}-1} \mathcal{H}_{ik}^r(p). \tag{5.44}$$

Based on (5.40) and (5.44), we have

$$\mathcal{H}_{ik}^r(p) \subseteq \mathcal{H}_{ik}^s(p) \text{ for } k = 1, \dots, n_{ao} - 1 \quad \Rightarrow \quad \mathcal{P}_i^r(p) \subseteq \mathcal{P}_i^s(p). \tag{5.45}$$

Now we prove $\mathcal{H}_{ik}^r(p) \subseteq \mathcal{H}_{ik}^s(p)$.

For $k = 1, \ldots, n_{ao} - 1$, denote

$$\mathcal{V}_i(l) = \{[A_i^r]_{q,:}^T : [A_i^r]_{q,:} l \geq c_A, q = 1, \ldots, n_l\} \tag{5.46}$$

for $l \in \mathbb{R}^n$ satisfying $|l| = 0$. Then, from the three properties of A_i^r below (5.31), $[A_i^s(p)]_{k,:}$ is a positive combination of some n elements of $\mathcal{V}_i([A_i^s(p)]_{k,:})$ [47, Theorem 3.3]. We use these n elements to form the rows of matrix C_{ik}^r, and define

$$\bar{\mathcal{H}}_{ik}^r(p) = \{[v_i^*; \delta_i] : C_{ik}^r v_i^* + C_{ik}^r [A_i^s(p)]_{k,:}^T [a_i^s(p)]_k \delta_i \leq 0\}. \tag{5.47}$$

Using the definitions of φ in (5.33) and $\mathcal{H}_{ik}^r(p)$ in (5.39), we have

$$\mathcal{H}_{ik}^r(p) \subseteq \bar{\mathcal{H}}_{ik}^r(p). \tag{5.48}$$

Since any n rows of A_i^r are linearly independent, the properties of positive combinations guarantee $[A_i^s(p)]_{k,:} C_{ik}^{r-1} \geq 0$. Multiplying both sides of the constraint inequality of $\bar{\mathcal{H}}_{ik}^r(p)$ in (5.47) by $[A_i^s(p)]_{k,:} C_{ik}^{r-1}$ yields

$$\begin{aligned}[A_i^s(p)]_{k,:} C_{ik}^{r-1} \left(C_{ik}^r v_i^* + C_{ik}^r [A_i^s(p)]_{k,:}^T [a_i^s(p)]_k \delta_i\right) &= [A_i^s(p)]_{k,:} v_i^* + [a_i^s(p)]_k \delta_i \\ &\leq 0.\end{aligned} \tag{5.49}$$

Clearly, the inequality is in accordance with the constraint inequality of $\mathcal{H}_{ik}^s(p)$ defined in (5.38), which means $\bar{\mathcal{H}}_{ik}^r(p) \subseteq \mathcal{H}_{ik}^s(p)$, and together with property (5.48) implies $\mathcal{H}_{ik}^r(p) \subseteq \mathcal{H}_{ik}^s(p)$. Recall (5.45). This completes the proof of Proposition 5.1.

5.4.2 Robustness of the Safety Property of the Nominal System

The following proposition gives the range of the RP δ_i, which is to be used for the robustness analysis later.

Proposition 5.2 *(Boundedness of the Relaxation Parameter)*: For any $\tilde{p}_{ij} \neq 0$ with $i \in \mathcal{N}_a$ and $j \in \mathcal{N}_{ao} \setminus \{i\}$, the solution $[v_i^*; \delta_i]$ to the QP (5.30)–(5.33) has the following properties:

1. If $\delta_i = 0$, then $v_i^* = 0$;
2. If $\delta_i > 0$, then $a_i^r(p)$ is bounded;
3. When δ is chosen large enough, $\delta_i > 0 \Rightarrow \delta_i \in [\delta/2, 3\delta/2]$.

Proof. The properties are proved one by one.

Property 1. For any specific $\delta_i \geq 0$ and any $\tilde{p}_{ij} \neq 0$ with $i \in \mathcal{N}_a$ and $j \in \mathcal{N}_{ao} \setminus \{i\}$, define

$$\bar{\mathcal{P}}_i^r(p) = \{v_i^* : A_i^r v_i^* \leq -a_i^r(p)\delta_i\}. \tag{5.50}$$

Then, the definition of A_i^r below (5.31) guarantees that $\bar{\mathcal{P}}_i^r$ is a bounded, closed, convex polyhedron.

Suppose that there exists some $d \neq 0$ such that $A_i^r d \leq 0$. Then, for any $v_i^* \in \bar{\mathcal{P}}_i^r(p)$ and any $\epsilon > 0$,

$$A_i^r(v_i^* + \epsilon d) = A_i^r v_i^* + \epsilon A_i^r d \leq -a_i^r(p)\delta_i, \tag{5.51}$$

that is $(v_i^* + \epsilon d) \in \bar{\mathcal{P}}_i^r(p)$. This means that $\bar{\mathcal{P}}_i^r(p)$ is not bounded.

By contradiction, v_i^* is the only solution corresponding to the constraint $A_i^r v_i^* \leq 0$. Property 1 is proved.

Property 2. Recall the definitions of $\mathcal{P}_i^s$, $\mathcal{P}_i^r$, and $\mathcal{H}_{ik}^s$ in (5.26), (5.31), and (5.38), respectively. From the proof of Proposition 5.1, we have

$$\mathcal{P}_i^r(p) \subseteq \mathcal{P}_i^s(p) \subseteq \mathcal{H}_{ik}^s(p). \tag{5.52}$$

For $k = 1, \dots, n_{ao} - 1$, from the properties of A_i^r given below (5.31), $-[A_i^s(p)]_{k,:}$ is a positive combination of some n elements of $\langle_i(-[A_i^s(p)]_{k,:})$. We define matrix C_{ik}^r with these n elements as the rows, define vector a_{ik}^r with the elements of $a_i^r(p)$ corresponding to these n rows, and define

$$\tilde{\mathcal{H}}_{ik}^r(p) = \{[v_i^*, \delta_i] : C_{ik}^r v_i^* + a_{ik}^r \delta_i \leq 0\}. \tag{5.53}$$

Using the definition of $\mathcal{P}_i^r$ in (5.31), we have

$$\mathcal{P}_i^r(p) \subseteq \tilde{\mathcal{H}}_{ik}^r(p). \tag{5.54}$$

Combining (5.52) and (5.54) implies

$$\mathcal{P}_i^r(p) \subseteq \mathcal{H}_{ik}^s(p) \cap \tilde{\mathcal{H}}_{ik}^r(p). \tag{5.55}$$

Since any n rows of A_i^r are linearly independent, using the property of positive combinations, we have

$$-[A_i^s(p)]_{k,:} C_{ik}^{r^{-1}} =: k_s \geq 0. \tag{5.56}$$

Multiplying both sides of the constraint inequality of $\tilde{\mathcal{H}}_{ik}^r(p)$ in (5.53) by the nonnegative k_s defined in (5.56) yields

$$-[A_i^s(p)]_{k,:} C_{ik}^{r^{-1}} C_{ik}^r v_i^* + k_s a_{ik}^r \delta_i = -[A_i^s(p)]_{k,:} v_i^* + k_s a_{ik}^r \delta_i \leq 0. \tag{5.57}$$

Also, the definition of $\mathcal{H}_{ik}^s(p)$ in (5.39) implies that

$$[A_i^s(p)]_{k,:} v_i^* \leq -[a_i^s(p)]_k \delta_i. \tag{5.58}$$

Properties (5.57) and (5.58) together guarantee that any $[v_i^*, \delta_i] \in \mathcal{H}_{ik}^s(p) \cap \tilde{\mathcal{H}}_{ik}^r(p)$ satisfies

$$k_s a_{ik}^r \delta_i \leq [A_i^s(p)]_{k,:} v_i^* \leq -[a_i^s(p)]_k \delta_i. \tag{5.59}$$

If $k_s a_{ik}^r > -[a_i^s(p)]_k$, then the only element of $\mathcal{H}_{ik}^s(p) \cap \tilde{\mathcal{H}}_{ik}^r(p)$ is 0, and thus, $\mathcal{P}_i^r(p) = \{0\}$. This contradicts with $\delta_i > 0$. Thus, we have

$$[a_i^s(p)]_k \leq -k_s a_{ik}^r. \tag{5.60}$$

Based on the definition of φ in (5.33), we rewrite

$$\begin{aligned}[\varphi(A_i^s, a_i^s, c_P/\delta)]_{j,k} = {} & -\frac{c_P}{\delta}\mathrm{sat}(c_K(c_A - [A_i^r A_i^{sT}]_{j,k})) \\ & + [A_i^r A_i^{sT}]_{j,k}[a_i^s]_k(1 - \mathrm{sat}(c_K(c_A - [A_i^r A_i^{sT}]_{j,k})))\end{aligned} \tag{5.61}$$

and then we have

$$\begin{aligned}[\varphi(A_i^s, a_i^s, c_P/\delta)]_{j,k} &\geq \min\left\{\left[A_i^r A_i^{sT}\right]_{j,k}\left[a_i^s\right]_k, -\frac{c_P}{\delta}\right\} \\ &\geq \frac{1}{\delta}\min\{\alpha_h(-\mu(D_s)), -c_P\}.\end{aligned} \tag{5.62}$$

This, together with (5.60) implies

$$\begin{aligned}[a_i^s(p)]_k &\leq -k_s a_{ik}^r \leq -k_s 1_{n\times 1} \min\{a_{ik}^r\}, \\ &\leq \frac{1}{\delta}\sqrt{n}|k_s| \max\{-\alpha_h(-\mu(D_s)), c_P\},\end{aligned} \tag{5.63}$$

where $1_{n\times 1}$ is the n-dimensional column vector of all ones.

On the other hand, the definitions of $a_i^o(p)$ in (5.23) and $a_i^s(p)$ in (5.27) imply

$$[a_i^s(p)]_k = \frac{1}{\delta}\alpha_h(h_{ik} - \mu(D_s)) \geq \frac{1}{\delta}\alpha_h(-\mu(D_s)). \tag{5.64}$$

Combining (5.63) and (5.64) yields

$$\frac{1}{\delta}\alpha_h(-\mu(D_s)) \leq [a_i^s(p)]_k \leq \frac{1}{\delta}|k_s|\sqrt{n}\max\{-\alpha_h(-\mu(D_s)), c_P\}. \tag{5.65}$$

The boundedness of $[a_i^s(p)]_k$ for all $k = 1, \dots, n_{ao} - 1$ guarantees the boundedness of $a_i^r(p)$. This completes the proof of property 2.

Property 3. If $[v_i^c; \delta] \in \mathcal{P}_i^r(p)$, then property 3 is obvious. Now, we consider the case of $[v_i^c; \delta] \notin \mathcal{P}_i^r(p)$. We use $M_i = [\breve{A}_i^r, \breve{a}_i^r]$ to represent the constraints that directly affect the optimal solution of the QP, with $\breve{A}_i^r$ and $\breve{a}_i^r$ being submatrices of

A_i^r and a_i^r, respectively. From [21, Example 2.1.5], the solution to the QP is

$$\begin{bmatrix} v_i^* \\ \delta_i \end{bmatrix} = \left(I - M_i^T (M_i M_i^T)^{-1} M_i\right) \begin{bmatrix} v_i^c \\ \delta \end{bmatrix}. \tag{5.66}$$

Then, using $M_i = [\breve{A}_i^r, \breve{a}_i^r]$, we have

$$\begin{aligned} \delta_i &= \delta - \breve{a}_i^{rT} (\breve{A}_i^r \breve{A}_i^{rT} + \breve{a}_i^r \breve{a}_i^{rT})^{-1} (\breve{a}_i^r \delta + \breve{A}_i^r v_i^c) \\ &= \frac{\delta - \breve{a}_i^{rT} (\breve{A}_i^r \breve{A}_i^{rT})^{-1} \breve{A}_i^r v_i^c}{1 + \breve{a}_i^{rT} (\breve{A}_i^r \breve{A}_i^{rT})^{-1} \breve{a}_i^r}, \end{aligned} \tag{5.67}$$

where Sherman–Morrison–Woodbury formula [76] is used for the second equality. Since $\breve{a}_i^r$ is a submatrix of a_i^r, according to property 2 of Proposition 5.2, there exists a positive constant τ_a such that

$$|\breve{a}_i^r| \leq \frac{\tau_a}{\delta}. \tag{5.68}$$

Since any n rows of A_i^r are chosen to be linearly independent as required after (5.31), there exists a positive constant c_M such that

$$\sup_{S_A \in \{[2^{S_p}]^n \setminus \{\emptyset\}\}} \left\{ \lambda_{\max}^{\frac{1}{2}} \left(([A_i^r]_{S_A,:} [A_i^r]_{S_A,:}^T)^{-1} \right) \right\} \leq c_M, \tag{5.69}$$

where $S_p = \{1, 2, \dots, n_p\}$, 2^{S_p} is the power set of S_p, and $[2^{S_p}]^n$ denotes the set of subsets of 2^{S_p} with cardinality not larger than n. Combining (5.68) and (5.69), we have

$$\delta_i \geq \frac{\delta - \bar{v}^c c_M |\breve{a}_i^r|}{1 + c_M^2 |\breve{a}_i^r|^2} \geq \frac{\delta - \bar{v}^c c_M \tau_a \delta^{-1}}{1 + c_M^2 \tau_a^2 \delta^{-2}} = \delta \frac{\delta^2 - \bar{v}^c c_M \tau_a}{\delta^2 + c_M^2 \tau_a^2}, \tag{5.70a}$$

$$\delta_i \leq \delta + \bar{v}^c c_M |\breve{a}_i^r| \leq \delta \left(1 + \frac{\bar{v}^c c_M \tau_a}{\delta^2} \right). \tag{5.70b}$$

If

$$\delta^2 \geq \max\{2\bar{v}^c c_M \tau_a + c_M^2 \tau_a^2, 2\bar{v}^c c_M \tau_a\}, \tag{5.71}$$

then (5.70a) directly implies $\delta_i \in [\delta/2, 3\delta/2]$. This completes the proof of Property 3.

Based on Proposition 5.2, the following proposition claims a robust safety property of the controlled nominal systems in the presence of velocity-tracking errors.

Proposition 5.3 (*The Influence of $\tilde{v}_i$ and $\tilde{v}_j$ on $\tilde{h}_{ij}$*): Consider the mobile agent defined in (5.8), and the controller defined in (5.30)–(5.34). Given any class $\mathcal{K}_\infty$ function $\gamma_h^{\tilde{v}}$ and any positive constant c_0, choose

$$\alpha_h(s) = 4(1+c_0)\left(\gamma_h^{\tilde{v}}\right)^{-1}(s) \tag{5.72}$$

for $s \geq 0$. Then, α_h is of class $\mathcal{K}^e$, and the following properties hold:

1. For any $\tilde{p}_{ij} \neq 0$ with $i \in \mathcal{N}_a$ and $j \in \mathcal{N}_{ao} \setminus \{i\}$, the QP (5.30)–(5.33) is feasible and has a unique solution;
2. There exist $\beta_h \in \mathcal{KL}$, $\theta > 0$ and $d_h^{\tilde{v}} = (1+\theta)\mu(D_s)$ such that for any $h_{ij}(0) \in \mathbb{R}_+$ and any piecewise continuous and bounded $\tilde{v}_i$, $\tilde{v}_j$ satisfying $\max_{k=i,j} \|\tilde{v}_k\|_t < \left(\gamma_h^{\tilde{v}}\right)^{-1}\left(\sup_{s\in\mathbb{R}_+} \mu(s) - d_h^{\tilde{v}}\right)$,

$$h_{ij}(t) \leq \beta_h(h_{ij}(0), t) + \gamma_h^{\tilde{v}}\left(\max_{k=i,j} \|\tilde{v}_k\|_t\right) + d_h^{\tilde{v}} \tag{5.73}$$

for all $0 \leq t < \max\{T_i, T_j\}$.

Proof. The properties are proved one by one.

Property 1. For any $\tilde{p}_{ij} \neq 0$ with $i \in \mathcal{N}_a$ and $j \in \mathcal{N}_{ao}$, the feasible set $\mathcal{P}_i^r(p)$ defined in (5.31) forms a convex, closed set [26, Section 2.2.4]. Since zero is always an element of $\mathcal{P}_i^r(p)$, the QP is feasible. The uniqueness of the solution is guaranteed by the projection theorem [21, Proposition B.11] (also see Proposition A.16).

Property 2. Recall $\tilde{p}_{ij} = p_i - p_j$ in (5.12) and $h_{ij} = h(\tilde{p}_{ij})$ in (5.19). Taking the derivative of h_{ij} along the trajectories of (5.8), for any $[v_i^*; \delta_i] \in \mathcal{P}_i^r(p)$, if $\tilde{p}_{ij} \neq 0$, we have

$$\begin{aligned}
\nabla h(\tilde{p}_{ij})\dot{\tilde{p}}_{ij} &= \nabla h(\tilde{p}_{ij})(v_i^* + \tilde{v}_i - v_j^* - \tilde{v}_j) \\
&= \alpha_\mu(h_{ij})\left(-\frac{\tilde{p}_{ij}^T}{|\tilde{p}_{ij}|}(v_i^* - v_j^*) - \frac{\tilde{p}_{ij}^T}{|\tilde{p}_{ij}|}(\tilde{v}_i - \tilde{v}_j)\right) \\
&\leq \alpha_\mu(h_{ij})\left(-\frac{\delta_{ij}}{\delta}\alpha_h(h_{ij} - \mu(D_s)) - \frac{\tilde{p}_{ij}^T}{|\tilde{p}_{ij}|}(\tilde{v}_i - \tilde{v}_j)\right),
\end{aligned} \tag{5.74}$$

where

$$\delta_{ij} = \begin{cases} \delta_i + \delta_j, & \text{for } j \in \mathcal{N}_a \setminus \{i\}, \\ \delta_i, & \text{for } j \in \mathcal{N}_o, \end{cases} \tag{5.75}$$

and

$$\alpha_\mu(s) = \begin{cases} -\dfrac{\partial\mu(\mu^{-1}(s))}{\partial\mu^{-1}(s)}, & \text{if } s > 0, \\ 0, & \text{if } s = 0. \end{cases} \tag{5.76}$$

For the inequality in (5.74), we used the constraint of the feasible set $\mathcal{P}_i^s(p)$ in (5.25) and the property that $\mathcal{P}_i^r(p) \subseteq \mathcal{P}_i^s(p)$ given by Proposition 5.1.

With α_h defined in (5.72), for any $\tilde{p}_{ij}$ satisfying $h(\tilde{p}_{ij}) \geq \mu(D_s)$, it holds that

$$-\alpha_h(h_{ij} - \mu(D_s)) = -4(1 + c_0)\left(\gamma_h^{\tilde{v}}\right)^{-1}(h_{ij} - \mu(D_s)). \tag{5.77}$$

From property 2 of Proposition 5.2, for all $0 \leq t < \max\{T_i, T_j\}$, it holds that

$$\frac{\delta_{ij}}{\delta} \geq \frac{1}{2}. \tag{5.78}$$

Then, (5.74), (5.77), and (5.78) together imply that

$$\nabla h(\tilde{p}_{ij})\dot{\tilde{p}}_{ij} \leq 2\alpha_\mu(h_{ij})(-(1 + c_0)(\gamma_h^{\tilde{v}})^{-1}(h_{ij} - \mu(D_s)) + \max_{k=i,j} \|\tilde{v}_k\|_t) \tag{5.79}$$

as long as $|\tilde{p}_{ij}| \in (0, D_s]$.

Denote $d_h^{\tilde{v}} = (1 + \theta)\mu(D_s)$. In the case of

$$\gamma_h^{\tilde{v}}\left(\max_{k=i,j} \|\tilde{v}_k\|_t\right) + d_h^{\tilde{v}} \leq h_{ij}, \tag{5.80}$$

it can be easily verified that

$$h_{ij} - \mu(D_s) \geq \gamma_h^{\tilde{v}}\left(\max_{k=i,j} \|\tilde{v}_k\|_t\right), \quad h_{ij} - \mu(D_s) \geq \frac{\theta}{1 + \theta} h_{ij}. \tag{5.81}$$

Substituting (5.81) into (5.79), we have that

$$\nabla h(\tilde{p}_{ij})\dot{\tilde{p}}_{ij} \leq -2c_0\alpha_\mu(h_{ij})\left(\gamma_h^{\tilde{v}}\right)^{-1}\left(\frac{\theta}{1 + \theta} h_{ij}\right) \tag{5.82}$$

holds in the case of (5.80).

Based on the discussion above, if $\alpha_\mu \in \mathcal{K}$, then there exists a $\beta_h \in \mathcal{KL}$ for property (5.73), following a similar argument as for ISS-Lyapunov functions [184, 188]. See also [110, Theorem 1.10.2] for related discussions on differential inequalities.

Now, we show $\alpha_\mu \in \mathcal{K}$. Using the properties of $\mathcal{M}^-\mathcal{C}$ functions and properties of limits of composition functions [23, Section 8.16], we have $\lim_{s\to\infty} \mu(s) = 0$, $\lim_{s\to 0} \mu^{-1}(s) = \infty$, $\lim_{s\to\infty} \partial\mu(s)/\partial s = 0$, and $\lim_{s\to 0} -\partial\mu(\mu^{-1}(s))/\partial\mu^{-1}(s) = 0$. This validates the right continuity of α_μ at the origin. Since μ is strictly decreasing, for any $s_2 > s_1 > 0$, it holds that $\mu^{-1}(s_1) > \mu^{-1}(s_2) > 0$. Also, recall that μ is strictly convex. Using [26, Equation 3.3], we have

$$\mu(\mu^{-1}(s_1)) > \mu(\mu^{-1}(s_2)) - \alpha_\mu(s_2)(\mu^{-1}(s_1) - \mu^{-1}(s_2)), \tag{5.83}$$

$$\mu(\mu^{-1}(s_2)) > \mu(\mu^{-1}(s_1)) - \alpha_\mu(s_1)(\mu^{-1}(s_2) - \mu^{-1}(s_1)). \tag{5.84}$$

Then, it can be verified that

$$\alpha_\mu(s_2) > \frac{s_2 - s_1}{\mu^{-1}(s_1) - \mu^{-1}(s_2)} > \alpha_\mu(s_1), \tag{5.85}$$

and thus α_μ is strictly increasing. This proves $\alpha_\mu \in \mathcal{K}$.

Proposition 5.3 employs the gain $\gamma_h^{\tilde{v}}$ to represent the influence of $\max\{|\tilde{v}_i|, |\tilde{v}_j|\}$ on $h(\tilde{p}_{ij})$, and accordingly, the robustness of $h(\tilde{p}_{ij})$ with respect to $\max\{|\tilde{v}_i|, |\tilde{v}_j|\}$. With v_i^* considered as the control input, Proposition 5.3 also shows how to choose α_h for a desired gain $\gamma_h^{\tilde{v}}$.

5.4.3 Response of the Uncertain Actuation System

In this section, we study the dynamic response of the actuation system to the velocity-reference input generated by the refined QP-based controller.

Proposition 5.4 (*The Influence of h_R on $\tilde{v}_i$*): Under Assumptions 5.1 and 5.2, consider the multi-agent system modeled by (5.3) and (5.4) and the controller defined in (5.30)–(5.34). Then, the following properties hold:

1. For $t \in [0, T_i)$, whenever the closed-loop signals are defined, the solution to the QP (5.30)–(5.33) is Lipschitz with respect to a_i^r and v_i^c;
2. There exists a class $\mathcal{K}$ function α_{v*}^h such that

$$|v_i^*(t)| \leq \alpha_{v*}^h(h_R(t)) + \bar{v}^c, \tag{5.86}$$

whenever h_R given in (5.37b) is defined;
3. There exist $\beta_{\tilde{v}}^h \in \mathcal{KL}$, $\gamma_{\tilde{v}}^h$, $\gamma_{\tilde{v}}^{\tilde{v}} \in \mathcal{K}$, and a constant $d_{\tilde{v}}^h \in \mathbb{R}_+$ such that for all $z_i(0) \in \mathbb{R}^m$ and $v_i^*(0) \in \mathbb{R}^n$, whenever the closed-loop signals are well-defined,

$$|\tilde{v}_i(t)| \leq \begin{cases} \max\left\{\beta_{\tilde{v}}^h(|z_i(0)| + |v_i^*(0)|, t) + \gamma_{\tilde{v}}^h(\|h_R\|_t) + d_{\tilde{v}}^h, \gamma_{\tilde{v}}^{\tilde{v}}(\|\tilde{v}_m\|_t)\right\}, & \text{for } t \in [0, T_i), \\ c_{\tilde{v}} e^{-\lambda(t - T_i)} |z_i(T_i)|, & \text{for } t \in [T_i, \infty). \end{cases} \tag{5.87}$$

Proof. Before the proofs, we rewrite the QP defined in (5.30)–(5.33) as

$$u = \underset{u \in \{x \in \mathbb{R}^{n+1}: M_F x \leq 0, [x]_{n+1} \geq 0\}}{\operatorname{argmin}} \quad 0.5u^T u + ru, \tag{5.88}$$

where

$$u = [v_i^*; \delta_i], \; M_F = [A_i^r, a_i^r], \quad r = -[v_i^c; \delta]. \tag{5.89}$$

As for the proof of property 3 of Proposition 5.2, we define $M_i = [\breve{A}_i^r, \breve{a}_i^r]$ to represent the constraints that directly affect the optimal solution, where $\breve{A}_i^r$ and $\breve{a}_i^r$ are submatrices of A_i^r and a_i^r, respectively.

Now we prove properties of Proposition 5.4 one by one.

Property 1. For $t \in [0, T_i)$, we prove the Lipschitz continuity of the solution to the QP by using Theorem B.1 as follows:

- As already proved for property 1 of Proposition 5.3, the QP has a unique solution.
- Since $\breve{a}_i^r$ is a submatrix of a_i^r, according to property 2 of Proposition 5.2, $\breve{a}_i^r$ is bounded; since $\breve{A}_i^r$ is composed of unit vectors, M_i is bounded.
- We use $\breve{n}$ to represent the number of the constraints that directly affect the optimal solution. Using the definition of T_i, we have $\breve{n} \leq n$ for all $t \in [0, T_i)$. Since any n rows of A_i^r are linearly independent and $\breve{n} \leq n$, $\breve{A}_i^r$ and M_i are full row rank, which means that there exists a $c_\lambda > 0$ such that $\lambda_{\min}^{1/2}(\breve{A}_i^r \breve{A}_i^{rT}) \geq c_\lambda$. As a direct consequence $|M_i^T \lambda| \geq \lambda_{\min}^{1/2}(M_i M_i^T)|\lambda| \geq \lambda_{\min}^{1/2}(\breve{A}_i^r \breve{A}_i^{rT})|\lambda| \geq c_\lambda |\lambda|$ for all λ.

Then, with all the conditions required by Theorem B.1 satisfied, we can prove the Lipschitz continuity of the solution with respect to M_F and r. Since δ and A_i^r are constant, property 1 can be proved based on the definitions of M_F and r in (5.89).

Property 2. When $t \geq T_i$, the controller (5.34) guarantees that $v_i^* \equiv 0$. When $t \in [0, T_i)$, we consider the cases of $[v_i^c; \delta] \notin \mathcal{P}_i^r$ and $[v_i^c; \delta] \in \mathcal{P}_i^r$ separately. In the case of $[v_i^c; \delta] \notin \mathcal{P}_i^r$, we have $v_i^* = v_i^c$.

Now we consider the case of $[v_i^c; \delta] \notin \mathcal{P}_i^r$. Define

$$q_i(v_i^c) = \underset{u_i \in \{x \in \mathbb{R}^n: A_i^r x + a_i^r \delta_i \leq 0\}}{\operatorname{argmin}} \quad 0.5u_i^T u_i - v_i^{cT} u_i. \tag{5.90}$$

We use $\breve{A}_i^r$ and $\breve{a}_i^r \delta_i$ to represent the constraints that directly affect the optimal solution of the QP (5.90). Clearly, $\breve{A}_i^r$ and $\breve{a}_i^r \delta_i$ are submatrices of A_i^r and $a_i^r \delta_i$, respectively. Using the projection theorem [21, Proposition B.11], $q_i(v_i^c)$ is continuous and nonexpansive, which means that

$$|q_i(v_i^c) - q_i(0)| \leq |v_i^c|. \tag{5.91}$$

From (5.90), we also have $\upsilon_i^* = q_i(\upsilon_i^c)$. Then, following [21, Example 2.1.5], we have

$$\begin{aligned} |\upsilon_i^*| &\le |\upsilon_i^c| + |q_i(0)| \\ &= \bar{\upsilon}^c + \left|\breve{A}_i^{rT}\left(\breve{A}_i^r\breve{A}_i^{rT}\right)^{-1}\breve{a}_i^r\delta_i\right| \\ &\le \bar{\upsilon}^c + \delta_i\sqrt{\breve{a}_i^{rT}\left(\breve{A}_i^r\breve{A}_i^{rT}\right)^{-1}\breve{a}_i^r}. \end{aligned} \tag{5.92}$$

Applying the Lagrange multiplier algorithms and Karush–Kuhn–Tucker optimality conditions [21], we have

$$\breve{a}_i^{rT}\left(\breve{A}_i^r\breve{A}_i^{rT}\right)^{-1} \ge 0. \tag{5.93}$$

Denote $\bar{a}_i = \max\{\breve{a}_i^r\}1_{n\times 1}$. It can be easily verified that

$$(\bar{a}_i - \breve{a}_i^r)^T\left(\breve{A}_i^r\breve{A}_i^{rT}\right)^{-1}(\bar{a}_i - \breve{a}_i^r) \ge 0, \tag{5.94}$$

$$\breve{a}_i^{rT}\left(\breve{A}_i^r\breve{A}_i^{rT}\right)^{-1}(\bar{a}_i - \breve{a}_i^r) \ge 0, \tag{5.95}$$

and thus,

$$\begin{aligned} \bar{a}_i^T\left(\breve{A}_i^r\breve{A}_i^{rT}\right)^{-1}\bar{a}_i &= (\bar{a}_i - \breve{a}_i^r)^T\left(\breve{A}_i^r\breve{A}_i^{rT}\right)^{-1}(\bar{a}_i - \breve{a}_i^r) \\ &\quad + 2\breve{a}_i^{rT}\left(\breve{A}_i^r\breve{A}_i^{rT}\right)^{-1}(\bar{a}_i - \breve{a}_i^r) + \breve{a}_i^{rT}\left(\breve{A}_i^r\breve{A}_i^{rT}\right)^{-1}\breve{a}_i^r \\ &\ge \breve{a}_i^{rT}\left(\breve{A}_i^r\breve{A}_i^{rT}\right)^{-1}\breve{a}_i^r, \end{aligned} \tag{5.96}$$

where $\bar{a}_i = \max\{\breve{a}_i^r\}1_{n\times 1}$. This, together with (5.92) implies

$$\begin{aligned} |\upsilon_i^*| &\le |\upsilon_i^c| + \delta_i\sqrt{\bar{a}_i^T(\breve{A}_i^r\breve{A}_i^r)^{-1}\bar{a}_i} \\ &\le \bar{\upsilon}^c + \frac{3c_M\sqrt{n}}{2}\max\{\breve{a}_i^r\delta\} \\ &\le \bar{\upsilon}^c + \frac{3c_M\sqrt{n}}{2}\max_{\substack{j\in\{1,\ldots,n_l\,:\,[A_i^r]_{j,:}\ \text{is a row of}\ \breve{A}_i^r\} \\ k\in\{1,\ldots,n_{ao}-1\}}}[\varphi(A_i^s, a_i^s\delta, c_P)]_{j,k} \\ &\le \bar{\upsilon}^c + \frac{3c_M\sqrt{n}}{2}\alpha_h(h_R - \mu(D_s)) \\ &\le \frac{3c_M\sqrt{n}}{2}\alpha_h(h_R) + \bar{\upsilon}^c, \end{aligned} \tag{5.97}$$

where we use (5.96) for the first inequality, use the definition of c_M in (5.69) and property 3 of Proposition 5.2 for the second inequality, and use the equivalent representation of φ in (5.61) for the fourth inequality.

Thus, property 2 is proved by defining $\alpha^h_{v*}(s) = 3c_M\sqrt{n}\alpha_h(s)/2$.

Property 3. When $t \geq T_i$, controller (5.34) gives $v_i^* \equiv 0$. Then, using the definition of $\tilde{v}_i$ in (5.7) and property (5.9), we have

$$|\tilde{v}_i(t)| \leq c_{\tilde{v}} e^{-\lambda(t-T_i)}|z_i(T_i)| \tag{5.98}$$

for all $t \geq T_i$.

Now, we consider the case of $t \in [0, T_i)$. Property 1 already shows the Lipschitz continuity of (5.34) with respect to a_i^r and v_i^c. To prove property 3, we first show the existence of two class $\mathcal{K}$ functions α^h_{v*d} and $\alpha^{\tilde{v}}_{v*d}$, and a positive constant c^h_{v*d} such that

$$|D^+ v_i^*(t)| \leq \alpha^{\tilde{v}}_{v*d}(|\tilde{v}_m(t)|) + \alpha^h_{v*d}(h_R(t)) + c^h_{v*d} \tag{5.99}$$

for all $t \in [0, T_i)$. Using the weak triangular inequality in [92], properties (5.9) and (5.99) together guarantee the first case in (5.87) with

$$d^h_{\tilde{v}} = (1 + k_{\tilde{v}})\gamma_{\tilde{v}}^{v*d} \circ \rho_{\tilde{v}}^{v*d}(c^h_{v*d}), \tag{5.100}$$

$$\gamma^h_{\tilde{v}}(s) = (1 + k_{\tilde{v}})\gamma_{\tilde{v}}^{v*d} \circ \rho_{\tilde{v}}^{v*d}(\alpha^h_{v*d}(s) + c^h_{v*d}) - d^h_{\tilde{v}}, \tag{5.101}$$

$$\beta^h_{\tilde{v}}(s, t) = (1 + k_{\tilde{v}})\beta_{\tilde{v}}(s, t), \tag{5.102}$$

$$\gamma^{\tilde{v}}_{\tilde{v}}(s) = (1 + k_{\tilde{v}}^{-1})\gamma_{\tilde{v}}^{v*d} \circ \rho_{\tilde{v}}^{v*d} \circ (\rho_{\tilde{v}}^{v*d} - \mathrm{Id})^{-1} \circ \alpha^{\tilde{v}}_{v*d}(s), \tag{5.103}$$

where $\rho_{\tilde{v}}^{v*d}$ is a function of class $\mathcal{K}_\infty$ such that $(\rho_{\tilde{v}}^{v*d} - \mathrm{Id})$ is of class $\mathcal{K}_\infty$.

In the case of $[v_i^c; \delta] \in \mathcal{P}_i^r$, v_i^c is the solution to the QP, and thus $|D^+ v_i^*| \leq \bar{v}^{cd}$. In this case, property (5.99) is obvious.

Now we consider the case of $[v_i^c; \delta] \notin \mathcal{P}_i^r$. Based on Theorem B.1, there exists a positive constant $c_{\mathcal{P}} \geq 1$ such that

$$\left|D^+ v_i^*\right| \leq c_{\mathcal{P}}\bar{v}^{cd} + 2c^2_{\mathcal{P}}\sqrt{\bar{v}^{c2} + \delta^2}\left|D^+ a_i^r(p(t))\right|. \tag{5.104}$$

If there exist two class $\mathcal{K}$ functions α^h_φ and $\alpha^{\tilde{v}}_\varphi$ such that

$$\left|D^+ a_i^r(p(t))\right| \leq \alpha^h_\varphi(h_R) + \alpha^{\tilde{v}}_\varphi(|\tilde{v}_m|), \tag{5.105}$$

then property (5.99) is established.

Now we prove inequality (5.105) holds for all $[v_i^c; \delta] \notin \mathcal{P}_i^r$. Taking derivatives of A_i^s and a_i^s with respect to t, we obtain

$$\frac{\partial A_i^s}{\partial t} = \left[A^d_{i1}, \dots, A^d_{i(i-1)}, A^d_{i(i+1)}, \dots, A^d_{in_{ao}}\right]^T, \tag{5.106}$$

$$\frac{\partial a_i^s}{\partial t} = \left[a^d_{i1}, \dots, a^d_{i(i-1)}, a^d_{i(i+1)}, \dots, a^d_{in_{ao}}\right]^T, \tag{5.107}$$

where

$$A_{ij}^d = -\left(I - \frac{\tilde{p}_{ij}\tilde{p}_{ij}^T}{|\tilde{p}_{ij}|^2}\right)(v_i - v_j)|\tilde{p}_{ij}|^{-1}, \tag{5.108}$$

$$a_{ij}^d = \delta^{-1}\alpha_\mu(h_{ij})\frac{\tilde{p}_{ij}^T}{|\tilde{p}_{ij}|}(v_i - v_j)\frac{\partial\alpha_h(h_{ij} - \mu(D_s))}{\partial(h_{ij} - \mu(D_s))}, \quad j \in \mathcal{N}_{ao} \setminus \{i\}. \tag{5.109}$$

Using the definition of velocity-tracking error in (5.7), the maximal velocity of agents satisfies

$$\begin{aligned} \max_{i\in\mathcal{N}_a} |v_i| &= |\tilde{v}_m| + \max_{i\in\mathcal{N}_a} |v_i^*| \\ &= |\tilde{v}_m| + \max_{i\in\mathcal{N}_a\setminus\mathcal{N}_s} |v_i^*| \\ &\leq |\tilde{v}_m| + \alpha_{v*}^h(h_R) + \bar{v}^c. \end{aligned} \tag{5.110}$$

The definition of α_h shows the lower bound of $\alpha_h(h_{ij} - \mu(D_s))$ and implies that there exists a class $\mathcal{K}$ function α_h^d and a constant $c_h^d \in \mathbb{R}_+$ such that

$$\left|\frac{\partial\alpha_h(h_{ij} - \mu(D_s))}{\partial(h_{ij} - \mu(D_s))}\right| \leq \alpha_h^d(h_R) + c_h^d. \tag{5.111}$$

Then, (5.106), (5.107), and (5.111) imply

$$\left|\frac{\partial A_i^s}{\partial t}\right| \leq 2\sqrt{n_{ao} - 1}\alpha_p(h_R) \max_{i\in\mathcal{N}_a} |v_i|, \tag{5.112}$$

$$\left|\frac{\partial a_i^s}{\partial t}\right| \leq \frac{2\sqrt{n_{ao} - 1}}{\delta}\alpha_\mu(h_R)(\alpha_h^d(h_R) + c_h^d) \max_{i\in\mathcal{N}_a} |v_i|, \tag{5.113}$$

where α_μ is a class $\mathcal{K}$ function defined in (5.76), and

$$\alpha_p(s) = \begin{cases} \dfrac{1}{\mu^{-1}(s)}, & \text{for } s > 0, \\ 0, & \text{for } s = 0. \end{cases} \tag{5.114}$$

Clearly, $\alpha_p(s)$ is a class $\mathcal{K}$ function. Each row of A_i^s is a unit vector, and a_i^s is bounded when $[v_i^c; \delta] \notin \mathcal{P}_i^r$ and $t \in [0, T_i)$ (see (5.65)). Using the definition of φ in (5.33), we have that φ is locally Lipschitz with respect to A_i^s and a_i^s, and thus, there exists a constant $c_\varphi > 0$ satisfying

$$\left|D^+ a_i^r(p(t))\right| \leq c_\varphi\left(\left|\frac{\partial A_i^s}{\partial t}\right| + \left|\frac{\partial a_i^s}{\partial t}\right|\right) \tag{5.115}$$

for all $t \in [0, T_i)$. Substituting (5.110), (5.112), and (5.113) into the inequality above, we can prove that (5.105) holds with

$$\alpha_{\varphi}^{h}(s) = \left(\alpha_{\upsilon*}^{h}(s) + \bar{\upsilon}^{c} + \frac{\alpha_{Aa}^{d}(s)}{4k_{\varphi}}\right)\alpha_{Aa}^{d}(s), \tag{5.116}$$

$$\alpha_{\varphi}^{\tilde{\upsilon}}(s) = k_{\varphi}s^{2}, \tag{5.117}$$

where k_{φ} is a positive constant and

$$\alpha_{Aa}^{d}(s) = 2c_{\varphi}(n_{ao} - 1)^{1/2}(\alpha_{p}(s) + \delta^{-1}\alpha_{\mu}(s)(\alpha_{h}^{d}(s) + c_{h}^{d})). \tag{5.118}$$

From (5.104), (5.105), and (5.117), we have that (5.99) holds for all $t \in [0, T_i)$. This together with (5.98) proves property 3. This ends the proof of Proposition 5.4.

5.5 Small-gain Analysis for Safety of the Multi-agent System

Propositions 5.3 and 5.4 naturally result in two interconnected subsystems, each of which admits a gain property (see Figure 5.6). We propose a small-gain analysis to guarantee the safety of the closed-loop system.

We suppose that the parameters are chosen to satisfy the following small-gain-type condition:

$$(\mathrm{Id} + \epsilon_1)\circ\gamma_{h}^{\tilde{\upsilon}}\circ(\mathrm{Id} + \epsilon_2)\circ\gamma_{\tilde{\upsilon}}^{h}(s) < s, \quad \forall s \in [\mu(D_s), \mu(D)], \tag{5.119}$$

$$\gamma_{\tilde{\upsilon}}^{\tilde{\upsilon}}(s) < s, \quad \forall s \in [d_{\tilde{\upsilon}}^{h}, \alpha_h(\mu(D) - \mu(D_s))] \tag{5.120}$$

with $\epsilon_1, \epsilon_2 \in \mathcal{K}_{\infty}$. A brief guideline is provided in Section 5.6 on how to choose the controller parameters to satisfy the above conditions.

In the following discussion, we first suppose that the closed-loop signals are right maximally defined on time-line $[0, T_{\max})$ with $T_{\max} \leq \infty$. We will finally

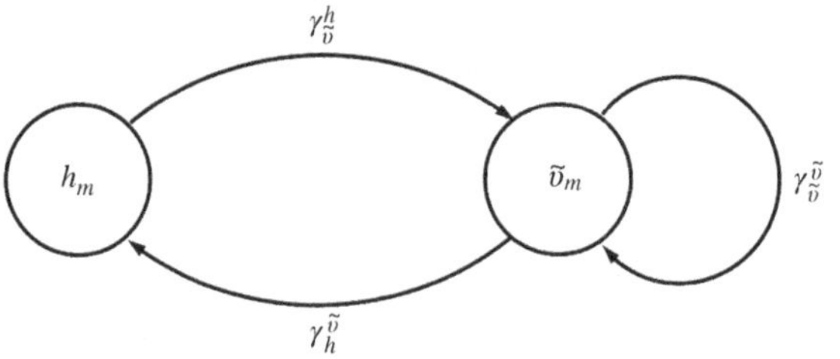

Figure 5.6 Gain interconnection between h_m and $\tilde{\upsilon}_m$.

prove $T_{\max} = +\infty$. For any agent $i \in \mathcal{N}_a$ and any agent or obstacle $j \in \mathcal{N}_{ao} \setminus \{i\}$, we consider the following two cases.

Case (A): $t < \min_{k \in \mathcal{N}_a} T_k$.

Recall the definitions of h_m, $\tilde{\upsilon}_m$, and z_m given before Theorem 5.1. In this case, properties (5.73) and (5.87) imply

$$|\tilde{\upsilon}_m(t)| \le \max\{\beta_{\tilde{\upsilon}}^h(|z_m(0)| + |\upsilon_m^*(0)|, t) + \gamma_{\tilde{\upsilon}}^h(\|h_m\|_t) + d_{\tilde{\upsilon}}^h, \gamma_{\tilde{\upsilon}}^{\tilde{\upsilon}}(\|\tilde{\upsilon}_m\|_t)\}, \tag{5.121}$$

$$h_m(t) \le \beta_h(h_m(0), t) + \gamma_h^{\tilde{\upsilon}}(\|\tilde{\upsilon}_m\|_t) + d_h^{\tilde{\upsilon}}. \tag{5.122}$$

Taking the supremum of the left-hand sides of the inequalities above and using the definition of class $\mathcal{KL}$ functions, we have

$$\|\tilde{\upsilon}_m\|_t \le \max\{\beta_{\tilde{\upsilon}}^h(|z_m(0)| + |\upsilon_m^*(0)|, 0) + \gamma_{\tilde{\upsilon}}^h(\|h_m\|_t) + d_{\tilde{\upsilon}}^h, \gamma_{\tilde{\upsilon}}^{\tilde{\upsilon}}(\|\tilde{\upsilon}_m\|_t)\}, \tag{5.123}$$

$$\|h_m\|_t \le \beta_h(h_m(0), 0) + \gamma_h^{\tilde{\upsilon}}(\|\tilde{\upsilon}_m\|_t) + d_h^{\tilde{\upsilon}}. \tag{5.124}$$

With $\gamma_{\tilde{\upsilon}}^{\tilde{\upsilon}}(s) < s$ for $d_{\tilde{\upsilon}}^h \le s \le \alpha_h(\mu(D) - \mu(D_s))$ given by (5.120), property (5.123) implies

$$\|\tilde{\upsilon}_m\|_t \le \beta_{\tilde{\upsilon}}^h(|z_m(0)| + |\upsilon_m^*(0)|, 0) + \gamma_{\tilde{\upsilon}}^h(\|h_m\|_t) + d_{\tilde{\upsilon}}^h \tag{5.125}$$

as long as $\|\tilde{\upsilon}_m\|_t \le \alpha_h(\mu(D) - \mu(D_s))$.

Substituting (5.124) into (5.125), we have

$$\|h_m\|_t \le \gamma_h^{\tilde{\upsilon}} \circ (\mathrm{Id} + \epsilon_2) \circ \gamma_{\tilde{\upsilon}}^h(\|h_m\|_t) + \Delta_h, \tag{5.126}$$

where

$$\Delta_h = \gamma_h^{\tilde{\upsilon}} \circ (\mathrm{Id} + \epsilon_2^{-1}) \circ (\beta_{\tilde{\upsilon}}^h(|z_m(0)| + |\upsilon_m^*(0)|, 0) + d_{\tilde{\upsilon}}^h) + \beta_h(h_m(0), 0) + d_h^{\tilde{\upsilon}} \tag{5.127}$$

with ϵ_2 being a class $\mathcal{K}_\infty$ function.

Condition (5.119) implies

$$\gamma_h^{\tilde{\upsilon}} \circ (\mathrm{Id} + \epsilon_2) \circ \gamma_{\tilde{\upsilon}}^h(s) \le (\mathrm{Id} + \epsilon_1)^{-1}(s), \quad \forall s \in [\mu(D_s), \mu(D)] \tag{5.128}$$

and thus

$$\gamma_h^{\tilde{\upsilon}} \circ (\mathrm{Id} + \epsilon_2) \circ \gamma_{\tilde{\upsilon}}^h(s) \le (\mathrm{Id} + \epsilon_1)^{-1}(s) + d_1, \quad \forall s \in [0, \mu(D)] \tag{5.129}$$

with $d_1 = \gamma_h^{\tilde{\upsilon}} \circ (\mathrm{Id} + \epsilon_2) \circ \gamma_{\tilde{\upsilon}}^h(\mu(D_s))$.

Substituting (5.129) into (5.126), we have

$$\|h_m\|_t \le (\mathrm{Id} + \epsilon_1)^{-1}(\|h_m\|_t) + d_1 + \Delta_h, \tag{5.130}$$

and thus

$$\|h_m\|_t \leq \left(\mathrm{Id} - (\mathrm{Id} + \epsilon_1)^{-1}\right)^{-1}(d_1 + \Delta_h) = (\mathrm{Id} + \epsilon_1^{-1})(d_1 + \Delta_h), \tag{5.131}$$

provided that $\|h_m\|_t \leq \mu(D)$. With (5.125), this means that

$$\|\tilde{v}_m\|_t \leq \beta_{\tilde{v}}^h(|z_m(0)| + |v_m^*(0)|, 0) + \gamma_{\tilde{v}}^h \circ (\mathrm{Id} + \epsilon_1^{-1})(d_1 + \Delta_h) + d_{\tilde{v}}^h. \tag{5.132}$$

It can be verified that, $\|h_m\|_t$ and $\|\tilde{v}_m\|_t$ are monotone with respect to $\mu(D_s)$, $\bar{v}^{cd}$ and the upper bounds of the initial states and the external inputs. Thus, all the conditions in the proof can be satisfied by appropriately choosing these values, and the boundedness of h_m and $\tilde{v}_m$ is proved. Then, directly applying properties (5.86) and (5.10), the maximal state z_m of the actuation systems is bounded. This also implies that $T_{\max} \geq \min_{k \in \mathcal{N}_a} T_k$.

Case (B): $t \geq \min_{k \in \mathcal{N}_a} T_k$.

In this case, $\mathcal{N}_S$ is not empty and the cardinality of $\mathcal{N}_S$ is nondecreasing with respect to t.

In accordance with the definitions of h_R and h_S in (5.37b) and (5.37c), we define

$$\tilde{v}_R = \underset{x \in \{\tilde{v}_i : i \in \mathcal{N}_a \setminus \mathcal{N}_S\}}{\operatorname{argmax}} |x|, \quad \tilde{v}_S = \underset{x \in \{\tilde{v}_i : i \in \mathcal{N}_S\}}{\operatorname{argmax}} |x|, \tag{5.133}$$

to represent the maximal velocity-tracking error of the agents belonging to $\mathcal{N}_a \setminus \mathcal{N}_S$ and $\mathcal{N}_S$, respectively. The definitions of h_m, h_R, h_S, $\tilde{v}_m$, $\tilde{v}_R$, and $\tilde{v}_S$ means that

$$h_m = \max\{h_R, h_S\}, \quad |\tilde{v}_m| = \max\{|\tilde{v}_R|, |\tilde{v}_S|\}. \tag{5.134}$$

Thus, the boundedness of h_m and $\tilde{v}_m$ is guaranteed if we can prove the boundedness of h_R, h_S, $\tilde{v}_R$, and $\tilde{v}_S$.

Denote

$$T_S = \max_{i \in \mathcal{N}_S} T_i. \tag{5.135}$$

(B1) Boundedness of $\tilde{v}_S$ and h_S. For any $i \in \mathcal{N}_S$ and $t \geq T_S$, we have $D^+ v_i^*(t) \equiv 0$, and the following property holds based on property (5.9):

$$|\tilde{v}_i(t)| \leq c_{\tilde{v}} |z_i(T_S)| e^{-\lambda(t - T_S)}, \tag{5.136}$$

which implies

$$|\tilde{v}_S(t)| \leq c_{\tilde{v}} |z_m(T_S)| e^{-\lambda(t - T_S)} \leq c_{\tilde{v}} |z_m(T_S)|. \tag{5.137}$$

This means the boundedness of $\tilde{v}_S$.

For any $i \in \mathcal{N}_S$ and any $j \in \mathcal{N}_S \cup \mathcal{N}_o \backslash \{i\}$, using (5.3) and (5.14), we have

$$\begin{aligned} |h_{ij}(t)| &= \mu\left(\left|\tilde{p}_{ij}(T_S) + \int_{T_S}^{t} (v_i(\tau) - v_j(\tau))d\tau\right|\right) \\ &\leq \mu\left(\mu^{-1}(h_{ij}(T_S)) - \int_{T_S}^{t} |\tilde{v}_i(\tau)| + |\tilde{v}_j(\tau)|d\tau\right) \\ &\leq \mu(\mu^{-1}(h_{ij}(T_S)) - c_{\tilde{v}}\lambda^{-1}(|z_i(T_S)| + |z_j(T_S)|)) \end{aligned} \tag{5.138}$$

for all $t \geq T_S$. We use (5.7) for the first inequality and use (5.9) for the last inequality above. Thus,

$$|h_S(t)| \leq \mu(\mu^{-1}(h_S(T_S)) - 2c_{\tilde{v}}\lambda^{-1}|z_m(T_S)|) \tag{5.139}$$

for all $t \geq T_S$. This proves the boundedness of h_S.

(B2) Boundedness of $\tilde{v}_R$ and h_R. Properties (5.73) and (5.87) imply that

$$\begin{aligned} |\tilde{v}_R(t)| \leq \max\{&\beta_{\tilde{v}}^h(|z_m(T_S)| + |v_m^*(T_S)|, t - T_S) + \gamma_{\tilde{v}}^h(\|h_R\|_{[T_S,t)}) \\ &+ d_{\tilde{v}}^h, \gamma_{\tilde{v}}^{\tilde{v}}(\|\tilde{v}_R\|_{[T_S,t)})\}, \end{aligned} \tag{5.140}$$

$$|h_R(t)| \leq \beta_h(h_R(T_S), t - T_S) + \gamma_h^{\tilde{v}}(\max\{\|\tilde{v}_R\|_{[T_S,t)} + d_h^{\tilde{v}}, \|\tilde{v}_S\|_{[T_S,t)}\}) \tag{5.141}$$

for all $t \geq T_S$. From (5.137), we have

$$\|\tilde{v}_S\|_{[T_S,t)} \leq c_{\tilde{v}}|z_m(T_S)|. \tag{5.142}$$

Combining (5.141) and (5.142), we have

$$\begin{aligned} |h_R(t)| &\leq \beta_h(h_R(T_S), t - T_S) + \gamma_h^{\tilde{v}}(\|\tilde{v}_R\|_{[T_S,t)}) + \gamma_h^{\tilde{v}}(c_{\tilde{v}}|z_m(T_S)|) + d_h^{\tilde{v}} \\ &= \beta_h(h_R(T_S), t - T_S) + \gamma_h^{\tilde{v}}(\|\tilde{v}_R\|_{[T_S,t)}) + d_{h_k}^{\tilde{v}} \end{aligned} \tag{5.143}$$

for all $t \geq T_S$, where

$$d_{h_k}^{\tilde{v}} = \gamma_h^{\tilde{v}}(c_{\tilde{v}}|z_m(T_S)|) + d_h^{\tilde{v}}. \tag{5.144}$$

Properties (5.140) and (5.143) result in an interconnection between $\tilde{v}_R$ and h_R, with a structure quite similar with the one between $\tilde{v}_m$ and h_m shown in Figure 5.6. The boundedness of $\tilde{v}_R$ and h_R can be proved following the small-gain analysis as for Case (A). The boundedness of h_m, $\tilde{v}_m$, and z_m can be proved based on the analysis in Cases (B1) and (B2). The boundedness of the closed-loop signals on $[0, T_{\max})$ means $T_{\max} = +\infty$.

5.6 Tuning the Safety-critical Controllers

This section provides a brief step-by-step guideline to choose controller parameters to satisfy the conditions required in the proofs above.

5.6.1 Choose the Functions Defining the Controller

For h defined in (5.14), by choosing $\mu(s) = 1/(s + D_s)$, we have $h(\tilde{p}) = |\tilde{p}|^{-1}$, $\mu^{-1}(s) = s^{-1}$, $\alpha_\mu(s) = s^2$, and $\alpha_p(s) = s$. For α_h defined in (5.72), by choosing $k_h^{\tilde{v}} > 0$ and $c_0 = 1/4$, we have $\alpha_h(s) = 5{k_h^{\tilde{v}}}^{-1} s$ and $\partial\alpha_h(s)/\partial s = 5{k_h^{\tilde{v}}}^{-1}$. Then, we choose a δ large enough to guarantee Property 3 of Proposition 5.2.

5.6.2 Calculate the Gains of the Subsystems

Based on the definition of the controller, properties (5.73) and (5.97) hold with

$$\gamma_h^{\tilde{v}}(s) = k_h^{\tilde{v}} s, \quad \alpha_{v*}^h(s) = 5c_M\sqrt{n}(k_h^{\tilde{v}})^{-1} s. \tag{5.145}$$

By choosing $k_\varphi = 1/4$, property (5.99) holds with

$$\alpha_{v*d}^h(s) = 2c_\varphi c_{\mathcal{P}}^2 \sqrt{\bar{v}^{c2} + \delta^2(\alpha_{v*}^h(s) + \bar{v}^c + \alpha_{Aa}^d(s))}\alpha_{Aa}^d(s), \tag{5.146}$$

$$\alpha_{v*d}^{\tilde{v}}(s) = c_\varphi c_{\mathcal{P}}^2 \sqrt{\bar{v}^{c2} + \delta^2 s^2/2}, \quad c_{v*d}^h = c_{\mathcal{P}} \bar{v}^{cd}, \tag{5.147}$$

where $\alpha_{Aa}^d(s) = 2c_\varphi\sqrt{n_{ao} - 1}\left(s + 5(k_h^{\tilde{v}}\delta)^{-1} s^2\right)$. Then, by choosing $\rho_{\tilde{v}}^{v*d}(s) = 2s$ and $k_{\tilde{v}} = 1$, properties (5.100)–(5.103) hold with

$$d_{\tilde{v}}^h = 2\gamma_{\tilde{v}}^{v*d}(2c_{v*d}^h), \quad \beta_{\tilde{v}}^h(s,t) = 2c_{\tilde{v}} e^{-\lambda t} s, \tag{5.148}$$

$$\gamma_{\tilde{v}}^h(s) = \alpha_{\tilde{v}}^{v*d} \circ \alpha_{v*d}^h(s), \tag{5.149}$$

$$\alpha_{\tilde{v}}^{v*d}(s) = 2(\gamma_{\tilde{v}}^{v*d}(2s + 2c_{v*d}^h) - d_{\tilde{v}}^h), \tag{5.150}$$

$$\gamma_{\tilde{v}}^{\tilde{v}}(s) = 2\gamma_{\tilde{v}}^{v*d}(2\alpha_{v*d}^{\tilde{v}}(s)). \tag{5.151}$$

By using the local Lipschitz property of $\gamma_{\tilde{v}}^{v*d}$ and the definition of $\alpha_{\tilde{v}}^{v*d}$ in (5.150), there exists $k_{\tilde{v}}^{v*d} \in \mathbb{R}_+$ such that

$$\gamma_{\tilde{v}}^{v*d}(s_1) \leq k_{\tilde{v}}^{v*d} s_1, \quad \alpha_{\tilde{v}}^{v*d}(s_2) \leq k_{\tilde{v}}^{v*d} s_2 \tag{5.152}$$

for all $s_1 \in [d_{\tilde{v}}^h, \alpha_h(\mu(D) - \mu(D_s))]$ and $s_2 \in [\alpha_{v*d}^h(\mu(D_s)), \alpha_{v*d}^h(\mu(D))]$.

5.6.3 Fine-tune the Controller Parameters to Satisfy the Small-gain-type Condition

By substituting (5.147) into (5.151), we have

$$\gamma_{\bar{\upsilon}}^{\bar{\upsilon}}(s) = 2\gamma_{\bar{\upsilon}}^{\upsilon*d}\left(c_{\varphi}c_{\mathcal{P}}^{2}\sqrt{\bar{\upsilon}^{c2} + \delta^{2}s^{2}}\right). \tag{5.153}$$

This, together with (5.152) implies

$$\gamma_{\bar{\upsilon}}^{\bar{\upsilon}}(s) \leq 2k_{\bar{\upsilon}}^{\upsilon*d}c_{\varphi}c_{\mathcal{P}}^{2}\sqrt{\bar{\upsilon}^{c2} + \delta^{2}s^{2}}. \tag{5.154}$$

Denote

$$\gamma_{c}(s) = (\text{Id} + \epsilon_{1})\circ\gamma_{h}^{\bar{\upsilon}}\circ(\text{Id} + \epsilon_{2})\circ\gamma_{\bar{\upsilon}}^{h}(s). \tag{5.155}$$

We choose

$$\epsilon_{1}(s) = s, \quad \epsilon_{2}(s) = s. \tag{5.156}$$

Then, from (5.155), we have

$$\begin{aligned}
\gamma_{c}(s) &= 8k_{h}^{\bar{\upsilon}}\left(\gamma_{\bar{\upsilon}}^{\upsilon*d}(2\alpha_{\upsilon*d}^{h}(s) + 2c_{\upsilon*d}^{h}) - d_{\bar{\upsilon}}^{h}\right) \leq 8k_{h}^{\bar{\upsilon}}k_{\bar{\upsilon}}^{\upsilon*d}\alpha_{\upsilon*d}^{h}(s) \\
&\leq 8k_{h}^{\bar{\upsilon}}k_{\bar{\upsilon}}^{\upsilon*d}2c_{\varphi}c_{\mathcal{P}}^{2}\sqrt{\overline{\upsilon}^{c2} + \delta^{2}\left(\alpha_{\upsilon*}^{h}(s) + \overline{\upsilon}^{c} + \alpha_{Aa}^{d}(s)\right)\alpha_{Aa}^{d}(s)} \\
&\leq 8k_{h}^{\bar{\upsilon}}k_{\bar{\upsilon}}^{\upsilon*d}2c_{\varphi}c_{\mathcal{P}}^{2}\sqrt{\overline{\upsilon}^{c2} + \delta^{2}\left(5c_{M}\sqrt{n}(k_{h}^{\bar{\upsilon}})^{-1}s + \overline{\upsilon}^{c}\right.} \\
&\quad \left. + 2c_{\varphi}\sqrt{n_{ao} - 1}(s + 5(k_{h}^{\bar{\upsilon}}\delta)^{-1}s^{2})\right) \\
&\quad \times 2c_{\varphi}\sqrt{n_{ao} - 1}(s + 5(k_{h}^{\bar{\upsilon}}\delta)^{-1}s^{2}).
\end{aligned} \tag{5.157}$$

We use the definitions of ϵ_1 and ϵ_2 in (5.156) for the first equality, use the property (5.152) for the first inequality, use the definition of $\alpha_{\upsilon*d}^{h}$ in (5.146) for the second equality, and use definitions of $\alpha_{\upsilon*}^{h}$ and α_{Aa}^{d} in (5.145) and (5.146), respectively, for the last inequality above.

Condition (5.120) is satisfied as

$$10k_{\bar{\upsilon}}^{\upsilon*d}c_{\varphi}c_{\mathcal{P}}^{2}\sqrt{\bar{\upsilon}^{c2} + \delta^{2}}k_{h}^{\bar{\upsilon}^{-1}}D^{-1} < 1 \tag{5.158}$$

and condition (5.124) is satisfied as

$$\begin{aligned}
&8k_{h}^{\bar{\upsilon}}k_{\bar{\upsilon}}^{\upsilon*d}2c_{\varphi}c_{\mathcal{P}}^{2}\sqrt{\overline{\upsilon}^{c2} + \delta^{2}\left(5c_{M}\sqrt{n}(k_{h}^{\bar{\upsilon}})^{-1}D^{-1} + \overline{\upsilon}^{c}\right.} \\
&\left. + 2c_{\varphi}\sqrt{n_{ao} - 1}(D^{-1} + 5(k_{h}^{\bar{\upsilon}}\delta)^{-1}D^{-2})\right) \\
&\times 2c_{\varphi}\sqrt{n_{ao} - 1}(1 + 5(k_{h}^{\bar{\upsilon}}\delta)^{-1}D^{-1}) \leq 1.
\end{aligned} \tag{5.159}$$

Based on (5.158) and (5.159), the conditions (5.119) and (5.120) are satisfied by choosing $1/k_h^{\tilde{v}}$, $1/D$, and $\bar{v}^c$ small enough. Then, safety is guaranteed by choosing D_s large enough.

This completes the proof of Theorem 5.1.

5.7 Numerical Simulation and Experiment

5.7.1 Numerical Simulation: Collision Avoidance in the Case of One Mobile Agent and Two Obstacles

In this section, we consider the scenario in Examples 5.2 and 5.3. The identified quadrotor model given in Example 1.2 is used for the numerical simulation.

The QP-based controller with a RP and reshaped feasible set (RPRF) defined in (5.30)–(5.34) is compared with the QP-based controller with RP (RP) defined in (5.25)–(5.27), to show the effectiveness of the proposed method.

We consider a constant velocity-command signal:

$$v_1^c(t) \equiv [2; -2]. \tag{5.160}$$

For both of the controllers, we choose

$$D = 0.6, \qquad D_s = 0.65, \qquad \delta = 100, \tag{5.161}$$

$$\mu(s) = s^{-1}, \qquad h(\tilde{p}) = |\tilde{p}|^{-1}, \qquad \alpha_h(s) = 0.75s. \tag{5.162}$$

For the QP-based controller with RPRF, we also choose

$$c_K = 1, \quad c_P = 2\sqrt{2}, \tag{5.163a}$$

$$[A_1^r]_{j,:} = \left[\cos\frac{2\pi j}{n_1}, \ \sin\frac{2\pi j}{n_1}\right], \quad j = 1, \dots, n_l \tag{5.163b}$$

with $n_l = 11$. Accordingly, $c_A = \cos(2\pi/11)$.

Figures 5.7 and 5.8 show the position trajectories of the controlled mobile agent and the velocity-reference inputs with the two controllers. Due to the uncertain actuation dynamics, the velocity-reference input generated by the QP-based controller with RP leads to an unexpected response and causes a collision. The QP-based controller with RPRF avoids collision.

5.7.2 Experiment: Safety-critical Control of Three Quadrotors

To verify the proposed method in practice, we consider a scenario of three quadrotors swapping positions.

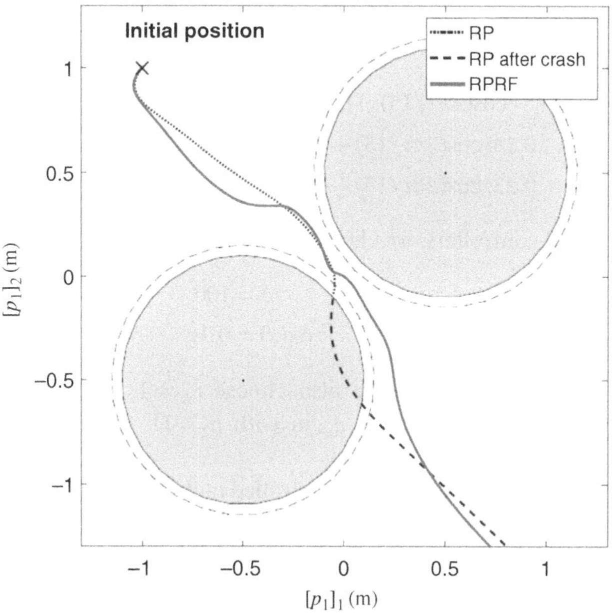

Figure 5.7 Trajectories of the controlled mobile agent under QP-based controllers in (5.30)–(5.34) and (5.25)–(5.27), respectively.

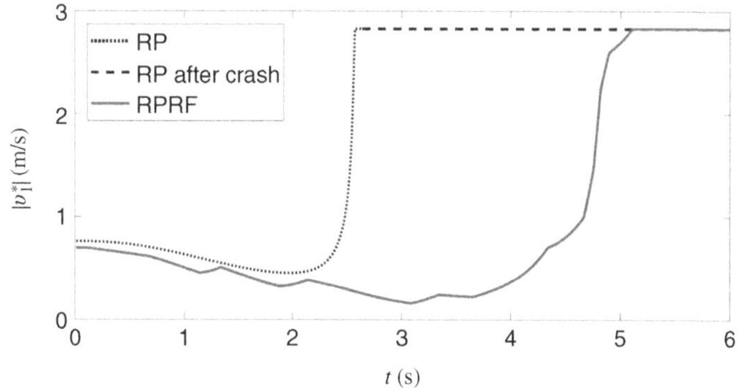

Figure 5.8 Velocity-reference inputs under QP-based controllers in (5.30)–(5.34) and (5.25)–(5.27), respectively.

The primary controller is designed for trajectory tracking. In particular, the velocity-command signals are generated by feedforward-feedback controllers:

$$v_i^c(t) = -1.7(p_i(t) - p_i^r(t)) + \dot{p}_i^r(t) \tag{5.164}$$

for $i = 1, 2, 3$, where the reference trajectories of the mobile agents are generated by sinusoidal functions:

$$p_1^r(t) = [-\cos(2\pi t/15); -\cos(2\pi t/15); 1], \tag{5.165}$$

$$p_2^r(t) = [\cos(2\pi t/15) - 0.23; \cos(2\pi t/15) + 0.23; 1], \tag{5.166}$$

$$p_3^r(t) = [\cos(2\pi t/15) + 0.23; \cos(2\pi t/15) - 0.23; 1]. \tag{5.167}$$

For both of the safety-critical controllers, we choose

$$D = 0.2, \qquad D_s = 0.3, \qquad \delta = 100, \tag{5.168}$$

$$\mu(s) = s^{-1}, \qquad h(\tilde{p}) = |\tilde{p}|^{-1}, \qquad \alpha_h(s) = 0.3s. \tag{5.169}$$

For the QP-based controller with RPRF, we also choose $c_K = 1$, $c_P = 1$ and $[A_1^r]_{j,:} = [\cos(2\pi j/n_l),\ \sin(2\pi j/n_l)]$ for $j = 1, \dots, n_l$ with $n_l = 11$. Accordingly, $c_A = \cos(2\pi/11)$.

Figures 5.9 and 5.10 show the trajectories of the controlled mobile agents and the norms of the velocity-reference inputs with the two controllers. Although collision avoidance is achieved in both of the cases, one may recognize a sudden change of agent 1's velocity-reference input at $t = 4.1$ when the QP-based controller without feasible-set reshaping is applied. The minimum distances between the agents under the two controllers are shown in Figure 5.11.

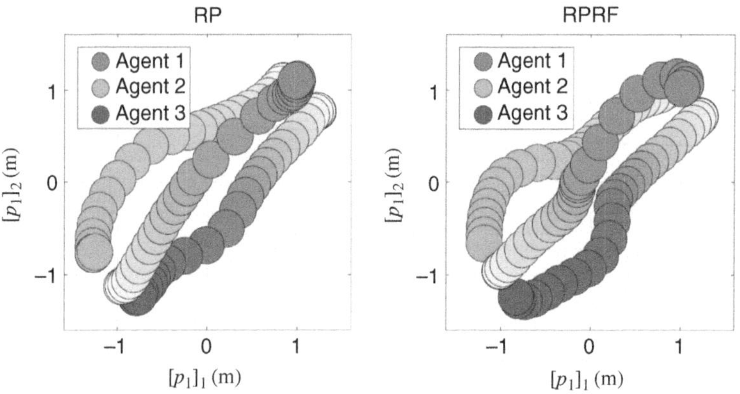

Figure 5.9 Trajectories of the agents under QP-based controllers in (5.30)–(5.34) and (5.25)–(5.27), respectively.

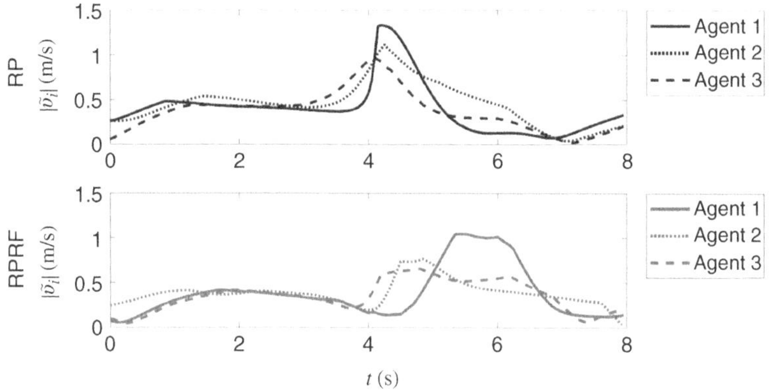

Figure 5.10 Norms of the velocity-reference inputs generated by QP-based controllers in (5.30)–(5.34) and (5.25)–(5.27), respectively.

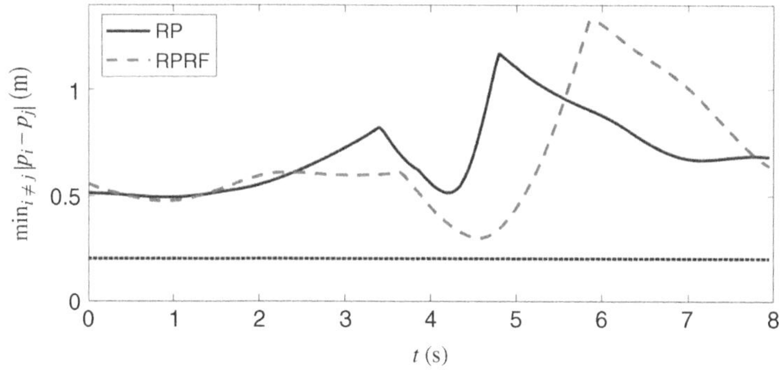

Figure 5.11 Minimum distances between the agents under QP-based controllers in (5.30)–(5.34) and (5.25)–(5.27), respectively.

5.8 Notes

Classical multi-robot cooperative control addresses formation control, area coverage, exploration, and boundary tracking. The theoretical foundations comprise distributed control, graph-theoretic coordination, and coverage optimization [20, 31, 32, 40, 136]. In much of the literature, safety requirements such as collision avoidance are incorporated via a hierarchical control architecture [14]. When the inter-robot distance falls below a prescribed threshold, a safety-critical controller modifies the nominal control law [31, 136, 166]. This separation-based design is effective when robots operate near a steady state, the population size is small, or obstacles are well separated. However, as the number of robots increases, interventions of the safety-critical controller become frequent and begin to dominate the closed-loop behavior, thereby impeding the realization of the primary control objectives [170].

Attaining primary objectives while satisfying motion constraints is an essential yet challenging task for vehicles and robotic systems. Multi-agent systems are one of the scenarios that most clearly illustrate the importance of safety-critical control. Reference [207] established strong safety guarantees using a Hamilton–Jacobi–Bellman–Isaacs framework, although the computational burden limited real-time scalability. To reduce computational complexity, References [2, 55, 209] developed geometric velocity-obstacle methods that compute safe velocity sets under constant-velocity and instantaneous-maneuverability assumptions. These approaches are widely used due to their low computational cost, but their assumptions on the kinematics model (including unbounded acceleration and piecewise-constant velocity) restrict applicability in highly dynamic environments. Complementarily, Reference [135] proposed an optimization-based method using mixed-integer QP to synthesize high-fidelity collision-free trajectories under constraints induced by stationary and moving agents. Reference [211] presented safety barrier certificates that ensure scalable and provably collision-free behaviors in multirobot systems by modifying the primary controllers to formally satisfy safety constraints.

6

Safety-critical Control of Euler–Lagrange Systems: Incorporating Barrier and Energy Functions

The preceding chapters have focused on mobile agents modeled as a cascade of a nominal kinematic system and an uncertain actuation system (representing the controlled dynamics). While the modeling approach based on uncertain actuation systems captures a broad class of controlled systems, it is of practical interest to investigate how the plant's intrinsic dynamics and their associated properties (e.g., energy conservation) can be directly incorporated into safety-critical controller design.

The Euler–Lagrange (EL) equation describes the motion of a diverse set of physical systems and has been widely employed in controller design for mechanical systems [158]. Developing a systematic solution for safety-critical control of EL systems remains a pressing need. For industrial robotic manipulators, safety fundamentally requires that every point on the manipulator body stay a sufficient distance away from both cooperative and non-cooperative objects [180]. A single obstacle point in the workspace generally corresponds to a set of obstacles in the configuration (joint) space. Compared with conventional stabilizing or tracking controllers, a well-designed safety-critical controller must address not only the nonlinear and uncertain dynamics of the plant but also various safety constraints, which introduce significant technical challenges. In the case of EL systems, it is particularly important to exploit the system's inherent energy-conservation properties in controller design, thereby reducing the controller's dependence on precise system modeling.

This chapter presents a systematic approach that integrates barrier and energy functions for the safety-critical control of EL systems. The proposed design naturally leads to a new class of nested-loop controllers formulated via quadratic programming (QP). By employing the feasible-set reshaping technique introduced in this book, the safety constraints are projected onto a suitably chosen constant matrix whose rows positively span the control input space, preserving feasibility while ensuring constraint satisfaction. Moreover, under mild conditions, the resulting control law is Lipschitz continuous with respect to the generalized coordinates of the EL system. Leveraging the inherent energy-conservation property of EL systems, a nonlinear proportional control law is developed for the inner loop to achieve velocity tracking. The safety property of the closed-loop system is ensured through a nontrivial integration between the safety indicator functions of the outer loop and the energy function of the inner loop. The proposed design also accommodates uncertain plant dynamics and incorporates velocity constraints to meet practical implementation requirements.

6.1 Problem Formulation

Consider the model of an EL system with n degrees of freedom (DOF) given by

$$M(q)\ddot{q} + C(q,\dot{q})\dot{q} + N(q,\dot{q}) = u, \tag{6.1}$$

where $q \in \mathbb{R}^n$ is the vector of generalized coordinates (positions), $M(q) \in \mathbb{R}^{n\times n}$ is the inertia matrix, $C(q,\dot{q})\dot{q}$ represents the Coriolis and centrifugal forces with $C(q,\dot{q}) \in \mathbb{R}^{n\times n}$, $N(q,\dot{q}) \in \mathbb{R}^n$ includes generalized resistance and gravity terms, and $u \in \mathbb{R}^n$ represents the vector of generalized forces. The study in this chapter does not rely on known system dynamics, but instead assumes the inherent energy conservation properties of EL systems; see [44, 149].

Assumption 6.1 (*Properties of the EL System*): The system (6.1) admits the following properties:

- Along the trajectories of the system (6.1), $\dot{M} - 2C$ is a skew-symmetric matrix, that is,

$$(\dot{M} - 2C) + (\dot{M} - 2C)^T = 0; \tag{6.2}$$

- $M(q)$ is an invertible, symmetric matrix for any $q \in \mathbb{R}^n$, and there exist positive constants μ_{m1} and μ_{m2} such that

$$\mu_{m1} I_{n\times n} < M(q) < \mu_{m2} I_{n\times n} \tag{6.3}$$

  for all $q \in \mathbb{R}^n$.

In our problem setting, u is considered as the control input. Given $v^c : \mathbb{R}_+ \to \mathbb{R}^n$ as the velocity-command signal, our objective is to design a controller for the plant (6.1) to satisfy the imposed safety constraints while minimally deviating from v^c. In practice, it is required that every point on the body (e.g., robotic manipulator)

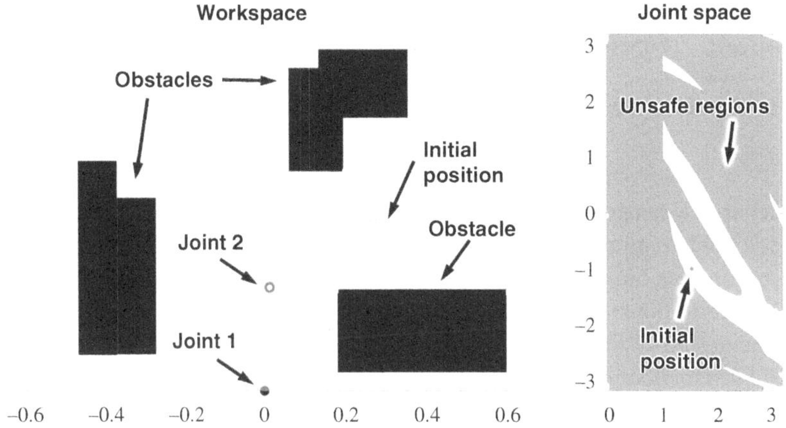

Figure 6.1 The obstacles in the workspace of a 2-DOF robotic manipulator and the corresponding obstacles in configuration space.

maintains a sufficient distance from all the points in the unsafe region in the workspace. This makes it quite difficult to explicitly represent all the safety constraints in the workspace. However, in the configuration space, with the generalized coordinate q considered as the state, it is much easier to use spherical obstacles to cover the unsafe region and define barrier functions. Figure 6.1 illustrates the obstacles in the workspace of a 2-DOF robotic manipulator and the corresponding obstacles in configuration space.

Specifically, the safety constraints on the generalized coordinates q are defined by spherical obstacles. It is desired that

$$h_i(q(t)) \geq 0, \quad i = 1, \dots , N, \tag{6.4}$$

for all $t \geq 0$, where

$$h_i(q) = |q - q_{oi}| - d_{si}, \tag{6.5}$$

with $q_{oi} \in \mathbb{R}^n$ and $d_{si} > 0$ representing the positions and radii of the spherical obstacles, respectively.

Moreover, the generalized velocities are required to stay within bounded ranges:

$$|\dot{q}(t)| \leq \bar{\upsilon} \tag{6.6}$$

for all $t \geq 0$, where $\bar{\upsilon}$ is a positive constant representing the velocity bound.

Without loss of generality, the velocity-command signal υ^c is assumed to be bounded and differentiable on the time-line.

Assumption 6.2 (*Boundedness of the Velocity-command Signal and Its Time Derivative*): There exist positive constants $\bar{\upsilon}^c$ and $\bar{\upsilon}^{cd}$ such that

$$|\upsilon^c(t)| \leq \bar{\upsilon}^c, \quad |\dot{\upsilon}^c(t)| \leq \bar{\upsilon}^{cd}, \tag{6.7}$$

for all $t \geq 0$.

In scenarios where a position feedback control objective needs to be achieved alongside safety requirements, a new feedback link should be established from q to υ^c. In this case, building on the results of this chapter, some relaxed Lipschitz continuity conditions on υ^c with respect to q are required for the closed-loop analysis of the overall system. Refer to Section 6.5.2 for an example.

A mild distance condition is assumed on the obstacles.

Assumption 6.3 (*Distances Between the Obstacles*): There exist constants d_a, d_b, and d_h satisfying

$$0 < d_a < \min_{i=1,\dots,N}\{d_{si}\}, \qquad d_b > 0, \qquad 0 < d_h < \min_{i=1,\dots,N}\{d_{si}\}, \tag{6.8}$$

such that for any q satisfying $h_i(q) \geq -d_h$ for all $i = 1, \dots, N$, if for some $j, k \in \{1, \dots, N\}$,

$$h_j(q) \leq \frac{d_b}{2}, \quad h_k(q) \leq \frac{d_b}{2}, \tag{6.9}$$

then

$$|q_{oj} - q_{ok}| \leq d_a. \tag{6.10}$$

Assumption 6.3 means that the spherical obstacles covering the unsafe region in the configuration space should either intersect sufficiently closely or disjoin. Given predetermined unsafe regions, one may first partition the configuration space into uniformly sized hypercubes and then place spherical obstacles with appropriate radii to cover the hypercubes. Assumption 6.3 can be ensured by choosing the hypercubes small enough and the radii of the spherical obstacles large enough. Figure 6.2 shows how spherical obstacles are employed to cover the unsafe region in the configuration space of a two-link planar manipulator.

The EL system model (6.1) exhibits a cascade structure, which motivates the application of a well-established constructive nonlinear control method (see, e.g., [174]) to address the safety-critical control problem. Based on this idea, we first treat $\dot{q}$ as the virtual control input for the kinematics part of the EL system and design a QP-based virtual control law that computes the velocity-reference input υ^* to fulfill the position constraints. Next, we design a velocity-tracking control law to tackle the dynamics part of the EL system, ensuring that the actual velocity

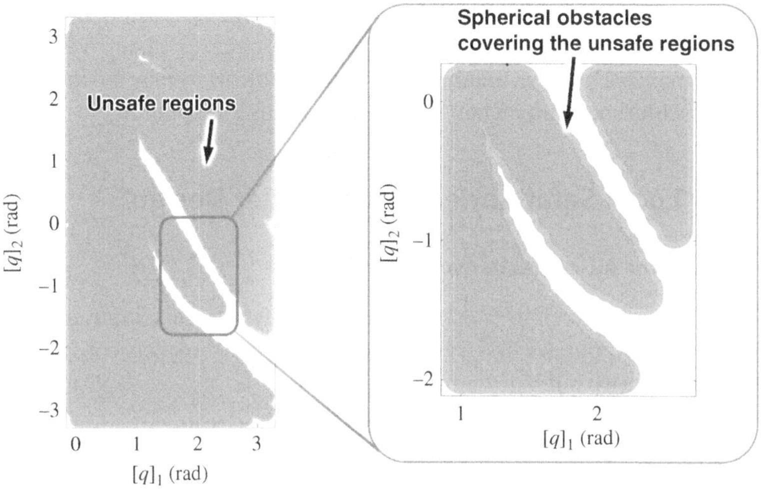

Figure 6.2 Spherical obstacles covering the unsafe region in the configuration space of a two-link planar manipulator.

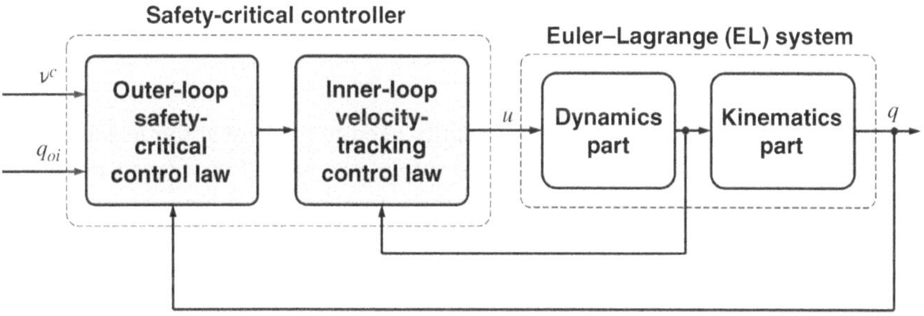

Figure 6.3 The structure of the proposed safety-critical control system.

$\dot{q}$ tracks υ^*. Figure 6.3 shows the structure of the proposed safety-critical control system.

With the velocity-tracking error defined by

$$\tilde{\upsilon} = \dot{q} - \upsilon^*, \tag{6.11}$$

the kinematics part of the EL system can be rewritten as

$$\dot{q} = \upsilon^* + \tilde{\upsilon}, \tag{6.12}$$

and the safety property should be carefully analyzed by fully taking into account the influence of $\tilde{\upsilon}$. Moreover, the velocity-tracking control performance is also influenced by the safety-critical control part. It is essential that the safety-oriented virtual control law, which generates υ^* is locally Lipschitz to ensure velocity-tracking performance. However, a standard QP-based control law may fail to admit the desired Lipschitz continuity when multiple constraints are present.

6.2 Outer Loop: Safety-oriented Controller Design

6.2.1 A Design for All-obstacle Avoidance

For the kinematics part given by (6.12), with the velocity-reference input υ^* considered as the control input, we first try using QP to integrate the safety constraints and the primary velocity-reference input:

$$\upsilon^* = \underset{\upsilon_o^* \in \mathbb{R}^n}{\operatorname{argmin}} |\upsilon_o^* - \upsilon^c|^2 \tag{6.13}$$

$$\text{s.t.} \quad -\nabla h_i(q)\upsilon_o^* \leq \alpha_p(h_i(q)) - \upsilon_r, \quad i = 1, \dots, N, \tag{6.14}$$

where α_p is of class $\mathcal{K}^e$, constant $\upsilon_r > 0$ is used as a robust term to handle the influence of the velocity-tracking error $\tilde{\upsilon}$, and according to the definition in (6.5),

$$\nabla h_i(q) = \frac{(q - q_{oi})^T}{|q - q_{oi}|}, \quad \forall q \neq q_{oi}. \tag{6.15}$$

Standard results such as [6] can be readily used to guarantee the feasibility of the QP (6.13) and (6.14) and analyze the safety property of the closed-loop system composed of (6.12)–(6.14) when $|\tilde{\upsilon}| \leq \upsilon_r$. In the case of $|\tilde{\upsilon}| \leq \upsilon_r$, condition (6.14) implies that along the trajectories of (6.12), the time-derivative of each $h_i(q)$, denoted by $\dot{h}_i(q, \upsilon)$, satisfies

$$\begin{aligned} \dot{h}_i(q, \upsilon) &= \nabla h_i(q)(\upsilon^* + \tilde{\upsilon}) \\ &\geq -\alpha_p(h_i(q)) + \upsilon_r - |\nabla h_i(q)\tilde{\upsilon}| \\ &\geq -\alpha_p(h_i(q)), \end{aligned} \tag{6.16}$$

which, under specific initial conditions, guarantees the satisfaction of the position constraints.

However, the velocity-reference input υ^* generated by the normal QP-based control law (6.13) and (6.14) may not be Lipschitz continuous when there is more than one constraint (i.e., $N \geq 2$). Moreover, the velocity constraint (6.6) cannot be represented in the affine form in general, and thus cannot be directly included as a new constraint of the QP (6.13) and (6.14). This means that the QP-based design (6.13) and (6.14) may not be readily used as an outer-loop control law.

We refine the feasible-set reshaping technique proposed in the previous chapters to solve this problem. In particular, the original safety constraints are projected onto appropriately chosen vectors positively spanning $\mathbb{R}^n$ such that the resulting constraints feature a constant constraint matrix which satisfies the full-row-rank condition required by [70, Theorem 3.1] (also see Theorem B.1) for Lipschitz continuity of solutions of constrained convex optimization problems. Moreover, with the positive span, we can represent the velocity constraint in an affine form.

The resulting QP-based control law with the reshaped feasible set is given by

$$v^* = \underset{v_o^* \in \mathbb{R}^n}{\mathrm{argmin}} |v_o^* - v^c|^2 \tag{6.17}$$

$$\text{s.t.} \quad l_k^T v_o^* \leq c_0 \alpha_c(r(q, l_k)) - v_r, \quad k = 1, \dots, m \tag{6.18}$$

$$l_k^T v_o^* \leq c_0(\bar{v} - v_r), \quad k = 1, \dots, m, \tag{6.19}$$

where α_c is chosen to be of class $\mathcal{K}^e$, c_0 is a positive constant less than 1 and

$$r(q, l_k) = \min_{i=1,\dots,N} \{h_i(q) + \phi(\nabla h_i(q) l_k)\} \tag{6.20}$$

is called a distance-regularization function, with $\phi : [-1, 1] \rightarrow \mathbb{R}_+$ being an appropriately chosen Lipschitz continuous, nonnegative, increasing function, $l_1, \dots, l_m \in \mathbb{R}^n$ are unit vectors positively span $\mathbb{R}^n$ such that any unit vector $l_o \in \mathbb{R}^n$ can be represented as a positive combination of the elements of $\{l_1, \dots, l_m : l_i^T l_o \geq c_0\}$, whose cardinality is not less than n. The existence of such vectors $l_1, \dots, l_m$ has been discussed in Appendix A.2. Moreover, as this chapter considers the case of obstacles intersecting, which is not within the scope of the previous chapters, additional conditions are attached to the unit vectors $l_1, \dots, l_m \in \mathbb{R}^n$, which positively span $\mathbb{R}^n$, such that the reshaped feasible set is still nonempty. The result is later given by Proposition 6.1.

Intuitively, the operation of $r(q, l_k)$ projects all the $\nabla h_i(q)$ for $i = 1, \dots, N$ to the unit vector l_k and takes their minimum. This, together with α_c of class $\mathcal{K}^e$ functions guarantees that any v_o^* satisfying the new constraints is within the original feasible set defined in (6.14). The function ϕ is used to enlarge the reshaped feasible set without violating the original safety constraints.

The advantage of the feasible-set reshaping technique lies in that the constraints (6.18) and (6.19), equivalently represented by

$$l_k^T v_o^* \leq \min\{c_0 \alpha_c(r(q, l_k)) - v_r, c_0(\bar{v} - v_r)\}, \quad k = 1, \dots, m, \tag{6.21}$$

features the constraint matrix $[l_1, \dots, l_m]^T$, any n rows of which can be guaranteed to be linearly independent by appropriately choosing the vectors $l_1, \dots, l_m$. As proved by [70], the full-row-rank condition is sufficient to guarantee the Lipschitz continuity of the solution to the QP.

We employ a numerical example to show the possible non-Lipschitz continuity of the solution to a QP and the basic idea of our feasible-set reshaping technique.

Example 6.1 (*Lipschitz Continuity of a QP-based Control Law with a Reshaped Feasible Set*): *Consider the kinematics part given by* (6.12) *with* $n = 2$. *Given velocity-command signal* $\upsilon^c = [0; 5]$ *and two disc-type obstacles with the same radius* $d_{si} = 0.096$ *but centered at* $q_{o1} = [0.1; 0]$, $q_{o2} = [-0.1; 0]$, *with the velocity-reference input* υ^* *considered as the virtual control input, we first design a control law based on the original QP* (6.13) and (6.14) *as*

$$\upsilon_1^* = \underset{\upsilon_o^* \in \mathbb{R}^n}{\operatorname{argmin}} |\upsilon_o^* - \upsilon^c|^2 \tag{6.22}$$

$$\text{s.t.} \quad -\nabla h_i(q)\upsilon_o^* \leq h_i(q) - \upsilon_r, \quad i = 1, 2 \tag{6.23}$$

with h_i *defined in* (6.5), *and* $\upsilon_r = 0.004$.

For comparison, we also design a control law based on the refined QP (6.17) and (6.18) *but neglect the velocity constraint* (6.19) *as*

$$\upsilon_2^* = \underset{\upsilon_o^* \in \mathbb{R}^n}{\operatorname{argmin}} |\upsilon_o^* - \upsilon^c|^2 \tag{6.24}$$

$$\text{s.t.} \quad l_k^T \upsilon_o^* \leq c_0 \alpha_c(r(q, l_k)) - \upsilon_r, \quad k = 1, \ldots, m \tag{6.25}$$

with $m = 21$, $l_k = [\cos(2(k-1)\pi/21); \sin(2(k-1)\pi/21)]$ *for* $k = 1, \ldots, m$, $c_0 = 0.9556$, $\alpha(s) = 6s$ *for* $s \in \mathbb{R}$, $\upsilon_r = 0.004$, *and*

$$r(q, l_k) = \min_{i=1,2}\{h_i(q) + \max\{0.0023\nabla h_i(q) l_k + 0.0015, 0\}\}. \tag{6.26}$$

Although Figure 6.4 only shows the map from $[q]_2$ *to* $[\upsilon^*]_2$, *one can observe that the normal QP-based control law results in a non-Lipschitz map, while the refined QP-based control law admits a Lipschitz map.*

Figure 6.5 shows the $q_1 - q_2$ *plane and the* $\nu_1 - \nu_2$ *plane simultaneously for an intuitive illustration of the feasible set reshaping technique in one single figure. Note that some of the vectors are scaled by* $1/20$ *to more effectively convey the basic idea.*

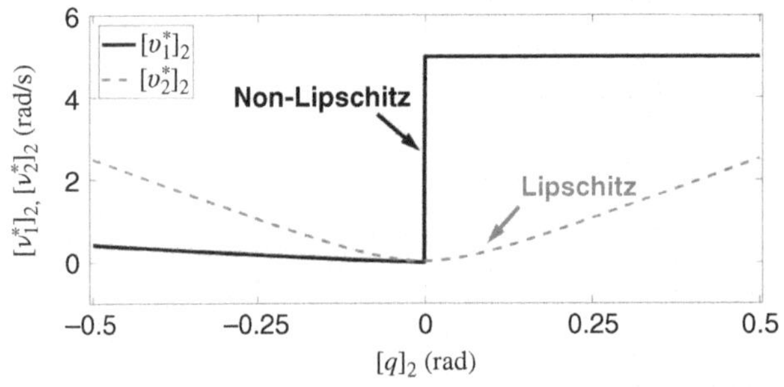

Figure 6.4 The maps from $[q]_2$ to $[\upsilon^*]_2$ of different QP-based control laws.

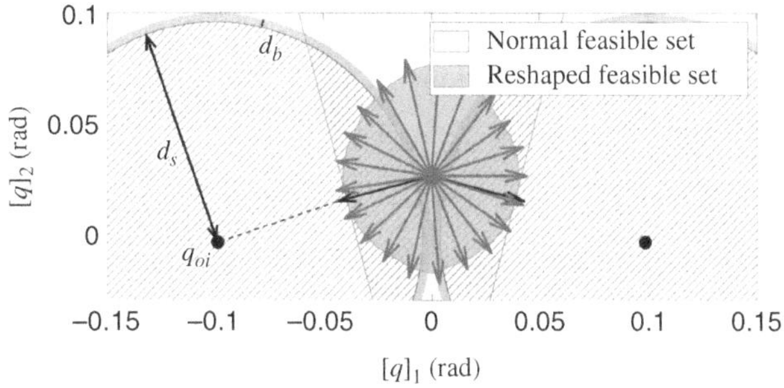

Figure 6.5 An illustration of the feasible-set reshaping technique.

If the refined QP (6.17)–(6.19) admits a unique solution, then we use $\varphi : \mathbb{R}^n \times \mathbb{R}^n \to \mathbb{R}^n$ to represent the resulting map from q and υ^c to υ^*, i.e.,

$$\upsilon^* = \varphi(q, \upsilon^c). \tag{6.27}$$

Denote

$$\underline{d}_s = \min_{i=1,\dots,N} \{d_{si}\}, \quad \bar{d}_s = \max_{i=1,\dots,N} \{d_{si}\}. \tag{6.28}$$

Proposition 6.1 shows the validity of the refined QP-based control law in dealing with multiple constraints while ensuring Lipschitz continuity of the function φ defined in (6.27).

Proposition 6.1 (*Safety Properties of the Outer Loop: All-obstacle Avoidance*): Consider the kinematics part (6.12) of the EL system (6.1), and set the velocity-reference input υ^* as the solution to the QP (6.17)–(6.19). Suppose that Assumptions (6.2) and (6.3) are satisfied. Under the condition that

$$\sqrt{2}\underline{d}_s > d_a, \tag{6.29}$$

$$\bar{\upsilon} > 2\upsilon_r, \tag{6.30}$$

$$\frac{2\underline{d}_s^2 - d_a^2}{2(\bar{d}_s + d_b/2)^2} > 1 - \frac{(\bar{\upsilon} - 2\upsilon_r)^2}{2(\bar{\upsilon} - \upsilon_r)^2} \tag{6.31}$$

with $\bar{\upsilon}$ defined right after (6.6), d_a and d_b defined in Assumption 6.3, and υ_r being a positive constant, one can find a Lipschitz continuous, nonnegative, increasing function $\phi : [-1, 1] \to \mathbb{R}_+$, a constant $0 < c_0 < 1$, a Lipschitz function $\alpha_c \in \mathcal{K}^e$ whose inverse function is also Lipschitz and a constant $\Delta_h > 0$ such that if

$$h_i(q) \geq -\Delta_h, \quad i = 1, \dots, N, \tag{6.32}$$

then

a. the QP (6.17)–(6.19) admits a unique solution;
b. the position trajectories satisfy

$$\nabla h_i(q)\dot{q} \geq -\alpha_p(h_i(q)) + \upsilon_r - |\tilde{\upsilon}|, \quad i = 1, \dots, N \tag{6.33}$$

with $\alpha_p(s) = \max\{\alpha_c(s), c_0\alpha_c(s)\}$, and the velocity-reference input υ^* satisfies

$$|\upsilon^*| \leq \bar{\upsilon} - \upsilon_r; \tag{6.34}$$

c. the function φ defined in (6.27) resulting from solving the QP (6.17)–(6.19) satisfies

$$|\varphi(q_1, \upsilon_{c1}) - \varphi(q_2, \upsilon_{c2})| \leq L(|q_1 - q_2| + |\upsilon_{c1} - \upsilon_{c2}|) \tag{6.35}$$

for all q_1, q_2 satisfying (6.32) with q replaced by q_1, q_2, and $\upsilon_{c1}, \upsilon_{c2} \in \mathbb{R}^n$, with constant $L > 0$.

Proof. Condition (6.29)–(6.31) guarantees the existence of a $c_0 \in (0, 1)$ satisfying

$$c_0 > \sqrt{c^*} + \sqrt{c^* + \frac{\upsilon_r}{\bar{\upsilon} - \upsilon_r}}, \tag{6.36}$$

with

$$c^* = \frac{(2\bar{d}_s + d_b)^2 - 4\underline{d}_s^2 + 2d_a^2}{2(2\bar{d}_s + d_b)^2}. \tag{6.37}$$

Then, we have

$$c_0(\bar{\upsilon} - \upsilon_r) > \frac{\upsilon_r}{\sqrt{c^* + \upsilon_r/(\bar{\upsilon} - \upsilon_r)} - \sqrt{c^*}}, \tag{6.38}$$

which means the existence of an $\alpha_c \in \mathcal{K}^e$ satisfying

$$c_0(\bar{\upsilon} - \upsilon_r) \geq c_0\alpha_c\left(\frac{d_b}{2}\right) - \upsilon_r > \frac{\upsilon_r - c_0\alpha_c(-d_h)}{\sqrt{c^* + \frac{\upsilon_r}{\bar{\upsilon} - \upsilon_r}} - \sqrt{c^*}}, \tag{6.39}$$

with d_h defined in Assumption 6.3. Moreover, for any c_0 satisfying (6.36), one can always find a ϕ satisfying

$$\phi(s) > \max_{p \in [0, d_h]} \left\{ \max_{K \in \left\{c_0(\bar{\upsilon} - \upsilon_r), \frac{\upsilon_r - c_0\alpha_c(-p)}{\sqrt{c^* + \frac{\upsilon_r}{\bar{\upsilon} - \upsilon_r}} - \sqrt{c^*}}\right\}} \left\{ \alpha_c^{-1}\left(\frac{K(s + c_0)}{c_0} + \frac{-K\left(\sqrt{c^* + \frac{\upsilon_r}{\bar{\upsilon} - \upsilon_r}} - \sqrt{c^*}\right) + \upsilon_r}{c_0} \right)\right\} + p \right\}, \quad s \in (-c_0, 1], \tag{6.40}$$

$$\phi(s) = 0, \quad s \in [-1, -c_0], \tag{6.41}$$

With c_0, α_c and ϕ chosen to satisfy (6.36), (6.37), and (6.39)–(6.41), we prove the three properties of the proposition one by one.

a. Feasibility of the QP

Under Assumption 6.3, with conditions (6.29)–(6.31), (6.36), (6.37), and (6.39)–(6.41) satisfied, we choose $\Delta_h \in (0, d_h]$, $K_v > 0$ and $c_M \in (0, 1)$ satisfying

$$\frac{2\left(\underline{d}_s - \Delta_h\right)^2 - d_a^2}{2\left(\bar{d}_s + d_b/2\right)^2} > c_M > 1 - \frac{(\bar{v} - 2v_r)^2}{2(\bar{v} - v_r)^2}, \tag{6.42}$$

$$c_0 > \sqrt{\frac{1 - c_M}{2}} + \sqrt{\frac{1 - c_M}{2} + \frac{v_r}{\bar{v} - v_r}}, \tag{6.43}$$

$$c_0(\bar{v} - v_r) \geq c_0\alpha_c\left(\frac{d_b}{2}\right) - v_r \geq K_v \geq \frac{-c_0\alpha_c(-\Delta_h) + v_r}{c_0 - \sqrt{2 - 2c_M}}, \tag{6.44}$$

$$c_0 - \sqrt{2 - 2c_M} > \sqrt{c^* + \frac{v_r}{\bar{v} - v_r}} - \sqrt{c^*}, \tag{6.45}$$

$$\phi(s) > \max_{K \in \left\{c_0(\bar{v} - v_r), \frac{v_r - c_0\alpha_c(-\Delta_h)}{\sqrt{c^* + \frac{v_r}{\bar{v} - v_r}} - \sqrt{c^*}}\right\}} \left\{\alpha_c^{-1}\left(\frac{K(s + c_0)}{c_0} + \frac{-K\left(\sqrt{c^* + \frac{v_r}{\bar{v} - v_r}} - \sqrt{c^*}\right) + v_r}{c_0}\right)\right\} + \Delta_h, \quad s \in (-c_0, 1]. \tag{6.46}$$

In accordance with Assumption 6.3, using condition (6.32) and $\Delta_h \in (0, d_h]$, the definition of the function r in (6.20) guarantees the existence of sets K_1 and K_2 satisfying

$$K_1 \cup K_2 = \{1, \dots, m\}, \quad K_1 \cap K_2 = \emptyset \tag{6.47}$$

such that

$$r(q, l_k) \geq d_b/2 \text{ for } k \in K_1 \text{ and } r(q, l_k) < d_b/2 \text{ for } k \in K_2. \tag{6.48}$$

Then, we discuss the following two cases separately.

- $k \in K_1$. In this case, due to (6.44), for any $v_s \in \mathbb{R}^n$ satisfying $|v_s| \leq K_v$, we have

$$l_k^T v_s \leq K_v \leq c_0\alpha_c(d_b/2) - v_r \leq c_0\alpha_c(r(q, l_k)) - v_r \tag{6.49}$$

for all $k \in K_1$.

- $k \in K_2$. Using (6.40)–(6.46), for $s \in [-1, 1]$, we have

$$\phi(s) \geq \max\left\{\alpha_c^{-1}\left(\frac{K_v(s+\sqrt{2-2c_M})+v_r}{c_0}\right)+\Delta_h, 0\right\}. \tag{6.50}$$

In this case, from the definition of $h_i(q)$ in (6.5) and the function r in (6.20), under conditions (6.32) and (6.50), there exists a $J \subseteq \{1, \dots, N\}$ such that for any $i \in J$,

$$-\Delta_h \leq |q_{oi} - q| - d_{si} < d_b/2, \tag{6.51}$$

and for any $k \in K_2$, there exists an $i^* \in J$ such that

$$r(q, l_k) = |q_{oi^*} - q| - d_{si^*} + \phi(\nabla h_{i^*}(q) l_k) \geq -\Delta_h. \tag{6.52}$$

Under Assumption 6.3, with $\Delta_h \in (0, d_h]$, using (6.5), (6.28), (6.29), (6.32), and (6.42), for any $i, i' \in J$, we have

$$|q_{oi} - q_{oi'}| \in [0, d_a], \tag{6.53}$$

$$\begin{aligned}\nabla h_i(q)\nabla h_{i'}^T(q) &= \frac{|q_{oi'}-q|^2+|q_{oi}-q|^2-|q_{oi}-q_{oi'}|^2}{2|q_{oi}-q||q_{oi'}-q|}\\ &\geq \frac{2(\underline{d}_s-\Delta_h)^2-d_a^2}{2(\bar{d}s+\frac{d_b}{2})^2} \geq c_M.\end{aligned} \tag{6.54}$$

Then, using the Cosine Theorem, for any $i, i' \in J$, we can prove that

$$|\nabla h_i(q) - \nabla h_{i'}(q)| \leq \sqrt{2-2c_M}. \tag{6.55}$$

Now, for all $i \in J$, we show that $v^* = K_v \nabla h_i(q)$ with K_v defined in (6.44) satisfies (6.18) for $k \in K_2$. Under conditions (6.41), (6.50)–(6.52), and (6.55), with q satisfying (6.32), we have

$$\begin{aligned}K_v\nabla h_i(q) l_k &= K_v(\nabla h_i(q) - \nabla h_{i^*}(q) + \nabla h_{i^*}(q)) l_k\\ &\leq K_v\sqrt{2-2c_M} - K_v \nabla h_{i^*}(q) l_k\\ &\leq c_0\alpha_c(\phi(\nabla h_i(q)l_k)-\Delta_h)-v_r\\ &\leq c_0\alpha_c(r(q,l_k))-v_r\end{aligned} \tag{6.56}$$

holds for any $i \in J$ and $k \in K_2$.

Thus, the QP (6.17)–(6.19) is always feasible.

A QP admits a unique solution as long as it is feasible (see, e.g., [21]).

b. Satisfaction of the position and velocity constraints

The vectors $l_1, \dots, l_m$ are chosen such that for each $i = 1, \dots, N$, there exist p elements of $\{l_1, \dots, l_m\}$, say $l_{i1}, \dots, l_{ip}$, and constants $\rho_{i1}, \dots, \rho_{ip} \geq 0$, with $p \geq n$, such that

$$-\nabla h_i^T(q) = \sum_{j=1}^{p} \rho_{ij} l_{ij}, \quad -\nabla h_i(q) l_{ij} \geq c_0 \tag{6.57}$$

for $j = 1, \dots, p$, which directly implies

$$1 \leq \sum_{j=1}^{p} \rho_{ij} \leq \frac{1}{c_0}. \tag{6.58}$$

With (6.57) satisfied, we also have

$$-\nabla h_i(q) v^* = \sum_{j=1}^{p} \rho_{ij} l_{ij}^T v^*, \quad i = 1, \dots, N. \tag{6.59}$$

Recall the definition of the function r in (6.20). With the satisfaction of conditions (6.18), (6.41), and (6.57), for any l_{ij} of $l_{i1}, \dots, l_{ip}$, we have

$$\begin{aligned} l_{ij}^T v^* &\leq c_0 \alpha_c(r(q, l_{ij})) - v_r \\ &= c_0 \alpha_c(\min_{w=1,\dots,N}\{h_w(q) + \phi(\nabla h_w(q) l_{ij})\}) - v_r \\ &\leq c_0 \alpha_c(h_i(q)) - v_r. \end{aligned} \tag{6.60}$$

Then, (6.18) and (6.58)–(6.60) together imply

$$\begin{aligned} -\nabla h_i(q) v^* &= \sum_{j=1}^{p} \rho_{ij} l_{ij}^T v^* \leq \sum_{j=1}^{p} \rho_{ij} c_0 \alpha_c(r(q, l_{ij})) - \sum_{j=1}^{p} \rho_{ij} v_r \\ &\leq \sum_{j=1}^{p} \rho_{ij} c_0 \alpha_c(h_i(q)) - v_r. \end{aligned} \tag{6.61}$$

From (6.57) and (6.61), we have that

$$-\nabla h_i(q) v^* \leq \begin{cases} \alpha_c(h_i(q)) - v_r, & \text{if } h_i(q) \geq 0, \\ c_0 \alpha_c(h_i(q)) - v_r, & \text{if } h_i(q) < 0. \end{cases} \tag{6.62}$$

Thus, we have

$$-\nabla h_i(q) v^* \leq \alpha_p(h_i(q)) - v_r \tag{6.63}$$

with $\alpha_p(s) = \max\{c_0 \alpha_c(s), \alpha_c(s)\}$ for $s \in \mathbb{R}$. It can be directly checked that $\alpha_p \in \mathcal{K}^e$. Then, using (6.5), (6.32), and (6.63), we have

$$\nabla h_i(q) v^* \geq -\alpha_p(h_i(q)) + v_r. \tag{6.64}$$

With each $\nabla h_i(q)$ being a unit vector, using (6.12) and (6.64), we can prove (6.33).

We rewrite any solution υ^* of the QP in the form of $\upsilon^* = |\upsilon^*| l_0$ with l_0 being a unit vector. Then, the selection of the vectors $\{l_1, \dots, l_m\}$ guarantees the existence of at least one element $l_i \in \{l_1, \dots, l_m\}$ satisfying $l_i^T l_0 \geq c_0$ such that

$$k_x l_i^T l_0 \leq c_0(\bar{\upsilon} - \upsilon_r), \tag{6.65}$$

which means

$$|\upsilon^*| = k_x \leq \frac{c_0(\bar{\upsilon} - \upsilon_r)}{l_i^T l_0} \leq \frac{c_0(\bar{\upsilon} - \upsilon_r)}{c_0} = \bar{\upsilon} - \upsilon_r. \tag{6.66}$$

c. Lipschitz continuity of the QP-based control law

Note that the constraints (6.18) and (6.19) can be equivalently represented by (6.21), which features the constant constraint matrix $[l_1, \dots, l_m]^T$, any n rows of which are guaranteed to be linearly independent. Then, in the region of q satisfying (6.32), by applying Theorem B.1, we can prove the Lipschitz continuity of the solution to the QP with respect to q and υ^c by showing that the right-hand sides of the constraints are Lipschitz continuous with respect to q. With α_c chosen to be Lipschitz continuous, this can be achieved by showing the Lipschitz continuity of $r(q, l_k)$ with respect to q.

With (6.5) and (6.20), we rewrite

$$r(q, l_k) = \min_{i=1,\dots,N} \{r_k(q, q_{oi}, d_{si})\} \tag{6.67}$$

with

$$r_k(q, q_{oi}, d_{si}) = |q - q_{oi}| - d_{si} + \phi(\nabla h_i(q) l_k). \tag{6.68}$$

With q satisfying (6.32), we can prove the Lipschitz continuity of $r_k(q, q_{oi}, d_{si})$ with respect to q, and thus that of $r(q, l_k)$ with respect to q. □

Through the discussion in this chapter, under Assumptions 6.2 and 6.3, with conditions (6.29)–(6.31) satisfied, one can construct a Lipschitz continuous QP-based safety-critical control law (6.17)–(6.19) by first appropriately choosing c_0, α_c and ϕ according to (6.36)–(6.41) and then defining a set of vectors $\{l_1, \dots, l_m\} \subset \mathbb{R}^n$ such that any unit vector $l_o \in \mathbb{R}^n$ is a positive combination of the elements of $\{l_1, \dots, l_m : l_i^T l_o \geq c_0, \ i = 1, \dots, m\}$ whose cardinality is not less than n. The existence of such $\{l_1, \dots, l_m\}$ is discussed in previous chapters.

6.2.2 Re-design for Close-obstacle Avoidance

The QP-based control law in the previous section takes into account all obstacles, the number of which could be very large. The computational complexity required by safety-critical control would be significantly increased as the number of obstacles becomes large. This section shows that the obstacles with positions far enough away from the plant position do not influence the position constraints much, and proposes a refined control law to reduce the computational complexity.

Recall the function ϕ and the unit vectors l_k for $k = 1, \dots, m$, defined right after (6.20). We replace the function r in (6.20) with

$$r_f(q, l_k, d_f) = \min\left\{ \min_{i \in J_N(q, d_f)} \{h_i(q) + \phi(\nabla h_i(q) l_k)\}, d_f \right\}, \tag{6.69}$$

where

$$J_N(q, d_f) = \{i \in \{1, \dots, N\} : h_i(q) \le d_f\} \tag{6.70}$$

with d_f being a positive constant to be determined later. Then, for $k = 1, \dots, m$, we define

$$r_k(q, d_f) = \begin{cases} r_f(q, l_k, d_f), & \text{if } J_N(q, d_f) \neq \emptyset, \\ d_f, & \text{if } J_N(q, d_f) = \emptyset, \end{cases} \tag{6.71}$$

and consider the following refined QP-based control law:

$$v^* = \underset{v_o^* \in \mathbb{R}^n}{\operatorname{argmin}} |v_o^* - v^c|^2 \tag{6.72}$$

$$\text{s.t.} \quad l_k^T v_o^* \le c_0 \alpha_c(r_k(q, d_f)) - v_r, \quad k = 1, \dots, m, \tag{6.73}$$

where α_c is a class $\mathcal{K}^e$ function.

With only the obstacles, the distances of which are smaller than or equal to an appropriately chosen positive constant d_f taken into account, the resulting feasible velocities are naturally restricted within the desired range. This means that the boundedness constraint on the velocity need not be given explicitly in the QP; see property (b) of Proposition 6.2.

Proposition 6.2 ***(Safety Properties of the Outer Loop: Close-obstacle Avoidance):*** Consider the kinematics part (6.12) of the EL system (6.1) with $v^* \in \mathbb{R}^n$ being the solution of the QP (6.72) and (6.73), and $\tilde{v} \in \mathbb{R}^n$ represents the generalized velocity-tracking error. Suppose that Assumptions 6.2 and 6.3 are satisfied. Under conditions (6.29)–(6.31), where $\bar{v}$ is defined right after (6.6), d_a and d_b are defined in Assumption 6.3, and v_r is a positive constant, there exist a Lipschitz continuous, nonnegative, increasing function $\phi : [-1, 1] \to \mathbb{R}_+$, a positive constant $0 < c_0 < 1$, a positive constant d_f, a Lipschitz function $\alpha_c \in \mathcal{K}^e$ whose inverse function is also Lipschitz, and a constant $\Delta_h > 0$ such that if

$$h_i(q) \ge -\Delta_h, \quad i = 1, \dots, N, \tag{6.74}$$

then

a. the QP (6.72) and (6.73) admits a unique solution;
b. the position trajectories satisfy

$$\nabla h_i(q)\dot{q} \geq -\alpha_p(h_i(q)) + \upsilon_r - |\bar{\upsilon}|, \quad i = 1, \dots, N \tag{6.75}$$

with

$$\alpha_p(s) = \max\{\alpha_c(s), c_0\alpha_c(s)\}, \tag{6.76}$$

and the velocity-reference input υ^* satisfies

$$|\upsilon^*| \leq \bar{\upsilon} - \upsilon_r; \tag{6.77}$$

c. the map φ in (6.27) generated by the QP (6.72) and (6.73) satisfies

$$|\varphi(q_1, \upsilon_{c1}) - \varphi(q_2, \upsilon_{c2})| \leq L(|q_1 - q_2| + |\upsilon_{c1} - \upsilon_{c2}|) \tag{6.78}$$

for all q_1, q_2 satisfying (6.74) with q replaced by q_1, q_2, and $\upsilon_{c1}, \upsilon_{c2} \in \mathbb{R}^n$, where L is a positive constant.

Proof. The parameters c_0, α_c, and ϕ can be chosen similarly as for Proposition 6.1 such that (6.36)–(6.41) are satisfied. Then, there exists a positive constant d_f satisfying

$$\begin{aligned} &\alpha_c^{-1}\left(\frac{-c_0\alpha_c(-d_h) + \left(1 + \sqrt{c^* + \frac{\upsilon_r}{\bar{\upsilon}-\upsilon_r}} - \sqrt{c^*}\right)\upsilon_r}{c_0\left(\sqrt{c^* + \frac{\upsilon_r}{\bar{\upsilon}-\upsilon_r}} - \sqrt{c^*}\right)}\right) \\ &< d_f \leq \alpha_c^{-1}\left(\bar{\upsilon} + (\frac{1}{c_0} - 1)\upsilon_r\right), \end{aligned} \tag{6.79}$$

with c^* defined in (6.37) and d_h defined in Assumption 6.3.

Then, the three properties can be proved one by one.

a. Feasibility of the QP
Conditions (6.29)–(6.31), (6.36), (6.37), (6.39)–(6.41), and (6.79) guarantee that there exist constants $K_\upsilon > 0$, $c_M \in (0, 1)$, and $\Delta_h \in (0, d_h]$ satisfying

$$\begin{aligned} c_0(\bar{\upsilon} - \upsilon_r) &\geq c_0\alpha_c\left(\max\left\{d_f, \frac{d_b}{2}\right\}\right) - \upsilon_r \\ &\geq c_0\alpha_c\left(\min\left\{d_f, \frac{d_b}{2}\right\}\right) - \upsilon_r \geq K_\upsilon \geq \frac{-c_0\alpha_c(-\Delta_h) + \upsilon_r}{c_0 - \sqrt{2 - 2c_M}}, \end{aligned} \tag{6.80}$$

$$\phi(s) \geq \alpha_c^{-1}\left(\frac{K_\upsilon(s + \sqrt{2 - 2c_M}) + \upsilon_r}{c_0}\right) + \Delta_h, \quad \forall s \in [-1, 1]. \tag{6.81}$$

With the satisfaction of conditions (6.71), (6.80), and (6.81), following the proof similar to Proposition 6.1, there exists a $\upsilon_x \in \mathbb{R}^n$ satisfying

$$|\upsilon_x| = K_\upsilon, \tag{6.82}$$

such that for all $k = 1, \dots, m$, if $J_N(q, d_f) \neq \emptyset$, then

$$l_k^T \upsilon_x \ \leq c_0 \alpha_c(r_f(q, l_k, d_f)) - \upsilon_r, \tag{6.83}$$

and if $J_N(q, d_f) = \emptyset$, then

$$l_k^T \upsilon_x \leq c_0 \alpha_c(d_f) - \upsilon_r \leq c_0(\bar{\upsilon} - \upsilon_r). \tag{6.84}$$

Thus, the QP (6.72) and (6.73) is always feasible.

A QP admits a unique solution as long as it is feasible (see, e.g., [21]).

b. Satisfaction of the position and velocity constraints

Suppose that $\upsilon^* = k_x l_0$, where k_x is a positive constant and $l_0 \in \mathbb{R}^n$ is some unit vector. Then, due to (6.70)–(6.73) and the positive span property right after (6.20), there exists at least one vector $l_k \in \{l_1, \dots, l_m\}$ satisfying $l_k^T l_0 \geq c_0$ such that

$$k_x l_k^T l_0 \leq c_0 \alpha_c(d_f) - \upsilon_r. \tag{6.85}$$

From (6.85), we have

$$|\upsilon^*| = k_x \leq \frac{c_0 \alpha_c(d_f) - \upsilon_r}{l_k^T l_0} \leq \alpha_c(d_f) - \frac{\upsilon_r}{c_0} = \bar{\upsilon} - \upsilon_r. \tag{6.86}$$

This obviously implies that the solution to the QP is bounded. Moreover, for any $i \in \{1, \dots, N\} \setminus J_N(q, d_f)$, by using (6.70), (6.76), (6.86), and $0 < c_0 < 1$, we have

$$\begin{aligned} -\nabla h_i(q)\upsilon^* \ &\leq \alpha_c(d_f) - \frac{\upsilon_r}{c_0} \leq \alpha_c(h_i(q)) - \upsilon_r \\ &= \alpha_p(h_i(q)) - \upsilon_r. \end{aligned} \tag{6.87}$$

Then, also using (6.12), we have

$$\nabla h_i(q)\dot{q} \geq -\alpha_p(h_i(q)) + \upsilon_r - |\tilde{\upsilon}| \tag{6.88}$$

for $i \in \{1, \dots, N\} \setminus J_N(q, d_f)$. Applying the same techniques as for the proof of Proposition 6.1, we have

$$-\nabla h_i(q)\upsilon^* \leq \alpha_p(|q_{oi} - q| - d_{si}) - \upsilon_r \tag{6.89}$$

for $i \in J_N(q, d_f)$. The satisfaction of (6.75) is a direct consequence of (6.5), (6.11), (6.12), (6.87), and (6.89).

c. Lipschitz continuity of the refined QP-based control law

From (6.20), (6.70), and (6.69), for any $q \in \mathbb{R}^n$, if $r_f(q, d_f, l_k) = d_f$, we have

$$r(q, l_k) \geq d_f, \tag{6.90}$$

and if $r_f(q, d_f, l_k) = \min_{i \in J_N(q, d_f)}\{h_i(q) + \phi(\nabla h_i(q) l_k)\}$, we have

$$r_f(q, d_f, l_k) = r(q, l_k) < d_f. \tag{6.91}$$

Thus, for any $q_1, q_2 \in \mathbb{R}^n$ satisfying (6.74), constant d_f satisfying (6.79) and l_k for $k = 1, \ldots, m$ defined right after (6.20),

$$|r_f(q_1, d_f) - r_f(q_2, d_f)| \leq |r(q_1, l_k) - r(q_2, l_k)|. \tag{6.92}$$

Then, we can prove the existence of a constant $L > 0$ for (6.78) based on the reasoning for the proof of Proposition 6.1. □

6.3 Inner Loop: Velocity-tracking Controller Design

Given the velocity-reference input υ^* generated by the proposed outer-loop control law, we design a velocity-tracking control law for the dynamics part of the system (6.1).

With the velocity-tracking error defined in (6.11), consider the following velocity-tracking control law

$$u = N(q, \dot{q}) + C(q, \dot{q})\upsilon^* - k_D \tilde{\upsilon} \tag{6.93}$$

with constant $k_D > 0$, and a Lyapunov function candidate

$$V(q, \tilde{\upsilon}) = \frac{1}{2}\tilde{\upsilon}^T M(q) \tilde{\upsilon}. \tag{6.94}$$

Recall (6.27) and (6.11). We equivalently rewrite $V(q, \tilde{\upsilon})$ as

$$\breve{V}(q, \dot{q}, \upsilon^c) = V(q, \tilde{\upsilon}) = \frac{1}{2}(\dot{q} - \varphi(q, \upsilon^c))^T M(q)(\dot{q} - \varphi(q, \upsilon^c)). \tag{6.95}$$

The following proposition shows that the controlled EL system admits a velocity-tracking capability.

Proposition 6.3 ***(Velocity-Tracking Property of the Inner Loop)*:** Under Assumptions 6.1 and 6.2, consider the system (6.1) and the control law (6.93). Suppose the existence of a positive constant L such that the outer-loop control law given by $\upsilon^* = \varphi(q, \upsilon^c)$ satisfies (6.35) for all $q_1, \upsilon_{c1}, q_2, \upsilon_{c2} \in \mathbb{R}^n$. Then,

$$\delta^T[\dot{q}; \ddot{q}; \dot{\upsilon}^c] \leq -\frac{2k_D}{\mu_{m2}}\breve{V}(q, \dot{q}, \upsilon^c) + 2nL\mu_{m2}\sqrt{\frac{2\breve{V}(q, \dot{q}, \upsilon^c)}{\mu_{m1}}}(\bar{\upsilon}^{cd} + |\dot{q}|) \tag{6.96}$$

holds for any $q, \dot{q}, \ddot{q}, \upsilon^c, \dot{\upsilon}^c \in \mathbb{R}^n$, and any $\delta \in \partial\breve{V}(q, \dot{q}, \upsilon^c)$.

Proof. Rewrite the control law $\varphi(q, \upsilon^c)$ as

$$\varphi(q, \upsilon^c) = [\varphi_{c1}(q, \upsilon^c); \ldots ; \varphi_{cn}(q, \upsilon^c)]. \tag{6.97}$$

With the existence of the positive constant L for the satisfaction of (6.35), using [37, Proposition 2.1.1], one can prove

$$|\varphi^{\circ}_{ci}(q, \upsilon_c, \upsilon)| \leq 2L|\upsilon|, \quad i = 1, \ldots, n \tag{6.98}$$

for all $q, \upsilon_c \in \mathbb{R}^n$ and $\upsilon \in \mathbb{R}^{2n}$, where $\varphi^{\circ}_{ci}(q, \upsilon_c, \upsilon)$ represents the directional derivative of $\varphi_{ci}(q, \upsilon^c)$. Then, according to the definition of generalized gradients,

$$2L \geq |\epsilon|, \quad \forall \epsilon \in \partial\varphi_{ci}(q, \upsilon^c), \quad i \in \{1, \ldots, n\} \tag{6.99}$$

for $q, \upsilon^c \in \mathbb{R}^n$.

We rewrite $\check{V}$ defined in (6.95) as

$$\check{V}(q, \dot{q}, \upsilon^c) = \frac{1}{2}V_1(q, \dot{q}, \upsilon^c) - V_2(q, \dot{q}, \upsilon^c) + \frac{1}{2}V_3(q, \dot{q}, \upsilon^c) \tag{6.100}$$

with

$$V_1(q, \dot{q}, \upsilon^c) = \dot{q}^T M(q)\dot{q}, \tag{6.101}$$
$$V_2(q, \dot{q}, \upsilon^c) = \dot{q}^T M(q)\varphi(q, \upsilon^c), \tag{6.102}$$
$$V_3(q, \dot{q}, \upsilon^c) = \varphi(q, \upsilon^c)^T M(q)\varphi(q, \upsilon^c). \tag{6.103}$$

Using the sum rule of generalized gradients (see [37, Proposition 2.3.3]) yields

$$\partial\check{V}(q, \dot{q}, \upsilon^c) \subset \frac{1}{2}\partial V_1(q, \dot{q}, \upsilon^c) - \partial V_2(q, \dot{q}, \upsilon^c) + \frac{1}{2}\partial V_3(q, \dot{q}, \upsilon^c). \tag{6.104}$$

Under Assumptions 6.1 and 6.2, with (6.27), (6.93), (6.95), and (6.99)–(6.104), by using the product rule of generalized gradients in [37, Proposition 2.3.13], we have

$$\begin{aligned}
&\delta^T[\dot{q}; \ddot{q}; \dot{\upsilon}^c] \\
&\leq \dot{q}^T M(q)\ddot{q} + \frac{1}{2}\dot{q}^T \dot{M}(q)\dot{q} - \dot{q}^T \dot{M}(q)\varphi(q, \upsilon^c) - \varphi^T(q, \upsilon^c)M(q)\ddot{q} \\
&\quad + 2nL\mu_{m2}|\dot{q} - \varphi(q, \upsilon^c)|(|\dot{q}| + |\dot{\upsilon}^c|) + \frac{1}{2}\varphi^T(q, \upsilon^c)\dot{M}(q)\varphi(q, \upsilon^c) \\
&\leq -k_D|\dot{q} - \varphi(q, \upsilon^c)|^2 + 2nL\mu_{m2}|\dot{q} - \varphi(q, \upsilon^c)|(|\dot{q}| + |\dot{\upsilon}^c|) \\
&\leq -\frac{2k_D}{\mu_{m2}}\check{V}(q, \dot{q}, \upsilon^c) + 2nL\mu_{m2}\sqrt{\frac{2\check{V}(q, \dot{q}, \upsilon^c)}{\mu_{m1}}}(\bar{\upsilon}^{cd} + |\dot{q}|),
\end{aligned} \tag{6.105}$$

for all $\delta \in \partial \breve{V}(q, \dot{q}, v^c)$. This proves the satisfaction of property (6.96) for any $q, \dot{q}, v^c \in \mathbb{R}^n$, and any $\delta \in \partial \breve{V}(q, \dot{q}, v^c)$. □

6.4 Safety Verification: Incorporating Barrier and Energy Functions

In this section, we show the validity of the safety-critical controller composed of the outer-loop safety-critical control law (6.17)–(6.19) in Section 6.2 and the inner-loop velocity-tracking control law (6.93) in Section 6.3. In particular, we construct a new max-type Lyapunov-like function to integrate the safety constraints and the velocity-tracking error, and guarantee the achievement of the safety-critical control objective.

Theorem 6.1 ***(Safety of the Closed-loop System: All-obstacle Avoidance)*****:** *Under Assumptions 6.1–6.3, the closed-loop system composed of the EL system* (6.1) *and the controller consisting of* (6.17)–(6.19) *and* (6.93) *admits the following properties:*

- *Under the condition* (6.29)–(6.31), *with $\bar{v}$ defined right after* (6.6), *d_a and d_b defined in Assumption 6.3, and v_r being a positive constant, there exist a Lipschitz continuous, nonnegative, increasing function $\phi : [-1, 1] \to \mathbb{R}_+$, a constant $0 < c_0 < 1$, a Lipschitz function $\alpha_c \in \mathcal{K}^e$ whose inverse function is also Lipschitz, and a positive constant Δ_h such that the map $v^* = \varphi(q, v^c)$ representing the solution of* (6.17)–(6.19) *satisfies*

$$|\varphi(q_1, v_{c1}) - \varphi(q_2, v_{c2})| \leq L(|q_1 - q_2| + |v_{c1} - v_{c2}|) \tag{6.106}$$

  for all q_1, q_2 satisfying (6.32) *with q replaced by q_1, q_2 and all $v_{c1}, v_{c2} \in \mathbb{R}^n$, with L being a positive constant;*
- *In addition, with k_D chosen such that*

$$k_D > 2nL\frac{\mu_{m2}^3(\bar{v}^{cd} + \bar{v})}{\mu_{m1}^2 v_r}, \tag{6.107}$$

  there exist a Lipschitz $\mathcal{K}^e$ function α_w and a positive constant d_w such that

$$\delta^T[\dot{q}; \ddot{q}; \dot{v}^c] \leq -\alpha_w(W(q, \dot{q}, v_v)), \quad \forall \delta \in \partial W(q, \dot{q}, v^c), \tag{6.108}$$

  holds for all $q, \dot{q}, v^c$ satisfying $W(q, \dot{q}, v^c) \leq d_w$, where

$$W(q, \dot{q}, v^c) = \max\left\{W_1(q, \dot{q}, v^c), \dots, W_{N+1}(q, \dot{q}, v^c)\right\}, \tag{6.109}$$

with

$$W_i(q, \dot{q}, v^c) = -h_i(q), \quad i = 1, \dots, N, \tag{6.110}$$

$$W_{N+1}(q, \dot{q}, v^c) = -\frac{nL\mu_{m1}\mu_{m2}^2(\bar{v}^{cd} + \bar{v} - v_r)v_r}{\mu_{m1}k_D - 2nL\mu_{m2}^2} + \frac{1}{2}(\dot{q} - \varphi(q, v^c))^T M(q)(\dot{q} - \varphi(q, v^c)). \tag{6.111}$$

Proof. Condition (6.106) is directly guaranteed by Proposition 6.1. Now, we prove the satisfaction of (6.108)–(6.111).

Define

$$J_w(q, \dot{q}, v^c) = \{i \in \{1, \dots, N+1\} : W_i(q, \dot{q}, v^c) = W(q, \dot{q}, v^c)\}. \tag{6.112}$$

Using the pointwise maxima rule and sum rule of generalized gradients (see, e.g., [37, Proposition 2.3.12]), we have

$$\partial W(q, \dot{q}, v^c) \subset \mathrm{conv}\{\partial W_i(q, \dot{q}, v^c),\ i \in J_w(q, \dot{q}, v^c)\}. \tag{6.113}$$

Under condition (6.113), using the definition of convex hull in [68], there exist appropriately chosen constants λ_i, for $i \in J_w(q, \dot{q}, v^c)$ satisfying

$$\sum_{i \in J_w(q,\dot{q},v^c)} \lambda_i = 1, \qquad \min_{i \in J_w(q,\dot{q},v^c)} \lambda_i \geq 0, \tag{6.114}$$

and appropriately chosen vectors $\delta_i \in \partial W_i(q, \dot{q}, v^c)$, $i \in J_w(q, \dot{q}, v^c)$ such that for any $\delta \in \partial W(q, \dot{q}, v^c)$,

$$\delta = \sum_{i \in J_w(q,\dot{q},v^c)} \lambda_i \delta_i. \tag{6.115}$$

The condition (6.107) leads to

$$\frac{\mu_{m1}^2 v_r^2}{2\mu_{m2}} - \frac{nL\mu_{m1}\mu_{m2}^2(\bar{v}^{cd} + \bar{v} - v_r)v_r}{\mu_{m1}k_D - 2nL\mu_{m2}^2} > 0. \tag{6.116}$$

Thus, we can choose d_w satisfying

$$d_w \leq \min\left\{\Delta_h, \frac{\mu_{m1}^2 v_r^2}{2\mu_{m2}} - \frac{nL\mu_{m1}\mu_{m2}^2(\bar{v}^{cd} + \bar{v} - v_r)v_r}{\mu_{m1}k_D - 2nL\mu_{m2}^2}\right\}. \tag{6.117}$$

Under the condition that

$$W(q, \dot{q}, v^c) \leq d_w, \tag{6.118}$$

with Assumption 6.1 satisfied, using (6.109), (6.111), and (6.118), we have

$$|\dot{q} - \varphi(q, \upsilon^c)| \leq \sqrt{\frac{\mu_{m1}}{\mu_{m2}}}\upsilon_r, \tag{6.119}$$

$$h_i(q) \geq -\Delta_h, \quad i = 1, \dots, N. \tag{6.120}$$

Consider the following two cases:

- $N + 1 \notin J_w(q, \dot{q}, \upsilon^c)$
  In this case, with the satisfaction of Assumption 6.1, from Proposition 6.1, under conditions (6.112)–(6.120) satisfied, there exists a Lipschitz, class $\mathcal{K}^e$ function α_{w1} such that

$$\begin{aligned} \delta^T[q, \ddot{q}, \dot{\upsilon}^c] &= \sum_{i \in J_w(q,\dot{q},\upsilon^c)} \lambda_i \nabla h_i(q)\dot{q} \\ &\leq \sum_{i \in J_w(q,\dot{q},\upsilon^c)} \lambda_i\left[\alpha_p(h_i(q)) - \upsilon_r + \left|\dot{q} - \varphi(q, \upsilon^c)\right|\right] \\ &\leq \sum_{i \in J_w(q,\dot{q},\upsilon^c)} \lambda_i \alpha_p(h_i(q)) \\ &= \sum_{i \in J_w(q,\dot{q},\upsilon^c)} \lambda_i \alpha_{w1}(W_i(q, \dot{q}, \upsilon^c)) \\ &= -\alpha_{w1}(W(q, \dot{q}, \upsilon^c)) \end{aligned} \tag{6.121}$$

  for any $\delta \in \partial W(q, \dot{q}, \upsilon^c)$;
- $N + 1 \in J_w(q, \dot{q}, \upsilon^c)$
  By using techniques similar to those in (6.121), we have for $\delta_i \in \partial W_i(q, \dot{q}, \upsilon^c)$, $i \in J_w(q, \dot{q}, \upsilon^c) \setminus \{N + 1\}$,

$$\delta_i^T[\dot{q}; \ddot{q}; \dot{\upsilon}^c] \leq -\alpha_{w1}(W(q, \dot{q}, \upsilon^c)). \tag{6.122}$$

  With Assumptions 6.1 and 6.2 satisfied, by using Propositions 6.1 and 6.3, there exists a Lipschitz, class $\mathcal{K}^e$ function α_{w2} such that

$$\begin{aligned} &\delta_{N+1}^T[\dot{q}; \ddot{q}; \dot{\upsilon}^c] \\ &\leq -\frac{2k_D}{\mu_{m2}}\check{V}(q, \dot{q}, \upsilon^c) + 2nL\mu_{m2}\sqrt{\frac{2\check{V}(q, \dot{q}, \upsilon^c)}{\mu_{m1}}}(\bar{\upsilon}^{cd} + |\dot{q}|) \\ &\leq -\frac{2k_D}{\mu_{m2}}\left(W_{N+1}(q, \dot{q}, \upsilon^c) + \frac{nL\mu_{m1}\mu_{m2}^2(\bar{\upsilon}^{cd} + \bar{\upsilon} - \upsilon_r)\upsilon_r}{\mu_{m1}k_D - 2nL\mu_{m2}^2}\right) \\ &\quad + 2nL\mu_{m2}\sqrt{\frac{2\check{V}(q, \dot{q}, \upsilon^c)}{\mu_{m1}}}\left(\bar{\upsilon}^{cd} + \bar{\upsilon} - \upsilon_r + \sqrt{\frac{2\check{V}(q, \dot{q}, \upsilon^c)}{\mu_{m1}}}\right) \end{aligned}$$

$$\begin{aligned}
&\leq -\frac{2k_D}{\mu_{m2}}\left(W_{N+1}(q,\dot{q},\upsilon^c) + \frac{nL\mu_{m1}\mu_{m2}^2(\bar{\upsilon}^{cd}+\bar{\upsilon}-\upsilon_r)\upsilon_r}{\mu_{m1}k_D - 2nL\mu_{m2}^2}\right) \qquad (6.123)\\
&+ 4nL\frac{\mu_{m2}}{\mu_{m1}}\left(W_{N+1}(q,\dot{q},\upsilon^c) + \frac{nL\mu_{m1}\mu_{m2}^2(\bar{\upsilon}^{cd}+\bar{\upsilon}-\upsilon_r)\upsilon_r}{\mu_{m1}k_D - 2nL\mu_{m2}^2}\right)\\
&+ 2nL\mu_{m2}(\bar{\upsilon}^{cd}+\bar{\upsilon}-\upsilon_r)\sqrt{\frac{2\check{V}(q,\dot{q},\upsilon^c)}{\mu_{m1}}}\\
&= -\left(\frac{2k_D}{\mu_{m2}} - 4nL\frac{\mu_{m2}}{\mu_{m1}}\right)W_{N+1}(q,\dot{q},\upsilon^c)\\
&- \left(\frac{2k_D}{\mu_{m2}} - 4nL\frac{\mu_{m2}}{\mu_{m1}}\right)\frac{nL\mu_{m1}\mu_{m2}^2(\bar{\upsilon}^{cd}+\bar{\upsilon}-\upsilon_r)\upsilon_r}{\mu_{m1}k_D - 2nL\mu_{m2}^2}\\
&+ 2nL\mu_{m2}(\bar{\upsilon}^{cd}+\bar{\upsilon}-\upsilon_r)\sqrt{\frac{2\check{V}(q,\dot{q},\upsilon^c)}{\mu_{m1}}}\\
&\leq -\left(\frac{2k_D}{\mu_{m2}} - 4nL\frac{\mu_{m2}}{\mu_{m1}}\right)W_{N+1}(q,\dot{q},\upsilon^c)\\
&+ 2nL\mu_{m2}(\bar{\upsilon}^{cd}+\bar{\upsilon}-\upsilon_r)\left(\sqrt{\frac{2\check{V}(q,\dot{q},\upsilon^c)}{\mu_{m1}}} - \upsilon_r\right)\\
&\leq -\left(\frac{2k_D}{\mu_{m2}} - 4nL\frac{\mu_{m2}}{\mu_{m1}}\right)W_{N+1}(q,\dot{q},\upsilon^c)\\
&\leq -\alpha_{w2}(W(q,\dot{q},\upsilon^c))
\end{aligned}$$

for any $\delta_{N+1} \in \partial W_{N+1}(q,\dot{q},\upsilon^c)$, where we have used conditions (6.11), (6.95), (6.106), (6.109)–(6.111), and (6.118)–(6.120) for the first inequality, used conditions (6.3), (6.34), (6.109)–(6.111), and (6.118)–(6.120) for the second inequality, used condition (6.111) for the third inequality, and used conditions (6.3), (6.107), (6.109), (6.118), and (6.119) for the fifth inequality.

Thus, for any $\delta_i \in W_i(q,\dot{q},\upsilon^c)$, $i \in J_w(q,\dot{q},\upsilon^c)$, we have

$$\delta_i^T[\dot{q};\ddot{q};\dot{\upsilon}^c] \leq -\alpha_w(W(q,\dot{q},\upsilon^c)) \qquad (6.124)$$

with

$$\alpha_w(s) = \min\{\alpha_{w1}(s), \alpha_{w2}(s)\} \qquad (6.125)$$

From (6.112)–(6.120) and (6.124), for any $\delta \in \partial W(q,\dot{q},\upsilon^c)$, we have

$$\delta^T[\dot{q};\ddot{q};\dot{\upsilon}^c] = \sum_{i\in J_w(q,\dot{q},\upsilon^c)} \lambda_i\delta_i^T[\dot{q};\ddot{q};\dot{\upsilon}^c] \leq -\alpha_w(W(q,\dot{q},\upsilon^c)). \qquad (6.126)$$

This ends the proof of Theorem 6.1.

Property (6.108) implies

$$\dot{W}(q(t), \dot{q}(t), \upsilon^c(t)) \leq -\alpha_w(W(q(t), \dot{q}(t), \upsilon^c(t))) \tag{6.127}$$

for almost every $t \geq 0$, as long as $W(q(t), \dot{q}(t), \upsilon^c(t)) \leq d_w$ (see, e.g., [147, Theorem 2]). Also with [110, Theorem 1.10.2], there exists a $\beta \in \mathcal{KL}$ satisfying $\beta(s, 0) = s$ for all $s \geq 0$ such that if initially $W(q(0), \dot{q}(0), \upsilon^c(0)) \leq d_w$, then

$$W(q(t), \dot{q}(t), \upsilon^c(t)) \leq \beta(\max\{W(q(0), \dot{q}(0), \upsilon^c(0)), 0\}, t) \tag{6.128}$$

for all $t \geq 0$. This means that

$$W(q(t), \dot{q}(t), \upsilon^c(t)) \leq 0, \quad \forall t \geq 0 \tag{6.129}$$

provided that $W(q(0), \dot{q}(0), \upsilon^c(0)) \leq 0$. Then, using the definition of W in (6.109) and (6.110), we can guarantee the achievement of the safety-critical control objectives (6.4) and (6.6).

The max-type combination (6.109) of the barrier functions and the Lyapunov function of different subsystems of the closed-loop system is somehow motivated by the Lyapunov-based nonlinear small-gain theorem [93], in which max-type Lyapunov functions are constructed for interconnected systems based on Lyapunov functions of the subsystems.

The following example shows how the safety-critical controller based on the refined QP is capable of guaranteeing the safety of the controlled EL system subject to multiple obstacles.

Example 6.2 (*Ensured Safety with the Proposed Design*): *This example still considers the case in Example 6.1 but also takes into account the dynamics part of the EL system* (6.1). *Suppose that*

$$M(q) = \frac{1}{100}\begin{bmatrix} 11 + 6\cos[q]_2 & 9 + 3\cos[q]_2 \\ 9 + 3\cos[q]_2 & 9 \end{bmatrix}, \tag{6.130}$$

$$C(q, \dot{q}) = \frac{1}{100}\begin{bmatrix} -6[\dot{q}]_2 \sin[q]_2 & -3[\dot{q}]_2 \sin[q]_2 \\ 3[\dot{q}]_1 \sin[q]_2 & 0 \end{bmatrix}, \tag{6.131}$$

$$N(q, \dot{q}) = \begin{bmatrix} 1.96\cos[q]_1 + 2.94\cos([q]_1 + [q]_2) \\ 2.94\cos([q]_1 + [q]_2) \end{bmatrix}, \tag{6.132}$$

and the control input $u \in \mathbb{R}^2$.

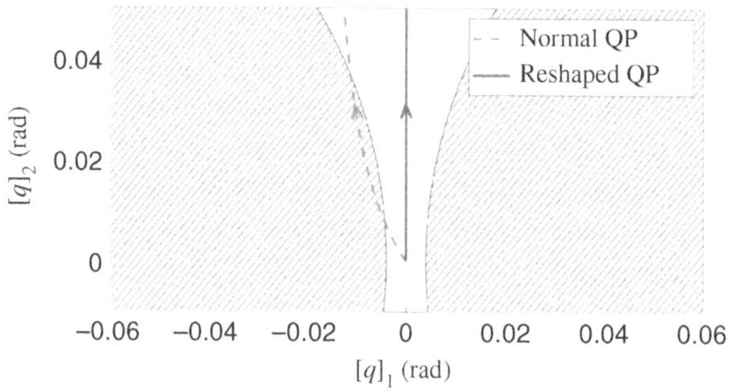

Figure 6.6 Position trajectories of the EL system under different controllers.

We propose two safety-critical control laws of the form in (6.93), *where* $k_D = 40$ *and* $\tilde{v} = v_i^* - \dot{q}$ *for* $i = 1, 2$. *Here,* v_i^* *for* $i = 1, 2$ *are the solutions to the original QP* (6.22) and (6.23) *and the refined QP* (6.24) and (6.25), *respectively.*

Figure 6.6 shows the position trajectories of the controlled EL system under the different controllers, depicted as a dashed line and a solid line, respectively. With the same velocity-tracking control law, a collision happens with the safety-critical controller based on the normal QP (6.13) *and* (6.14), *while safety is guaranteed by the one based on the refined QP* (6.17)–(6.19).

The following theorem shows the effectiveness of the refined safety-critical controller with a reduced computational complexity.

Theorem 6.2 ***(Safety of the Closed-loop System: Close-obstacle Avoidance)***: *Under Assumptions 6.1–6.3, the closed-loop system composed of the EL system* (6.1) *and inner-outer-loop controller consisting of* (6.72), (6.73), *and* (6.93) *admits the following properties:*

- *Under the condition* (6.29)–(6.31), *where* $\bar{v}$ *is defined right after* (6.6), d_a *and* d_b *are defined in Assumption 6.3, and* v_r *is a positive constant, there exist a Lipschitz continuous, nonnegative, increasing function* $\phi : [-1, 1] \to \mathbb{R}_+$, *a positive constant* $0 < c_0 < 1$, *a positive constant* d_f *and a Lipschitz function* $\alpha_c \in \mathcal{K}^e$ *whose inverse function is also Lipschitz such that there exists a positive constant* $\Delta_h > 0$ *for which if* (6.74) *holds, the map* $v^* = \varphi(q, v^c)$ *representing the solution of* (6.72) and (6.73) *satisfies* (6.106) *for all* $v_{c1}, v_{c2} \in \mathbb{R}^n$, *with L being a positive constant;*
- *In addition, with* k_D *satisfying* (6.107), *there exists a Lipschitz* $\mathcal{K}^e$ *function* α_w *and a positive constant* d_w *such that* (6.108)–(6.111) *holds for all* $q, \dot{q}, v^c \in \mathbb{R}^n$.

6.5 Numerical Simulation and Experiment

We consider a safety-critical control scenario for a two-link planar manipulator, as illustrated in Figure 6.7. Such scenarios are common in practice. It is required that every point on the body of the manipulator maintain a sufficient distance from obstacles. Moreover, with $P_2 \in \mathbb{R}^2$ and $P_e \in \mathbb{R}^2$ denoting the positions of joint 2 and the end effector, safety also requires that $[P_2]_2 \geq 0$ and $[P_e]_2 \geq 0$. Link 1 is a uniform rod with width 0.07 m, length 0.25 m, and mass 2 kg; link 2 is a uniform rod with width 0.07 m, length 0.4 m, and mass 3 kg. SI units are used throughout this section, and units are omitted where clear from context.

6.5.1 Safety-critical Control Scenario and Controller Design

The positions q_{oi} of the ball obstacles in the joint (configuration) space are generated according to the following procedure. The configuration space is first partitioned into uniformly sized hypercubes, and balls with identical radius are assigned to these hypercubes to cover the unsafe region. In particular, the side length of each hypercube is chosen as 0.0698 rad, and the radius of each ball is 0.1396 rad.

We design two controllers, whose outer-loop safety-critical control laws take the form of (6.17)–(6.19) and (6.72) and (6.73), respectively. For both controllers, and following Propositions 6.1 and 6.2, we select

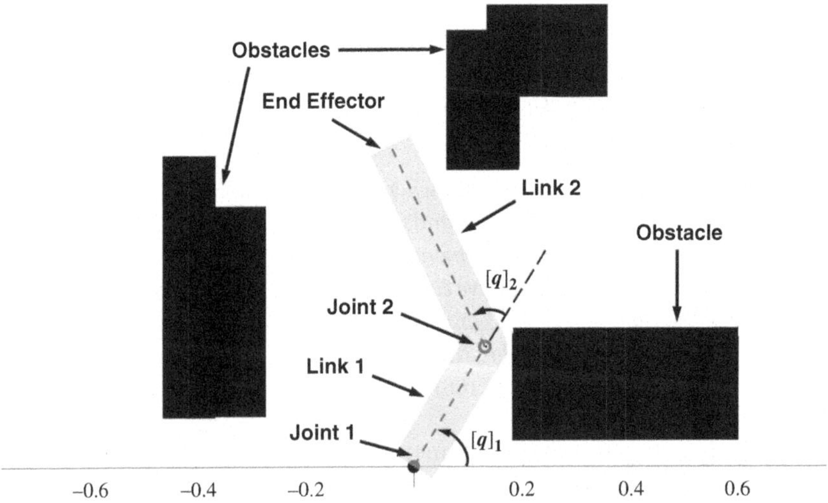

Figure 6.7 A scenario of safety-critical control of a two-link robotic manipulator.

$$d_a = 0.1561, \qquad d_b = 0.0182, \qquad \upsilon_r = 0.0105, \qquad d_h = 0.00002,$$
$$d_{si} = 0.1745, \qquad c_0 = 0.9965, \qquad \bar{\upsilon} = 0.3142,$$
$$\alpha_c(r) = \begin{cases} 0.9r, & \text{for } r \leq 0, \\ 34.5506r, & \text{for } 0 < r \leq 0.0091, \\ 0.9(r - 0.0091) + 0.3136, & \text{for } 0.0091 < r, \end{cases}$$
$$\phi(r) = \max\{-0.3362s + 0.3350, 0\}, \quad r \in [-1, 1].$$

Moreover, for the controller whose outer-loop safety-critical control law takes the form of (6.72) and (6.73), we choose

$$d_f = 0.0098.$$

With these choices, Assumption 6.3 can be verified.

6.5.2 Numerical Simulation

The coefficients of the EL model (6.1) for the robotic manipulator are readily calculated following the standard modeling approach in [44]. For the two-link planar manipulator considered here, the relevant coefficients are available in [128]. We design the inner-loop velocity-tracking control law in the form (6.93) with $k_D = 800.0000$.

The primary controller is designed based on a saturated proportional feedback law and an appropriately chosen waypoint, to ensure the primary velocity-command signal remains within the desired range and that deadlock is avoided:

$$\upsilon_{ci} = (q - q_{ri}) \max\left\{-0.5236, -\frac{\bar{\upsilon}^c}{|q - q_{ri}|}\right\}, \tag{6.133}$$

where $\bar{\upsilon}^c$ is the upper bound, q_{r1} is the waypoint, and q_{r2} is the target point. In the numerical simulation, the state q progresses from the initial state $q(0) = [1.5208, -1]^T$ toward the target $q_{r2} = [1.7208, 0]^T$ through the waypoint $q_{r1} = [2.6, -1.6]^T$. Here, we set $\bar{\upsilon}^c = 0.2618$.

Note that υ^c, as defined in (6.133), depends explicitly on q, which means that its time-derivative $\dot{\upsilon}^c$ (when defined) also depends on $\dot{q}$. Consequently, the system setup in the numerical simulation differs from that considered in the main result. In this case, an intuitive approach is to consider replacing the constant $\bar{\upsilon}^{cd}$ in property (6.7) with a function $\bar{\upsilon}^{cd}(|\dot{q}|)$. If the function $\bar{\upsilon}^{cd}$ is sufficiently small, then the reasoning in the proof of Theorem 6.1 remains valid. The effectiveness of the proposed controller is demonstrated through the simulation results for this system setup. However, a rigorous proof remains nontrivial.

Figure 6.8 shows the trajectories of the velocity-reference input υ^* for both safety-critical controllers: one consisting of (6.17)–(6.19) and (6.93), and the other consisting of (6.72), (6.73), and (6.93). Both velocity-reference inputs are kept within the desired range and coincide with each other. Figures 6.9 and 6.10 depict the motion in the workspace and in the joint space of the manipulator using controller (6.72), (6.73), and (6.93), respectively. It can be observed that the manipulator remains sufficiently distant from the ball obstacles. Since the velocity-reference

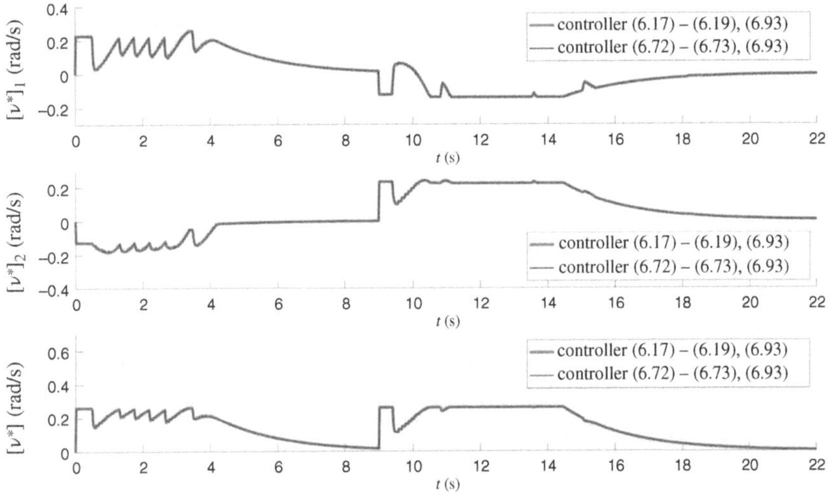

Figure 6.8 Trajectories of the velocity-reference signal υ^* in the numerical simulation.

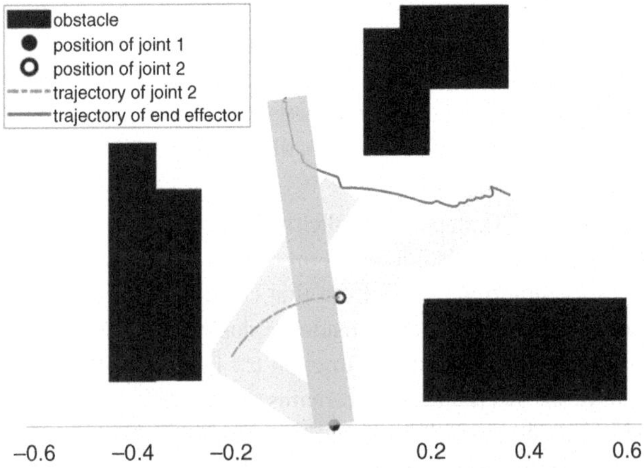

Figure 6.9 The motion of the two-link robotic manipulator in the workspace.

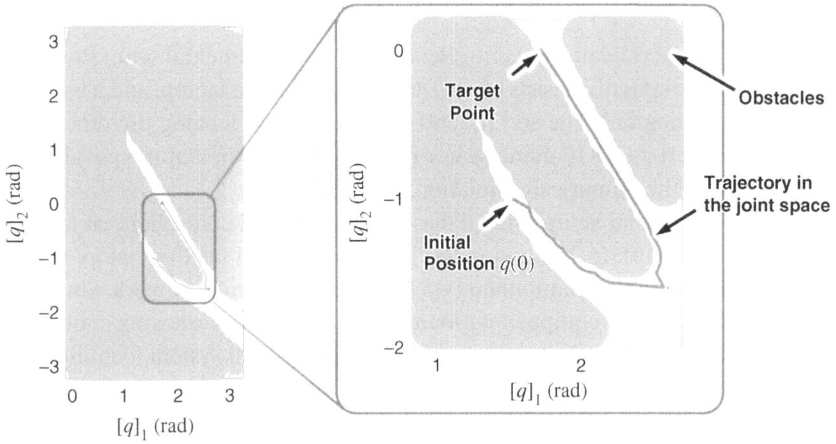

Figure 6.10 Unsafe regions and the motion of the two-link robotic manipulator in the joint space.

Table 6.1 Computation time of the controllers (ms).

	Type of controller	
N	**Controller A**	**Controller B**
3457	15.5	6.7
8747	38.9	6.9
13 617	46.5	8.3

inputs v^* generated by the two controllers are close to each other, the first controller can also guarantee the safety of the manipulator. The corresponding simulation result is omitted here due to space limitations.

The computation times for both controllers were also tested using different numbers of ball obstacles to represent the unsafe regions. Following the discussions in Section 6.1 and at the beginning of Section 6.5.1, by setting the side length of the hypercubes to 0.0698, 0.0436, and 0.0349 rad, the unsafe region in configuration space is covered by 3457, 8747, and 13 617 ball obstacles, respectively. MATLAB-based numerical simulations were performed on a Microsoft Windows laptop with an Intel Core i7-10510U CPU @ 1.80 GHz. The computation times per iteration for the two controllers are shown in Table 6.1. It can be seen that reducing the number of ball obstacles helps decrease computation time.

6.5.3 Experiment

In this section, we validate our controllers using the experimental setup shown in Figure 6.11. The system consists of a 6-DOF manipulator, a laptop, and a wireless router. By utilizing only the second and third joints and locking the other four joints, we convert a 6-DOF manipulator into a 2-DOF manipulator equivalent to the one used in the numerical simulation.

In our experimental setup, the QP-based safety-critical controllers taking the form of (6.17)–(6.19), (6.72), and (6.73) are implemented on the laptop, which communicates with the manipulator via a wireless local area network. Since the manipulator is already equipped with an inner-loop velocity-tracking controller, only the outer-loop QP-based virtual control law is verified. System identification for the velocity-tracking loop is performed using the MATLAB System Identification Toolbox, with υ^* as the input and $\dot{q}$ as the output. Then, following Propositions 6.1, 6.2, and the discussion after the proof of Proposition 6.1, certain controller parameters are modified as follows:

$$\upsilon_r = 0.0209, \quad \bar{\upsilon} = 0.5585, \quad \bar{\upsilon}^c = 0.2094,$$
$$d_f = 0.0091, \quad d_h = 0.000002,$$
$$\alpha_c(r) = \begin{cases} 1.8r, & \text{for } r \leq 0, \\ 61.5382r, & \text{for } 0 < r \leq 0.0091, \\ 1.8(r - 0.0091) + 0.5585, & \text{for } 0.0091 < r, \end{cases}$$
$$\phi(r) = \max\{-1.4881s + 1.4828, 0\}, \quad r \in [-1, 1].$$

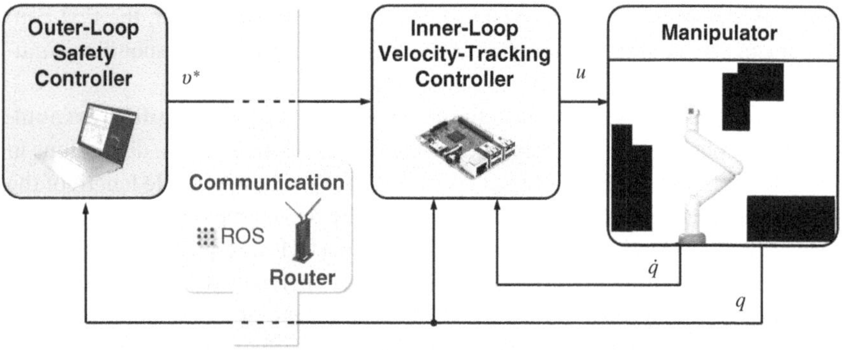

Figure 6.11 Block diagram of the experimental system for a manipulator in an environment containing multiple obstacles.

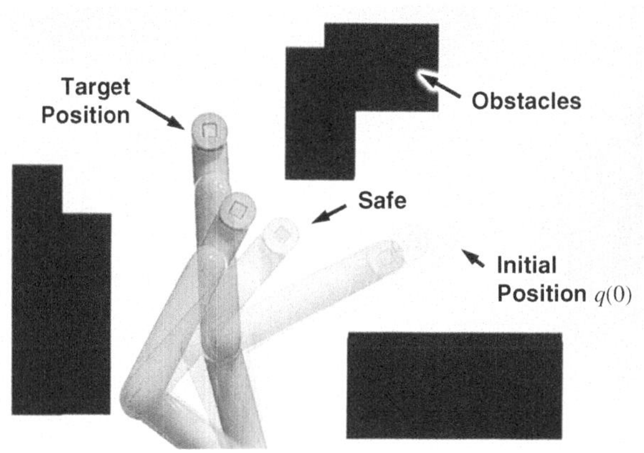

Figure 6.12 The motion of the manipulator in the experiment.

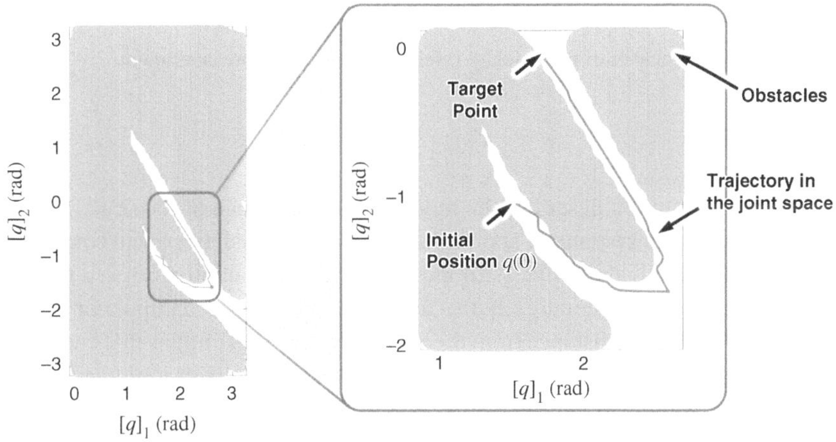

Figure 6.13 Unsafe regions and the motion of the six-link robotic manipulator in the joint space with the safety-critical controller (6.72) and (6.73).

Figure 6.12 shows the motion of the manipulator in the experiment. Figure 6.13 illustrates the motion of the manipulator in the joint space with controller (6.72) and (6.73). Figure 6.14 shows the trajectories of the velocity-reference input υ^* generated by controllers (6.17)–(6.19), (6.72), and (6.73), respectively. It can be observed that for both controllers, the velocity-reference inputs remain within the desired range, and the manipulator keeps a sufficient distance from the ball obstacles.

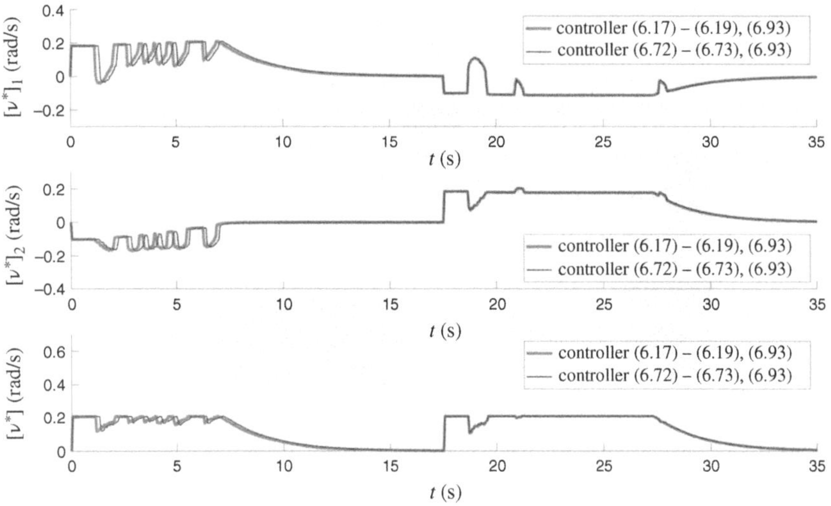

Figure 6.14 Trajectories of the velocity-reference input v^* in the experiment.

6.6 Notes

Since the EL equation describes the motion of a wide range of physical systems [158], developing a systematic approach to ensuring the safety-critical control of EL systems is highly desirable. With industrial robotic manipulators as a typical example, safety fundamentally requires that every point on the manipulator's body maintains a sufficient distance from the unsafe region. This implies that each single point in the unsafe region in the workspace often results in multiple forbidden postures, leading to multiple obstacle points in the configuration space (joint space) [194, 218].

One approach is to design upper-level safety mechanisms in advance to constrain the postures of EL systems within predetermined safe regions [51, 122, 230]. However, such methods may restrict real-time performance in cluttered environments. On the other hand, artificial potential field methods [99] can integrate environmental sensing feedback directly into feedback control loop, but may fail to fully account for the effects of the nonlinear uncertain dynamics.

Recently, QP algorithms and CBFs have shown great promise in addressing safety-critical control problems for EL systems. In [181], energy-based CBFs were introduced to extend purely kinematic CBFs by leveraging the inherent energy conservation property of EL systems. Reference [145] proposed a two-step approach: first, a desired safe velocity is generated using a nonsmooth CBF, and then a tracking controller is designed to ensure that the actual velocity follows the desired safe velocity. The design naturally results in an inner-outer-loop structure. The study in [175] focused on the scenario, where the states and inputs of the EL system are required to be kept constrained within generalized axis-aligned bounding boxes and proposed a correct-by-design algorithm to construct multiple, non-conflicting CBFs satisfying safety regulations and a safety-critical controller with sampled-data feedback. Reference [7] proposed safety barrier certificates in the closed form of path integrals for collisions-free distributed optimal coordination for multiple EL systems.

Although the safety-critical control of EL systems has attracted considerable attention, several open challenges remain unaddressed. Most recent studies have focused on scenarios involving stationary obstacles. The problem becomes more complex when the shapes and sizes of obstacles vary over time. Furthermore, there is still no systematic solution for safety-critical control of underactuated EL systems. In typical applications of EL systems (e.g., robotic grasping), the need to simultaneously satisfy position, velocity, and torque constraints further intensified the challenge.

7

Safety-critical Control of Cascade Systems: Towards a Constructive Control Framework

This chapter extends our study to the safety-critical control problem for nonlinear uncertain systems subject to multiple safety constraints. Specifically, the systems considered here are modeled with a cascade structure consisting of fully actuated subsystems, and the safety constraints are characterized by safety indicator functions.

In this chapter, the feasible-set reshaping technique is further refined for quadratically constrained quadratic programming (QCQP) arising from robust safety-critical control, enabling construction of Lipschitz continuous virtual controllers for the subsystems, and allowing their interconnections to be described by gain functions. In addition, a stepwise constructive control design approach is proposed, incorporating a refined nonlinear small-gain synthesis to address the interconnections between subsystems and ensure achievement of the safety-critical control objective.

More specifically, the safety-critical control problem for cascade systems is addressed through the following steps:

- First, leveraging the cascade structure of the plant, we consider the first subsystem with the state of the second subsystem treated as a virtual control input, and design a controller using QCQP to enforce the safety constraints. This guarantees that the controlled subsystem exhibits a robust safety property, accounting for the influence of the other subsystems.
- Next, we introduce a novel feasible-set reshaping technique for the QCQP-based safety-critical controller, which makes it possible to design Lipschitz continuous virtual controllers based on quadratic programming (QP) for the other subsystems, and allows the interconnections between controlled subsystems to be characterized by gain functions.
- Finally, we propose a stepwise constructive control design incorporating nonlinear small-gain synthesis to effectively address interconnections between the subsystems and ensure achievement of the safety-critical control objective.

Under the assumption that plant dynamics are bounded by monotone functions and the safety constraints satisfy a disjointness condition, the proposed controller can practically guarantee satisfaction of all safety constraints. The effectiveness of the proposed safety-critical controller is experimentally validated using a testbed involving a vertical takeoff and landing (VTOL) vehicle operating in narrow spaces.

7.1 Problem Formulation

This section introduces the class of plants under consideration and formulates the safety-critical control problem to be studied in this chapter.

7.1.1 Plant

We consider nonlinear plants in cascade form:

$$\dot{x}_i = f_i(z_i) + (g_i + \delta_i(z_i))x_{i+1}, \qquad i = 1, \dots, m-1 \tag{7.1a}$$

$$\dot{x}_m = f_m(z_m) + (g_m + \delta_m(z_m))u, \tag{7.1b}$$

where $x_i \in \mathbb{R}^{n_{x_i}}$ for $i = 1, \dots, m$ are the subsystem states, $z_i = [x_1; \dots; x_i] \in \mathbb{R}^{n_{z_i}}$ with $n_{z_i} := \sum_{j=1}^{i} n_{x_j}$, $u \in \mathbb{R}^{n_u}$ is the control input, $g_i \in \mathbb{R}^{n_{x_i} \times n_{x_{i+1}}}$ is a constant matrix, and $f_i : \mathbb{R}^{n_{z_i}} \to \mathbb{R}^{n_{x_i}}$, $\delta_i : \mathbb{R}^{n_{z_i}} \to \mathbb{R}^{n_{x_i} \times n_{x_{i+1}}}$ are unknown, locally Lipschitz functions, with $n_{x_{m+1}} = n_u$. The first state x_1 is considered the system output. Figure 7.1 illustrates the cascade structure of the plant (7.1).

For convenience of notation, define

$$\underline{g}_i = \lambda_{\min}^{1/2}(g_i g_i^T), \qquad \bar{g}_i = \lambda_{\max}^{1/2}(g_i g_i^T) \tag{7.2}$$

for $i = 1, \dots, m$. The following assumption is imposed on the plant.

Assumption 7.1 (*Bounds on the Plant Dynamics*): For each $i = 1, \dots, m$, there exists a function $\bar{f}_i \in \mathcal{K} \cup \{0\}$ and a nonnegative constant $\bar{\delta}_i$ such that

$$|f_i(z_i)| \le \bar{f}_i(|z_i|), \qquad |\delta_i(z_i)| \le \bar{\delta}_i < \underline{g}_i, \tag{7.3}$$

for all $z_i \in \mathbb{R}^{n_{z_i}}$.

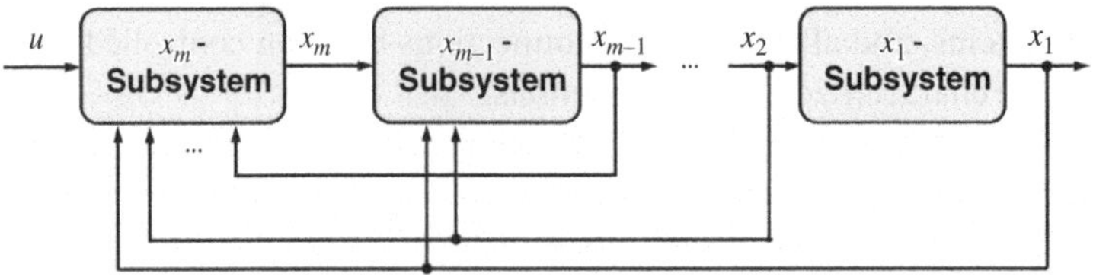

Figure 7.1 Plant: cascade connection of multiple subsystems.

The boundedness of δ_i assumed in (7.3) ensures (right) invertibility of $g_i + \delta_i(\cdot)$, implying that each subsystem is fully actuated. Typical examples of (7.1) satisfying (7.3) include fully actuated manipulators and aerial vehicles, which have been extensively studied in constructive nonlinear control [174].

7.1.2 Safety Indicator Functions

In this chapter, we focus primarily on the safety of the state x_1, characterized by safety indicator functions $h_j : \mathrm{Cl}(\mathcal{X}) \to \mathbb{R}_+$ for $j = 1, \dots, n_c$. Here, $\mathcal{X} \subseteq \mathbb{R}^{n_{x_1}}$ is a nonempty open set representing the admissible range for x_1.

In line with intuition, the plant is said to be safe if the values of all the safety indicator functions remain below specified thresholds. Taking into account transient performance, we require that $x_1(t)$ remains within $\mathcal{X}$, and that there exist $\breve{\beta}_1, \dots, \breve{\beta}_m \in \mathcal{KL}$, constants $c_1, \dots, c_{n_c}, \breve{c}_2, \dots, \breve{c}_m \geq 0$, and $\bar{X} > 0$ such that, under the initial condition $X(0) \leq \bar{X}$,

$$h_j(x_1(t)) \leq \max\{\breve{\beta}_1(X(0), t),\ c_j\}, \qquad j = 1, \dots, n_c \tag{7.4a}$$

$$|x_i(t)| \leq \max\{\breve{\beta}_i(X(0), t),\ \breve{c}_i\}, \qquad i = 2, \dots, m \tag{7.4b}$$

where $X = \max\{h_1(x_1), \dots, h_{n_c}(x_1), |x_2|, \dots, |x_m|\}$, whenever $[x_1(t); \dots; x_m(t)]$ is well-defined. The $\breve{\beta}$ terms characterize the transient performance.

The following assumption is made on the safety indicator functions.

Assumption 7.2 (*Disjointness and Gradient Conditions for Safety Indicator Functions*): For $j = 1, \dots, n_c$, there exist constants $\upsilon_j > 0$ such that

$$\sup\{h_j(x_1) : x_1 \in \mathrm{Cl}(\mathcal{X})\} > \upsilon_j, \tag{7.5}$$

$$\sup\{h_j(x_1) : x_1 \in \mathrm{Cl}(\mathcal{X}), h_{j'}(x_1) \geq \upsilon_{j'}\} < \upsilon_j, \forall j' = j, \tag{7.6}$$

$$h_j(x_1) \geq \upsilon_j \Rightarrow h_j(x_1) \geq \psi(\bar{f}_1(|x_1|)),\ \forall x_1 \in \mathcal{X} \tag{7.7}$$

and h_j is continuous on $\mathrm{Cl}(\mathcal{X})$, continuously differentiable on $\mathcal{X}$, and satisfies

$$\frac{\partial h_j(x_1)}{\partial x_1} \neq 0,\ \ \forall x_1 \in \mathcal{X}, \tag{7.8}$$

$$\left|\frac{\partial h_j(x_1)}{\partial x_1}\right| \geq \eta,\ \ \forall x_1 \in \mathcal{X} \text{ with } h_j(x_1) \geq \upsilon_j \tag{7.9}$$

with $\eta > 0$. Moreover, for each $x_1 \in \mathrm{Cl}(\mathcal{X}) \setminus \mathcal{X}$, there exists a $j \in \{1, \dots, n_c\}$ such that

$$h_j(x_1) > h_j(x_1'), \qquad \forall x_1' \in \mathcal{X}. \tag{7.10}$$

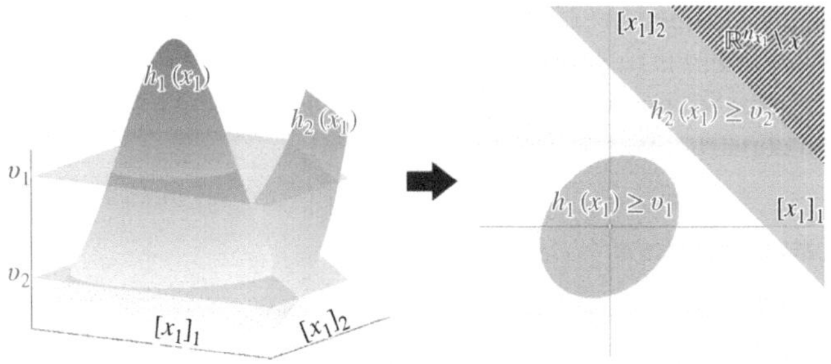

Figure 7.2 Safety indicator functions satisfying Assumption 7.2 ($n_{x_1} = 2$).

Condition (7.6) means the pairwise disjointness between the sets $\{x_1 \in \mathcal{X} : h_j(x_1) \geq v_j\}$, $j = 1, \dots, n_c$. An intuitive illustration of two safety indicator functions and their associated superlevel sets is shown in Figure 7.2. Here, we impose the disjointness condition to ensure the feasibility of the safety-critical controller; see the proof of property (a) in Theorem 7.1 for details. It is worth noting that similar non-conflicting conditions have been employed in related works, e.g., [41].

Under Assumption 7.2, when the plant reduces to a control-affine system without unknown dynamics and satisfies mild controllability conditions, one can design a safety-critical controller using existing methods, e.g., CBFs, so that the sets $\{x_1 \in \mathcal{X} : h_j(x_1) \geq v_j\}$, $j = 1, \dots, n_c$, are strictly safe in the sense of set invariance; see Section 1.1.1 for the definition of set invariance. When x_1 constitutes only a subset of the full state of the plant (7.1), strict safety in the sense of set invariance may be unattainable, and the safety-critical control objective (7.4) would be meaningful.

Some properties of the safety indicator functions h_j for $j = 1, \dots, n_c$ under Assumption 7.2 are summarized in Proposition 7.1.

Proposition 7.1 (*Bounds of Safety Indicator Functions via Signed Distance Functions*): Consider the safety indicator function h_j and the corresponding constant v_j for $j = 1, \dots, n_c$. Under Assumption 7.2, with $D_j : \mathrm{Cl}(\mathcal{X}) \to (-a_j, b_j)$ defined by

$$D_j(x_1) = \mathrm{sign}(h_j(x_1) - v_j) \inf_{s: h_j(s) = v_j} |x_1 - s|, \tag{7.11}$$

there exist class $\mathcal{K}^e$ functions $\underline{\alpha}_j, \bar{\alpha}_j : (-a_j, b_j) \to (-v_j, \infty)$ such that

$$\underline{\alpha}_j(D_j(x_1)) \leq h_j(x_1) - v_j \leq \bar{\alpha}_j(D_j(x_1)), \quad \forall x_1 \in \mathcal{X}. \tag{7.12}$$

Proof. Define

$$\underline{\alpha}'_j(s) = \inf_{x_1 \in \{x_1 \in \text{Cl}(\mathcal{X}): D_j(x_1) \geq s\}} h_j(x_1) - v_j, \tag{7.13}$$

$$\bar{\alpha}'_j(s) = \sup_{x_1 \in \{x_1 \in \text{Cl}(\mathcal{X}): D_j(x_1) \leq s\}} h_j(x_1) - v_j, \tag{7.14}$$

for $j = 1, \ldots, n_c$ and $s \in (-a_j, b_j)$. Then, the proposition is proved by defining functions $\underline{\alpha}_j, \bar{\alpha}_j : (-a_j, b_j) \to (-v_j, \infty)$ as follows:

$$\bar{\alpha}_j(s) = \left(1 + \frac{\tau(s)+1}{2}\text{sign}(s)\right)\bar{\alpha}'_j(s), \quad \text{for } s \in (-a_j, b_j), \tag{7.15}$$

$$\underline{\alpha}_j(s) = \begin{cases} \frac{1}{2}(\tau(s)+1)\underline{\alpha}'_j(s), & \text{for } s \in [0, b_j), \\ \underline{\alpha}'_j(s) + (v_j + \underline{\alpha}'_j(s))\tau(s), & \text{for } s \in (-a_j, 0), \end{cases} \tag{7.16}$$

where $\tau : (-a_j, b_j) \to (-1, 1)$ is a strictly increasing function satisfying $\lim_{s \to -a_j} \tau(s) = -1$, $\lim_{s \to b_j} \tau(s) = 1$, and $\tau(0) = 0$. □

The safety property (7.4a) coincides with the notion of ISSf [104], in the sense that bounded disturbances in the dynamics lead to bounded deviations of the controlled output/state from the safety boundary. However, in this chapter, we are primarily concerned with whether the first state x_1 satisfies the safety constraints defined by the safety indicator functions, while the other states $x_2, \ldots, x_m$ are only required to remain bounded. Intuitively, if one considers ISSf as a generalization of input-to-state stability (ISS) [188], we may view our safety property as an extension of input-to-output stability (IOS) [192, 92].

7.1.3 Predefined Primary Controller

In practice, it is crucial not only to enforce safety constraints, but also to minimize interference with a given primary controller (which typically encodes the primary control objective). In our problem setting, the primary controller is assumed to have the form

$$u_0 = \rho_0(x_1), \tag{7.17}$$

where $u_0 \in \mathbb{R}^{n_{x_2}}$ is the primary control input for the x_1-subsystem, and $\rho_0 : \mathbb{R}^{n_{x_1}} \to \mathbb{R}^{n_{x_2}}$.

The following assumption is made regarding the primary controller.

Assumption 7.3 (*Continuous Differentiability and Boundedness of the Primary Controller*): The function $\rho_0 : \mathbb{R}^{n_{x_1}} \to \mathbb{R}^{n_{x_2}}$ is continuously differentiable, and there exists a constant $\bar{\rho}_0 > 0$ such that

$$|\rho_0(x_1)| \leq \bar{\rho}_0 \quad \forall x_1 \in \mathbb{R}^{n_{x_1}}. \tag{7.18}$$

For example, consider a mobile robot modeled by (7.1), where x_1 and x_2 represent the position and velocity, respectively. A primary controller can generate a velocity-command signal u_0 based on position feedback to achieve a reference position. In this case, the safety constraints must be met while ensuring that the velocity x_2 remains as close as possible to the command u_0. It is natural to require ρ_0 to be bounded so that the generated velocity command always stays within a desired range, even when the robot is far from the target. For simplicity, we do not consider the case where ρ_0 explicitly depends on time, but our approach could be extended provided ρ_0 remains bounded and continuously differentiable.

7.1.4 Expected Safety-critical Controller

Given safety indicator functions $h_j, j = 1, \dots, n_c$ and the primary controller (7.17), we seek to design a continuous safety-critical controller,

$$u = \rho(x_1, \dots, x_m) \tag{7.19}$$

for the plant (7.1), such that the closed-loop system exhibits the safety properties described in (7.4) and x_2 minimally deviates from u_0.

Consistent with constructive nonlinear control [174], ρ is expected to be recursively defined as

$$x_2^* = \rho_1(x_1), \tag{7.20a}$$

$$x_{i+1}^* = \rho_i(x_i - x_i^*), \qquad i = 2, \dots, m, \tag{7.20b}$$

$$u = x_{i+1}^*, \tag{7.20c}$$

where $\rho_i : \mathbb{R}^{n_{x_i}} \to \mathbb{R}^{n_{x_{i+1}}}$ for $i = 1, \dots, m$.

The overall block diagram of the expected safety-critical control system is illustrated in Figure 7.3.

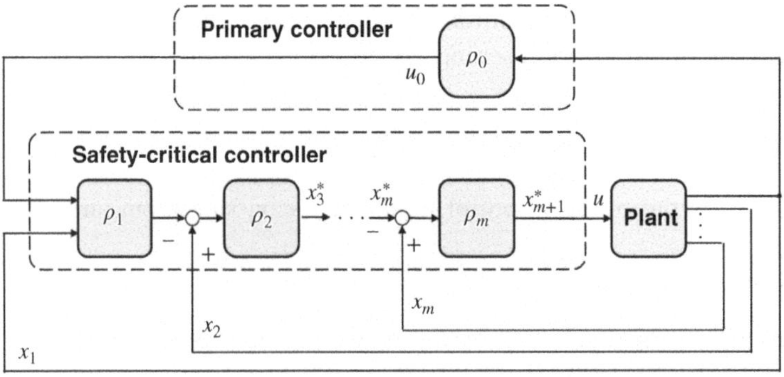

Figure 7.3 The overall block diagram of the recursively designed safety-critical control system.

7.2 Design Ingredient: Plants with Relative-degree-one

In this section, we propose a QCQP-based safety-critical controller for a class of nonlinear uncertain plants with relative-degree-one, in which multiple safety constraints must be addressed simultaneously. This QCQP-based controller ensures that the controlled x_1-subsystem possesses robust safety properties, while explicitly accounting for the interactions with other subsystems. The results derived herein provide a foundational basis for the subsequent development of our main result for nonlinear cascaded systems in Section 7.4.

For the x_1-subsystem of the plant (7.1), we treat x_2 as a virtual control input and denote x_2^* as its ideal value. The x_1-subsystem is thus given by

$$\dot{x}_1 = f_1(x_1) + (g_1 + \delta_1(x_1))(x_2^* + \tilde{x}_2), \tag{7.21}$$

where

$$\tilde{x}_2 = x_2 - x_2^* \tag{7.22}$$

is the tracking error, which is treated as an external input in the design of the virtual controller for the x_1-subsystem.

If the function f_1 in the x_1-subsystem was known, one would construct safety constraints that are affine in the virtual control input x_2^*, following standard CBF-based designs; see [3]. In the present case, when the dynamics are unknown, motivated by robust CBF formulations [87, 42], we augment the safety constraints with quadratic terms to accommodate uncertainties. Accordingly, we consider a QCQP-based safety-critical controller:

$$x_2^* = \underset{x_2^*}{\operatorname{argmin}} |x_2^* - \rho_0(x_1)|^2, \tag{7.23a}$$

$$\text{s.t.} \quad x_2^* \in \mathcal{U}_c(x_1), \tag{7.23b}$$

where ρ_0 represents the primary controller (7.17) and

$$\mathcal{U}_c(x_1) = \left\{ x_2^* \in \mathbb{R}^{n_{x_2}} : A_c(x_1)x_2^* + c_c|x_2^*| \leq b_c(x_1) \right\} \tag{7.24}$$

is the feasible set with

$$[A_c(x_1)]_{j,:} = \frac{\partial h_j(x_1)}{\partial x_1} g_1 \left| \frac{\partial h_j(x_1)}{\partial x_1} g_1 \right|^{-1}, \tag{7.25a}$$

$$[c_c]_j = \frac{\bar{\delta}_1}{\underline{g}_1}, \tag{7.25b}$$

$$[b_c(x_1)]_j = -\alpha_j(h_j(x_1) - \upsilon_j), \tag{7.25c}$$

for $j = 1, \dots, n_c$ with $\alpha_j \in \mathcal{K}^e$. Under (7.3) and (7.8), $(\partial h_j(x_1)/\partial x_1)g_1 \neq 0$ holds for all $x_1 \in \mathcal{X}$ and $j \in \{1, \dots, n_c\}$, which guarantees that A_c is well-defined on $\mathcal{X}$.

The following theorem shows the validity of the QCQP-based controller design.

Theorem 7.1 (*Feasibility and Transient-aware Safety for the x_1-subsystem*): *For the plant (7.21), given the safety indicator functions h_j for $j = 1, \dots, n_c$ and the primary controller (7.17), consider the QCQP-based controller (7.23)–(7.25). Suppose the satisfaction of Assumptions 7.1–7.3. For $j = 1, \dots, n_c$, choose*

$$\alpha_j(s) = \alpha \circ \bar{\alpha}_j^{-1}(s), \quad \forall s \in (-\upsilon_j, \infty), \tag{7.26}$$

with $\alpha \in \mathcal{K}^e$ satisfying

$$\alpha(s) + \frac{\underline{g}_1 + \bar{\delta}_1}{\underline{g}_1 - \bar{\delta}_1}\alpha(-s) \leq 0, \quad \forall s \leq 0 \tag{7.27}$$

and functions $\underline{\alpha}_j, \bar{\alpha}_j \in \mathcal{K}^e$ given by Proposition 7.1. Then, it holds that

1. *$\mathcal{U}_c(x_1)$ defined in (7.24) is non-empty for each $x_1 \in \mathcal{X}$;*
2. *for $j = 1, \dots, n_c$, given any constant c_j satisfying $\upsilon_j < c_j < \sup_{x_1 \in \mathrm{Cl}(\mathcal{X})} h_j(x_1)$, any class $\mathcal{K}_\infty$ function $\gamma_{1,2}$ and any continuous, positive definite function σ, with α_j in (7.26) chosen to further satisfy*

$$\alpha_j\left(\frac{c_j - \upsilon_j}{c_j}s\right) \geq \frac{\psi^{-1}(s)}{\underline{g}_1} + \frac{\underline{g}_1 + \bar{\delta}_1}{\underline{g}_1}\gamma_{1,2}^{-1}(s) + \sigma(s), \quad \forall s \geq c_j, \tag{7.28}$$

there exists a $\beta_1 \in \mathcal{KL}$ satisfying $\beta_1(s, 0) = s$ for all $s \geq 0$ such that for any initial state $x_1(0) \in \mathcal{X}$ and any piecewise continuous $\tilde{x}_2$ satisfying $\|\tilde{x}_2\|_\infty < \gamma_{1,2}^{-1}(\sup_{x_1 \in \mathrm{Cl}(\mathcal{X})} h_j(x_1))$,

$$h_j(x_1(t)) \leq \max\{\beta_1(h_j(x_1(0)), t), \gamma_{1,2}(\|\tilde{x}_2\|_t), c_j\}, \tag{7.29}$$

whenever $x_1(t)$ is defined.

Proof. **Property 1. Nonemptiness of $\mathcal{U}_c(x_1)$**

We prove nonemptiness of $\mathcal{U}_c(x_1)$ as defined in (7.24) by considering two distinct cases:

- Case 1: $\min_{j=1,\dots,n_c}[b_c(x_1)]_j \geq 0$. In this case, $x_2^* = 0$ always belongs to $\mathcal{U}_c(x_1)$.
- Case 2: $\min_{j=1,\dots,n_c}[b_c(x_1)]_j < 0$. Define

$$x_{2s}^*(x_1) = [A_c(x_1)]_{\underline{j},:}^T \frac{\underline{g}_1 \min\{[b_c(x_1)]_{\underline{j}}, 0\}}{\underline{g}_1 - \bar{\delta}_1}, \tag{7.30}$$

for $x_1 \in \mathcal{X}$, where $\underline{j}$ is the index of any minimal entry of $b_c(x_1)$, that is, $[b_c(x_1)]_{\underline{j}} = \min_{j=1,\dots,n_c}[b_c(x_1)]_j$. We show that $x_{2s}^*(x_1) \in \mathcal{U}_c(x_1)$ by verifying all constraints in $\mathcal{U}_c(x_1)$.

It is immediate that $x_{2s}^*(x_1)$ satisfies the $\underline{j}$th constraint in $\mathcal{U}_c(x_1)$.

Next, we show that $x_{2s}^*(x_1)$ satisfies all other constraints. From (7.6) and the triangle inequality [13, Theorem 3.3], D_j defined in (7.11) satisfies

$$\max\{D_j(x_1), D_{\underline{j}}(x_1)\} + \min\{D_j(x_1), D_{\underline{j}}(x_1)\} \leq 0, \forall x_1 \in \mathbb{R}^{n_{x_1}}. \tag{7.31}$$

Define

$$\Delta(x_1) = -\frac{\underline{g}_1 + \bar{\delta}_1}{\underline{g}_1 - \bar{\delta}_1}[b_c(x_1)]_{\underline{j}} - [b_c(x_1)]_j. \tag{7.32}$$

Then,

$$\Delta(x_1) \leq \frac{\underline{g}_1 + \bar{\delta}_1}{\underline{g}_1 - \bar{\delta}_1}\alpha(D_{\underline{j}}(x_1)) + \alpha(D_j(x_1)) \leq 0, \tag{7.33}$$

where the first inequality uses (7.25c) and (7.12), and the last step uses (7.27) and (7.31).

By substituting $x_{2s}^*(x_1)$ for x_2^* in the jth constraint (for $j \neq \underline{j}$), we obtain

$$\begin{aligned} &[A_c(x_1)]_{j,:}x_{2s}^*(x_1) + \frac{\bar{\delta}_1}{\underline{g}_1}|x_{2s}^*(x_1)| \leq \frac{\underline{g}_1 + \bar{\delta}_1}{\underline{g}_1}|x_{2s}^*(x_1)| \\ &= \Delta(x_1) + [b_c(x_1)]_j \leq [b_c(x_1)]_j, \end{aligned} \tag{7.34}$$

where we have used the triangle inequality and the definition of x_{2s}^* in (7.30) for the first equality, and (7.33) for the last inequality.

Property 2. Safety

For any $x_2^* \in \mathcal{U}_c(x_1)$, if $h_j(x_1) \geq c_j$, then

$$h_j(x_1) - \upsilon_j \geq \frac{c_j - \upsilon_j}{c_j}h_j(x_1). \tag{7.35}$$

Taking the time derivative of $h_j(x_1(t))$ along the trajectories of the closed-loop system formed by (7.21) and (7.23), and using (7.7), (7.28) and (7.35), we obtain

$$\begin{aligned} \nabla h_j \dot{x}_1 &= \frac{\partial h_j(x_1)}{\partial x_1}\Big((g_1 + \delta_1(x_1))(x_2^* + \tilde{x}_2) + f_1(x_1)\Big) \\ &\leq -\left|\frac{\partial h_j(x_1)}{\partial x_1}g_1\right|\left(\alpha_j(h_j(x_1) - \upsilon_j) - \left(1 + \frac{\bar{\delta}_1}{\underline{g}_1}\right)|\tilde{x}_2| - \frac{1}{\underline{g}_1}\bar{f}_1(|x_1|)\right) \\ &\leq -\left|\frac{\partial h_j(x_1)}{\partial x_1}g_1\right|\left((1 + \frac{\bar{\delta}_1}{\underline{g}_1})(\gamma_{1,2}^{-1}(h_j(x_1)) - |\tilde{x}_2|) + \sigma(h_j(x_1))\right). \end{aligned} \tag{7.36}$$

Thus,

$$h_j(x_1) \geq \max\{\gamma_{1,2}(|\tilde{x}_2|), c_j\} \Rightarrow \nabla h_j \dot{x}_1 \leq -\eta \underline{g}_1 \sigma(h_j(x_1)). \tag{7.37}$$

Therefore, there exists $\beta_1 \in \mathcal{KL}$ with $\beta_1(s, 0) = 0$ for all $s \in \mathbb{R}_+$, such that

$$h_j(x_1(t)) \leq \beta_1(h_j(x_1(0)), t) \tag{7.38}$$

as long as $h_j(x_1(t)) \geq \max\{\gamma_{1,2}(\|\tilde{x}_2\|_\infty), c_j\}$. This implies that for any $x_1(0) \in \mathcal{X}$ and any piecewise continuous $\tilde{x}_2$, property (7.29) holds whenever $x_1(t)$ is defined.

This concludes the proof of Theorem 7.1. □

For the simultaneous satisfaction of conditions (7.26)–(7.28), one may first determine the value of $\alpha_j(s)$ for $s \geq c_j - v_j$ to satisfy condition (7.28), and arbitrarily choose the value of $\alpha_j(s)$ for $0 \leq s < c_j - v_j$ as long as α_j is guaranteed to be of class $\mathcal{K}^e$. Then, to satisfy (7.27), we choose

$$\alpha(s) = \begin{cases} \alpha_j \circ \bar{\alpha}_j(s) & \text{for } s \geq 0, \\ -\dfrac{\underline{g}_1 + \bar{\delta}_1}{\underline{g}_1 - \bar{\delta}_1} \alpha_j \circ \bar{\alpha}_j(-s) & \text{for } s < 0. \end{cases} \tag{7.39}$$

Finally, the value of $\alpha_j(s)$ for $-v_j \leq s < 0$ can be determined by (7.26).

The following example illustrates both the feasibility and associated Lipschitz continuity issues of the proposed method.

Example 7.1 (*Feasibility of the QCQP-based Controller and the Lipschitz Continuity Issue*): *Consider a special case of the plant (7.21) in which* $\dot{x}_1 = x_2^* + \tilde{x}_2$, $x_1 \in \mathbb{R}^2$, $x_2^*, \tilde{x}_2 \in \mathbb{R}^2$. *Suppose there are two disc-type obstacles with centers located at* $o_1 = [0; 1]$ *and* $o_2 = [0; -1]$, *both having the same radius* 0.5. *A primary controller takes the form of* (7.17) *with* $\rho_0(x_1) \equiv [1; 0]$. *The scenario is illustrated in Figure 7.4.*

To verify the effectiveness of Theorem 7.1, we choose $h_j(x_1) = e^{-|o_j - x_1|}$, $c_j = e^{-0.5}$, $v_1 = v_2 \in (e^{-1}, e^{-0.5})$, $\alpha(s) = s$ *and* $\alpha_j(s) = \ln(s + v_j) - \ln v_j$ *for* $j = 1, 2$. *This results in a safety-critical controller as in* (7.23) *and* (7.24) *with*

$$[A_c(x_1)]_{j,:} = \frac{(o_j - x_1)^T}{|o_j - x_1|}, \tag{7.40a}$$

$$[b_c(x_1)]_j = |o_j - x_1| + \ln v_j, \quad [c_c]_j = 0 \tag{7.40b}$$

for $j = 1, 2$ *and* $x_1 \in \mathcal{X} := \{x_1 \in \mathbb{R}^2 : |x_1 - o_j| > 0, j = 1, 2\}$. *It can be verified that for each* $x_1 \in \mathcal{X}$, $\mathcal{U}_c(x_1)$ *defined in* (7.24) *with* (7.40) *is non-empty.*

We try the method in [144] to compose $h_{z,j}(x_1) := |o_j - x_1| + \ln v_j$ *for* $j = 1, 2$ *as*

$$h^c(x_1) = -\frac{1}{\kappa} \ln(e^{-\kappa h_{z,1}(x_1)} + e^{-\kappa h_{z,2}(x_1)}), \tag{7.41}$$

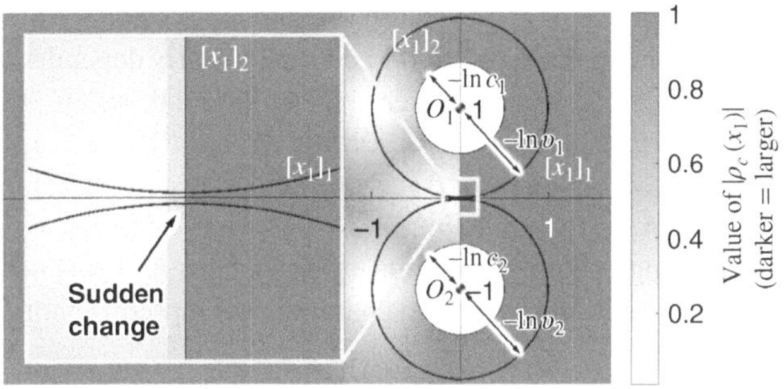

Figure 7.4 $|\rho_c(x_1)|$ with respect to different x_1: ρ_c may admit a Lipschitz constant depending on the configuration of the obstacles.

with constant $\kappa > 0$. The resulting safety-critical controller is in the form of (7.23) and (7.24) with

$$A_c(x_1) = -\frac{\partial h^c(x_1)}{\partial x_1}, \; b_c(x_1) = h^c(x_1), \; c_c = 0. \tag{7.42}$$

The resulting QCQP is infeasible at $x_1 = 0$ unless $\kappa \geq \ln(2)/(1 + \ln v_1)$. This means that the constant κ should be chosen in accordance with the constant v_j of the barrier functions.

We reconsider the map from x_1 to x_2^* generated by the QCQP (7.23) and (7.24) with (7.40), denoted by ρ_c. A Lipschitz constant for ρ_c independent of v_j may not exist. For example, by restricting $[x_1]_2 = 0$ and $\rho_0(x_1) \notin \mathcal{U}_c(x_1)$, we have

$$\rho_c(x_1) = \begin{bmatrix} -\dfrac{1 + [x_1]_1^2 + \sqrt{[x_1]_1^2 + 1}\ln v_1}{[x_1]_1} \\ 0 \end{bmatrix}, \quad \rho_c(0) = \begin{bmatrix} 1 \\ 0 \end{bmatrix}. \tag{7.43}$$

Consider $x_1' = [-\sqrt{1 + \ln v_1}; 0]$. For $v_1 \in (e^{-1}, e^{-0.9})$, we can verify that $\rho_0(x_1') \notin \mathcal{U}_c(x_1)$, and

$$\frac{|\rho_c(x_1') - \rho_c(0)|}{|x_1' - 0|} = \frac{1}{\sqrt{1 + \ln v_1}} - \frac{2 + (1 + \sqrt{2 + \ln v_1})\ln v_1}{1 + \ln v_1}, \tag{7.44}$$

which means that any Lipschitz constant of ρ_c is at least as large as the value on the right-hand side of (7.44), and arbitrarily large as v_j may be arbitrarily close to e^{-1}. Figure 7.4 depicts the dependence of $|\rho_c(x_1)|$ on x_1 for $v_j = e^{-0.99}$, where darker shading indicates larger values of $|\rho_c(x_1)|$. One can observe that the value of $|\rho_c(x_1)|$ exhibits a sudden change near $x_1 = [0; 0]$.

Moreover, an inappropriate choice of α may cause the gradient vectors of the constraints that directly affect the optimal solution to become linearly dependent at specific states. In particular, we consider the feasible set in (7.24), where A_c and c_c are defined in (7.40), and b_c is defined in (7.25c) with $\alpha_j(s) = \alpha(\ln(s + \upsilon_j) - \ln \upsilon_j)$. Choose $\alpha(s) = s$ for $s < 0$, $\alpha(s) = 0.8s$ for $0 \leq s < 0.1$ and $\alpha(s) = s - 0.02$ for $s \geq 0.1$. Then, $[A_c(x_1)]_{1,:} = -[A_c(x_1)]_{2,:}$ and $[b_c(x_1)]_1 = -[b_c(x_1)]_2$ for $[x_1]_1 = 0$ and $|[x_1]_2| \in (0.09, 1)$. Accordingly, both constraints are active and $A_c(x_1)$ is not of full row rank, violating the condition required to guarantee the Lipschitz continuity of the map from x_1 to x_2^*.

Strict safety is sometimes desired, meaning that $h_j(x_1(0)) \leq \upsilon_j$ for $j = 1, \dots, n_c$ implies $h_j(x_1(t)) \leq \upsilon_j$ for $j = 1, \dots, n_c$ whenever $x_1(t)$ is defined. In the case of $m = 1$ (i.e., $\tilde{x}_2 \equiv 0$) and $f_1(x_1) \equiv 0$, following the derivations of (7.36) and (7.37), we obtain

$$\nabla h_j \dot{x}_1 \leq -\left|\frac{\partial h_j(x_1)}{\partial x_1} g_1\right| \alpha_j(h_j(x_1) - \upsilon_j), \tag{7.45}$$

and consequently,

$$h_j(x_1) = \upsilon_j \Rightarrow \nabla h_j \dot{x}_1 \leq 0. \tag{7.46}$$

This, together with condition (7.9), ensures that

$$h_j(x_1(0)) \leq \upsilon_j \Rightarrow h_j(x_1(t)) \leq \upsilon_j, \quad \forall t \geq 0, \tag{7.47}$$

which guarantees strict safety. However, this reasoning cannot be readily extended to the case where $m > 1$ and/or $\bar{f}_1(|x_1|) \neq 0$, as $\tilde{x}_2$ and $f_1(x_1)$ introduce perturbations to the closed-loop system, and may violate the strict safety property when the plant state approaches the safety boundary.

7.3 Design Ingredient: Refined Feasible-set Reshaping

In this section, we propose a refined feasible-set reshaping technique for QCQP-based safety-critical controllers, which enables designing Lipschitz continuous virtual controllers for the subsystems, while describing their interconnections with gain functions.

According to [70, Theorem 3.1] (also see Section 1.3.3), the coefficient matrix of the constraints that directly affect the optimal solution is required to be of full row rank to guarantee the Lipschitz continuity of the solution to a constrained optimization problem with respect to the parameters.

Our basic idea is to project the quadratic constraints involving uncertainties onto a predefined constant matrix [47], which results in a reshaped feasible set with linear constraints and a QP. Under mild conditions, by appropriately choosing the constant matrix, we can guarantee that the coefficient matrix of the constraints that directly affect the optimal solution is never singular and prove that the solution to the resulting QP is Lipschitz.

Suppose that $\mathcal{U}_c : \mathcal{X} \to \mathbb{R}^{n_{x_2}}$ admits a selection $\rho_s : \mathcal{X} \to \mathbb{R}^{n_{x_2}}$. Define a set-valued map $\mathcal{U}_L : \mathcal{X} \rightsquigarrow \mathbb{R}^{n_{x_2}}$ as follows:

$$\mathcal{U}_L(x_1) := \{x_2^* \in \mathbb{R}^{n_{x_2}} : A_L x_2^* \leq b_L(x_1)\}, \tag{7.48}$$

where $A_L \in \mathbb{R}^{n_l \times n_{x_2}}$ satisfies that

1. For $q = 1, \dots, n_l$, $[A_L]_{q,:}$ is a unit vector,
2. Any n_{x_2} rows of A_L are linearly independent, and
3. Any unit vector $l_0 \in \mathbb{R}^{n_{x_2}}$ is a positive combination of the elements of $\{[A_L]_{q,:}^T : [A_L]_{q,:} l_0 \geq c_A, q = 1, \dots, n_l\}$, whose cardinality is not less than n_{x_2}, with $c_A \in (0, 1)$ being a positive constant,

and $b_L : \mathcal{X} \to \mathbb{R}^{n_l}$ is chosen such that the $\mathcal{U}_L$ defined in (7.48) satisfies

$$\rho_s(x_1) \in \mathcal{U}_L(x_1) \subseteq \mathcal{U}_c(x_1), \quad \forall x_1 \in \mathcal{X}. \tag{7.49}$$

The set $\mathcal{U}_L$ in (7.48) is referred to as the reshaped feasible set. The existence of such A_L is guaranteed by Proposition A.14 in Appendix A.2. The existence of b_L is by Lemma B.1 in Appendix B.

Replacing $\mathcal{U}_c$ in (7.23) with $\mathcal{U}_L$ leads to the following QP:

$$x_2^* = \underset{x_2^*}{\operatorname{argmin}} |x_2^* - \rho_0(x_1)|^2 \tag{7.50a}$$

$$\text{s.t.} \quad x_2^* \in \mathcal{U}_L(x_1). \tag{7.50b}$$

Theorem 7.2 gives the boundedness and Lipschitz continuity of the QP-based controller with the reshaped feasible set.

Theorem 7.2 (*Boundedness and Lipschitz Continuity of* ρ_L): *Given the primary controller (7.17) defined by ρ_0 and the QCQP-based controller (7.23) with original feasible set $\mathcal{U}_c$ defined in (7.24), suppose that $\mathcal{U}_c : \mathcal{X} \to \mathbb{R}^{n_{x_2}}$ admits a selection $\rho_s : \mathcal{X} \to \mathbb{R}^{n_{x_2}}$. Then, the QP-based controller (7.50) admits a unique solution for each $x_1 \in \mathcal{X}$, and the function $\rho_L : \mathcal{X} \to \mathbb{R}^{n_{x_2}}$ representing the map from x_1 to x_2^* generated by the QP-based controller (7.50) admits*

1. *Boundedness property:*

$$|\rho_L(x_1)| \leq |\rho_s(x_1)| + |\rho_0(x_1)| \tag{7.51}$$

for all $x_1 \in \mathcal{X}$;

2. *Lipschitz continuity:*

$$|\rho_L(x_1) - \rho_L(x_1')| \leq (1 + L + L|A_L|)|\rho_s(x_1) - \rho_s(x_1')| + L|\rho_0(x_1) - \rho_0(x_1')| + L|b_L(x_1) - b_L(x_1')|, \tag{7.52}$$

for all $x_1, x_1' \in \mathcal{X}$, *where*

$$L = 1 + \frac{3}{c_{A_L}} + \frac{5|A_L|}{c_{A_L}^2}, \tag{7.53}$$

with positive constant c_{A_L} *defined by*[1]

$$c_{A_L} = \min_{\substack{I \subseteq \{1, \dots, n_l\}, \\ \mathrm{card}(I) \leq n_u}} \sqrt{\lambda_{\min}([A_L]_{I,:}[A_L]_{I,:}^T)}. \tag{7.54}$$

Furthermore, under Assumption 7.3, if ρ_s *and* b_L *are Lipschitz on* $\mathcal{X}$, *then there exists a positive constant* L_{ρ_L} *such that*

$$|\rho_L(x_1) - \rho_L(x_1')| \leq L_{\rho_L}|x_1 - x_1'| \tag{7.55}$$

for all $x_1, x_1' \in \mathcal{X}$.

Proof. With Lemma B.1, for each $x_1 \in \mathcal{X}$, the properties $\rho_s(x_1) \in \mathcal{U}_c(x_1)$ and $\rho_s(x_1) \in \mathcal{U}_L(x_1)$ ensure that $\mathcal{U}_L(x_1)$ is non-empty. It can be observed that $\mathcal{U}_L(x_1)$ is a convex set for each $x_1 \in \mathcal{X}$. Then, using the projection theorem [21, Proposition B.11] (also see Proposition A.16), we conclude that the QP (7.50) admits a unique solution for each $x_1 \in \mathcal{X}$.

Boundedness property

For each $x_1 \in \mathcal{X}$, with the projection theorem (see Proposition A.16), $\rho_s(x_1) \in \mathcal{U}_L(x_1)$ implies

$$(\rho_s(x_1) - \rho_L(x_1))^T(\rho_0(x_1) - \rho_L(x_1)) \leq 0, \tag{7.56}$$

which can be rewritten as

$$\left|\rho_L(x_1) - \frac{\rho_0(x_1) + \rho_s(x_1)}{2}\right|^2 - \left|\frac{\rho_0(x_1) - \rho_s(x_1)}{2}\right|^2 \leq 0. \tag{7.57}$$

Applying the triangle inequality [13, Theorem 3.3] to the inequality (7.57) guarantees (7.51) for all $x_1 \in \mathcal{X}$. This ends the proof of Property 1.

1 Note that card(I) denotes the cardinality of the set I. For $I = \{i_1, \dots, i_k\}$, the submatrix $[A_L]_{I,:}$ is given by $[A_L]_{I,:} = [[A_L]_{i_1,:}; \dots; [A_L]_{i_k,:}]$.

Lipschitz continuity

We first invoke B.1 to establish the Lipschitz continuity of the QP-based safety-critical controller (7.50). For $x_1 \in \mathcal{X}$, define a new QP

$$x_2^{*\prime} = \underset{x_2^*}{\operatorname{argmin}} |x_2^* - \rho_0'(x_1)|^2 \tag{7.58a}$$

$$\text{s.t.} \quad x_2^* \in \mathcal{U}_L'(x_1), \tag{7.58b}$$

where $\rho_0'(x_1) = \rho_0(x_1) - \rho_s(x_1)$ and $\mathcal{U}_L'(x_1) = \{x_2^* : A_L x_2^* \leq b_L'(x_1)\}$ with $b_L'(x_1) = b_L(x_1) - A_L \rho_s(x_1)$. It can be verified that $\mathcal{U}_L'(x_1) \neq \emptyset$ by using $\rho_s(x_1) \in \mathcal{U}_L(x_1)$. Then,

$$\rho_L(x_1) = \rho_s(x_1) + x_2^{*\prime}, \tag{7.59}$$

where $x_2^{*\prime}$ is the solution to QP (7.58).

Use $\breve{A}_L x_2^* \leq \breve{b}_L'(x_1)$ to represent the constraints that directly affect the optimal solution of the QP (7.58). Let $\breve{A}_L x_2^* \leq \breve{b}_L'(x_1)$ represent the constraints of the QP (7.58) that directly affect the optimal solution. Note that the number of rows of $\breve{A}_L$ cannot exceed n_{x_2}, since otherwise the rows of $\breve{A}_L$ would be linearly dependent, contradicting the fact that removing any one of them changes the solution.

For any $x_1 \in \mathcal{X}$, $\rho_r'(x_1)$, A_L, and $b_L'(x_1)$ are elements of $\mathbb{R}^{n_u}$, $\{A_L\}$ and $\mathbb{R}_+^{n_l}$, respectively, and all the conditions required by Theorem B.1 are checked as follows:

- $\mathbb{R}^{n_u}$, $\{A_L\}$ and $\mathbb{R}_+^{n_l}$ are convex;
- for each $x_1 \in \mathcal{X}, 0 \in \mathcal{U}_L'(x_1)$ and the projection theorem (see Proposition A.16) guarantee the existence and uniqueness of the solution to QP (7.59), respectively;
- condition 1 of A_L, given below (7.48), guarantees the boundedness of $|\breve{A}_L|$;
- condition 2 of A_L, given below (7.48), guarantees that c_{A_L} defined in (7.54) is a positive constant and that $\lambda_{\min}^{1/2}(\breve{A}_L \breve{A}_L^T) \geq c_{A_L}$, and thus $|\breve{A}_L^T \xi| \geq c_{A_L} |\xi|, \forall \xi$.

Then, the function $\rho_L' : \mathcal{X} \rightarrow \mathbb{R}^{n_{x_2}}$ representing the map from x_1 to $x_2^{*\prime}$ generated by the QP (7.58) satisfies

$$\begin{aligned}
|\rho_L'(x_1) - \rho_L'(x_1')| &\leq L(|\rho_0'(x_1) - \rho_0'(x_1')| + |b_L'(x_1) - b_L'(x_1')|), \\
&\leq L(1 + |A_L|)|\rho_s(x_1) - \rho_s(x_1')| \\
&\quad + L|\rho_0(x_1) - \rho_0(x_1')| + L|b_L(x_1) - b_L(x_1')|
\end{aligned} \tag{7.60}$$

for all $x_1, x_1' \in \mathcal{X}$, where we have used Theorem B.1 for the first inequality with $L = \alpha^{-1} + 2\kappa_1\beta^{-1} + 4\kappa_1\kappa_2\kappa_3$ and used the definitions of ρ_0' and b_L' below (7.58) for the second inequality. By applying the computational method outlined in [70] to the QP (7.58), we obtain the following parameter values: $\alpha = 1$, $\beta = c_{A_L}$, $\kappa_1 = \Gamma$, $\kappa_2 = \Gamma|A_L|/c_{A_L}$, and $\kappa_3 = \Gamma/c_{A_L}$, where $\Gamma = (5/4)^{1/3}$.

Consequently, by considering the form of ρ_L in (7.59), the inequality in (7.60) and applying the algebraic properties of Lipschitz functions [38], it follows that (7.52) holds for all $x_1, x_1' \in \mathcal{X}$.

By Assumption 7.3, ρ_0 is Lipschitz continuous on $\mathcal{X}$. Inequality (7.52), together with the Lipschitz continuity of ρ_0, ρ_s, and b_L, guarantees (7.55). This ends the proof of Property 2. □

It is of practical interest to give an explicit construction of A_L and b_L, and thus $\mathcal{U}_L$ for feasible-set reshaping.

Proposition 7.2 (*Practical Feasible Set Reshaping for QCQPs*): Suppose that $\mathcal{U}_c : \mathcal{X} \rightsquigarrow \mathbb{R}^{n_{x_2}}$ admits a selection $\rho_s : \mathcal{X} \to \mathbb{R}^{n_{x_2}}$. One can construct $\mathcal{U}_L : \mathcal{X} \rightsquigarrow \mathbb{R}^{n_{x_2}}$ in the form of (7.48) to satisfy (7.49) by choosing $A_L \in \mathbb{R}^{n_l \times n_{x_2}}$ to satisfy the conditions below (7.48) with

$$c_A > \cos\left(\pi/2 - \text{acos}\sqrt{1 - \bar{\delta}_1^2/\underline{g}_1^2}\right), \tag{7.61}$$

and choosing $b_L : \mathcal{X} \to \mathbb{R}^{n_l}$ as

$$b_L(x_1) = \phi(\rho_s(x_1), A_c(x_1), b_c(x_1), c_c), \tag{7.62}$$

with

$$\phi(s, A, b, c) = A_L s + \min(\phi_1(s, A, b, c) + \phi_2(A)), \tag{7.63a}$$

$$\phi_1(s, A, b, c) = \max\{A_L A^T, \bar{c}_A\} \odot \frac{(b - As - c|s|)^T}{1 + c^T}, \tag{7.63b}$$

$$\phi_2(A) = \max\{k_\phi(\bar{c}_A - A_L A^T), 0\}, \tag{7.63c}$$

where $\bar{c}_A = \cos(\text{acos}\sqrt{1 - \bar{\delta}_1^2/\underline{g}_1^2} + \text{acos}\, c_A)$ and $k_\phi \geq 0$.

Proof. To prove (7.49), we first prove $\rho_s(x_1) \in \mathcal{U}_L(x_1)$ for all $x_1 \in \mathcal{X}$. Substituting $\rho_s(x_1)$ for x_2^* in the constraints of $\mathcal{U}_L(x_1)$, it is easy to check that $A_L \rho_s(x_1) \leq b_L(x_1)$ holds for all $x_1 \in \mathcal{X}$ by using the fact that ϕ_1 and ϕ_2 are nonnegative functions.

Then, we show that every element of $\mathcal{U}_L(x_1)$ is contained in $\mathcal{U}_c(x_1)$ for all $x_1 \in \mathcal{X}$. Rewrite $\mathcal{U}_c(x_1)$ as

$$\mathcal{U}_c(x_1) = \bigcap_{j=1,\dots,n_c} \; \bigcap_{c \in \{c \in \mathbb{R}^{1 \times n_u} : |c| \leq [c_c]_j\}} \mathcal{S}_{j,c}(x_1), \tag{7.64}$$

where

$$\mathcal{S}_{j,c}(x_1) = \left\{u : l_{j,c}^T(x_1) u \leq \frac{[b_c(x_1)]_j}{|[A_c(x_1)]_{j,:} + c|}\right\} \tag{7.65}$$

with $l_{j,c}^T(x_1) = ([A_c(x_1)]_{j,:} + c)/|[A_c(x_1)]_{j,:} + c|$. Clearly,

$$\begin{aligned} &\mathcal{U}_L(x_1) \subseteq \mathcal{S}_{j,c}(x_1), \quad \forall |c| \leq [c_c]_j,\ j = 1, \dots, n_c, \\ &\Rightarrow \mathcal{U}_L(x_1) \subseteq \mathcal{U}_c(x_1). \end{aligned} \tag{7.66}$$

Using Proposition A.14, for any vector $l_{j,c}$, there exist at least n_u vectors $l_{c_1}, \dots, l_{c_{n_u}}$ in $\mathcal{L}_c := \{l_i \in \{l_1, \dots, l_{n_l}\} : l_i^T l_{j,c} \geq c_A\}$ such that $l_{j,c}$ is a positive combination of $\{l_{c_1}, \dots, l_{c_{n_u}}\}$. Denote the constraints in $\mathcal{U}_L$ corresponding to $l_{c_1}, \dots, l_{c_{n_u}}$ as $A_{L_c} u \leq b_{L_c}$. Utilizing the definition of the positive combination [47], there exists a $\iota \in \mathbb{R}_+^{n_u}$ (with nonnegative elements) satisfying $\iota^T A_{L_c} = l_{j,c}^T$.

For any $x_{2s}^* \in \mathcal{U}_L(x_1)$, we have $A_{L_c} x_{2s}^* \leq b_{L_c}$. This together with $\iota \geq 0$, implies

$$\begin{aligned} l_{j,c}^T(x_1) x_{2s}^* &= \iota^T A_{L_c} x_{2s}^* \leq \iota^T A_{L_c} \rho_s(x_1) + \iota^T A_{L_c} [A_c(x_1)]_{j,:}^T \\ &\quad \cdot \frac{[b_c(x_1)]_j - [A_c(x_1)]_{j,:} \rho_s(x_1) - [c_c]_j |\rho_s(x_1)|}{1 + [c_c]_j} \\ &\leq l_{j,c}^T(x_1) \rho_s(x_1) + \frac{[b_c(x_1)]_j - [A_c(x_1)]_{j,:} \rho_s(x_1) - c\rho_s(x_1)}{|[A_c(x_1)]_{j,:} + c|} \\ &\leq \frac{[b_c(x_1)]_j}{|[A_c(x_1)]_{j,:} + c|}, \end{aligned} \tag{7.67}$$

where we have used the definition $b_L(x_1)$ in (7.62) for the first inequality, used $\iota^T A_{L_c} = l_{j,c}(x_1)$, $\iota^T A_{L_c} [A_c(x_1)]_{j,:}^T \in (0, 1)$, $\rho_s(x_1) \in \mathcal{U}_c(x_1)$, and $|c| \leq [c_c]_j$ for the second inequality, and used the definition of $l_{j,c}(x_1)$ for the last inequality. This proves the satisfaction of $\mathcal{U}_L(x_1) \subseteq \mathcal{S}_{j,c}(x_1)$ for all $j = 1, \dots, n_c$ and $c \in \mathbb{R}^{n_u}$ satisfying $|c| \leq [c_c]_j$. Recalling (7.66), we can prove $\mathcal{U}_L(x_1) \subseteq \mathcal{U}_c(x_1)$. This ends the proof of Proposition 7.2. □

Constructing a selection ρ_s of the set-valued map $\mathcal{U}_c$ plays a crucial role for feasible-set reshaping. The following lemma gives an explicit construction of ρ_s based on A_c, b_c, and c_c defining $\mathcal{U}_c$.

Lemma 7.1 (*Constructing a Selection of* $\mathcal{U}_c(x_1)$): *Consider $\mathcal{U}_c : \mathcal{X} \to \mathbb{R}^{n_{x_2}}$ in the form of (7.24) defined by A_c, b_c, and c_c. Suppose that A_c, b_c, and c_c satisfy*

$$\frac{[b_c(x_1)]_j}{1 + \text{sign}([b_c(x_1)]_j)[c_c]_j} \geq \frac{-[b_c(x_1)]_k}{1 + \text{sign}([b_c(x_1)]_k)[c_c]_k} \tag{7.68}$$

for any $j, k = 1, \dots, n_c$ and $j \neq k$. Define

$$\rho_s(x_1) = [A_c(x_1)]_{\underline{j},:}^T \min\left\{\frac{[b_c(x_1)]_{\underline{j}}}{1 - [c_c]_{\underline{j}}}, 0\right\}, \tag{7.69}$$

where $\underline{j}$ represents the index of any one of the smallest elements of $b_c(x_1)$. Then, ρ_s satisfies $\rho_s(x_1) \in \mathcal{U}_c(x_1)$ for all $x_1 \in \mathcal{X}$.

This lemma can be proved based on a similar idea used for the proof of Theorem 7.1.

Then, any original feasible set $\mathcal{U}_c(x_1)$ with $x_1 \in \mathcal{X}$ can be reshaped following the steps:

1. Constructing a selection ρ_s of the set-valued map $\mathcal{U}_c$ (see Lemma 7.1);
2. Determine a constant matrix A_L that satisfies the conditions below (7.48);[2]
3. Enlarge the set by introducing an appropriate neighborhood around the selection ρ_s along each row of A_L, as captured by the term $\min\left(\phi_1(s, A, b, c) + \phi_2(A)\right)$ in (7.63) in Proposition 7.2).

The feasible-set reshaping technique ensures the (local) Lipschitz continuity of the QP-based controller (7.50), but this comes at the cost of the reshaped feasible set being a subset of the original feasible set. This typically introduces an "optimality gap" between the QCQP-based controller (7.23) and the QP-based controller (7.50). However, this "optimality gap" can be reduced by appropriately selecting the parameters of feasible-set reshaping. As shown in equations (7.62) and (7.63), larger values of the parameters k_ϕ and c_A result in larger values of the functions ϕ_1 and ϕ_2, thereby expanding the feasible set around ρ_s and reducing the "optimality gap." This observation is validated by Example 7.2.

Example 7.2 *(Illustration of Feasible-set Reshaping for Ensuring Lipschitz Continuity)*: *Continue Example 7.1. We apply the feasible-set reshaping technique given by Proposition 7.2 to the original feasible set* (7.24) *with* A_c, b_c, *and* c_c *defined in* (7.40). *Set* $\rho_s(x_1) = 0$ *for all* x_1 *such that* $|x_1 - o_j| \geq -\ln v_j$ *for* $j = 1, 2$, *and define* b_L *according to* (7.62), *with* $c_A = \cos(2\pi/n_l)$, *where* $n_l = 5$ *and* $k_\phi = 0$. *Then, we can obtain* $\mathcal{U}_L$ *in the form of* (7.48) *with*

$$[A_L]_{q,:} = \left[\cos\frac{2\pi q}{n_l},\ \sin\frac{2\pi q}{n_l}\right],\ q = 0, \dots, n_l - 1, \tag{7.70a}$$

$$b_L(x_1) = \min(\max\{A_L A_c^T(x_1), c_A\} \odot b_c^T(x_1)). \tag{7.70b}$$

For the QP (7.50) *with* A_L *and* b_L *defined in* (7.70), *by restricting* $[x_1]_2 = 0$ *and* $\rho_0(x_1) \notin \mathcal{U}_L(x_1)$, *we define the function* $\rho_L : \mathcal{X} \to \mathbb{R}^{n_{x_2}}$ *that represents the map from* x_1 *to* x_2^* *as*

$$\rho_L(x_1) = \left[\max\left\{\frac{-[x_1]_1}{\sqrt{[x_1]_1^2 + 1}}, c_A\right\}\left(\sqrt{[x_1]_1^2 + 1} - D\right); 0\right]. \tag{7.71}$$

---

2 The existence of A_L satisfying the specific conditions is guaranteed by Proposition A.14 in Appendix A.2, and a script developed to generate the required A_L is available at https://github.com/EXPSIN/constructive_safety_critical_control.

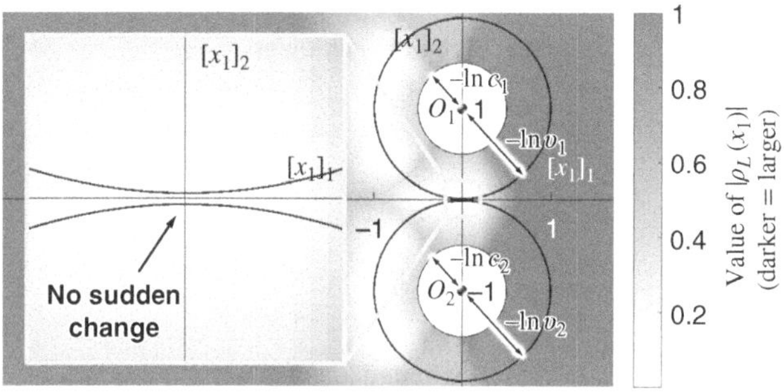

Figure 7.5 $|\rho_L(x_1)|$ with respect to different x_1. In the scenario of Example 7.1, the Lipschitz continuity of the solution to the QP (7.50) can be guaranteed by reshaping the feasible set.

For $[x_1]_1 \in (-0.3, 0)$ *and* $[x_1]_2 \equiv 0$, *we have*

$$\frac{\partial \rho_L(x_1)}{\partial [x_1]_1} = \left[\frac{c_A [x_1]_1}{\sqrt{[x_1]_1^2 + 1}}; 0 \right]. \tag{7.72}$$

This somehow verifies the Lipschitz continuity described by (7.55). *Moreover, the Lipschitz constant does not depend on D.*

Figure 7.5 illustrates the dependence of $|\rho_L(x_1)|$ *on* x_1, *where* $\rho_L(x_1)$ *denotes the map from* x_1 *to* x_2^* *obtained by solving the QP* (7.50) *with constraints defined in* (7.40), (7.48), (7.62), (7.63), *and* (7.70a). *The parameters are chosen as* $\upsilon_1 = \upsilon_2 = e^{-0.99}$, $n_l = 11$, *and* $k_\phi = 1.0$. *This outcome is consistent with our theoretical analysis of Lipschitz continuity.*

Figure 7.6 illustrates the original feasible set and the reshaped feasible sets at $x_1 = [-2; 0]$. *In this figure, the light-gray area represents the original feasible set, the dark-gray area corresponds to the reshaped feasible set with* $k_\phi = 1$ *and* $c_A = \cos(2\pi/5)$, *and the medium-gray area corresponds to the reshaped feasible set with* $k_\phi = 8$ *and* $c_A = \cos(2\pi/27)$. *It can be observed that larger values of parameters* k_ϕ *and* c_A *result in a larger reshaped feasible set.*

7.4 Constructive Design for Plants in the Cascade Form

In this section, building on the methods introduced in Sections 7.2 and 7.3, we propose a recursive design procedure for safety-critical control of nonlinear plants in the cascade form. The proposed design results in an interconnected system comprising the controlled subsystems of the plant and utilizes a nonlinear small-gain

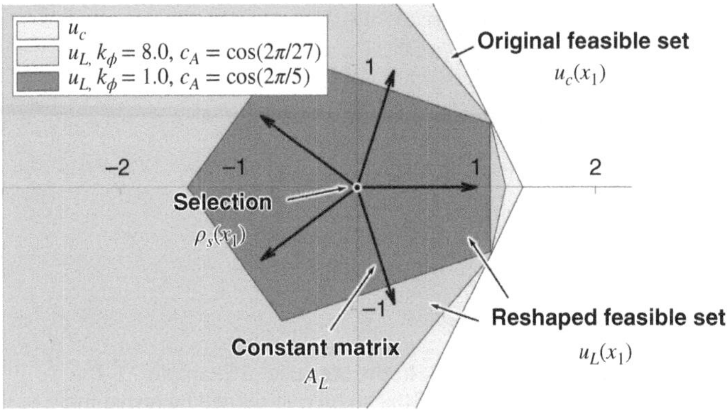

Figure 7.6 Original feasible set (7.24) and reshaped feasible sets (7.48) with different k_ϕ and c_A.

synthesis to fine-tune the controller parameters, ensuring the safety of the closed-loop system.

7.4.1 Constructive Controller Design Procedure

7.4.1.1 Initial Step: Safety-critical Control of the x_1-subsystem

Recall that the x_1-subsystem of the plant (7.1) has been expressed in the form (7.21), with x_2^* denoting the ideal virtual control input. We initiate the constructive control design from the x_1-subsystem. We restate the x_1-subsystem here:

$$\dot{x}_1 = f_1(x_1) + (g_1 + \delta_1(x_1))(x_2^* + \tilde{x}_2). \tag{7.73}$$

Given the primary controller (7.17) defined by ρ_0 and the safety indicator functions h_j and constants υ_j for $j = 1, \dots, n_c$, under Assumptions 7.1 and 7.2, we apply the techniques of Sections 7.2 and 7.3 to design a virtual control law of the form (7.50):

$$x_2^* = \underset{x_2^*}{\operatorname{argmin}} |x_2^* - \rho_0(x_1)|^2 \tag{7.74a}$$

$$\text{s.t.} \quad A_L x_2^* \leq b_L(x_1), \tag{7.74b}$$

where $A_L \in \mathbb{R}^{n_l \times n_{x_2}}$ is chosen according to the conditions below (7.48), with a constant c_A satisfying (7.61), and $b_L : \mathcal{X} \to \mathbb{R}^{n_l}$ is defined by

$$b_L(x_1) = \phi(\rho_s(x_1), A_c(x_1), b_c(x_1), c_c) \tag{7.75}$$

with

$$[A_c(x_1)]_{j,:} = \frac{\partial h_j(x_1)}{\partial x_1} g_1 \left| \frac{\partial h_j(x_1)}{\partial x_1} g_1 \right|^{-1}, \tag{7.76a}$$

$$[b_c(x_1)]_j = -\alpha_j(h_j(x_1) - v_j), \qquad [c_c]_j = \frac{\bar{\delta}_1}{\underline{g}_1}, \tag{7.76b}$$

$$\rho_s(x_1) = [A_c(x_1)]^T_{\underline{j},:} \min \left\{ \frac{[b_c(x_1)]_{\underline{j}}}{1 - [c_c]_{\underline{j}}}, 0 \right\}, \tag{7.76c}$$

$$\phi(s, A, b, c) = A_L s + \min(\phi_1(s, A, b, c) + \phi_2(A)) \tag{7.76d}$$

$$\phi_1(s, A, b, c) = \max\{A_L A^T, \bar{c}_A\} \odot \frac{(b - As - c|s|)^T}{1 + c^T} \tag{7.76e}$$

$$\phi_2(A) = \max\{k_\phi(\bar{c}_A - A_L A^T), 0\} \tag{7.76f}$$

for $j = 1, \dots, n_c$, where $\bar{c}_A = \cos(\arccos \sqrt{1 - \bar{\delta}_1^2/\underline{g}_1^2} + \arccos c_A)$, $k_\phi \geq 0$ is a constant, and $\underline{j}$ is the index of any of the smallest elements of $b_c(x_1)$.

By selecting α_j to satisfy (7.26) and (7.28), it follows that the QP (7.74) admits a unique solution for each $x_1 \in \mathcal{X}$, and the safety indicator functions of the closed-loop x_1-subsystem attain Property 2 in Theorem 7.1.

In addition, by property (7.51) and the definition of ρ_s in (7.76c), there exists a function $\gamma_{x_2^*,h} \in \mathcal{K}$ such that

$$|x_2^*| \leq \gamma_{x_2^*,h}(\breve{h}(x_1)) + |\rho_0(x_1)|, \tag{7.77}$$

for all $x_1 \in \mathcal{X}$, where

$$\breve{h}(x_1) = \max \left\{0, \max_{j=1,\dots,n_c}\{h_j(x_1) - v_j\}\right\}. \tag{7.78}$$

The following upper bound property of $|D^+ x_2^*(t)|$ is useful for the recursive design procedure provided later.

Claim 7.1 (*Local Lipschitz Continuity of* $x_2^*(t)$): If A_c and b_c are Lipschitz functions on $\mathcal{X}$, then there exists a monotonically increasing function $k_1 : \mathbb{R}_+ \to \mathbb{R}_+$ such that for any $x_1 \in \mathcal{X}$ and any piecewise continuous $\tilde{x}_2$,

$$|D^+ x_2^*(t)| \leq k_1(\breve{h}(x_1(t)))(\bar{f}_1(|x_1(t)|) + (\bar{g}_1 + \bar{\delta}_1)(|x_2^*(t)| + |\tilde{x}_2(t)|)) \tag{7.79}$$

whenever $x_1(t)$ and $\tilde{x}_2(t)$ are defined.

Proof. Inequality (7.79) can be proved by using the Lipschitz property (7.52) in Theorem 7.2 and by demonstrating the (local) Lipschitz continuity of ρ_0, ρ_s, and b_L on $\mathcal{X}$.

Specifically, Assumption 7.3 guarantees that ρ_0 is Lipschitz continuous on $\mathcal{X}$.

If $[b_c(x_1)]_{\underline{j}} \geq 2\bar{\rho}_0/\bar{c}_A$, then $\rho_0(x_1)$ is the solution to the QP (7.74). Otherwise, based on the definitions of ρ_s and b_L in (7.69) and (7.62), and using the Lipschitz properties of A_c and b_c, along with the fundamental properties of algebraic operations involving Lipschitz functions as outlined in [38, Section 2.3], it follows that there exist constants $L', L'' \geq 0$ and functions $k_1', k_1'' \in \mathcal{K}$ such that

$$|\rho_s(x_1) - \rho_s(x_1')| \leq (L' + k_1'(\check{V}(x_1)))|x_1 - x_1'| \tag{7.80}$$

$$|b_L(x_1) - b_L(x_1')| \leq (L'' + k_1''(\check{V}(x_1)))|x_1 - x_1'| \tag{7.81}$$

for all $x_1, x_1' \in \{x_1 \in \mathcal{X} : [b_c(x_1)]_{\underline{j}} < 2\bar{\rho}_0/\bar{c}_A\}$.

Based on the discussion above and the property (7.52), there exists a monotonically increasing function k_1 such that (7.79) holds whenever x_1 and $\tilde{x}_2$ are defined. □

7.4.1.2 Recursive Steps: Control of the x_i-subsystems ($i = 2, \dots, m$)

For the x_i-subsystem of the plant (7.1), we consider x_{i+1} as the virtual control input. Define the error between the state x_i and the ideal virtual control input x_i^* of the x_{i-1}-subsystem as

$$\tilde{x}_i = x_i - x_i^*, \tag{7.82}$$

for $i = 2, \dots, m+1$, with $x_{m+1} = x_{m+1}^* = u$. Then, we have

$$D^+\tilde{x}_i = f_i(z_i) + (g_i + \delta_i(z_i))(x_{i+1}^* + \tilde{x}_{i+1}) - D^+x_i^*, \tag{7.83}$$

where x_{i+1}^* is considered as the ideal virtual control input of the x_i-subsystem, and $\tilde{x}_{i+1}, D^+x_i^*$, and z_i are considered as external inputs of the subsystem.

Using condition (7.3) in Assumption 7.1, properties (7.77) and (7.79), the definition in (7.82), and condition (7.84), suppose the existence of a constant $c_{x_1} \geq 0$ and a function $\bar{f}_i^o \in \mathcal{K} \cup \{0\}$ such that

$$\bar{f}_i(|z_i|) \leq c_{x_1} + \bar{f}_i^o(|[x_2; \dots; x_i]|), \quad \forall z_i \in \mathbb{R}^{n_{z_i}}. \tag{7.84}$$

Then, there exists a $\kappa_i^* \in \mathcal{K}_\infty$ such that

$$|f_i(z_i)| + |D^+x_i^*| + (\underline{g}_i + \bar{\delta}_i)|\tilde{x}_{i+1}| \leq \kappa_i^*(X_i), \tag{7.85}$$

where $X_i = \max_{k=2,\dots,i+1}\{\breve{h}(x_1), |\tilde{x}_k|, \bar{\rho}_0, c_{x_1}\}$.[3]

---

3 This is due to the fact that any continuous function $f_1 : \mathbb{R}^n \to \mathbb{R}^m$ satisfies $|f_1(x)| \leq f_2(|x|)$ for all $x \in \mathbb{R}^n$ with $f_2(s) := \sup_{|x|\leq s}|f(x)| + s$ for $s \geq 0$ being of class $\mathcal{K}_\infty$.

The control problem for the $\tilde{x}_i$-subsystem is solved by directly considering $|\tilde{x}_i|$ as a safety-indicator-like function and applying the method in Section 7.2. In particular, the virtual controller is designed as

$$x^*_{i+1} = \underset{x^*_{i+1}}{\operatorname{argmin}} |x^*_{i+1}|^2 \tag{7.86a}$$

$$\text{s.t.} \quad \tilde{x}_i^T g_i x^*_{i+1} + \frac{\bar{\delta}_i}{\underline{g}_i} |\tilde{x}_i^T g_i||x^*_{i+1}| \leq -|\tilde{x}_i^T g_i| \kappa_i(|\tilde{x}_i|), \tag{7.86b}$$

where $\kappa_i \in \mathcal{K}_\infty$ is continuously differentiable and satisfies

$$\kappa_i(s) \geq \sigma(s) + \frac{2}{\underline{g}_i} \max\{\kappa_i^* \circ \gamma_i^{-1}(s), \kappa_i^* \circ \chi_i^{-1}(s)\}, \tag{7.87}$$

for all $s \geq \underline{c}$, with $\underline{c}$ being a positive constant, σ being any continuous, positive definite function, $\chi \in \mathcal{K}_\infty$, and $\gamma_i \in \mathcal{K}_\infty$ satisfying

$$\gamma_i \circ \gamma_{1,2} < \mathrm{Id} \ \text{ and } \gamma_i < \mathrm{Id}. \tag{7.88}$$

The above design results in the following property of $|\tilde{x}_i(t)|$.

Claim 7.2 (*The Influences of* $\breve{h}(x_1)$ *and* $\tilde{x}_k$ *for* $k = 2, \dots, i+1$ *on* $\tilde{x}_i$): There exists a $\beta_i \in \mathcal{KL}$ such that for any specific initial state $\tilde{x}_i(0)$ and any piecewise continuous $\tilde{x}_2, \dots, \tilde{x}_{i-1}, \tilde{x}_{i+1}$ and x_1 satisfying $\|h_j(x_1)\|_\infty < \sup_{x_1 \in \mathrm{Cl}(\mathcal{X})} h_j(x_1)$ for $j = 1, \dots, n_c$,

$$|\tilde{x}_i(t)| \leq \max_{k=2,\dots,i+1, k\neq i} \left\{ \beta_i(|\tilde{x}_i(0)|, t), \gamma_i(\|\breve{h}(x_1)\|_t), \gamma_i(\| \tilde{x}_k \|_t), c_{\tilde{x}_i} \right\} \tag{7.89}$$

whenever $\tilde{x}_i(t)$ is defined, where $c_{\tilde{x}_i} = \max\{\chi_i(c_{x_1}), \chi_i(\bar{\rho}_0), \underline{c}\}$.

Proof. Taking the upper right Dini derivative of $|\tilde{x}_i(t)|$ along the trajectories of the $\tilde{x}_i$-subsystem defined in (7.83) and (7.86), we have

$$\begin{aligned} D^+|\tilde{x}_i(t)| \leq & \frac{|\tilde{x}_i^T(t) g_i|}{|\tilde{x}_i(t)| \underline{g}_i} \big(|f_i(z_i(t))| + |D^+ x_i^*(t)| \\ & + (\underline{g}_i + \bar{\delta}_i)|\tilde{x}_{i+1}(t)| - \underline{g}_i \kappa_i(|\tilde{x}_i(t)|) \big), \end{aligned} \tag{7.90}$$

whenever $\tilde{x}_i(t)$ is defined and $\tilde{x}_i(t) \neq 0$. Substituting (7.85) and (7.87) into (7.90), we have

$$\begin{aligned} & |\tilde{x}_i(t)| \geq \max_{\substack{k = 2, \dots, i+1, \\ k \neq i}} \{\gamma_i(|\breve{V}(x_1(t))|), \gamma_i(|\tilde{x}_k(t)|), c_{\tilde{x}_i}\} \\ & \Rightarrow D^+|\tilde{x}_i(t)| \leq -\underline{g}_i \sigma(|\tilde{x}_i(t)|), \end{aligned} \tag{7.91}$$

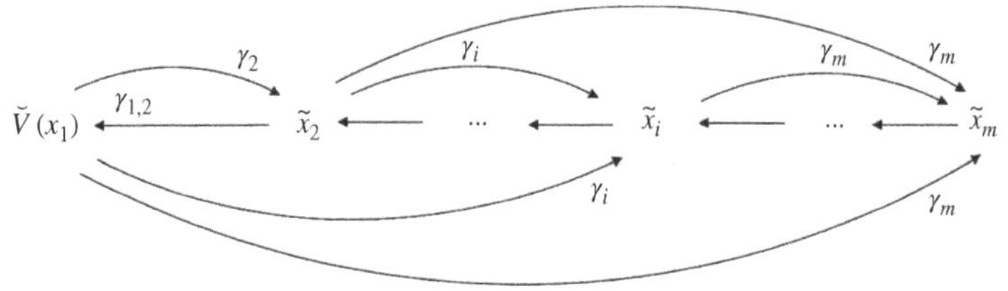

Figure 7.7 Gain interconnection between $\breve{V}(x_1)$ and $\tilde{x}_2, \dots, \tilde{x}_m$.

where $c_{\tilde{x}_i}$ is a positive constant defined below (7.89). This implies the existence of a $\beta_i \in \mathcal{KL}$ such that

$$|\tilde{x}_i(t)| \le \beta_i(|\tilde{x}_i(0)|, t), \tag{7.92}$$

whenever $|\tilde{x}_i(t)| \ge \max_{k=2,\dots,i+1,k\neq i}\{\gamma_i(\|\breve{V}(x_1)\|_\infty), \gamma_i(\|\tilde{x}_k\|_\infty), c_{\tilde{x}_i}\}$. This ensures the satisfaction of property (7.89), thereby concluding the proof of Claim 7.2. □

The recursive design transforms the closed-loop system into an interconnection of controlled subsystems with their interaction described by gain functions, as shown in Figure 7.7.

7.4.2 Main Result

By fine-tuning the controller parameters, we have the following main result on the safety-critical control of nonlinear cascaded systems subject to multiple constraints.

Theorem 7.3 *(Small-Gain-Ensured Transient-Aware Safety)*: *For the plant* (7.1), *given the primary controller* (7.17) *defined by* ρ_0 *and the safety indicator functions* $h_1, \dots, h_{n_c}$, *consider the controller defined in* (7.74) *and* (7.86). *Suppose that Assumptions 7.1, 7.2 and 7.3, as well as conditions* (7.7) *and* (7.84) *are satisfied. By appropriately choosing* $\alpha_1, \dots, \alpha_{n_c}$, A_L, c_A, k_ϕ *and* $\kappa_2, \dots, \kappa_m$, *there exist* $\breve{\beta}_1, \dots, \breve{\beta}_m \in \mathcal{KL}$, *constants* $c_1, \dots, c_{n_c}, \breve{c}_2, \dots, \breve{c}_m \ge 0$ *and* $\bar{X} > 0$ *such that for any initial state satisfying* $\max\{X(0), |\rho_0(x_1(0))|\} \le \bar{X}$, $x_1(t)$ *keeps inside* $\mathcal{X}$, *and property* (7.4) *holds whenever* $z_m(t)$ *is defined.*

Proof. By transforming the closed-loop system into an interconnected system, as illustrated in Figure 7.7, and with the subsystems satisfying properties (7.29) and (7.89), we conduct a nonlinear small-gain analysis to prove the achievement of the safety-critical control objective.

Step 1: boundedness of $h_j(x_1)$ for $j = 1, \dots, n_c$ and x_i for $i = 2, \dots, m$
For any initial state such that $x_1(0) \in \mathcal{X}$ and $x_i(0) \in \mathbb{R}^{n_{x_i}}$ for $i = 2, \dots, m$, suppose that $[x_1(t); \dots; x_m(t)]$ is right maximally defined on $[0, T)$ with $0 < T \le \infty$,

and that $[h_1(x_1(t)); \dots ; h_{n_c}(x_1(t))]$ is right maximally defined on $[0, T')$ with $0 < T' \le \infty$.

Using condition (7.5), property (7.29), and the definition (7.78), we have

$$\breve{h}(x_1(t)) \le \max\{\beta_1(X'(0), t), \gamma_{1,2}(\|\tilde{x}_2\|_{T'}), v_\delta\}, \tag{7.93}$$

for $t \in [0, T')$, where

$$X' = \max\{X, |\rho_0(x_1)|\} \tag{7.94}$$

with X defined below (7.4), and constant v_δ satisfies

$$0 < v_\delta < \sup_{x_1 \in \mathrm{Cl}(\mathcal{X})} h_j(x_1) - v_j, \quad \forall j = 1, \dots, n_c. \tag{7.95}$$

Recall property (7.89). For $i = 2, \dots, m$ and any positive constants c_{x_1} and $\bar{\rho}_0$, by choosing γ_i, χ_i, and $\underline{c}$ small enough, we have

$$|\tilde{x}_i(t)| \le \max_{k=2,\dots,i+1,k\ne i}\{\beta_i(\alpha_X(X'(0)), t), \gamma_i(\|\breve{h}(x_1)\|_{T'}), \gamma_i(\|\tilde{x}_k\|_{T'}), v_\delta\}, \tag{7.96}$$

for $t \in [0, T')$, where $\alpha_X \in \mathcal{K}$ satisfies

$$|\tilde{x}_i(0)| \le \alpha_X(X'(0)). \tag{7.97}$$

Now, we prove the boundedness of the safety indicator functions. Denote

$$W_m = \max\{\breve{h}(x_1), \breve{\gamma}_{1,2}(|\tilde{x}_2|), \dots, \breve{\gamma}_{1,m}(|\tilde{x}_m|)\}, \tag{7.98}$$

where $\breve{\gamma}_{1,i} = \breve{\gamma}_1 \circ \cdots \circ \breve{\gamma}_{i-1}$ with $\breve{\gamma}_i \in \mathcal{K}_\infty$ satisfying

$$\breve{\gamma}_1 > \gamma_{1,2}, \quad \gamma_i \circ \breve{\gamma}_1 < \mathrm{Id}, \quad \breve{\gamma}_i > \gamma_i, \quad \breve{\gamma}_i \circ \gamma_i < \mathrm{Id} \tag{7.99}$$

for $i = 2, \dots, m$. This means that

$$|\breve{h}(x_1)| \le W_m, \quad \text{and} \quad |\tilde{x}_i| \le \breve{\gamma}_{1,i}^{-1}(W_m), \quad \forall i = 2, \dots, m. \tag{7.100}$$

By substituting (7.93) and (7.96) into the right-hand side of (7.98), it is achieved that

$$\begin{aligned} W_m(t) &\le \max_{i,k}\{\beta(X'(0), t), v_\delta, \gamma_{1,2}(\|\tilde{x}_2\|_{T'}), \\ &\qquad \breve{\gamma}_{1,i} \circ \gamma_i(\|\breve{h}(x_1)\|_{T'}), \breve{\gamma}_{1,i} \circ \gamma_i(\|\tilde{x}_k\|_{T'})\} \\ &\le \max_{i,k}\{\beta(X'(0), t), v_\delta, \gamma_{1,2} \circ \breve{\gamma}_{1,2}^{-1}(\|W_m\|_{T'}), \\ &\qquad \breve{\gamma}_{1,i} \circ \gamma_i(\|W_m\|_{T'}), \breve{\gamma}_{1,i} \circ \gamma_i \circ \breve{\gamma}_{1,k}^{-1}(\|W_m\|_{T'})\} \\ &\le \max\{\beta(X'(0), t), \gamma(\|W_m\|_{T'}), v_\delta\} \end{aligned} \tag{7.101}$$

for $i = 2, \dots, m$, $k = 1, \dots, i+1$ satisfying $k \neq i$ and $k \leq m$, and $t \in [0, T')$, where we have used (7.100) for the second inequality, and used condition (7.88) for the last inequality, with $\gamma \in \mathcal{K}_\infty$ satisfying $\gamma < \mathrm{Id}$, and

$$\beta(s,t) = \max_{i=1,\dots,m} \breve{\gamma}_{1,i}(\beta_i(\alpha_X(s), t)). \tag{7.102}$$

By taking the supremum of $|W_m(t)|$ over $[0, T')$ and choosing a positive constant $\bar{X}$ to satisfy $\beta(\bar{X}, 0) \leq \upsilon_\delta$, we have that for any initial state satisfying $X'(0) \leq \bar{X}$

$$\|W_m(t)\|_{T'} \leq \max\{\beta(X'(0), 0), \upsilon_\delta\} \leq \upsilon_\delta, \tag{7.103}$$

for $t \in [0, T')$. And thus, we have

$$h_j(x_1(t)) \leq \|W_m(t)\|_{T'} + \upsilon_j \leq \upsilon_\delta + \upsilon_j < \sup_{x_1 \in \mathrm{Cl}(\mathcal{X})} h_j(x_1), \quad \forall j = 1, \dots, n_c, \tag{7.104}$$

for all $t \in [0, T')$, where we have used (7.95) for the last inequality. By combining (7.104) with condition (7.10), we have that $x_1(t)$ keeps inside $\mathcal{X}$ for all $t \in [0, T)$.

Recall the property (7.77) and the definitions (7.22), (7.82) and (7.86). Direct calculation yields that

$$|x_2(t)| \leq |\tilde{x}_2(t)| + \gamma_{x_2^*,h}(\breve{h}(x_1(t))) + \bar{\rho}_0, \tag{7.105a}$$

$$|x_i(t)| \leq |\tilde{x}_i(t)| + \frac{\underline{g}_{i-1}}{\underline{g}_{i-1} - \bar{\delta}_{i-1}} \kappa_{i-1}(|\tilde{x}_{i-1}(t)|), \tag{7.105b}$$

for $i = 3, \dots, m$ and $t \in [0, T)$. Substituting (7.103) into (7.105) ensures that, for any initial state satisfying $X'(0) \leq \bar{X}$, the solutions $x_2(t), \dots, x_m(t)$ are bounded on $[0, T)$.

Step 2: safety property of the closed-loop system

By using the boundedness of $h_j(x_1(t))$ for $j = 1, \dots, n_c$ and $x_i(t)$ for $i = 1, \dots, m$, we have that there exist $\alpha_X \in \mathcal{K}_\infty$ and c_X such that

$$X(t) \leq \max\{\alpha_X(X(0)), c_X\} \tag{7.106}$$

whenever $x_1(t)$ is defined.

By substituting (7.94) into (7.101), we have

$$|W_m(t)| \leq \max\{\beta(X(0), t), \gamma(\|W_m\|_T), \upsilon_\delta'\} \tag{7.107}$$

with $\upsilon_\delta' = \max\{\beta(|\rho_0(x_1(0))|, 0), \upsilon_\delta\}$. By means of time invariance and causality, (7.107) and (7.106) imply that

$$\begin{aligned} |W_m(t)| &\leq \max\{\beta(X(t/2), t/2), \gamma(\|W_m\|_{[t/2,t]}), \upsilon_\delta'\}, \\ &\leq \max\{\beta(\alpha_X(X(0)), t/2), \gamma(\|W_m\|_{[t/2,t]}), \upsilon_\delta''\} \end{aligned} \tag{7.108}$$

with $\upsilon_\delta'' = \max\{\beta(c_X, 0), \upsilon_\delta'\}$. By [120, Lemma D.1], it can be proved that there exists $\beta' \in \mathcal{KL}$ such that

$$W_m(t) \leq \max\{\beta'(X(0), t), \upsilon_\delta''\}, \tag{7.109}$$

whenever $x_1(t)$ is defined. This implies that

$$\begin{aligned} h_j(x_1(t)) &\leq W_m(t) + \upsilon_j \leq \max\{\beta'(X(0), t), \upsilon_\delta''\} + \upsilon_j \\ &\leq \max\left\{\frac{\upsilon_\delta'' + \upsilon_j}{\upsilon_\delta''}\beta'(X(0), t), \upsilon_\delta'' + \upsilon_j\right\} \end{aligned} \tag{7.110}$$

where we have used the fact that $a + b \leq \max\{(1 + 1/\delta)a, (1 + \delta)b\}, \forall a, b \geq 0$, $\delta > 0$ for the last inequality. This verifies property (7.4a) for all $t \in [0, T)$. Substituting (7.100) and (7.109) into (7.105) proves property (7.4b) for all $t \in [0, T)$. This ends the proof of Theorem 7.3. □

Based on the discussions above, the controller parameters can be tuned to ensure the safety of the plant according to the following guidelines.

- **Step 1 - Design the virtual control law (7.74) for the x_1-subsystem:**
  - *Step 1.1:* For $j = 1, \dots, n_c$, given the safety indicator function h_j and its corresponding constant υ_j, choose functions $\underline{\alpha}_j, \bar{\alpha}_j \in \mathcal{K}^e$ satisfying (7.12) (following Proposition 7.1 and its proof);
  - *Step 1.2:* For $j = 1, \dots, n_c$, given any class $\mathcal{K}_\infty$ function $\gamma_{1,2}$, any continuous, positive definite function σ, and any constant c_j satisfying $\upsilon_j < c_j < \sup_{x_1 \in \mathrm{Cl}(\mathcal{X})} h_j(x_1)$, choose a class $\mathcal{K}^e$ function α_j satisfying conditions (7.26), (7.27) and (7.28) (following the discussion following Theorem 7.1);
  - *Step 1.3:* Choose a constant matrix A_L satisfying the conditions below (7.48) (the existence of such A_L is guaranteed by Proposition A.14 in Appendix A.2, and a script developed to generate the required A_L is available at https://github.com/EXPSIN/constructive_safety_critical_control);
  - *Step 1.4:* Choose a class $\mathcal{K}$ function $\gamma_{x_2^*,h}$ and a monotonically increasing function k_1 to satisfy conditions (7.77) and (7.79).
- **Step 2 - Recursively design the virtual controllers (7.86) for the x_i-subsystem ($i = 2, \dots, m$):** Based on the class $\mathcal{K}_\infty$ function $\gamma_{1,2}$ specified in Step 1.2, as well as the gain function $\gamma_{x_2^*,h}$ and the monotonically increasing function k_1 determined in Step 1, and given any continuous, positive definite function σ and any class $\mathcal{K}_\infty$ function χ_i, proceed as follows:
  - *Step 2.1:* Choose a class $\mathcal{K}^e$ function κ_i^* whose gradient is sufficiently large over its domain to satisfy condition (7.85);
  - *Step 2.2:* Choose a class $\mathcal{K}_\infty$ function γ_i to satisfy condition (7.88);
  - *Step 2.3:* Based on the selected κ_i^* and γ_i, choose a continuously differentiable, class $\mathcal{K}_\infty$ function κ_i to satisfy condition (7.87).

It is of practical interest to investigate safety-critical control with saturated control inputs. By appropriately selecting the safety indicator functions, it is possible to confine the control input within the desired range under specific initial conditions. In particular, properties (7.100) and (7.103), as established in the proof of Theorem 7.3, ensure the boundedness of $\tilde{x}_m$. This, together with (7.86), further guarantees the boundedness of the resulting control input. However, in general, due to the presence of nonlinear uncertain dynamics, directly imposing saturation constraints on the admissible set of control inputs may easily compromise feasibility.

7.5 Experiment: VTOL Taking Off in a Narrow Space

Numerical simulations and physical experiments are conducted to validate the proposed safety-critical control method and demonstrate its application to a vertical takeoff and landing (VTOL) vehicle that moves in a narrow space.

7.5.1 Dynamic Modeling of a VTOL Vehicle and Dynamic Feedback Linearization

A simplified dynamic model of a VTOL is given by

$$\ddot{p} = \begin{bmatrix} 0 \\ -g \end{bmatrix} + \begin{bmatrix} -\sin\theta \\ \cos\theta \end{bmatrix} a_1, \quad \ddot{\theta} = a_2, \tag{7.111a}$$

where $p \in \mathbb{R}^2$ represents the horizontal and vertical positions of the center of mass, θ is the roll angle, and the thrust a_1 (directed out the bottom of the aircraft) and the angular acceleration a_2 (rolling moment) are used as the control inputs [54]. Figure 7.8 shows the VTOL vehicle used in the experiment.

As long as $a_1 \neq 0$, the dynamic model can be transformed into a fourth-order integrator

$$\frac{\mathrm{d}^4 x_1(t)}{\mathrm{d}t^4} = u(t), \tag{7.112}$$

through the dynamic state feedback [54]:

$$\begin{bmatrix} \ddot{a}_1 \\ a_2 \end{bmatrix} = \begin{bmatrix} \dot{\theta}^2 a_1 \\ -\dfrac{2\dot{\theta}\dot{a}_1}{a_1} \end{bmatrix} + \begin{bmatrix} -\sin\theta, & \cos\theta \\ -\dfrac{\cos\theta}{a_1}, & -\dfrac{\sin\theta}{a_1} \end{bmatrix} u, \tag{7.113}$$

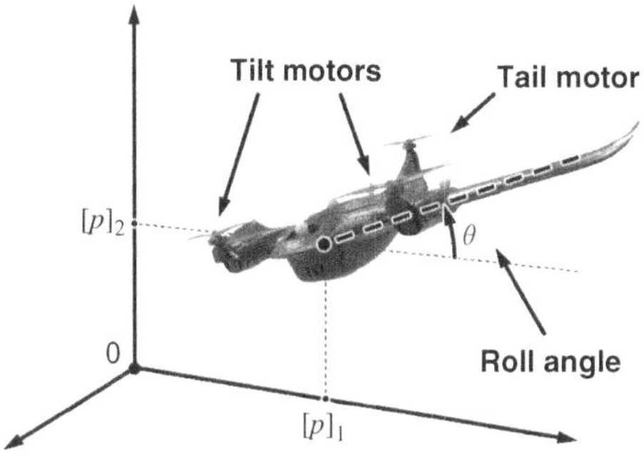

Figure 7.8 The VTOL vehicle and its coordinates in the experiment.

where $x_1 = p$ is the position vector, and $u = d^4p/dt^4$ is the snap. In accordance with our system setup, we rewrite (7.112) as

$$\dot{x}_i = x_{i+1} = x_{i+1}^* + \tilde{x}_{i+1}, \quad i = 1, \dots, 4 \tag{7.114}$$

where x_i^* represents the virtual control inputs, and $\tilde{x}_{i+1}$ represents the tracking errors. Define $x_5^* = u$ and $\tilde{x}_5 = 0$. Obviously, the linearized model (7.114) is a chain of four integrators and satisfies Assumption 7.1 with $\bar{f}_i = 0$, $\underline{g}_i = 1$, $\bar{g}_i = 1$ and $\bar{\delta}_i = 0$ for $i = 1, \dots, 4$. We consider (7.114) as the plant model for controller design in the following section.

7.5.2 The Scenario for Simulation and Experiment

Consider a scenario with n_c obstacles, each represented by a line segment with ending points $o_{j_1}, o_{j_2} \in \mathbb{R}^2$. Accordingly, the safety indicator functions are defined by $h_j(x_1) = \mu(h_j(x_1))$ with $\mu(s) = e^{-s}$ and

$$h_j(x_1) = \begin{cases} |x_1 - o_{j_1}| - D_s, & \text{if } (x_1 - o_{j1})^T(o_{j2} - o_{j1}) < 0 \\ |x_1 - o_{j_2}| - D_s, & \text{if } (x_1 - o_{j2})^T(o_{j1} - o_{j2}) < 0 \\ \dfrac{2S(x_1)}{|o_{j_1} - o_{j_2}|} - D_s, & \text{otherwise} \end{cases} \tag{7.115}$$

where $D_s > 0$ is the safe distance,

$$S(p) = \sqrt{l(p)(l(p) - |p - o_{j_1}|)(l(p) - |p - o_{j_2}|)(l(p) - |o_{j_1} - o_{j_2}|)} \tag{7.116}$$

with $l(p) = (|p - o_{j_1}| + |p - o_{j_2}| + |o_{j_1} - o_{j_2}|)/2$. Note that $S(p)$ represents the area of the triangle with corner points p, o_{j_1} and o_{j_2}, and the area is calculated using Heron's formula [43]. So, $h_j(x_1)$ represents the distance from x_1 to the j-th line segment (o_{j_1}, o_{j_2}), and satisfies $\left|\partial h_j(x_1)/\partial x_1\right| = 1$ when $h_j(x_1) \neq -D_s$.

In both numerical simulation and experiment, we consider $n_c = 2$, $o_{1_1} = [-2.5; 1.5]$, $o_{1_2} = [1.5; 2.0]$, $o_{2_1} = [-2.5; 0.5]$, $o_{2_2} = [2.5; 0.5]$ and $D_s = 0.35$. Direct calculation verifies Assumption 7.2 with $\upsilon_j = 1$ for $j = 1, 2$. Then, using Proposition 7.1, we have $\underline{\alpha}_j(s) = \bar{\alpha}_j(s) = e^s - 1$ for $j = 1, 2$.

7.5.3 Controller Design and Numerical Simulation

We consider the primary controller (7.17) defined by $\rho_0(x_1) \equiv [0.6; 1]$ for taking-off, which obviously satisfies Assumption 7.3.

The control system composed of (7.74), (7.86) and (7.112) is shown in Figure 7.9.

For the virtual controller (7.74), we choose

$$[A_L]_{q,:} = \left[\cos\frac{2\pi q}{n_l}, \sin\frac{2\pi q}{n_l}\right], \qquad k_\phi = 2, \tag{7.117a}$$

$$[A_c(x_1)]_{j,:} = \frac{\partial h_j(x_1)}{\partial x_1}, \qquad c_A = \cos\frac{2\pi}{n_l}, \tag{7.117b}$$

$$[b_c(x_1)]_j = k_\alpha h_j(x_1), \qquad [c_c]_j = 0, \tag{7.117c}$$

where $k_\alpha = 1.0$, $q = 1, \dots, n_l$ and $j = 1, \dots, n_c$ with $n_l = 11$. It can be verified that conditions (7.27) and (7.28) required by Theorem 7.1 are satisfied with $\underline{g}_1 = 1$, $\bar{\delta}_1 = 0$, $\alpha(s) = k_\alpha s$, $\bar{f}_1 = 0$, $c_j = 1.5$ for $j = 1, 2$, $\sigma(s) = 0.001s$ and $\gamma_{1,2}(s) = 4s$. According to (7.26), we choose $\alpha_j(s) = k_\alpha \bar{\alpha}_j^{-1}(s)$ for $j = 1, 2$.

For the virtual controller (7.86), following the guideline in Section 7.4.2, we set $\kappa_i(s) = K_i s$, and choose

$$K_2 = 11.81, \quad K_3 = 24.73 \quad K_4 = 662.70. \tag{7.118}$$

These choices ensure that the conditions (7.84) and (7.88) required by Theorem 7.3 are satisfied. In computing K_i, we use $\gamma_{x_2^*,V}(s) = k_\alpha s/4$, $k_1(s) \equiv 3.49$ and $\gamma_i(s) = 0.249s$. Moreover, the gains K_i can be reduced by decreasing k_α and k_ϕ, since smaller values of k_α and k_ϕ yield a smaller Lipschitz constant for the control law

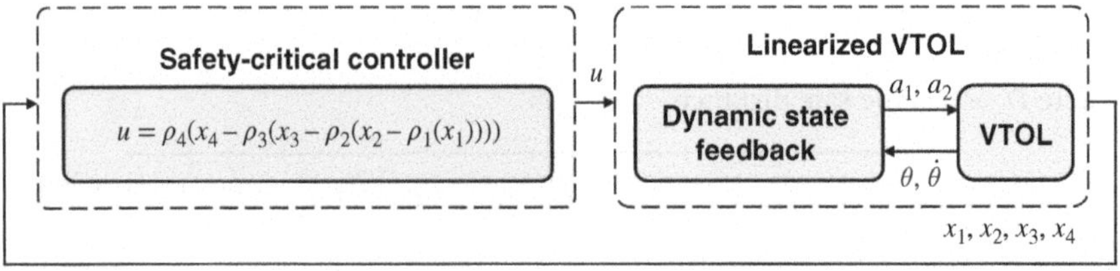

Figure 7.9 The block diagram of the controlled VTOL.

ρ_1 (see (7.52) and (7.75)–(7.76)). The techniques of [217] are employed to estimate the constant k_1 associated with ρ_1.

For comparison, with the same safety-critical controller parameters as given by (7.117), we also consider another set of controller parameters

$$K_2 = 11.78, \quad K_3 = 11.78, \quad K_4 = 11.78, \tag{7.119}$$

corresponding to the tracking controller. With this set of controller parameters, one cannot find γ_i for $i = 2, \dots, 4$ to satisfy (7.87) and (7.88) required by Theorem 7.3 at the same time, since condition (7.87) can only be satisfied when $K_{i+1} > K_i$.

Figure 7.10 shows the simulation result with $x_1(0) = [-2.0; 1.0]$, and $x_i = [0; 0]$ for $i = 2, \dots, 4$. The position trajectory shown by the solid line corresponds to the first parameter set and maintains far enough away from the obstacles as expected, while the other trajectory violates the safety constraints.

7.5.4 Experiment

This subsection employs an experimental system to further verify the validity of the proposed method. In particular, the plant is a FIMI Manta tiltrotor VTOL fixed-wing. The real-time position and attitude of the VTOL are measured by OptiTrack. The controller is implemented on a laptop with an Intel Core i7-8565U processor. The communication from the laptop to the VTOL is established with a combination of a USB-to-PPM transmitter module (based on a modified FrSky DJT) and a PPM-to-SBUS onboard receiver module (based on a modified FrSky V8FR-II). Figure 7.11 shows the hardware diagram.

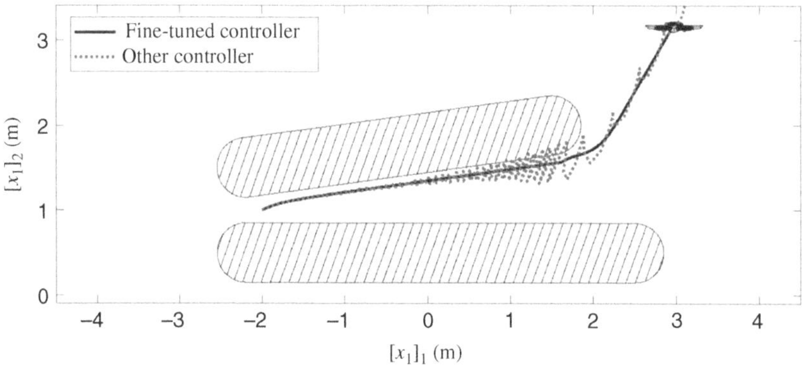

Figure 7.10 Trajectories of the controlled VTOL with different controller parameters.

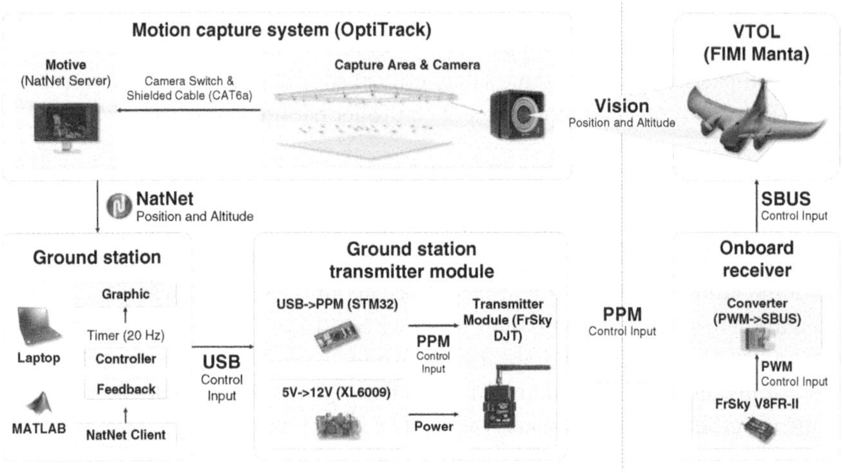

Figure 7.11 The hardware diagram of the experimental system based on VTOL.

The VTOL is already equipped with a velocity controller. We directly use it instead of designing a new one. The identified model of the velocity loop is given as follows:

$$\dot{x}_4 = T_4(T_3(T_2(x_2^* - x_2) - x_3) - x_4) \tag{7.120}$$

where

$$T_2 = \text{diag}(0.2928,\ 2.6711), \tag{7.121a}$$

$$T_3 = \text{diag}(1.2231,\ 29.7555), \tag{7.121b}$$

$$T_4 = \text{diag}(4.1709,\ 113.3872). \tag{7.121c}$$

We note that the identified model is in accordance with the cascade controller proposed in this chapter.

In the experiment, most of the parameters are the same as those used for the numerical simulation, except n_l, $\rho_0(x_1)$ and k_α. We choose $n_l = 21$ and $\rho_0(x_1) \equiv [1; 1]$, and try different values of k_α for the experiment. Following the analysis in Theorem 7.3, the value of k_α should be small enough to satisfy the conditions required by Theorem 7.3.

Figures 7.12–7.14 show the trajectories of the controlled VTOL, the minimal distance, and the velocity-reference input x_2^* corresponding to different values of the parameter k_α. It can be observed that the position trajectory shown by the solid line corresponding to the smaller $k_\alpha = 8.0$ maintains far enough away from the obstacles as expected, while the other two position trajectories corresponding to $k_\alpha = 12.0$ and $k_\alpha = 16.0$ violate the safety constraints.

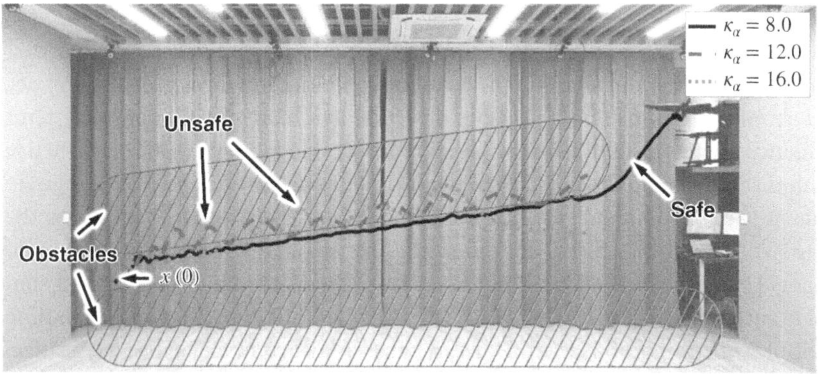

Figure 7.12 Position trajectories of the controlled VTOL (larger values of the parameter k_α of the safety-critical controller cause collisions).

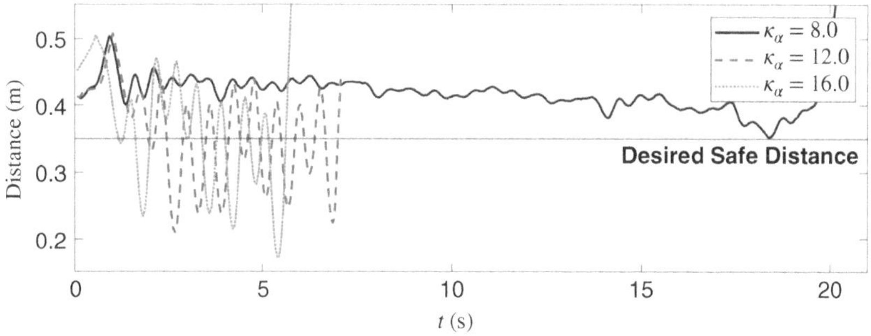

Figure 7.13 The minimum distance between the VTOL and the obstacles corresponding to different values of k_α.

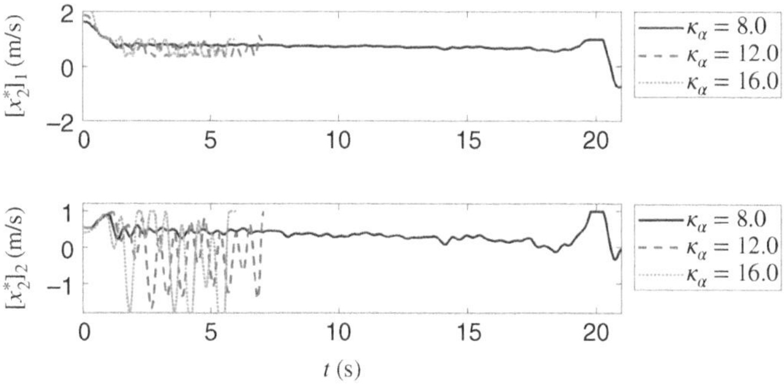

Figure 7.14 The velocity-reference signal x_2^* corresponding to different values of k_α.

7.6 Notes

Many engineering control systems, including robotic manipulators, mobile robots, and aerial vehicles, exhibit a cascaded structure in which lower-order subsystems influence higher-order dynamics. The field has developed systematic constructive nonlinear control methods, particularly backstepping-based controller design, to address stabilization and tracking for such systems. Backstepping leverages the recursive structure of the system to synthesize stabilizing and/or tracking controllers [174, 96, 102, 108, 130, 58, 174, 107, 48, 80]. Extending safety-critical control to such uncertain nonlinear cascaded systems, while simultaneously handling multiple constraints and external disturbances, is a current focus in safety-critical control.

The idea of constructive control is consistent with the cascaded strategies commonly used in control engineering, but it targets general uncertain nonlinear systems. Typical recursive designs include backstepping and forwarding, which synthesize controllers for lower-triangular, upper-triangular, and normal-form nonlinear systems [102, 108, 130, 58, 174, 107, 48, 80, 132, 201]. In recent years, backstepping-based constructive methods have been extensively studied in safety-critical control [199]. Reference [154] proposed a recursive safety-critical controller design for higher-order nonlinear dynamics based on barrier functions. Reference [212] ensures the safety of a strict-feedback system by integrating a barrier-based and backstepping-based design. References [198] and [222] employed exponential control barrier functions and higher-order control barrier functions, respectively, to extend safety-critical controller design to systems with relative degree exceeding one. In parallel, safe backstepping integrates the recursive design with barrier functions by embedding safety barrier functions into the virtual control design [78, 199, 101].

Within this line of research, two issues merit particular attention:

- First, ensuring Lipschitz continuity of both the virtual controller and the physical controller is critical for recursive design. In QP-based safety-critical control (including formulations using control Lyapunov functions and control barrier functions), continuity of the optimizer depends on constraint qualifications, in particular the linear independence of the gradients of the constraints that directly affect the optimal solution [161]. However, this condition may fail in the presence of multiple simultaneously active constraints, particularly when the constraints depend on the real-time state of the plant. Recent sensitivity and continuity analyses for QP-based controllers study these phenomena and their implications for regularity [137, 219, 157, 33]. Guaranteeing Lipschitz continuity under multiple potentially competing constraints remains a core obstacle to broadly deployable safe backstepping.

- Second, constructive handling of cascaded structures under dynamic uncertainties remains challenging. Standard input-to-state stability and small-gain methods provide strong stability analysis tools for cascaded systems [89, 92], but they do not explicitly consider safety. Recent advances in safety verification for interconnected systems [125, 126] provided concise and effective sufficient conditions for safety of cascaded and interconnected systems via barrier-function constructions, yet they do not directly capture the interplay between uncertain dynamics and safety. Moving from verification to constructive synthesis that exploits the cascaded structure requires harmonizing barrier-function-based safety conditions with recursive virtual-control design, while maintaining robustness to cascade-induced uncertainties and ensuring feasibility and regularity at each recursive step.

A

Mathematical Preliminaries

This chapter presents the mathematical concepts used throughout the book and reviews relevant preliminary results.

A.1 Real Vectors and Matrices

The material in this section can be found in standard linear algebra textbooks; see, e.g., [196]. It is also presented in standard texts on control and optimization; see, e.g., [21].

A.1.1 Euclidean Norm of Real Vectors

The Euclidean norm of a real vector $x \in \mathbb{R}^n$ is defined as

$$|x| = (x^T x)^{1/2}. \tag{A.1}$$

Some useful properties of the Euclidean norm are summarized in the following proposition.

Proposition A.1: The Euclidean norm satisfies the following properties:

1. For any $x, y \in \mathbb{R}^n$, if $x^T y = 0$, then

$$|x + y|^2 = |x|^2 + |y|^2; \tag{A.2}$$

2. For any $x, y \in \mathbb{R}^n$,

$$|x^T y| \leq |x||y| \tag{A.3}$$

   where equality holds if and only if x and y are linearly dependent, or at least one of the vectors is the zero vector.

A.1.2 Induced 2-Norm of Real Matrices

The induced 2-norm of a matrix $A \in \mathbb{R}^{m\times n}$ is defined by

$$|A| = \sup_{x\neq 0} \frac{|Ax|}{|x|} = \max_{|x|=1} |Ax|. \tag{A.4}$$

From this definition, it follows that

$$|Ax| \leq |A||x|, \tag{A.5}$$

for all $A \in \mathbb{R}^{m\times n}$ and $x \in \mathbb{R}^n$. The induced 2-norm is also known as the spectral norm or operator norm, intuitively representing the maximum factor by which A can stretch the magnitude of a vector x.

A.1.3 Square Real Matrices and Eigenvalues

Definition A.1: A matrix $A \in \mathbb{R}^{n\times n}$ is said to be singular if its determinant is zero; otherwise, it is termed nonsingular or invertible.

Proposition A.2: For $A \in \mathbb{R}^{n\times n}$, the following statements are equivalent:

1. A is nonsingular;
2. A^T is nonsingular;
3. $Ax \neq 0$ for any nonzero $x \in \mathbb{R}^n$;
4. For any $y \in \mathbb{R}^n$, there exists a unique $x \in \mathbb{R}^n$ such that $Ax = y$;
5. There exists a unique $n \times n$ real matrix, denoted A^{-1}, such that $AA^{-1} = I_n = A^{-1}A$;
6. The columns of A are linearly independent;
7. The rows of A are linearly independent.

For nonsingular matrices $A, B \in \mathbb{R}^{n\times n}$, it holds that $(AB)^{-1} = B^{-1}A^{-1}$.

The characteristic polynomial ϕ of $A \in \mathbb{R}^{n\times n}$ is defined by $\phi(\lambda) = \det(\lambda I_n - A)$. The n (possibly repeated and possibly complex) roots of ϕ are called the eigenvalues of A. A vector x (possibly with complex entries) that satisfies $Ax = \lambda x$, where λ is an eigenvalue, is called an eigenvector of A associated with λ.

Proposition A.3: The following facts hold:

1. A complex number λ is an eigenvalue of $A \in \mathbb{R}^{n\times n}$ if and only if there exists a nonzero eigenvector associated with λ;
2. $A \in \mathbb{R}^{n\times n}$ is singular if and only if it has a zero eigenvalue;
3. The eigenvalues of $A \in \mathbb{R}^{n\times n}$ vary continuously with the entries of A;
4. The eigenvalues of a triangular matrix are exactly its diagonal entries;
5. The eigenvalues of $A \in \mathbb{R}^{n\times n}$ and A^T coincide;

6. For any nonsingular $M \in \mathbb{R}^{n\times n}$, the eigenvalues of $A \in \mathbb{R}^{n\times n}$ and $M^{-1}AM$ are identical.

The spectral radius of $A \in \mathbb{R}^{n\times n}$, denoted $\rho(A)$, is defined as the largest one of the absolute values of its eigenvalues. The function $\rho(A)$ varies continuously with A.

Proposition A.4: For $A \in \mathbb{R}^{n\times n}$, $\lim_{k\to\infty} A^k = 0$ if and only if $\rho(A) < 1$.

It is also useful to observe that

$$|A| = \lambda_{\max}^{1/2}(A^T A). \tag{A.6}$$

Proposition A.5: The eigenvalues of any symmetric matrix $A \in \mathbb{R}^{n\times n}$ are real.

Proposition A.6: Let $\lambda_1 \leq \cdots \leq \lambda_n$ be the (real) eigenvalues of the symmetric matrix $A \in \mathbb{R}^{n\times n}$. Then,

1. $|A| = \rho(A) = \max\{|\lambda_1|, |\lambda_n|\}$;
2. For all $x \in \mathbb{R}^n$, $\lambda_1|x|^2 \leq x^T Ax \leq \lambda_n|x|^2$.

Proposition A.7: For $A \in \mathbb{R}^{n\times n}$, the following properties hold:

1. If A is symmetric, then $|A^k| = |A|^k$ for any positive integer k;
2. $|A|^2 = |A^T A| = |AA^T|$;
3. If A is symmetric and nonsingular, then $|A^{-1}|$ equals the reciprocal of the smallest absolute value among the eigenvalues of A.

Definition A.2: A symmetric matrix $A \in \mathbb{R}^{n\times n}$ is said to be positive definite if $x^T Ax > 0$ for all nonzero $x \in \mathbb{R}^n$. It is said to be positive semidefinite (or nonnegative definite) if $x^T Ax \geq 0$ for all $x \in \mathbb{R}^n$.

For any $A \in \mathbb{R}^{m\times n}$, $A^T A$ is symmetric and positive semidefinite. $A^T A$ is positive definite if and only if A has rank n. In particular, when $m = n$, $A^T A$ is positive definite if and only if A is nonsingular. It is also noteworthy that a square symmetric matrix is positive definite (respectively, positive semidefinite) if and only if all of its eigenvalues are positive (respectively, nonnegative). The inverse of a symmetric positive definite matrix is itself symmetric and positive definite.

A.2 Basis and Positive Basis

The concepts and results related to bases can be found in standard linear algebra texts; see, e.g., [196], while material on positive bases is based on [47].

Definition A.3: A subset $\mathcal{S}$ of $\mathbb{R}^n$ is called a subspace of $\mathbb{R}^n$ if $a_1x_1 + a_2x_2 \in \mathcal{S}$ for any $x_1, x_2 \in \mathcal{S}$ and any $a_1, a_2 \in \mathbb{R}$.

The span of a finite set $\{x_1, \dots, x_m\}$ in $\mathbb{R}^n$ is the subspace consisting of all vectors x expressible as $x = \sum_{k=1}^{m} a_k x_k$ for some real scalars a_k. By definition, any set that contains a subset which spans $\mathbb{R}^n$ also spans $\mathbb{R}^n$.

Definition A.4: Vectors $x_1, \dots, x_m \in \mathbb{R}^n$ are said to be linearly independent if there do not exist scalars $a_1, \dots, a_m$, not all zero, such that $\sum_{k=1}^{m} a_k x_k = 0$.

Definition A.5: Given a subspace $\mathcal{S} \subseteq \mathbb{R}^n$ containing at least one nonzero vector, a basis of $\mathcal{S}$ is a set of linearly independent vectors whose span is $\mathcal{S}$.

Every basis of a subspace $\mathcal{S}$ of $\mathbb{R}^n$ contains the same number of vectors, known as the dimension of $\mathcal{S}$. By convention, the subspace $\{0\}$ has dimension zero. Importantly, every subspace of nonzero dimension admits an orthogonal basis, that is, a basis consisting of mutually orthogonal vectors.

Definition A.6: A positive combination of vectors $\{x_i \in \mathbb{R}^n : i = 1, \dots, m\}$ is a linear combination $a_1x_1 + \cdots + a_mx_m$ with $a_i \geq 0$ for $i = 1, \dots, m$; it is called strictly positive if $a_i > 0$ for all i.

Definition A.7: A set of vectors $\{x_1, \dots, x_m\}$ is said to be positively dependent if some x_i is a positive combination of the others; otherwise, the set is said to be positively independent.

A set $\{x_i \in \mathbb{R}^n : i = 1, \dots, m\}$ is said to positively span the set (i.e., the convex cone) $\{a_1x_1 + \cdots + a_mx_m : a_i \geq 0 \text{ for } i = 1, \dots, m\}$, which may not be a subspace of $\mathbb{R}^n$. A positive basis for a subspace $\mathcal{S} \subseteq \mathbb{R}^n$ is a positively independent set of vectors that positively spans $\mathcal{S}$.

Proposition A.8: A vector x is a positive combination of $\{x_1, \dots, x_m\}$ if and only if, for every z with $z^T x > 0$, there exists $i = 1, \dots, m$ such that $z^T x_i > 0$.

Proposition A.9: Any subset of a positively independent set of vectors is positively independent.

Proposition A.10: Suppose any n of the nonzero vectors $x_1, \dots, x_m \in \mathbb{R}^n$ with $m \geq n$ are linearly independent. For any $x_0 \in \mathbb{R}^n$ and any $\epsilon > 0$, there exists $x_{m+1} \in \mathbb{R}^n$ with $|x_{m+1} - x_0| \leq \epsilon$ such that any n vectors among $x_1, \dots, x_{m+1}$ are linearly independent.

Proof. Denote $p = m!/(n!(n-m)!)$. For $i = 1, \dots, p$, define $M_i \in \mathbb{R}^{n\times n}$ with columns selected from $x_1, \dots, x_m$, $\bar{M}_i = M_i^{-1}$, and

$$a_i^* = [a_{i1}^*, \dots, a_{in}^*]^T = \bar{M}_i x^*. \tag{A.7}$$

The existence of M_i^{-1} is guaranteed by the condition that any n of the vectors $x_1, \dots, x_m$ are linearly independent. Denote $\bar{M}_{ij}$ as the j-th row of $\bar{M}_i$.

We find x_{m+1} through a "perturbation" approach. Suppose that

$$a_{ij}^* = \bar{M}_{ij} x^* = 0. \tag{A.8}$$

Then, one can always find an arbitrarily small $\delta_0 \in \mathbb{R}^n$ such that all the nonzero elements of $a_1^*, \dots, a_p^*$ keep nonzero, and

$$a_{ij}^* = \bar{M}_{ij}(x^* + \delta_0) \neq 0. \tag{A.9}$$

By addressing the nonzero elements of $a_1^*, \dots, a_p^*$ one-by-one, we can get $a_1, \dots, a_p$ with all the elements nonzero such that

$$a_i = \bar{M}_i(x^* + \delta) \tag{A.10}$$

where δ can be chosen arbitrarily small.

Denote $x_{m+1} = x^* + \delta$. Based on the treatment above, for any n of the vectors $x_1, \dots, x_m$, say $x_{k_1}, \dots, x_{k_n}$, there exist nonzero constants $\hat{a}_{k_1}, \dots, \hat{a}_{k_n}$ such that

$$x_{m+1} = \sum_{i=1}^{n} \hat{a}_{k_i} x_{k_i}, \tag{A.11}$$

and thus any n of the vectors $x_{k_1}, \dots, x_{k_n}, x_{m+1}$ are linearly independent. This ends the proof of Proposition A.10. □

Proposition A.11: Any set of vectors containing a subset which positively spans $\mathbb{R}^n$ also positively spans $\mathbb{R}^n$.

Proposition A.12: A set $\{x_1, \dots, x_m\} \subset \mathbb{R}^n$ positively spans $\mathbb{R}^n$ if and only if for every nonzero $x \in \mathbb{R}^n$, there exists at least one $i = 1, \dots, m$ such that $x^T x_i > 0$.

Proposition A.13: There exists a set $\{x_1, \dots, x_m\} \subset \mathbb{R}^n$ with $m \geq n+1$, such that any n elements are linearly independent and the set positively spans $\mathbb{R}^n$.

Proof. Proposition A.13 can be established by constructing vectors that positively span $\mathbb{R}^n$ as in [47, Theorem 3.8], followed by a slight perturbation (cf. Proposition A.10) to ensure linear independence. □

The following proposition follows from Propositions A.10 and A.13.

Proposition A.14: Given any $0 < c_A < 1$, there exists a set $\{x_1, \dots, x_m\} \subset \mathbb{R}^n$ with $m > n$ such that

1. Each vector x_i ($i = 1, \dots, m$) is a unit vector, i.e., $|x_i| = 1$;
2. Any n vectors in $\{x_1, \dots, x_m\}$ are linearly independent;
3. For any unit vector $x_0 \in \mathbb{R}^n$, there exists a subset $\{x_i : x_i^T x_0 \geq c_A, i = 1, \dots, m\}$, of cardinality at least n, such that x_0 is a positive combination of its elements.

Proof. We first show the existence of a set of vectors satisfying conditions 1 and 2.

For any positive constant o_0, we find unit vectors $x_1', \dots, x_m'$ to positively span $\mathbb{R}^n$ and at the same time satisfy the following "density" condition: for any unit vector $x_0 \in \mathbb{R}^n$, $\min_{i=1,\dots,m} |x_i' - x_0| \leq o_0$. Since $x_1', \dots, x_m'$ positively span $\mathbb{R}^n$, there are at least n linearly independent vectors, say $x_1, \dots, x_n$. For convenience of notations, denote $x_i = x_i'$ for $i = 1, \dots, n$. Then, given any positive constant o_1, by using Proposition A.10, we modify $x_{n+1}', \dots, x_m'$ one-by-one to get new unit vectors, denoted by $x_{n+1}, \dots, x_m$, such that any n of the vectors are linearly independent and $\max_{i=n+1,\dots,m} |x_i - x_i'| \leq o_1$. It is a direct consequence that $\min_{i=1,\dots,m} |x_i - x_0| \leq o_0 + o_1$ for any unit vector $x_0 \in \mathbb{R}^n$. This implies that $\{x_1, \dots, x_m\}$ satisfies conditions 1 and 2.

Then, we show that the set $\{x_1, \dots, x_m\}$ satisfies the cardinality condition in condition 3 if there exists a positive constant $o_2 \in (0, 1)$ depending on c_A such that for any unit vector x_0, there are at least n vectors from $x_1, \dots, x_m$, say $x_{k_1}, \dots, x_{k_n}$, such that

$$|x_{k_i} - x_0| \leq o_2 \tag{A.12}$$

for $i = 1, \dots, n$. This is achievable by choosing o_0 and o_1 small enough.

Finally, we prove that the positive combination conditions in condition 3 can be satisfied. For any unit vector x_0 and any unit vector z satisfying $z^T x_0 > 0$, we define an auxiliary unit vector

$$v_a = k_{o_2} x_0 + o_2 z \tag{A.13}$$

with

$$k_{o_2} = \sqrt{1 - o_2^2 + (o_2 z^T x_0)^2} - o_2 z^T x_0. \tag{A.14}$$

By direct calculation, we have

$$
\begin{aligned}
z^T v_a &= k_{o_2} z^T x_0 + o_2 \\
&= \sqrt{1 - o_2^2 + (o_2 z^T x_0)^2} z^T x_0 - o_2 (z^T x_0)^2 + o_2 \\
&> \sqrt{(o_2 z^T x_0)^2} z^T x_0 - o_2 (z^T x_0)^2 + o_2 \\
&> o_2.
\end{aligned} \tag{A.15}
$$

We select $x_{l_1}, \dots, x_{l_r}$ in $\{x_1, \dots, x_m\}$ satisfying

$$
|x_{l_i} - x_0| \leq o_3, \quad \forall i = 1, \dots, r, \tag{A.16}
$$

where

$$
o_3 = o_2 + \sqrt{2(1 - k_{o_2} - o_2 z^T x_0)}. \tag{A.17}
$$

Then, we have $|v_a - x_0| = o_3 - o_2$. This, together with (A.12), implies that there exists $x_{l_*} \in \{x_{l_1}, \dots, x_{l_r}\}$ such that

$$
|x_{l_*} - v_a| \leq o_2. \tag{A.18}
$$

It can be verified that

$$
\begin{aligned}
z^T x_{l_*} &= z^T (v_a + x_{l_*} - v_a) \\
&> o_2 + z^T (x_{l_*} - v_a) \\
&\geq o_2 - |x_{l_*} - v_a| \\
&\geq o_2 - o_2 \\
&\geq 0,
\end{aligned} \tag{A.19}
$$

where we have used inequality (A.15) for the first inequality, and used Cauchy–Schwarz inequality for the second inequality.

Using Proposition A.8, inequality (A.19) implies that x_0 can be represented by a positive combination of $x_{l_1}, \dots, x_{l_r}$. Thus, the satisfaction of the third condition is proved. □

A.3 Sets and Convexity

Basic concepts of sets and convexity can be found in standard analysis texts; see, e.g., [171]. Material related to nonsmooth analysis can be found in [16, 37].

Definition A.8: A set $\mathcal{S} \subseteq \mathbb{R}^n$ is said to be closed if it contains all of its limit points.

Definition A.9: A set $\mathcal{S} \subseteq \mathbb{R}^n$ is said to be open if its complement $\{x : x \notin \mathcal{S}\}$ is closed.

Definition A.10: A set $\mathcal{S} \subseteq \mathbb{R}^n$ is bounded if there exists $c > 0$ such that $|x| < c$ for all $x \in \mathcal{S}$.

Definition A.11: A set $\mathcal{S} \subseteq \mathbb{R}^n$ is compact if every sequence of elements in $\mathcal{S}$ has a subsequence converging to an element of $\mathcal{S}$.

A neighborhood of a vector x is an open set containing x.

Definition A.12: A vector x is said to be an interior point of $\mathcal{S}$ if there exists a neighborhood of x that is contained within $\mathcal{S}$.

Conversely, a vector $x \in \mathbb{R}^n$ that belongs to $\mathcal{S}$ but is not an interior point is called a boundary point of $\mathcal{S}$.

Proposition A.15: The following facts on sets hold:

1. The union of a finite number of closed sets is closed;
2. The intersection of closed sets is closed;
3. The union of open sets is open;
4. The intersection of a finite number of open sets is open;
5. A set is open if and only if all of its elements are interior points;
6. A subset of $\mathbb{R}^n$ is compact if and only if it is closed and bounded.

Given a closed set $\mathcal{S} \subseteq \mathbb{R}^n$, the tangent cone to $\mathcal{S}$ at $x \in \mathbb{R}^n$ is defined as

$$\mathcal{T}_{\mathcal{S}}(x) = \left\{ z \in \mathbb{R}^n : \liminf_{\tau \downarrow 0} \frac{\text{dist}(x + \tau z, \mathcal{S})}{\tau} = 0 \right\}. \tag{A.20}$$

Consider a closed set $\mathcal{S} \subseteq \mathbb{R}^n$ defined by a finite number of inequalities:

$$\mathcal{S} = \{x : g_k(x) \leq 0, k = 1, \dots, m\} \tag{A.21}$$

where $g_k : \mathcal{X} \to \mathbb{R}$ for $k = 1, \dots, m$ are continuously differentiable functions with $\mathcal{X}$ containing $\mathcal{S}$. The set is called a practical set if

1. For each $x \in \mathcal{S}$, there exists a $z \in \mathbb{R}^n$ such that

$$g_k(x) + \nabla g_k(x) z < 0 \tag{A.22}$$

   for all $k = 1, \dots, m$;
2. There exists a Lipschitz continuous vector field $\phi(x)$ such that for all $x \in \partial\mathcal{S}$,

$$\nabla g_k(x)\phi(x) < 0, \quad k = 1, \dots, m. \tag{A.23}$$

For the practical set $\mathcal{S}$ defined above, the tangent cone at $x \in \mathcal{S}$ is given by

$$\mathcal{T}_{\mathcal{S}}(x) = \{z : \nabla g_k(x)z \leq 0,\ i \in Act(x)\}, \tag{A.24}$$

where

$$Act(x) = \{k = 1, \ldots, m : g_k(x) = 0\}. \tag{A.25}$$

Definition A.13: A set $\mathcal{S} \subseteq \mathbb{R}^n$ is said to be convex if

$$\lambda x_1 + (1 - \lambda)x_2 \in \mathcal{S} \tag{A.26}$$

for any $0 < \lambda < 1$ and any $x_1, x_2 \in \mathcal{S}$.

Here gives the projection theorem.

Proposition A.16: The following facts hold for any closed, convex set $\mathcal{S} \subseteq \mathbb{R}^n$:

- For any $x \in \mathbb{R}^n$, there exists a unique $x^* \in \mathcal{S}$ (called the projection of x on $\mathcal{S}$) such that

$$x^* = \operatorname*{argmin}_{x^* \in \mathcal{S}} |x^* - x|^2; \tag{A.27}$$

- For any $x \in \mathbb{R}^n$, $x^* \in \mathcal{S}$ is the projection of x on $\mathcal{S}$ if and only if

$$(x - x^*)^T (x' - x^*) \leq 0 \quad \forall x' \in \mathcal{S}; \tag{A.28}$$

- The function $f : \mathbb{R}^n \to \mathcal{S}$ representing the mapping from $x \in \mathbb{R}^n$ to its projection on $\mathcal{S}$ is continuous and nonexpansive, i.e.,

$$|f(x_1) - f(x_2)| \leq |x_1 - x_2| \quad \forall x_1, x_2 \in \mathbb{R}^n. \tag{A.29}$$

The convex hull of set $\mathcal{S} \subseteq \mathbb{R}^n$, denoted by conv($\mathcal{S}$), is intersection of all convex sets that contain all the elements of $\mathcal{S}$. Intuitively, conv($\mathcal{S}$) is the "smallest" convex set that contains $\mathcal{S}$.

A.4 Continuity, Differentiability, and Convexity of Functions

This section briefly reviews the basic properties of continuity, differentiability, and convexity of functions, which are commonly used in the study of safety-critical control for nonlinear systems. The material presented here is based on standard analysis texts; see, e.g., [171].

Definition A.14: Consider a function $f : \mathcal{X} \to \mathcal{Y}$, with $\mathcal{X} \subseteq \mathbb{R}^n$ and $\mathcal{Y} \subseteq \mathbb{R}^m$. Given $x \in \mathcal{X}$, if for every sequence $\{x_k\}$ in $\mathcal{X}$ and converging to x, the sequence

$f(x_k)$ converges to $f(x)$, then the function f is said to be continuous at x. If f is continuous at every point in $\mathcal{X}$, it is said to be continuous on $\mathcal{X}$.

A.-L. Cauchy defined continuity using the "ϵ-δ" language: if for every $\epsilon > 0$, there exists a $\delta > 0$ such that for any $x' \in \mathcal{X}$ satisfying $|x' - x| \leq \delta$, it holds that $|f(x') - f(x)| \leq \epsilon$, then the function f is continuous at x.

Definition A.15: Consider a function $f : \mathcal{X} \to \mathcal{Y}$, with $\mathcal{X} \subseteq \mathbb{R}^n$ and $\mathcal{Y} \subseteq \mathbb{R}^m$. If for every $\epsilon > 0$, there exists a $\delta > 0$ such that for any $x, x' \in \mathcal{X}$ satisfying $|x - x'| \leq \delta$, it holds that $|f(x') - f(x)| \leq \epsilon$, then the function f is uniformly continuous on $\mathcal{X}$.

Clearly, uniform continuity implies continuity, but the converse is not necessarily true. For example, the function $f(x) = x^2$ is continuous but not uniformly continuous.

Given two (uniformly) continuous functions f_1 and f_2 defined on the same domain, and any scalar constants a_1 and a_2, the function $a_1 f_1 + a_2 f_2$ is still (uniformly) continuous. This means that the linear combination of (uniformly) continuous functions remains (uniformly) continuous. Additionally, the composition of (uniformly) continuous functions defined on appropriate domains is also (uniformly) continuous.

Definition A.16: Consider a function $f : \mathcal{X} \to \mathcal{Y}$, with $\mathcal{X} \subseteq \mathbb{R}$ and $\mathcal{Y} \subseteq \mathbb{R}^m$. If f is continuous at all points in any bounded interval of $\mathcal{X}$, except at a finite number of points, then it is said to be piecewise continuous on $\mathcal{X}$.

Definition A.17: Consider a function $f : \mathcal{X} \to \mathcal{Y}$, with $\mathcal{X} \subseteq \mathbb{R}^n$ and $\mathcal{Y} \subseteq \mathbb{R}^m$. If there exists a constant $L \geq 0$ such that

$$|f(x_1) - f(x_2)| \leq L|x_1 - x_2| \tag{A.30}$$

holds for any $x_1, x_2 \in \mathcal{X}$, then f is said to be Lipschitz on $\mathcal{X}$. The constant L is called the Lipschitz constant.

Definition A.18: Consider a function $f : \mathcal{X} \to \mathcal{Y}$, with $\mathcal{X} \subseteq \mathbb{R}^n$ being an open-connected set, and $\mathcal{Y} \subseteq \mathbb{R}^m$. If for some $x \in \mathcal{X}$, there exists a neighborhood $\mathcal{X}_0 \subseteq \mathcal{X}$ such that f is Lipschitz on $\mathcal{X}_0$, then f is said to be (locally) Lipschitz at x.

Definition A.19: Consider a function $f : \mathcal{X} \to \mathcal{Y}$, with $\mathcal{X} \subseteq \mathbb{R}^n$ being an open-connected set, and $\mathcal{Y} \subseteq \mathbb{R}^m$. If for every $x \in \mathcal{X}$, there exists a neighborhood $\mathcal{X}_0 \subseteq \mathcal{X}$ such that f is Lipschitz on $\mathcal{X}_0$, then f is said to be locally Lipschitz on $\mathcal{X}$.

Definition A.20: Consider a function $f : \mathcal{X} \to \mathcal{Y}$, with $\mathcal{X} \subseteq \mathbb{R}^n$ being an open set, and $\mathcal{Y} \subseteq \mathbb{R}^m$. For $x \in \mathcal{X}$, if there exists an $A \in \mathbb{R}^{n\times m}$ such that

$$\lim_{h\to 0} \frac{|f(x+h) - f(x) - Ah|}{|h|} = 0, \tag{A.31}$$

then f is said to be differentiable at x, and A is called the derivative of f at x, denoted by $f'(x) = A$. If $f : \mathcal{X} \to \mathcal{Y}$ is differentiable at every $x \in \mathcal{X}$, then it is said to be differentiable on $\mathcal{X}$.

If a function f is differentiable at x, then its derivative is unique. If in Definition A.20, $\mathcal{X} \subseteq \mathbb{R}$ and $\mathcal{Y} \subseteq \mathbb{R}^m$, then the derivative of f at x is reduced to

$$f'(x) = \lim_{h\to 0} \frac{f(x+h) - f(x)}{h}. \tag{A.32}$$

Moreover, if $\mathcal{X} \subseteq \mathbb{R}^n$ and $\mathcal{Y} \subseteq \mathbb{R}$ in Definition A.20, then the derivative of f at x is also called gradient, denoted by $\nabla f(x)$.

If a function $f : \mathcal{X} \to \mathcal{Y}$ is differentiable on $\mathcal{X}$, then its derivatives corresponding to different $x \in \mathcal{X}$ form the derivative function $f' : \mathcal{X} \to \mathbb{R}^{n\times m}$.

Consider functions $f : \mathcal{X} \to \mathcal{Y}$ and $g : \mathcal{Y} \to \mathcal{Z}$, with $\mathcal{X} \subseteq \mathbb{R}^n$, $\mathcal{Y} \subseteq \mathbb{R}^m$, and $\mathcal{Z} \subseteq \mathbb{R}^k$. Define $F : \mathcal{X} \to \mathcal{Z}$ as follows:

$$F(x) = g(f(x)), \tag{A.33}$$

that is,

$$F = g \circ f, \tag{A.34}$$

If f is differentiable at $x \in \mathcal{X}$ and g is differentiable at $f(x)$, then F is differentiable at x, and

$$F'(x) = g'(f(x))f'(x). \tag{A.35}$$

This is the chain rule for differentiation.

Express the function f and its derivative f' as follows:

$$f(x) = \begin{bmatrix} f_1(x) \\ f_2(x) \\ \vdots \\ f_m(x) \end{bmatrix}, \quad f'(x) = \begin{bmatrix} f'_{11}(x) & \cdots & f'_{1n}(x) \\ f'_{21}(x) & \cdots & f'_{2n}(x) \\ \vdots & \ddots & \vdots \\ f'_{m1}(x) & \cdots & f'_{mn}(x) \end{bmatrix}. \tag{A.36}$$

Then,

$$f'_{ij}(x) = \lim_{h\to 0} \frac{f_i(x + he_j) - f_i(x)}{h}, \tag{A.37}$$

where e_j is the n-dimensional unit vector with the j-th element being 1 and all other elements being zero. At point x, denote

$$f'_{ij}(x) = \frac{\partial f_i(x)}{\partial x_j}, \tag{A.38}$$

where x_j is the j-th component of the vector x. The term $\partial f_i(x)/\partial x_j$ is also known as the partial derivative of the function f_i with respect to its j-th variable.

Definition A.21: If a function $f : \mathcal{X} \to \mathcal{Y}$ is differentiable on $\mathcal{X}$ and its derivative function $f' : \mathcal{X} \to \mathbb{R}^{n\times m}$ is continuous, then f is said to be continuously differentiable on $\mathcal{X}$.

Definition A.22: A continuous function $f : \mathcal{X} \to \mathbb{R}$ with $\mathcal{X} \subseteq \mathbb{R}^n$ being convex is said to be convex if

$$f(\lambda x_1 + (1-\lambda)x_2) \le \lambda f(x_1) + (1-\lambda)f(x_2) \tag{A.39}$$

for any $0 < \lambda < 1$ and any $x_1, x_2 \in \mathcal{X}$; it is said to be strictly convex if the inequality in (A.39) is strict for any $0 < \lambda < 1$ and any $x_1, x_2 \in \mathcal{X}$ satisfying $x_1 \neq x_2$.

Proposition A.17: The following facts hold to verify convex functions:

1. A linear function is convex;
2. Any vector norm is convex;
3. The weighted sum of convex functions, with positive weights, is convex;
4. If $f_i : \mathcal{X} \to \mathbb{R}$ is convex for each $i = 1, \dots, N$ with $\mathcal{X}$ being a convex set, then $f : \mathcal{X} \to \mathbb{R}$ defined by

$$f(x) = \max_{i=1,\dots,N} f_i(x) \tag{A.40}$$

for $x \in \mathcal{X}$, is also convex.

Proposition A.18: For a differentiable function $f : \mathcal{X} \to \mathbb{R}$ with $\mathcal{X} \subseteq \mathbb{R}^n$ being open and convex, the following facts hold:

1. The function f is convex over $\mathcal{X}$ if and only if

$$f(z) \ge f(x) + \nabla f(x)(z - x), \quad \forall x, z \in \mathcal{X}; \tag{A.41}$$

2. The function f is strictly convex over $\mathcal{X}$ if the inequality (A.41) is strict whenever $x \neq z$.

Proposition A.19: Consider $f : \mathcal{X} \to \mathbb{R}$ with $\mathcal{X} \subseteq \mathbb{R}^n$ being open and convex, suppose that f is twice continuously differentiable over $\mathcal{X}$. Then, the following facts hold:

1. If $\nabla^2 f(x)$ is positive semidefinite for $x \in \mathcal{X}$, then f is convex over $\mathcal{X}$;
2. If $\nabla^2 f(x)$ is positive definite for $x \in \mathcal{X}$, then f is strictly convex over $\mathcal{X}$;
3. If $\mathcal{X} = \mathbb{R}^n$ and f is convex, then $\nabla^2 f(x)$ is positive semidefinite for $x \in \mathcal{X}$.

The quadratic function $f(x) = x^T Qx$ with Q being a symmetric real matrix, is convex if and only if Q is positive (semi-)definite. Furthermore, f is strictly convex if and only if Q is positive definite.

A.5 Comparison Functions

Comparison functions provide an intuitive and concise method to describe the dynamic behaviors of nonlinear systems. This section presents the definitions of several classes of comparison functions that are frequently used in the safety-critical control of nonlinear systems. Standard comparison functions widely used to analyze the dynamical behavior of nonlinear systems can be found in, e.g., [71, 98].

Definition A.23: A function $\alpha : \mathbb{R}_+ \to \mathbb{R}_+$ is said to be positive definite, if $\alpha(0) = 0$ and $\alpha(s) > 0$ for $s > 0$.

Definition A.24: A function $\alpha : \mathbb{R}_+ \to \mathbb{R}_+$ is said to be of class $\mathcal{K}$, denoted by $\alpha \in \mathcal{K}$, if it is continuous, strictly increasing, and satisfies $\alpha(0) = 0$.

Definition A.25: A function $\alpha : \mathbb{R}_+ \to \mathbb{R}_+$ is said to be of class $\mathcal{K}_\infty$, denoted by $\alpha \in \mathcal{K}_\infty$, if it is of class $\mathcal{K}$ and $\alpha(s) \to \infty$ as $s \to \infty$.

Definition A.26: A function $\alpha : (-a, b) \to (-c, \infty)$ with constants $a, b, c \in \mathbb{R}_+ \cup \{\infty\}$ is said to be of class $\mathcal{K}^e$, denoted by $\alpha \in \mathcal{K}^e$, if it is continuous, strictly increasing, and satisfies $\alpha(0) = 0$.

Definition A.27: A function $\alpha : \mathbb{R} \to \mathbb{R}$ is said to be of class $\mathcal{K}^e_\infty$, denoted by $\alpha \in \mathcal{K}^e_\infty$, if it is of class $\mathcal{K}^e$ and $\alpha(r) \to \pm\infty$ as $r \to \pm\infty$.

Definition A.28: A function $\mu : (-a, \infty) \to (0, b)$ with constants $a, b \in \mathbb{R}_+ \cup \{\infty\}$ is said to be of class $\mathcal{M}^-\mathcal{C}$, denoted by $\mu \in \mathcal{M}^-\mathcal{C}$, if it is strictly decreasing, strictly convex and continuously differentiable, and satisfies $\lim_{r\to\infty} \mu(r) = 0$ and $\lim_{r\to\infty} \mathrm{d}\mu(r)/\mathrm{d}r = 0$.

Definition A.29: A function $\beta : \mathbb{R}_+ \times \mathbb{R}_+ \to \mathbb{R}_+$ is said to be of class $\mathcal{KL}$, denoted by $\beta \in \mathcal{KL}$, if it is continuous and satisfies the following two conditions:

- For any fixed $t \geq 0$, $\beta(\cdot, t)$ is of class $\mathcal{K}$;
- For any fixed $s > 0$, $\beta(s, t)$ is monotonically decreasing with respect to t and $\lim_{t\to\infty} \beta(s, t) = 0$.

Definition A.30: A function $\beta : \mathbb{R} \times \mathbb{R}_+ \to \mathbb{R}$ is said to be of class $\mathcal{K}^e\mathcal{L}$, denoted by $\beta \in \mathcal{K}^e\mathcal{L}$, if it is continuous and satisfies the following two conditions:

- For any fixed $t \geq 0$, $\beta(\cdot, t)$ is of class $\mathcal{K}^e$;
- For any fixed r, $|\beta(r, t)|$ is monotonically decreasing with respect to t and $\lim_{t\to\infty} |\beta(r, t)| = 0$.

A.6 Nonsmooth Analysis

This section briefly reviews some useful concepts of nonsmooth and set-valued analysis. For detailed discussions of the relevant concepts, see, e.g., [37].

Definition A.31: The generalized directional derivative of a locally Lipschitz function $f : \mathcal{X} \to \mathbb{R}$ at $x \in \mathcal{X}$ ($\mathcal{X} \subseteq \mathbb{R}^n$) with a vector $v \in \mathbb{R}^n$ is defined by

$$f^{\circ}(x, v) = \limsup_{y\to x,\, \lambda\to 0+} \frac{f(y + \lambda v) - f(y)}{\lambda}. \tag{A.42}$$

Definition A.32: The generalized gradient of a locally Lipschitz function $f : \mathcal{X} \to \mathbb{R}$ at $x \in \mathcal{X}$ ($\mathcal{X} \subseteq \mathbb{R}^n$) is defined by

$$\partial f(x) = \{\epsilon \in \mathbb{R}^n : f^{\circ}(x, v) \geq \epsilon^T v, \forall v \in \mathbb{R}^n\}. \tag{A.43}$$

Here gives some useful properties of generalized gradients.

Proposition A.20: If $f : \mathcal{X} \to \mathbb{R}$ is Lipschitz at $x \in \mathcal{X}$, then the function $a \cdot f$ with constant $a \in \mathbb{R}$ is Lipschitz at x, and

$$\partial(a \cdot f)(x) = a \cdot \partial f(x). \tag{A.44}$$

Proposition A.21: If $f_1, f_2 : \mathcal{X} \to \mathbb{R}$ is Lipschitz at $x \in \mathcal{X}$ with $\mathcal{X} \subseteq \mathbb{R}^n$, then the function $a_1 \cdot f_1 + a_2 \cdot f_2$ with constant $a_1, a_2 \in \mathbb{R}$ is Lipschitz at x, and

$$\partial(a_1 \cdot f_1 + a_2 \cdot f_2)(x) \subseteq a_1 \cdot \partial f_1(x) + a_2 \cdot \partial f_2(x), \tag{A.45}$$

where the sum of two sets $A_1, A_2 \subseteq \mathbb{R}^n$ is defined as $A_1 + A_2 = \{a_1 + a_2 : a_1 \in A_1, a_2 \in A_2\}$.

Proposition A.22: If $f_1, f_2 : \mathcal{X} \to \mathbb{R}$ is Lipschitz at $x \in \mathcal{X}$, then the function $f_1 \cdot f_2$ is Lipschitz at x, and

$$\partial(f_1 \cdot f_2)(x) \subseteq f_2(x) \cdot \partial f_1(x) + f_1(x) \cdot \partial f_2(x). \tag{A.46}$$

Proposition A.23: If $h = [h_1, \dots, h_m]^T : \mathbb{R}^n \to \mathbb{R}^m$ is Lipschitz at $x \in \mathbb{R}^n$ and $g : \mathbb{R}^m \to \mathbb{R}$ is Lipschitz at $h(x) \in \mathbb{R}^m$, then $g \circ h$ is Lipschitz at x, and

$$\begin{aligned}\partial(g \circ h(x)) \subseteq \mathrm{conv}\Big\{ \sum_{k=1}^{m} \alpha_k \beta_k : (\alpha_1, \dots, \alpha_m) \in \partial g(h(x)) \\ (\beta_1, \dots, \beta_m) \in \partial h_1(x) \times \dots \times \partial h_m(x) \Big\}.\end{aligned} \tag{A.47}$$

Proposition A.24: For $f_{\max} : \mathbb{R}^n \to \mathbb{R}$ defined by

$$f_{\max}(x) = \max\{f_i(x) : i \in \{1, \dots, m\}\} \tag{A.48}$$

with $f_i : \mathbb{R}^n \to \mathbb{R}$, suppose that each f_i for $i = 1, \dots, m$ is Lipschitz at x. Then, the following statements hold:

- $f_{\max}$ is Lipschitz at x;
- With $I_{\max}(x)$ representing the set of indices i for which $f_i(x) = f_{\max}(x)$,

$$\partial f_{\max}(x) \subseteq \mathrm{conv}\{\partial f_i(x) : i \in I_{\max}(x)\}. \tag{A.49}$$

Definition A.33: Let $f(t)$ be a real-valued function defined over an open interval (a, b). The upper right Dini derivative of $f(t)$ at $t_0 \in (a, b)$ is defined as

$$D^+ f(t_0) = \limsup_{t \to t_0^+} \frac{f(t) - f(t_0)}{t - t_0} \tag{A.50}$$

Proposition A.25: Let $f : \mathcal{X} \to \mathbb{R}^{n_f}$ be a Lipschitz continuous function defined on an interval $\mathcal{X} \subseteq \mathbb{R}$. Then, for any $x \in \mathcal{X}$, the upper-right Dini derivative of f satisfies

$$|D^+ f(x)| \leq \sqrt{n_f} D_L f(x) \leq \sqrt{n_f} L_{\mathcal{X}}(f), \tag{A.51}$$

where $D_L(f)(x)$ and $L_{\mathcal{X}}(f)$ denote the Lipschitz derivative of f at x and the Lipschitz norm of f over $\mathcal{X}$, defined by

$$D_L f(x) = \limsup_{x' \to x} \frac{|f(x') - f(x)|}{|x' - x|}, \tag{A.52}$$

$$L_{\mathcal{X}}(f) = \sup\left\{\frac{|f(x_1) - f(x_2)|}{|x_1 - x_2|} : x_1, x_2 \in \mathcal{X},\ x_1 \neq x_2\right\}. \tag{A.53}$$

Proof. Direct calculation yields

$$\begin{aligned}
|D^+ f(x)| &= \left|\limsup_{x' \to x+} \frac{f(x') - f(x)}{x' - x}\right| \\
&\leq \sqrt{\sum_{i=1}^{n_f} \left|\limsup_{x' \to x+} \frac{[f(x')]_i - [f(x)]_i}{x' - x}\right|^2} \\
&\leq \sqrt{\sum_{i=1}^{n_f} \left(\limsup_{x' \to x+} \frac{|[f(x')]_i - [f(x)]_i|}{|x' - x|}\right)^2} \\
&\leq \sqrt{n_f} \max_{i=1,\ldots,n_f} \limsup_{x' \to x+} \frac{|[f(x')]_i - [f(x)]_i|}{|x' - x|} \\
&\leq \sqrt{n_f} \limsup_{x' \to x+} \frac{|f(x') - f(x)|}{|x' - x|} \\
&= \sqrt{n_f}\, D_L f(x) \leq \sqrt{n_f} L_{\mathcal{X}}(f),
\end{aligned} \tag{A.54}$$

where we have used Definition A.33 to component-wisely define the upper-right Dini derivative of f for the first equality, and used the Lipschitz continuity of f and the definition of $L_{\mathcal{X}}(f)$ in (A.53) for the last equality. □

Proposition A.26: Let $g_1 : \mathbb{R} \to \mathbb{R}^{n_g}$ be continuously differentiable, let $g_2 : \mathbb{R} \to \mathbb{R}^{n_g}$ be Lipschitz continuous, and let $f : \mathbb{R}^{n_g} \to \mathbb{R}$ be continuously differentiable. Define $g(x) = g_1(x) + g_2(x)$. Then, the upper right Dini derivative of $f(g(x))$ is given by

$$D^+ f(g(x)) = \frac{\partial f(g(x))}{\partial g^T(x)} \frac{\partial g_1(x)}{\partial x} + \limsup_{\Delta \to 0+} \frac{\partial f(g(x))}{\partial g^T(x)} \frac{g_2(x + \Delta) - g_2(x)}{\Delta}. \tag{A.55}$$

Proof. For functions $f_1 : \mathbb{R} \to \mathbb{R}$ and $f_2 : \mathbb{R} \to \mathbb{R}$ satisfying

$$\lim_{x \to x_0^+} f_2(x) = c \tag{A.56}$$

for some $c \in \mathbb{R}$, we have that

$$\begin{aligned}\limsup_{x\to x_0^+}(f_1(x)+f_2(x)) &\leq \limsup_{x\to x_0^+} f_1(x) + \limsup_{x\to x_0^+} f_2(x)\\ &= \limsup_{x\to x_0^+} f_1(x) + c, \qquad \text{(A.57a)}\end{aligned}$$

$$\begin{aligned}\limsup_{x\to x_0^+} f_1(x) &= \limsup_{x\to x_0^+}(f_1(x)+f_2(x)-f_2(x))\\ &\leq \limsup_{x\to x_0^+}(f_1(x)+f_2(x)) + \limsup_{x\to x_0^+}(-f_2(x))\\ &= \limsup_{x\to x_0^+}(f_1(x)+f_2(x)) - \liminf_{x\to x_0^+} f_2(x)\\ &= \limsup_{x\to x_0^+}(f_1(x)+f_2(x)) - c, \qquad \text{(A.57b)}\end{aligned}$$

where we have used the subadditivity of lim sup for the first inequality in (A.57a) and the first inequality in (A.57b), and used (A.56) for the last equality in (A.57a) and (A.57b). Combining (A.57a) and (A.57b) yields

$$\limsup_{x\to x_0^+}(f_1(x)+f_2(x)) = \limsup_{x\to x_0^+} f_1(x) + c. \qquad \text{(A.58)}$$

Since $g(x) = g_1(x) + g_2(x)$ for all $x \in \mathbb{R}$, where g_1 is continuously differentiable and g_2 is Lipschitz continuous, we have that $|g(x+\Delta) - g(x)|\Delta$ is bounded for all sufficiently small $\Delta > 0$. Then, direct calculation yields

$$\begin{aligned}D^+ f(g(x)) &= \limsup_{\Delta\to 0^+}\frac{f(g(x+\Delta))-f(g(x))}{\Delta}\\ &= \limsup_{\Delta\to 0^+}\left(\frac{\partial f(g(x))}{\partial g^T(x)}\frac{g_1(x+\Delta)-g_1(x)}{\Delta} + \frac{\partial f(g(x))}{\partial g^T(x)}\frac{g_2(x+\Delta)-g_2(x)}{\Delta}\right.\\ &\quad\left. + \frac{E_{g(x)}(g(x+\Delta)-g(x))|g(x+\Delta)-g(x)|}{\Delta}\right)\\ &= \limsup_{\Delta\to 0^+}\left(\frac{\partial f(g(x))}{\partial g^T(x)}\frac{g_1(x+\Delta)-g_1(x)}{\Delta} + \frac{\partial f(g(x))}{\partial g^T(x)}\frac{g_2(x+\Delta)-g_2(x)}{\Delta}\right)\\ &= \limsup_{\Delta\to 0^+}\frac{\partial f(g(x))}{\partial g^T(x)}\frac{g_2(x+\Delta)-g_2(x)}{\Delta} + \lim_{\Delta\to 0^+}\frac{\partial f(g(x))}{\partial g^T(x)}\frac{g_1(x+\Delta)-g_1(x)}{\Delta}\\ &= \frac{\partial f(g(x))}{\partial g^T(x)}\frac{\partial g_1(x)}{\partial x} + \limsup_{\Delta\to 0^+}\frac{\partial f(g(x))}{\partial g^T(x)}\frac{g_2(x+\Delta)-g_2(x)}{\Delta}.\end{aligned}$$

(A.59)

where we have used the definition of upper right Dini derivative for the first equality, used the Taylor formula with $E_{g(x)}(\cdot)$ such that $\lim_{g(x+\Delta)\to g(x)} E_{g(x)}(g(x+\Delta)-g(x))=0$ [13, Chapter 12.4 Equation (7) and Theorem 12.5] for the second equality, used (A.58) and the fact that the remainder term divided by Δ tends to zero for the third equality, used (A.58) together with the fact that the term involving g_1 admits a finite limit for the fourth equality, and used the continuous differentiability of g_1 at x for the last equality. □

A.7 Set Invariance

This section provides fundamental definitions and key results related to invariant sets in control theory. The concept of invariance is fundamental to safety-critical control of dynamical systems. For detailed discussions on solving control problems using set-invariance principles, see, e.g., [25].

Consider an autonomous system:

$$\dot{x} = f(x) \tag{A.60}$$

where $x \in \mathbb{R}^n$ is the state, and $f : \mathbb{R}^n \to \mathbb{R}^n$ is a locally Lipschitz function.

Definition A.34: A set $\mathcal{S} \subseteq \mathbb{R}^n$ is said to be positively invariant with respect to the system (A.60), if every trajectory of the system with initial condition $x(0) \in \mathcal{S}$ is defined and satisfies $x(t) \in \mathcal{S}$ for all $t \geq 0$.

Nagumo's theorem is of a fundamental importance in the characterization of positively invariant sets for continuous-time systems. Given the local Lipschitz continuity of the system dynamics, here presents the "strict" result of Nagumo's theorem for positive invariance of $\mathcal{S}$.

Proposition A.27: Consider the system (A.60) and assume that for each initial condition $x(0)$ in an open set $\mathcal{D}$ it admits a unique solution defined for all $t \geq 0$. Let $\mathcal{S} \subset \mathcal{D}$ be a closed set. Then, $\mathcal{S}$ is positively invariant for the system if and only if the system dynamics satisfy Nagumo's condition:

$$f(x) \in \mathcal{T}_{\mathcal{S}}(x), \quad \forall x \in \mathcal{S}. \tag{A.61}$$

Note that Nagumo's condition is meaningful only for $x \in \partial\mathcal{S}$, since for any interior point x, $\mathcal{T}_{\mathcal{S}}(x) = \mathbb{R}^n$. Detailed discussions of Nagumo's theorem can be found in [25].

Specifically, consider the case in which a closed set $\mathcal{S}$ is defined in the form of

$$\mathcal{S} = \{x \in \mathcal{D} : h(x) \leq 0\} \tag{A.62}$$

where $h : \mathcal{D} \to \mathbb{R}$ is a continuously differentiable function satisfying

1. For each $x \in \mathcal{S}$, there exists a $z \in \mathbb{R}^n$ such that

$$h(x) + \nabla h(x)z < 0; \tag{A.63}$$

2. There exists a Lipschitz continuous vector field $\phi(x)$ such that for all $x \in \partial\mathcal{S}$,

$$\nabla h(x)\phi(x) < 0. \tag{A.64}$$

In this case, the tangent cone to $\mathcal{S}$ at $x \in \mathcal{S}$ is given by

$$\mathcal{T}_{\mathcal{S}}(x) = \{z : \nabla h(x)z \leq 0\}, \tag{A.65}$$

and the Nagumo's condition is reduced to

$$\nabla h(x)f(x) \leq 0, \quad \forall x \in \partial\mathcal{S}. \tag{A.66}$$

For dynamical systems with control inputs, the notion of control invariance arises naturally. Intuitively, a set $\mathcal{S} \subseteq \mathbb{R}^n$ is said to be control invariant with respect to a plant $\dot{x} = f(x, u)$ if there exists an admissible control law $u = \kappa(x)$ that renders $\mathcal{S}$ forward invariant with respect to the closed-loop system $\dot{x} = f(x, \kappa(x))$. See [24, Chapter 8] for a systematic discussion of the concept and [75] for an application to safety-oriented control scenarios.

B

Quadratic Programming

B.1 Quadratic Optimization Problems

The material discussed in this section is standard and may be found in, e.g., [21].

A quadratic programming (QP) problem takes the following general form:

$$u = \underset{u}{\operatorname{argmin}} \frac{1}{2} u^T P u + q^T u \tag{B.1a}$$

$$\text{s.t.} \quad Au \leq b \tag{B.1b}$$

where $P \in \mathbb{R}^{n \times n}$ is a symmetric positive semidefinite matrix, $A \in \mathbb{R}^{m \times n}$, $q \in \mathbb{R}^n$, $b \in \mathbb{R}^m$, and $u \in \mathbb{R}^n$ is the optimization variable. The objective function

$$\frac{1}{2} u^T P u + q^T u \tag{B.2}$$

is quadratic (and, provided P is positive semidefinite, convex), and the constraints are affine in u. By convention, the feasible set $\{u \in \mathbb{R}^n : Au \leq b\}$ is called the feasible region. The QP problem is said to be feasible if the feasible set is nonempty. Note also that equality constraints are equivalently rewritten as a pair of inequality constraints (i.e., $x = y$ is enforced by $x \geq y$ and $x \leq y$). A constraint is nonredundant if its removal alters the feasible set. At a solution u^* to the QP problem, a constraint is said to be active if equality holds at u^* [26].

If the feasible set is nonempty and P is positive definite, then the QP problem (B.1) admits a unique solution (which may be shown, for example, by setting $v = P^{1/2}u$ and applying the projection theorem). Moreover, if the constraints that directly affect the optimal solution are denoted by

$$\breve{A}u = \breve{b}, \tag{B.3}$$

then the unique solution is given by

$$u = -P^{-1}\left(q - \breve{A}^T(\breve{A}P^{-1}\breve{A}^T)^{-1}\breve{A}P^{-1}q - \breve{A}^T(\breve{A}P^{-1}\breve{A}^T)^{-1}\breve{b}\right). \tag{B.4}$$

When $P = I_n$, the objective function simplifies:

$$\frac{1}{2}u^T u + q^T u = \frac{1}{2}|u + q|^2 - \frac{1}{2}|q|^2, \tag{B.5}$$

and the QP problem (B.1) becomes

$$u = \underset{u}{\operatorname{argmin}} |u + q|^2 \tag{B.6a}$$

$$\text{s.t.} \quad Au \leq b, \tag{B.6b}$$

which frequently arises in safety-critical control as a means to enforce both primary performance and safety constraints.

When the affine constraints are replaced by quadratic constraints, we obtain the so-called quadratically constrained quadratic programming (QCQP) problem:

$$u = \underset{u}{\operatorname{argmin}} \frac{1}{2}u^T P u + q^T u \tag{B.7a}$$

$$\text{s.t.} \quad a_i^T u + u^T P_i u \leq b_i, \qquad i = 1, \dots, m \tag{B.7b}$$

where $a_i \in \mathbb{R}^n$, $P_i \in \mathbb{R}^{n \times n}$, and $b_i \in \mathbb{R}$ for $i = 1, \dots, m$. If all matrices P_i are symmetric and positive definite, and the feasible set is nonempty, the feasible region corresponds to the intersection of ellipsoids.

B.2 Lipschitz Continuity of QP Solutions

For applications such as safety-critical control, one often considers QP problems whose data depend on an exogenous state vector. An investigation of Lipschitz continuity of solutions to optimization problems can be found in [70].

Consider the following QP parameterized by x:

$$u = \underset{u}{\operatorname{argmin}} |u - \rho_0(x)|^2 \tag{B.8a}$$

$$\text{s.t.} \quad A_c(x)u \leq b_c(x) \tag{B.8b}$$

where $u \in \mathbb{R}^{n_u}$ is the optimization variable, $x \in \mathcal{X} \subseteq \mathbb{R}^{n_x}$ is an exogenous state, and $\rho_0 : \mathcal{X} \to \mathbb{R}^{n_u}$, $A_c : \mathcal{X} \to \mathbb{R}^{n_c \times n_u}$, $b_c : \mathcal{X} \to \mathbb{R}^{n_c}$ are given functions. For each $x \in \mathcal{X}$, denote the constraints that directly affect the optimal solution as $\breve{A}_c(x)u = \breve{b}_c(x)$.

We recall below [70, Theorem 3.1], which provides conditions for Lipschitz continuity of the QP solution with respect to x.

Theorem B.1: *Consider the QP problem* (B.8). *Suppose:*

- $\{\rho_0(x) : x \in \mathcal{X}\}$, $\{A_c(x) : x \in \mathcal{X}\}$, *and* $\{b_c(x) : x \in \mathcal{X}\}$ *are convex valued;*
- *For each* $x \in \mathcal{X}$, *the QP has a unique solution, denoted* $\rho_L(x)$*;*

- *There exists* $\overline{A}_c > 0$ *with* $|A_c^T(x)| < \overline{A}_c$ *for all* $x \in \mathcal{X}$;
- *There exists* $\underline{A}_c > 0$ *such that for each* $x \in \mathcal{X}$ *and all* λ, $|\breve{A}_c^T(x)\lambda| \geq \underline{A}_c|\lambda|$.

Then, there exists $L > 0$ *with* $L \leq 1 + 2\underline{A}_c^{-1}(1 + 2\overline{A}_c \max\{\underline{A}_c^{-1}, 1\})$ *such that*

$$\begin{aligned}|\rho_L(x_1) - \rho_L(x_2)| \leq\ & L(|\rho_0(x_1) - \rho_0(x_2)| + |b_c(x_1) - b_c(x_2)|)\\ & + L^2(|A_c(x_1) - A_c(x_2)| + |A_c^T(x_1) - A_c^T(x_2)|)\\ & \times (|\rho_0(x_1)| + |\rho_0(x_2)| + |b_c(x_1)| + |b_c(x_2)|)\end{aligned} \tag{B.9}$$

for all $x_1, x_2 \in \mathcal{X}$.

For QP problems with a single constraint, the solutions admit continuity properties even if the constraint matrix becomes singular at some points.

Theorem B.2: *Consider the QP problem:*

$$u = \text{argmin}|u|^2 \tag{B.10}$$

$$\text{s.t.}\quad a(x)u \leq b(x) \tag{B.11}$$

with $u \in \mathbb{R}^{n_u}$, $x \in \mathcal{X} \subseteq \mathbb{R}^{n_x}$, $a : \mathbb{R}^{n_x} \to \mathbb{R}^{1\times n_u}$, *and* $b : \mathbb{R}^{n_x} \to \mathbb{R}$. *Suppose that*

$$\lim_{x\to x^*} \frac{|b(x)|}{|a(x)|} = 0 \tag{B.12}$$

for any x^* *such that* $a(x^*) = 0$. *Then, the QP problem is feasible for all* x, *and the solution map* ρ *from* x *to* u *given by*

$$u = \begin{cases} a^T(x)\dfrac{b(x)}{|a(x)|^2} & if\ a(x) \neq 0\ and\ b(x) < 0 \\ 0 & otherwise \end{cases} \tag{B.13}$$

is continuous on $\mathbb{R}^{n_x}$.

Proof. Consider the following three cases:

- If $a(x) = 0$, then by (B.12) and continuity of a and b, the solution is $u = 0$;
- If $a(x) \neq 0,\ b(x) \geq 0$, then the solution is also $u = 0$;
- If $a(x) \neq 0,\ b(x) < 0$, then the constraint is active, hence the optimal u is $a^T(x)b(x)/|a(x)|^2$.

For $\mathcal{S} = \{x : a(x) \neq 0,\ b(x) < 0\}$ and $\overline{\mathcal{S}} = \{x : a(x) = 0 \text{ or } b(x) \geq 0\}$, direct analysis shows continuity of ρ in the interior of each region. At points x^* satisfying $a(x^*) = 0$, for $x_n \to x^*$ in $\mathcal{S}$, we have

$$\lim_{n\to\infty} |\rho(x_n) - \rho(x^*)| = \lim_{n\to\infty} \left| \frac{a^T(x_n)}{|a(x_n)|^2} b(x_n) \right| = \lim_{n\to\infty} \left| \frac{b(x_n)}{|a(x_n)|} \right| = 0, \tag{B.14}$$

where the last equality uses (B.12). Hence, ρ is continuous everywhere. □

It is of independent interest that Lipschitz continuous selections may be obtained from certain set-valued maps described by quadratic constraints, by solving a QP.

Consider

$$\mathcal{U}_c(x) = \{u \in \mathbb{R}^{n_u} : A_c(x)u + c_c(x)|u| \leq b_c(x)\} \tag{B.15}$$

where $A_c : \mathcal{X} \to \mathbb{R}^{n_c \times n_u}$, $b_c : \mathcal{X} \to \mathbb{R}^{n_c}$, and $c_c : \mathcal{X} \to \mathbb{R}_+^{n_c}$, with $\mathcal{X} \subseteq \mathbb{R}^{n_x}$.

Proposition B.1: Consider the set-valued map $\mathcal{U}_c$ defined in (B.15). Suppose that A_c, b_c, and c_c are Lipschitz continuous on $\mathcal{X}$ and that

$$|[A_c(x)]_{i,:}| = 1, \qquad i = 1, \dots, n_c \tag{B.16}$$

$$|[c_c(x)]_i| < 1, \qquad i = 1, \dots, n_c \tag{B.17}$$

$$\sum_{i=j,k} \frac{[b_c(x)]_i}{1 + \text{sign}([b_c(x)]_i)[c_c(x)]_i} \geq 0, \qquad j, k = 1, \dots, n_c, \ j \neq k. \tag{B.18}$$

Then, for each $x \in \mathcal{X}$, the QP

$$u = \underset{u}{\text{argmin}} |u|^2 \tag{B.19a}$$

$$\text{s.t.} \quad [A_c(x)]_{i,:}\, u \leq \frac{[b_c(x)]_i}{1 - [c_c(x)]_i}, \qquad i = 1, \dots, n_c \tag{B.19b}$$

admits a unique solution $\rho_s : \mathcal{X} \to \mathbb{R}^{n_u}$, which is locally Lipschitz continuous and satisfies

$$\rho_s(x) \in \mathcal{U}_c(x) \tag{B.20}$$

for all $x \in \mathcal{X}$.

Proof. By the given conditions, the QP problem (B.19) admits a unique solution in two cases:

- If $\min_{j=1,\dots,n_c} [b_c(x)]_j \geq 0$, then $u = 0$ is optimal, and $0 \in \mathcal{U}_c(x)$.
- If $\min_{j=1,\dots,n_c} [b_c(x)]_j < 0$, suppose $\underline{j} = \text{argmin}_{j=1,\dots,n_c} [b_c(x)]_j$. The active constraint is the $\underline{j}$-th, so

$$\rho_s(x) = [A_c(x)]_{\underline{j},:}^T \frac{[b_c(x)]_{\underline{j}}}{1 - [c_c(x)]_{\underline{j}}}. \tag{B.21}$$

Substituting this into the constraints of (B.15) and applying (B.18), we confirm

$$\begin{aligned}
&[A_c(x)]_{k,:}[A_c(x)]_{\underline{j},:}^T \frac{[b_c(x)]_{\underline{j}}}{1-[c_c(x)]_{\underline{j}}} + [c_c(x)]_k \left| [A_c(x)]_{\underline{j},:}^T \frac{[b_c(x)]_{\underline{j}}}{1-[c_c(x)]_{\underline{j}}} \right| \\
&\leq (1+[c_c(x)]_k)\frac{-[b_c(x)]_{\underline{j}}}{1-[c_c(x)]_{\underline{j}}} \\
&= (1+[c_c(x)]_k)\frac{-[b_c(x)]_{\underline{j}}}{1+\text{sign}([b_c(x)]_{\underline{j}})[c_c(x)]_{\underline{j}}} \\
&\leq (1+[c_c(x)]_k)\frac{[b_c(x)]_k}{1+\text{sign}([b_c(x)]_k)[c_c(x)]_k} \\
&= [b_c(x)]_k
\end{aligned} \tag{B.22}$$

for $k = 1, \dots, n_c, k \neq \underline{j}$. Thus, the solution lies in $\mathcal{U}_c(x)$.

Since A_c, b_c, and c_c are Lipschitz, so ρ_s is locally Lipschitz continuous on $\mathcal{X}$. □

Lemma B.1: *Consider a set-valued map $\mathcal{U}_c : \mathcal{X} \rightsquigarrow \mathbb{R}^{n_{x_2}}$ with a selection $\rho_s : \mathcal{X} \to \mathbb{R}^{n_{x_2}}$, i.e., $\rho_s(x_1) \in \mathcal{U}_c(x_1)$ for all $x_1 \in \mathcal{X}$. For any $A_L = [l_1, \dots, l_{n_l}]^T \in \mathbb{R}^{n_l \times n_{x_2}}$ where $\{l_i\}_{i=1}^{n_l}$ positively span $\mathbb{R}^{b_{x_2}}$, there exists a function $b_L : \mathcal{X} \to \mathbb{R}^{n_l}$ such that*

$$\mathcal{U}_L(x_1) := \{x_2^* \in \mathbb{R}^{n_{x_2}} : A_L x_2^* \leq b_L(x_1)\}, \tag{B.23}$$

is nonempty and satisfies

$$\rho_s(x_1) \in \mathcal{U}_L(x_1) \subseteq \mathcal{U}_c(x_1), \qquad \forall x_1 \in \mathcal{X}. \tag{B.24}$$

Moreover, if ρ_s is (locally) Lipschitz, then b_L can be chosen to be (locally) Lipschitz as well.

Proof. Define $b_L(x_1) = A_L \rho_s(x_1)$. Then $\mathcal{U}_L(x_1) = \{\rho_s(x_1)\}$ for each $x_1 \in \mathcal{X}$. Since the rows of A_L positively span $\mathbb{R}^{n_{x_2}}$, if $A_L(\rho_s(x_1) + d) \leq b_L(x_1)$ for some $d \neq 0$, then $A_L d \leq 0$, contradicting the positive spanning property [47, Theorem 3.1]. So, $\rho_s(x_1)$ is uniquely in $\mathcal{U}_L(x_1) \subseteq \mathcal{U}_c(x_1)$. The local Lipschitz continuity of ρ_s implies that of b_L. □

C

Lyapunov Stability, Input-to-state Stability, and the Nonlinear Small-gain Theorem

C.1 Lyapunov Stability Theory

A.M. Lyapunov defined stability based on the continuous dependence of the trajectory amplitudes on initial states. Lyapunov stability theory is widely acknowledged as essential for the analysis and control of nonlinear systems [98].

Consider a nonlinear dynamic system in the following form:

$$\dot{x} = f(x) \tag{C.1}$$

where $x \in \mathbb{R}^n$ represents the state, and $f : \mathbb{R}^n \to \mathbb{R}^n$ is a locally Lipschitz function that describes the system dynamics. The assumption that the function f is locally Lipschitz ensures that the initial-value problem [171] corresponding to (C.1) has a unique solution, or in other words, that the system state trajectory is uniquely defined (at least on a short time interval). If the state trajectory is defined, it indicates that the system model is valid; if the state trajectory is uniquely defined, it further indicates that the system model is repeatable. For a more detailed discussion, see the textbook [98].

A state point x^e is called an equilibrium if it satisfies

$$f(x^e) = 0. \tag{C.2}$$

For a given equilibrium x^e, a new state can be defined through a coordinate transformation:

$$\tilde{x} = x - x^e. \tag{C.3}$$

This transformation converts the original system (C.1) into

$$\dot{\tilde{x}} = f(x) = f(\tilde{x} + x^e) =: \tilde{f}(\tilde{x}), \tag{C.4}$$

i.e.,

$$\dot{\tilde{x}} = \tilde{f}(\tilde{x}). \tag{C.5}$$

Clearly, the system (C.5) is still in the form of (C.1), except that the state x has been replaced with $\tilde{x}$, and the corresponding equilibrium has been shifted to the origin ($\tilde{f}(0) = f(x^e) = 0$).

In other words, if the equilibrium x^e under consideration is not the origin, it can be moved to the origin by defining a new error state. Therefore, it is without loss of generality to consider the origin as an equilibrium, i.e., $x^e = 0$.

The function f representing the dynamics of (C.1) depends only on the state x and does not explicitly depend on time t, nor does it consider the influence of other external inputs. Such systems are commonly referred to as autonomous or time-invariant systems. For these systems, regardless of the initial time, as long as the initial states are the same, the state trajectories will have the same form (merely requiring a translation along the time axis to accommodate different initial times). Therefore, when discussing the stability of autonomous systems, it is reasonable to consider the initial time to be 0.

C.1.1 Stability in the Sense of Lyapunov

Given the initial time $t = 0$ and the initial state $x(0)$, let $x(t)$ denote the state trajectory of system (C.1). Lyapunov defined the stability of a nonlinear system at a specific equilibrium using the continuous dependence of the upper bounds of the state trajectory $x(t)$ on the upper bounds of the initial state $x(0)$. Asymptotic stability (AS) additionally requires the convergence of $x(t)$ to the equilibrium at t goes to infinity. Global asymptotic stability (GAS) extends the region of stability to the entire state space.

Lyapunov initially characterized the continuous dependence in stability using the "ϵ-δ" language [123].

Definition C.1: The system (C.1) is

- stable at the origin, if for any $\epsilon > 0$, there exists a $\delta > 0$ such that

$$|x(0)| < \delta \quad \Rightarrow \quad |x(t)| < \epsilon \quad \forall t \geq 0 \tag{C.6}$$

- AS at the origin, if for any $\epsilon > 0$, there exists a $\delta > 0$ such that (C.6) holds and

$$|x(0)| < \delta \quad \Rightarrow \quad \lim_{t \to \infty} x(t) = 0 \tag{C.7}$$

- GAS at the origin, if the system is stable at the origin and for any initial state $x(0)$, it holds that

$$\lim_{t \to \infty} x(t) = 0 \tag{C.8}$$

Definition C.2: The system (C.1) is

- stable at the origin, if there exist a constant $c > 0$ and $\alpha \in \mathcal{K}$ such that for any initial state $x(0) \in \mathbb{R}^n$ satisfying $|x(0)| \leq c$, it holds that

$$|x(t)| \leq \alpha(|x(0)|) \quad \forall t \geq 0; \tag{C.9}$$

- AS at the origin, if there exist a constant $c > 0$ and $\beta \in \mathcal{KL}$ such that for any initial state $x(0) \in \mathbb{R}^n$ satisfying $|x(0)| \leq c$, it holds that

$$|x(t)| \leq \beta(|x(0)|, t) \quad \forall t \geq 0; \tag{C.10}$$

- GAS at the origin, if property (C.10) holds for any initial state $x(0) \in \mathbb{R}^n$.

C.1.2 Lyapunov Stability Theorems

The state trajectories of nonlinear systems are often difficult to explicitly solve or accurately estimate in advance, and disturbances and uncertainties are inevitable during system operation. The Lyapunov stability theorem employs Lyapunov functions to characterize stability.

Theorem C.1: *Suppose that the origin is an equilibrium of the system* (C.1). *If there exists a continuously differentiable function* $V : \Omega \to \mathbb{R}_+$ *(where* $\Omega \subseteq \mathbb{R}^n$ *is an open neighborhood of the origin) satisfying*

$$V(0) = 0, \tag{C.11}$$

$$V(x) > 0 \quad \forall x \in \Omega \setminus \{0\}, \tag{C.12}$$

$$\nabla V(x) f(x) \leq 0 \quad \forall x \in \Omega, \tag{C.13}$$

then the system (C.1) *is stable at the origin; if the function* V *further satisfies*

$$\nabla V(x) f(x) < 0 \quad \forall x \in \Omega \setminus \{0\} \tag{C.14}$$

then the system (C.1) *is AS at the origin.*

In Theorem C.1, $\nabla V(x) f(x)$ is the derivative of $V(x(t))$ with respect to time t along the state trajectory $x(t)$ of the system (C.1). A function V satisfying conditions (C.11)–(C.13) is called a Lyapunov function. If it further satisfies condition (C.14), it is called a strict Lyapunov function [18]. Clearly, like the concept of stability, the Lyapunov function is also associated with a specific equilibrium. The method of using the Lyapunov stability theorem to check stability is known as the direct method of Lyapunov or the second method.

The Lyapunov stability theorem reformulates stability analysis as the task of identifying or constructing a suitable Lyapunov function. Conversely, the existence of a Lyapunov function is not only sufficient but, according to the Lyapunov converse theorem, also necessary for establishing system stability.

To further ensure GAS on the basis of the Lyapunov function V satisfying the conditions for AS in Theorem C.1, in addition to replacing Ω with $\mathbb{R}^n$, it is also required that the Lyapunov function be radially unbounded, i.e., $|x| \to \infty \Rightarrow V(x) \to \infty$, which ensures that $V(x)$ and $|x|$ are somehow equivalent.

Theorem C.2: *Suppose that the origin is an equilibrium of the system* (C.1). *If there exists a continuously differentiable function* $V : \mathbb{R}^n \to \mathbb{R}_+$ *satisfying*

$$V(0) = 0, \tag{C.15}$$

$$V(x) > 0 \quad \forall x \neq 0, \tag{C.16}$$

$$|x| \to \infty \quad \Rightarrow \quad V(x) \to \infty, \tag{C.17}$$

$$\nabla V(x) f(x) < 0 \quad \forall x \neq 0, \tag{C.18}$$

then the system (C.1) *is GAS at the origin.*

The key to guaranteeing GAS is the inclusion of the radially unbounded condition (C.17) for the Lyapunov function V. If $V(x)$ is radially unbounded with respect to the state x, then the boundedness of $V(x)$ implies the boundedness of x. Moreover, a monotonically decreasing $V(x(t))$ with respect to time t ensures that $x(t)$ converges as $t \to \infty$.

It is important to note that, for a function $V : \mathbb{R}^n \to \mathbb{R}$, the following statements are equivalent:

- V satisfies conditions (C.15)–(C.17);
- V is positive definite and radially unbounded;
- There exist comparison functions $\underline{\alpha}, \overline{\alpha} \in \mathcal{K}_\infty$ such that

$$\underline{\alpha}(|x|) \leq V(x) \leq \overline{\alpha}(|x|), \quad \forall x \in \mathbb{R}^n. \tag{C.19}$$

The relevant definitions of comparison functions are provided in Appendix A. The equivalence between the second and third statements above is established in [98, Lemma 4.3]. Condition (C.19) offers a more intuitive characterization of the relationship between $V(x)$ and $|x|$. Furthermore, if $V(x)$ is defined for all $x \in \mathbb{R}^n$, satisfies $V(0) = 0$, and fulfills the left inequality in (C.19), then the right inequality also holds. Therefore, given the equivalent formulations above, replacing conditions (C.15)–(C.17) with condition (C.19) does not affect the validity of Theorem C.2.

C.2 Input-to-state Stability

In the late 1980s, E.D. Sontag introduced the concept of input-to-state stability (ISS) in [184], unifying two classical notions: input/output stability and Lyapunov stability. This seminal work also established methods for feedback controller redesign to achieve ISS in the presence of actuator errors, along with a sufficiency test via ISS-Lyapunov functions. The necessity of the Lyapunov characterization of ISS was further examined in [189], while the asymptotic gain characterizations of ISS were developed in [190]. Over the past three decades, the ISS framework has been extended to a wide variety of nonlinear systems modeled in different ways. ISS has also inspired numerous related stability notions, including input-to-output stability (IOS) [92, 192, 193], integral-ISS [8, 186], and differential-ISS [9]. For a comprehensive survey and tutorial on ISS, see [188].

C.2.1 Definition of Input-to-state Stability

Consider the general nonlinear system:

$$\dot{x} = f(x, d) \tag{C.20}$$

where $x \in \mathbb{R}^n$ denotes the state, $d \in \mathbb{R}^m$ represents the external input, and $f : \mathbb{R}^n \times \mathbb{R}^m \to \mathbb{R}^n$ is a locally Lipschitz function with $f(0, 0) = 0$. The input d is viewed as a (possibly time-dependent) signal, typically assumed to be piecewise continuous and bounded.

With regard to the existence and uniqueness of solutions, the regularity assumptions on f and d can be further relaxed. Specifically, reformulating the system as $\dot{x}(t) = f(x(t), d(t)) =: \overline{f}(x(t), t)$ and requiring d to be piecewise continuous and bounded, it suffices for f to be locally Lipschitz in x and continuous in d in order to guarantee that $\overline{f}$ is locally Lipschitz in x and piecewise continuous in t, thereby ensuring local existence and uniqueness of solutions. Moreover, the assumption on d can be weakened so that d is merely measurable and locally essentially bounded.[1]

The concept of ISS captures both the influence of initial conditions and external inputs on the system:

- If $d \equiv 0$, then the system (C.20) is GAS at the origin;
- If d is arbitrary (but satisfies the aforementioned piecewise continuity and boundedness condition), all trajectories remain bounded and ultimately converge to a neighborhood of the origin, the size of which is determined by the magnitude of d.

---

1 A measurable function $d : \mathbb{R}_+ \to \mathbb{R}^m$ is essentially bounded if $\text{ess sup}\{|d(t)| : t \geq 0\} < \infty$. If this holds over every finite interval $I \subset \mathbb{R}_+$, then d is called locally essentially bounded.

Definition C.3: System (C.20) is said to be ISS if there exist functions $\beta \in \mathcal{KL}$ and $\gamma \in \mathcal{K}$ such that for any initial state $x(0)$ and any piecewise continuous and bounded input d, the corresponding solution satisfies

$$|x(t)| \leq \max\{\beta(|x(0)|, t),\ \gamma(\|d\|_\infty)\}, \quad \forall\, t \geq 0, \tag{C.21}$$

where $\|d\|_\infty := \sup_{t\geq 0} |d(t)|$.

Intuitively, $\beta(|x(0)|, t)$ quantifies the transient effect due to the initial state, decaying to zero as $t \to \infty$, while $\gamma(\|d\|_\infty)$ quantifies the steady-state effect of the input, ensuring that the state ultimately enters a neighborhood of the origin whose size is determined by the magnitude of the input. Notably, the ISS property generalizes the dynamic response of linear systems. For causal systems, $\|d\|_\infty$ may be replaced by $\|d\|_{[0,t)}$ in (C.21).

For a fixed $\|d\|_\infty$, larger values of γ correspond to a larger steady-state bound on $|x(t)|$, while smaller γ yield tighter bounds. Therefore, γ is often interpreted as an ISS gain, representing the "proportionality" between the input size and the ultimate state bound.

Evidently, if the system (C.20) is ISS, then the unforced system

$$\dot{x} = f(x, 0) \tag{C.22}$$

is GAS at the origin.

The use of the max operator in Definition C.3 simultaneously accounts for the effects of the initial condition and the input. In Sontag's original formulation [184], a sum operator was used instead:

$$|x(t)| \leq \beta'(|x(0)|, t) + \gamma'(\|d\|_\infty), \tag{C.23}$$

where $\beta' \in \mathcal{KL}$ and $\gamma' \in \mathcal{K}$. Note that for any $a, b \geq 0$, $\max\{a, b\} \leq a + b \leq 2 \max\{a, b\}$; hence, property (C.21) is equivalent to (C.23) (possibly after scaling β' and γ').

From (C.23), two key properties immediately follow:

- **GAS in the absence of input:** If $d \equiv 0$, then $|x(t)| \leq \beta'(|x(0)|, t)$ for all $t \geq 0$;
- **Asymptotic gain property:** For any admissible input d,

$$\limsup_{t\to\infty} |x(t)| \leq \gamma'\left(\limsup_{t\to\infty} |d(t)|\right), \tag{C.24}$$

indicating that the asymptotic bound on the state $x(t)$ is determined by the asymptotic bound of the input d, as described by γ'. The function γ' is therefore referred to as the asymptotic gain.

For linear time-invariant systems, the ISS property coincides with classical (internal) stability.

Theorem C.3: *A linear time-invariant system $\dot{x} = Ax + Bd$ is ISS if and only if the matrix A is Hurwitz.*

C.2.2 Lyapunov Characterization of Input-to-state Stability

For the system (C.20), the property of ISS is equivalent to the existence of an appropriate ISS-Lyapunov function.

Theorem C.4: *System (C.20) is ISS if and only if there exists a continuously differentiable function $V : \mathbb{R}^n \to \mathbb{R}_+$ satisfying the following conditions:*

1. *There exist class $\mathcal{K}_\infty$ functions $\underline{\alpha}, \overline{\alpha}$ such that for all $x \in \mathbb{R}^n$,*

$$\underline{\alpha}(|x|) \le V(x) \le \overline{\alpha}(|x|); \tag{C.25}$$

2. *There exist a function $\gamma \in \mathcal{K}$ and a continuous, positive definite function $\alpha : \mathbb{R}_+ \to \mathbb{R}_+$ such that for all $x \in \mathbb{R}^n$ and $d \in \mathbb{R}^m$,*

$$V(x) \ge \gamma(|d|) \Rightarrow \nabla V(x) f(x, d) \le -\alpha(V(x)). \tag{C.26}$$

A function V satisfying these conditions is referred to as an *ISS-Lyapunov function*. When $d \equiv 0$, Theorem C.4 coincides with the classical Lyapunov characterization of global asymptotic stability, in which case the ISS-Lyapunov function becomes an ordinary Lyapunov function for the autonomous system.

Condition (C.26) ensures that $V(x)$ strictly decreases along trajectories whenever $V(x) \ge \gamma(\|d\|_\infty)$, thus guaranteeing that the state $x(t)$ eventually enters and remains in a set determined by the input magnitude $\|d\|_\infty$. For this reason, (C.26) is often termed the *gain margin condition* for ISS-Lyapunov functions, and γ is called the *Lyapunov-based ISS gain*.

Proofs of the sufficiency and necessity statements in Theorem C.4 can be found in [184] and [189], respectively.

From a control design perspective, the ISS property naturally leads to the concept of input-to-state stabilization. Consider the plant

$$\dot{x} = f(x, u, d), \tag{C.27}$$

where x is the system state, u is the control input, and d is an external disturbance. The goal of input-to-state stabilization is to design a feedback controller of the form

$$u = \varphi(x) \tag{C.28}$$

such that the closed-loop system

$$\dot{x} = f(x, \varphi(x), d) \tag{C.29}$$

is ISS with respect to the input d. In this regard, the construction and analysis of ISS-Lyapunov functions are central to both theoretical analysis and controller synthesis.

Example C.1: *Consider the plant*

$$\dot{x} = f(x, d) + g(x, d)u, \tag{C.30}$$

$$x^m = x + w, \tag{C.31}$$

where $x \in \mathbb{R}$ is the state, $u \in \mathbb{R}$ the control input, $d \in \mathbb{R}$ an external disturbance, $w \in \mathbb{R}$ a measurement noise, and x^m is the measured state. The functions $f : \mathbb{R} \times \mathbb{R} \to \mathbb{R}$ and $g : \mathbb{R} \times \mathbb{R} \to \mathbb{R}$ are locally Lipschitz. Assume the existence of $\psi \in \mathcal{K}$ and constant $\underline{g} > 0$ such that for all $x, d \in \mathbb{R}$,

$$|f(x, d)| \leq \psi(|x| + |d|), \tag{C.32}$$

$$g(x, d) \geq \underline{g}. \tag{C.33}$$

Consider the candidate Lyapunov function

$$V(x) = |x|. \tag{C.34}$$

For $x \neq 0$,

$$\begin{aligned} \nabla V(x)(f(x, d) + g(x, d)u) &= \text{sign}(x)(f(x, d) + g(x, d)u) \\ &\leq |f(x, d)| + \text{sign}(x)g(x, d)u \\ &\leq \psi(|x| + |d|) + \text{sign}(x)g(x, d)u. \end{aligned} \tag{C.35}$$

Consider the feedback controller

$$\begin{aligned} u &= -\kappa(x^m) \\ &= -\frac{1}{\underline{g}}\text{sign}(x^m)\left[\psi\left(\frac{1+\delta}{\delta}|x^m| + \gamma^{-1}\left(\frac{1+\delta}{\delta}|x^m|\right)\right) + \sigma\left(\frac{1+\delta}{\delta}|x^m|\right)\right], \end{aligned} \tag{C.36}$$

where $\delta > 0$ is a constant, and $\gamma \in \mathcal{K}_\infty$, and $\sigma : \mathbb{R}_+ \to \mathbb{R}_+$ is continuous and positive definite.

To verify that V is an ISS-Lyapunov function for the closed-loop system, consider the case

$$V(x) \geq \max\{\gamma(|d|), (1 + \delta)|w|\}. \tag{C.37}$$

For $x \neq 0$, $V(x) = |x|$ *implies* $|d| \leq \gamma^{-1}(|x|)$ *and* $|x^m| \geq ||x| - |w|| \geq \frac{\delta}{1+\delta}|x|$. *Thus,*

$$\psi(|x| + |d|) \leq \psi(|x| + \gamma^{-1}(|x|)), \tag{C.38}$$

$$\text{sign}(x)g(x,d)u \leq -\psi(|x| + \gamma^{-1}(|x|)) - \sigma(|x|). \tag{C.39}$$

Substituting (C.38) *and* (C.39) *into* (C.35) *yields*

$$\nabla V(x)(f(x,d) - g(x,d)\kappa(x^m)) \leq -\sigma(V(x)) \tag{C.40}$$

whenever

$$V(x) \geq \max\{\gamma(|d|), \chi(|w|)\} \tag{C.41}$$

with $\chi(s) = (1+\delta)s$ *for* $s \geq 0$.

By Theorem C.4, the closed-loop system given by (C.30)–(C.31) *together with the feedback law* (C.36) *is ISS, with* V *as an ISS-Lyapunov function. The ISS gains with respect to* d *and* w *are* γ *and* χ*, respectively. Notably, through controller design, the gain for* d *can be made arbitrarily small, but the gain for* w *cannot be reduced below the identity function.*

In general, the extension of control Lyapunov function theory to ISS yields necessary and sufficient conditions for input-to-state stabilization of control-affine systems; see [205].

C.3 The Nonlinear Small-gain Theorem

The overall stability of an interconnected system is not generally preserved by the stability properties of its individual subsystems, even in the case of linear systems. The small-gain principle—specifically, the requirement that the loop gain be less than unity—constitutes a foundational tool for the stability analysis and control of interconnected systems. The original formulation of the small-gain theorem focused on the feedback interconnection of two finite-gain stable systems, with the gain property characterized in a linear or affine manner, to establish input-output stability properties for feedback systems (see [50, 173, 232]; for recent developments, see [30, 69]). The pivotal role of the small-gain theorem in the evolution of robust control theory has been well documented (see, e.g., [235]).

Subsequent generalizations have extended the classical small-gain results to nonlinear feedback systems with non-affine gain characteristics, formulated within the input-output framework [74, 129]. Building on Sontag's foundational work on input-to-state stability (ISS) [184, 185], a nonlinear ISS small-gain theorem was introduced in [92]. Various further developments include small-gain results incorporating input-to-state practical stability (ISpS) and input-to-output stability (IOS) [92], as well as a Lyapunov-based reformulation of the ISS small-gain theorem [93]. Extensive extensions of the nonlinear small-gain theorem for diverse classes of nonlinear dynamical systems have been presented in the literature (see, e.g., [45, 46, 64, 73, 82–85, 90, 91, 94, 115–118, 141, 152, 202]). The ISS small-gain theorem has accordingly become a standard element in advanced textbooks on nonlinear systems (see, e.g., [80, 98]). For additional recent developments on ISS small-gain and related results, see [88, 96, 102] and the references therein.

C.3.1 Trajectory-based Nonlinear Small-gain Theorem

Consider the following interconnected system consisting of two subsystems:

$$\dot{x}_1 = f_1(x, d_1), \tag{C.42}$$

$$\dot{x}_2 = f_2(x, d_2), \tag{C.43}$$

where $x_1 \in \mathbb{R}^{n_1}$ and $x_2 \in \mathbb{R}^{n_2}$ are the states of the respective subsystems, $x = [x_1^T, x_2^T]^T$, $d_1 \in \mathbb{R}^{m_1}$ and $d_2 \in \mathbb{R}^{m_2}$ are the external inputs to the subsystems, and $f_1 : \mathbb{R}^{n_1+n_2} \times \mathbb{R}^{m_1} \to \mathbb{R}^{n_1}$ and $f_2 : \mathbb{R}^{n_1+n_2} \times \mathbb{R}^{m_2} \to \mathbb{R}^{n_2}$ are locally Lipschitz functions satisfying $f_1(0,0) = 0$ and $f_2(0,0) = 0$. For notational convenience, define $d = [d_1^T, d_2^T]^T$. The external input d is assumed to be piecewise continuous and bounded as a function of time.

Suppose that each subsystem is ISS. Specifically, for each $i = 1, 2$, there exist functions $\beta_i \in \mathcal{KL}$, $\gamma_{i(3-i)} \in \mathcal{K}$, and $\chi_i \in \mathcal{K}$ such that, for any initial state $x_i(0)$ and any piecewise continuous and bounded inputs x_{3-i} and d_i, the state trajectory of the x_i-subsystem satisfies

$$|x_i(t)| \le \max\{\beta_i(|x_i(0)|, t),\ \gamma_{i(3-i)}(\|x_{3-i}\|_\infty),\ \chi_i(\|d_i\|_\infty)\}, \tag{C.44}$$

for all $t \ge 0$. Here, each $\gamma_{i(3-i)}$ characterizes the gain from x_{3-i} to x_i.

The following theorem states the trajectory-based nonlinear small-gain theorem [92].

Theorem C.5: *Consider the interconnected system* (C.42)–(C.43), *with state x and input d. Assume each x_i-subsystem ($i = 1, 2$) is ISS and satisfies* (C.44). *If*

$$\gamma_{12}(\gamma_{21}(s)) < s \quad \forall s > 0, \tag{C.45}$$

that is,

$$\gamma_{12} \circ \gamma_{21} < \mathrm{Id}, \tag{C.46}$$

then the interconnected system is ISS; that is, there exist $\beta \in \mathcal{KL}$ and $\chi \in \mathcal{K}$ such that, for any initial state $x(0)$ and any piecewise continuous and bounded external input d,

$$|x(t)| \le \max\{\beta(|x(0)|, t),\ \chi(\|d\|_\infty)\} \tag{C.47}$$

for all $t \ge 0$.

Condition (C.46) requires that the composition of the interconnection gain functions is strictly less than the identity map, and is referred to as the nonlinear small-gain condition. If all external inputs are identically zero, i.e., $d_1 \equiv 0$ and $d_2 \equiv 0$, this condition guarantees global asymptotic stability of the interconnected system at the origin.

It is noteworthy that, although in general $\gamma_{12} \circ \gamma_{21} \neq \gamma_{21} \circ \gamma_{12}$, the following equivalence holds:

$$\gamma_{12} \circ \gamma_{21} < \mathrm{Id} \quad \Leftrightarrow \quad \gamma_{21} \circ \gamma_{12} < \mathrm{Id}, \tag{C.48}$$

which implies that the validity of the small-gain condition remains unchanged under interchanging γ_{12} and γ_{21}.

If the gains γ_{12} and γ_{21} are linear, i.e.,

$$\gamma_{12}(s) = k_{12}s, \quad \gamma_{21}(s) = k_{21}s \quad \forall s \ge 0, \tag{C.49}$$

where k_{12} and k_{21} are non-negative constants, then the small-gain condition (C.46) reduces to

$$k_{12} \cdot k_{21} < 1. \tag{C.50}$$

In this case, k_{12} and k_{21} are termed the gain coefficients.

A special case of the interconnected system (C.42)–(C.43) is the cascade system

$$\dot{x}_1 = f_1(x_1, x_2, d_1), \tag{C.51}$$
$$\dot{x}_2 = f_2(x_2, d_2), \tag{C.52}$$

where the variables and functions are defined as previously. Since this system forms a cascade connection and contains no feedback loop, the small-gain condition is automatically satisfied.

Corollary C.1: *Consider the system* (C.51)–(C.52), *with state x and input d. If each subsystem is ISS and possesses the property* (C.44), *and furthermore,* $\gamma_{21} = 0$, *then the interconnected system is ISS.*

C.3.2 Lyapunov-based ISS Small-gain Theorem

This section focuses on interconnected systems whose subsystems possess the ISS property characterized by ISS-Lyapunov functions. The Lyapunov-based nonlinear small-gain theorem [93] not only facilitates the assessment of the overall ISS property of the interconnected system in terms of loop gains, but also provides a systematic methodology for constructing an explicit Lyapunov function for the entire system. Such a Lyapunov function is particularly valuable for quantitatively describing the stability characteristics of the interconnected system and for facilitating controller design.

Assume that each x_i-subsystem ($i = 1, 2$) of the interconnected system (C.42)–(C.43) is ISS and admits a continuously differentiable ISS-Lyapunov function $V_i : \mathbb{R}^{n_i} \to \mathbb{R}_+$ satisfying:

1. There exist $\underline{\alpha}_i, \overline{\alpha}_i \in \mathcal{K}_\infty$ such that

$$\underline{\alpha}_i(|x_i|) \leq V_i(x_i) \leq \overline{\alpha}_i(|x_i|), \tag{C.53}$$

   for all x_i;
2. There exists $\gamma_{i(3-i)}, \chi_i \in \mathcal{K}$ and a continuous, positive definite function $\alpha_i : \mathbb{R}_+ \to \mathbb{R}_+$ such that

$$\begin{aligned} & V_i(x_i) \geq \max\{\gamma_{i(3-i)}(V_{3-i}(x_{3-i})), \chi_i(|d_i|)\} \\ \Rightarrow\ & \nabla V_i(x_i) f_i(x, d_i) \leq -\alpha_i(V_i(x_i)) \end{aligned} \tag{C.54}$$

   for all x and d_i.

For notational convenience, the dynamics of the overall interconnected system can be written as

$$f(x, d) = [f_1^T(x, d_1),\ f_2^T(x, d_2)]^T. \tag{C.55}$$

The Lyapunov formulation of the nonlinear small-gain theorem [93] is given as follows.

Theorem C.6: *Consider the interconnected system* (C.42)–(C.43), *where each subsystem admits an ISS-Lyapunov function* V_i *satisfying* (C.53)–(C.54). *Suppose further that*

$$\gamma_{12} \circ \gamma_{21} < \mathrm{Id}, \tag{C.56}$$

where Id *denotes the identity mapping. Then:*

- *The interconnected system is ISS;*
- *For any* $\sigma \in \mathcal{K}_\infty$ *that is continuously differentiable on* $(0, \infty)$ *and satisfies*

$$\gamma_{12} \circ \sigma < \mathrm{Id}, \qquad \sigma > \gamma_{21}, \tag{C.57}$$

  an ISS-Lyapunov function for the interconnected system can be constructed as

$$V(x) = \max\{\sigma(V_1(x_1)),\ V_2(x_2)\}, \tag{C.58}$$

which satisfies

$$V(x) \geq \max\{\sigma\circ\chi_1(|d_1|),\ \chi_2(|d_2|)\} \ \Rightarrow\ \nabla V(x)f(x,d) \leq -\alpha(V(x)), \tag{C.59}$$

wherever ∇V *is defined, where* $\alpha : \mathbb{R}_+ \to \mathbb{R}_+$ *is a continuous, positive definite function.*

C.3.3 Nonlinear Cyclic-small-gain Theorem for Large-scale Systems

Due to renewed interest in large-scale nonlinear systems, Teel [203] was the first to state an extension of the nonlinear small-gain theorem for networks of discrete-time ISS systems. Shortly thereafter, Dashkovskiy, Rüffer, and Wirth [45, 46] developed a matrix-based small-gain criterion for dynamic networks. In [91] and [94], more general cyclic small-gain theorems were established for networks of IOS systems described by either ordinary differential equations or difference equations. Corresponding Lyapunov-based formulations were provided in [118, 119]. The nonlinear small-gain theorem for large-scale systems has since been extended to various classes of nonlinear systems.

Consider a large-scale system consisting of N subsystems:

$$\dot{x}_i = f_i(x_1, \ldots, x_N, d_i), \quad i = 1, \ldots, N, \tag{C.60}$$

where $x_i \in \mathbb{R}^{n_i}$ is the state of subsystem i, $d_i \in \mathbb{R}^{m_i}$ is the external input to subsystem i, and $f_i : \mathbb{R}^{n_1} \times \cdots \times \mathbb{R}^{n_N} \times \mathbb{R}^{m_i} \to \mathbb{R}^{n_i}$ is a locally Lipschitz function satisfying $f_i(0, \ldots, 0) = 0$. For notational simplicity, let $x = [x_1^T, \ldots, x_N^T]^T$ and $d = [d_1^T, \ldots, d_N^T]^T$ denote the overall state and input, respectively. The external input d is assumed to be piecewise continuous and bounded as a function of time.

Assume that each x_i-subsystem ($i = 1, \ldots, N$) of system (C.60) is ISS. That is, there exist $\beta_i \in \mathcal{KL}$, $\gamma_{ij} \in \mathcal{K}$ (for $j \neq i$), and $\chi_i \in \mathcal{K}$ such that for any initial state $x_i(0)$, any piecewise continuous and bounded inputs x_j (for $j \neq i$) and d_i,

$$|x_i(t)| \leq \max_{j\neq i}\{\beta_i(|x_i(0)|, t),\ \gamma_{ij}(\|x_j\|_\infty),\ \chi_i(\|d_i\|_\infty)\} \tag{C.61}$$

for all $t \geq 0$.

Theorem C.7 presents the cyclic small-gain theorem for large-scale nonlinear systems [91].

Theorem C.7: *Consider the large-scale system* (C.60). *Assume that each* x_i*-subsystem* ($i = 1, \ldots, N$) *is ISS and satisfies* (C.61). *If*

$$\gamma_{i_1 i_2} \circ \gamma_{i_2 i_3} \circ \cdots \circ \gamma_{i_r i_1} < \mathrm{Id} \tag{C.62}$$

for every simple cycle $(i_1, i_2, \dots, i_r, i_1)$ *in the system, then the large-scale system is ISS. Specifically, there exist* $\beta \in \mathcal{KL}$ *and* $\chi \in \mathcal{K}$ *such that, for any initial state* $x(0)$ *and any piecewise continuous and bounded input* d,

$$|x(t)| \le \max\{\beta(|x(0)|, t),\ \chi(\|d\|_\infty)\} \tag{C.63}$$

holds for all $t \ge 0$.

Condition (C.62) requires that the composition of the gains along every simple cycle in the system is less than the identity function. For interconnected systems with two subsystems, this result coincides with Theorem C.5.

Following the Lyapunov formulation of the nonlinear small-gain theorem (Theorem C.6), if the ISS property of each subsystem in (C.60) is described by a Lyapunov function, then the Lyapunov-based cyclic small-gain theorem not only ensures ISS, but also yields an explicit Lyapunov function for the entire large-scale system.

Assume that each x_i-subsystem ($i = 1, \dots, N$) of system (C.60) is ISS and admits a continuously differentiable ISS-Lyapunov function $V_i : \mathbb{R}^{n_i} \to \mathbb{R}_+$ satisfying:

1. There exist $\underline{\alpha}_i, \overline{\alpha}_i \in \mathcal{K}_\infty$ such that

$$\underline{\alpha}_i(|x_i|) \le V_i(x_i) \le \overline{\alpha}_i(|x_i|), \tag{C.64}$$

   for all x_i;
2. There exist $\gamma_{ij} \in \mathcal{K}$ (for $j \ne i$), $\chi_i \in \mathcal{K}$, and a continuous, positive definite function $\alpha_i : \mathbb{R}_+ \to \mathbb{R}_+$ such that

$$V_i(x_i) \ge \max_{j \ne i}\{\gamma_{ij}(V_j(x_j)),\ \chi_i(|d_i|)\} \tag{C.65}$$
$$\Rightarrow \quad \nabla V_i(x_i) f_i(x_1, \dots, x_N, d_i) \le -\alpha_i(V_i(x_i))$$

   for all x and d_i.

For convenience, write the overall system dynamics as

$$f(x, d) = [f_1^T(x, d_1), \dots, f_N^T(x, d_N)]^T. \tag{C.66}$$

Theorem C.8 provides the Lyapunov formulation of the cyclic small-gain theorem [118].

Theorem C.8: *Consider the large-scale system* (C.60), *where each* x_i*-subsystem admits an ISS-Lyapunov function* V_i *satisfying* (C.64)–(C.65). *If*

$$\gamma_{i_1 i_2} \circ \gamma_{i_2 i_3} \circ \cdots \circ \gamma_{i_r i_1} < \mathrm{Id} \tag{C.67}$$

for every simple cycle $(i_1, i_2, \dots, i_r, i_1)$ *within the system, then the following properties hold for the large-scale system:*

- *The system is ISS;*
- *If the interconnection digraph among the subsystems is connected, then, by choosing continuously differentiable $\hat{\gamma}_{ij} \in \mathcal{K}_\infty$ such that replacing γ_{ij} with $\hat{\gamma}_{ij}$ still satisfies* (C.67)*, and defining*

$$\sigma_{i^*}(s) = s, \tag{C.68}$$
$$\sigma_j(s) = \max_{(i^*, i_2, \ldots, i_r, j) \in \mathcal{P}_{i^* j}} \{\hat{\gamma}_{i^* i_2} \circ \hat{\gamma}_{i_2 i_3} \circ \cdots \circ \hat{\gamma}_{i_r j}(s)\},$$

where $\mathcal{P}_{i^* j}$ is the set of all paths from subsystem x_j to x_{i^*}, then

$$V(x) = \max\{\sigma_i(V_i(x_i))\} \tag{C.69}$$

is an ISS-Lyapunov function for the entire system, satisfying

$$V(x) \geq \max_{i=1,\ldots,N} \{\sigma_i \circ \chi_i(|d_i|)\} \quad \Rightarrow \quad \nabla V(x) f(x, d) \leq -\alpha(V(x)) \tag{C.70}$$

wherever ∇V is defined, and $\alpha : \mathbb{R}_+ \to \mathbb{R}_+$ is a continuous positive definite function.

We propose an algorithm that constructs the gain digraph of an interconnected system from specified inter-subsystem gains, allowing the gains to be expressed as symbolic functions. The algorithm then computes the gain compositions along all simple cycles in the digraph and assesses stability by testing the cyclic small-gain condition. A MATLAB implementation is available at https://github.com/EXPSIN/gains_of_interconnected_systems.

References

1 A. Alan, A. J. Taylor, C. R. He, A. D. Ames, and G. Orosz. Control barrier functions and input-to-state safety with application to automated vehicles. *IEEE Transactions on Control Systems Technology*, 31(6): 2744–2759, 2023.

2 J. Alonso-Mora, A. Breitenmoser, M. Rufli, P. Beardsley, and R. Siegwart. Optimal reciprocal collision avoidance for multiple non-holonomic robots. In *Distributed Autonomous Robotic Systems*, pages 203–216. New York, NY, USA: Springer, 2013.

3 A. Ames, S. Coogan, M. Egerstedt, G. Notomista, K. Sreenath, and P. Tabuada. Control barrier functions: theory and applications. In *Proceedings of the 18th European Control Conference*, pages 3420–3431, 2019.

4 A. D. Ames and M. Powell. Towards the unification of locomotion and manipulation through control Lyapunov functions and quadratic programs. In D. Tarraf, editor, *Control of Cyber-physical Systems*, pages 219–240. Springer, 2013.

5 A. D. Ames, J. W. Grizzle, and P. Tabuada. Control barrier function based quadratic programs with application to adaptive cruise control. In *Proceedings of the 53rd IEEE Conference on Decision and Control*, pages 6271–6278, 2014.

6 A. D. Ames, X. Xu, J. W. Grizzle, and P. Tabuada. Control barrier function based quadratic programs for safety critical systems. *IEEE Transactions on Automatic Control*, 62: 3861–3876, 2017.

7 L. An and G. Yang. Collisions-free distributed optimal coordination for multiple Euler-Lagrangian systems. *IEEE Transactions on Automatic Control*, 67(1): 460–467, 2021.

8 D. Angeli, E. D. Sontag, and Y. Wang. A characterization of integral input to state stability. *IEEE Transactions on Automatic Control*, 45: 1082–1097, 2000.

9 D. Angeli, E. D. Sontag, and Y. Wang. Input-to-state stability with respect to inputs and their derivatives. *International Journal of Robust and Nonlinear Control*, 13: 1035–1056, 2003.

10 Z. Angeliki, K. Ioannis, G. Antonios, and D. Ioannis. Safety bounds in human robot interaction: A survey. *Safety Science*, 127: 104667, 2020.

11 A. M. Annaswamy, K. H. Johansson, and G. J. Pappas, (eds.). *Control for Societal-scale Challenges: Road Map 2030*. IEEE Control Systems Society Publication, 2023.

12 A. Annichini, A. Bouajjani, and M. Sighireanu. Trex: A tool for reachability analysis of complex systems. In *Computer Aided Verification: 13th International Conference, CAV 2001 Paris, France, July 18–22, 2001 Proceedings 13*, pages 368–372. Springer, 2001.

13 T. M. Apostol. *Mathematical Analysis*, 2nd edition. Pearson, 1973.

14 R. C. Arkin. *Behavior-Based Robotics*. MIT Press, 1998.

15 Z. Artstein. Stabilization with relaxed controls. *Nonlinear Analysis: Theory, Methods & Applications*, 7: 1163–1173, 1983.

16 J. Aubin and H. Frankowska. *Set-valued Analysis*. Springer Science & Business Media, 2009.

17 S. Axler. *Measure, Integration & Real Analysis*. Springer, 2020.

18 A. Bacciotti and L. Rosier. *Liapunov Functions and Stability in Control Theory*, 2nd edition. Berlin: Springer-Verlag, 2005.

19 A. Bajcsy, S. Bansal, E. Bronstein, V. Tolani, and C. J. Tomlin. An efficient reachability-based framework for provably safe autonomous navigation in unknown environments. In *Proceedings of the 58th Conference on Decision and Control*, pages 1758–1765. IEEE, 2019.

20 T. Balch and R. C. Arkin. Behavior-based formation control for multirobot teams. *IEEE Transactions on Robotics and Automation*, 14(6): 926–939, 1998.

21 D. P. Bertsekas. *Nonlinear Programming*, 2nd edition. Athena Scientific, 1999.

22 A. Bicchi, G. Casalino, and C. Santilli. Planning shortest bounded-curvature paths for a class of nonholonomic vehicles among obstacles. In *Proceedings of 1995 IEEE International Conference on Robotics and Automation*, volume 2, pages 1349–1354. IEEE, 1995.

23 K. G. Binmore. *Mathematical Analysis: A Straightforward Approach*. Cambridge University Press, 1982.

24 G. Bitsoris. *Comparison Methods in Control*. Springer, 2025.

25 F. Blanchini and S. Miani. *Set-Theoretic Methods in Control*. Springer, 2008.

26 S. P. Boyd and L. Vandenberghe. *Convex Optimization*. Cambridge University Press, 2004.

27 J. Breeden and D. Panagou. Compositions of multiple control barrier functions under input constraints. In *Proceedings of the 2023 American Control Conference*, pages 3688–3695. IEEE, 2023.

28 J. Breeden and D. Panagou. Robust control barrier functions under high relative degree and input constraints for satellite trajectories. *Automatica*, 155: 111109, 2023.

29 B. Brogliato, R. Lozano, B. Maschke, and O. Egeland. *Dissipative Systems Analysis and Control: Theory and Applications*, 2nd edition. London: Springer-Verlag, 2007.

30 F. Bullo, J. Cortés, and S. Martinez. *Distributed Control of Robotic Networks: A Mathematical Approach to Motion Coordination Algorithms*. Princeton University Press, 2009.

31 W. Burgard, M. Moors, D. Fox, R. Simmons, and S. Thrun. Collaborative multi-robot exploration. In *Proceedings of the IEEE International Conference on Robotics and Automation*, volume 1, pages 476–481, 2000.

32 T. C. Y. Chan and P. A. Mar. Stability and continuity in robust optimization. *SIAM Journal on Optimization*, 27(2): 817–841, 2017.

33 C. T. Chen. *Linear System Theory and Design*, 3rd edition. New York Oxford: Oxford University Press, 1999.

34 M. Chen, S. L. Herbert, H. Hu, Y. Pu, J. F. Fisac, S. Bansal, S. Han, and C. J. Tomlin. Fastrack: A modular framework for real-time motion planning and guaranteed safe tracking. *IEEE Transactions on Automatic Control*, 66(12): 5861–5876, 2021.

35 H. Choset, K. M. Lynch, S. Hutchinson, G. A. Kantor, W. Burgard, L. E. Kavraki, and S. Thrun. *Principles of Robot Motion: Theory, Algorithms, and Implementations*. MIT Press, 2005.

36 F. H. Clarke. *Optimization and Nonsmooth Analysis*. SIAM, 1990.

37 Ş. Cobzaş, R. Miculescu, and A. Nicolae. *Lipschitz Functions*. Springer, 2019.

38 J. Cortés. Discontinuous dynamical systems. *IEEE Control Systems Magazine*, 28(3): 36–73, 2008.

39 J. Cortes, S. Martinez, T. Karatas, and F. Bullo. Coverage control for mobile sensing networks. In *Proceedings of the IEEE International Conference on Robotics and Automation*, volume 2, pages 1327–1332, 2002.

40 W. Cortez Shaw, X. Tan, and D. V. Dimarogonas. A robust, multiple control barrier function framework for input constrained systems. *IEEE Control Systems Letters*, 6: 1742–1747, 2021.

41 R. K. Cosner, A. W. Singletary, T. G. Taylor, T. G. Molnar, K. L. Bouman, and A. D. Ames. Measurement-robust control barrier functions: Certainty in safety with uncertainty in state. In *Proceedings of 2021 IEEE/RSJ International Conference on Intelligent Robots and Systems*, pages 6286–6291, 2021.

42 H. S. M. Coxeter. *Introduction to Geometry*, 2nd edition. John Wiley & Sons, Inc., 1969.

43 J. J. Craig. *Introduction to Robotics: Mechanics and Control*, 3rd edition. Pearson Education International, 2005.

44 S. Dashkovskiy, B. S. Rüffer, and F. R. Wirth. An ISS small-gain theorem for general networks. *Mathematics of Control, Signals and Systems*, 19: 93–122, 2007.

45 S. Dashkovskiy, B. S. Rüffer, and F. R. Wirth. Small gain theorems for large scale systems and construction of ISS Lyapunov functions. *SIAM Journal on Control and Optimization*, 48: 4089–4118, 2010.

46 C. Davis. Theory of positive linear dependence. *American Journal of Mathematics*, 76: 733–746, 1954.

47 D. M. Dawson, J. Hu, and T. C. Burg. *Nonlinear Control of Electric Machinery*. Marcel Dekker, Inc., 1998.

48 G. Delimpaltadakis, J. Cortés, and W. P. M. H. Heemels. Continuous approximations of projected dynamical systems via control barrier functions. *IEEE Transactions on Automatic Control*, 70(1): 681–688, 2025.

49 C. A. Desoer and M. Vidyasagar. *Feedback Systems: Input-Output Properties*. Academic Press, 1975.

50 A. Dietrich, T. Wimbock, A. Albu-Schäffer, and G. Hirzinger. Reactive whole-body control: Dynamic mobile manipulation using a large number of actuated degrees of freedom. *IEEE Robotics & Automation Magazine*, 19: 20–33, 2012.

51 Y. Dong, X. Wang, and Y. Hong. Safety critical control design for nonlinear system with tracking and safety objectives. *Automatica*, 159: 111365, 2024.

52 A. Escande, N. Mansard, and P.-B. Wieber. Hierarchical quadratic programming: Fast online humanoid-robot motion generation. *International Journal of Robotics Research*, 33: 1006–1028, 2014.

53 I. Fantoni and R. Lozano. Control of nonlinear mechanical systems. *European Journal of Control*, 7(2–3): 328–348, 2001.

54 P. Fiorini and Z. Shiller. Motion planning in dynamic environments using velocity obstacles. *International Journal of Robotics Research*, 17: 760–772, 1998.

55 J. F. Fisac, M. Chen, C. J. Tomlin, and S. S. Sastry. Reach-avoid problems with time-varying dynamics, targets and constraints. In *Proceedings of the 18th International Conference on Hybrid Systems: Computation and Control*, pages 11–20, 2015.

56 D. Fox, W. Burgard, and S. Thrun. The dynamic window approach to collision avoidance. *IEEE Robotics & Automation Magazine*, 4: 23–33, 1997.

57 R. Freeman and P. V. Kokotović. *Robust Nonlinear Control Design: State-Space and Lyapunov Techniques*. Boston: Birkhäuser, 2008.

58 F. Gao, L. Wang, B. Zhou, X. Zhou, J. Pan, and S. Shen. Teach-repeat-replan: A complete and robust system for aggressive flight in complex environments. *IEEE Transactions on Robotics*, 36(5): 1526–1545, 2020.

59 Y. Gao, K. H. Johansson, and L. Xie. Computing probabilistic controlled invariant sets. *IEEE Transactions on Automatic Control*, 66(7): 3138–3151, 2020.

60 G. Giorgi and S. Komlósi. Dini derivatives in optimization—Part I. *Rivista di Matematica per le Scienze Economiche e Sociali*, 15: 3–30, 1992.

61 S. Glavaski, A. Papachristodoulou, and K. Ariyur. Safety verification of controlled advanced life support system using barrier certificates. In *International Workshop on Hybrid Systems: Computation and Control*, pages 306–321. Springer, 2005.

62 P. Glotfelter, J. Cortés, and M. Egerstedt. A nonsmooth approach to controller synthesis for boolean specifications. *IEEE Transactions on Automatic Control*, 66(11): 5160–5174, 2020.

63 R. Goebel, R. G. Sanfelice, and A. R. Teel. *Hybrid Dynamical Systems: Modeling, Stability, and Robustness.* Princeton University Press, 2012.

64 D. Goldfarb and A. Idnani. A numerically stable dual method for solving strictly convex quadratic programs. *Mathematical Programming*, 27: 1–33, 1983.

65 R. Grandia, A. J. Taylor, A. D. Ames, and M. Hutter. Multi-layered safety for legged robots via control barrier functions and model predictive control. In *Proceedings of 2021 IEEE International Conference on Robotics and Automation*, pages 8352–8358, 2021.

66 B. Grünbaum, V. Klee, M. A. Perles, and G. C. Shephard. *Convex Polytopes.* Springer, 1967.

67 W. M. Haddad and V. Chellaboina. *Nonlinear Dynamical Systems and Control: A Lyapunov-Based Approach.* Princeton, New Jersey, USA: Princeton University Press, 2008.

68 W. W. Hager. Lipschitz continuity for constrained processes. *SIAM Journal on Control and Optimization*, 17: 321–338, 1979.

69 W. Hahn. *Stability of Motion.* Heidelberg: Springer Berlin, 1967.

70 A. Haraldsen, M. S. Wiig, A. D. Ames, and K. V. Pattersen. Safety-critical control of nonholonomic vehicles in dynamic environments using velocity obstacles. In *Proceedings of the 2024 American Control Conference*, pages 3152–3159. IEEE, 2024.

71 W. P. M. H. Heemels and S. Weiland. Input-to-state stability and interconnections of discontinuous dynamical systems. *Automatica*, 44: 3079–3086, 2008.

72 D. J. Hill. A generalization of the small-gain theorem for nonlinear feedback systems. *Automatica*, 27: 1043–1045, 1991.

73 K. L. Hobbs, M. L. Mote, M. C. L. Abate, S. D. Coogan, and E. M. Feron. Runtime assurance for safety-critical systems: An introduction to safety filtering approaches for complex control systems. *IEEE Control Systems Magazine*, 43(2): 28–65, 2023.

74 R. A. Horn and C. R. Johnson. *Matrix Analysis.* Cambridge University Press, 2012.

75 M. Hoy, A. S. Matveev, and A. V. Savkin. Collision free cooperative navigation of multiple wheeled robots in unknown cluttered environments. *Robotics and Autonomous Systems*, 60(10): 1253–1266, 2012.

76 S. C. Hsu, X. Xu, and A. D. Ames. Control barrier function based quadratic programs with application to bipedal robotic walking. In *Proceedings of 2015 American Control Conference*, pages 4542–4548, 2015.

77 A. Isaly, M. Ghanbarpour, R. G. Sanfelice, and W. E. Dixon. On the feasibility and continuity of feedback controllers defined by multiple control barrier functions. *IEEE Transactions on Automatic Control*, 69(11): 7326–7339, 2024.

78 A. Isidori. *Nonlinear Control Systems II.* Springer, 1999.

79 H. Ito. State-dependent scaling problems and stability of interconnected iISS and ISS systems. *IEEE Transactions on Automatic Control*, 51: 1626–1643, 2006.

80 H. Ito and Z. P. Jiang. Necessary and sufficient small gain conditions for integral input-to-state stable systems: A Lyapunov perspective. *IEEE Transactions on Automatic Control*, 54: 2389–2404, 2009.

81 H. Ito, Z. P. Jiang, and P. Pepe. A small-gain condition for iISS of interconnected retarded systems based on Lyapunov–Krasovskii functionals. *Automatica*, 46: 1646–1656, 2010.

82 H. Ito, Z. P. Jiang, and P. Pepe. Construction of Lyapunov–Krasovskii functionals for networks of iISS retarded systems in small-gain formulation. *Automatica*, 49: 3246–3257, 2013.

83 I. Jang and H. J. Kim. Safe control for navigation in cluttered space using multiple Lyapunov-based control barrier functions. *IEEE Robotics and Automation Letters*, 9(3): 2056–2063, 2024.

84 M. Jankovic. Robust control barrier functions for constrained stabilization of nonlinear systems. *Automatica*, 96: 359–367, 2018.

85 Z. P. Jiang and T. Liu. Small-gain theory for stability and control of dynamical networks: A survey. *Annual Reviews in Control*, 46: 58–79, 2018.

86 Z. P. Jiang and I. Mareels. A small-gain control method for nonlinear cascaded systems with dynamic uncertainties. *IEEE Transactions on Automatic Control*, 42(3): 292–308, 1997.

87 Z. P. Jiang and Y. Wang. Input-to-state stability for discrete-time nonlinear systems. *Automatica*, 37: 857–869, 2001.

88 Z. P. Jiang and Y. Wang. A generalization of the nonlinear small-gain theorem for large-scale complex systems. In *Proceedings of the 7th World Congress on Intelligent Control and Automation*, pages 1188–1193, 2008.

89 Z. P. Jiang, A. R. Teel, and L. Praly. Small-gain theorem for ISS systems and applications. *Mathematics of Control, Signals, and Systems*, 7: 95–120, 1994.

90 Z. P. Jiang, I. M. Y. Mareels, and Y. Wang. A Lyapunov formulation of the nonlinear small-gain theorem for interconnected ISS systems. *Automatica*, 32(8): 1211–1215, 1996.

91 Z. P. Jiang, Y. Lin, and Y. Wang. Nonlinear small-gain theorems for discrete-time large-scale systems. In *Proceedings of the 27th Chinese Control Conference*, pages 704–708, 2008.

92 R. Kannan and C. K. Krueger. *Advanced Analysis: on the Real Line*. Springer Science & Business Media, 2012.

93 I. Karafyllis and Z. P. Jiang. *Stability and Stabilization of Nonlinear Systems*. Springer Science & Business Media, 2011.

94 H. K. Khalil. *Nonlinear Systems*, 3rd edition. New Jersey: Prentice-Hall, 2002.

95 O. Khatib. Real-time obstacle avoidance for manipulators and mobile robots. *International Journal of Robotics Research*, 5: 90–98, 1986.

96 S. Kim, K. Jang, S. Park, Y. Lee, S. Y. Lee, and J. Park. Continuous task transition approach for robot controller based on hierarchical quadratic programming. *IEEE Robotics and Automation Letters*, 4: 1603–1610, 2019.

97 S. Koga and M. Krstic. Safe PDE backstepping QP control with high relative degree CBFs: Stefan model with actuator dynamics. *IEEE Transactions on Automatic Control*, 68(12): 7195–7208, 2023.

98 P. Kokotović and M. Arcak. Constructive nonlinear control: A historical perspective. *Automatica*, 37(5): 637–662, 2001.

99 S. Kolathaya and A. D. Ames. Input-to-state safety with control barrier functions. *IEEE Control Systems Letters*, 3(1): 108–113, 2019.

100 M. Krstic. Inverse optimal safety filters. *IEEE Transactions on Automatic Control*, 69(1): 16–31, 2023.

101 M. Krstić and H. Deng. *Stabilization of Nonlinear Uncertain Systems*. Springer, 1998.

102 M. Krstić, I. Kanellakopoulos, and P. V. Kokotović. *Nonlinear and Adaptive Control Design*. NY: John Wiley & Sons, 1995.

103 V. Lakshmikantham and S. Leela. *Differential and Integral Inequalities: Theory and Applications: Volume I: Ordinary Differential Equations*. Academic Press, 1969.

104 V. Lakshmikantham, S. Leela, and A. A. Martynyuk. *Practical Stability of Nonlinear Systems*. World Scientific, 1990.

105 J.-C. Latombe. *Robot Motion Planning*. Springer, 1991.

106 S. M. LaValle. *Planning Algorithms*. Cambridge University Press, 2: 3671–3678, 2006.

107 J. Lee, N. Mansard, and J. Park. Intermediate desired value approach for task transition of robots in kinematic control. *IEEE Transactions on Robotics*, 28: 1260–1277, 2012.

108 D. Liberzon and D. Nešić. A small-gain approach to stability analysis of hybrid systems. In *Proceedings of the 44th IEEE Conference on Decision and Control*, pages 5409–5414, 2005.

109 D. Liberzon and D. Nešić. Stability analysis of hybrid systems via small-gain theorems. In J. P. Hespanha and A. Tiwari, editors, *Proceedings of the 9th International Workshop on Hybrid Systems: Computation and Control, Lecture Notes in Computer Science*. Springer, 2006.

110 D. Liberzon, D. Nešić, and A. R. Teel. Lyapunov-based small-gain theorems for hybrid systems. *IEEE Transactions on Automatic Control*, 59: 1395–1410, 2014.

111 T. Liu, D. J. Hill, and Z. P. Jiang. Lyapunov formulation of ISS cyclic-small-gain in continuous-time dynamical networks. *Automatica*, 47: 2088–2093, 2011.

112 T. Liu, D. J. Hill, and Z. P. Jiang. Lyapunov formulation of the large-scale, ISS cyclic-small-gain theorem: The discrete-time case. *Systems & Control Letters*, 61: 266–272, 2012.

113 T. Liu, Z. P. Jiang, and D. J. Hill. *Nonlinear Control of Dynamic Networks*. CRC Press, 2018.

114 L. Long, C. Huang, and Z. Sun. Safety control of switched systems via multiple barrier functions. *IEEE Transactions on Automatic Control*, 70: 5989–6004, 2025.

115 T. Lozano-Perez. Automatic planning of manipulator transfer movements. *IEEE Transactions on Systems, Man, and Cybernetics*, 11: 681–698, 1981.

116 A. M. Lyapunov. The general problem of the stability of motion. *International Journal of Control*, 55: 531–773, 1992.

117 K. M. Lynch and F. C. Park. *Modern Robotics: Mechanics, Planning, and Control*. Cambridge University Press, 2017.

118 Z. Lyu, X. Xu, and Y. Hong. Small-gain theorem for safety verification of interconnected systems. *Automatica*, 139: 110178, 2022.

119 Z. Lyu, X. Xu, and Y. Hong. Small-gain theorem for safety verification under high-relative-degree constraints. *IEEE Transactions on Automatic Control*, 69(6): 3717–3731, 2024.

120 Z. Lyu, X. Xu, Y. Hong, and L. Xie. On converse zeroing barrier functions. *Automatica*, 172: 112011, 2025.

121 S. M. Mahil and A. Al-Durra. Modeling analysis and simulation of 2-DOF robotic manipulator. In *Proceedings of 2016 IEEE 59th International Midwest Symposium on Circuits and Systems*, pages 1–4, 2016.

122 I. M. Y. Mareels and D. J. Hill. Monotone stability of nonlinear feedback systems. *Journal of Mathematical Systems, Estimation, and Control*, 2: 275–291, 1992.

123 R. Marino and P. Tomei. *Nonlinear Control Design: Geometric, Adaptive and Robust*. Prentice Hall, 1996.

124 J. Marzat, S. Bertrand, A. Eudes, M. Sanfourche, and J. Moras. Reactive MPC for autonomous MAV navigation in indoor cluttered environments: Flight experiments. *IFAC-PapersOnLine*, 50(1): 15996–16002, 2017.

125 F. Mazenc and L. Praly. Adding integrations, saturated controls, and stabilization for feedforward systems. *IEEE Transactions on Automatic Control*, 41(11): 1559–1578, 1996.

126 E. J. McShane. *Integration*. Princeton University Press, 1947.

127 D. Mellinger and V. Kumar. Minimum snap trajectory generation and control for quadrotors. In *Proceedings of the 2011 IEEE International Conference on Robotics and Automation*, pages 2520–2525, 2011.

128 D. Mellinger, A. Kushleyev, and V. Kumar. Mixed-integer quadratic program trajectory generation for heterogeneous quadrotor teams. In *Proceedings of the IEEE International Conference on Robotics and Automation*, pages 477–483, 2012.

129 M. Mesbahi and M. Egerstedt. *Graph Theoretic Methods in Multiagent Networks*. Princeton University Press, 2010.

130 P. Mestres and J. Cortés. Feasibility and regularity analysis of safe stabilizing controllers under uncertainty. *Automatica*, 167: 111800, 2024.

131 P. Mestres, A. Allibhoy, and J. Cortés. Regularity properties of optimization-based controllers. *European Journal of Control*, 81: 101098, 2025.

132 X. Min, S. Baldi, Y. Shi, and W. Yu. Safe control of multiagent systems via low-complexity control barrier functions. *IEEE Transactions on Automatic Control*, 70(10): 6831–6845, 2025.

133 J. Minguez and L. Montano. Nearness diagram (nd) navigation: collision avoidance in troublesome scenarios. *IEEE Transactions on Robotics and Automation*, 20(1): 45–59, 2004.

134 A. Mironchenko, G. Yang, and D. Liberzon. Lyapunov small-gain theorems for networks of not necessarily ISS hybrid systems. *Automatica*, 88: 10–20, 2018.

135 I. M. Mitchell. A toolbox of level set methods. *UBC Department of Computer Science Technical Report TR-2007-11*, 1: 6, 2007.

136 I. M. Mitchell, A. M. Bayen, and C. J. Tomlin. A time-dependent Hamilton-Jacobi formulation of reachable sets for continuous dynamic games. *IEEE Transactions on Automatic Control*, 50(7): 947–957, 2005.

137 T. G. Molnar and A. D. Ames. Composing control barrier functions for complex safety specifications. *IEEE Control Systems Letters*, 7: 3615–3620, 2023.

138 T. G. Molnar, R. K. Cosner, A. W. Singletary, W. Ubellacker, and A. D. Ames. Model-free safety-critical control for robotic systems. *IEEE Robotics and Automation Letters*, 7(2): 944–951, 2022.

139 J. J. Moreau. Proximité et dualité dans un espace hilbertien. *Bulletin de la Société Mathématique de France*, 93: 273–299, 1965.

140 J. J. Moreau and M. Valadier. A chain rule involving vector functions of bounded variation. *Journal of Functional Analysis*, 74: 333–345, 1987.

141 B. J. Morris, M. J. Powell, and A. D. Ames. Continuity and smoothness properties of nonlinear optimization-based feedback controllers. In *Proceedings of the 54th IEEE Conference on Decision and Control*, pages 151–158, 2015.

142 R. M. Murray, Z. Li, and S. S. Sastry. *A Mathematical Introduction to Robotic Manipulation*. CRC Press, 1994.

143 M. Nagumo. Über die lage der integralkurven gewöhnlicher differentialgleichungen. *Proceedings of the Physico-Mathematical Society of Japan*, 24: 551–559, 1942.

144 Y. Nakamura. *Advanced Robotics: Redundancy and Optimization*. Addison-Wesley Longman Publishing Co., Inc., 1990.

145 D. Nešić and A. R. Teel. A Lyapunov-based small-gain theorem for hybrid ISS systems. In *Proceedings of the 47th IEEE Conference on Decision and Control*, pages 3380–3385, 2008.

146 K. B. Ngo, R. Mahony, and Z. P. Jiang. Integrator backstepping using barrier functions for systems with multiple state constraints. In *Proceedings of the 44th IEEE Conference on Decision and Control*, pages 8306–8312, 2005.

147 Q. Nguyen and K. Sreenath. Exponential control barrier functions for enforcing high relative-degree safety-critical constraints. In *Proceedings of 2016 American Control Conference*, pages 322–328, 2016.

148 Q. Nguyen and K. Sreenath. Optimal robust control for constrained nonlinear hybrid systems with application to bipedal locomotion. In *Proceedings of 2016 American Control Conference*, pages 4807–4813, 2016.

149 Q. Nguyen and K. Sreenath. L_1 adaptive control barrier functions for nonlinear underactuated systems. In *Proceedings of 2022 American Control Conference*, pages 721–728, 2022.

150 P. Ong and J. Cortés. Universal formula for smooth safe stabilization. In *Proceedings of the 58th IEEE Conference on Decision and Control*, pages 2373–2378, 2019.

151 R. Ortega, A. Loria, P. J. Nicklasson, and H. Sira-Ramirez. *Passivity-based Control of Euler–Lagrange Systems: Mechanical, Electrical and Electromechanical Applications*. Springer, 1998.

152 Z. Peng, C. Wang, Y. Yin, and J. Wang. Safety-certified constrained control of maritime autonomous surface ships for automatic berthing. *IEEE Transactions on Vehicular Technology*, 72(7): 8541–8552, 2023.

153 D. W. Peterson. A review of constraint qualifications in finite-dimensional spaces. *SIAM Review*, 15: 639–654, 1973.

154 E. Polak, T. H. Yang, and D. Q. Mayne. A method of centers based on barrier functions for solving optimal control problems with continuum state and control constraints. *SIAM Journal on Control and Optimization*, 31: 159–179, 1993.

155 S. Prajna, A. Jadbabaie, and G. J. Pappas. A framework for worst-case and stochastic safety verification using barrier certificates. *IEEE Transactions on Automatic Control*, 52: 1415–1428, 2007.

156 Q. Quan. *Introduction to Multicopter Design and Control*. Springer, 2017.

157 P. Rabiee and J. B. Hoagg. Soft-minimum and soft-maximum barrier functions for safety with actuation constraints. *Automatica*, 171: 111921, 2025.

158 W. Ren and R. W. Beard. *Distributed Consensus in Multi-vehicle Cooperative Control: Theory and Applications*. Springer, 2008.

159 M. Z. Romdlony and B. Jayawardhana. Stabilization with guaranteed safety using control Lyapunov-barrier function. *Automatica*, 66: 39–47, 2016.

160 M. Z. Romdlony and B. Jayawardhana. On the new notion of input-to-state safety. In *Proceedings of the 54th IEEE Conference on Decision and Control*, pages 6403–6409. IEEE, 2016.

161 M. Z. Romdlony and B. Jayawardhana. Robustness analysis of systems' safety through a new notion of input-to-state safety. *International Journal of Robust and Nonlinear Control*, 29(7): 2125–2136, 2019.

162 S. I. Roumeliotis and M. J. Mataric. "Small-world" networks of mobile robots. In *Proceedings of the 17th National Conference on Artificial Intelligence and 12th*

Conference on Innovative Applications of Artificial Intelligence, page 1093. AAAI Press, 2000.

163 W. Rudin. *Principles of Mathematical Analysis*, 3rd edition. McGraw-Hill, 1976.

164 M. Rufli, J. Alonso-Mora, and R. Siegwart. Reciprocal collision avoidance with motion continuity constraints. *IEEE Transactions on Robotics*, 29: 899–912, 2013.

165 I. W. Sandberg. On the L_2 boundedness of solutions of nonlinear functional equations. *Bell System Technical Journal*, 43: 99–104, 1964.

166 R. Sepulchre, M. Janković, and P. V. Kokotović. *Constructive Nonlinear Control*. Springer, 1997.

167 W. Shaw Cortez and D. V. Dimarogonas. Safe-by-design control for Euler–Lagrange systems. *Automatica*, 146: 110620, 2022.

168 W. Shaw Cortez, D. Oetomo, C. Manzie, and P. Choong. Control barrier functions for mechanical systems: Theory and application to robotic grasping. *IEEE Transactions on Control Systems Technology*, 29: 530–545, 2021.

169 S. Singh, A. Majumdar, J. Slotine, and M. Pavone. Robust online motion planning via contraction theory and convex optimization. In *Proceedings of 2017 IEEE International Conference on Robotics and Automation*, pages 5883–5890, 2017.

170 A. Singletary, P. Nilsson, T. Gurriet, and A. D. Ames. Online active safety for robotic manipulators. In *Proceedings of 2019 IEEE/RSJ International Conference on Intelligent Robots and Systems (IROS)*, pages 173–178, 2019.

171 A. Singletary, K. Klingebiel, J. Bourne, A. Browning, P. Tokumaru, and A. D. Ames. Comparative analysis of control barrier functions and artificial potential fields for obstacle avoidance. In *Proceedings of 2021 IEEE/RSJ International Conference on Intelligent Robots and Systems*, pages 8129–8136, 2021.

172 A. Singletary, W. Guffey, T. G. Molnar, R. Sinnet, and A. D. Ames. Safety-critical manipulation for collision-free food preparation. *IEEE Robotics and Automation Letters*, 7: 10954–10961, 2022.

173 A. Singletary, S. Kolathaya, and A. D. Ames. Safety-critical kinematic control of robotic systems. *IEEE Control Systems Letters*, 6: 139–144, 2022.

174 J.-J. E. Slotine and B. Siciliano. A general framework for managing multiple tasks in highly redundant robotic systems. In *Proceeding of the 5th International Conference on Advanced Robotics*, volume 2, pages 1211–1216, 1991.

175 E. D. Sontag. A "universal" construction of Artstein's theorem on nonlinear stabilization. *Systems & Control Letters*, 13(2): 117–123, 1989.

176 E. D. Sontag. Smooth stabilization implies coprime factorization. *IEEE Transactions on Automatic Control*, 34: 435–443, 1989.

177 E. D. Sontag. Further facts about input to state stabilization. *IEEE Transactions on Automatic Control*, 35: 473–476, 1990.

178 E. D. Sontag. Comments on integral variants of ISS. *Systems & Control Letters*, 34: 93–100, 1998.

179 E. D. Sontag. *Mathematical Control Theory: Deterministic Finite Dimensional Systems*. New York, NY: Springer, 1998.

180 E. D. Sontag. Input to state stability: Basic concepts and results. In *Nonlinear and Optimal Control Theory*, pages 163–220. Berlin: Springer-Verlag, 2008.

181 E. D. Sontag and Y. Wang. On characterizations of the input-to-state stability property. *Systems & Control Letters*, 24: 351–359, 1995.

182 E. D. Sontag and Y. Wang. New characterizations of input-to-state stability. *IEEE Transactions on Automatic Control*, 41(9): 1283–1294, 1996.

183 E. D. Sontag and Y. Wang. Notions of input to output stability. *Systems & Control Letters*, 38: 235–248, 1999.

184 E. D. Sontag and Y. Wang. Lyapunov characterizations of input to output stability. *SIAM Journal on Control and Optimization*, 39: 226–249, 2000.

185 M. W. Spong and M. Vidyasagar. *Robot dynamics and control*. John Wiley & Sons, 2008.

186 B. L. Stevens, F. L. Lewis, and E. N. Johnson. *Aircraft Control and Simulation: Dynamics, Controls Design, and Autonomous Systems*. John Wiley & Sons, 2015.

187 G. Strang. *Linear Algebra and Its Applications*. Thomson Learning, Inc., 1988.

188 J. Sun, J. Yang, and Z. Zeng. Safety-critical control with control barrier function based on disturbance observer. *IEEE Transactions on Automatic Control*, 69(7): 4750–4756, 2024.

189 X. Tan, W. S. Cortez, and D. V. Dimarogonas. High-order barrier functions: Robustness, safety, and performance-critical control. *IEEE Transactions on Automatic Control*, 67(6): 3021–3028, 2022.

190 A. J. Taylor, P. Ong, T. G. Molnar, and A. D. Ames. Safe backstepping with control barrier functions. In *Proceedings of the 61st IEEE Conference on Decision and Control*, pages 5775–5782, 2022.

191 K. P. Tee, S. S. Ge, and E. H. Tay. Barrier Lyapunov functions for the control of output-constrained nonlinear systems. *Automatica*, 45: 918–927, 2009.

192 A. R. Teel. Using saturation to stabilize a class of single-input partially linear composite systems. In *Nonlinear Control Systems Design 1992*, pages 379–384. Elsevier, 1993.

193 A. R. Teel. A nonlinear small gain theorem for the analysis of control systems with saturation. *IEEE Transactions on Automatic Control*, 41: 1256–1270, 1996.

194 A. R. Teel. Input-to-state stability and the nonlinear small-gain theorem, 2003. Private communications.

195 A. R. Teel and L. Praly. A smooth Lyapunov function from a class-$\mathcal{KL}$ estimate involving two positive semidefinite functions. *ESAIM: Control, Optimisation and Calculus of Variations*, 5: 313–367, 2000.

196 A. R. Teel and L. Praly. On assigning the derivative of a disturbance attenuation control. *Mathematics of Control, Signals, and Systems*, 3: 95–124, 2000.

197 G. Teschl. *Ordinary Differential Equations and Dynamical Systems*. American Mathematical Society, 2012.

198 C. Tomlin, G. J. Pappas, and S. Sastry. Conflict resolution for air traffic management: A study in multiagent hybrid systems. *IEEE Transactions on Automatic Control*, 43(4): 509–521, 1998.

199 J. van den Berg, S. J. Guy, M. Lin, and D. Manocha. Reciprocal n-body collision avoidance. In B. Siciliano, O. Khatib, and F. Groen, editors, *Robotics Research*, pages 3–19. Springer-Verlag, 2011.

200 J. van den Berg, J. Snape, S. J. Guy, and D. Manocha. Reciprocal collision avoidance with acceleration-velocity obstacles. In *Proceedings of the IEEE International Conference on Robotics and Automation*, pages 3475–3482, 2011.

201 K. P. Wabersich, A. J. Taylor, J. J. Choi, K. Sreenath, C. J. Tomlin, A. D. Ames, and M. N. Zeilinger. Data-driven safety filters: Hamilton-jacobi reachability, control barrier functions, and predictive methods for uncertain systems. *IEEE Control Systems Magazine*, 43(5): 137–177, 2023.

202 L. Wang, A. D. Ames, and M. Egerstedt. Safety barrier certificates for collisions-free multirobot systems. *IEEE Transactions on Robotics*, 33: 661–674, 2017.

203 Y. Wang and X. Xu. Proxy control barrier functions: Integrating barrier-based and Lyapunov-based safety-critical control design. *Automatica*, 178: 112364, 2025.

204 P. Wieland and F. Allgower. Constructive safety using control barrier functions. In *Proceedings of the 7th IFAC Symposium on Nonlinear Control System*, pages 462–467, 2007.

205 A. G. Wills and W. P. Heath. Barrier function based model predictive control. *Automatica*, 40: 1415–1422, 2004.

206 S. Wilson, P. Glotfelter, L. Wang, S. Mayya, G. Notomista, M. Mote, and M. Egerstedt. The Robotarium: Globally impactful opportunities, challenges, and lessons learned in remote-access, distributed control of multirobot systems. *IEEE Control Systems Magazine*, 40: 26–44, 2020.

207 R. Wisniewski and C. Sloth. Converse barrier certificate theorems. *IEEE Transactions on Automatic Control*, 61: 1356–1361, 2016.

208 G. R. Wood and B. P. Zhang. Estimation of the Lipschitz constant of a function. *Journal of Global Optimization*, 8: 91–103, 1996.

209 Q. Wu, Y. Wang, Y. Fu, T. Yang, Y. Fang, and N. Sun. Design and kinematic modeling of wrist-inspired joints for restricted operating spaces. *Journal of Field Robotics*, 42(6): 2878–2891, 2025.

210 S. Wu, T. Liu, M. Egerstedt, and Z. P. Jiang. Quadratic programming for continuous control of safety-critical multi-agent systems under uncertainty. *IEEE Transactions on Automatic Control*, 68(11): 6664–6679, 2023.

211 S. Wu, B. Lu, Y. Fang, and N. Sun. Safety filter for underactuated mechanical systems with time-varying constraints. In *IEEE Transactions on Systems, Man, and Cybernetics: Systems*, pages 1–13, 2025.

212 X. Wu, Z. Li, Z. Kan, and H. Gao. Reference trajectory reshaping optimization and control of robotic exoskeletons for human-robot co-manipulation. *IEEE Transactions on Cybernetics*, 50(8): 3740–3751, 2019.

213 W. Xiao and C. Belta. High-order control barrier functions. *IEEE Transactions on Automatic Control*, 67(7): 3655–3662, 2022.

214 W. Xiao, C. Belta, and C. G. Cassandras. Adaptive control barrier functions. *IEEE Transactions on Automatic Control*, 67(5): 2267–2281, 2022.

215 X. Xiong and A. D. Ames. Slip walking over rough terrain via h-lip stepping and backstepping-barrier function inspired quadratic program. *IEEE Robotics and Automation Letters*, 6: 2122–2129, 2021.

216 X. Xu, P. Tabuada, J. W. Grizzle, and A. D. Ames. Robustness of control barrier functions for safety critical control. In *Proceedings of the 19th IFAC World Congress*, pages 054–061, 2014.

217 X. Xu, J. W. Grizzle, P. Tabuada, and A. D. Ames. Correctness guarantees for the composition of lane keeping and adaptive cruise control. *IEEE Transactions on Automation Science and Engineering*, 15(3): 1216–1229, 2017.

218 Y. Yang, Y. Zhang, W. Zou, J. Chen, Y. Yin, and S. E. Li. Synthesizing control barrier functions with feasible region iteration for safe reinforcement learning. *IEEE Transactions on Automatic Control*, 69(4): 2713–2720, 2023.

219 J. A. Yorke. Invariance for ordinary differential equations. *Mathematical Systems Theory*, 1(4): 353–372, 1967.

220 K. Yosida. *Functional Analysis*. Berlin, Heidelberg: Springer, 1965.

221 D. Youakim, P. Ridao, N. Palomeras, F. Spadafora, D. Ribas, and M. Muzzupappa. MoveIt!: Autonomous underwater free-floating manipulation. *IEEE Robotics & Automation Magazine*, 24: 41–51, 2017.

222 X. Yu, L. Guo, Y. Zhang, and J. Jiang. *Autonomous Safety Control of Flight Vehicles*. CRC Press, 2021.

223 G. Zames. On the input-output stability of time-varying nonlinear feedback systems Part one: Conditions derived using concepts of loop gain, conicity, and positivity. *IEEE Transactions on Automatic Control*, 11: 228–238, 1962.

224 C. Zhao, L. An, and L. Zhang. Collisions-free distributed cooperative tracking control for nonlinear mass with limited data rate. *IEEE Transactions on Automatic Control*, 70: 8250–8257, 2025.

225 Z. Zheng, S. Tong, Y. Zhang, Y. Zhu, T. Li, and J. Shao. Robust safe control for nonlinear quadrotor with a cable-suspended payload systems via control barrier function and disturbance estimator. *Control Engineering Practice*, 165: 106564, 2025.

226 K. Zhou, J. C. Doyle, and K. Glover. *Robust and Optimal Control*. Prentice Hall, 1995.

227 X. Zhou, X. Wen, Z. Wang, Y. Gao, H. Li, Q. Wang, T. Yang, H. Lu, Y. Cao, C. Xu, and F. Gao. Swarm of micro flying robots in the wild. *Science Robotics*, 7(66): eabm5954, 2022.

Index

Wiley The manufacturer's authorized representative according to the EU General Product Safety Regulation is Wiley-VCH GmbH, Boschstr. 12, 69469 Weinheim, Germany, e-mail: Product_Safety@wiley.com.

Printed and bound by CPI Group (UK) Ltd, Croydon, CR0 4YY

29/09/2026

02224912-0002